AF819756

Previous Years' Paper

Himachal Pradesh Police Constable

Recruitment Exam, 2025

(Exam held on 15-06-2025)

1. 'गुरु गुड़ ही रहे, चेले शक्कर'– लोकोक्ति का अर्थ है:

A. गुरु चेले से आगे बढ़ गए।

B. चेला गुरु से भी आगे बढ़ गया।

C. चेले का व्यवहार गुरु से भी मधुर हो गया।

D. गुरु का व्यवहार यथावत् रह गया।

2. मुझे साँप से बहुत डर लगता है। रेखांकित पद संज्ञा का प्रकार है:

A. व्यक्तिवाचक B. भाववाचक

C. जातिवाचक D. द्रव्यवाचक

3. मैं घर जाकर पढ़ लिया करता हूँ। इस वाक्य में मुख्य क्रिया है:

A. जाकर B. पढ़

C. लिया D. करता हूँ

4. एक तुम ही थे जिस पर मैं भरोसा कर सकता था। रेखांकित पद अव्यय का प्रकार है:

A. निषेधार्थक निपात B. बलदायक निपात

C. समुच्चयबोधक D. संबंधबोधक

5. किस शब्द में संयुक्त स्वर का प्रयोग नहीं हुआ है?

A. एकड़ B. ओषधि

C. अंगद D. औघड़

6. मैं इस समय कुछ कहना-सुनना नहीं चाहता। इस वाक्य में मुख्य क्रिया है:

A. कहना B. सुनना

C. कहना-सुनना D. चाहता

7. 'पक्षी' शब्द का सही पर्यायवाची चुनिए:

A. रात्रिचर B. नभचर

C. दिनकर D. पयोधर

8. सही विलोम चुनिए:

A. अपेक्षा – उपेक्षा B. एक – दो

C. शीत – शीतोष्ण D. सामिश्र – असमिश्र

9. 'सोना, धतूरा, गेहूँ' का अनेकार्थी शब्द बताइये:

A. खग B. आली

C. कर D. कनक

10. 'मोर नाचता है' वाक्य में कौन-सी क्रिया प्रयुक्त हुई है?

A. क्रिया विशेषण B. अकर्मक क्रिया

C. सकर्मक क्रिया D. इनमें से कोई नहीं

11. 'अपने पांव पर खड़े होना' मुहावरे का सही अर्थ चुनिए:

A. एक पैर पर खड़ा होना

B. स्वार्थ सिद्ध करना

C. आत्मनिर्भर होना

D. इनमें से कोई नहीं

12. 'हाथ कंगन को आरसी क्या' लोकोक्ति का सही अर्थ चुनिए:

A. स्वयं अयोग्य होना, दोष दूसरों को देना

B. प्रत्यक्ष को प्रमाण की आवश्यकता नहीं

C. सामर्थ्य के अनुसार कार्य करना चाहिए

D. परिश्रम अधिक, फल कम

1. B	**2.** B	**3.** B	**4.** B	**5.** C	**6.** D	**7.** B	**8.** A	**9.** D	**10.** B	**11.** C	**12.** B

13. भाषा की लघुतम इकाई चुनिए:

A. ध्वनि B. स्वर
C. व्यंजन D. वर्ण

14. 'चाँद' का एकार्थी शब्द चुनिए:

A. मयंक B. अनुपम
C. बटोही D. भुजंग

15. जो शब्द लिंग, वचन, कारक, काल, पुरुष के कारण परिवर्तित नहीं होते हैं, उन्हें **क्या कहते हैं**?

A. विशेषण B. **समास**
C. विकारी शब्द D. **अव्यय**

16. हिन्दी में कितने स्वर हैं?

A. 9 B. 7
C. 8 D. 11

17. समुच्चयबोधक अव्यय के कितने भेद हैं?

A. दो B. तीन
C. चार D. पाँच

18. 'हार मान लेना' के लिए कौन-सा मुहावरा प्रयुक्त होगा?

A. गले पड़ना B. कलेजा फटना
C. घुटने टेकना D. जान पर खेलना

19. निम्नलिखित में से विशेषण छाँटिए:

A. मूर्धन्य B. यज्ञ
C. सत्य D. मधु

20. सोना-चाँदी शब्द किस प्रकार की संज्ञा है?

A. व्यक्तिवाचक B. भाववाचक
C. द्रव्यवाचक D. समूहवाचक

21. The area of the trapezium is 105 cm^2 and its height is 7 cm. If one of the parallel sides is longer than the other by 6 cm, then the sum of the parallel sides is:

A. 25 B. 30
C. 35 D. 40

22. If one cubic meter of ice weighs 720 kg, then the weight of cuboidal block of ice 50 cm in length is:

A. 75 B. 80
C. 85 D. 90

23. A shopkeeper allows a discount of 10% to its customers and still gains 20% on a product. If the cost price of the product is ₹ 450, the marked price is:

A. 500 B. 540
C. 600 D. 640

24. The mean of *a*, *b*, *c*, *d* and *e* is 28. If the mean of *a*, *c* and *e* is 24, then mean of *b* and *d* is:

A. 31 B. 32
C. 33 D. 34

25. In a cricket match, a batsman hits a boundary 8 times out of 42 balls he played. The probability that he did not hit a boundary is:

A. $\frac{4}{21}$ B. $\frac{7}{21}$
C. $\frac{12}{21}$ D. $\frac{17}{21}$

26. The arithmetic mean and mode of a data are 24 and 12 respectively, then its median is:

A. 18 B. 20
C. 22 D. 25

27. Mina buys a fish from a shop for her aquarium. The shopkeeper takes out one fish at random from a tank containing 5 male fish and 7 female fish. The probability that the fish taken out is a female fish is:

A. $\frac{2}{12}$ B. $\frac{5}{12}$
C. $\frac{6}{12}$ D. $\frac{7}{12}$

13. D	**14.** A	**15.** D	**16.** D	**17.** A	**18.** C	**19.** A	**20.** C
21. B	**22.** D	**23.** C	**24.** D	**25.** D	**26.** B	**27.** D	

R. Gupta's®

POPULAR MASTER GUIDE

Himachal Pradesh Police

CONSTABLE

Recruitment Exam

- Sufficient Theory & Solved Questions for Practice
- Strictly According to Current Exam Pattern

by

RPH Editorial Board

2027
EDITION

RAMESH PUBLISHING HOUSE, NEW DELHI

Published by
O.P. Gupta *for* Ramesh Publishing House

Admin. Office
12-H, New Daryaganj Road, Opp. Officer's Mess,
New Delhi-110002 ✆ 23275224, 23245124

E-mail: info@rameshpublishinghouse.com
For Online Shopping: www.rameshpublishinghouse.com

Showroom
• Balaji Market, Nai Sarak, Delhi-110006 ✆ 23282525 📱 9354373464
• 4457, Nai Sarak, Delhi-110006

© Reserved with the Publisher

No Part of this book may be reproduced or transmitted in any form or by any means, electronic or mechanical including photocopying, recording or by any transformation storage and retrieval system without written permission from the Publisher.

Indemnification Clause: This book is being sold/distributed subject to the exclusive condition that neither the author nor the publishers, individually or collectively, shall be responsible to indemnify the buyer/user/possessor of this book beyond the selling price of this book for any reason under any circumstances. If you do not agree to it, please do not buy/accept/use/possess this book.

Book Code: R-1803

ISBN: 978-93-5012-773-5

Price: ₹ 370

Printed at: Deepak Offset, Delhi

CONTENTS

R. Gupta's®

General Knowledge Books

Book Name	Code	Price (₹)
• Quick General Knowledge 2026	R-1716	60
• General Knowledge for All 2026	R-1641	35
• R. Gupta's® GK & Current Affairs *including Latest Who's Who*	R-1	50
• General Knowledge Digest	R-1739	395
• General Knowledge & Current Affairs	R-5	75
• Popular General Knowledge	R-9	210
• General Knowledge Encyclopaedia	R-11	330
• Delhi General Knowledge	R-464	95
• Objective General Knowledge	R-177	210
• Comprehensive J&K and Ladakh (UTs) General Knowledge	R-564	130
• J&K and Ladakh GK (with latest Facts & Data)	R-1605	70
• J&K and Ladakh General Knowledge – At a Glance	R-1066	110
• Haryana General Knowledge	R-505	130
• Himachal Pradesh General Knowledge	R-415	160
• Uttarakhand General Knowledge	R-469	110
• Odisha General Knowledge	R-518	195
• West Bengal General Knowledge	R-1070	85
• Arunachal Pradesh General Knowledge	R-2560	210
• Manipur General Knowledge	R-1864	160
• Manipur GK Handbook *(with Multiple Choice Questions)*	R-954	90
• Maharashtra General Knowledge	R-2818	240

Ramesh Publishing House

2601

4457, Nai Sarak, Delhi-6

For Online Shopping: www.rameshpublishinghouse.com

28. If two acute angles of a right-angled triangle are equal, then each acute angle is:

A. 30° B. 45°
C. 60° D. 90°

29. A bus travels first 100 km at a speed of 100 km/h. It covers next 150 km at a speed of 90 km/h. The average speed of the bus is:

A. 93.75 B. 113.25
C. 115.50 D. 117.75

30. The number in $0.00\overline{273}$ in the form $\frac{p}{q}$, where p and q are integers, and $q \neq 0$, is:

A. $\frac{261}{99000}$ B. $\frac{271}{99000}$
C. $\frac{281}{99000}$ D. $\frac{291}{99000}$

31. In decimal form, $\frac{65}{16}$ equals:

A. 4.0625 B. 4.0725
C. 4.0655 D. 4.0175

32. The sum of length, breadth and height of a cuboid is 20 cm and the length of its diagonal is 10 cm. The surface area of the cuboid is:

A. 280 B. 300
C. 320 D. 340

33. A rectangular sheet of paper 88 cm (length) and 28 cm (breadth) is rolled along its length and a cylinder is formed. The radius of the cylinder is:

A. 11 B. 14
C. 16 D. 22

34. A shopkeeper allows a discount of 20% to its customers and still gains 10% on a product. If the cost price of the product is ₹ 500, then the marked price is:

A. 683.5 B. 685.5
C. 687.5 D. 689.5

35. If the difference of mode and median of a data is 24, then the difference of median and mean is:

A. 8 B. 12
C. 24 D. 36

36. An exterior angle of a triangle is equal to 100° and two interior opposite angles are equal. Then, each of these angles is equal to:

A. 40° B. 50°
C. 75° D. 80°

37. The rational number between $\sqrt{2}$ and $\sqrt{3}$ is:

A. 1.5 B. 1.8
C. $\frac{\sqrt{2}+\sqrt{3}}{2}$ D. $\frac{\sqrt{2}\times\sqrt{3}}{2}$

38. The value of $32^{\frac{2}{5}}$ is:

A. 4 B. 6
C. 8 D. 16

39. The curved surface area of a right circular cone whose slant height is 10 cm and base is 7 cm is:

A. 220 cm^2 B. 240 cm^2
C. 260 cm^2 D. 280 cm^2

40. The decimal form of $4\frac{1}{8}$ is:

A. 4.115 B. 4.125
C. 4.135 D. 4.145

41. Find the wrong number in the series:

3, 8, 15, 24, 34, 48, 63

A. 8 B. 24
C. 34 D. 63

28. B	29. A	30. B	31. A	32. B	33. B	34. C
35. B	36. B	37. A	38. A	39. A	40. B	41. C

42. In the given series of letters, how many T's are preceded and followed by T?

PTPTTPPTPTPPPTTPTPTTPPPT

A. Nil B. One
C. Two D. Three

43. Which of the images A to D is next in the sequence?

A. 

B. 

C. 

D. 

44. An aquarium contains 17 goldfish. All but eight died. How many goldfish is the aquarium left with?

A. 0 B. 8
C. 9 D. 17

45. Pointing towards a boy, Mina said, "He is the son of only son of my grandfather". How is the boy related to Mina?

A. Uncle B. Brother
C. Cousin D. None of these

46. If today is Wednesday, then what will be the day after 56 days?

A. Wednesday B. Thursday
C. Friday D. Saturday

47. How many cubes are there in the given figure?

A. 6 B. 8
C. 10 D. 12

48. A introduced B as the son of the only brother of his father's wife. How is A related to B?

A. Cousin B. Son
C. Brother D. Uncle

49. Select the related word from the given alternatives:

Medicine : Patient :: Education : ?

A. Teacher B. School
C. Student D. Tuition

50. In a certain code language, "TIRED" is written as "56" and "BRAIN" is written as "44". How is "LAZY" written in that code language?

A. 43 B. 58
C. 61 D. 64

51. Who has invented the Mercury Thermometer?

A. Daniel Gabriel Fahrenheit
B. Marie Curie
C. Sir Isacc Newton
D. Pierre Curie

52. Identify from the following cities, where was the first National Institute of Designs established in India?

A. Mumbai B. Ahmedabad
C. Bengaluru D. Kolkata

53. The headquarters of NATO is in:

A. Berlin B. Paris
C. Athens D. Brussels

54. Identify the author of book, "Kulut Desh ki Kahani", from the following:

A. Lal Chand Prarthi
B. Vidya Stokes
C. Sunil Dutt Gautam
D. Shanta Kumar

42. A	**43.** A	**44.** B	**45.** B	**46.** A	**47.** C	**48.** A
49. C	**50.** D	**51.** A	**52.** B	**53.** D	**54.** A	

55. Identify the date of International Yoga Day:

A. July, 10 B. June, 21
C. July, 25 D. June, 15

56. What does the abbreviation IMF stands for?

A. International Money Fund
B. Indian Monetary Fund
C. Irani Military Force
D. International Monetary Fund

57. In which of the following district of Himachal Pradesh, the Kumarwah lake is located?

A. Mandi B. Chamba
C. Kullu D. Kangra

58. Which of the following pass of Himachal Pradesh is located at highest altitude?

A. Talang B. Singoor
C. Waru D. Kugti

59. Identify from the following months when the Minjar Fair is held in Himachal Pradesh?

A. June B. August
C. July D. September

60. Which of the following has been introduced to replace the IPC (Indian Penal Code)?

A. BNS (Bhartiya Nyaya Sanhita)
B. BNSS (Bhartiya Nagarik Suraksha Sanhita)
C. BSA (Bhartiya Sakshya Adhiniyam)
D. BSN (Bhartiya Suraksha Niyam)

61. Which of the following countries emerged winner of the Men's Hockey Asian Championsip Trophy-2024?

A. China B. India
C. Japna D. South Korea

62. Which of the following is the largest river of Himachal Pradesh in terms of water volume?

A. Beas B. Chenab
C. Sutlej D. Ravi

63. Where is headquarters of 'UNESCO' situated?

A. Geneva B. New Delhi
C. Paris D. Berlin

64. 'Vande-Matram' is part of which of the following books?

A. Geetanjali B. Anandmath
C. Bhagwat Geeta D. Bharat Bharti

65. Who amongst the following has been awarded the Jnanpith Award-2023?

A. Rambhadracharya
B. Gaurav Pandey
C. Devender Kumar
D. Nandini Sen Gupta

66. The capital of United Arab Emirates, known for its futuristic architecture and luxury shopping is:

A. Al Ain B. Abu Dbhabi
C. Dubai D. Sharjah

67. The 'Best State in Horticulture 2024' was conferred on to which of the following states in the Agriculture Leadership Award-2024?

A. Nagaland B. Himachal Pradesh
C. Maharashtra D. Jammu & Kashmir

68. Which of the following is the largest Monastery in Spiti?

A. Tabo B. Lha Kun
C. Gemur D. Kee

69. In which of the following districts of H.P. a 'Centre of Excellence' is going to be established under Rashtriya Gokul Mission?

A. Kangra B. Sirmaur
C. Bilaspur D. Una

70. Netaji Subhash Chandra National Institute of Sports is located in which of the following places?

A. Kolkata B. Patiala
C. Bengaluru D. Ahmedabad

55. B	**56.** D	**57.** A, D	**58.** D	**59.** B, C	**60.** A	**61.** B	**62.** B
63. C	**64.** B	**65.** A	**66.** B	**67.** A	**68.** D	**69.** D	**70.** B

71. You should not _____ the worst.

A. assumed B. assuming
C. assume D. assumes

72. The teacher said, 'Be honest' (Direct to Indirect speech)

A. The teacher ordered me to be honest.
B. The teacher advised me to be honest.
C. The teacher said to be honest.
D. The teacher asked to be honest.

73. "The police arrested the thief." (Active to Passive voice)

A. The thief is arrested by the police.
B. The thief has been arrested by the police.
C. The thief was arrested by the police.
D. The thief will be arrested by the police.

74. Find the incorrect sentence:

A. The sun rises in the east.
B. She goes to school everyday.
C. They are go to the market now.
D. We have completed our homework.

75. He is _____ best player in our team.

A. a B. an
C. the D. no article

76. She has only a _____ time left before the exam.

A. many B. little
C. few D. more

77. This book is mine, but that one is _____.

A. her B. she
C. theirs D. they

78. By the next month, we shall _____, the project.

A. has completed B. completing
C. completed D. have completed

79. She said, "Do you like ice cream?" (Direct to Indirect speech)

A. She said if I like ice cream.
B. She asked if I liked ice cream.
C. She asked that I liked ice cream.
D. She asked if I like ice creams.

80. He said, "May God bless you!" (Direct to Indirect speech)

A. He prayed that God might bless me.
B. He said that God may bless me.
C. He told that God will bless me.
D. He wished that God could bless me.

81. "Open the door!" (Active to Passive voice)

A. The door is opened.
B. Let the door be opened.
C. The door was opened.
D. The door has been opened.

82. "She must complete this work by Monday." (Active to Passive voice)

A. This work must be completed by her by Monday.
B. This work should be completed by her by Monday.
C. This work will be completed by her by Monday.
D. This work has to be completed by her by Monday.

83. Identify the incorrect sentence:

A. We are listening to music.
B. They was going to school.
C. She has completed her work.
D. He is learning French.

84. Would you like _____ sugar in your tea?

A. some B. any
C. much D. few

85. They _____ a new car last week.

A. buy B. buys
C. bought D. buying

71. C	**72.** B	**73.** C	**74.** C	**75.** C	**76.** B	**77.** C	**78.** D
79. B	**80.** A	**81.** B	**82.** A	**83.** B	**84.** A	**85.** C	

86. This is an _____ book.

A. interesting
B. quickly
C. sadly
D. slowly

87. From the choices given below, pick out the correct one to complete the following sentence:

We would like to inform you _____.

A. that you have been selected for the job
B. that you will have been selected for the job.
C. that you had been selected for the job.
D. that you are been selected for the job.

88. Pick out the rightly spelt word:

A. Allowence
B. Accuracy
C. Occurrance
D. Commitee

89. Pick out the correct sentence among the following:

A. I have lived here for ten years.
B. I have been living here since ten years.
C. I am living here since 2014.
D. I am living here for ten years.

90. Fill in the blank in the given sentence:

Rising prices are _____ universal phenomenon.

A. an
B. the
C. a
D. None of these

EXPLANATORY ANSWERS

1. 'गुरु गुड़ ही रहे, चेले शक्कर' का भाव यह है कि गुरु तो जैसे-का-तैसा (गुड़) रहा, लेकिन चेला उससे भी अधिक श्रेष्ठ/उन्नत (शक्कर) हो गया। यहाँ तुलना मिठास के माध्यम से "शिष्य का गुरु से आगे निकल जाना" दिखाती है, इसलिए विकल्प B सही है।

2. वाक्य "मुझे साँप से बहुत डर लगता है।" में रेखांकित पद 'डर' है। 'डर' मन की एक अवस्था/भाव को व्यक्त करता है। जो संज्ञा किसी भाव, अवस्था, गुण या अनुभूति का बोध कराए, उसे भाववाचक संज्ञा कहते हैं। यद्यपि 'साँप' जातिवाचक संज्ञा है, परंतु यहाँ प्रश्न में रेखांकित पद 'डर' होने के कारण सही उत्तर भाववाचक संज्ञा (विकल्प B) ही है।

3. वाक्य "मैं घर जाकर पढ़ लिया करता हूँ" में 'जाकर' क्रिया का अव्यय/क्रियाविशेषणात्मक रूप है (मुख्य क्रिया नहीं)। 'करता हूँ' आदतन/नियमितता बताने वाली सहायक क्रिया है और 'लिया' पूर्णता/समापन का भाव जोड़ता है, जबकि वास्तविक कार्य "पढ़" है; इसलिए मुख्य क्रिया 'पढ़' (विकल्प B) है।

4. इस वाक्य में रेखांकित पद "ही" (एक तुम ही थे) जोर देकर विशेष रूप से "केवल तुम" का अर्थ स्पष्ट करता है। जो अव्यय वाक्य में बल/जोर/निश्चय बढ़ाए, वह बलदायक निपात कहलाता है; इसलिए विकल्प B सही है।

5. संयुक्त स्वर (ए, ऐ, ओ, औ) का प्रयोग जिन शब्दों में होता है, उनमें ये स्वर आते हैं–जैसे "एकड़" में 'ए', "ओषधि" में 'ओ', "औघड़" में 'औ'। "अंगद" में इनमें से कोई संयुक्त स्वर नहीं है, इसलिए विकल्प C सही है।

6. वाक्य "मैं इस समय कुछ कहना-सुनना नहीं चाहता" में वास्तविक क्रिया 'चाहना' है, जो इच्छा या अभिलाषा प्रकट करती है। 'कहना' और 'सुनना' यहाँ क्रियार्थक संज्ञा के रूप में प्रयुक्त हैं और 'नहीं चाहता' के आश्रित हैं, इसलिए मुख्य क्रिया 'चाहता' है।

7. 'पक्षी' वह प्राणी है जो आकाश में उड़ता है। 'नभ' का अर्थ आकाश और 'चर' का अर्थ चलने वाला होता है, इसलिए 'नभचर' पक्षी का सही पर्यायवाची है। अन्य विकल्प या तो असंबंधित हैं या भिन्न अर्थ रखते हैं।

8. 'अपेक्षा' का अर्थ है इच्छा, चाह या आवश्यकता, जबकि 'उपेक्षा' का अर्थ है अनदेखा करना, तिरस्कार करना। अर्थ की दृष्टि से ये दोनों शब्द एक-दूसरे के स्पष्ट और स्वीकृत विलोम हैं।

अन्य विकल्प सही विलोम युग्म नहीं बनाते–
'एक' का विलोम 'दो' नहीं बल्कि 'अनेक' होता है;
'शीत' का विलोम 'उष्ण' होता है, न कि 'शीतोष्ण';
और 'सामिश्र' का अर्थ मिला-जुला होता है, जिसका विलोम 'असमिश्र' शब्दकोशीय रूप से मान्य नहीं है (सामिश का विलोम निरामिष होता है, जो भिन्न संदर्भ का शब्द है)।

9. 'सोना' (धातु), 'धतूरा' (एक पौधा) और 'गेहूँ'–तीनों के लिए 'कनक' शब्द प्रयुक्त होता है। इसी कारण 'कनक'

86. A	87. A	88. B	89. A	90. C

एक अनेकार्थी शब्द है, जो संदर्भ के अनुसार अलग-अलग अर्थ देता है।

10. वाक्य ''मोर नाचता है'' में क्रिया 'नाचता है' का कोई कर्म नहीं है, अर्थात् क्रिया का प्रभाव किसी वस्तु पर नहीं पड़ता। जो क्रिया बिना कर्म के पूरी हो जाए, वह अकर्मक क्रिया कहलाती है; इसलिए सही उत्तर विकल्प B है।

11. 'अपने पांव पर खड़े होना' मुहावरे का भावार्थ किसी दूसरे पर निर्भर न रहकर स्वयं अपनी आजीविका, निर्णय और जीवन का संचालन करने की क्षमता प्राप्त करना है। इसका शाब्दिक अर्थ एक पैर पर खड़े होना नहीं होता, बल्कि सामाजिक-आर्थिक स्वतंत्रता और स्वावलंबन को व्यक्त करता है, इसलिए विकल्प C पूर्णतः सही है।

12. 'हाथ कंगन को आरसी क्या' लोकोक्ति का अर्थ है कि जो बात प्रत्यक्ष रूप से सामने हो, उसके लिए अलग से प्रमाण या साक्ष्य की जरूरत नहीं होती। जैसे हाथ में कंगन हो तो उसे देखने के लिए दर्पण नहीं चाहिए, उसी प्रकार स्पष्ट सत्य को सिद्ध करने की आवश्यकता नहीं होती; अतः विकल्प B सही है।

13. भाषा की लघुतम इकाई वर्ण होती है, क्योंकि वर्ण भाषा का वह सबसे छोटा अविभाज्य तत्व है जिसे और छोटे भागों में विभाजित नहीं किया जा सकता। भाषा का लेखन और संरचना वर्णों पर ही आधारित होती है।

ध्वनि भाषा की मूल श्रव्य इकाई अवश्य है, लेकिन व्याकरण की दृष्टि से वह अमूर्त (abstract) होती है, जबकि वर्ण ध्वनियों का लिखित और निश्चित रूप है। स्वर और व्यंजन, दोनों ही वर्ण के प्रकार हैं, स्वतंत्र इकाइयाँ नहीं।

भारतीय व्याकरण परंपरा में, विशेषकर पाणिनि जैसे आचार्यों ने भी वर्ण को ही भाषा की मूल एवं लघुतम इकाई के रूप में स्वीकार किया है।

14. 'चाँद' का एकार्थी (पर्यायवाची) शब्द 'मयंक' है, जो केवल चंद्रमा के अर्थ में ही प्रयुक्त होता है। अन्य विकल्पों के अर्थ भिन्न हैं—अनुपम (श्रेष्ठ), बटोही (पथिक), भुजंग (साँप)—इसलिए सही उत्तर विकल्प A है।

15. जो शब्द लिंग, वचन, कारक, काल और पुरुष के कारण अपने रूप में कोई परिवर्तन नहीं करते, उन्हें अव्यय कहा जाता है। जैसे—ही, भी, और, नहीं आदि। ये सदैव अपरिवर्तित रहते हैं, इसलिए विकल्प D पूर्णतः सही है।

16. हिंदी वर्णमाला में मुख्य स्वर कुल 11 माने जाते हैं— अ, आ, इ, ई, उ, ऊ, ऋ, ए, ऐ, ओ, औ।

'अं' (अनुस्वार) और 'अः' (विसर्ग) को अयोगवाह कहा जाता है। ये स्वर के सहायक चिह्न हैं, मुख्य स्वर नहीं, इसलिए स्वरों की मानक गणना में इन्हें शामिल नहीं किया जाता।

इसी कारण परीक्षाओं और पाठ्यपुस्तकों में हिंदी के स्वरों की संख्या 11 मानी जाती है।

17. समुच्चयबोधक अव्यय के सामान्यतः दो भेद माने जाते हैं—समन्वयबोधक (जैसेः और, तथा) तथा विरोधबोधक (जैसेः लेकिन, परंतु)। अतः विकल्प A सही है।

18. 'हार मान लेना' की स्थिति में व्यक्ति प्रतिरोध छोड़ देता है और पराजय स्वीकार कर लेता है। इस भाव को व्यक्त करने वाला मुहावरा 'घुटने टेकना' है, इसलिए विकल्प C पूर्णतः उपयुक्त है।

19. 'मूर्धन्य' शब्द किसी संज्ञा की विशेषता बताता है, जैसे—मूर्धन्य विद्वान। अतः यह विशेषण है। अन्य विकल्प या तो संज्ञा हैं या स्वतंत्र अर्थ वाले शब्द हैं, इसलिए सही उत्तर विकल्प A है।

20. 'सोना-चाँदी' भौतिक पदार्थों/धातुओं के नाम हैं, जिनका प्रयोग द्रव्य के रूप में होता है। इस प्रकार की संज्ञा द्रव्यवाचक कहलाती है, इसलिए विकल्प C सही है।

21. Area of trapezium $= \frac{1}{2} \times$ (sum of parallel sides) $\times$ height

$$105 = \frac{1}{2} \times S \times 7 = \frac{7S}{2}$$

$$210 = 7S \Rightarrow S = \frac{210}{7} = 30.$$

22. 1 m^3 of ice weighs 720 kg

50 cm = 0.5 m

Volume of cuboid $= (0.5)^3 = 0.125\ m^3$

Weight $= 720 \times 0.125 = 90$ kg.

23. Cost Price = 450

Gain = 20%

$$\text{Selling Price} = 450 \times \frac{120}{100} = 540$$

Discount = 10%

Selling Price = 90% of Marked Price

$$\frac{90}{100} \times MP = 540$$

$$MP = 540 \times \frac{100}{90} = 600.$$

24. Mean of $a, b, c, d, e = 28$

$a + b + c + d + e = 28 \times 5 = 140$

Mean of $a, c, e = 24$

$a + c + e = 24 \times 3 = 72$

$$b + d = 140 - 72 = 68$$

$$\text{Mean of } b \text{ and } d = \frac{68}{2} = 34.$$

25. Total number of balls = 42

Number of boundaries hit = 8

Number of times boundary not hit

$$= 42 - 8 = 34$$

$$\text{Required probability} = \frac{34}{42} = \frac{17}{21}.$$

26. Mean = 24

Mode = 12

$$\text{Median} = \frac{2 \times \text{Mean} + \text{Mode}}{3} = \frac{2 \times 24 + 12}{3}$$

$$= \frac{48 + 12}{3} = \frac{60}{3} = 20.$$

27. Number of male fish = 5

Numbe of female fish = 7

Total number of fish = 5 + 7 = 12

$$\text{Required probability} = \frac{\text{Number of female fish}}{\text{Total number of fish}}$$

$$= \frac{7}{12}.$$

28. Sum of angles of a triangle = 180°

One angle of right angled triangle = 90°

Sum of remaining two acute angles

$$= 180° - 90° = 90°$$

Given both acute angles are equal

$$\text{Each acute angle} = \frac{90°}{2} = 45°.$$

29. Distance = 100 km,

Speed = 100 km/h

$$\text{Time} = \frac{100}{100} = 1 \text{ hour}$$

Distance = 150 km,

Speed = 90 km/h

$$\text{Time} = \frac{150}{90} = \frac{5}{3} \text{ hours}$$

Total distance = 100 + 150 = 250 km

$$\text{Total time} = 1 + \frac{5}{3} = \frac{8}{3} \text{ hours}$$

$$\text{Average speed} = \frac{250}{\frac{8}{3}} = 250 \times \frac{3}{8}$$

$$= 93.75 \text{ km/h}.$$

30. Let,

$$x = 0.002\overline{73}$$
$$100x = 0.27\overline{373}$$
$$10000x = 27.3\overline{73}$$
$$10000x - 100x = 27.3\overline{73} - 0.27\overline{373}$$
$$9900x = 27.1$$
$$x = \frac{27.1}{9900} = \frac{271}{99000}.$$

31.

$$\frac{65}{16} = \frac{64+1}{16} = \frac{64}{16} + \frac{1}{16} = 4 + \frac{1}{16}$$

$$= 4 + 0.0625 = 4.0625.$$

32. $l + b + h = 20$

Diagonal of cuboid $d = 10 \Rightarrow l^2 + b^2 + h^2 = 10^2 = 100$

$$(l + b + h)^2 = l^2 + b^2 + h^2 + 2(lb + bh + hl)$$
$$20^2 = 100 + 2(lb + bh + hl)$$
$$400 = 100 + 2(lb + bh + hl)$$
$$2(lb + bh + hl) = 300$$
$$lb + bh + hl = 150$$
$$\text{Surface area} = 2(lb + bh + hl) = 2 \times 150 = 300.$$

33. Rolled along its length ⇒ Circumference = length = 88

$$2\pi r = 88$$

$$r = \frac{88}{2\pi} = \frac{44}{\pi}$$

$$\pi = \frac{22}{7} \Rightarrow r = \frac{44}{\frac{22}{7}} = 44 \times \frac{7}{22} = 14.$$

34. CP = 500, Gain = 10%

$$\Rightarrow \quad \text{SP} = 500 \times \frac{110}{100} = 550$$

Discount = 20% ⇒ SP = 80% MP

$$\frac{80}{100} \times \text{MP} = 550$$

$$\text{MP} = 550 \times \frac{100}{80} = 687.5.$$

35. Empirical relation:

Mode = 3(Median) − 2(Mean)

Mode − Median = 2(Median − Mean)

Given: Mode − Media = 24

24 = 2(Median − Mean)

Median − Mean = 12.

36. Exterior angle of a triangle = sum of the two interior opposite angles

Given exterior angle = 100°

Let each interior opposite angle = x

$$x + x = 100°$$
$$2x = 100°$$
$$x = \frac{100°}{2} = 50°.$$

37. $\sqrt{2} \approx 1.414$

$\sqrt{3} \approx 1.732$

$1.414 < 1.5 < 1.732$

Hence, 1.5 lies between $\sqrt{2}$ and $\sqrt{3}$

Also, $1.5 = \frac{3}{2}$, which is a rational number.

38. $32^{\frac{2}{5}} = (2^5)^{\frac{2}{5}} = 2^{5\times\frac{2}{5}} = 22 = 4.$

39. Radius $r = 7$ cm

Slant height $= l = 10$ cm

Curved surface area of cone $= \pi rl$

$= \frac{22}{7} \times 7 \times 10 = 22 \times 10 = 220 \text{ cm}^2.$

40. $4\frac{1}{8} = 4 + \frac{1}{8} \Rightarrow \frac{1}{8} = 0.125$

$4 + 0.125 = 4.125.$

41. Given series: 3, 8, 15, 24, 34, 48, 63

Required pattern: $n^2 + 2$

$1^2 + 2 = 3$

$2^2 + 2 = 6$

(but series has $8 = 2^2 + 4$)

Alternatively,observe differences:

$8 - 3 = 5$

$15 - 8 = 7$

$24 - 15 = 9$

$34 - 24 = 10$

$48 - 34 = 14$

$63 - 48 = 15$

Correct increasing odd differences should be: 5, 7, 9, 11, 13, 15

$24 + 11 = 35 \neq 34$

34 is the wrong term.

42. Series:

PTPTTPPTPTPPPTTPTPTTPPPT

Check each T for condition: preceded by T and followed by T

At every position,each T has at least one adjacent P

No T is both preceded and followed by T

Number of such T = 0.

43. The correct image to follow the sequence is Option A.

The sequence is based on two simultaneous patterns:

Outer shape pattern (number and type of sides):

The outer shapes follow a structured progression where the number of sides first increases and then decreases, with one intentionally irregular shape included in the sequence:

Figure 1: Square → 4 sides

Figure 2: Flag/arrow-like shape → treated as a 5-sided figure

Figure 3: Hexagon → 6 sides

Figure 4: Pentagon → 5 sides

This establishes the side sequence as 4 → 5 → 6 → 5, so the next logical outer figure should return to a 4-sided figure, such as a trapezium or quadrilateral.

Shading pattern:

The shading alternates consistently between the outer and inner shapes:

Figure 1: Outer shaded, inner unshaded

Figure 2: Outer unshaded, inner shaded

Figure 3: Outer shaded, inner unshaded

Figure 4: Outer unshaded, inner shaded

Therefore, the next figure must have the outer shape shaded and the inner shape unshaded.

Matching both conditions, Option A is the only choice that:

Uses a 4-sided outer figure, and

Has the outer shape shaded with the inner shape unshaded.

Hence, the correct continuation of the sequence is Option A.

44. Total goldfish = 17

"All but eight died" ⇒ Only 8 did not die

Goldfish left = 8.

45. "Only son of my grandfather" = Mina's father

"Son of Mina's father" = Mina's brother (or Mina herself if Mina were male,but given Mina is female)

Boy is Mina's brother

46. $56 \equiv 0 \pmod{7}$

Day after 56 days = same day Wednesday.

47. Rule: Every cube in an upper layer must be supported by a cube below

Now calculate cubes according to heights

One stack is 3 cubes high (central stack)

Two stacks are 2 cubes high (supporting the middle layer)

Three stacks are 1 cube high (base-only cubes)

Total cubes $= (1 \times 3) + (2 \times 2) + (3 \times 1)$

$= 3 + 4 + 3 = 10$

Therefore, total no. of cubes = 10 and the correct option is C(10).

48. Father's wife = mother; only brother of mother = maternal uncle; son of maternal uncle = cousin; therefore A is B's cousin.

49. Medicine is for a patient (receiver/beneficiary); similarly education is for a student.

50. TIRED
T(20) + I(9) + R(18) + E(5) + D(4) = 56
BRAIN
B(2) + R(18) + A(1) + I(9) + N(14) = 44
LAZY
L(12) + A(1) + Z(26) + Y(25) = 64.

51. The mercury thermometer was invented by Daniel Gabriel Fahrenheit in 1714. He introduced mercury as a reliable thermometric liquid due to its uniform expansion and also developed the Fahrenheit temperature scale.

52. The first National Institute of Design (NID) in India was established in 1961 at Ahmedabad, Gujarat. It was set up to promote design education and industrial innovation in the country.

53. The headquarters of NATO (North Atlantic Treaty Organization) is located in Brussels, Belgium. It has been headquartered there since 1967.

54. The book "Kulut Desh ki Kahani" was written by Lal Chand Prarthi, who is known for his works related to the history and culture of Himachal Pradesh.

55. International Yoga Day is celebrated every year on 21st June. The date was adopted by the United Nations in 2014 following India's proposal.

56. IMF stands for International Monetary Fund. It is an international financial institution established in 1944 to promote global monetary cooperation and financial stability.

57. Kumarwah Lake is located in Kangra district of Himachal Pradesh. After careful factual verification, there is no reliable geographical or administrative evidence placing Kumarwah Lake in Mandi district.

58. Compare the given passes by altitude (approx.)

Talang Pass ≈ 4640 m
Waru Pass ≈ 3870 m
Singoor Pass ≈ 4310 m
Kugti Pass ≈ 5050 m

5050 > 4640, 4310, 3870
⇒ Highest altitude pass = Kugti Pass.

59. Minjar Fair of Himachal Pradesh (celebrated mainly in Chamba district) is a week-long festival that begins in the last week of July and continues into early August.

Therefore, depending on the calendar year and dates, the fair is observed across both months. Since the question asks to identify the month when the Minjar Fair is held and both July and August are factually correct, the correct answers are:

C. July (starting period)
B. August (continuation period)

Hence, both options (B) and (C) are correct.

60. The Indian Penal Code (IPC) has been replaced by the Bhartiya Nyaya Sanhita (BNS) as part of the new criminal law reforms introduced by the Government of India.

61. India emerged as the winner of the Men's Hockey Asian Champions Trophy 2024, showcasing a strong performance throughout the tournament.

62. In terms of water volume, the Chenab River is the largest river of Himachal Pradesh. It carries a greater discharge compared to other rivers in the state.

63. The headquarters of UNESCO (United Nations Educational, Scientific and Cultural Organization) is situated in Paris, France.

64. "Vande Mataram" is part of the novel Anandmath, written by Bankim Chandra Chattopadhyay. The song later became a national song of India.

65. The Jnanpith Award 2023 was awarded to Jagadguru Rambhadracharya for his outstanding contribution to Indian literature, particularly in Sanskrit and Hindi.

66. Abu Dhabi is the capital of the United Arab Emirates. It is internationally known for its modern skyline, futuristic architecture, luxury shopping destinations, and as the political and administrative center of the UAE.

67. The 'Best State in Horticulture 2024' award under the Agriculture Leadership Award-2024 was conferred on Nagaland. The state was recognised for its outstanding work in horticulture development through innovative programmes and policies, particularly for securing Geographical Indication (GI) registration for indigenous crops such as Naga Mircha, Naga Tree Tomato, and Naga Sweet Cucumber, along with strengthening value chains and farmer participation.

68. Kee (Key) Monastery is the largest monastery in the Spiti Valley. It is a major center of Buddhist learning and religious activity and is located at a prominent hilltop position overlooking the Spiti River.

69. A 'Centre of Excellence' under the Rashtriya Gokul Mission is going to be established in Una district of Himachal Pradesh. The mission focuses on conservation and development of indigenous cattle breeds and scientific livestock management.

70. Netaji Subhash Chandra National Institute of Sports (NIS) is located in Patiala, Punjab. It is India's premier institute for sports training, coaching education, and sports science.

71. After the modal expression "should not," the base form of the verb is required. Hence, "assume" is grammatically correct, while the other forms are incorrect in this structure.

72. The direct speech "Be honest" is an imperative sentence giving advice. In indirect speech, such sentences are best reported using verbs like advised, making option B correct.

73. The given sentence is in the simple past tense active voice. Its correct passive form must also be in the simple past tense, which is "was arrested."

74. This sentence is grammatically incorrect because the present continuous tense requires the verb in "-ing" form. It should be "They are going to the market now."

75. Superlative adjectives like "best" are always preceded by the definite article "the." Therefore, "He is the best player in our team" is grammatically correct.

76. The noun "time" is uncountable, and the expression "only a little time" correctly indicates a small amount. Options like many and few are used with countable nouns, while more does not fit the structure.

77. The sentence requires a possessive pronoun to replace "their book." "Theirs" is the correct possessive pronoun, whereas her, she, and they are not suitable here.

78. The phrase "By the next month" indicates completion before a future time, which requires the future perfect tense. Hence, "shall have completed" (option D) is grammatically correct.

79. The direct sentence is a yes/no question, so in indirect speech it uses "asked if/whether," and the tense shifts from present to past (like → liked).

80. This is an optative sentence expressing a prayer or wish. In indirect speech, such sentences are correctly reported using "prayed that" with might replacing may.

81. An imperative sentence in the active voice is converted into the passive voice by using the structure "Let + object + be + past participle." Therefore, "Open the door!" correctly becomes "Let the door be opened."

82. The modal verb "must" remains unchanged in passive voice. The object "this work" becomes the subject, and the structure must + be + past participle is correctly used, making option A grammatically accurate.

83. The subject "they" is plural and must take the auxiliary verb "were," not "was." Hence, this sentence is grammatically incorrect, while the other options are correct.

84. In polite offers and requests, "some" is used instead of "any." Since the sentence is a polite question offering sugar, "some" is the correct choice.

85. The time expression "last week" indicates the simple past tense. The past form of "buy" is "bought," making option C the correct answer.

86. The blank requires an adjective to describe the noun "book." "Interesting" is an adjective, whereas "quickly," "sadly," and "slowly" are adverbs, so they cannot modify a noun directly.

87. The sentence is used to convey official information with relevance to the present. The present perfect tense "have been selected" is correct here. The other options either use incorrect tense or incorrect verb structure.

88. "Accuracy" is the correctly spelt word. The other options contain spelling errors: Allowence (Allowance), Occurrance (Occurrence), and Commitee (Committee).

89. This sentence correctly uses the present perfect tense with "for" to show duration up to the present. The other options incorrectly combine tense with "since/for."

90. "Universal" begins with a consonant sound /ju:/ (not a vowel sound), so the correct article is "a," not "an." Hence, "a universal phenomenon" is grammatically correct.

Previous Paper (Solved)

Himachal Pradesh Police Constable

Recruitment Exam, 2022*

1. Which of the states ranked first in the Sustainable Development Goals India Index, 2020-21 released by NITI Aayog?

A. Himachal Pradesh
B. Tamil Nadu
C. Andhra Pradesh
D. Kerala

2. Consider the following quote:

"On 26th January, 1950, we are going to enter a life of contradictions. In politics, we will have equality and in social and economic life we will have inequality."

To whom among the following is this quote attributed?

A. Mahatma Gandhi
B. Babasaheb Dr. Bhimrao Ambedkar
C. Sardar Vallabhbhai Patel
D. Lal Bahadur Shastri

3. The Electoral College for electing the President of India includes which of the following?

(*i*) Elected members of Rajya Sabha
(*ii*) Elected members of the Legislative Assemblies of the States
(*iii*) Elected members of the Legislative Councils of the States

A. (*iii*) only B. (*ii*) only
C. (*ii*) and (*iii*) D. (*i*) and (*ii*)

4. The state bird of Himachal Pradesh is ______.

A. Monal
B. Western Tragopan
C. Himalayan Bulbul
D. Great Barbet

5. Who among the following fixes the date of election of the Deputy Speaker of the Lok Sabha?

A. The Secretary General of the Lok Sabha
B. The Protem Speaker of the Lok Sabha
C. The President of India
D. The Speaker of the Lok Sabha

6. Which river is the Kol Dam in Himachal Pradesh built across?

A. Ravi B. Beas
C. Sutlej D. Sainj

7. Because of its high clay content, the soil develops wide cracks in dry season. It is poor in humus yet highly moisture-retentive, thus responding well to irrigation. Cotton is the most traditional crop where this soil is found. Identify the soil type.

A. Red Soil B. Alluvial Soil
C. Laterite Soil D. Black Soil

8. The first 5G call in India was recently tested at:

A. IIT Kanpur B. IISc Bangalore
C. IIT Madras D. IIT Delhi

9. _______ is aimed at building an extra decentralized web that puts users in control of their data and identity.

A. Web 2.0 B. Web 5.0
C. Web 3.0 D. Web 4.0

10. What is the architectural style of the temple built on the edge of the Prashar lake?

A. Pyramidal shaped B. Nagara
C. Pagoda D. Cone shaped

* *Exam held on 03 July, 2022*

11. The Cripps Mission was sent by the British Government to visit India in the year:
A. 1946 B. 1935
C. 1942 D. 1939

12. Which provision of law did the *Navtej Singh Johar vs Union of India* case of the Supreme Court deal with?
A. Section 124A of IPC
B. Section 377 of IPC
C. Section 66A of IT Act
D. Section 497 of IPC

13. Which among the following books was authored by Mahatma Gandhi?
A. My Truth
B. Hindu View of Life
C. Hind Swaraj
D. Discovery of India

14. The 'Police Commemoration Day' is observed in India on:
A. January 15 B. November 26
C. July 26 D. October 21

15. In which district is Bandli Wildlife Sanctuary located?
A. Kangra B. Sirmaur
C. Mandi D. Kullu

16. Which mountain pass provides access between Lahaul and Spiti valleys?
A. Kugti B. Ghasutri
C. Inderhar D. Kunzum

Directions (Qs. No. 17-19): *For these questions, choose the most appropriate meaning of the following idioms:*

17. Forty winks
A. Sleep disorders
B. Eye sight related issue
C. A short sleep during the day
D. Long sleeping hours

18. Raise some hackles
A. To do a great task
B. To annoy
C. To make someone happy
D. To empathise with others

19. Throw in the towel
A. To give up B. To resist
C. To have a bath D. To fight

Directions (Qs. No. 20-22): *For these questions, choose the most appropriate synonyms of the following words:*

20. Shocked
A. Pacified B. Fascinated
C. Impeded D. Appalled

21. Didactic
A. Enlightening B. Frightening
C. Disgusting D. Sensational

22. Spurious
A. Honest B. Spoiled
C. Counterfeit D Genuine

Directions (Qs. No. 23-25): *For these questions, choose the most appropriate antonyms of the following words:*

23. Pandemonium
A. Noisy B. Confusion
C. Protest D. Peace

24. Modesty
A. Grandeur B. Sobriety
C. Propriety D. Fairness

25. Concise
A. Brief B. Lengthy
C. Abridged D. Laconic

Directions (Qs. No. 26-29): *For these questions, fill in the blanks with the most appropriate word:*

26. We must not shy ______ taking risks in life.
A. upon B. with
C. away from D. to

27. Due to her illness, she could not finish the work _______ time.
A. to B. by
C. upon D. on

28. The police was directed to ________ his business dealings.
A. look on B. look into
C. look up D. look to

29. Despite the injuries, Neeraj managed to ______ the gold medal in the tournament.
A. pull out B. pull off
C. pull in D. put in

30. Select the option which best expresses the sentence in active/passive voice:

I remember my sister taking me to the museum.
A. I remember taken to the museum by my sister.
B. I remember being taken to the museum by my sister.
C. I remember myself being taken to the museum by my sister.
D. I remember I was taken to the museum by my sister.

Directions (Qs. No. 31-32): *For these questions, select the appropriate option to change the sentence from direct to indirect speech and vice versa.*

31. I asked my sister if she had returned the mobile phone to her friend.
A. I said to my sister, 'Have you return the mobile phone to your friend?'
B. I asked my sister, 'Did you return the mobile phone to my friend?'
C. I said to my sister, 'Have you returned the mobile phone to my friend?'
D. I asked my sister, 'Have you returned the mobile phone to your friend?'

32. 'Where will you be tomorrow', she said, 'in case I have to call you?'
A. She enquired about his whereabouts the next day in case she would have to call him.
B. She asked where he would be the next day in case she had to call him.
C. She asked him where he will be the next day in case she had to call him.
D. She said to him where he would be tomorrow in case she would have to call him.

33. जिसे वशवर्ती बनाना कठिन हो :
A. स्वावलंबी B. दुर्लभ
C. दुर्धर्ष D. होनहार

34. जो किसी पर अभियोग लाता हो :
A. अभियन्ता B. प्रतिवादी
C. वादी D. याचक

35. तैरने की इच्छा :
A. पिपासा B. बुभुक्षा
C. जिगीषा D. तितीर्षा

36. सांझ और रात के बीच का समय :
A. मार्तंड B. पूर्वाह्न
C. गोधूलि D. ऊष्मा

निर्देश (प्र.सं. 37 से 42 तक): *निम्नलिखित प्रश्नों में वाक्य-खण्ड के स्थान पर एक शब्द बताइए।*

37. जिसका विभाजन न किया जा सके
A. अखण्डित B. अविभाज्य
C. अविभक्त D. अखण्ड

38. जहाँ पहुँचना कठिन हो
A. दुर्गम B. अगम
C. सुगम D. अगेय

39. विनयपूर्वक किया गया हठ है :
A. अनुरोध B. विनम्रता
C. अनुबोध D. आग्रह

40. 'मन को लुभाने वाली वस्तु' :
A. सुन्दर B. चारू
C. रूचिर D. मनोहर

41. 'जिसका अनुभव किया गया हो' :
A. अनुभूत B. अद्‌भुत
C. आचार D. विचार

42. 'तीन माह में एक बार होने वाला' :
A. तिगुना B. त्रैमासिक
C. द्विमासिक D. वार्षिक

43. भाषा का प्रयोग दो रूपों में किया जा सकता है—एक तो सामान्य जिससे लोक ______ में होता है तथा दूसरा साहित्य रचना के लिए, जिसमें प्रायः ______ भाषा का प्रयोग किया जाता है।
A. कार्य, रचनात्मकता B. विनिमय, काव्यात्मक
C. व्यवहार, आलंकारिक D. संचालन, भावात्मक

44. 'चादर के बाहर पैर पसारना' मुहावरे का अर्थ है :
A. क्षमा माँगना
B. परामर्श देना
C. क्षमता से अधिक व्यय करना
D. पोल खोलना

45. इंटरनेट विज्ञान एवं प्रौद्योगिकी की श्रेष्ठतम सौगातों में से एक है, लेकिन ________ यह है कि जैसे-जैसे इंटरनेट हमारे जीवन को सुगम व गतिशील बना रहा है, वैसे-वैसे इससे जुड़े खतरों की ________ भी बढ़ती जा रही है।
A. विवाद, परिभाषा B. यथार्थ, संख्या
C. विडम्बना, आशंका D. विकृति, स्थिति

46. 'आकाश से बातें करना' मुहावरे का अर्थ है :
A. अंग भंग करना B. बहुत ऊँचा होना
C. भयभीत होना D. इनमें से कोई नहीं

47. निम्नलिखित शब्दों में से कौन-सा कान्ति का पर्यायवाची नहीं है :
A. द्युति B. आलोक
C. समृद्धि D. आभा

48. निम्नलिखित शब्दों में से कौन-सा अग्नि का पर्यायवाची नहीं है?
A. दहन B. वैश्वानर
C. अनल D. जलज

49. How many times does the digit 6 appear while writing integers from 400 to 900?
A. 201 B. 150
C. 170 D. 200

50. A competitive examination was attended by male and female candidates. Out of the candidates who applied 60% are female. 18% of the candidates have passed the examination. 22.22% of the candidates who cleared are male. What percentage of female candidates has not passed the exam?
A. 76.67%
B. 33.33%
C. 40%
D. Cannot be determined

51. Ramesh buys 20 kgs of wheat every month for the family. The cost of wheat is increased from ₹ 14 per kg to ₹ 16 per kg. If Ramesh does not want to increase his expenditure on wheat, then what quantity of wheat should he buy after the price increase?
A. 12.5 kg B. 16 kg
C. 17.5 kg D. 16.5 kg

52. A train of 150 m length travelling at 90 kmph can cross a tunnel of length 250 m in:
A. 12 seconds
B. 15 seconds
C. 16 seconds
D. 18 seconds

53. What is the length of the longest pole that can be placed in a room 24 m long, 16 m wide and 18 m high?
A. 24 m B. 28 m
C. 34 m D. 42 m

54. The surface area of two spherical balls is in the ratio 4 : 9. Find the radius of the bigger ball, if the radius of the smaller ball is 4 cm.
A. 5 cm B. 7.5 cm
C. 6 cm D. 9 cm

55. A fish tank is in the shape of cuboid. Shyam who wants to increase the volume of the tank so as to have more fish, increased the length, width and depth of the tank by 10%, 15% and 20% respectively. By what percent has the tank's volume increased?
A. 46.2% B. 33.1%
C. 51.8% D. 62.0%

56. James can do a piece of work in 50 days. Peter can do the same piece of work in 40 days. How long will they take to complete 45% of the work when working together?
A. 5 days B. 9 days
C. 7 days D. 10 days

57. The Earth's atmosphere is mainly heated by:
A. Short wave solar radiation
B. Long wave terrestrial radiation
C. Reflected solar radiation
D. Scattered radiation

58. How are evergreen plants with woody stems having naked seed classified?
A. Angiosperms B. Pteridophytes
C. Gymnosperms D. Bryophytes

59. Which of the following organelles is not found in animal cells?
A. Lysosome
B. Cell wall
C. Endoplasmic reticulum
D. Cell membrane

60. The stars twinkle in the night because:
A. They emit light intermittently
B. The earth's atmosphere absorbs light intermittently
C. The star's atmosphere absorbs light intermittently
D. The refractive index of air in the atmosphere fluctuates

61. Which one of the following is called the King of Chemicals?
A. Sodium chloride B. Nitric acid
C. Sulphuric acid D. Sodium carbonate

62. Vinegar is the trade name for _______ .
A. Formic acid
B. Phenol
C. Carbon tetrachloride
D. Acetic acid

63. Water in plants is transported by _______.
A. Xylem B. Phloem
C. Epidermis D. Cambium

64. During the process of respiration in human beings, the exchange of gases takes place in _______ .
A. Alveoli B. Bronchiole
C. Bronchi D. Pleura

65. What is the value of X in the sequence:
40, 20, 20, 30, 60, 150, X?
A. 300 B. 450
C. 600 D. 250

66. Find the next term in the given series:
369, 387, 351, 360, 342, ______
A. 343 B. 351
C. 363 D. 376

67. If in a certain code language 'FORMAL' is written as 'IRUJXI', then how will 'BETTER' be written in that language?
A. EHQWBO B. EHWOBQ
C. EHWQBO D. EHWQOB

Directions (Qs. No. 68-70): *Read the following information and answer these questions.*

K, L, M, N, O, P and Q are seven students studying in three different colleges X, Y and Z. There are three girls among them, one in each of these colleges. Two of them study mechanical engineering, two study medicine and one each study biotechnology, pharmacy and electrical engineering. M studies with only her best friend K who studies pharmacy in college Y. No girl studies either biotechnology or electrical engineering. O studies mechanical engineering in college X and his brother P studies electrical engineering in college Z. None of the two who are studying medicine are in college Y. N studies biotechnology along with O and Q.

68. In which of the colleges do three of them study?
A. Z B. Y
C. X D. None of these

69. Which of the following pairs of students study medicine?
A. N, Q B. Q, P
C. Q, L D. O, L

70. Apart from O, who studies mechanical engineering?
A. L B. M
C. Q D. None of these

71. Museum is related to curator in the same way as Prison is related to _______ ?
A. Manager B. Monitor
C. Jailor D. Warden

72. Choose the alternative which closely resembles the mirror image of the given combination.

ANS43Q12

A. 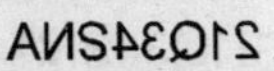 B. 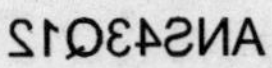
C. 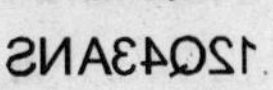 D. 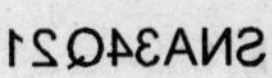

Directions (Qs. No. 73-77): *Read the following information and answer these questions.*

Five professors Dr. Joshi, Dr. Davar, Dr. Natrajan, Dr. Choudhary and Dr. Zia teach five different subjects Zoology, Physics, Botany, Geology and History in four Universities Delhi, Gujarat, Bombay and Osmania.

I. Dr. Choudhary teaches Zoology in Bombay University.

II. Dr. Natrajan is neither in Osmania University nor in Delhi University and he neither teaches Geology nor History.

III. Dr. Zia teaches Physics but neither in Bombay University nor in Osmania University.

IV. Dr. Joshi teaches History in Delhi University.

V. Two professors are from Gujarat University.

73. Who teaches Geology?
A. Dr Natrajan B. Dr. Zia
C. Dr. Davar D. Dr. Joshi

74. Dr. Zia is from which University?
A. Gujarat B. Bombay
C. Delhi D. Osmania

75. Who teaches Botany?
A. Dr. Zia B. Dr. Davar
C. Dr. Joshi D. Dr. Natrajan

76. Who is from Osmania University?
A. Dr. Natrajan B. Dr. Davar
C. Dr. Joshi D. Dr. Zia

77. Which of the following combinations is correct?
A. Dr. Zia – Delhi University
B. Dr. Choudhary – Geology
C. Dr. Davar – Bombay University
D. Dr. Natrajan – Gujarat University

78. If in a certain language MYSTIFY is coded as NZTUJGZ, how is NEMESIS coded in that language?
A. MDLHRDR B. OFNFTJT
C. ODNHTDR D. PGOKUGU

79. Pointing to a man, a woman said: "His mother is the only daughter of my mother." How is the woman related to the man?
A. Mother B. Daughter
C. Sister D. Grandmother

80. If M + N means M is the brother of N; M % N means M is the father of N and M × N means M is the sister of N. Which of the following means A is the uncle of C?
A. A % B × C
B. B × C % A
C. A + D % E % C
D. A + F % G × C

ANSWERS

1. (D) **2. (B)** **3. (D)**
4. (B) **5. (D)** **6. (C)**
7. (D) **8. (C)** **9. (B)**
10. (C) **11. (C)** **12. (B)**
13. (C) **14. (D)** **15. (C)**
16. (D) **17. (C)** **18. (C)**
19. (A) **20. (D)** **21. (A)**
22. (C) **23. (D)** **24. (A)**
25. (B) **26. (D)** **27. (D)**
28. (A) **29. (A)** **30. (B)**
31. (A) **32. (B)** **33. (C)**
34. (C) **35. (D)** **36. (C)**
37. (B) **38. (A)** **39. (D)**
40. (D) **41. (A)** **42. (B)**
43. (C) **44. (C)** **45. (C)**
46. (B) **47. (C)** **48. (D)**

49. (D): The digit 6 appear from 400 to 500
⇒ 406, 416, 426, 436, 446, 456, 460, 461, 462, 463, 464, 465, 466, 467, 468, 469, 476, 486, 496

∴ The number of digit 6 appear from 400 to 500 = 20

∴ The number of digit 6 appear from 600 to 700 = 100 + 20 = 120

∴ The number of digit 6 appear from 400 to 900 = 20 + 20 + 120 + 20 + 20

= 80 + 120 = 200.

50. (A): Let the male and female candidates are 100

Then, number of female applied = 60

and number of male applied = 40

∵ Number of candidates who passed the exam

= 18

∴ Number of male candidates who passed the exam

$$= \frac{18 \times 22.22}{100} = \frac{399.96}{100}$$

= 3.9996 = 4

and number of female candidates who passed the exam = 18 – 4 = 14

∴ % of female candidates has not passed the exam

$$= \frac{60-14}{60} \times 100$$

$$= 46 \times \frac{5}{3} = \frac{230}{3} = 76.67\%.$$

51. (C): The cost of 20 kg wheat

= ₹ 14 × 20 = ₹ 280

∴ Ramesh should buy quantity of wheat after the price increase$= \frac{280}{16} = 17.5$ kg.

52. (C): Here, Speed of train = 90 kmph

$$= 90 \times \frac{5}{18} = 5 \times 5 = 25 \text{ mps}$$

$$\because \quad \text{Time} = \frac{\text{Distance}}{\text{Speed}}$$

$$= \frac{150+250}{25} = \frac{400}{25}$$

= 16 seconds

∴ Required time = 16 seconds.

53. (C): Given, l = 24 m, b = 16 m and h = 18 m

The length of the longest pole that can be placed in a room

$$= \sqrt{l^2+b^2+h^2}$$

$$= \sqrt{(24)^2+(16)^2+(18)^2}$$

$$= \sqrt{576+256+324}$$

$$= \sqrt{1156}$$

= 34 m.

54. (C): The surface area of two spherical ball in the ratio 4 : 9

$$\Rightarrow \quad \frac{4\pi r_1^2}{4\pi r_2^2} = \frac{4}{9}$$

$$\Rightarrow \quad \frac{(4)^2}{r_2^2} = \frac{4}{9}$$

$$\Rightarrow \quad \frac{16}{r_2^2} = \frac{4}{9}$$

$$\Rightarrow \quad r_2^2 = \frac{16 \times 9}{4}$$

$$\Rightarrow \quad r_2^2 = 36 = (6)^2$$

$$\Rightarrow \quad r_2 = 6 \text{ cm}$$

∴ The radius of the bigger ball = r_2

= 6 cm.

55. (C): Volume of a tank (cuboid shape) = lbh

and volume of a tank after increasing the length, width and depth

$$= l \times \frac{110}{100} \times b \times \frac{115}{100} \times h \times \frac{120}{100}$$

$$= \frac{11}{10} \times \frac{23}{20} \times \frac{6}{5} lbh$$

$$= \frac{11}{10} \times \frac{23}{10} \times \frac{3}{5} lbh$$

$$= \frac{11 \times 69}{500} = \frac{759}{500} lbh$$

= 1.518 lbh

The tanks volume increased %

$$= \frac{1.518\,lbh - lbh}{lbh} \times 100\%$$

$$= \frac{0.518\,lbh}{lbh} \times 100\%$$

$= 0.518 \times 100 = 51.8\%$.

56. (D): (James + Peter)'s 1 day's work

$$= \frac{1}{50} + \frac{1}{40} = \frac{4+5}{200} = \frac{9}{200}$$

Now, 45% work = $\frac{45}{100} = \frac{9}{20}$

$\therefore$ They will take $\frac{9}{20} / \frac{9}{200}$

$$= \frac{9}{20} \times \frac{200}{9} = 10 \text{ days}$$

to complete 45% of the work.

57. (B) **58. (C)** **59. (D)**

60. (D) **61. (C)** **62. (D)**

63. (A) **64. (A)**

65. (B):

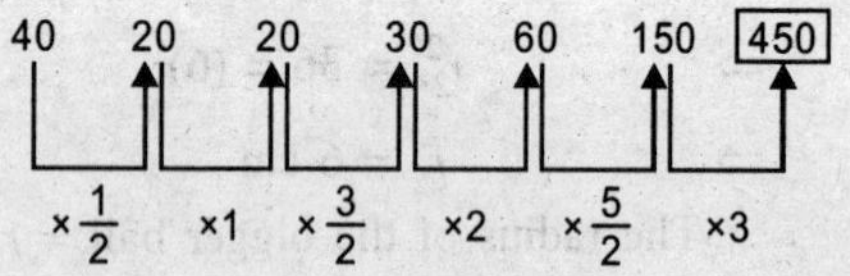

Hence, the value of X in the sequence = 450.

66. (B)

67. (C): Given,

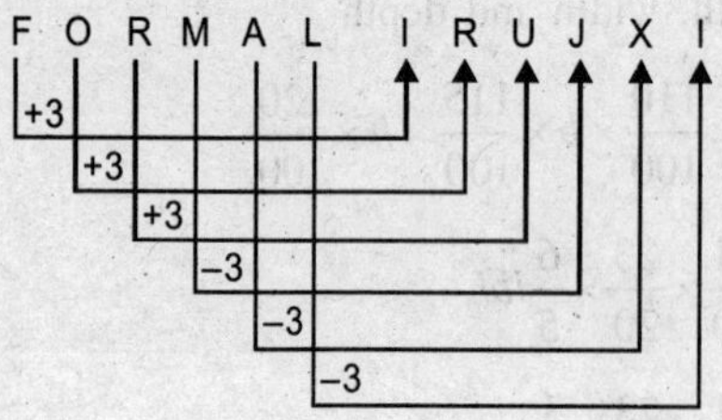

Similarly,

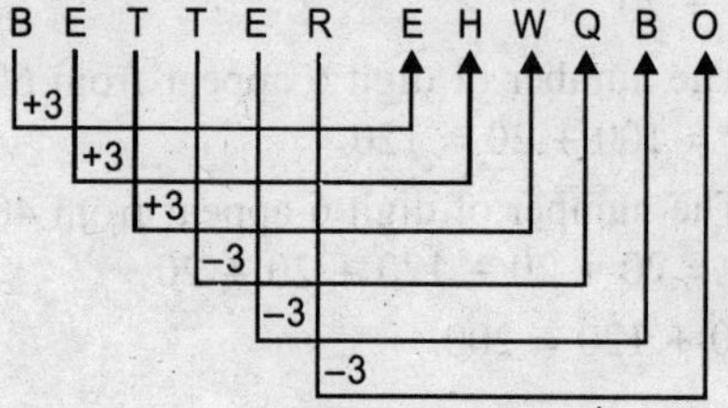

Therefore, BETTER will be written as EHWQBO.

For Qs. No. 68-70.

According to given information:

Students	Colleges	Courses	
K	Y	Pharmacy	Boy/Girl
L	Z	Medicine	Girl
M	Y	Mechanical Engineering	Boy/Girl
N	X	Biotechnology	Boy
O	X	Mechanical Engineering	Boy
P	Z	Electrical Engineering	Boy
Q	X	Medicine	Girl

68. (C): Three of them do study in College X.

69. (C): The pair (Q, L) study Medicine.

70. (B): Apart O, M studies Mechanical Engineering.

71. (C) **72. (B)** **73. (C)**

74. (A) **75. (D)** **76. (B)**

77. (D) **78. (B)** **79. (A)**

80. (D)

Previous Paper (Solved)

Himachal Pradesh Police Constable
Recruitment Exam, 2019*

1. Softwares such as Explorer and Firefox are also called as :
A. System Softwares B. Utility Softwares
C. Browsers D. Internet tools

2. During diving, the gas used for breathing is a mixture of oxygen and ______.
A. Nitrogen and Helium
B. Helium
C. Argon
D. Carbon dioxide

3. Junk email is also called as :
A. Sniffer script B. Spam
C. Spool D. Spoof

4. The Sankalp Project is related to the elimination of
A. HIV-AIDS B. Polio
C. Tuberculosis D. Leprosy

5. The density of water is :
A. Minimum at 4-degree Celcius
B. Maximum at 4-degree Celcius
C. Maximum at 0-degree Celcius
D. Minimum at 0-degree Celcius

6. Human skin is :
A. An organ B. A tissue
C. A cell D. A respiratory system

7. In India, a newborn baby is vaccinated with the vaccine :
A. B.C.G. B. Hepatitis
C. Tetanus D. Polio

8. Why is it easy to cook food in a pressure cooker?
A. It creates high pressure and high tension
B. More steam is generated inside the cooker
C. The boiling point of water increases
D. The boiling point of water decreases

9. Which of the following sectors in India does **not** belong to 'Service Sector'?
A. Insurance
B. Transport
C. Construction
D. Hotel & Restaurant

10. Which of the following district in Himachal Pradesh has the least forest cover area wise?
A. Kinnaur (623 sq. km)
B. Kullu (1987 sq. km)
C. Lahaul & Spiti (193 sq. km)
D. Una (556 sq. km)

11. What is the representation of 1-degree latitude in a kilometer?
A. 111 km B. 222 km
C. 1111 km D. 2222 km

12. What is the length of the Rohtang Tunnel?
A. 10 km B. 8.8 km
C. 9.2 km D. 8.0 km

13. Upanishads are books on :
A. Philosophy B. Yoga
C. Theology D. Law

14. Prior to Kullu Sultanpur, what was the capital of Kullu princely state?
A. Bajaura B. Naggar
C. Bajiri Paraul D. Bajiri Rupi

15. 'Parushni' was the mythological name of which river?
A. Beas B. Ravi
C. Yamuna D. Satluj

* *Held on 08-09-2019.*

16. When was Shimla made the summer capital of India?
A. 1905 B. 1919
C. 1864 D. 1885

17. Of the following, which sportsperson was awarded the First 'Rajiv Gandhi Khel Ratna'?
A. Geet Sethi
B. Vishwanathan Anand
C. Karnam Malleswari
D. Sachin Tendulkar

18. Who founded the Ramakrishna Mission?
A. Rama Krishna Paramhans
B. Swami Dayanand Saraswati
C. Swami Vivekanand
D. Mr. Keshav Chandra Sen

19. Himachal's most aged voter who voted in the Lok Sabha elections-2019 died recently.
A. Shari Devi B. Bhuri Singh Negi
C. Karam Devi D. Manjari Devi

20. The 'Tropic of Cancer' passes through which of the following states?
A. Gujarat, Madhya Pradesh, Chattisgarh, Manipur
B. Uttar Pradesh, Bihar, Jharkhand
C. Rajasthan, Jharkhand, West Bengal, Mizoram
D. Maharashtra, Chattisgarh, Odisha, Andhra Pradesh

21. Which of the following articles of the Indian constitution has the provision to enforce "President's Rule"?
A. Article 352 B. Article 356
C. Article 360 D. Article 342

22. During the freedom struggle who gave the slogan "Do or Die"?
A. Subhash Chander Bose
B. Mahatma Gandhi
C. Lala Lajpat Rai
D. Chandrashekhar Azad

23. When were the first Lok Sabha elections held in Himachal Pradesh?
A. 1950 B. 1953
C. 1951 D. 1952

24. During Akbar's reign, who worked on the permanent settlement system?
A. Birbal B. Man Singh
C. Todar Mal D. None of the above

Directions (Qs. No. 25) : *Choose the word closest in meaning to the word written in capital letters.*

25. TO JETTISON
A. To go on a track B. To fly
C. To abandon D. To fire a gun

Directions (Qs. No. 26 and 27) : *In the given sentences, choose the word which is opposite to the underlined word.*

26. People are willing to <u>follow</u> the rules.
A. Waive B. Neglect
C. Dispose D. Disregard

27. His appearance on the scene was <u>fortuitous</u>.
A. Circumstantial B. Unfortunate
C. Sudden D. Calculated

Directions (Qs. No. 28-34) : *In the passage below, a choice of four words marked A, B, C and D are suggested. Choose the best word to fit in the blank marked with numbers.*

You probably know about instant coffee and instant tea. They are a part of modern man's life. However, have you heard __(28)__ instant trees? Yes, Mr. Mohan __(29)__ Mumbai has achieved this feat by a __(30)__ pole planting technique. By this new __(31)__ a tree can be easily grown __(32)__ three months to a size which __(33)__ normally have taken three years to __(34)__.

28. A. of B. with respect to
C. at D. from

29. A. belonging from B. within
C. from D. on

30. A. fanciful B. revolutionary
C. classical D. bridge

31. A. strategy B. method
C. environment D. diameter

32. A. within B. during
C. after D. from

33. A. shall B. would
C. will D. regularly

34. A. plant B. grow
C. attain D. birth

Directions (Qs. No. 35-38) : *A sentence has been given with one underlined part. There are three possible substitutions for the underlined part written as A, B and C to correct/improve the sentence. If the sentence does not need improvement, then you can indicate D as your response.*

35. Whenever my students come across a new word, I ask them to look for them in the dictionary.

A. To look it up B. to look them up
C. to look at them D. no improvement

36. He insisted on he was innocent.

A. Insisted on that B. Insisted that
C. Insisted with D. No improvement

37. Each furniture on display in this hall is on the sale.

A. each of the furniture
B. each piece of furniture
C. each one of the furniture
D. no improvement

38. The building is a prime example of the 18th century.

A. Primary B. Paramount
C. Primitive D. No improvement

Directions (Qs. No. 39 and 40) : *Correct the word to fill in the blanks.*

39. Climbing Mount Everest is a remarkable ______.

A. feet B. feat
C. foot D. fete

40. The loss of his father ______ him badly.

A. Affect B. Effect
C. Affected D. Effected

निर्देश (प्र. सं. 41 से 43) : *नीचे लिखे वाक्यों में क्रिया विशेषण को चिन्हित करें।*

41. हादसे के बाद मैं वहाँ से सरपट भागा।

A. बाद B. वहाँ
C. सरपट D. भागा

42. रेलगाड़ी धीरे-धीरे पहुँच ही गई।

A. धीरे-धीरे B. पहुँच
C. ही D. गई

43. रमेश इतना तेज दौड़ा कि बहुत आगे निकल गया।

A. इतना B. तेज
C. कि D. बहुत

निर्देश (प्र. सं. 44 एवं 45) : *निम्न वाक्यों में क्रिया को चिन्हित करें।*

44. गया शहर किस प्रदेश में है?

A. शहर B. किस
C. में D. है

45. तुम अभी चुप रहो।

A. तुम B. अभी
C. चुप D. रहो

निर्देश (प्र. सं. 46 एवं 47) : *इन मुहावरों का अर्थ क्या है?*

46. छत्तीस का आँकड़ा

A. गहरी दोस्ती B. पक्की दुश्मनी
C. गणित में ज्ञानी D. थोक में भाव करना

47. आसमान सिर पर उठाना

A. नंगे पैर चलना
B. सब को तंग करना
C. छत पर जा कर चिल्लाना
D. बारिश में बचाव करना

निर्देश (प्र. सं. 48 एवं 49) : *निम्नलिखित शब्द समूह में उस शब्द को चुनें जो अन्य से मेल नहीं रखता है।*

48. A. जूता B. चप्पल
C. मोजे D. बेल्ट

49. A. नदी B. झील
C. वर्षा D. तालाब

निर्देश (प्र. सं. 50 एवं 51) : *निम्नलिखित में विशेषण लिखे।*

50. लड़के ने लाल कमीज पहनी है।

A. ने B. लाल
C. पहनी D. है

51. झील की गहराई का अनुमान लगाना कठिन है।

A. गहराई B. अनुमान
C. लगाना D. कठिन

निर्देश (प्र. सं. 52 से 56) : *निम्नलिखित लोकोक्तियों का अर्थ बताएं।*

52. सफेद झूठ
A. जिसे पकड़ा न जा सके।
B. जो साफ पता चले कि झूठ है।
C. जो सरकारी कागजों में गलत लिखा है।
D. बच्चों द्वारा बोला गया झूठ।

53. लाल-पीला होना
A. रंग बदलना
B. मारपीट करना
C. होली का निमंत्रण देना
D. गुस्सा आना

54. सही शब्द चुनें :
A. मात्री भूमि B. मात्र भूमि
C. मातृ भूमि D. मातृत्री भूमि

55. सही शब्द चुनें :
A. सूर्यगृहण B. सूर्यग्रहण
C. सुर्यगृहन D. सूर्यग्रहिन्

56. अवनि का विपरीतार्थक शब्द चुनें :
A. आकाश B. अम्बर
C. नभ D. आसमान

Directions (Qs. No. 57-61) : *Six persons A, B, C, D, E and F bought different chocolates i.e., Snickers, Perk, Munch, Gems and Cadbury, Every person bought these packets in different numbers 1, 2, 3, 4 and 5. It is not necessary that all the information is in one sequence. More than two persons did not buy the same item or the same numbers of packets.*

- 'C' bought packets of Munch.
- 'A' did not buy Cadbury packets.
- 'B' bought one packet.
- 'A' and 'D' bought the same number of packets.
- Two persons bought 5 packet of Gems.
- Only one person bought 5 Perk packets.
- 'E' bought two packets of Gems.
- Packets of Cadbury bought were more than those of Snickers but less than those of Munch.

Based on the above information, answer the following five questions.

57. Of the following, who bought Cadbury Chocolate?
A. B B. D
C. E D. F

58. Of the following pairs, who bought the equal number of packets?
A. A – B B. D – C
C. E – B D. A – D

59. Of the following, who bought Perk chocolate?
A. B B. D
C. E D. F

60. What is the difference in the number of packets bought by C and D?
A. 1 B. 2
C. 3 D. 4

61. What is the average of packets bought by F, C and D together.
A. 3 B. 4
C. 5 D. 2

Directions (Qs. No. 62-65) : *Four questions given below are based on the five three-digit numbers given below :*

851, 375, 638, 249, 526

62. If the digits of every number are arranged from left to right in ascending order then the numbers are arranged from left to right in descending order, which of the following will be third from the end.
A. 375 B. 526
C. 638 D. 249

63. If 2 is added to the middle digit of all odd numbers and 3 is subtracted from the first digit of all even numbers then what will be the difference between the biggest & second-biggest numbers of the newly created numbers.
A. 525 B. 729
C. 476 D. 582

64. What will be the product (multiplication) of the third digit of the third number from the left and second number from the right?
A. 27 B. 36
C. 28 D. 32

65. If the first and last digit of every number is interchanged then which of the following will become the second-largest number.

A. 526 B. 638
C. 851 D. 375

66. Choose the odd one out.

A. Japan
B. China
C. Kuala Lampur
D. Indonesia

67. If TOGETHER is coded as RQEGRJCT in one code then PAROLE will be coded as ______ in the same code.

A. RCTQNG B. RCPQJK
C. NCQPJG D. NCPQJG

68. If the third day of a month is Monday then what will be the 5th day after the 21st day of the same month.

A. Monday
B. Wednesday
C. Tuesday
D. None of these

69. Among five boys, Basant is taller than Manohar but not as much as Raju. Jayant is taller than Pradeep but smaller than Manohar. Who is the tallest

A. Raju
B. Manohar
C. Basant
D. Cannot be determined

70. In the English Dictionary which of the following will come in the third place.

A. Monarchy B. Monastic
C. Monetary D. Moneyed

71. Choose the odd one out :

A. PRT B. QOM
C. CEG D. UWY

72. How many meaningful English words can be made with the second, fourth, sixth and seventh letters of the word STUMBLE using each letter only once in each word?

A. One B. Two
C. Three D. None

73. $\left[\sqrt{4}\right]^3 \times \left[\sqrt{16}\right]^4 \div 8^2 = 2^?$

A. 8 B. 5
C. 9 D. 7

74. The average of Ram's five different scores in the test is 46.5. It was learnt latter his two scoes were written as 40 in place of 38 and 32 in place of 36. What is his correct average?

A. 42.1 B. 46.9
C. 43.9 D. 47.5

75. 'A' completes a piece of work in 12 days. 'B' is 20% more efficient than 'A', 'C' completes the same work taking 6 more days than 'B'. What will be the time (days) taken by 'B' & 'C' jointly to complete the work?

A. $3\frac{3}{13}$ B. $5\frac{2}{13}$

C. $4\frac{1}{13}$ D. $6\frac{2}{13}$

76. The ratio of the biggest and second-biggest angle of a triangle is 3 : 2. The smallest angle is 20% of the sum of the biggest & second-biggest angle. What is the sum of the smallest & second-biggest angle?

A. 100 degree B. 90 degree
C. 80 degree D. 105 degree

77. In the following series, identify the wrong number.

2269, 2284, 2319, 2376, 2539, 2760

A. 2760 B. 2284
C. 2319 D. 2376

78. A certain amount of money from ₹ 5000 is lent at 10% interest per annum while the remaining amount is lent at 20% interest per annum. In next two years an amount of ₹ 1700 is earned as simple interest on these two amounts. What is the amount that has been lent at 10% interest per annum?

A. ₹ 1500 B. ₹ 1900
C. ₹ 2100 D. ₹ 1345

79. The ratio of the ages of father and mother at the time of the birth of their son is 9 : 8. The ratio of ages of father and mother would be 17 : 16 when their son's age would be double of his present age. What is ratio of present ages of father and mother.

A. 15 : 14 B. 13 : 12
C. 10 : 9 D. 16 : 15

80. A train crosses the platform in 25 seconds. The length of the platform is 240 meters. What is the length of the train?

A. 140 meter
B. 200 meter
C. Cannot be determined
D. None of the above

ANSWERS

1	2	3	4	5	6	7	8	9	10
C	B	B	A	B	A	A	C	C	C
11	**12**	**13**	**14**	**15**	**16**	**17**	**18**	**19**	**20**
A	C	A	B	B	C	B	C	A	C
21	**22**	**23**	**24**	**25**	**26**	**27**	**28**	**29**	**30**
B	B	C	C	C	D	D	A	C	B
31	**32**	**33**	**34**	**35**	**36**	**37**	**38**	**39**	**40**
B	A	B	C	A	B	B	D	B	C
41	**42**	**43**	**44**	**45**	**46**	**47**	**48**	**49**	**50**
C	A	B	B	C	B	B	D	C	B
51	**52**	**53**	**54**	**55**	**56**	**57**	**58**	**59**	**60**
A	B	D	C	B	B	B	D	D	A
61	**62**	**63**	**64**	**65**	**66**	**67**	**68**	**69**	**70**
B	B	C	D	B	C	D	B	A	C
71	**72**	**73**	**74**	**75**	**76**	**77**	**78**	**79**	**80**
B	A	B	B	D	B	C	A	B	C

EXPLANATORY ANSWERS

For Questions (57-61) :

By given information.

Person	Chocolate	Number of Packet
A	Gems	3
B	Snickers	1
C	Munch	4
D	Cadbury	3
E	Gems	2
F	Perk	5

57. D bought Cadbury.

58. A and D bought the equal number of packets.

59. F bought Perk.

60. The difference in the number of packets bought by C and D = 4 – 3 = 1.

61. Average of packets bought by F, C and D

$$= \frac{5+4+3}{3} = 4.$$

For Questions (62-65) :

851, 375, 638, 249, 526

Given, the digits of every number are arrange in ascending order *i.e.*, 158, 357, 368, 249, 256

Again, the number are arrange in descending order

368, 357, 256, 249, 158

62. Third from the end = 256 *i.e.*, 526.

63. 851, 375, 638, 249, 526

Given, 2 is added to the middle digits of all odd numbers

i.e., 871, 395, 638, 269, 526

and 3 is subtracted from the first digit of all even numbers

i.e., 871, 395, 338, 269, 226

Here, biggest number = 871

and second biggest number = 395

Hence, Required difference = 871 − 395 = 476.

64. Here, the third number from the left = 638

and the second number from the right = 249

∴ Required product = 8 × 4 = 32.

65. Given, 851, 375, 638, 249, 526

The first and last digit of every number is interchanged

i.e., 158, 573, 836, 942, 625

Here, second largest number = 836

Hence, 638 will become the second-largest number.

66. Kuala Lampur is the capital of Malesia. Japan, China and Indonesia are country.

67.

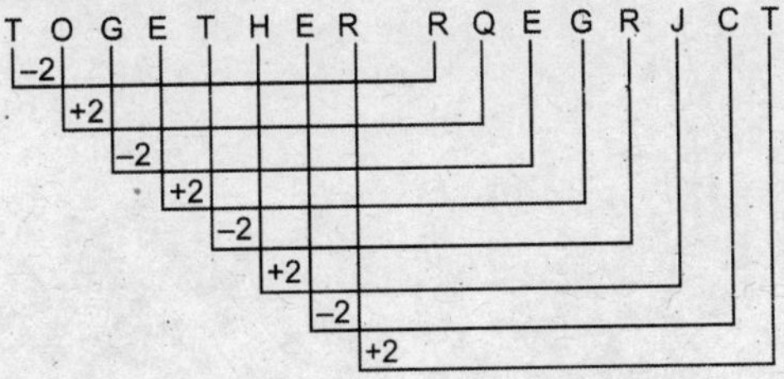

Similarly,

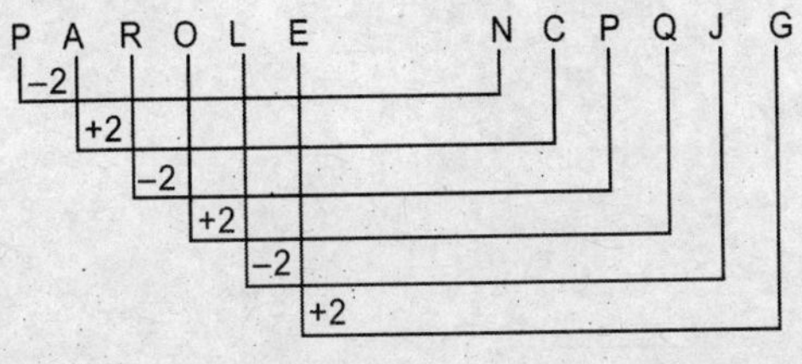

68. Given, the third day of a month = Monday

∴ 7th day = 14th day

= 21st day = Friday

Hence, the 5th day after the 21st day of the same month

= Friday + 5 day

= Wednesday.

69. Here, Raju > Basant > Manohar

Manohar > Jayant > Pradeep

∴ Raju > Basant > Manohar > Jayant > Pradeep

Hence, Raju is the tallest.

70. According to the english dictionary.

Monarchy, Monastic, Monetary, Moneyed

Here, Monetary will come in the third place.

71. A.

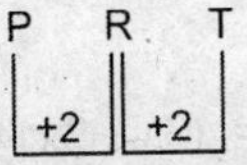

B.

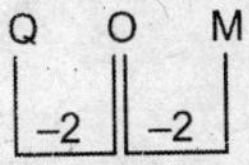

C.

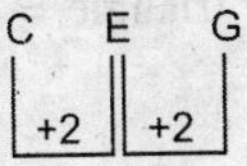

D.

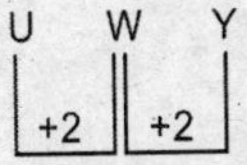

72. The second, fourth, sixth and seventh lettere of the word STUMBLE

i.e., TMLE

Meaning word = MELT.

73. $\left[\sqrt{4}\right]^3 \times \left[\sqrt{16}\right]^4 \div 8^2 = 2^?$

$\Rightarrow 4\sqrt{4} \times 16 \times 16 \div 64 = 2^?$

$\Rightarrow 4\sqrt{4} \times 16 \times 16 \times \frac{1}{64} = 2^?$

$\Rightarrow 2 \times 16 = 2^?$

$\Rightarrow 32 = 2^?$

$\Rightarrow (2)^5 = 2^?$

$\Rightarrow 5 = ?$

$\Rightarrow ? = 5.$

74. The total of Ram's five different scores in the test

$= 5 \times 46.5$

$= 232.5$

$\Rightarrow$ Total correct scoring

$= 232.5 + (38 - 40) + (36 - 32)$

$= 232.5 - 2 + 4$

$= 232.5 + 2$

$= 234.5$

Hence, his correct average

$= \dfrac{234.5}{5}$

$= 46.9.$

76. Let the biggest and second-biggest angle of a triangle is $3x$ and $2x$

Then, the smallest angle $= (3x+2x)\times\dfrac{20}{100}$

$= 5x\times\dfrac{1}{5} = x$

$\because$ Sum of the angles of a triangle = 180°

$\therefore \quad 3x + 2x + x = 180°$

$\Rightarrow \quad 6x = 180°$

$\Rightarrow \quad x = 30°$

Hence, the sum of the smallest and second-biggest angle

$= x + 2x$

$= 3x = 3 \times 30°$

$= 90°.$

78. Let ₹ x is the amount that has been lent at 10% interest per annum

Then, $\dfrac{x\times10\times2}{100}+\dfrac{(5000-x)\times20\times2}{100} = 1700$

$\Rightarrow \dfrac{x}{5}+\dfrac{2}{5}(5000-x) = 1700$

$\Rightarrow \dfrac{x}{5}+2000-\dfrac{2}{5}x = 1700$

$\Rightarrow 2000-\dfrac{x}{5} = 1700$

$\Rightarrow \dfrac{x}{5} = 2000 - 1700$

$\Rightarrow \quad x = 5 \times 300$

$\Rightarrow \quad x =$ ₹ 1500.

Previous Paper (Solved)

Himachal Pradesh Police Constable

Recruitment Exam, 2017*

1. How is the word 'enough' used in these two sentences?
   (*i*) There is time 'enough' and to spare.
   (*ii*) You know well 'enough' what I mean
   A. Adjective & Adverb
   B. Noun & Verb
   C. Conjunction & Preposition
   D. Adverb & Preposition

Directions (Qs. No. 2 & 3) : *In each question below choose the correct meaning of the given IDIOMS.*

2. His behaviour compelled me to "given him a piece of my mind"
   A. Scold him
   B. Pardon him
   C. Make him my friend
   D. Take him into confidence
3. "In black and white"
   A. In short B. Useless
   C. In writing D. In full swing

Directions (Qs. No. 4 & 5) : *Out of the four given alternatives, choose the one which correctly stands for each expression.*

4. Public declaration by a political party, ruler, etc. of principles and policy:
   A. Promise
   B. Advertisement
   C. Manifesto
   D. Blue book
5. Custom of having more than one husband at the same time.
   A. Polyandry B. Polygamy
   C. Monogamy D. Bigamy

Directions (Qs. No. 6 & 7) : *Choose the word/phrase which is most opposite in meaning of the word printed in BOLD.*

6. ESTABLISHED
   A. Small B. New
   C. Orthodox D. Modern
7. AFFLUENT
   A. Affected B. Poor
   C. Uneducated D. Usual

Directions (Qs. No. 8 & 9) : *In each of the following questions, a sentence contains a blank space. You have to choose from options (A), (B), (C) and (D) and fill the blank in such a manner that it completes the sentence in the most meaningful and grammatically appropriate manner.*

8. Tonight's game was .... because of the rain.
   A. struck off B. called off
   C. winning D. played
9. .... having worked really hard in office, Vikas did not get the much expected promotion.
   A. In spite of B. On
   C. Since D. Despite off

Directions (Qs. No. 10 & 11) : *Choose the word/phrase below which is most nearly the same in meaning to the word/phrase in BOLD.*

10. PREMIUM
    A. Superior B. Bonus
    C. Payable D. Promotional
11. Exhort
    A. Threaten B. Show
    C. Encourage D. Alert

* *Held on 02-10-2017.*

Directions (Qs. No. 12 & 13) : *In each question below a sentence with four words printed in bold type is given. They are numbered as (A), (B), (C) and (D). One of these words printed in bold may be either wrongly spelt or inappropriate in the context of the sentence. Find out this word and the number of the word is your answer.*

12. It is better to Seek (A) / Advice from a Financial (B) / Consultant on how to (C) / Safe your business / (D).

13. On two Consecutive nights two greatest (A) / Icones of show business were honoured with (B) / Unprecedented (C) / Affection / (D).

Directions (Qs. No. 14-16) : *In the following passage, there are blank spaces which have been numbered. These numbers are printed below the passage and against each, four words are suggested one of which fits appropriately.*

The emperor of China had .... 14 .... some peaches to the king of the Turkey with a note .... 15 ... that the fruit gives long life to anyone who eats them. As the fruits were being shown to the ruler Ram giving into the temptation .... 16 .... up one of the luscious peaches and bit into it.

14. A. parcel B. grown
C. bought D. sent

15. A. stating B. attach
C. stuck D. telling

16. A. reached B. picked
C. take D. secured

17. निम्नलिखित में से अशुद्ध वाक्य कौन-सा है?
A. बाघ बकरी एक घाट में पानी पीते हैं
B. वहाँ बहुत भीड़ है
C. श्रीकृष्ण के अनेक नाम हैं
D. हमारे शिक्षक बहुत अच्छे हैं

18. निम्न में से 'कुसुम' का पर्यायवाची शब्द नहीं है :
A. कमल B. पुष्प
C. सुमन D. प्रसून

19. 'ताप' शब्द का विलोम .... होता है।
A. तम B. तामसिक
C. शरद D. शीत

20. 'लकीर का फकीर' होना :
A. सरल जीवन यापन करना
B. परम्परावादी होना
C. झाड़फूक पर विश्वास करना
D. आडम्बर विरोधी होना

21. 'क्रूर' शब्द है :
A. सर्वनाम B. विशेषण
C. संज्ञा D. क्रिया

22. 'शांति' शब्द का समानार्थ नहीं है :
A. चुप्पी B. मौन
C. नीरवता D. आकाश

23. ''जो सब कुछ जानता है'' इस वाक्यांश के लिये सही शब्द क्या है?
A. बहुज B. अल्पज्ञ
C. सर्वज्ञ D. अभिज्ञ

24. ''दाता' शब्द का स्त्रीलिंग होता है।
A. दातृ B. दानी
C. दार्त D. दात्री

25. ''उल्लास'' का सन्धिविच्छेद होगा :
A. उत् + लास B. उल् + लास
C. उल + लास D. उल्ल + आस

26. ''जो अच्छे कुल में पैदा हुआ हो'' कहलाता है :
A. कुलीन B. संस्कारी
C. सर्वज्ञ D. बहुज्ञ

27. वृद्धा ने बौद्ध भिक्षु को .... दी :
A. दीक्षा B. परीक्षा
C. भिक्षा D. बुभुक्षा

28. ''जीतने की इच्छा रखने वाला'' कहलाता है :
A. उन्माद B. जिगीषु
C. आकांक्षी D. जिगिषा

29. बहुत सी भाषाओं को जानने वाला .... कहलाता है।
A. बहुभाषाविद् B. बहुभाषाभाषी
C. बहुश्रुत D. बहुदर्शी

30. ''उत्कृष्ट'' शब्द का विलोम है :
A. अपकर्ष B. व्यर्थ
C. निकृष्ट D. विकराल

31. 'यथार्थ' का विलोम है :

A. कृत्रिम B. कल्पित

C. उचित D. अनुचित

32. 'नाक में दम कर देना' मुहावरे का अर्थ बताइये :

A. बहुत प्रसन्न होना

B. बहुत परेशान होना

C. जिज्ञासा शांत करना

D. निंदा करना

33. अगर P का अर्थ है 'भाग'; R का अर्थ 'जमा'; T का अर्थ 'घटाना'; V का अर्थ 'गुणा'; तब 12 V 4 R 16 P 8 T 6 = ?

A. 138 B. 50

C. 44 D. 72

34. इस क्रमांक में आगे क्या आयेगा?

ABCD PQRS ABCDE PQRST ABCDEF PQRST?

A. A B. V

C. U D. W

निर्देश (प्र. सं. 35 से 39) : *उपरोक्त के सम्बन्ध में निम्न प्रश्नों का सही उत्तर दें :*

A, B, C, D, E, F & G एक गोलाकार में बीच की तरफ मुँह करके बैठे हैं (जरूरी नहीं वह उसी क्रम में बैठें) D, F के बाएँ है; D, A के दाएँ में दूसरे नम्बर पर है; C, A के बाएँ पर तीसरे नम्बर पर है; C, G के बाएँ में दूसरे नम्बर पर है; B, G का एकदम पड़ोसी है।

35. C के बाएँ पर दूसरे नम्बर पर कौन है?

A. B B. G

C. F D. D

36. C से एकदम दाएँ पर कौन है?

A. D B. G

C. E D. B

37. A एवं B के बीच में कौन है?

A. F B. D

C. G D. E

38. D के एकदम बाएँ पर कौन है?

A. B B. E

C. A D. नहीं जाना जा सकता

39. E का स्थान D के मुकाबले कहाँ है?

A. एमदम बाएँ

B. दाएँ से तीसरे

C. दाएँ से दूसरे

D. बाएँ से तीसरे

40. NSIK से कितने सार्थक अंग्रेजी शब्द बनाये जा सकते हैं, जो 'S' से शुरू होते हैं?

A. One B. Two

C. Three D. Four

41. 'K, N' का रिश्ता 'Q, T' से वही है जो 'D, G' का .... से है।

A. JN B. IM

C. JM D. IN

42. रोहन उत्तर दिशा में 10 किमी. चला फिर वह बाएँ मुड़कर 20 किमी. चला है। वह फिर बाएँ मुड़कर 10 किमी. चला है। वह फिर दाएँ मुड़ा और 5 किमी. चला। वह शुरुआती जगह से कितनी दूर है?

A. 10 किमी. B. 20 किमी.

C. 30 किमी. D. 25 किमी.

43. चार में से तीन एक समान हैं तथा एक समूह बनाते हैं। कौन समूह से बाहर है?

A. ताँबा B. चाँदी

C. सोना D. हीरा

44. चार में से तीन समान हैं ताकि एक समूह बन सके। कौन समूह से बाहर है?

A. नीला B. लाल

C. बैंगनी D. धूसर

45. NREA से कितने सार्थक अंग्रेजी शब्द बनाए जा सकते हैं। एक अक्षर का प्रयोग केवल एक ही बार करना है?

A. कोई नहीं B. एक

C. दो D. तीन

46. इस क्रमांक में आगे क्या आयेगा?

311, 300, 278, 245, 201, 146

A. 70 B. 90

C. 80 D. 110

47. भारतीय सेना का सेना प्रमुख कौन है?

A. श्री विक्रम सिंह राठौर

B. श्री बिपिन रावत

C. श्री वेलू नायर

D. श्री वीरेन्द्र सिंह

48. किसी निश्चित भाषा में 'GUEST' को 'HVFTU' के रूप में लिखा जाता है, तो 'NEST' को लिखा जायेगा।

A. IWTU B. XWTU

C. OFTU D. MDTU

49. अपराध उसी प्रकार पुलिस से सम्बन्धित है जिस प्रकार बाढ़ सम्बन्धित है :

A. नदी से B. तालाब से

C. क्रूज से D. बाँध से

50. भारत में पहली Technicolour film .... 1950 में .... द्वारा निर्मित की गई थी?

A. झांसी की रानी – सोहराब मोदी

B. झांसी की रानी – सैयद मोदी

C. मिर्जा गालिब – सोहराब मोदी

D. मिर्जा गालिब – मुंशी प्रेमचंद

51. विश्व मानव अधिकार दिवस कब मनाया जाता है?

A. 24 फरवरी B. 10 दिसम्बर

C. 15 मई D. 21 जुलाई

52. भारत की पहली यूरेनियम (Uranium) खान कहाँ स्थित है?

A. जादुगोडा B. तुमल्ला पुल्ले

C. पिचली D. दलभूम

53. किस मौसम में हमें ज्यादा चर्बी की जरूरत होती है?

A. वर्षा B. बसन्त

C. सर्दी D. गर्मी

54. भारत में सबसे अधिक भण्डार किस खनिज के हैं?

A. सोना B. ताँबा

C. माइका (mica) D. इनमें से कोई नहीं

55. ताबो मठ किस राज्य में स्थित है?

A. अरुणाचल प्रदेश

B. हिमाचल प्रदेश

C. जम्मू व कश्मीर

D. सिक्किम

56. प्रसिद्ध वैज्ञानिक प्रोफेसर यशपाल किन संगठनों से जुड़े थे?

A. इसरो (ISRO)

B. जवाहरलाल नेहरू विश्वविद्यालय

C. University Grants Commision

D. उपरोक्त सभी

57. भारतीय वायुसेना ने कब अपनी स्वर्ण जयंती मनायी थी?

A. 1962 B. 1972

C. 1982 D. 1992

58. Hygrometer क्या नापता है?

A. सापेक्षित आद्रता (Relative humidity)

B. दूध की शुद्धता

C. किसी भी तरल पदार्थ का विशिष्ट गुरुत्व

D. इनमें से कोई नहीं

59. आखिरी शीतकालीन ओलम्पिक कहां खेले गए?

A. अलबर्टवाइल

B. लाइफ हैमर

C. सोची (Sochi-Russia)

D. साल्ट लेक सिटी (Salt Lake City-USA)

60. भारत का पहला परमाणु Reactor कहाँ स्थापित किया गया?

A. सूरत B. तारापुर

C. ट्राम्बे D. शोलापुर

61. अन्तर्राष्ट्रीय न्यायालय का मुख्यालय कहाँ स्थित है?

A. हेग (Hague)

B. एडीस अबाबा (Addis Ababa)

C. पेरिस (Paris)

D. न्यूयॉर्क (New York)

62. भूमिगत जल के अधिगम प्रयोग से क्या समस्या उत्पन्न हुई है?

A. खारापन

B. जल स्तर का नीचे गिरना

C. जल भराव

D. ऊपर सभी

63. शक संवत का अंतिम महीना कौन-सा है?

A. फाल्गुन B. चैत्र
C. आषाढ़ D. पौष

64. मुगल साम्राज्य का अंतिम शासक कौन था?

A. बाबर
B. बहादुर शाह जफर
C. अकबर
D. इनमें से कोई नहीं

65. 258 का 13% – ? = 10

A. 23.45 B. 24.53
C. 23.54 D. 24.35

66. एक आयत की लम्बाई उसकी चौड़ाई से 7 cm अधिक है। अगर आयत की परिधि 126 cm है तो आयत की चौड़ाई क्या होगी?

A. 56 cm B. 38 cm
C. 28 cm D. 32 cm

67. $5\frac{1}{5}+2\frac{3}{5}+1\frac{2}{5}=?$

A. $7\frac{5}{4}$ B. $8\frac{3}{5}$
C. $6\frac{2}{5}$ D. $9\frac{1}{5}$

68. 5437 – 3153 + 2284 = ? × 50

A. 96.66 B. 91.36
C. 96.13 D. 93.16

69. राजू ने एक वस्तु ₹ 4500/- में खरीदी और उसे 15% के लाभ पर बेच दिया। इस पैसे से उसने एक और वस्तु खरीदी और उसे 10% के नुकसान पर बेच दिया। उसका कुल लाभ या हानि क्या है?

A. ₹ 151.60 का लाभ
B. ₹ 157.50 का लाभ
C. ₹ 165 की हानि
D. न कोई लाभ न हानि

70. 27 टोसटर और 18 मिक्सर का दाम 80,100/- है। 12 टोसटर और 8 मिक्सर का दाम मिलाकर कितना होगा?

A. 36,000 B. 36,500
C. 35,600 D. नहीं जाना जा सकता

71. 10 आदमी और 8 औरतें एक काम को मिलकर 5 दिन में खत्म करते हैं। औरत द्वारा एक दिन में किया गया काम आदमी द्वारा एक दिन में किये गये काम का आधा है। 4 आदमी और 6 औरतें इस काम को करने में कितने दिन लेंगे।

A. 12 दिन B. 10 दिन
C. $8\frac{2}{3}$ दिन D. $9\frac{3}{4}$ दिन

72. ₹ 16,500/- के मूलधन पर 16% की दर से चार साल में साधारण ब्याज कितना होगा?

A. 11,560 B. 10,560
C. 12,500 D. 9,980

73. सहेजे गये दस्तावेज (saved document) का मतलब क्या है?

A. फाइल (File) B. शब्द (Word)
C. फोल्डर (Folder) D. प्रोजेक्ट (Project)

74. अलेक्जेंडर फ्लेमिंग ने .... की खोज की।

A. पेनिसिलीन (Penicillin)
B. एक्स-रे (X-Ray)
C. टेलीफोन (Telephone)
D. वायरलेस (Wireless)

75. प्रकाश वर्ष निम्नलिखित में किसकी माप है?

A. तारकीय दूरी
B. हवाई जहाज की गति
C. प्रकाश की गति
D. रॉकेट की गति

76. कोरल (coral) क्या है?

A. पौधा B. कवक (Fungi)
C. जानवर D. प्रर्णग (Fern)

77. भोजन के पाचन की प्रक्रिया, मनुष्य के किस अंग से शुरू होती है?

A. पेट B. भोजन नली
C. मुँह D. छोटी आँत

78. निम्नलिखित में से कौन-सी वस्तु (Pencil) बनाने के लिए इस्तेमाल होती है?

A. ग्रेफाइट (graphite)

B. सिलिकॉन (silicon)

C. कटकोयला (char coal)

D. भास्वर (phosphorus)

79. निम्नलिखित में से किस रक्त कोष को शरीर का सिपाही (Soldier) कहा जाता है?

A. सफेद रक्त कोशिका

B. प्लैटिलैट्स

C. लाल रक्त कोशिका

D. ऊपर के सभी

80. HINI FLU निम्नलिखित में से किसकी वजह से होता है?

A. विषाणु B. जीवाणु

C. सर्दी D. कवक

ANSWERS

1	**2**	**3**	**4**	**5**	**6**	**7**	**8**	**9**	**10**
A	A	C	C	A	B	B	B	A	A
11	**12**	**13**	**14**	**15**	**16**	**17**	**18**	**19**	**20**
C	D	B	D	A	B	A	A	D	B
21	**22**	**23**	**24**	**25**	**26**	**27**	**28**	**29**	**30**
B	D	C	D	A	A	C	B	A	C
31	**32**	**33**	**34**	**35**	**36**	**37**	**38**	**39**	**40**
B	B	C	C	D	D	C	B	A	B
41	**42**	**43**	**44**	**45**	**46**	**47**	**48**	**49**	**50**
C	D	D	D	C	C	B	C	D	A
51	**52**	**53**	**54**	**55**	**56**	**57**	**58**	**59**	**60**
B	A	C	C	B	C	C	A	C	B
61	**62**	**63**	**64**	**65**	**66**	**67**	**68**	**69**	**70**
A	B	A	B	C	C	D	B	B	C
71	**72**	**73**	**74**	**75**	**76**	**77**	**78**	**79**	**80**
B	B	A	A	A	C	C	A	A	A

EXPLANATORY ANSWERS

33. 12 V 4 R 16 P 8 T 6

$12 \times 4 + \underbrace{16 \div 8} - 6$

BODMAS नियमानुसार,

$= 12 \times 4 + 2 - 6$

$= 48 + 2 - 6$

$= 44$

34. दी गई श्रृंखला में क्रमागत + 1 के क्रमानुसार एक-एक अंग्रेजी वर्णमाला का अक्षर बढ़ रहा है।

35-39.

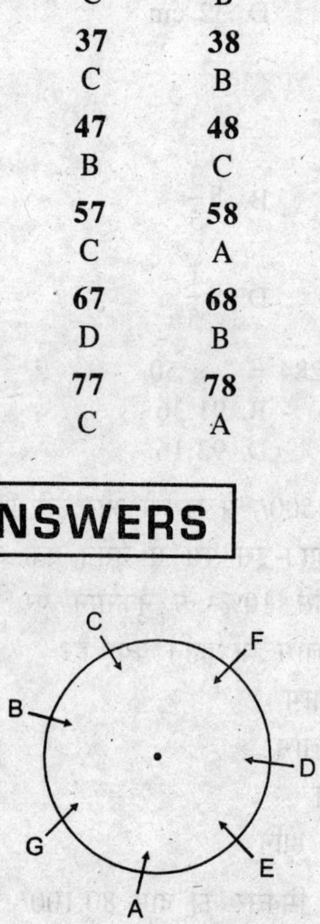

40. 'S' से शुरू निम्न सार्थक शब्द बनाये जा सकते हैं।

SINK, SKIN

41. जिस प्रकार, उसी प्रकार,

42.

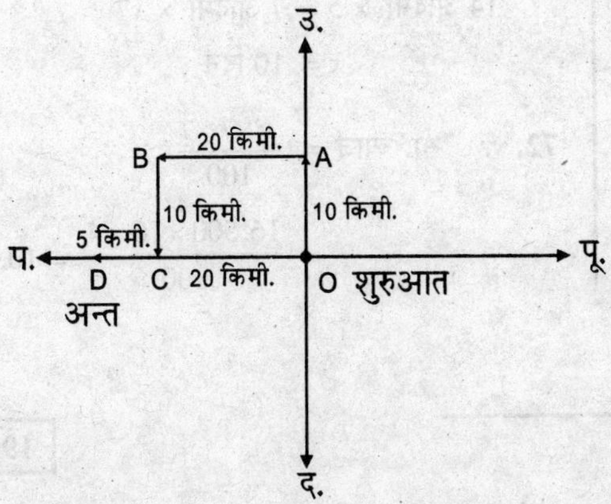

अतः शुरुआत से 25 किमी. की दूरी पर है।

43. हीरा के अतिरिक्त अन्य सभी धातुएँ हैं।

44. धूसर (Grey) के अतिरिक्त अन्य सभी इन्द्रधनुष के सात रंगों में से एक है।

45. सार्थक शब्द, EARN, NEAR

46.

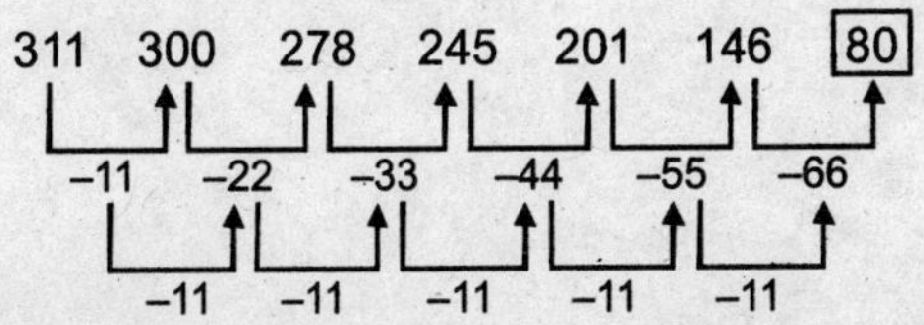

48. जिस प्रकार,

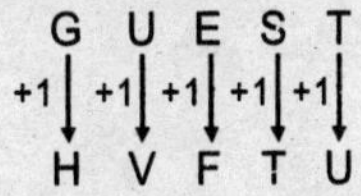

उसी प्रकार,

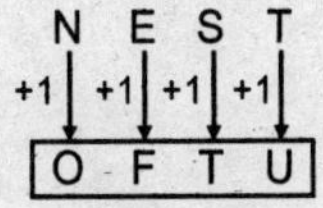

65. 258 का 13% – ?

$$\frac{13 \times 258}{100} - ? = 10$$

$$? = \frac{3354}{100} - 10$$

$$= \frac{3354 - 1000}{1000} = \frac{2354}{100}$$

$$? = 23.54$$

66. माना आयत की चौड़ाई $= x$ cm

$\therefore$ आयत की लम्बाई $= (x + 7)$ cm

$\because$ आयत की परिधि = 2 (ल. + चौ.)

$$2(x + 7 + x) = 126 \text{ cm}$$

$$2(2x + 7) = 126$$

$$4x + 14 = 126$$

$$4x = 112$$

$$x = 28 \text{ cm}$$

$\therefore$ आयत की चौड़ाई 28 cm है।

67. $$5\frac{1}{5} + 2\frac{3}{5} + 1\frac{2}{5} = \frac{26}{5} + \frac{13}{5} + \frac{7}{5}$$

$$= \frac{26 + 13 + 7}{5}$$

$$= \frac{46}{5} = 9\frac{1}{5}$$

68. $5437 - 3153 + 2284 = ? \times 50$

$$2284 + 2284 = ? \times 50$$

$$? = \frac{4568}{50}$$

$$? = 91.36$$

69. विक्रय मूल्य $= 4500\left(\frac{100 + 15}{100}\right)\left(\frac{100 - 10}{100}\right)$

$$= 4500 \times \frac{115}{100} \times \frac{90}{100}$$

$$= 4657.50$$

लाभ = वि. मूल्य – क्रय मूल्य

$= 4657.50 - 4500$

= ₹ 157.50 का लाभ

70. दिया है,

27 टोसटर + 18 मिक्सर = 80,100/-

9 से भाग करने पर,

3 टोसटर + 2 मिक्सर = 8,900/-

4 से गुणा करने पर,

12 टोसटर + 8 मिक्सर = 35,600/-

71. एक औरत का काम = $\frac{1}{2}$ (एक आदमी का काम)

$M_1 \times D_1 = M_2 \times D_2$

(10 आदमी + 8 औरत) × 5

= (4 आदमी + 6 औरत) × x

(10 आदमी + $8 \times \frac{1}{2}$ आदमी) × 5

= (4 आदमी + $6 \times \frac{1}{2}$ आदमी) × x

14 आदमी × 5 = 7 आदमी × x

x = 10 दिन

72. ∵ सा. ब्याज = $\frac{p \times r \times t}{100}$

= $\frac{16,500 \times 16 \times 4}{100}$ = 10,560/-

Previous Paper (Solved)

Himachal Pradesh Police Constable

Recruitment Exam, 2016*

1. Which is not a synonym of DISASTER?
A. Misfortune B. Calamity
C. Prosperity D. Mishap

2. Opposite of the word CONCUR is:
A. Disagree B. Disappear
C. Discourage D. Damage

Directions (Qs. No. 3-5) : *Choose the correct meaning of the idiom from the four given options A, B, C & D.*

3. To die in harness:
A. to die young in an accident
B. planned murder
C. to die while in service
D. to be taken by surprise

4. A cock and bull story:
A. Long story B. Factual story
C. True story D. A lie

5. To miss the bus:
A. to miss an opportunity
B. to miss the daily bus to work
C. to find fault with others
D. to argue without reason

Directions (Qs. No. 6-8) : *Fill in the blank with correct word.*

6. I have been living here ______ 2009.
A. from B. since
C. for D. between

7. She fell prey ______ malaria.
A. of B. for
C. into D. to

8. Rohan is good _______ mathematics.
A. in B. for
C. at D. on

9. Choose the correctly spelt word:
A. Argument B. Arguement
C. Argumant D. Arguemant

Directions (Qs. No. 10 & 11) : *Find out incorrect part of sentence.*

10. My Father (A)/ deals (B)/ with garments (C)/ No error (D).

11. Knowledge of (A)/ at least two languages (B)/ are required to pass the examination (C)/ No error (D).

12. Choose the correctly spelt word:
A. Aluminium B. Alminium
C. Elminium D. Alumenium

13. The passing on of physical or mental characteristics from one generation to another is known as:
A. Heritage B. Pedigree
C. Heredity D. Legacy

14. A person who has no money to pay his debt is called:
A. Poor B. Pauper
C. Destitute D. Insolvent

15. A doctor who treats diseases of the eye is known as:
A. Radiologist B. Ophthalmologist
C. Cardiologist D. Dermatologist

16. What will be past indefinite tense of "I play cricket":
A. I have been playing cricket
B. I played cricket.
C. I had played cricket.
D. I did not play cricket.

* *Held on 29-05-2016.*

17. विलोम शब्द छाँटिए–

उत्कर्ष

A. उपकर्ष B. ह्रास

C. पतन D. अपकर्ष

18. "आहार" शब्द का विपरीतार्थक शब्द है–

A. विहार B. साहार

C. अनाहार D. निराहार

19. "अधजल गगरी छलकत जाय" मुहावरे/लोकोक्ति का क्या अर्थ है?

A. बड़े आदमी अधिक दिखावा करते हैं

B. आधा पानी से भरा गागर

C. छोटे आदमी अधिक दिखावा करते हैं

D. गागर के साथ दिखावा करना

20. इनमें से भाववाचक संज्ञा कौन-सी है?

A. मीठा B. मिठाई

C. मिठास D. मिष्ठान

21. "बिल्ली के भागों छींका टूटा" का अर्थ है–

A. बिल्ली की उछल-कूद से नुकसान होना

B. आने वाला दुख आकर ही रहता है

C. लाभ के बजाय हानि होना

D. अचानक लाभ होना

22. शुद्ध संधि का चयन कीजिए–

आकृष्ट

A. आ + कृष्ट B. आक्र + रिष्ट

C. आकृष + त D. आकृष + ट

23. वह का बहुवचन क्या है?

A. वोह B. वह सब

C. वे D. उन

24. शुद्ध संधि का चयन कीजिए–

परीक्षक

A. पर् + वीक्षक B. परि + इक्षक

C. परि + अक्षक D. पर + इक्षक

25. शुद्ध वर्तनी का चयन कीजिए–

A. निरीक्षण B. निरिक्षण

C. नीरिक्षण D. निरीषण

26. निम्नलिखित में से स्त्रीलिंग है–

A. माली B. खत्री

C. चौधरी D. धनवती

27. "प्रलय" का विलोम क्या है?

A. विलय B. आलय

C. सृष्टि D. पुण्य

28. निम्नलिखित में से कौन-सा शब्द बिजली का पर्यायवाची नहीं है?

A. चपला B. चंचला

C. तड़ित D. ज्योत्सना

29. समानार्थी शब्द का चयन कीजिए–

कैवल्य

A. निर्वाण B. केशव

C. केवल D. दण्ड

30. "मिलन" का विलोम क्या है?

A. अमिलन B. विरह

C. मिलनी D. समिलन

31. "सारी फसल" वाक्यांश में कौन-सा विशेषण प्रयुक्त हुआ है?

A. गुणवाचक B. संख्यावाचक

C. परिमाणवाचक D. सार्वनामिक

32. "कुंजर" का पर्यायवाची है–

A. नर B. गज

C. वानर D. गिलहरी

33. पैरालिम्पिक (Paralympic) खेलों का संबंध है–

A. केवल बर्फीले और शीतकालीन खेलों से

B. विशेष रूप से शारीरिक विकलांगता वाले एथलीटों से

C. केवल किशोर एथलीटों से

D. शौकिया युवाओं से

34. राष्ट्रीय मतदाता दिवस प्रतिवर्ष ______ को मनाया जाता है।

A. 25 नवम्बर B. 25 अक्टूबर

C. 25 दिसम्बर D. 25 जनवरी

35. "कांगड़ा वधू" एक चित्रकला कृति है–

A. निकोलस रोरिक की B. सरदार शोभा सिंह की

C. अमृता शेरगिल की D. एम.एफ. हुसैन की

36. धर्मगुरु दलाई लामा को इनमें से कौन-सा पुरस्कार मिला है?

A. भारत रत्न
B. मैगसेसे पुरस्कार
C. नोबेल शान्ति पुरस्कार
D. बुकर पुरस्कार

37. Social Networking Site "FACEBOOK" का संस्थापक कौन है?

A. बिल गेट्स
B. बिल क्लिंटन
C. स्टीव जॉब्स
D. मार्क जुकरबर्ग

38. इनमें से किस देश ने क्योटो प्रोटोकॉल पर हस्ताक्षर करने से मना किया है?

A. जापान
B. चीन
C. भारत
D. अमरीका

39. नीति आयोग क्या कार्य करता है?

A. खेलकूद को प्रोत्साहन
B. अन्तर्राष्ट्रीय संबंधों को दृढ़ करना
C. राज्यों के लिए वित्त का प्रावधान एवं आर्थिक उन्नति के संसाधन जुटाना
D. आयात-निर्यात नीति तय करना

40. निम्नलिखित में से कौन संयुक्त राष्ट्र सुरक्षा परिषद का स्थायी सदस्य नहीं है?

A. भारत
B. चीन
C. रूस
D. फ्रांस

41. भारतीय उच्च अध्ययन संस्थान पूर्व में ______ नाम से जाना जाता था।

A. वाइस रीगल लॉज
B. बोनी मून
C. वाइल्ड पलावर हाल
D. ऑकलैंड हाउस

42. खिलाड़ी जीव मिल्खा सिंह किस खेल से जुड़े हैं?

A. एथलेटिक्स
B. गोल्फ
C. हॉकी
D. फुटबॉल

43. CNG क्या है?

A. Conduced Natural Gas
B. Converted Natural Gas
C. Compressed Natural Gas
D. Common Natural Gas

44. चन्द्रताल झील किस जिले में स्थित है?

A. किन्नौर
B. लाहौल एवं स्पीति
C. कुल्लू
D. मण्डी

45. भारत की प्रथम महिला जिमनास्ट जिसने ओलम्पिक खेलों के लिए क्वालिफाई किया है–

A. पी.टी. ऊषा
B. साइना नेहवाल
C. दीपा करमाकर
D. दीपिका सालगांवकर

46. रोरिक आर्ट गैलरी कहाँ स्थित है?

A. नग्गर
B. सोलन
C. राजबन
D. गुलेर

47. राम श्याम से छोटा है, लेकिन गौतम से बड़ा है। गोविन्द मोहन से बड़ा है, लेकिन गौतम से छोटा है। यदि महेश इन सबसे बड़ा हो तो बताइए सबसे छोटा कौन है?

A. राम
B. गौतम
C. मोहन
D. गोविन्द

48. पंचतंत्र के लेखक कौन हैं?

A. विष्णु शर्मा
B. कर्नल रंजीत
C. वी.के. शर्मा
D. मुंशी प्रेमचंद

49. श्रेणी को पूर्ण करें–

7, 10, 8, 11, 9, 12, ?

A. 11
B. 7
C. 10
D. 13

50. गणितीय चिह्न $\propto$ का अर्थ है–

A. अनन्त संख्या
B. इससे गुणित किया गया
C. इसके आनुपातिक
D. इसके सर्वसम समान

51. इनमें से विषक को चुनें–

A. केला
B. सेब
C. गाजर
D. संतरा

52. दी गई श्रेणी का लुप्त पद ज्ञात कीजिए–

AQ, DR, GS, ______, MU, PV

A. HT
B. IT
C. TJ
D. JT

53. दिए गए विकल्पों में से एक सही उत्तर का चयन कीजिए जो निम्न श्रेणी को पूरा करे–

EMS, DLR, CKQ, ______ AIO

A. KBP
B. CBP
C. BJP
D. PIB

54. वायुमण्डल : वायुयान : समुद्र : ?
A. किनारा
B. पनडुब्बी
C. जहाज
D. किश्ती

55. रवि पूर्व दिशा में 15 कि.मी. गया तब वह बाएँ मुड़कर 5 कि.मी. चला। फिर वह बाएँ मुड़कर 15 कि.मी. चला। तो बताइए वह प्रारंभिक स्थान से कितनी दूर है?
A. 30 कि.मी. B. 6 कि.मी.
C. 35 कि.मी. D. 15 कि.मी.

56. एक पिक्चर हाल में चार सीटें खाली हैं। इन चारों सीटों पर चार महिलाओं को कितनी तरह से बैठाया जा सकता है?
A. 16 B. 20
C. 24 D. 28

57. नीचे दिए गए शब्दों को तर्कसंगत एवं अर्थयुक्त क्रम से क्रमबद्ध करें, फिर उसके नीचे दिए गए विकल्प से सही विकल्प चुनें।
1. दही
2. घास
3. मक्खन
4. दूध
5. गाय
A. 5, 2, 4, 1, 3 B. 5, 2, 3, 4, 1
C. 4, 2, 5, 3, 1 D. 2, 5, 4, 3, 1

58. यदि किसी भाषा में RACE = 4793. FACT = 1795, FORCE = 16493 लिखा जाता है तो उसी भाषा में REACT को क्या लिखा जाएगा?
A. 43759 B. 43975
C. 43795 D. 59734

59. दिए गए शब्दों को शब्दकोष (Dictionary) में उनके क्रम के अनुसार क्रमबद्ध करें फिर निम्नलिखित में से क्रम चुनें।
1. Wound
2. Writer
3. White
4. Worst
5. Worked
A. 5, 3, 2, 1, 4 B. 1, 4, 3, 5, 2
C. 3, 2, 5, 4, 1 D. 2, 1, 3, 4, 5

60. राहुल का स्थान अपनी कक्षा में ऊपर से 9वाँ है तथा नीचे से 38वाँ है। उसकी कक्षा में कुल कितने छात्र हैं?
A. 45 B. 46
C. 47 D. 48

61. यदि आज 24 जनवरी, 1994 को दिन सोमवार है तो 24 जनवरी, 1995 को कौन-सा दिन होगा?
A. सोमवार B. मंगलवार
C. बुधवार D. रविवार

62. कोल डैम परियोजना किस संगठन से संबंधित है?
A. NHPC B. NTPC
C. J.P. HYDRO D. HCC

63. दिए गए वैकल्पिक शब्दों में से उस शब्द को चुनिए जो नीचे दिए गए शब्द के अक्षरों से नहीं बनाया जा सकता है–

LEGISLATURE
A. Salute B. Gesture
C. Serial D. Slaughter

64. एड्स रोग के द्वारा कौन-सा तंत्र प्रभावित होता है?
A. पाचन तंत्र
B. श्वसन तंत्र
C. केन्द्रीय तंत्रिका तंत्र
D. प्रतिरक्षा तंत्र

65. खाने के सोडे का रासायनिक सूत्र है–
A. NaCL B. $NaHCO_3$
C. NaOH D. KNO_3

66. यदि किसी घर के मूल्य के 2/7 हिस्से की कीमत ₹ 28000 है तो पूरे घर की कीमत क्या होगी?
A. ₹ 9,60,000 B. ₹ 9,70,000
C. ₹ 9,80,000 D. इनमें से कोई नहीं

67. नेत्रदान में नेत्र का कौन-सा हिस्सा दान दिया जाता है?
A. कॉर्निया B. लेन्स
C. रेटिना D. पूरा नेत्र

68. गुर्दों का मुख्य कार्य क्या है?
A. रक्तचाप को नियंत्रण में रखना
B. शरीर के तापमान का नियंत्रण
C. शरीर से बेकार चीजों (Waste Products) को बाहर करना
D. भोजन के पाचन में सहायता करना

69. निम्नलिखित में से किसे मास्टर ग्रंथि के नाम से जाना जाता है?

A. पियूष ग्रंथि B. अवटू ग्रंथि
C. जनन ग्रंथि D. अधिवृक्क ग्रंथि

70. एक बैग का अंकित मूल्य ₹ 80 है परन्तु इसे ₹ 68 में बेचा जाता है। इस बैग पर कितने प्रतिशत डिस्काउंट दिया जा रहा है?

A. 12% B. 15%
C. $17\frac{11}{17}\%$ D. 20%

71. इनमें से कौन-सा रासायनिक परिवर्तन है?

A. नाई द्वारा बाल काटना
B. ब्लीचिंग पाउडर का पानी में घुलना
C. रेशमी कीड़ों द्वारा शहतूत के पत्तों को रेशम में परिवर्तित करना
D. ऊन का धागा बनाना

72. URL से तात्पर्य है?

A. Uniform Resource Locator
B. Uniform Research Link
C. Uniform Resource Link
D. Unified Registered Link

73. $1\frac{3}{4}+5\frac{1}{3}+3\frac{2}{5}=?$

A. $9\frac{2}{5}$ B. $9\frac{29}{60}$
C. $10\frac{2}{5}$ D. $10\frac{29}{60}$

74. Hepatitis किसका प्रदाह (Inflammation) है?

A. उदर B. गुर्दे
C. फेफड़े D. लिवर

75. रक्त कोशिका का कौन-सा भाग प्रतिरक्षण (Immunity) प्रदान करता है?

A. RBC B. WBC
C. PLATELET D. रक्त प्लाज्मा

76. $54 \div 66 \div 33 = ?$

A. 27 B. 37
C. 47 D. 57

77. पृथ्वी के वायुमंडल का मुख्य घटक क्या है?

A. नाइट्रोजन
B. ऑक्सीजन
C. कार्बन डाइऑक्साइड
D. हाइड्रोजन

78. यदि A : B = 2 : 3 तथा B : C = 4 : 5 है, तब C : A क्या होगा?

A. 15 : 8 B. 12 : 10
C. 8 : 5 D. 8 : 15

79. प्रकाश वर्ष निम्नलिखित में किसका मात्रक है?

A. विद्युत धारा
B. ज्योति तीव्रता
C. दूरी
D. ताप

80. यदि 18 : X = X : 8 हो, तो X = ?

A. 144 B. 72
C. 26 D. 12

उत्तरमाला

1	2	3	4	5	6	7	8	9	10
C	A	C	D	A	B	D	C	A	C
11	**12**	**13**	**14**	**15**	**16**	**17**	**18**	**19**	**20**
C	A	C	D	B	B	D	D	C	C
21	**22**	**23**	**24**	**25**	**26**	**27**	**28**	**29**	**30**
D	D	C	D	A	D	C	D	A	B
31	**32**	**33**	**34**	**35**	**36**	**37**	**38**	**39**	**40**
C	B	B	D	B	C	D	D	C	A

41	42	43	44	45	46	47	48	49	50
A	B	C	B	C	A	C	A	C	C
51	**52**	**53**	**54**	**55**	**56**	**57**	**58**	**59**	**60**
C	D	C	C	B	C	A	C	C	B
61	**62**	**63**	**64**	**65**	**66**	**67**	**68**	**69**	**70**
B	B	D	D	B	C	A	C	A	B
71	**72**	**73**	**74**	**75**	**76**	**77**	**78**	**79**	**80**
B	A	D	D	B	A	A	A	C	D

व्याख्यात्मक उत्तर

39. नीति आयोग (राष्ट्रीय भारत परिवर्तन संस्थान्) भारत सरकार द्वारा योजना आयोग के स्थान पर गठित एक नया संस्थान है। इसका गठन 1 जनवरी, 2015 में किया गया। नीति आयोग का उद्देश्य ऐसे दृढ़ राज्यों का निर्माण करना है जो आपस में एकजुट होकर एक सुदृढ़ भारत का निर्माण करे। राष्ट्रीय उद्देश्यों को दृष्टिगत रखते हुए राज्यों की सक्रिय भागीदारी के साथ राष्ट्रीय विकास प्राथमिकताओं, क्षेत्रों और रणनीतियों का एक साझा दृष्टिकोण विकसित करना है। नीति आयोग का विजन बल प्रदान करने के लिए प्रधानमंत्री और मुख्यमंत्रियों को 'राष्ट्रीय एजेंडा' का प्रारूप उपलब्ध कराना है। भारत के प्रधानमंत्री इस आयोग के अध्यक्ष होते हैं। साथ ही गवर्निंग काउंसिल में राज्यों के मुख्यमंत्री और केन्द्रशासित प्रदेशों के उपराज्यपाल शामिल होते हैं।

47. महेश ← श्याम ← राम ← गौतम ← गोविन्द ← मोहन

अतः मोहन सबसे छोटा है।

48. 'पंचतंत्र' के लेखक विष्णु शर्मा हैं। संस्कृत भाषा में लिखित 'पंचतंत्र का नीति-कथाओं में प्रथम स्थान माना जाता है। यद्यपि यह पुस्तक मूल रूप में नहीं है फिर भी इसकी रचना तीसरी शताब्दी ईसा पूर्व निर्धारित की गई है। पंचतंत्र में पाँच तंत्र या विभाग है। विभाग को तंत्र इसलिए कहा गया है क्योंकि नैतिकतापूर्ण शासन की विधियाँ बतायी गई है। ये तंत्र हैं–

1. मित्रभेद
2. मित्रलाभ
3. काकोलुकीयम्
4. लब्धप्रणाश
5. अपरीक्षित कारक

49.

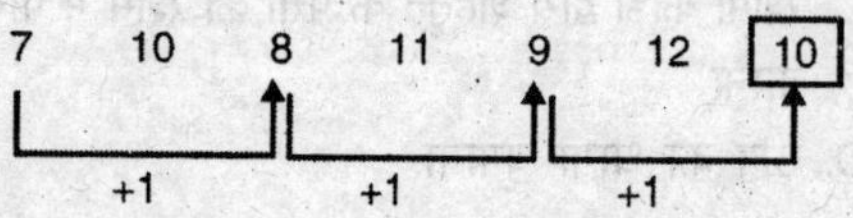

अतः प्रश्नचिह्न के स्थान पर 10 होगा।

50. गणितीय चिह्न ∝ का अर्थ है इसके आनुपातिक।

51. केला, सेब, संतरा फल हैं जबकि गाजर सब्जी।

अतः गाजर विषम है।

52.

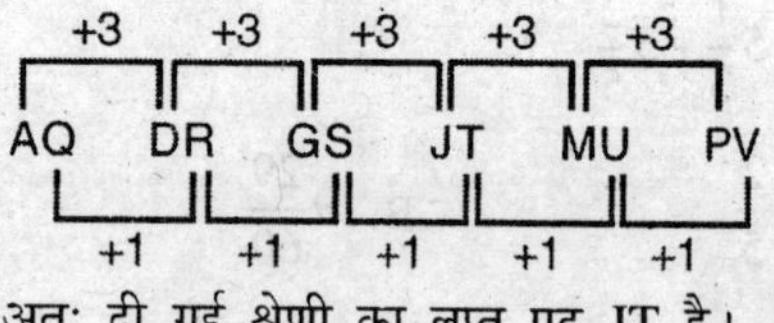

अतः दी गई श्रेणी का लुप्त पद JT है।

53.

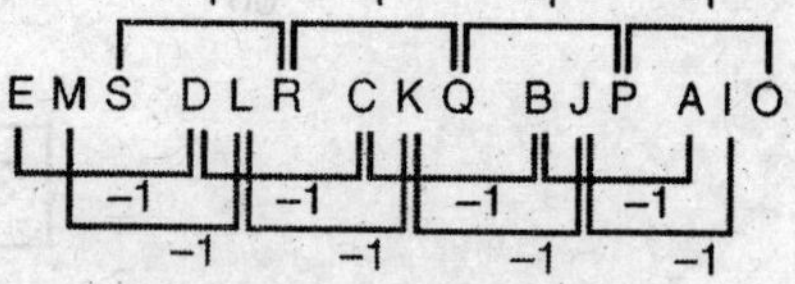

अतः रिक्त स्थान पर BJP होगा।

55.

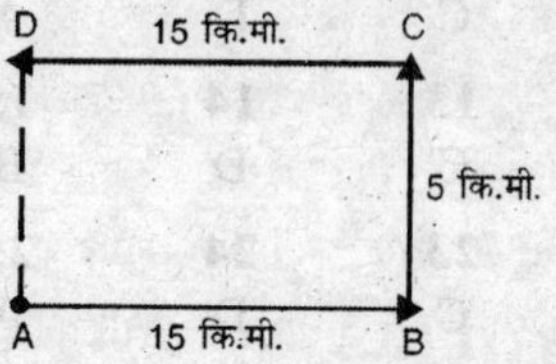

∴ AD = 5 कि.मी.

अतः रवि प्रारम्भिक स्थान से 5 किमी. दूर है।

56. बैठाने के तरीकों की संख्या = $^4P_4$

$$= \frac{4!}{\lfloor 4-4}$$

$$= \frac{4\times3\times2\times1}{\lfloor 0}$$

$$= \frac{4\times3\times2\times1}{1} = 24.$$

57.

गाय	घास	दूध	दही	मक्खन
↓	↓	↓	↓	↓
5	2	4	1	3

अतः सही विकल्प (A) है।

58. दिया गया है :

R A C E   F A C T   F O R C E
↓ ↓ ↓ ↓   ↓ ↓ ↓ ↓   ↓ ↓ ↓ ↓ ↓
4 7 9 3   1 7 9 5   1 6 4 9 3

इसी प्रकार,

R E A C T
↓ ↓ ↓ ↓ ↓
4 3 7 9 5

अतः उसी भाषा में REACT को 43795 लिखा जाएगा।

60. कक्षा में कुल छात्रों की संख्या

$$= (38 + 9) - 1$$
$$= 47 - 1 = 46$$

अतः कुल छात्रों की संख्या 46 है।

64. एड्स (AIDS) : इस रोग का विषाणु एच.आई.वी. (HIV) है जिसका पूरा नाम 'एक्वायर्ड इम्यूनो डिफिसिएन्सी सिन्ड्रोम' (Acquired Immuno Deficiency Syndrome) है। यह रोग प्रतिरक्षा तंत्र को प्रभावित करता है। यह रोग यौन सम्बन्धों के कारण, रक्तधान में अनियमितता से और नशीले पदार्थों के अत्यधिक सेवन करने से फैलता है। इस रोग से ग्रसित रोगी की रोग प्रतिरोधक क्षमता समाप्त हो जाती है। रोगी का शरीर जगह-जगह फूल जाता है, खून का संचार अव्यवस्थित हो जाता है और अंततः रोगी की मृत्यु हो जाती है।

65. सोडियम बाइकार्बोनेट (Sodium Bicarbonate) : सोडियम बाइकार्बोनेट का दूसरा नाम बेकिंग सोडा (Baking Soda) है। सोडियम बाइकार्बोनेट ($NaHCO_3$) को खाने वाला सोडा भी कहते हैं। आटा में खाने वाला सोडा मिलाने पर रोटी अच्छी तरह फूलती है, क्योंकि इस दौरान कार्बन डाइऑक्साइड गैस (CO_2) निकलती है। सोडियम बाइकार्बोनेट का उपयोग औषधि के रूप में, पेट की अम्लता (Acidity) दूर करने में, बेकिंग पाउडर (Baking Powder) बनाने में तथा अग्निशामक यंत्रों में होता है।

66. x का $\frac{2}{7}$ = ₹ 28000

$\Rightarrow$ $2x$ = ₹ 7 × 28000

$\Rightarrow$ x = ₹ $\frac{7\times28000}{2}$

= ₹ 7 × 14000

= ₹ 98000.

67. नेत्र गोलक एक प्रकार के द्रव से भरी एक गोलाकार रचना है, जिसका अगला भाग आगे की ओर उभरा एवं पारदर्शक होता है। इस भाग को कॉर्निया (Cornea) कहते हैं। नेत्र-दान में इसी भाग को दान किया जाता है। नेत्र पलकों (Eye lids) का भीतरी स्तर कॉर्निया के ऊपर एक पतला पारदर्शक आवरण या झिल्ली बना देता है, जिसे कंजक्टाइवा (Conjuctiva) कहते हैं।

68. वृक्क (Kidney) : मनुष्य एवं अन्य स्तनधारियों में मुख्य उत्सर्जी अंग एक जोड़ा वृक्क होता है, जो रुधिर-परिसंचरण से बेकार चीजों को हटाने, साथ ही साथ रुधिर में लाभदायक तत्वों को बनाए रखने के लिए भली-भाँति अनुकूलित होते हैं। वृक्क सेम के बीज के आकार के होते हैं। उदरगुहा में पीठ की ओर कमर के क्षेत्र में, कशेरुक दंड के दोनों ओर एक-एक वृक्क स्थित होते हैं। इसके चारों ओर पेरिटोनियम (Peritoneum) नामक झिल्ली पायी जाती है।

69. पीयूष ग्रंथि (Pituitary Gland) : यह कपाल की स्फेनाइड (Sphenoid) हड्डी में एक गड्ढे में स्थित होती है। इसको सेलाटर्सिका (Sellaturcica) कहते हैं। इसका भार लगभग 0.6 gm होता है। इसे मास्टर ग्रंथि (Master Gland) के रूप में भी जाना जाता है।

74. हिपैटाइटिस या पीलिया या जॉन्डिस (Jaundice) : यह एक यकृत रोग है, जिसमें रक्त में पित्त वर्णक (Bile Pigment) अधिक मात्रा में चला आता है। इसमें यकृत में पित्त वर्णक का निर्माण अधिक मात्रा में होने लगता है, परन्तु यकृत की कोशिकाएँ इसका उत्सर्जन निम्न मात्रा में करती हैं। फलतः पित्त वर्णक यकृत-शिरा के माध्यम से रक्त में प्रवेश कर जाता है। पेशाब भी पीला हो जाता है। खून में पित्त (Bile) बढ़ जाता है।

70. अंकित मूल्य = ₹ 80

विक्रय मूल्य = ₹ 68

छूट = 80 – 68 = ₹ 12

$$\text{प्रतिशत छूट} = \frac{12}{80}\times 100$$

$$= 15\%.$$

73.

$$\frac{7}{4}+\frac{16}{3}+\frac{17}{5} = \frac{105+320+204}{60}$$

$$= \frac{629}{60} = 10\frac{29}{60}.$$

76.

$$\frac{54}{\left(\frac{66}{33}\right)} = \frac{54\times 33}{66}$$

$$= \frac{27\times 33}{33} = 27.$$

78. $\because$ $\frac{A}{B} = \frac{2}{3}$

$\Rightarrow$ $3A = 2B$

$\therefore$ $A = \frac{2}{3}B$

पुनः $\frac{B}{C} = \frac{4}{5}$

$\Rightarrow$ $4C = 5B$

$$C = \frac{5B}{4}$$

अब

$$\frac{C}{A} = \frac{\frac{5B}{4}}{\frac{2B}{3}} = \frac{5B}{4}\times\frac{3}{2B}$$

$$= \frac{15}{8}$$

अतः C : A = 15 : 8 होगा।

80. $\because$ $\frac{18}{x} = \frac{x}{8}$

$\Rightarrow$ $x^2 = 18 \times 8$

$= 144$

$\Rightarrow$ $x = \sqrt{144} = 12$

अतः x का मान 12 होगा।

Previous Paper (Solved)

Himachal Pradesh Police Constable Recruitment Exam, 2015*

1. नूतन का विलोम क्या है?

A. अनूतन B. पुराना

C. पुरातन D. पुरातत्व

2. 'जो बहुत बोलता है', के लिए एक शब्द क्या होगा?

A. बड़बोला B. आचाल

C. वक्ता D. वाचाल

3. चतुर की भावनात्मक संज्ञा क्या है?

A. चतुराई B. चालाक

C. चतुर्थ D. तेज

4. निम्नलिखित मुहावरे में रिक्त स्थान पर क्या आएगा? बहती गंगा में .... धोना।

A. पैर B. कपड़े

C. हाथ D. सिर

5. निम्नलिखित में कौन-सा मुहावरा नहीं है?

A. नाक काटना B. नाक रख लेना

C. नाक रगड़ना D. नाक साफ करना

6. 'कान भरना' मुहावरे का क्या अर्थ है?

A. धोखा देना B. चाणक होना

C. चुगली करना D. असर न होना

7. With which game Vijay Kumar is associated with?

A. Swimming B. Shooting

C. Archery D. Volleyball

8. Patliputra is the name of which old city?

A. Allahabad B. Varanasi

C. Patna D. Kolkata

9. Sattellite station is located at?

A. Sri Hari Kota

B. Sholapur

C. Vishakhapattnam

D. Wargal

10. Which is correct?

A. I take tea every morning.

B. tea take every morning.

C. Tea is taken by me every morning.

D. A and C

11. Which one of them is correct?

A. The examination had been passed by her.

B. Her pass the exam.

C. She exam the pass.

D. Exam her pass.

12. Change the sentence – "He does his duty" to a negative one by ticking the correct options:

A. Duty not him

B. Duty not done

C. He cannot his duty

D. He does not do his duty.

13. What will be future indefinite tense of— I know him?

A. I know him.

B. I known him.

C. I shall have known him.

D. I will know him

14. "How dare you .... my cupboard?"

A. to open B. open

C. opening D. opened

15. विद्यालय का सही संधि विच्छेद क्या है?

A. विद्य + आलय

B. विद्या + आलय

C. विद्या + लय

D. इनमें से कोई नहीं

* Held on 21-06-2015 (Based on Memory)

16. The arithmetic mean of 2, 4, 6, 8, 10 is:
A. 4 B. 6
C. 5 D. 3

17. Who is capital of Goa?
A. Panaji B. Shillong
C. Aizawl D. Dispur

18. What is the probability of getting one head tossed a coin ?
A. 0 B. 1
C. 1/2 D. 1/3

19. If the height of the tower and length of its shadow is equal, then final the angle of elevation of the sun.
A. 30° B. 60°
C. 90° D. 45°

20. The rate of photosynthesis is maximum in:
A. Red light B. Green light
C. Violet light D. White light

21. Curd is made by the phenomen of ....
A. fast reaction
B. slow reaction
C. cogulating
D. fermentation

22. What is the Nearest point of clear vision from normal human eye?
A. 20 cm B. 25 cm
C. 10 cm D. 30 cm

23. रात को अचानक आँगन में ढक-ढक की आवाज सुनकर ....।
A. मेरे रोंगटे खड़े हो गए
B. रोंगटे खड़े हो गए मेरे
C. खड़े हो गए मेरे रोंगटे
D. मेरे खड़े हो गए रोंगटे

24. निम्न शब्दों में कौन भिन्न है?
A. यश B. कीर्ति
C. निष्ठा D. गौरव

25. Combine the two sentences using in spite of— "he failed. He did not lose heart".
A. He did not lose heart in spite of he failed.
B. In spite of having failed, he did not lose heart.
C. He failed in spite of he losing heart.
D. He failed in spite of the lost heart.

26. The plural of mouse is:
A. Mouses B. Messes
C. Mice D. Mices

27. The feminine for gentleman is:
A. Woman B. Madam
C. Lady D. Simple

28. She .... me to walk straight.
A. tell B. speak
C. told D. Telled

29. 'to hang one's boots' means':
A. To clean one's shoes
B. To hang them to dry
C. To retire from work
D. To change one's shoes

30. The synonym for kind is:
A. Benevolent B. Loving
C. Affectionate D. patient

31. In the field some Swans and Goats. If the number of heads be 77 and the number of feet equals 224. Then find the number of Swans.
A. 42 B. 30
C. 32 D. 47

32. Rahul travels 1 km in 4 hrs. He takes rest for 20 minutes after every km. What time will take for covering 3.5 km?
A. 14 B. 13
C. 15 D. 12

33. When did Constitution of India come into force?
A. 15 August, 1947
B. 26 January, 1947
C. 15 August, 1950
D. 26 January, 1950

34. Before 1947, Shimla was the Capital of?

A. Undivided Punjab
B. Undivided India
C. North India region
D. Hill State

35. What was the name of the first chief Minister of Himachal Pradesh?

A. Sri Veerbhadra Singh
B. Sri Ram Lal
C. Sri Yashvant Singh Parmar
D. Sri Preem Kumar Dhumal

36. Who composed Ram Charit Manas?

A. Valmiki
B. Tulsidas
C. Sant Ravidas
D. Swami Vivekananda

37. Which city is not situated on the bank of Gangas?

A. Allahabad B. Haridwar
C. Mathura D. Banaras

38. Red Delicious is a type of ......

A. Apple B. Guava
C. Mango D. Papaya

39. First Indian who got gold medal in Olympics is:

A. Saina Nehwal
B. Abhinav Bindra
C. Sushil Kumar
D. Rajyavardhan Rathore

40. Who said, "Swaraj is my birth right"?

A. Lala Lajpat Rai
B. Bal Gangadhar Tilak
C. Bipin Chandra Pal
D. Subhash Chandra Bose

41. Where is the headquarters of SAARC?

A. New Delhi B. Colombo
C. Kathmandu D. Lahore

42. How many languages are affiliated in Indian Constitution?

A. 15 B. 20
C. 22 D. 28

43. What is meant for KYC?

A. Know your company
B. Know your customer
C. Know your facts
D. None of these

44. Who is the Speaker of Himachal Vidhan Sabha?

A. Raja Veerbhadra Singh
B. Sri Kaul Singh
C. Sri Braj Bihari Lal Butal
D. Sri G.S. Wali

45. Which number will come in place of question mark (?)?

7::49; 6::36; 4::16; 9::?

A. 47 B. 64
C. 81 D. 121

46. What is measured by RICHTER SCALE?

A. Density of Milk
B. Temperature
C. River flow
D. Intensity of Earthquake

47. What is the full form of IPL?

A. Indian Policy League
B. Indian Premier League
C. International Police League
D. India Police Labour

48. Who is the Health Minister of India?

A. Jagat Prakash Nadda
B. Rajeev Pratap Rudi
C. Gulam Nabi Azad
D. Smriti Irani

49. What is the full form of BCCI?

A. Board of Custom Control of India
B. Board of Common Wealth Countries of India
C. Board of Control for Cricket in India
D. Board for Control of Cricket in India

50. Some friends decided to go on a picnic cost ₹ 96. But out of them 4 did not go. At the result they have to pay ₹ 4 more each. Find the number of people to go on picnic.

A. 8 B. 16

C. 12 D. 24

51. Which instrument is associated with Amjad Ali Khan?

A. Violin B. Sarod

C. Veena D. Shehnai

52. Make meaningful order :

(a) Mobile (b) Network

(c) Number (d) Talking

A. (b) (c) (d) (a) B. (d) (a) (b) (c)

C. (a) (c) (b) (d) D. (b) (a) (d) (c)

53. Make meaningful order :

(a) Suit (b) Quarrel

(c) Court (d) Justice

A. (a) (d) (b) (c) B. (b) (c) (d) (a)

C. (a) (b) (c) (d) D. (b) (a) (c) (d)

54. Three traffic lights flashes after 10, 15 and 20 minutes respectively. All together they flash at 6.10 AM. After then, when they will flash together?

A. 7:00 AM B. 7:20 AM

C. 7:30 AM D. 7:10 AM

55. A is the sister of B, B is the brother of C and D is father of C. Then, what is the relation of A with D?

A. Mother B. Daughter

C. Son D. Uncle

56. If A = 2, M = 26 and Z = 52, then BET = ?

A. 44 B. 54

C. 64 D. 72

57. If CENTRAL is coded as ABCDEFG and PLANETARIUM is coded as HGFCBDFEIJK. Then what is the code of LANTERN?

A. GFCDFEG B. GFCDBEC

C. GFCDEFG D. GFCDBEB

58. Who invented Telephone?

A. Addison

B. Graham Bell

C. Marconi

D. J.L. Baird

59. What does RAM stand for?

A. Read and Memories

B. Rapid and Memories

C. Random Access Memory

D. Running Access Memory

60. Which is the largest-district (in term of area) of Himachal Pradesh?

A. Kangara B. Shimla

C. Lahol-Spiti D. Mandi

61. Cost of 3 chairs and 2 tables is ₹ 700, while cost of 5 chairs and 3 tables is ₹ 1100. Find the cost of 2 chairs and 2 tables.

A. ₹ 300 B. ₹ 50

C. ₹ 450 D. ₹ 500

62. Some rupees were divided between two persons A and B in the ratio of 4 : 5. A got ₹ 5 less than B. Find the total money.

A. 45 B. 600

C. 90 D. 250

63. Add the following

7.007, 70.7 and 7.007:

A. 84.074 B. 84.714

C. 84.741 D. 80.714

64. A shopkeeper sold an article ₹ 6.750 at the discount of 10%. If he did not give discount, he get 50% profit. Find his gain percent.

A. 36 B. 40

C. 35 D. 41

65. In a bag 5 red ball, 8 blue ball, 4 green ball and 7 black ball. One ball is dranwn, find the probability to not get green ball.

A. 5/6 B. 1/4

C. 1/6 D. 7/4

66. 'ईश्वर को नहीं मानने वाला' के लिए एक शब्द होगा–

A. आस्तिक B. अधर्मवान

C. बंदा D. नास्तिक

67. चकित का समानार्थक शब्द निम्न में से कौन नहीं है?

A. हैरान B. उदासीन

C. विस्मित D. भौंचक्का

68. लखन उतर आहुति सरिन भृगवर कोपु कृसानु।
बढ़त देखि जलसन्न बयनबोले राधुकुल भानु।।

उपरोक्त काव्यांश में कोपु और कृसानु का क्या अर्थ है?

A. क्रोध, आग

B. समान, कडना

C. दीवार, दर्पण

D. बहुत अधिक, उमडना

69. In theif is spotted by a policeman from a distance of 500 metres. When the policeman starts the chase, the thief also starts running. If the speed of the thief be 6 km/hr and that of the police man 8 km/hr, how for the thief will have run before he is over taken?

A. 3 km B. 4 km

C. 2 km D. 1 km

70. Shyam bought 20 dozen toys at the cost of ₹ 375 per dozen. He sold each toy at the cost of ₹ 33. Find profit per cent.

A. 3.5 B. 4.5

C. 5.6 D. 6.5

71. What will come in the next term:

9, 11, 33, 13, 15, 33, 17, ...

A. 19, 33 B. 33, 35

C. 33, 19 D. 15, 33

72. 'वीथि' शब्द का अर्थ क्या है?

A. सूर्य B. किरण

C. गली D. रास्ता

73. मेरी कमीज में ढ़ाई मीटर कपड़ा है। वाक्य में विशेषण है :

A. मेरी B. ढ़ाई मीटर

C. कपड़ा D. लगता है

74. बालकों ने अखबार पढ़ा और .... ने पत्रिका। रेखांकित शब्द के विपरीत लिंग वाले शब्द से वाक्य पूरा कीजिए :

A. बालिकाओं B. अध्यापिका

C. विदुषी D. नर्तकी

75. राष्ट्र की भाववाचक संज्ञा है :

A. राष्ट्र B. राष्ट्रीय

C. सौराष्ट्र D. राष्ट्रीयता

76. देश की सरहदों पर डटे सुरक्षा कर्मी कफन सिर पर बाँधकर लड़ते हैं। वाक्य के रेखांकित अंश का अर्थ है :

A. मरने को तैयार रहना

B. कठिनाइयों का सामना करना

C. डटकर मुकाबला करना

D. इनमें से कोई नहीं

77. When he was young he .... cross the river.

A. can B. could

C. may D. shall

78. He will not leave the place .... I come back.

A. until B. because

C. as D. on

79. (*a*) study / (*b*) is / (*c*) chemicals / (*d*) chemistry / (*e*) the / (*f*) of.

A. abcdefgh B. bcdefa

C. dbeafc D. none

80. (*a*) basic / (*b*) elements / (*c*) hundred / (*d*) gold / (*e*) there / (*f*) are / (*g*) such as / (*h*) oxygen and.

A. abcdefgh B. fedcbahg

C. efcabghd D. none

ANSWERS

1	**2**	**3**	**4**	**5**	**6**	**7**	**8**	**9**	**10**
C	D	A	C	D	C	B	C	A	D
11	**12**	**13**	**14**	**15**	**16**	**17**	**18**	**19**	**20**
A	D	D	A	B	B	A	C	D	B
21	**22**	**23**	**24**	**25**	**26**	**27**	**28**	**29**	**30**
B	B	A	C	B	C	C	C	C	A
31	**32**	**33**	**34**	**35**	**36**	**37**	**38**	**39**	**40**
A	C	D	D	C	B	C	A	B	B
41	**42**	**43**	**44**	**45**	**46**	**47**	**48**	**49**	**50**
C	C	B	C	C	D	B	A	C	A
51	**52**	**53**	**54**	**55**	**56**	**57**	**58**	**59**	**60**
B	C	D	D	B	B	B	B	C	C
61	**62**	**63**	**64**	**65**	**66**	**67**	**68**	**69**	**70**
B	A	B	C	A	D	B	A	C	C
71	**72**	**73**	**74**	**75**	**76**	**77**	**78**	**79**	**80**
A	B	B	A	D	A	B	A	C	C

SOME SELECTED EXPLANATORY ANSWERS

16. $$\text{Average} = \frac{2+4+6+8+10}{5}$$

$$= \frac{30}{5} = 6$$

18. $P(\text{head}) = \dfrac{1}{2}$

$$\text{Required probability} = \frac{1}{2}$$

19.

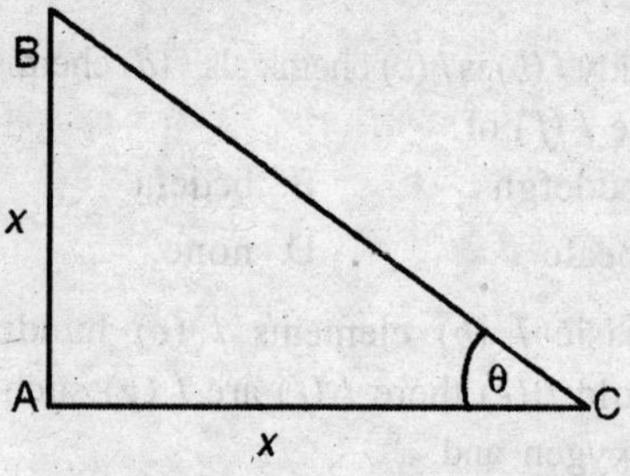

$$\tan\theta = \frac{x}{x} = 1 = \tan 45°$$

$$\Rightarrow \quad \theta = 45°$$

31.
$$x + y = 77 \quad \text{... (i)]} \times 2$$
$$2x + 4y = 224 \quad \text{... (ii)]} \times 1$$
$$2x + 2y = 154$$
$$2x + 4y = 224$$
$$- \quad - \quad -$$
$$2y = 70$$
$$\Rightarrow \quad y = 35$$
$$x = 77 - 35 = 42$$

Hence, the number of Swans = 42

45. 9 : : 81

Hence, 81 will come at the place of question mark.

50. According to the question,

$$\frac{96}{x-4} = \frac{96}{x} + 4$$

$$\Rightarrow \quad \frac{96}{x-4} = \frac{96+4x}{x}$$

$\Rightarrow \quad 96x = (x - 4)(96 + 4x)$

$\Rightarrow \quad 96x = 96x + 4x^2 - 384 + 16x$

$\Rightarrow \quad 4x^2 - 16x - 384 = 0$

$\Rightarrow \quad x^2 - 4x - 96 = 0$

$\Rightarrow \quad x^2 - 12x + 8x - 96 = 0$

$\Rightarrow \quad x(x - 12) + 8(x - 12) = 0$

$\Rightarrow \quad (x - 12)(x + 8) = 0$

$\Rightarrow \quad x = -12 \text{ or } x = -8$

$\therefore \quad 12 - 4 = 8$

Hence no. of students who attained the picnic = 8.

54. L.C.M. of 10, 15 and 20 = 60 minutes.
Hence, they will ring 7:10 am together.

61. $3x + 2y = 700$ ...(i)] × 3

$5x + 3y = 1100$ ...(ii)] × 2

$9x + 6y = 2100$ ...(iii)

$10x + 6y = 2200$ ...(iv)

Subtract (iii) from (iv)

$x = 100$

$3(100) + 2y = 700$

$\Rightarrow \quad 2y = 400$

$\Rightarrow \quad y = 200$

$\therefore \quad 2x + 2y = 2(100) + 2(200)$

$= 200 + 400 = 600$

$\therefore$ Cost of 2 chairs and 2 tables
= ₹ 600.

62. Let A = ₹ $4x$ and B = ₹ $5x$
According to the question,

$4x + 5 = 5x$

$\Rightarrow \quad x = 5$

Total money $= 4 \times 5 + 5 \times 5$

$= 20 + 25 =$ ₹ 45

63.
```
  7.007
 70.7
  7.007
 ------
 84.714
```

65. $P(\text{not green}) = \frac{20}{24} = \frac{5}{6}$.

1602

R. Gupta's®

GENERAL KNOWLEDGE BOOKS

Book Name	*Code*	*Price (₹)*
• General Knowledge 2017	R-1716	38
• General Knowledge For All 2017	R-1641	24
• R. Gupta's® GK & Current Affairs including Latest Who's Who	R-1	32
• General Knowledge Hand Book (Junior)	R-3	48
• General Knowledge & Current Affairs	R-5	54
• General Knowledge At a Glance	R-7	65
• Popular General Knowledge	R-9	145
• General Knowledge Encyclopaedia	R-11	240
• Delhi General Knowledge	R-464	70
• Kerala General Knowledge	R-1588	80
• Comprehensive J&K GK, Current Affairs & Who's Who	R-564	90
• J & K General Knowledge (small)	R-12	40
• J & K General Knowledge – At a Glance	R-1066	50
• Haryana General Knowledge	R-505	80
• Himachal Pradesh General Knowledge	R-415	90
• Uttarakhand General Knowledge	R-469	65
• Odisha General Knowledge	R-518	95
• West Bengal General Knowledge	R-1070	50
• Arunachal Pradesh General Knowledge	R-1067	60
• India At a Glance *(with Description of All States/Union Territories)*	R-489	75
• Manipur General Knowledge	R-822	95
• Manipur GK Handbook (with Multiple Choice Questions)	R-954	50
• Maharashtra General Knowledge	R-1043	75

For Cash on Delivery (COD)

E-mail your order to: **order@rameshpublishinghouse.com**

1603

Ramesh Publishing House, 4457, Nai Sarak, Delhi-6

For Online Shopping: www.rameshpublishinghouse.com

HIMACHAL PRADESH GENERAL KNOWLEDGE

Multiple Choice Questions

HISTORY

1. Ancient King Prithu, on the name of whom the earth is named **Prithvi,** basically be longed to

A. Kullu (HP) B. Mathura (UP)
C. Jalandhar (Punjab) D. Jind (Haryana)

2. Who discovered places near Himalaya at right side of river Sirsa which is tributary of river Satluj in Nalagarh near Shimla?

A. Sri Brajwasilal
B. Sri Aulaj Prajar
C. Dr. Radhakumud Mukherji
D. Aashirwadlal Srivastava

3. Who discovered equipments of **Sohan** variety in valley of Vyas and Banganga in district Kangra in 1955?

A. Sri Sohan Lal
B. Sri Prafull Mukherji
C. Sri Brajwasi Lal
D. Sri Manas Prasad

4. Who discovered more than 500 remains in Sirsa river valley (Kangra) in latter stone age?

A. Dr. G.C. Mahapatra
B. Sri Krishna Swami
C. Amlendu Guha
D. P.C. Khanna

5. Ancient stone equipments in Makand river valley of district Sirmaur were discovered in

A. 1909 B. 1914
C. 1945 D. 1974

6. Who first of all discovered ancient historical stone instruments in 1951 in Nalagarh of Shivalik mountain range?

A. Olaf Prajar
B. Dr. Santosh Chandra
C. Fradrick
D. George Patro

7. When did Human habitation started is Himachal on the basis of historical remains

A. Iron era B. Copper-stone era
C. Pre stone era D. Latter stone era

8. Who lived in early Vedic age in Shivalik Valley?

A. Arya B. Dasya
C. Mangol D. Gorkha

9. Which was the oldest princely state of Himachal?

A. Trigart B. Vilaspur
C. Thiyog D. Kehloor

10. In the Panini era (300BC), Himachal Pradesh was divided into two parts, one part was called Trigart Gansangh, what was the name of other Gansangh?

A. Aayas B. Kunind
C. Bhadra D. Raghav

11. Which of the following epic book gave information about ancient Himachal first of all?

A. Aaranyak B. Upnishad
C. Rigveda D. Puran

12. Which of the following district was established in unknown historical period?
A. Kangra B. Kullu
C. Rampur-Bushar D. All of these

13. In the great war of Mahabharata, which of the following Kachotvanshi of Kangra took part from the side of Kauravas?
A. Susharmchandra
B. Jagatchandra
C. Suchendra
D. Ganesh Chandra

14. Whose was the most powerful King of Anarya tribes, living in Himachal?
A. Veer chandra B. Shambar
C. Suketu D. Kachot

15. With which Arya King did Anaarya King Shambar of the state had several wars?
A. Dragendra B. Divodaas
C. Shashank D. Prithu

16. Who of the following was most famous Vedic era Arya King of the state
A. Sudaas B. Ravidas
C. Bhejbahes D. Amodhvarsh

17. In the Mahabharat period, with which monster girl did Bheem get-married – who lates on became **Kul-devi** of district Kullu?
A. Devi Mahamaya
B. Devi Handoli
C. Devi Rajbheema
D. Devi Hidimba

18. How many states were under Trigart Gansangh of Himachal?
A. 6 B. 7
C. 12 D. 16

19. Which of the following republic of **Panini** era was union territory of Mahasu, Shimla and Nalagarh states?
A. Aayudh B. Kunand
C. Chamba D. Brahmaur

20. Which of the following historical book mentions that Kulinda people were used to live near Shalda river of Himachal?
A. Ramayan B. Upnishad
C. Mahabharat D. Ashtadhyayi

21. Anirudha, the grand son of Srikrishna tied a knot with usha after an affair - at which place of the state?
A. Kinnaur B. Chamba
C. Kangra D. Kehloor

22. Which of the following King, who also established Gupta-Dynasty, in the beginning of fourth century, won over various districts of Himalaya and took the command of all of them?
A. Chandragupta Vikramaditya
B. Samudragupt
C. Chandragupta
D. Kumargupta

23. Which tribe of Himachal used to defeat Kirat and Nag?
A. Coal B. Doom
C. Khash D. Haali

24. Which is the oldest ruling custom of the state?
A. Mavna ruling custom/mode
B. Kunden ruling custom/mode
C. Thati ruling custom/mode
D. Savahi ruling custom/mode

25. Begore the Rajsuya yajna, during his victory trip, Arjun traveled which republic of Himachal?
A. Trigart B. Kulut
C. Kulind D. All of the above

26. Which historical book of princely poet-Vakrapati of King Yashovarman gives the information that Yashovarman conquered over Himalaya portion?
A. Jandvah B. Davnaal
C. Mahopati D. Kakdal

27. Kinyothal state was established by whom in 765?
A. Harihar Chand B. Vijay Chand
C. Girisen D. Devbhooti

28. Which King of Kangra was a regular visitor of royal court and was famous as Deewan?
A. Bheem Chand
B. Suraj Chand
C. Shyam Singh
D. Pratap Singh

29. Where was the capital of state chamba in ancient times?
A. Satpura B. Bahavpura
C. Brahmapura D. Chamora

30. When was popular government established after changing regional council to HP legislative council?
A. 1st February, 1963
B. 4th August, 1963
C. 10th June, 1963
D. 1st July, 1963

31. Ancient Kullu state was established in following year in Himachal by Vihangam Manipaal—
A. 1300 B. 1400
C. 1500 D. 1600

32. Traveller Bernier of France origin visited Himachal in time of which Mughal emperor?
A. Aurangjeb B. Humayun
C. Akbar D. Jahangeer

33. Which chineese travellers articles describes about life style in Kangra, Kullu and Lahaul district of Himachal?
A. Fahyan B. It-sing
C. Huent-sang D. Yuwanchwang

34. Opposition leader Mahammad Junaidi of Rajiya Sultana took shelter in which district of Himachal in 13th century?
A. Sirmaur B. Chamba
C. Kangda D. Nalagarh

35. When did Kangra King Vidhichand had a war against Akbar by making a union of all emperors of hilly area?
A. 1489–90 B. 1516–17
C. 1588–89 D. 1590–91

36. Who was the ruler of Nagarkoat while Mahmood Gajnavi attacked over it in 1009.
A. Jai Chand
B. Kalyan Chand
C. Vijay Chand
D. Jagdish Chand

37. Who established Mandi princely state of Himachal?
A. Surendra Singh B. Veersen
C. Vijay Chand D. Duni Chand

38. Which King of Kullu got married to ruler **Roop-Sundari** of Kothi Barsai and included that area into his empire?
A. Padma Singh
B. Kalyaan Chand
C. Rajender Pal
D. Jai Chand

39. Which King established city Mandi in 1527?
A. Ajbar Sen
B. Darshan Sen
C. Shyam Singh
D. Bahadur Singh

40. Who was the last ruler of Sirmaur state?
A. Rajendra Prakash
B. Maan Singh
C. Naurang Singh
D. Padam Singh

41. When did Sher Shah Suri send his commander Khawas Khan to Nagar Koat and other hilly states to take command?
A. 1450 B. 1504
C. 1505 D. 1540

42. Which area of the state was won by Sher Shah Suri?
A. Kangda B. Sirmaur
C. Chamba D. Shimla

43. Which King of Himachal revolted against Mughal emperor in 1641?
A. Jagat Singh B. Padam Singh
C. Gyan Singh D. Bahingpaal

44. What was the ancient name of Kangra city?
A. Kalsi B. Kamra
C. Trigart D. Sitami

45. Who was the Himachal emperor who revolted against Mughal emperor Akbar by making a union of hilly princeley states in 1588-89
A. Darshan Sen
B. Ram Prakash
C. Vidhi Chand
D. Gyan Singh

46. Mughal emperor Jahangir got victory over Kangra Fort with the help of following King of Himachal of related princely state

A. Chamba, King Charat Singh
B. Kangra, King Harichand
C. Kangra, King Roopchand
D. Noorpur, King Jagat Singh

47. Noorpur sub-zone of Kangra district was named **Noorpur** from **Dhameli** at the time of which Mughal emperor?

A. Babar B. Jahangir
C. Akbar D. Aurangjeb

48. What was the title given to King Kehri Singh of Rampur-Bushar by Mughals after being fascinated by his bravery?

A. Chatrapati B. Vikramditya
C. Chatrasaal D. Suaiputra

49. Which King of Himachal supported Aurangjeb in South campaign?

A. King Kchri Singh of Rampur-Bushar
B. King Karm Prakash of Sirmaur
C. King Deep Chand of Bilaspur
D. King Chatar Singh of Chamba

50. Guru Govind Singh travelled Sirmaur in rulership of which King?

A. Medani Prakash
B. Ravirao
C. Chandra Varman
D. Prakash Chandra

ANSWERS

1 A	2 B	3 C	4 A	5 D	6 A	7 C	8 B	9 A	10 B
11 C	12 D	13 A	14 B	15 B	16 A	17 D	18 A	19 B	20 C
21 A	22 C	23 C	24 A	25 D	26 A	27 C	28 A	29 C	30 B
31 C	32 A	33 C	34 A	35 C	36 D	37 B	38 C	39 A	40 A
41 A	42 A	43 A	44 A	45 C	46 D	47 B	48 A	49 C	50 A

GEOGRAPHY

1. What is the average height of Himachal Pradesh from sea level?
A. 300 m to 4,300 m
B. 350 m to 7,026 m
C. 460 m to 5,200 m
D. 580 m to 7,200 m

2. Himachal Pradesh is situated between—
A. 30° 22′ and 30° 12′ Northern Latitude
B. 30° 12′ and 30° 15′ Northern Latitude
C. 40° 17′ and 40° 25′ Northern Latitude
D. 40° 22′ and 40° 20′ Northern Latitude

3. Which of the following hills fall under outer-Himalaya or Shivalik range of the state?
A. High hills B. Jaskar hills
C. Low hills D. None of these

4. Low hills of outer Himalaya or Shivalik range of the state are situated at which height from sea level?
A. 500 m B. 600 m
C. 700 m D. 800 m

5. How much average rain-fall is recorded in the region of outer Himalaya or Shivalik range?
A. 1500 mm to 2000 mm
B. 1800 mm to 1000 mm
C. 2000 mm to 3000 mm
D. 3000 mm to 4000 mm

6. Rain increases with increasing height in the state up to:
A. 1000 m B. 1500 m
C. 2000 m D. 3000 m

7. Lower Himalaya or middle area based Dhauladhar mountain range is having an average height of:
A. 2,440 m B. 3,300 m
C. 4,200 m D. 4,550 m

8. Lower Himalaya or middle area has an average annual rain fall of:
A. 75 cm to 100 cm
B. 110 cm to 200 cm
C. 150 cm to 200 cm
D. 200 cm to 225 cm

9. Upper Himalaya mountain range is situated at:
A. 4,000 m to 5,000 m
B. 5,000 m to 6,000 m
C. 6,000 m to 7,000 m
D. 7,000 m to 8,000 m

10. What is the height of Pin Parvati pass situated in upper Himalayan area?
A. 3,250 m B. 3,600 m
C. 4,802 m D. 5,250 m

11. Jaskar mountain range separates which of the following to Kinnaur and Spiti?
A. Tibet B. Myanmar
C. China D. Kashmir

12. Peak named 'Shilla' in Jaskar of the state has a height of:
A. 6,021 m B. 7,026 m
C. 8,030 m D. 9,029 m

13. Peak 'Rivo Fargyul' in Jaskar of the state has a height of:
A. 4,200 m B. 4,600 m
C. 5,700 m D. 6,500 m

14. What do you call glacier in local language of Himachal?
A. Shigadi B. Chikati
C. Shipka D. Shaapi

15. Kinnar Kailash mountain is situated in which district of Himachal?
A. Kinnaur B. Lahaul
C. Kullu D. Chamba

16. Which of the following peak is not found in district Kinnaur?
A. Shila B. Shipki
C. Shingrila D. Liyoparzil

17. Kinnar Kailash mountain of Kinnaur district is situated at the height of:
A. 19,824 ft B. 19,500 ft
C. 18,600 ft D. 18,210 ft

18. Which of the following mountain is situated in district Lahaul-Spiti?
A. Mani-Rang B. Mul-Quila
C. Lachhalangla D. All of the above

19. 'Gephang' mountain in Lahaul-Spiti is at what height from sea level?
A. 19,824 ft B. 18,200 ft
C. 20,373 ft D. 21,075 ft

20. 'Shingrila' mountain peak is situated in which district of Himachal?
A. Kinnaur B. Kullu
C. Lahaul-Spiti D. Kangra

21. Which of the following mountain is not in district Lahaul-Spiti?
A. Shingrila B. Patalsu
C. Hargaran D. Mukarbah

22. 'Shaldu-da-par' mountain peak is situated in the district:
A. Lahaul-Spiti B. Kinnaur
C. Kangra D. Mandi

23. 'Murangala' named mountain peak in Lahaul-spiti is at the height from sea level of:
A. 15,180 ft B. 18,690 ft
C. 16,950 ft D. 19,781 ft

24. 'Solang' named mountain peak is in which the following district of Himachal?
A. Lahaul B. Spiti
C. Kullu D. Kangra

25. Which of the following mountain peak is in district Kullu?
A. Dibivokari B. Indrakila
C. Diyotibba D. All of the above

26. 'Umashila' mountain peak in district Kullu is at what height from the sea level?
A. 17,925 ft B. 19,200 ft
C. 15,882 ft D. 18,003 ft

27. Mountain peak Saacha is in district:
A. Kangra B. Kullu
C. Manali D. None of these

28. Which of the following mountain is not in district Kullu?
A. Meva Kandinu B. Paragala
C. Shrikhanda D. Kailash

29. 'Hanuman Tibba' named mountain peak of Kullu in Kangra district is at what height from the sea level?
A. 17,580 ft B. 19,200 ft
C. 15,546 ft D. 10,620 ft

30. Which of the following mountain is in district Kullu and Kangra?
A. Indra kila B. Ghora Tantanu
C. Tamsaar D. Shikarbah

31. 'Narsingh Tibba' peak of Chamba district is situated at the height from sea-level of:
A. 9,810 ft B. 14,820 ft
C. 11,190 ft D. 13,410 ft

32. Which of the following mountain is not in district Chamba?
A. Kailash B. Solang
C. Tamsaar D. Bada-Khanda

33. 'Peer Panjal' of Chamba district is situated at the height from sea level of:
A. 17,916 B. 16,731
C. 11,190 D. 14,640

34. 'Lo-chang' mountain peak is in which district of Himachal?
A. Chamba B. Kullu
C. Kangra D. Kinnaur

35. 'Hamta' cultivated land is related to which district of Himachal?
A. Kangra
B. Chamba, Kullu and Spiti
C. Kinnaur
D. Mandi

36. 'Gairu' the cultivated land of Kangra district is situated at the height of:
A. 13,980 ft B. 13,620 ft
C. 12,810 ft D. 15,000 ft

37. 'Bheem Dhasutadi' cultivated land is related to which district of Himachal?
A. Lahaul-spiti B. Mandi
C. Kangra & Chamba D. Kullu

38. Which of the following cultivated land is not located in district Kangra and Chamba?
A. Tori B. Duggi
C. Baleni D. Jalsu

39. 'Laluji' cultivated land is situated in which district of Himachal?
A. Lahaul-Spiti
B. Kullu
C. Kangra
D. Kangra & Chamba

40. What is the length of the Atal Tunnel, Rohtang?
A. 10 km B. 8.8 km
C. 9.02 km D. 12.5 km

41. 'Gulari' cultivated land is related to which district of Himachal?
A. Chamba B. Lahaul
C. Kangra D. Kullu

42. Which of the following cultivated land is in district Kullu?
A. Shee B. Rasaul
C. Gadhu D. All of the above

43. 'Tainti' the cultivated land in Kullu is at what height from the sea level?
A. 9,690 ft B. 10,800 ft
C. 11,190 ft D. 10,320 ft

44. Basodan pass is situated in district:
A. Chamba B. Kangra
C. Kinnaur D. Lahaul

45. Karhi Kukdi pass is related to which district of Himachal?
A. Bharmaur and Kangra
B. Lahaul and Spiti
C. Lahaul Spiti and Bharmaur
D. Kullu and Kangra

46. Which of the following pass is situated in district Kangra and Chamba?
A. Kalichho B. Indrahar
C. Chouri D. Sipki-la

47. Where Bhootnath temple is situated?
A. Mandi B. Bhunter
C. Sarahan D. Manali

48. Kugati pass is in which districts of Himachal?
A. Kullu and Kangra
B. Kangra and Chamba
C. Lahaul-Spiti and Bharmour
D. Lahaul and Kullu

49. Which of the following pass is situated in Kangra and Bharmaur district?
A. Nikoda B. Dulli
C. Jalori D. Padri

50. Which of the following city of Himachal Pradesh does not fall under Kangra valley?
A. Dharmshala B. Bharmaur
C. Noorpur D. Baijnaath

51. Which of the following is an important feature of Kangra valley of HP?
A. Paintings B. Jute-production
C. Sculpture D. None of these

52. Chamba valley is known by another name in the state which is:
A. Satluj valley B. Bait valley
C. Raavi valley D. Kaithi valley

53. Minimum height of Chamba valley from sea level is 750 m. What is its maximum height?
A. 4,057 m B. 6,025 m
C. 6,200 m D. 7,035 m

54. Which one of the following city is not in Chamba Valley of Himachal?
A. Dalhousie B. Chuwadi
C. Gagal D. Khajiyaar

55. Kullu valley in Himachal has a length and width of:
A. 75 km long, 2-4 km wide
B. 80 km long, 8-12 km wide
C. 100 km long, 12-15 km wide
D. 105 km long, 20-22 km wide

56. Kullu valley of Himachal is also known as
A. Ramghati B. Devghati
C. Chetaghati D. Shivghati

57. Which of the following city is in Kullu valley in Himachal?
A. Manali B. Naagar
C. Banjaar D. All of the above

58. Roerich art museum is in which valley of Himachal?
A. Kullu B. Kangra
C. Paunta D. Sangalya

59. Paunta valley is in which district of Himachal?
A. Kangra B. Mandi
C. Kinnaur D. Kullu

60. From which river other than Giri in Paunta valley, water is taken for irrigation?
A. Bata B. Yamuna
C. Godawari D. Chinab

61. Which of the following valley is in district Mandi of Himachal?
A. Kangra B. Balh
C. Chamba D. Kullu

62. Average height of Spiti in Lahaul-Spiti valley is:
A. 1,000 m B. 2,000 m
C. 3,000 m D. 4,000 m

63. Average height of Balh valley in district Mandi is:
A. 800 m B. 900 m
C. 1000 m D. 1200 m

64. Lahaul of Lahaul-Spiti valley of Himachal is situated to which side of Chandrabhaga (Chinab)?
A. East B. West
C. North D. South

65. Which of the following valley was benefitted in Himachal by the implementation of Indo-German joint agricultural project in 1962?
A. Kullu B. Balh
C. Kangra D. Pabbar

66. Pabbar valley of Himachal is known by which other name?
A. Rohadu B. Baagi
C. Setu D. Pabbar

67. Which of the following depression is main in Pabbar valley?
A. Pejor khand B. Andhra khand
C. Shikri khand D. All of the above

68. Which of the following valley is built from **Shipki** to **Bilaspur** by river Satluj?
A. Satluj B. Balh
C. Sangla D. Chamba

69. Alpine type trees are found in which valley of HP?
A. Balh B. Spiti
C. Sangla D. Chamba

70. Which of the following river is related to HP?
A. Raavi B. Satluj
C. Chinab D. All of the above

71. Raavi River related to HP is known by which other name?
A. Irawati B. Satwami
C. Chirutha D. Banchali

72. How long is river Raavi in HP?
A. 100 km B. 125 km
C. 158 km D. 182 km

73. Which river of Himachal Pradesh is the tributary of **river Raavi**?
A. Khadde Chidchand B. Chhatradi
C. Bodhil D. All of the above

74. What is the epic/ancient name of river Satluj in HP ?
A. Chandrabhaga B. Shatakshi
C. Sutudri D. Chhitadri

75. Chinab river is known by which other name in HP?
A. Chandrakala B. Charuda
C. Chapla D. Chandrabhaga

76. What is the flow area (in km) of Chinab in HP?
A. 112 km B. 115 km
C. 122 km D. 135 km

77. How long is the flow area of Vyas in HP?
A. 265 km B. 356 km
C. 390 km D. 415 km

78. Which of the following is not a tributary of river Vyas?
A. Bhaga B. Chaki
C. Parvati D. Suketi

79. How much is the water catchment area of Yamuna in HP?
A. 1,255 km B. 3,115 km
C. 2,320 km D. 2,388 km

80. Which of the following river is not related to district Shimla?
A. River Satluj B. Vyas
C. Pabbar D. Giri

81. Vyas river is not related to which of the following district?

A. Kullu B. Mandi
C. Una D. Kangra

82. Sainj, Tirthan, Malad, Nalan and other digs are in which district of the state?

A. Kullu B. Hamirpur
C. Kangra D. Chamba

83. Maan, Kunah and other famous digs are in which district of HP?

A. Kinnaur B. Solan
C. Bilaspur D. Hamirpur

84. What is the height of Dull lake in district Kangra (11 km form Dharmshala)?

A. 1,500 ft B. 2,800 ft
C. 2,500 ft D. 3,110 ft

85. Lake 'Nako' is in which district of HP?

A. Kinnaur B. Chamba
C. Shimla D. Mandi

86. Which of the following lake is in district Mandi?

A. Chandrataal B. Kamrunaag
C. Lama D. Renuka

87. Which of the following lake is not in district Chamba?

A. Manimahesh B. Kamarwah
C. Mahakali D. Lama

88. Which of the following **Himnad** is situated in HP?

A. Parvati (Kullu)
B. Big Shigadi Himnad of Lahaul
C. Miyar Himanad (Lahaul)
D. All of the above

89. Which of the following hot water fall is not in district Kullu?

A. Khirganga B. Manikarn
C. Jyori D. Vashishtha

90. Point out the incorrectly matched pair

Lake	**Height**
A. Kaveri	1. 3048 m
B. Mani Mahesh	2. 3950 m
C. Dull	3. 5321 m
D. Mahakali	4. 3657 m

91. 'Rivalsar lake' known as floating island is in which district of HP?

A. Kangra B. Mandi
C. Chamba D. Bilaspur

92. Which of the famous lake is found in district Kangra near Dharmshala?

A. Naako lake B. Lama lake
C. Dull lake D. Kamarvah lake

93. 22 miles from Mandi, Parashar lake has a height of .... from sea level.

A. 1,000 ft B. 4,000 ft
C. 3,000 ft D. 6,000 ft

94. Which of the following lake is not found in district Mandi?

A. Kamarvah lake B. Naako lake
C. Kamrunaag lake D. Rivalsar lake

95. Which of the following is biggest artificial/ lake of HP?

A. Govindsagar lake B. Pong lake
C. Mani-Mahesh lake D. Rivalsar lake

96. Biggest natural lake of HP is:

A. Parashar B. Kamrunaag
C. Naako D. Renuka

97. Area of Govindsagar lake, which is largest artificial lake and is in Bilaspur district is:

A. 50 miles^2 B. 66 mile^2
C. 88 miles^2 D. 95 miles^2

98. Which of the lake is actually a group of 7 lakes in HP?

A. Lama B. Khajiyaar
C. Dull D. Mani-Mahesh

99. Which lake in HP is at maximum height?

A. Mahakali B. Dull
C. Mani-Mahesh D. Chandrataal

100. Sarkund or Darrshaeer lake of Kullu is at what height from sea level?

A. 500 m B. 1000 m
C. 12,100 m D. 14,500 m

101. Surajtaal and Chandrataal named lakes are in which district of HP?

A. Lahaul-Spiti B. Kullu
C. Chamba D. Mandi

102. 'Dhekarchoh' lake in Lahaul-spiti is at what height from sea-level?
A. 1,200 m B. 2,500 m
C. 3,500 m D. 3,800 m

103. Point out the correct pair:

Lake	Height
A. Lama	1. 2,700 m
B. Mahakali	2. 3,000 m
C. Chandrataal	3. 4,883 m
D. Naako	4. 4,000 m

104. Lake named 'Yunamatso' is at which place in Shimla?,
A. Jubbal B. Thiyog
C. Rohadu D. Chaupal

105. 'Rohla Waterfall' is in which district of HP?
A. Bilaspur B. Shimla
C. Kullu D. Una

106. Which of the following district does not have hot water falls/stream in HP?
A. Una B. Mandi
C. Kullu D. Kangra

107. Satdhaar Waterfall is near which city of the state?
A. Kinnaur B. Dalhousi
C. Una D. Hamirpur

108. Famous 'Chadvik Waterfall' is near which of the following place?
A. Samarhil B. Naaldhera
C. Kufri D. Mashotara

109. Jwalamukhi named waterfall is at which place in the state?
A. Kullu B. Badsar
C. Nadaon D. Chamba

110. Soil of the state has been divided into how many parts in HP by agriculture department of the state?
A. 2 B. 3
C. 5 D. 6

111. Low mountain soil area fall under the range of what height from sea level?
A. upto 1000 m B. upto 1500 m
C. upto 2000 m D. upto 2300 m

112. Which soil region in HP is found to have carbon & nitrogen ratio as 10:1
A. Low mountain soil area
B. Middle mountain soil area
C. High mountain soil area
D. Dry mountain soil area

113. Which of the following is grown in low mountain soil area?
A. Paddy (rice) B. Sugarcane
C. Corn D. All of these

114. High mountain soil area are at what height from sea level?
A. 1000 to 1100 m B. 1000 to 1500 m
C. 1500 to 2100 m D. 2000 to 3000 m

115. High to middle clam nitrogen is found in which soil zone of the state?
A. Middle mountain soil area
B. High mountain soil area
C. Mountaneous soil area
D. Low mountain soil area

116. Upper area of Shimla, Sirmaur and Chamba fall into which soil zone
A. Low mountaneous soil zone
B. High mountaneous soil zone
C. Dry mountaneous soil zone
D. Mountaneous soil zone

117. Which of the following does not comes under dry mountains soil zone in the state?
A. Shimla B. Lahaul-Spiti
C. Kinnaur D. Panga

118. 'Chaih soil' type is irrigated by which method in the state?
A. By Dams B. By Wells
C. By rivers D. By rain water

119. Which of the crop is grown in 'Naad' soil type in the state?
A. Sugarcane B. Wheat
C. Paddy (rice) D. Black gram

120. Which of the soil is found in middle Himalayan area?
A. Alluvial soil
B. Sandy soil
C. Black-brown and slippery soil
D. All of the above

121. In Shivalik region of the state, which soil type's found?
A. Stony slippery soil
B. Kaanp soil
C. Alluvial soil
D. Sandy soil

122. 'Ballah valley of Mandi' and 'Kunihaar valley of Solan' falls under which mountain soil area of the state?
A. Middle mountain in soil area
B. Mountain soil area
C. Dry mountain soil area
D. Low mountain soil area

123. Which of the following part is most fertile in the state which falls in Shivalik region?
A. Kullu valley B. Balghati
C. Khaziyaar valley D. All of the above

124. Which of the following can be well grown in middle mountain soil zone?
A. Gram & Jowar B. Rice and Gandam
C. Potato & Maize D. Lemon & Mango

125. Which of the following historians named Raavi river as 'High draster' and 'Rahoaadis'?
A. Mughals historians
B. Greek historians
C. Pahadi historians
D. British historians

ANSWERS

1	**2**	**3**	**4**	**5**	**6**	**7**	**8**	**9**	**10**
B	A	C	B	A	B	D	A	B	C
11	**12**	**13**	**14**	**15**	**16**	**17**	**18**	**19**	**20**
A	B	D	A	A	C	B	D	B	C
21	**22**	**23**	**24**	**25**	**26**	**27**	**28**	**29**	**30**
B	A	A	C	D	C	B	D	A	B
31	**32**	**33**	**34**	**35**	**36**	**37**	**38**	**39**	**40**
C	B	A	C	B	A	C	B	A	C
41	**42**	**43**	**44**	**45**	**46**	**47**	**48**	**49**	**50**
B	D	B	A	D	C	A	C	A	B
51	**52**	**53**	**54**	**55**	**56**	**57**	**58**	**59**	**60**
A	C	B	C	A	B	D	A	C	A
61	**62**	**63**	**64**	**65**	**66**	**67**	**68**	**69**	**70**
B	D	A	C	B	A	D	A	B	D
71	**72**	**73**	**74**	**75**	**76**	**77**	**78**	**79**	**80**
A	C	D	C	D	C	B	A	C	B
81	**82**	**83**	**84**	**85**	**86**	**87**	**88**	**89**	**90**
C	A	D	C	A	B	B	D	C	C
91	**92**	**93**	**94**	**95**	**96**	**97**	**98**	**99**	**100**
B	C	C	B	A	D	B	A	C	D
101	**102**	**103**	**104**	**105**	**106**	**107**	**108**	**109**	**110**
A	C	B	C	C	A	B	A	C	C
111	**112**	**113**	**114**	**115**	**116**	**117**	**118**	**119**	**120**
A	A	D	C	B	D	A	B	C	A
121	**122**	**123**	**124**	**125**					
A	D	B	C	B					

ADMINISTRATION

1. What was the population of HP according to 2011 census?
A. 6,864,602 B. 6,110,877
C. 7,505,766 D. 6,150,458

2. What is the density of population of HP?
A. 112 persons / km^2 B. 140 persons / km^2
C. 123 persons / km^2 D. 130 persons / km^2

3. What is the no. of females per 1000 males of HP according to 2011 census?
A. 870 B. 796
C. 976 D. 972

4. What is the percentage of population inhabitating the cities of HP of the state?
A. 6.64% B. 7.72%
C. 8.22% D. 10.0%

5. What is the population of Kinnaur district (census, 2011)?
A. 81640 B. 73324
C. 84121 D. 82750

6. In which of the city of state maximum population of schedule tribes is inhabitating?
A. Chamba B. Una
C. Shimla D. Hamirpur

7. What is the population of literate people in the state according to 2011 census?
A. 5,10,400 B. 4,016,058
C. 5,039,736 D. 4,035,068

8. Ancient 'Tharoch & Dadi' princely states are now a part of which district of Himachal?
A. Solan B. Bilaspur
C. Shimla D. Kangra

9. Which district of HP has least population of schedule cast?
A. Lahaul-Spiti B. Hamirpur
C. Kangra D. Shimla

10. What is the population of district Sirmaur according to 2011 census?
A. 558,292 B. 542,842
C. 587,602 D. 529,855

11. Which district of the state has maximum population of schedule caste?
A. Kullu B. Mandi
C. Kangra D. Una

12. Population of males is 192,764 in district Bilaspur according to 2011 census, what would be population of females in the same?
A. 189,192 B. 150,445
C. 165,078 D. 195,106

13. What is the total population of district Una according to 2011 census?
A. 562,680 B. 521,173
C. 302,865 D. 410,115

14. Which district of the state has maximum number of females per 1000 males?
A. Chamba B. Una
C. Hamirpur D. Kullu

15. Which district of HP has least population density?
A. Kangra B. Lahaul-Spiti
C. Shimla D. Solan

16. Which district of the state has most flourshing villages?
A. Hamirpur B. Chamha
C. Bilaspur D. Kangra

17. What is the percentage of population raise in the state during 2001 to 2011?
A. 10.86% B. 12.94%
C. 25.89% D. 30.277%

18. Which district of the state has least population of schedule tribe?
A. Una B. Sirmaur
C. Solan D. Mandi

19. Where is the head office of district Lahaul-Spiti of HP?
A. Nahan B. Solan
C. Kelang D. Kalpa

20. Which district of HP has a population lesser than 50,000 according to 2011 census?
A. Sirmaur B. Mandi
C. Lahaul-Spiti D. Solan

21. Kandaghat sub-division is located in which district?
A. Solan B. Kangra
C. Kullu D. Bilashpur

22. Which city besides Shimla has maximum population?
A. Solan B. Mandi
C. Kullu D. Kangra

23. What is the population of male according to 2011 census in the state?
A. 3,154,295 B. 3,168,952
C. 24,018,188 D. 3,481,873

24. What is the total female population in the state according to 2011 census?
A. 3,502,650 B. 3,664,155
C. 3,382,729 D. 3,007,529

25. What is the children (0-6 years) population in the state according to 2011 census?
A. 777,898 B. 769,524
C. 765,428 D. 748,356

26. What is the population of literate men in the state according to 2011 census?
A. 2,366,103 B. 2,752,590
C. 2,970,508 D. 3,366,402

27. What is the percentage of literate persons in the state of total population according to 2011 census?
A. 80.51% B. 88.26%
C. 82.80% D. 82.24%

28. What is the percentage of children (0-6 years) population of the state according to 2011 census?
A. 10.67 B. 16.24
C. 12.24 D. 11.3

29. What is the population of Nahan city according to 2011 census?
A. 28899 B. 27450
C. 21432 D. 35821

30. What is the total area of HP?
A. 44,575 km^2 B. 50,281 km^2
C. 55,673 km^2 D. 61,177 km^2

31. What is the total area of district Kinnaur of the state?
A. 6002 km^2 B. 6401 km^2
C. 5503 km^2 D. 4805 km^2

32. What is the area of district Sirmaur of the state?
A. 2825 km^2 B. 3375 km^2
C. 1288 km^2 D. 4228 km^2

33. What is the total area of district Lahaul Spiti?
A. 18325 km^2 B. 13835 km^2
C. 29416 km^2 D. 10045 km^2

34. What is the area of district Mandi?
A. 3,950 km^2 B. 3,440 km^2
C. 2,1000 km^2 D. 4,150 km^2

35. Match the columns:

List I *(District)*	**List II** *(Total area)*
(*a*) Chamba	1. 1936 km^2
(*b*) Bilaspur	2. 6528 km^2
(*c*) Solan	3. 5739 km^2
(*d*) Kangra	4. 1167 km^2

	(*a*)	(*b*)	(*c*)	(*d*)
A.	2	4	1	3
B.	1	2	4	3
C.	2	3	1	4
D.	3	1	4	2

36. Which of the following district does not belong to Shimla division of HP?
A. Kinnaur B. Hamirpur
C. Solan D. Sirmaur

37. Which of the following district belong to Dharmshala division?
A. Kangra B. Sirmaur
C. Bilaspur D. Kullu

38. Which of the following district belongs to Mandi division.
A. Hamirpur B. Bilaspur
C. Lahaul Spiti D. All of these

39. Which of the following sub-division belongs to district Shimla?
A. Thiyog B. Joginder Nagar
C. Nalagarh D. Sarkaghat

40. **Rohru** sub-division belongs to which of the following district?

A. Solan B. Una
C. Shimla D. Mandi

41. Which of the following **Tehsil** does not belong to district Solan?
A. Kasauli B. Chadgaon
C. Arki D. Kandaghat

42. 'Amb' Tehsil of the state belongs to following district?
A. Sirmaur B. Solan
C. Hamirpur D. Una

43. Which of the following developmental block belongs to district Kinnaur?
A. Nahan B. Gagrate
C. Rampur D. None of these

44. 'Nohra Dhar' Tehsil belongs to following district
A. Sirmaur B. Kinnaur
C. Una D. Bilaspur

45. Which of the following sub-division belongs to district lahaul spiti?
A. Palampur B. Udaipur
C. Noorpur D. Rampur

46. Which of the following Tehsil does not belong to district Kangra?
A. Palampur B. Baijnaath
C. Kumarsen D. Indaura

47. 'Sainz' sub-Tehsil belongs to following district—
A. Kullu B. Shimla
C. Kangra D. Una

48. Which of the following Tehsil belongs to district Kangra of the state?
A. Badoh B. Jwali
C. Jaisinghpur D. Banjar

49. Tahsil named 'Baalichowki' belongs to following district of Himachal—
A. Kullu B. Mandi
C. Lahaul Spiti D. Kangra

50. 'Kelang' developmental block belongs to which district of the state?
A. Solan B. Mandi
C. Lahaul Spiti D. Chamba

51. Which of the following Tehsil belongs to district Kinnaur?
A. Mooram B. Rajgarh
C. Renuka D. Pachhad

52. Under which law was Panchayat established first of all in HP?
A. Panchayat law 1949
B. Panchayat law 1950
C. Panchayat law 1952
D. Panchayat law 1962

53. Panchayati Raj organizations were formed under which system in the state?
A. Single Tier B. Two Tier
C. Three Tier D. All of these

54. Banjar Tehsil belongs to which district?
A. Una B. Hamirpur
C. Kullu D. Shimla

55. What is the number of members of panchayat for the population of 2000-3500?
A. 4 B. 5
C. 7 D. 9

56. When did HP represented council of States (Rajyasabha) first time?
A. 1952 B. 1948
C. 1951 D. 1966

57. From which place of the state, Hindi weekly magzine 'Giriraaj' is published?
A. Solan B. Una
C. Shimla D. Bilaspur

58. Which was the most popular and old bilingual fortnightly newspaper of HP?
A. Himalaya Dhwani B. Kshatriya Tej
C. Uncha Himalaya D. None of these

59. Which of the following newspaper is publised from Chamba?
A. Chamba News B. Him Samvahak
C. Udai Bharat D. Him Rakshak

60. Manali is located in which district?
A. Solan B. Shimla
C. Kullu D. Una

61. News paper 'Uncha Himalaya' is published from which place of the state?
A. Una B. Bilaspur
C. Solan D. Shimla

62. Newspaper 'Himachal Bramhastra' is published in following language from Shimla—

A. Hindi B. Urdu

C. Sanskrit D. Punjabi

63. Which of the following newspaper is not weekly?

A. Himachal Brahmastra

B. Chamba News

C. Himachal Dhwani

D. Him Satta

64. A Grade Hotel 'Oberai-Clark's is in following city of the state —

A. Solan B. Manali

C. Kullu D. Shimla

65. What is the area of Kinnaur district?

A. 5739 km^2 B. 6401 km^2

C. 5503 km^2 D. 6528 km^2

66. Who founded first central school in Shimla in the year 1948?

A. Edward B. John Marshel

C. Alfred D. Smith

67. Where is the 'Government Ayurvedic College' of the state?

A. Solan B. Shimla

C. Kangra D. Joginder Nagar

68. When was first primary school started in Chamba?

A. 1810 B. 1821

C. 1863 D. 1895

69. When first primary school was started in Kaja of Spiti?

A. 1899 B. 1932

C. 1926 D. 1955

70. Who was the founder of Bishop cotton school in Himachal in 1863?

A. John Lorens B. John Rizard

C. Edward D. Sir Henry

71. When was first regular school was established in Lahaul valley by Kangra educational board?

A. 1842 B. 1865

C. 1901 D. 1919

72. At which place of HP is situated Medical and Ayurvedic college?

A. Papraula B. Joginder Nagar

C. Shimla D. All of these

73. At which place was agriculture university founded on 1st November, 1978?

A. Palampur (Kangra) B. Mandi

C. Mashobara (Shimla) D. Chamba

74. When was Dr. Yashwant Singh Parmar Park & Forestry University (Naavi, district solan) established?

A. 1st January, 1985

B. 5th April, 1985

C. 1st December, 1985

D. 7th May, 1985

75. **Una** was a part of which district before it got merged into HP, 1966.

A. Chamba B. Shimla

C. Hoshiyaarpur D. Kangra

76. At which place of Himachal Pradesh B.Ed. college is situated?

A. Dharmshala B. Bilaspur

C. Kangra D. Kullu

77. N.C.E.R.T educational institute is situated at which place of the state?

A. Bharmaur B. Bilaspur

C. Chamba D. Solan

78. Where is the head office of 'educational board' related to high school and senior secondary education?

A. Dharmshala B. Mandi

C. Bilaspur D. Kullu

79. When was HP University, Shimla established?

A. 1966 B. 1974

C. 1971 D. 1985

80. Where is Indira Gandhi Medical College situated in HP?

A. Solan B. Hamirpur

C. Kangra D. Shimla

81. Where is the Indian Institute of Advance Studies' in HP?

A. Una B. Kinnaur

C. Shimla D. Kangra

82. Which district of HP is having maximum illiteracy?
A. Chamba B. Kangra
C. Kullu D. Bilaspur

83. Himachal Pradesh peoples administrative educational institute was established in 1974, where is this institute in the state?
A. Una B. Chamba
C. Fare lance D. Bilaspur

84. What is the number of seats of Kullu district in states legislative assembly?
A. 4 B. 5
C. 6 D. 12

85. Where is the National Biological Laboratory in HP?
A. Nahan B. Palampur
C. Shimla D. Solan

86. Odambur tribe of ancient times used to inhability between which two rivers of HP?
A. Vyas & Satluj
B. Raavi & Jhelum
C. Vyas and Raavi
D. Chinab & Satluj

87. Gujjar inhability in HP are supposed of family origin
A. Kshastriya B. Rajput
C. Hoon D. Khas

88. What is the population of tribes of HP according to 2011 census?
A. 1,24,214 B. 2,25,445
C. 3,92,126 D. 3,50,257

89. Population wise, which district is richest about tribes?
A. Mandi B. Una
C. Kullu D. Chamba

90. What is the percentage of schedule tribe of the total population of HP?
A. 5.71% B. 7.12%
C. 4.56% D. 6.44%

91. What is the name of township of 'Gaddi' tribe of the state?
A. Gapparan B. Galhop
C. Gadderan D. Gachhila

92. Which tribe of HP is also known as 'Khosia'?
A. Gaddi B. Pangwaal
C. Gujjar D. Kinnar

93. Shon, Bukum, Jahru etc folk songs and dances are popular in which tribe of the state?
A. Gaddi
B. Lahaulial and Spitian
C. Gujjar
D. Pangwaal

94. What is the population of the tribes of district Hamirpur according to 2011 census?
A. 3,044 B. 1,591
C. 2,658 D. 4,662

95. What is the other name of Spitian tribe of state?
A. Bhot B. Paagi
C. Chara D. Silani

96. Which regions of the state have popular 'Jind funk' or 'Jarad Funki' marriage traditions?
A. Kangra & Chamba
B. Sirmaur & Hamirpur
C. Bharmaur & Bilaspur
D. Kullu & Kangra

97. What is the meaning of following terms popular in Kinnaur district?
Darosh / Dahdali / Nayamash Dopang / Nayamash Leemod / Aashish / Huchi Shadi
A. Love Marriage
B. Forced or agreed marriage
C. Widow Marriage
D. Group Marriage

98. What is the meaning of 'Janji' or 'Jaani' method of marriage, which is popular in Pangwaal tribe of the state?
A. Excellent marriage
B. Self choosen marriage
C. Kidnapped marriage
D. Love marriage

99. 'Jaad' tribe is found in which area of the state?
A. Lahaul B. Kullu
C. Paangi D. None of these

100. What is the meaning of 'Jaanikang' or 'Jaanitang' marriage popular in Kinnaur district?
A. Love marriage
B. Marriage with wife of other person
C. Kidnapping marriage
D. Arranged marriage

101. Two kinds of marriages are popular in Khas caste of HP, one is named ''Haara'' and what is the name of other kind of marriage?
A. Saai B. Mangani
C. Huchi D. Darosh

102. Rajgarh sub division is located in which district?
A. Shimla B. Solan
C. Kullu D. Sirmaur

103. In which areas does Gaddi tribe found in maximum number?
A. Bilaspur, Kinnaur
B. Bharmaur, Chamba
C. Bajaur, Kullu
D. None of these

104. Gujjar tribe is related to which of the following religion?
A. Hindu B. Muslim
C. Christian D. Both A & B

105. **Gharasani** custom is related to which kind of marriage of HP?
A. Jhajhara, Gaddar or Paraina
B. Janertang
C. Jhanjrada
D. Reet

106. What is the other name of **Paraina Marriage** in Kinnaur and other places?
A. Reet B. Haar
C. Janertang D. Jhanghrada

107. Barad fuk / Jarad fuk / Jhindifuk marriage is related to which area of the state?
A. Low B. Middle
C. Chamba D. All of these

108. ''Haar'' marriage of middle HP is known by which of the following names in Kinnaur?
A. Dabdub B. Chuchis
C. Khutkima D. All of the above

109. In ancient times of HP, polyandry tradition was popular in which of the following region?
A. Upper region
B. Trans Giri of Sirmaur
C. Saraj region
D. All of these

110. Shiv Puja of Gaadi tribe is done by which tradition in the state?
A. Nuala B. Sutan
C. Nacha D. Toda

111. What is the name of the dress from neck to knees, wore by people of Pabbar valley (Rohadu Tahseel)?
A. Sultan B. Chapkan
C. Chura or Jhukadi D. Dhayat

112. Which of the following tree is worshipped in Himachal Pradesh?
A. Vat B. Jaredi (Berl)
C. Pomegranate D. All of these

113. By the time of second century, various small empires were established in HP which used to fight among themselves, due to this their relations are till date known as
A. Chather tradition B. Boru tradition
C. Boir tradition D. Saarath tradition

114. Which of the following caste of HP is suppose of the time of Sindhu civilization?
A. Koal B. Kinnar
C. Naag D. All of the above

115. Which of the following caste superseed in the state?
A. Rajput B. Vaishya
C. Brahmin D. Schedule caste

116. In which area of HP Kanet caste is found in excess?
A. Western Himachal
B. Northern Himachal
C. Eastern Himachal
D. South Himachal

117. What is the name of people of Kinnaur and Lahaul-Spiti are also related to people of western Tibet?

A. Bhot B. Kharvar
C. Vishen D. Jatang

118. Which of the following class of HP is not related to business class
A. Karad B. Sood
C. Jeripal D. Handa

119. Khasia and Kanet Rajpoot (Kuninde of Mahabharat) basically belongs to
A. Aryans B. Brahmin
C. Haal D. Khas

120. Gujjar and Jat families living in lower Shivalik range of the state are supposed to be having following ancesteral origin
A. Saith B. Anarya
C. Arya D. Ghogi

121. What is the name of Carpenter and Blacksmith of district Kinnaur?
A. Kiral B. Chanal
C. Saval D. Barwaal

122. People living in western Himachal which are Koli, Haali, Doom, Chanal, Rehad, Baadhi are supposed to be related to which of the following ancestral tribe?
A. Agney tribe
B. Kinnar tribe
C. Naag tribe
D. Dravin tribe

123. What was the level of prayer of Khash people which are still popular in HP?
A. Istita Devta Prayer
B. Gram Devta Prayer
C. Grih Devta Prayer
D. All of these

124. Original Inhabitant of Himachal, description of whom is also found in Rigveda, are known today as :
A. Koli B. Doom
C. Haali D. All of these

125. Sujanpur sub division is located in which district?
A. Kangra B. Chamba
C. Bilaspur D. Hamirpur

126. From the administrative convenience point of view, when was HP divided into Kangra and Shimla?
A. 1966 B. 1970
C. 1973 D. 1979

127. Who was choosen first member of Rajyasabha from HP
A. Shivcharan Daas
B. Vidyachand Paaliwal
C. Chiranji Lal Verma
D. Harish Bharadwaj

128. Who was made the first Governor of the state in Jan, 1954 when in 1948 Himachal came into existence
A. Sri Bajrang Bahadur Bhadri
B. Sri C. Raj Gopalachari
C. Sri Veerbhadra Singh
D. Sri Yashwant Singh Parmaar

129. Who was made the governor of Himachal in 1971 when the state got the status of union state?
A. Sri C.V. Vaidya
B. Sri S. Chakrahorty
C. Sri Yashwant Singh Parmaar
D. Sri E. Paidar lamoon

130. Which of the following place is Head office of Tibet Government in HP?
A. Dharmshala B. Shimla
C. Dalhousie D. Nahan

131. What is the no. of population fixed for legislative assembly elections in the state
A. 65,000 B. 86,000
C. 75,000 D. 96,000

132. In 4th Lok Sabha, 1967 for how many seats in HP there was an election?
A. 5 B. 6
C. 7 D. 8

133. When was 'administrative - authority' formed in HP?
A. 1986 B. 1989
C. 1990 D. 1992

134. Which of the following persons has been a speaker of state legislative assembly?
A. Sri Sravan Kumar
B. Sri Jaivantram
C. Sri Thakur Sen Negi
D. All of the above

135. What should be the minimum age of a person to be a governor of HP?
A. 30 yrs B. 35 yrs
C. 25 yrs D. 18 yrs

136. Where is the office of HP public service commission?
A. Shimla B. Kinnaur
C. Solan D. Una

137. Who was elected as 1st 'Lokayukt' in 1983 in HP?
A. Justice G.S. Pandey
B. Jutice Kedarnaath Singh
C. Justice T.V.R Tatachari
D. Justice R.S. Sarkaria

138. Tell the name of first chief minister of the state
A. Lalbahadur Shastri
B. Dr. Yashwant Singh Parmar
C. Thakur Ramlal
D. Sri Veerbhadra Singh

139. When did Dr. Y.S. Parmar become chief minister of the state?
A. 24th March, 1952
B. 30th March, 1953
C. 26th January, 1954
D. 23rd April, 1959

140. Which of the following has never been the CM of HP?
A. Sri Veerbhadra Singh
B. Sri Shanta Kumar
C. Sri Satya Prakash Thakur
D. Sri Prem Kumar Dhumal

141. When was Municipal corporation established at the place of Municipal Committee in Shimla city?
A. 1978 B. 1980
C. 1982 D. 1985

142. Who was appointed as first Governor of Kangra region by Maharaja Ranjeet Singh in 1809?
A. Desasingh Majithiya
B. Sir Anand Daas
C. Bheema Choudhary
D. Anniberent

143. When was High Court established in HP?
A. 5th January, 1966
B. 7th January, 1870
C. 25th January, 1871
D. 26th January, 1977

144. What is the retirement age of presidents and vice-presidents of HP administrative officers?
A. 65 yrs B. 68 yrs
C. 62 yrs D. 70 yrs

145. National Navy cadet unit was established in which district of state in 1963?
A. Bilaspur B. Shimla
C. Ura D. Mandi

146. When was Shimla made the summer capital of India?
A. 1905 B. 1919
C. 1864 D. 1885

147. When was Army head office shifted to Delhi from Shimla?
A. 1924 B. 1941
C. 1948 D. 1950

148. Who of the following was Army chief related to HP?
A. C.S. Sharma B. G.V. Kaul
C. C.G. Vaidya D. B.N. Sharma

149. Which of the following district was scatterd in Raavi, Vyas, Satluj Valleys and Jalandhar in ancient times?
A. Trigart Sangh (Kangra)
B. Chamba
C. Una
D. Shimla

150. Which of the following city of HP was known as **Vyaspur** in ancient times
A. Una B. Shimla
C. Bilaspur D. Solan

ANSWERS

1	2	3	4	5	6	7	8	9	10
A	C	D	D	C	A	C	C	A	D
11	12	13	14	15	16	17	18	19	20
C	A	B	C	B	D	B	A	C	C
21	22	23	24	25	26	27	28	29	30
A	A	D	C	A	B	C	D	A	C
31	32	33	34	35	36	37	38	39	40
B	A	B	A	A	B	A	D	A	C
41	42	43	44	45	46	47	48	49	50
B	D	D	A	B	C	A	D	B	C
51	52	53	54	55	56	57	58	59	60
A	C	C	C	D	A	C	B	A	C
61	62	63	64	65	66	67	68	69	70
D	A	C	D	B	A	D	C	B	A
71	72	73	74	75	76	77	78	79	80
D	D	A	C	C	A	D	A	C	D
81	82	83	84	85	86	87	88	89	90
C	A	C	A	B	A	C	C	D	A
91	92	93	94	95	96	97	98	99	100
C	D	B	A	A	A	B	A	C	D
101	102	103	104	105	106	107	108	109	110
B	D	B	D	A	C	D	D	D	A
111	112	113	114	115	116	117	118	119	120
C	D	C	D	A	C	A	B	D	A
121	122	123	124	125	126	127	128	129	130
B	A	D	D	D	D	C	A	B	A
131	132	133	134	135	136	137	138	139	140
C	B	A	D	B	A	C	B	A	C
141	142	143	144	145	146	147	148	149	150
A	A	C	A	A	C	B	D	A	C

ECONOMICS

1. Nearby in how many hectares agricultural practices are done in HP?
A. 5.12 Lakh hectare
B. 9.44 Lakh hectare
C. 12.16 Lakh hectare
D. 15.18 Lakh hectare

2. What percentage land of Lahaul-spiti district is used for agriculture?
A. 0.3% B. 0.5%
C. 10.4% D. 8.14%

3. In which district of the state maximum agricultural practices are performed?
A. Hamirpur B. Kangda
C. Manali D. Kullu

4. When are Khareef crops grown in the state?
A. March-April
B. August-September
C. December-January
D. May-June

5. What percentage of total land is used for paddy cultivation in HP?
A. 10% B. 20%
C. 40% D. 70%

6. Which district of the state has maximum paddy production?
A. Shimla B. Solan
C. Kangra D. Chamba

7. Kinnaur & Lahaul-Spiti produces following crop in excessive amount—
A. Maize B. Wheat
C. Barley D. Gram

8. Maize is grown in which district of the state?
A. Shimla B. Hamirpur
C. Solan D. All of these

9. Maximum production of Jowar, millet, Ragi and other small cereals is from the following district
A. Una B. Chamba
C. Kinnaur D. Kangra

10. How many metric tonnes of pulses are produced in HP on an average annually?
A. 54800 mt. B. 40000 mt.
C. 12000 mt. D. 25000 mt.

11. At what time potato crop was cultivated in the state for the first time?
A. During 2nd world war
B. During war of India & China
C. During 1st world war
D. During war between India & Pakistan

12. What was the per capita income at current prices of Himachal Pradesh in 2021-22?
A. 201854 B. 140360
C. 160580 D. 180440

13. Which variety of potato is grown in HP?
A. Kufri Chandramukhi
B. Kufri Jyoti
C. Kufri Jeewan
D. All of the above

14. Seed of beet root is produced at which place of the state?
A. Kinnaur B. Una
C. Bilaspur D. Kangra

15. At which place 'Kala-Jeera' (caraway seed) is produced inHP?
A. Chamba & Kangra
B. Solan & Shimla
C. Kinnaur & Lahaul-spiti
D. Una & Bilaspur

16. 'Kuth' medicinal herb is exported to which country from India, which is cultivated in HP?
A. America B. Canada
C. France D. All of the above

17. Where was first-Apple farm planted in HP?
A. Shimla
B. Kangra
C. Bundoral in Kullu valley
D. Lahaul-spiti

18. Who planted first apple farm in HP?
A. Captain A.A. Lee
B. John Crystal
C. Sir Henry
D. Lady Mount batten

19. When was first apple crop produced in Mashobara of Shimla Hills?
A. 1850 B. 1855
C. 1887 D. 1865

20. Who started potato crop production first of all in Shimla Hills in 1823?
A. Major Henry B. A.O. Hume
C. Sir Charles D. Major Candy

21. What is the position of HP on national level for ginger production?
A. 2nd B. 7th
C. 8th D. 9th

22. Who started Land-improvement in 1876?
A. Sir Henry B. King Raisen
C. Colonel Peter D. Colonel Reed

23. Which of the following is not cultivated in HP?
A. Cotton B. Paddy (rice)
C. Corn D. Mushroom

24. 'Kalyan Sona', 'Sonalika' and R.R.21 are varieties of which crop of the state?
A. Wheat B. Rice
C. Barley D. Sugar Cane

25. What is the percentage of land used for farming in the state?
A. 10 B. 16.95
C. 30 D. 35

26. In which year 'land-law' was passed in HP?
A. 1950 B. 1953
C. 1972 D. 1981

27. Where are oranges grown in the state?
A. Shimla & Manali B. Kullu & Kangra
C. Lahaul & Kinnaur D. Kasauli

28. Maximum apple production is from—
A. Bilaspur B. Sirmaur
C. Solan D. Shimla

29. At which place in Sirmaur district did Indian Government established food procesing unit?
A. Dhaula Kuan B. Sirmaur
C. Solan D. Shimla

30. Which part of the state is best for citrus fruit production?
A. Nalagarh area B. Manali
C. Chamba D. Shivalik Valley

31. HP's largest fruit procesing unit is at which place?
A. Chamba B. Badsar
C. Bharmaur D. Parvanu

32. Which of the following is not a variety of apple produced in the state?
A. Shervaji B. Jonathan
C. Beauty of Bath D. Roam Beauty

33. In which zone, grazier, Gaddi, Kinnar & Gujjar people depends upon animal husbandry in the state?
A. Kinnaur B. Lahaul-Spiti
C. Paangi D. All of the above

34. As per Livestock Census-2019, what is the number of total Livestock in the state?
A. 20 Lakh B. 40 Lakh
C. 44.13 Lakh D. 70 Lakh

35. Gulmarg special is species of which crop?
A. Potato B. Apple
C. Oranges D. Cherry

36. In which district of the state, 7 units are established to improve the bread of Angora rabbit?
A. Chamba B. Shimla
C. Kangra D. Bilaspur

37. At which place of HP, sheep fertility centre is opened?
A. Juri (Shimla)
B. Nagwai (Manali)
C. Taal (Hamirpur)
D. All of the above

38. At which place of the state is Angora Rabbit Farm?
A. Kandvadi (Kangra)
B. Aani (Kullu)
C. Taal (Hamirpur)
D. Rampur (Shimla)

39. Fish fertility centre is established at following place by state government—
A. Jagat Khana (Nalagarh)
B. Aalsu (Manali)
C. Milwa (Kangra)
D. All of the above

40. A special centre for **Traut** fish rearing is opened at
A. Katrai
B. Barot
C. Chadgaon
D. All of the above

41. At which place of the state is biggest fish fertility centre of Asia?
A. Dayoli (Bilaspur)
B. Jagat Khana (Nalagarh)
C. Aalsoo (Manali)
D. Milawa (Kangra)

42. Annual fish production of the state is as
A. 5000 metric tonnes
B. 5100 metric tonnes
C. 9000 metric tonnes
D. 6500 metric tonnes

43. Which of the following variety of fish is found in HP?
A. Mahasheer B. Mirr
C. Traut D. All of the above

44. At which place of Chamba, sheep fertility centre is opened?
A. Paangi B. Choori
C. Bhatiyaat D. Salooni

45. Dayoli where largest fish fertility centre of Asia is based, falls under the following district
A. Bilaspur B. Kangra
C. Una D. Shimla

46. What percentage land of the state is pasture land?
A. 5% B. 8%
C. 32.89% D. 21%

ANSWERS

1	**2**	**3**	**4**	**5**	**6**	**7**	**8**	**9**	**10**
B	A	C	D	A	C	C	D	C	A
11	**12**	**13**	**14**	**15**	**16**	**17**	**18**	**19**	**20**
A	A	D	A	C	D	C	A	C	D
21	**22**	**23**	**24**	**25**	**26**	**27**	**28**	**29**	**30**
A	D	A	A	B	C	B	D	A	D
31	**32**	**33**	**34**	**35**	**36**	**37**	**38**	**39**	**40**
D	A	D	C	A	C	D	A	D	D
41	**42**	**43**	**44**	**45**	**46**				
D	C	D	B	A	C				

ART AND CULTURE

1. What is the height of 'Nandi' standing in the premises of Mani-Mahesh temple of Bharmaur?

A. 5" B. 6"
C. 7" D. 8"

2. In which year Ms J.E. Dunken discovered Mrukula Devi slate hand print?

A. 1905 B. 1906
C. 1907 D. 1908

3. Which King's Coronation date is calculated from 'Luj Panghat Rock inscription'?

A. Nagra B. Jasath
C. Bhatli D. Meruvarman

4. From various temples and Rock inscription of Chamba about the period of which of King rulership information is obtained?

A. Meruvarman (680–700)
B. Chandravarman (650–708)
C. Jaivarman (800–830)
D. Mukteshwar (775–800)

5. Inscription of Buddha statue obtained from Kangra is perhaps from following century—

A. 9th or 10th B. 8th or 9th
C. 5th or 6th D. 6th or 7th

6. Near Pathiyaar a little distant from Kunihara of Kangra district two Rock inscription obtained were of which period?

A. Maurya Period B. Gupt Period
C. Kushan Period D. Rajpoot Period

7. How many lines are there in Bharmaur copper sheet article of Yugakar varman?

A. 16 B. 17
C. 18 D. 19

8. In which Rock inscription, Lord Ganesh is not sitting on rat but on lion?

A. Luj Panghat Stone print
B. Sehli Panghat Stone print
C. Mithala Mata print
D. Mrukula Devi state print

9. 'Rock inscription' obtained near 'Loh tikri' Churah is related to rulership period of which King?

A. Asata Varman B. Jasata Varman
C. Rana Paal D. Anant Devi

10. 'Divri Kothi' and 'Saiyu Nala' Paanji stone prints are related to time period of King

A. Lalit Barman B. Udai Barman
C. Prithvi Barman D. Dala Barman

11. Which festival of Kinnaur district is famous as 'festival of flowers'?

A. Losar B. Fulaich
C. Ukhyaang D. Bhunda

12. At which place in Kinnaur the family having son presents a goat to Gram-devta at ukhyang festival?

A. Poddar valley B. Ropa village
C. Sangla valley D. Ranka

13. Who started 'Mandi Shivraatri fare' in the state?

A. King Aamer Singh
B. King Anand Paal
C. King Mohar Singh
D. King Ajber Sen

14. Point out the wrong match

A. Nalwadi fare – Bilaspur
B. Minchar fare – Kullu
C. Renuka fare – Sirmaur
D. Lavi fare – Rampur

15. Which is the festival of HP?

A. Cherwaal B. Jagraata
C. Barlaj D. All of these

16. Which festival of Kinnaur district is organised by only young males?

A. Toshin B. Halda
C. Losar D. Fulaich

17. At which place of the state a fare named 'Boodhi-Diwali' is organized?

A. Mandi B. Riwalsar
C. Nirmad D. Bilaspur

18. Gandhi fare in Sirmaur district is organised at which place on 30th January?

A. Amri B. Ambora
C. Maangarh D. Dadaher

19. Which fare of Manali district is declared to be **National-level**?

A. Rivalsar fare B. Bhangrotu fare
C. Kao fare D. Shivratri fare

20. Winter-Carniwal of the state is organised at
A. Chandrabhaga valley
B. Kullu
C. Kufri
D. Mahasu

21. Which festival is celebrated in remembrance of devi Hidimba in Kullu district?
A. Doongari fare B. Cintapoorni fare
C. Brajeshwari fare D. Durga fare

22. Baba Daya geer fare of Kangra district is organised at
A. Daulatpur B. Maidi
C. Mahasu D. Kangra

23. Which fare is declared to be of state level in district Bilaspur?
A. Nalwadi fare B. Shiv fare
C. Chintpoorni fare D. Rewalsar fare

24. At which place of the state famous 'Stone-game' fare is organised?
A. Kinnaur B. Halog
C. Lahaul D. Kangra

25. Which festival is celebrated in Sirmaur on the day of Baisakhi?
A. Bishu festival B. Halda
C. Fulaich D. Bees Bhadon

26. Dassehara of which place of Himachal is famous?
A. Kullu B. Shimla
C. Mandi D. Solan

27. Which fare of Bilaspur is famous from business point of view?
A. Luhnu fare B. Chinz
C. Agricultural fare D. Fare of Nalwadi

28. Which is the largest fare of eastern Himachal
A. Renuka B. Holi
C. Kahik D. Mizar

29. At Nahan of Himachal at the time of Sawan Dwadashi and Dassehara, which fare is organised?
A. Teej Mela
B. Baha Badbhag Singh Mela
C. Dayot Siddh Mela
D. Chadiyon ka Mela

30. Which fare is organised at Paota of Himachal during Holi?
A. Holi Mela
B. Chadiyon ka Mela
C. Jhanda Sahib Mela
D. Dayot Siddh Mela

31. Bala Sundari fare at Tilokpu is organised in the month of
A. Maagh B. Srawan
C. Chait D. Bhado

32. In which festival of the state, people from abroad and cultural origin taken part?
A. Dassehara of Kullu
B. Holi Mela of Kangra & Sujanpur
C. Nalwadi fare of Bilaspur
D. Minjar fare of Chamba

33. Which fare is organised in Chamba on the day of full moon of Bhadrapad month?
A. Rath-rathadi
B. Brajeshwari fare
C. Vishnu rathyatra fare
D. Minjar fare

34. Which festival is celebrated by Gaddi tribe of Himachal?
A. Basoa B. Patrodu
C. Sair D. All of these

35. Which fare is organized in Kinnaur in the month of Baisakh?
A. Saanjhi fare B. Soohi fare
C. Animal fare D. Ukhyad fare

36. Which fare is organized in the month of Fagun in Rampur?
A. Faag fare B. Holi Mela
C. Devi Mela D. Animal fare

37. Which person of the state is not recorded in Guinness book of World records?
A. Tilak Raaj B. Ranjeet Singh
C. Madam Singh D. Gurinder Jeet Aaasi

38. Short story art style was started in rulership of which King in Baghal princely state's capital Arki?
A. Rana Sabha Chand
B. Rana Jagat Singh
C. Rana Abhay Chand
D. Rana Kishan Chand

39. In remembrance of queen Chambiyaali in Chamba, which fare is organised from 15 Chaitra to 1st Baisakh?

A. Markand fare B. Soohi fare
C. Shiv fare D. Dayot Siddh fare

40. At which place near Bharmaur a fare is organised on Sukla Astami of Bhadrapad month?
A. Mani Mahesh B. Bhalai
C. Paangi D. Salooni

41. Which is the famous festival of HP which is organised every year on 25 to 27 Kartik Vikrami in Rampur (Mahasu)?
A. Markand fare B. Shiv fare
C. Lavi fare D. Devi fare

42. Which cultural event is given special space in Sirmaur?
A. Lochar B. Sanjhi celebration
C. Halda D. Falaich

43. Which of the following writer does not belong to HP?
A. Shanta Kumar
B. Shivpoojan Shahi
C. P.N. Sibbal
D. Dr. Bariyaam Singh

44. From which creation of Ganesh Singh Bedi are get information about history of HP?
A. Shashivansh Vinod
B. Vinod Mantra
C. History of Himachal
D. None of these

45. Himachal state was divided into various small rulers in 1st century. There rulers were called Rana, Thakur, Maavi. This is an opinion of famous historian?
A. Alberuni B. It-sing
C. Farishta D. None of these

46. Kangra Kingdom of HP was discovered for the first time by which historian?
A. Farishta B. It-sing
C. Ptolemy D. Alberuni

47. First Pahadi Gandhi Baba Kanshi Ram prize in the year 1989 was given to
A. Sri Sharad Upadhyaya
B. Sri Jaidev Kiran
C. Sri Shyam Chand hari
D. Sri Prakash Jha

48. In the ancient times, pahari language was written in
A. Tankari B. Dravin
C. Devnagri D. Brahmi

49. Where is Kehloori language spoken in the state?
A. Mandi B. Kullu
C. Bilaspur D. None of these

50. Bhagati language is spoken in which part of the state?
A. Kangra B. Una
C. Bilaspur D. Solan

ANSWERS

1	2	3	4	5	6	7	8	9	10
A	C	B	A	D	A	D	B	B	A
11	12	13	14	15	16	17	18	19	20
C	B	D	B	D	A	C	B	D	C
21	22	23	24	25	26	27	28	29	30
A	A	A	B	A	A	D	A	D	C
31	32	33	34	35	36	37	38	39	40
C	A	A	D	D	A	A	A	B	A
41	42	43	44	45	46	47	48	49	50
C	B	B	A	C	A	B	A	C	D

Miscellaneous

1. What is the Vedic name of river Raavi?
A. Parushni B. Shutudri
C. Askini D. Arjikiya

2. Which is the smallest city in HP?
A. Dharmshala B. Naina devi
C. Rampur D. Noorpur

3. Which of the following district does not fall under Shimla Mandal in HP?
A. Kinnaur B. Hamirpur
C. Solan D. Sirmaur

4. Which King of Gupta Dynasty in beginning of 4th century won over Himachal and imprisoned the people of the state?
A. Chandragupta Vikramaditya
B. Chandragupta
C. Samudragupta
D. Kumargupta

5. Who was the ruler of Nagarkot when Mahmood Gajnavi attacked there in 1009?
A. Jaichand B. Kalyaanchand
C. Vijaychand D. Jagdishchand

6. Where was the capital of Chamba in ancient time?
A. Satpura B. Bahavpura
C. Brahmapura D. Chamora

7. Which of the following ruler captured Kangra Library and got all the books translated in Farsi?
A. Aadil Shah
B. Firoz Shah Tughlaq
C. Mohammad Tughlaq
D. Humayun

8. Freedom movement was started at following place in HP in 1857
A. Kasauli Sainik Chhavni
B. Nalagarh
C. Kullu
D. Bushahar

9. Panzhauta movement against which of the following took place in HP?
A. British ruler B. Mandi Riyasat
C. Sikh D. Gorkha

10. Who was the leader of 'Quit India Movement' in Shimla?
A. Somnaath
B. Rajkumari Amrit Kaur
C. Bhavkar Nand
D. Baba Kanshiram

11. Who first of all demanded for Himachal to be declared as Pahadi State in 1946?
A. Hazara Singh
B. Raja Maansingh
C. Veerbhadra Singh
D. Jeewan Lal

12. Legislative assembly was formed in HP under following amendment of Indian constitution
A. 12th B. 14th
C. 16th D. 20th

13. Shingrila mountain peak is in which district of HP?
A. Kinnaur B. Kullu
C. Lahaul-Spiti D. Kangra

14. Kullu valley of HP is known by which other name?
A. Raam B. Dev
C. Cheta D. Shiv

15. In which districts of HP; various programmes were run to popularize modern techniques with help of Germany?
A. Mandi & Kullu
B. Kangra & Chamba
C. Hamirpur and Shimla
D. Bilaspur and Una

16. Uranium is found in which part of HP?
A. Una, Hamirpur B. Kangra-Kullu
C. Shimla, Kullu D. Bilaspur, Solan

17. Which is major industrial city of HP?
A. Nahan B. Shimla
C. Bilaspur D. Una

18. Which river is considered most sacred by Gaddi tribes of HP?
A. Yamuna B. Raavi
C. Ganga D. Satluj

19. Who was the leader of Buddhism followers (deciples) whom king Ashoka send for popularisation of Buddhism in Himalaya?
A. Mazzhima B. Mahendra
C. Charudatt D. Sanghmitra

20. Which city of HP was known as 'Vyaspur' in ancient times?
A. Una B. Shimla
C. Bilaspur D. Solan

21. Which is the biggest fair in eastern Himalaya?
A. Renuka B. Holi
C. Jwalamukhi D. Minzer

22. Which of the following is the biggest irrigation plant in HP?
A. Shah Canal Project
B. Singpur Canal Project
C. Jalalpur Canal Project
D. Ishtapami Canal Project

23. Famous 'Jhanjhar Dance' is related to which district of HP?
A. Kangra B. Lahaul
C. Bilaspur D. Chamba

24. Riwalsar is the birth place of whom of the following?
A. Padm Sambhav B. Mahaveer Swami
C. Gautam Budh D. Raja Sansar Chand

25. World famous 'Roomal Art' is related with the district .... of HP.
A. Chamba B. Kangra
C. Bilaspur D. Una

26. Renukaji lake is in which district?
A. Shimla B. Chamba
C. Mandi D. Sirmaur

27. Which is the main fruit of Himachal Pradesh?
A. Peach B. Apple
C. Pears D. None of these

28. Bandli sanctuary located in—
A. Una B. Mandi
C. Kullu D. None of these

29. The book 'Kangra Paintings' is written by—
A. R.K. Kaushal B. M.S. Randhawa
C. L.C. Paranthi D. Bal Govind

30. Moti Mahal located at—
A. Nahan B. Una
C. Mandi D. Shimla

31. The Book 'Prachin Himachal' is written by—
A. Moor Craft B. Shanta Kumar
C. L.C. Parathi D. Ram Rahul

32. The book 'History of Mandi State' is written by—
A. Manmohan Singh B. A.K. Kaushal
C. A.K. Randhawa D. None of these

33. Which is birth place of Prem kumar Dhumal?
A. Hamirpur B. Samirpur
C. Mehatpur D. None of these

34. Literacy rate of Una district is—
A. 70.50% B. 86.53%
C. 80.54% D. 89.65%

35. The book 'Pahar Begane Nahin Honge' is written by—
A. Vikram Kayasth B. Shanta Kumar
C. Anand Chand D. Ranzor Singh

36. Pathankot to Mandi is a NH of No.—
A. 21 B. 20
C. 23 D. 24

37. Tirthan Sanctury is located in—
A. Shimla B. Kullu
C. Una D. None of these

38. What is overall literacy rate of H.P.?
A. 82.80% B. 76%
C. 79% D. None of these

39. What is Literacy rate of Female in H.P.?
A. 66% B. 75.93%
C. 69% D. None of these

40. Who built Gouari Shanker Temple in Chamba?
A. Bataloo B. Meru Verma
C. Yuzankar Verma D. None of these

41. Who built Hidimba Temple in Manali?
A. R.B. Singh B. R.S. Singh
C. R.N. Singh D. None of these

42. What is height of Shimla above sea Level?
A. 2205 B. 2206
C. 2208 D. None of these

43. How many district are in H.P.?
A. 13 B. 14
C. 12 D. 19

44. Who is district head of Medical Services?
A. DMO B. CMO
C. SMO D. None of these

45. In Himachal Pradesh number of members elected for Rajya Sabha are:
A. 3 B. 2
C. 4 D. 5

46. Who is Officer Incharge of Headquarter?
A. IG B. DIG
C. DSP D. None of these

47. Shri Naina Devi Ji is a Tehsile of Which district?
A. Bilaspur B. Una
C. Shimla D. None of these

48. Battle of Haloti fought in which year?
A. 1650 AD B. 1670 AD
C. 1690 AD D. None of these

49. Who is Founder of Chamba State?
A. Veer Sen B. Meru Varma
C. Hati Chand D. None of these

50. Who is founder of Jubbel ?
A. Karan B. Karan Chand
C. K.P. D. None of these

51. Dr. Y.S. Parmar University was established in—
A. 1980 B. 1985
C. 1987 D. None of these

52. Dr. Y.S. Parmar University located in H.P.—
A. Shimla B. Nanni
C. Sundernagar D. None of these

53. Where is place of Publication of Newspaper Ooncha Himalaya?
A. Una B. Shimla
C. Delhi D. None of these

54. Lahauli Language is Spoken in which area—
A. Lahaul Spiti B. Shimla
C. Una D. None of these

55. Gujjar are .... in HP.
A. SC B. ST
C. OBC D. None of these

56. Lahaulis are—
A. ST B. SC
C. OBC D. None of these

57. What is area of Una district?
A. 1550 sq. km B. 1540 sq. km
C. 1550 D. None of these

58. Which district is maximum literate?
A. Hamirpur B. Una
C. Shimla D. None of these

59. What is sex ratio in H.P?
A. 870:1000 B. 972:1000
C. 900:1000 D. None of these

60. Dal Lake is located in—
A. Una B. Kangra
C. Chamba D. Shimla

61. Pong Dam is in—
A. Kangra district B. Una district
C. Shimla D. None of these

62. What is height of Shilla Peak ?
A. 7020 m B. 7050 m
C. 7051 m D. None of these

63. Who built Maukot fort?
A. Salim B. Salim Shah Sur
C. A & B D. None of these

64. Who is the founder of Hamirpur?
A. Hamir chand B. Raja Ram Singh
C. Deep chand D. None of these

65. Who was the first C.M. of H.P.?
A. Y.S. Parmar B. Y.S. Singh
C. Y.S. Bhoot D. N.C. Mehta

66. In area wise, which is the smallest district?
A. Una B. Hamirpur
C. Bilaspur D. None of these

67. Highest rain occur at—
A. Una B. Dharamshala
C. Shimla D. None of these

68. In Himachal Pradesh who is called Pahari Gandhi?
A. B. Pratap Singh B. Baba Kanshi Ram
C. L.C. Prarthi D. None of these

69. Himachal Pradesh Agriculture University is situated in—
A. Jogindernagar B. Palampur
C. Kandaghat D. Rohru

70. The first primary school was opened at Keylong in—
A. 1861 B. 1890
C. 1885 D. 1910

71. Every year 'Lavi fair' is celebrated at—
A. Rampur Bushahr B. Kangra
C. Chamba D. Mashobra

72. The book 'Prachin Himachal' is written by—
A. L.C. Sharma B. L.C. Parathi
C. Gharib Khan D. None of these

73. Which is the birth place of Shanta Kumar?
A. Samirpur B. Una
C. Gharjumla D. None of these

74. Himachal Pradesh High Court was established in—
A. 1970 B. 1971
C. 1972 D. 1973

75. Himachal Pradesh High Court is located in which district?
A. Shimla B. Mandi
C. Kangra D. Kullu

76. How many mountain ranges are there in Himachal Pradesh?
A. Four B. Three
C. Two D. One

77. In which mountain range 'Hamirpur and Una' Districts are located?
A. Outer Himalayas B. Inner Himalayas
C. Great Himalayas D. None of these

78. Outer Himalayas is known as—
A. Lower Himalayas B. Shivalik
C. Manak D. All of these

79. Where is 'Dashahar Lake' Situated?
A. Near Mandali (Kullu)
B. Rewalsar Town (Mandi)
C. Dankhar (Sirmaur)
D. None of these

80. Which district has been declared as the Mushroom District of Himachal Pradesh?
A. Shimla B. Solan
C. Bilaspur D. Una

81. In which District of Himachal Pradesh to produce Sugar beet?
A. Kullu B. Sirmaur
C. Kinnaur D. Kangra

82. The State Day of Himachal Pradesh is—
A. 5th April B. 15th January
C. 25 March D. 15 May

83. The High Court of Himachal Pradesh is in—
A. Una B. Hamirpur
C. Shimla D. Mandi

84. How many Divisions are there in Himachal Pradesh?
A. 4 B. 5
C. 2 D. 3

85. Which of the following is a tributary of Beas river—
A. Chandra B. Kunah
C. Htli D. Baira

86. The location of Himachal Pradesh is—
A. 32022' to 34012' North latitude and 750 47' to 780 04' East Longitude
B. 30022' to 33012' North latitude and 75047' to 79004' East Longitude
C. 31022' to 30012' North longitude and 75047' to 79004' east longitude
D. None of these

87. The area of Himachal Pradesh is—
A. 55673 sq km B. 55574 sq km
C. 55373 sq km D. 55272 sq km

88. Which of the following district is Renuka lake situated?
A. Mandi B. Una
C. Sirmour D. Shimla

89. In which district Mani Mahesh Lake situated?
A. Kangra B. Una
C. Chamba D. Palampur

90. The river Satluj arise from which of the following Lake—
A. Bradonsar Lake
B. Kamru Nag Lake
C. Mani Mahesh Lake
D. Man Sarover Lake

91. In which district a Budha monastry was established?
A. Kangra B. Lahaul Siti
C. Una D. Shimla

92. The Idol of Raghu Nath was brought to Kulu from Ayodhya in—
A. 1651 A.D. B. 1751 A.D.
C. 1851 A.D. D. 1951 A.D.

93. Mandi Town was established by—
A. Raja Suraj Sen B. Raja Ajmer Sen
C. Raja Ber Sen D. None of these

94. When was Mandi town established?
A. 1512 B. 1517
C. 1527 D. 1530

95. Where was Ras Bihari Bose Stayed in 1913 A.D.—
A. Kullu B. Kangra
C. Lahaul Spiti D. Palampur

96. The greatest Ruler Raja Rattan Chand ruled over—
A. Kahloor B. Bilaspur
C. Kullu D. None of these

97. In which district the highest pass of Himachal Pradesh is located?
A. Kangra B. Kullu
C. Shimla D. Lahaul Spiti

98. Banganga is tributary of which of the following rivers?
A. Beas B. Yamuna
C. Ganga D. None of these

99. National Institute of Technology is in—
A. Shimla B. Chamba
C. Hamirpur D. Kullu

100. The height of District Shimla is—
A. 2205 m B. 2305 m
C. 2405 m D. 2505 m

101. Which is the largest city of Himachal Pradesh?
A. Shimla B. Hamirpur
C. Kullu D. Chama

102. Find out the following Place is called 'Mini Lahasa'
A. Solan B. Kinnaur
C. Sirmor D. Dharamshala

103. The longest river of Himachal Pradesh is—
A. Jehlem B. Beas
C. Chenab D. Satluj

104. The main religion of People of Lahul Spiti?
A. Hinduism B. Christian
C. Budhism D. None of these

105. Who was the first Assembly Speaker of the State?
A. Thakur Himmat Singh
B. Pandit Jaiwant Ram
C. D.R. Mahajan
D. K.C. Rana

106. Who was the first chief Justice of H.P.?
A. M.H. Beg B. R.S. Pathak
C. T.U. Mehta D. None of these

107. When was the first General Election held in Himachal Pradesh—
A. 1953 B. 1954
C. 1952 D. 1951

108. The old name of Ravi is—
A. Ravati B. Ramani
C. Kalindi D. Iravati

109. Which of the following districts is the biggest in area wise?
A. Shimla B. Una
C. Lahaul Spiti D. Palampur

110. On which river 'Bhakra Dam' Project is located?
A. Satluj B. Ganga
C. Ravi D. Beas

111. Which was the first Capital of Nurpur State?
A. Niyajpur B. Trigarta
C. Pathan Kot D. Shahpur

112. When was the battle of Bhagini fought?
A. 1586 A.D. B. 1686 A.D.
C. 1786 A.D. D. 1886 A.D.

113. The battle of Bhangini was fought between—
A. Guru Gobind Singh & Sansar Chand
B. Siks & Chande Bhan
C. Ishwar Sen & Siks
D. Guru Gobind Singh & Raja Bhi Chand of Bilaspur

114. When was Gandhi Ji visited Shimla?
A. 1916 B. 1917
C. 1918 D. 1921

115. Gandhi ji Visited Shimla and he stayed at—
A. Peterhaff B. Chauki
C. Shanti Kutir D. None of these

116. Who was the Great General of Ranjit Singh King?
A. Hari Singh Nalwa B. Gorkhas
C. Bhagat Singh D. None of these

117. The book 'Country Life' written by—
A. M. Pallis B. U.S. Kumar
C. Nora Richard D. None of these

118. 'H.P. Area and Languages' is written by—
A. Shanta Kumar B. Dr. Y.S. Parmar
C. Hari Ram Jasta D. None of these

119. Palampur Sub Division is located in which district?
A. Hamirpur B. Chamba
C. Kangra D. Bilaspur

120. Which is the State Bird of Himachal Pradesh?
A. Sparrow B. Western Tragopan
C. Peacock D. None of these

121. On which river a bridge was constructed in 1894?
A. Satluj B. Ravi
C. Beas D. Chenow

122. Which was the ancient name of Kangra?
A. Trigarta B. Nagar
C. Triartan D. None of these

123. The Capital of Trigarta was—
A. Nagoori B. Nagar
C. Nagarcot D. Narvani

124. When was Dharam Chand ascended the Kangra Throne—
A. 1516 B. 1518
C. 1524 D. 1528

125. Hamirpur town was established by—
A. Alam B. Hamir chand
C. Bhim Chand D. Sansar Chand

ANSWERS

1	**2**	**3**	**4**	**5**	**6**	**7**	**8**	**9**	**10**
A	B	B	C	D	C	B	A	A	B
11	**12**	**13**	**14**	**15**	**16**	**17**	**18**	**19**	**20**
A	B	C	B	B	C	A	B	A	C
21	**22**	**23**	**24**	**25**	**26**	**27**	**28**	**29**	**30**
A	A	D	A	A	D	B	B	B	A
31	**32**	**33**	**34**	**35**	**36**	**37**	**38**	**39**	**40**
C	A	B	B	B	B	B	A	B	C
41	**42**	**43**	**44**	**45**	**46**	**47**	**48**	**49**	**50**
A	B	C	A	A	A	A	B	B	B
51	**52**	**53**	**54**	**55**	**56**	**57**	**58**	**59**	**60**
B	B	B	A	B	A	B	A	B	B
61	**62**	**63**	**64**	**65**	**66**	**67**	**68**	**69**	**70**
A	B	B	A	A	B	B	B	B	A
71	**72**	**73**	**74**	**75**	**76**	**77**	**78**	**79**	**80**
A	B	C	B	A	B	A	D	A	B
81	**82**	**83**	**84**	**85**	**86**	**87**	**88**	**89**	**90**
C	A	C	D	B	B	A	C	C	D
91	**92**	**93**	**94**	**95**	**96**	**97**	**98**	**99**	**100**
B	A	B	C	C	A	D	A	C	A
101	**102**	**103**	**104**	**105**	**106**	**107**	**108**	**109**	**110**
A	D	D	C	B	A	C	D	C	A
111	**112**	**113**	**114**	**115**	**116**	**117**	**118**	**119**	**120**
C	B	D	D	C	A	C	B	C	B
121	**122**	**123**	**124**	**125**					
B	A	B	D	B					

OBJECTIVE
GENERAL KNOWLEDGE

History of World

1. Abraham Lincon was elected the President of United States in:
A. 1862 B. 1860
C. 1875 D. 1855
2. D-Day is the day when:
A. Germany declared war on Britain
B. US dropped the atom bomb on Hiroshima.
C. Allied Troops landed in Normandy
D. Germany surrendered to the allies
3. Whose teachings inspired the French Revolution?
A. Locke B. Rousseau
C. Hegel D. Plato
4. At a time when empires in Europe were crumbling before the might of Napoleon which *one* of the following Governor-Generals kept the British flag flying high in India?
A. Warren Hastings
B. Lord Cornwallis
C. Lord Wellesley
D. Lord Hastings
5. Which one of the following statements regarding Fascism in Italy is *not* true?
A. The Fascists came to power as a result of popular uprising
B. In 1926, all political parties except Mussolini's party were banned
C. The Fascists suppressed the Socialist movement
D. The Fascists were hostile to the Communists
6. The fall of Czar Nicholas-II is known as:
A. Bloody Sunday
B. Bolshevik Revolution
C. February Revolution
D. October Revolution
7. Industrial Revolution took place first in:
A. France
B. Germany
C. United Kingdom
D. Japan
8. The British Prime Minister at the outbreak of World War II was
A. Churchill
B. Baldwin
C. Attlee
D. Chemberlain
9. The slogan "No taxation without representation" was raised during the:
A. American War of Independence
B. Russian Revolution
C. French Revolution
D. Indian Freedom struggle
10. In the nineteenth century the people of Europe started moving from the villages to the cities due to the impact of
A. Epidemics
B. War
C. Industrialisation
D. Population explosion in villages
11. The important cause of the Civil War in America was:
A. Abolition of slavery
B. Quest for freedom
C. Industrialisation
D. Rebellion by the native Americans
12. Industrial Revolution could not have come about without:
A. Merchant capitalism
B. The Enclosure Movement
C. The services of the proletariat class
D. An agricultural revolution
13. Consider the following statements
The French Revolution came about mainly due to the
1. Extreme poverty of the people
2. Impact of the works of great writers
3. Cruelty of the rulers
4. Impact of impulsive reaction
Which of the above statements are correct?
A. 1, 2 and 4
B. 2 and 3
C. 1, 3 and 4
D. All of the above
14. Asia's oldest and largest Buddhist monastery is situated in:

A. Tawang (Arunachal Pradesh)
B. Lhasa (Tibet)
C. Trincomallee (Sri Lanka)
D. Ulan Bator (Mongolia)

15. Who was the main architect of the Russian Revolution?
A. Karl Marx
B. Lenin
C. Stalin
D. Tolstoy

16. Lenin is associated with:
A. Russian Revolution of 1917
B. Chinese Revolution of 1949
C. German Revolution
D. French Revolution of 1789

17. Which one of the following statements is *not* correct?
A. Voltaire believed in Natural Religion
B. Rousseau wrote *Social Contract*
C. Montesquieu authored *The Spirit of Laws*
D. Necker believed in 'General Will'

18. The Nihilists were responsible for the:
A. American Revolution
B. French Revolution
C. Industrial Revolution
D. Russian Revolution

19. The British Prime Minister at the time of India's Independence was :
A. Winston Churchill
B. Clement Attlee
C. Anthony Eden
D. Harold Macmillan

20. Mesopotamian civilization was bound by Persian Gulf in the—
A. South B. North
C. East D. West

21. Which part of the Mesopotamian civilization is called Babylonia?
A. North B. East
C. West D. South

22. In which civilization cities used to fight among themselves for the territorial or water irrigation?
A. Indus valley civilization
B. Egyptian civilization
C. Mesopotamian civilization
D. Greek civilization

23. Hieroglyphic is a script developed by the people of which civilization?
A. Indus valley civilization
B. Egyptian civilization
C. Chinese civilization
D. Roman civilization

24. Chinese rulers made the great wall to protect their empire from—
A. Huns B. Kushans
C. Greeks D. Romans

25. Which among the following was not a part of Roman civilization?
A. South Europe
B. North Africa
C. South-east Asia
D. West Asia

26. Which among the following civilizations was famous for its city-states?
A. Greek civilization
B. Roman civilization
C. Chinese civilization
D. Indus valley civilization

27. Solar calendar based on 365 days was developed by..........
A. Egyptian B. Greek
C. Chinese D. Roman

28. Papyrus, a technique of making paper is developed by ....
A. Chinese B. Roman
C. Egyptian D. Greek

ANSWERS

1	**2**	**3**	**4**	**5**	**6**	**7**	**8**	**9**	**10**
B	C	B	C	A	B	C	A	A	C
11	**12**	**13**	**14**	**15**	**16**	**17**	**18**	**19**	**20**
A	A	D	A	B	A	D	D	B	A
21	**22**	**23**	**24**	**25**	**26**	**27**	**28**		
D	C	B	A	C	A	A	C		

HISTORY OF INDIA

1. 6th April, 1930 is well known in the history of India because this date is associated with...........
   A. Dandi March by Mahatma Gandhi
   B. Quit India Movement
   C. Partition of Bengal
   D. Partition of India
2. Which ruler enforced the system of 'Price Control' in India?
   A. Mohammad Tughlak
   B. Razia Begum
   C. Alauddin Khilji
   D. Sher Shah Suri
3. The concept of 'Din-e-Elahi' was founded by which king?
   A. Dara Shikoh
   B. Akbar
   C. Sher Shah Suri
   D. Shahjahan
4. Who are supposed to be the earliest inhabitants of India? Where did they come from?
   A. Aryans from Central Asia
   B. Dravidians from Mediterranean
   C. Negroids from Africa
   D. Bhils and the Santhals from West Asia
5. The one chief characteristic of temple architecture of the Gupta Age was :
   A. Absence of dome
   B. Huge size
   C. Beautiful carvings
   D. absence of a covered courtyard for the gathering of worshippers
6. The Rigveda consists of :
   A. 1000 hymns
   B. 2028 hymns
   C. 1028 hymns
   D. 1038 hymns
7. The central point in Ashoka's dharma was:
   A. royalty to kings
   B. peace and non-violence
   C. respect to elders
   D. religious toleration
8. The social evil which was conspicuously absent during ancient India was :
   A. *Sati*-System
   B. *Devadasi*-System
   C. Polygamy
   D. *Purdah*-System
9. Which, among the following, can be accepted as a novelty introduced by Mughal emperors to their buildings?
   A. Domes
   B. Minarets
   C. Arches
   D. Attached gardens
10. The first ruler of India who defeated Muhammad of Ghur was :
    A. Mularaja II of Gujarat
    B. Prithviraja Chauhan of Delhi
    C. Jayachand of Kannauj
    D. Parmaldeva of Bundelkhand
11. What important event happened in India in 1911?
    A. Bengal was partitioned
    B. Non-Cooperation movement was launched
    C. India's capital was shifted from Calcutta to Delhi
    D. Mahatma Gandhi presided over, the Congress session
12. The first phase of the Congress Party (1885-1905) was characterized by its efforts to secure
    A. limited independence
    B. complete freedom
    C. Indianization of services
    D. constitutional reforms
13. The Muslim League demanded a separate homeland for the Indian Muslims openly for the first time at its annual session held in Lahore in the year :
    A. 1931 A.D. B. 1936 A.D.
    C. 1940 A.D. D. 1941 A.D.
14. Under whose governorship did the East India Company secure the Diwani Rights in Bengal, Bihar and Orissa (Odisha) from Emperor Shah Alam?
    A. Lord Cornwallis
    B. Lord William Bentinck
    C. Lord Clive
    D. Lord Wellesley

15. The Simon Commission was generally boycotted by the Indian political parties. What was the reason for this general non-cooperation?
A. the Commission aimed at dividing the people
B. it was an 'all white' Commission
C. it came after the Jallian-wala Bagh carnage
D. it was an eye wash

16. Aligarh Muslim University was founded by :
A. Dr. Saifuddin Kitchlu
B. Mohammad Ali Jinnah
C. Sir Syed Ahmed Khan
D. Maulana Mohammad Ali

17. Ibn Batutah was an African traveller visiting India during the time of :
A. Alivardi Khan
B. Ala-ud-din Khilji
C. Iltutmish
D. Mohammad-bin-Tughlaq

18. The battle of Wandiawash was fought in :
A. 1726 B. 1760
C. 1818 D. 1857

19. The abolition of *Sati* by government regulation was implemented at the time of:
A. Warren Hastings
B. Lord Wellesley
C. Lord Bentinck
D. Lord Ahmerst

20. Pick out the wrong combination :
A. Dilwara Temple : Mt. Abu
B. Pashupati Temple : Kathmandu
C. Padmanabha Temple : Bangalore
D. Minakshi Temple : Madurai

21. Match the following:
(*a*) Chanhu-daro
(*b*) Kalibangan
(*c*) Lothal
(*d*) Surkotoda
1. Alleged discovery of the skeleton of horse.
2. Bead making.
3. Traces of a dock and ship on seal.
4. Evidence of ploughing the fields.

Codes :

	(*a*)	(*b*)	(*c*)	(*d*)
A.	2	4	3	1
B.	2	1	3	4
C.	1	2	3	4
D.	2	1	4	3

22. Match the Harappan settlements with the banks of rivers on which they were located :
(*a*) Harappa 1. Ravi
(*b*) Mohenjo-daro 2. Indus
(*c*) Ropar 3. Sutlej
(*d*) Kalibangan 4. Ghaggar
(*e*) Lothal 5. Bhogava

Codes :

	(*a*)	(*b*)	(*c*)	(*d*)	(*e*)
A.	1	2	3	4	5
B.	1	2	3	5	4
C.	2	1	3	5	4
D.	2	1	4	3	5

23. The Goddess 'Kannagi' whose many temples were erected during the 'Sangam Age' was the goddess of :
A. Chastity B. Love
C. Prowess D. Wisdom

24. The Jain goal of life is to attain deliverance from the fetters of mudane existence, the way to which lies through three jewels. Which one of the following was not included among the 'three jewels' of Jainism?
A. Right faith
B. Right action
C. Right knowledge
D. Right conduct

25. The most striking feature of the Ashokan pillar is polish. Name the Ashokan pillar which is considered to be the most graceful of all Ashokan pillars.
A. Sarnath
B. Rampurva
C. Laurya-Nandangarh
D. Rummindei

26. Which are the correct statements?
1. The land grants, started in Satavahana period, paved the way for feudal developments in India.
2. Silk and spices were the Chief Indian export articles of Indo-Roman trade.
3. The Guptas issued the largest number of gold coins in ancient India.
4. The first memorial of a 'SATI' dated 510 A.D. is found at Eran in Madhya Pradesh.
A. 1 and 2
B. 1, 3 and 4
C. 1 and 4
D. All of the above

27. Who among the following patronised the 'Gandhara' (Indo-Greek style) School of Art?
A. Ashoka, the Great
B. Harsha Vardhana
C. Kanishka
D. Chandragupta Vikramaditya

28. The Sultanate of Delhi had five ruling dynasties. The dynasty having longest and shortest period were :
A. Ilbari and Khalji
B. Tughlaq and Khalji
C. Tughlaq and Sayyid
D. Ilbari and Lodis

29. Which one of the following events took place at the last during reign of Muhammad-bin-Tughlaq?
A. Introduction of token currency
B. Increase of land-revenue in Doab
C. Transfer of Capital from Delhi to Devagiri.
D. Conquest of Khurasan and Iraq

30. The most learned medieval Muslim ruler who was well versed in various branches of learning including astronomy, mathematics and medicine was :
A. Jalaluddin Khilji
B. Sikander Lodi
C. Ghiyasuddin Tughlaq
D. Muhammad-bin-Tughlaq

31. The 'Sufis' had 12 silsilas. They propounded the idea of Union with God through:
A. Love B. Rituals
C. Fasts D. Prayers

32. Match the following:

(*a*) Peshwa	1. Foreign affairs
(*b*) Panditrao	2. Audit and accounts
(*c*) Amatya	3. Providing grants to scholars
(*d*) Sumant	4. General supervision
	5. Military affairs

Codes :

	(*a*)	(*b*)	(*c*)	(*d*)
A.	2	3	4	5
B.	4	1	2	3
C.	4	3	2	1
D.	3	1	4	2

33. The Regulating Act of 1773 can be regarded as the first measure to :
A. assert the right of British Parliament to legislate for India
B. separate the legislature from the executive
C. separate the judiciary from the executive
D. centralise law-making

34. What was the exact constitutional status of the Indian Republic on 26th January, 1950?
A. A Democratic Republic
B. A Sovereign Democratic Republic
C. A Sovereign Secular Democratic Republic
D. A Sovereign Socialist Secular Democratic Republic

35. When the British obtained the grant of Diwani of Bengal, Bihar and Orissa (Odisha) they acquired the right to :
A. maintain law and order in these territories
B. administer civil justice and collect revenue in these territories
C. collect revenue and establish revenue administration in these territories
D. militarily defend these territories

36. Which of the following were responsible for the growth of nationalism in India during the British rule?
1. Economic exploitation of India.
2. Impact of Western education.
3. Role of the Press.
Select the correct answer using the codes given below :
Codes:
A. 1, 2 and 3 B. 1 and 2,
C. 2 and 3 D. 1 and 3

37. Which one of the following nationalist leaders has been described as being radical in politics but conservative on social issues?
A. G.K. Gokhale
B. B.G. Tilak
C. Lala Lajpat Rai
D. Madan Mohan Malviya

38. Provincial Autonomy in British India was envisaged by the :
A. Act of 1909
B. Act of 1919
C. Act of 1935
D. Act of 1947

39. Dyarchy means:
A. double government
B. a government in which the centre is very powerful
C. a government based on division of power between centre and provinces
D. None of the above

40. The Indian National Congress observed 'Independence Day' for the first time on 26th January in :

A. 1920 B. 1925
C. 1930 D. 1947

41. The Ghadar Party was organised in USA by:
A. Raja Mahendra Pratap
B. Lala Hardayal
C. Abul Kalam Azad
D. M.A. Jinnah

42. Mahatma Gandhi for the first time practised his Satyagraha in India at :
A. Chauri-Chaura
B. Ahmedabad
C. Champaran
D. Navakholi

43. The non-cooperation movement was suspended by Gandhiji because :
A. The response of the people was poor
B. The Muslims kept aloof from the movement
C. The British government agreed to concede the demands of the Congress
D. Violence broke out at Chauri-Chaura

44. In 1911, the British annulled the partition of Bengal with a view to :
A. provide better administration of the province
B. to placate the Indians
C. to win over the Muslims to its side
D. reduce expenditure on administration

45. There was no Congress representative in the :
A. First Round Table Conference
B. Second Round Table Conference
C. Third Round Table Conference
D. First and Third Round Table Conferences

46. Who among the following transformed the Shivaji and Ganapati festival into a national festival?
A. Lala Lajpat Rai
B. Bal Gangadhar Tilak
C. Veer Savarkar
D. Gopal Krishna Gokhale

47. The Rowlatt Act stood for :
A. compulsory economic support to war efforts
B. imprisonment without trial and summary procedures for trial
C. suppression of Khilafat Movement
D. imposition of restrictions on freedom of the Press

48. Which one of the following finally alienated the Muslims and crystallized the demand for Pakistan?
A. The introduction of separate electorates for the Muslims
B. The establishment of the Muslim League
C. The non-inclusion of Muslims in the provincial governments
D. The federal provisions envisaged under the Government of India Act of 1935

49. At which session of Congress in 1907 the first split in the party occurred?
A. Surat session
B. Pune session
C. Nagpur session
D. Ahmedabad session

50. Consider the following :
1. Ghadar Party
2. Khilafat Movement
3. Dandi March
4. Champaran Satyagraha
The correct chronological sequence is:
A. 4, 1, 2, 3 B. 1, 4, 3, 2
C. 4, 1, 3, 2 D. 1, 4, 2, 3

51. The first effective attempt by the nationalists for drafting the Constitution of Independent India may be traced back to :
A. the Poona Pact
B. Sapru Report
C. Nehru Report
D. Jinnah's Fourteen Points

52. People of the Indus Valley Civilization were:
A. warlike
B. vindictive
C. uncompromising
D. None of these

53. The women of Indus Valley Civilization used:
A. face powder
B. lip stick
C. elaborate hair styles
D. eye make-up

54. What importance does the year 563 B.C. have in Indian History?
A. Gautam Buddha was born
B. Indus Valley Civilization was made known
C. Chandragupta Maurya came to the throne
D. Rig Veda was written

55. The Great Hindu laws was given by :
A. Kapil
B. Kautilya
C. Manu
D. None of these

56. Which of the following is not one of the features of the economic regulations of Alauddin Khilji?
A. Use of correct measures
B. Prices fixed being calculated on the basis of production cost
C. Total curbing of black marketing
D. Organisation of separate markets for separate commodities

57. Who among the following was not an exponent of Bhakti movement?
A. Ramananda
B. Kabir
C. Shankaracharya
D. Nanak

58. Consider the following four saints :
1. Kabir
2. Nanak
3. Chaitanya
4. Tulsidas
What is the correct chronological order in which they flourished?
A. 1, 2, 3, 4
B. 2, 3, 4, 1
C. 3, 1, 2, 4
D. 3, 2, 4, 1

59. Brahmo Samaj mainly insisted upon:
A. Abolition of sati
B. Abolition of child marriage
C. Monotheism
D. Reintroduction of converted Hindus

60. Who among the early nationalists worked in England to mobilize public opinion in favour of the Indian National Movement?
A. Gopal Krishna Gokhale
B. D.E. Wacha
C. Lala Lajpat Rai
D. Dadabhai Naoroji

61. Sir Charles Wood despatch of 1854 dealt primarily with:
A. administrative reforms
B. social reforms
C. economic reforms
D. educational reforms

62. The most important feature of the Government of India Act of 1919 was the introduction of:
A. Dyarchy
B. Provincial autonomy
C. Separate electorates
D. Adult franchise

63. The leader of the Young Bengal Movement was:
A. Dwarkanath Tagore
B. Chandrashekhar Deb
C. Ishwar Chandra Vidyasagar
D. Henry Vivian Derozio

64. Indian National Congress found wide acceptance initially among:
A. peasants and working class
B. landlords
C. educated middle class
D. businessmen

65. Arrange the following in chronological order who administered as Governor-Generals in India.
1. Wellesley
2. Cornwallis
3. Warren Hastings
4. Dalhousie
A. 3, 2, 1, 4 B. 1, 2, 4, 3
C. 4, 2, 3, 1 D. 4, 1, 2, 3

66. The Legislative Council can delay the enactment of a Bill passed by the Legislative Assembly for a maximum period of :
A. one month
B. four months
C. six months
D. one year

67. The Sufi Saint, who founded the Chisti order was :
A. Nizamuddin Auliya
B. Khwaja Moinuddin
C. Nasiruddin Chiragh-i-Delhi
D. Homidud-Din Nagori

68. Akbar's mausoleum is situated at :
A. Lucknow
B. New Delhi
C. Sikandara
D. Sasaram

69. Who was the founder of the Sunga Dynasty?
A. Agnimitra
B. Divakarmaitra
C. Pushyamitra
D. Vasumitra

70. Where did Babar die?
A. Agra B. Delhi
C. Kabul D. Lahore

71. Jainism differed from Buddhism in which of the following aspects?
A. Doctrine of Ahimsa
B. Faith in Karma
C. Belief in Fasting
D. Rejection of Yajna

72. "Go back to the Vedas" was the motto of :
A. Raja Ram Mohan Roy
B. Swami Vivekananda
C. Swami Dayanand Saraswati
D. M.G. Ranade

73. Which of the following were not one of the royal patrons of Jainism?
A. Satvahanas
B. Gangas

C. Chalukyas of Gujarat
D. Rashtrakutas

74. Match List-I (Name of the revolutionary tried in a conspiracy case) with List-II (Name of conspiracy case) and select the correct answer using the codes given below the Lists :

List I
(*a*) Ram Prasad Bismil
(*b*) Surya Sen
(*c*) Aurobindo Ghosh
(*d*) Bhagat Singh

List II
1. Lahore Conspiracy Case
2. Kakori Conspiracy Case
3. Chittagong Armoury Raid
4. Alipore Bomb Case

Codes :

	(*a*)	(*b*)	(*c*)	(*d*)
A.	4	2	3	1
B.	2	3	4	1
C.	3	4	1	2
D.	4	1	2	3

75. The Mathura School of Art was influenced by :
A. Amaravati School of Art
B. Bodh Gaya School of Art
C. Roman School of Art
D. Gandhara School of Art

76. Which one of the following has been the main feature of the South Indian Temple architecture?
A. Sikhara B. Gopuram
C. Vimana D. Mandapa

77. Amir Khusrau was the famous poet in the court of :
A. Akbar
B. Shahjahan
C. Ibrahim Lodi
D. Alauddin Khilji

78. Who among the following, destroyed the "Group of Forty" Nobles?
A. Baharam Shah
B. Iltutmish
C. Sultana Razia
D. Balban

79. Which of the following states was not annexed by Lord Dalhousie under the Doctrine of Lapse?
A. Jammu
B. Oudh
C. Udaipur
D. Nagpur

80. The *Ashtapradhan* was the council of ministers during the reign of :
A. Krishnadeva Rai
B. Tipu Sultan
C. Shivaji
D. Akbar

81. Arrange the following in chronological order:
1. Dandi March
2. Simon Commission
3. Poona Pact
4. Gandhi-Irwin Pact
A. 2, 1, 3, 4 B. 2, 1, 4, 3
C. 4, 3, 1, 2 D. 4, 3, 2, 1

82. Which of the contemporary Muslim writers criticized Alauddin for his disregard of religion :
A. Barani
B. Amir Khusrau
C. Al-beruni
D. Minhaj Siraj

83. Which of the following statements is false?
A. The third battle of Panipat sealed the fate of Maratha supermacy in India
B. The foreign invasion in the Punjab failed to suppress the authority of the Sikh Chiefs
C. Guru Arjun Dev developed the Gurumukhi script
D. The Sikh Misls were organised on the principles of autonomy

84. Which of the following Act formally introduced the principle of elections for the first time?
A. The Indian Councils Act, 1909
B. Government of India Act, 1919
C. The 1935 Act
D. India Independence Act, 1947

85. Match the following :
(*a*). C.R. Das
(*b*) Vallabhbhai Patel
(*c*) Khan Abdul Ghaffar Khan
(*d*) Maulana A.K. Azad
1. Bardoli Satygaraha
2. Swarajist
3. Khilafatist
4. Khudai Khidmatgar

Codes:

	(*a*)	(*b*)	(*c*)	(*d*)
A.	2	1	4	3
B.	2	4	1	3
C.	4	1	3	2
D.	2	1	3	4

86. The object of Alauddin Khalji's economic regulations was mainly :
A. to encourage trade
B. to maintain a strong army
C. to punish shopkeepers
D. the welfare of the people

87. Harihar and Bukka laid the foundation of the Vijayanagar empire under the influence of :
A. Jnaneshvara
B. Tukaram
C. Ramanuj
D. Vidyaranya

88. The practice of 'Jharokha darshan' to the public was stopped by :
A. Jehangir
B. Shahjahan
C. Aurangzeb
D. None of these

89. Who among the following Mughal commanders compelled Shivaji to sign the Treaty of Purandar (1665)?
A. Shayesta Khan
B. Bahadur Khan
C. Mirza Raja Jai Singh
D. Raja Jaswant Singh

90. Which one of the following Mughal emperors gave permission to East India Company to build a factory at Surat?
A. Jehangir
B. Shahjahan
C. Farrukhsiyar
D. Bahadurshah II

91. Which one of the following proved to be Dalhousie's worst political blunder?
A. Annexation of Punjab
B. Occupation of lower Burma (Myanmar)
C. 'Doctrine of Lapse'
D. Annexation of Oudh

92. Arrange the following events in chronological order on the basis of codes given below :
1. The Surat Congress
2. March from Sabarmati Ashram to Dandi
3. Rowlatt Act
4. Gandhi-Irwin Pact

Codes :
A. 3, 2, 1, 4 B. 1, 3, 2, 4
C. 2, 1, 3, 4 D. 1, 2, 4, 3

93. Which one of the following statements about untouchability is *not* correct?
A. It was widely practised in the Indus Valley civilization
B. The Rigveda does not show any acquaintance with it
C. It is clearly referred to in the Buddhist Jatakas
D. It came to be applied to several castes only in the post-Gupta period

94. The minister in charge of organisation of military contingents in early Delhi Sultanate was known as:
A. Sadr-us-sudur
B. Diwan-i-arz
C. Naib-i-mumlikat
D. Amir-i-Kohi

95. Alauddin Khalji levied land revenue on the basis of:
A. crop sharing
B. arbitrary assessment
C. measurement
D. a fixed money tribute

ANSWERS

1	**2**	**3**	**4**	**5**	**6**	**7**	**8**	**9**	**10**
A	C	B	C	D	C	B	D	D	A
11	**12**	**13**	**14**	**15**	**16**	**17**	**18**	**19**	**20**
C	D	C	C	B	C	D	B	C	C
21	**22**	**23**	**24**	**25**	**26**	**27**	**28**	**29**	**30**
A	A	A	B	C	D	C	B	D	D
31	**32**	**33**	**34**	**35**	**36**	**37**	**38**	**39**	**40**
A	C	A	B	B	A	B	C	A	C
41	**42**	**43**	**44**	**45**	**46**	**47**	**48**	**49**	**50**
B	C	D	B	D	B	B	C	A	D
51	**52**	**53**	**54**	**55**	**56**	**57**	**58**	**59**	**60**
C	D	A	A	C	D	C	A	C	D
61	**62**	**63**	**64**	**65**	**66**	**67**	**68**	**69**	**70**
D	A	D	C	A	B	B	C	C	A
71	**72**	**73**	**74**	**75**	**76**	**77**	**78**	**79**	**80**
B	C	A	B	D	B	D	D	A	C
81	**82**	**83**	**84**	**85**	**86**	**87**	**88**	**89**	**90**
B	A	C	A	A	B	D	C	C	A
91	**92**	**93**	**94**	**95**					
D	B	A	B	C					

GEOGRAPHY

1. ....is situated near the banks of Sabarmati River.
   A. Bhavnagar
   B. Aurangabad
   C. Ahmedabad
   D. Rajkot
2. Sericulture is:
   A. science of the various kinds of serum
   B. artificial rearing of fish
   C. art of silkworm breeding
   D. study of various cultures of a community
3. The leading producers of groundnut in India are :
   A. Tamil Nadu and Karnataka
   B. Gujarat and Deccan Plateau
   C. Bihar and Haryana
   D. Punjab and Gujarat
4. Indian Standard Time is based on:
   A. 80°E longitude
   B. 82½°E longitude
   C. 110°E longitude
   D. 25°E longitude
5. Tides in the oceans are caused by :
   A. Gravitational pull of the moon on the earth's surface including sea water
   B. Gravitational pull of the sun on the earth's surface only and not on the sea water
   C. Gravitational pull of the moon and the sun on the earth's surface including the sea water
   D. None of these
6. Nagarjunasagar Project is situated on the river:
   A. Tungabhadra
   B. Cauvery
   C. Krishna
   D. Godavari
7. The difference between the Indian Standard Time and the Greenwich Mean Time is:
   A. – 3½ hours
   B. + 3½ hours
   C. – 5½ hours
   D. + 5½ hours
8. Which of the following dams is not on Narmada river?
   A. Indira-Sagar Project
   B. Maheshwar Hydel Power Project
   C. Jobat Project
   D. Koyna Power Project
9. Which of the following statements is **not true** about the availability of water on the earth, the crisis for which is going to increase in the years to come?
   A. About 97.5 per cent of the total volume of water available on the earth is salty
   B. 80 per cent of the water available to us for use comes in bursts as monsoons
   C. About 2.5 per cent of the total water available on the earth is polluted water and cannot be used for human activities
   D. Possibility is that some big glaciers will melt in the coming ten-fifteen years and sea level will rise by 3-4 metres all over the earth
10. Which of the following is **not** a cash crop?
    A. Jute
    B. Paddy
    C. Cashewnut
    D. Sugarcane
11. Through which States does Cauvery River flow?
    A. Gujarat, M.P., Tamil Nadu
    B. Karnataka, Kerala, Tamil Nadu
    C. Karnataka, Kerala, Andhra Pradesh
    D. M.P., Maharashtra, Tamil Nadu
12. Indian Standard Time is the local time of 82½°E which passes through :
    A. Guntur
    B. Delhi
    C. Allahabad
    D. Kolkata
13. The 17th parallel defines the boundary between:
    A. North and South Korea
    B. USA and Canada

C. North and South Vietnam
D. China and Russia

14. During the period of south-west monsoon, Tamil Nadu remains dry because:
A. the winds do not reach this area
B. there are no mountains in this area
C. it lies in the rain shadow area
D. the temperature is too high to let the winds cool down

15. Which country does top in producing cocoa?
A. Ghana
B. Brazil
C. Cote d'Ivoire
D. Nigeria

16. 'Aeroflot' is the name of the airline of:
A. Russia B. China
C. Thailand D. U.S.A.

17. The Girnar Hills are situated in which of the following states?
A. Gujarat
B. Karnataka
C. Madhya Pradesh
D. Maharashtra

18. During December 22nd the sun is vertically over:
A. Tropic of Cancer
B. Tropic of Capricorn
C. The Equator
D. None of the above

19. Photosphere is described as the :
A. Lower layer of atmosphere
B. Visible surface of the sun from which radiation emanates
C. Wavelength of solar spectrum
D. None of the above

20. Broadly, there are three layers of the earth of the crust, the mantle and the core. The crust forms what percentage of the volume of the earth?
A. 0.5% B. 2.5%
C. 7.5% D. 12.5%

21. The grassland of Argentina is known as :
A. Pampas
B. Campos
C. Savanna
D. None of the above

22. Different seasons are formed because
A. Sun is moving around the earth
B. of revolution of the earth around the Sun on its orbit
C. of rotation of the earth around its axis
D. All of the above

23. Eskers and Drumlins are features formed by:
A. underground water
B. running water
C. the action of wind
D. glacial action

24. Match List-I and List-II and select the correct answer using the codes given below the Lists :

List-I
(Rivers)
(*a*) Saryu
(*b*) Brahmaputra
(*c*) Narmada
(*d*) Sabarmati

List-II
(Towns)
1. Lucknow
2. Hoshangabad
3. Ahmedabad
4. Guwahati
5. Ayodhya

Codes:

	(*a*)	(*b*)	(*c*)	(*d*)
A.	4	5	1	2
B.	5	4	2	3
C.	5	4	3	1
D.	3	5	2	1

25. Which one of the following is the appropriate reason for considering the Gondwana rocks as most important rock systems of India?
A. More than 90% of limestone reserves of India are found in them.
B. More than 90% of India's coal reserves are found in them.
C. More than 90% of fertile black cotton soils are spread over them.
D. None of the reasons given above is appropriate in this context.

26. The world is divided into :
A. 12 time zones
B. 20 time zones
C. 24 time zones
D. 36 time zones

27. The 'Kiel' canal links the :
A. Pacific and Atlantic Oceans
B. Mediterranean Sea and Red Sea
C. Mediterranean Sea and Black Sea
D. North Sea and Baltic Sea

28. Match the following :
(*a*) Himadri 1. Outer Himalayas
(*b*) Shivalik 2. Great Himalayas
(*c*) Himachal 3. Middle Himalayas

(*d*) Sahyadri 4. Western Ghats

	(*a*)	(*b*)	(*c*)	(*d*)
A.	1	2	3	4
B.	4	2	3	1
C.	2	1	3	4
D.	1	2	3	4

29. The term 'Regur' refers to:
A. Laterite soils
B. Black Cotton soils
C. Red Soils
D. Deltaic Alluvial Soils

30. Location of sugar industry in India is shifting from north to south because of:
A. cheap labour
B. expanding regional market
C. cheap and abundant supply of power
D. high yield and high sugar content in sugarcane

31. Consider the following statements :
1. Ozone is found mostly in the Stratosphere.
2. Ozone layer lies 55-75 km above the surface of the earth.
3. Ozone absorbs ultra-violet radiation from the Sun.
4. Ozone layer has no significance for life on the earth.

Which of the above statements are correct?
A. 1 and 3 B. 2 and 4
C. 2 and 3 D. 1 and 4

32. Match List I with List II and select the correct answer using the codes given below the Lists :

List-I *(Crops)*	**List-II** *(Producer)*
(*a*) Banana	1. Brazil
(*b*) Cocoa	2. Cote d'Ivoire
(*c*) Coffee	3. India
(*d*) Cotton	4. China

Codes :

	(*a*)	(*b*)	(*c*)	(*d*)
A.	2	3	1	4
B.	3	2	1	4
C.	3	2	4	1
D.	2	3	4	1

33. Darjeeling and Dharamsala would be the right places to visit if one wanted to get a clear view respectively of:
A. Kanchanjunga and Dhauladhar ranges
B. Nandadevi and Dhauladhar ranges
C. Kanchanjunga and Nandadevi ranges
D. Nandadevi and Nanga Parvot

34. Atmosphere exists because:
A. The Gravitational force of the Earth
B. Revolution of the Earth
C. Rotation of the Earth
D. Weight of the gases of atmosphere

35. Victoria lake is located in the continent:
A. Africa
B. Asia
C. North America
D. South America

36. The famous Lagoon Lake of India is :
A. Dal Lake
B. Chilka Lake
C. Pulicat Lake
D. Mansarover

37. Where are most of the earth's active volcanoes concentrated?
A. Europe
B. Pacific Ocean
C. Africa
D. South America

38. Through which of the following states does the river Chambal flow?
A. U.P., M.P., Rajasthan
B. M.P., Gujarat, U.P.
C. Rajasthan, M.P., Bihar
D. Gujarat, M.P., U.P.

39. Which country is called the sugar bowl of the world?
A. Cuba
B. India
C. Argentina
D. USA

40. The area covered by forest in India is about:
A. 46% B. 33%
C. 23% D. 21.71%

41. In India, there are three crop seasons. Two of them are Kharif and Rabi, name the third one?
A. Barsati B. Garama
C. Zaid D. Khari

42. In India agriculture of Jute is maximum on which Delta region?
A. Ganga
B. Mahanadi
C. Brahamputra
D. Godavari

43. The natural vegetation of Savana consists of:
A. Tall grass
B. Scrub jungle
C. Short grass
D. Trees

44. The zone of excessively dry climate with very cold temperature throughout the year correspond to:
A. Arctic deserts
B. Tundra

C. Alpine meadouss
D. Antarctica

45. The International Date Line is represented by:
A. 100° Meridian
B. 0° Meridian
C. 180° Meridian
D. 90° Meridian

46. Adam's bridge connects:
A. Israel and Jerusalem
B. Amman and Damascus
C. Persian Gulf and Gulf of Oman
D. Dhanushkoti (Rameswaram) and Talaimannar

47. In May-June each year, the monsoon winds approach the southern tip of India from:
A. Northly direction
B. North-easterly direction
C. North-westerly direction
D. South-westerly direction

48. Sahayadri is the traditional name of the:
A. Western Ghats
B. Eastern Ghats
C. Aravallis
D. Barabar and Nagarjun hills

49. The fertility of the soil can be increased by growing:
A. Cereals
B. Fibre Crops
C. Legumes
D. Root Crops

50. India's Oil bearing areas are mostly associated with the:
A. Plutonic rocks
B. Volcanic rocks
C. Sedimentary rocks
D. Metamorphic rocks

51. Which one of the following pairs is *not* correctly matched?

	Places	Minerals
A.	Kudremukh	Iron Ore
B.	Singhbhum	Manganese
C.	Hazaribagh	Silver
D.	Khetri	Copper

52. The much discussed Tehri Dam Project is located in which of the following states?
A. Madhya Pradesh
B. Rajasthan
C. Haryana
D. Uttarakhand

53. Which of the following States has abundant black soil?
A. Karnataka
B. Maharashtra
C. Tamil Nadu
D. Kerala

54. Match the following:

List-I
(*a*) Kumaon Himalayas
(*b*) Nepal Himalayas
(*c*) Punjab Himalayas
(*d*) Assam Himalayas

List-II
1. Between Indus and Sutlej
2. Between Kali and Tista
3. Between Tista and Brahmaputra (Dihang)
4. Between Sutlej and Kali

Codes:

	(*a*)	(*b*)	(*c*)	(*d*)
A.	1	2	3	4
B.	2	3	1	4
C.	4	2	3	1
D.	4	2	1	3

55. The largest irrigation canal in India is the:
A. Yamuna Canal (West)
B. Indira Gandhi Canal
C. Lower Ganga Canal
D. Upper Ganga Canal

56. Laterite soil develop as a result of:
A. deposits of alluvial
B. deposition of loess
C. leaching
D. continued vegetation cover

57. The planet which is called twin sister of Earth is:
A. Mercury
B. Mars
C. Venus
D. Jupiter

58. On which of the following rivers is Almatti Dam located?
A. Mahanadi B. Cauvery
C. Krishna D. Penganga

59. Ursa Minor is:
A. the name of a satellite
B. the name of an island
C. a group of stars that form the little dipper in the most northern constellation
D. the name of a disease in USA

60. Which of the following is a block mountain?
A. Rocky B. Vosgas
C. Alps D. Andes

61. Which is the shortest route from Moscow to San Francisco?
A. via Canada
B. over land
C. over to South Pole
D. over to North Pole

62. Cash crops of India include:
A. paddy and jowar
B. maize, jowar and paddy
C. cotton and sugarcane
D. bajra and paddy

63. The equator is a parallel or

63. The equator is a parallel or latitude of:

A. 23½° B. 0°
C. 66½° D. 90°

64. To complete one revolution in its orbit, the earth takes:

A. one month
B. two years
C. 6 months
D. 12 months

65. Which strait separates Europe from Africa?

A. Bosperus
B. Gibraltar
C. Dover
D. Bering

66. The beneficiary States of Sardar Sarovar Project are :

A. Gujarat, Maharashtra, MP and Rajasthan
B. AP, MP, Gujarat and Maharashtra
C. Odisha, MP, Gujarat and Maharashtra
D. MP, Gujarat, Karnataka and Maharashtra

67. 'Horn of Africa' consists of:

A. Algeria, Morocco and West Sahara
B. Libya, Sudan and Egypt
C. Somalia, Ethiopia and Djibouti
D. Zimbabwe, Botswana and Angola

68. New York is situated on the river bank of:

A. Rhine
B. Thames
C. Amazon
D. Hudson

69. Match List-I with List-II and select the correct answer from the code given below:

List-I *(Town)*	**List-II** *(River)*
(*a*) Berlin	1. Tiber
(*b*) Lahore	2. Hudson
(*c*) New York	3. Ravi
(*d*) Rome	4. Spree

Codes :

	(*a*)	(*b*)	(*c*)	(*d*)
A.	1	2	3	4
B.	4	3	2	1
C.	3	4	1	2
D.	1	4	2	3

70. The Kullu Valley is situated between the mountain ranges of :

A. Dhauladhar and Pir Panjal
B. Ranjoti and Nagtibba
C. Ladakh and Pir Panjal
D. Middle Himalayas and Shivalik

71. Which one of the following towns is nearest to the Tropic of Cancer?

A. Agartala
B. Gandhinagar
C. Jabalpur
D. Ujjain

72. Which one of the following pairs is not correctly matched?

A. Kota—Chambal
B. Bhubaneshwar—Mahanadi
C. Jabalpur—Narmada
D. Surat—Tapti

73. The first three largest sugar producing States in India are :

A. Bihar, UP, Maharashtra
B. UP, Maharashtra, Tamil Nadu
C. UP, Maharashtra, Karnataka
D. Bihar, UP, Andhra Pradesh

74. Indira Gandhi Canal has its source at :

A. Gandhi Sagar Dam
B. Bhakra Dam
C. Harike Barrage
D. Govind Ballabh Sagar

75. Consider the following statements :

1. Tides are of great help in navigation and fishing.
2. High tide enables big ships to enter or leave the harbour safely.
3. Tide prevents siltation in the harbours.
4. Kandla and Diamond Harbour are tidal ports.

A. 1 and 4
B. 2, 3, and 4
C. 1, 2 and 3
D. All of these

76. Which of the following countries is not a South American country?

A. Argentina B. Bolivia
C. Colombia D. Mexico

77. Which of the following is the biggest fresh water lake in India?

A. Dal Lake
B. Sukhna Lake
C. Loktak Lake
D. Wular Lake

78. Which of the following rivers is not a tributory of the Indus?

A. Sutlej
B. Jhelum
C. Bhagirathi
D. Chenab

79. Which of the following pairs of the river dam project and the State in which it is located, is **not** correct?

A. Gandhi Sagar–Madhya Pradesh
B. Tungabhadra–Tamil Nadu
C. Bhakra Nangal–Punjab
D. Hirakud–Odisha
E. All are correct

80. If it is 10.00 a.m. I.S.T., then what would be the local time at Shillong on 92°E longitude?
A. 9.38 a.m.
B. 10.38 a.m.
C. 10.22 a.m.
D. 9.22 a.m.

81. Match List-I with List-II and select the *correct* answer using the codes given below the Lists :

List-I
(Rivers)
(*a*) Cauvery
(*b*) Krishna
(*c*) Narmada
(*d*) Chambal

List-II
(Dams)
1. Alamatti
2. Mettur
3. Gandhi Sagar
4. Sardar Sarovar

Codes :

	(*a*)	(*b*)	(*c*)	(*d*)
A.	1	4	2	3
B.	2	1	4	3
C.	2	1	3	4
D.	1	3	4	2

82. The Brahmaputra empties into:
A. Ganga
B. Jamuna
C. Bay of Bengal
D. None of these

83. The State which produces the largest quantity of wheat is:
A. Haryana
B. Rajasthan
C. Uttar Pradesh
D. Punjab

84. Moscow is situated on the bank of:
A. Moskva
B. Spree
C. Volga
D. Tagus

85. When does the moon come between the sun and the earth?
A. Lunar eclipse
B. Solar eclipse
C. Sidereal day
D. Full moon day

86. Which of the following statements about Kharif and Rabi is *not* correct?
A. Kharif season begins with the onset of monsoon season and is harvested in late Spring
B. Kharif season begins with the onset of monsoon season and is harvested in Autumn
C. Rabi season begins in Autumn after the rains and harvested in late Spring
D. Important Kharif crops are rice, millets, jute, maize and cotton; important Rabi crops are wheat, gram, barley and linseed

87. Raniganj Coal Mine is situated in:
A. Jharkhand
B. Madhya Pradesh
C. West Bengal
D. Maharashtra

88. The latitude of a place is expressed by its angular distance in relation to:
A. Equator
B. South Pole
C. Axis of the Earth
D. North Pole

89. The southern tip of India is:
A. Cape Camorin
B. Point Calimere
C. Indira Point in Nicobar Islands
D. Kovalam in Trivandrum

90. Which is India's largest saline water lake?
A. Nainital
B. Sambhar
C. Sishram
D. Chilka

91. During winter, the northern half of India is warmer than areas of similar latitudinal location by 3° to 8° because:
A. India is essentially a tropical country
B. The surface wind blows in a particular direction in one season
C. The Great Himalayas check the penetration of cold polar air into India effectively
D. Of winter rains

92. When rivers carrying a load enter the sea, their flow gets checked, and much of the material so carried is deposited offshore. Such deposits result in the formation of :
A. An atoll
B. A delta
C. A harbour
D. A lake

93. Which one of the following can one come across if one travels through the strait of Malacca?
A. Bali B. Brunei
C. Java D. Singapore

94. In India, which one of the following states has the largest inland saline wetland?
A. Gujarat
B. Haryana
C. Madhya Pradesh
D. Rajasthan

95. In which of the following places is the shompen tribe found?
A. Nilgiri Hills
B. Nicobar Islands
C. Spiti Valley
D. Lakshadweep Islands

96. Consider the following statements:
1. India does not have any deposits of Thorium.
2. Kerala's monazitosands contain Uranium.
Which of the statements given above is/are correct.
A. 1 only
B. 2 only
C. Both 1 and 2
D. Neither 1 nor 2

97. Which ocean is reducing due to plate tectonic movement?
A. Pacific Ocean
B. Atlantic Ocean
C. Indian Ocean
D. Arctic Ocean

98. The new folded mountain system is known as
A. Alpine system
B. Alps system
C. Rocky system
D. Penine system

99. Core of the earth is made of
A. Solid materials
B. Liquid material
C. Gaseous material
D. None of these

100. The deepest rift valley in the world is
A. Death valley
B. Jorden valley
C. Dead sea
D. Narmada valley

ANSWERS

1	**2**	**3**	**4**	**5**	**6**	**7**	**8**	**9**	**10**
C	C	B	B	C	C	D	D	D	B
11	**12**	**13**	**14**	**15**	**16**	**17**	**18**	**19**	**20**
B	C	C	C	C	A	A	B	B	A
21	**22**	**23**	**24**	**25**	**26**	**27**	**28**	**29**	**30**
A	B	D	B	B	C	D	C	B	D
31	**32**	**33**	**34**	**35**	**36**	**37**	**38**	**39**	**40**
A	B	A	A	A	B	B	A	A	D
41	**42**	**43**	**44**	**45**	**46**	**47**	**48**	**49**	**50**
C	A	A	A	C	D	D	A	C	C
51	**52**	**53**	**54**	**55**	**56**	**57**	**58**	**59**	**60**
C	D	B	D	B	C	C	C	B	B
61	**62**	**63**	**64**	**65**	**66**	**67**	**68**	**69**	**70**
A	C	B	D	B	A	C	D	B	D
71	**72**	**73**	**74**	**75**	**76**	**77**	**78**	**79**	**80**
B	B	C	C	D	D	D	C	B	B
81	**82**	**83**	**84**	**85**	**86**	**87**	**88**	**89**	**90**
B	C	C	A	B	A	C	A	C	D
91	**92**	**93**	**94**	**95**	**96**	**97**	**98**	**99**	**100**
C	B	D	D	B	B	A	A	B	C

ECONOMICS

1. A closed economy is the one which :
A. does not permit emigration or immigration
B. permits emigration but no immigration
C. engages in no foreign trade
D. engages in no foreign and domestic trade or transit

2. In a developed economy the major share of employment originates in the :
A. primary sector
B. tertiary sector
C. secondary sector
D. any of the above

3. The Economic and Social Commission for Asia and Pacific (ESCAP) is located at:
A. Bangkok
B. Kuala Lumpur
C. Manila
D. Singapore

4. Commercial vehicles are not produced by which of the following companies in India?
A. TELCO
B. Ashok Leyland
C. DCM Daewoo
D. Birla Yamaha

5. In India, the Public Sector is most dominant in:
A. transport
B. steel production
C. commercial banking
D. organised term-lending financial institutions

6. The main argument advanced in favour of small scale and cottage industries in India is that:
A. cost of production is low
B. they require small capital investment
C. they advance the goal of equitable distribution of wealth
D. they generate a large volume of employment

7. The most serious economic problems of India are:
A. Poverty and unemployment
B. Stagnation, not poverty
C. Unemployment, not poverty
D. Underdevelopment, not poverty

8. Which of the following is not one of the three central problems of an economy?
A. What to produce
B. How to produce
C. When to produce
D. For whom to produce

9. If saving exceeds investment, the national income will:
A. fall
B. rise
C. fluctuate
D. remain constant

10. In which of the following industries in India are the maximum number of workers employed?
A. Sugar
B. Jute
C. Textiles
D. Iron and Steel

11. Terrace Cultivation is practiced mostly:
A. in urban areas
B. on slopes of mountains
C. on tops of hills
D. in undulating tracts

12. Which of the following is a selective Credit Control method?
A. Bank Rate
B. RBI directives
C. Cash Reserve Ratio
D. Open market operations

13. Which tax can be levied by Gram Panchayat?
A. Sales Tax
B. Tax on Local Fairs
C. Custom Duty
D. Land Revenue

14. ICICI is the name of a:
A. Financial Institution
B. Chemical Industry
C. Cotton Industry
D. Chamber of Commerce and Industry

15. The new share Price Index (in dollar value) of Mumbai share Market is—
A. DOLEX
B. UREX
C. FOREX
D. SENSEX

16. 'Smart Money' is a term used for:
A. Internet Banking
B. Cash with Bank
C. Credit Card
D. Cash with Public

17. The largest public sector bank in India is:
A. Central Bank of India
B. Punjab National Bank
C. State Bank of India
D. Indian Overseas Bank

18. Index 'Residex' is associated with—
A. Share Prices
B. Mutual Fund Prices
C. Price Inflation Index
D. Land Prices

19. Price in the market is fixed by:
A. Stock exchange rates
B. The demand and supply ruling in the market at a particular time
C. The Finance Minister
D. None of the above

20. Devaluation of currency helps to promote:
A. National Income
B. Savings
C. Imports at lower cost
D. Exports

21. GST has been implemented from:
A. January 1, 2017
B. January 1, 2018
C. July 1, 2017
D. April 1, 2018

22. Project 'Sankalp' is associated with the elimination of—
A. Illiteracy
B. Polio
C. Unemployment
D. AIDS/HIV

23. UNDP has introduced a new poverty index known as—
A. Human Poverty Index
B. Poorest among Poor Index
C. Social Poverty Index
D. Multi-dimensional Poverty Index

24. 'KUSUM' scheme launched by Government of India is associated with:
A. Female child protection
B. Solar power plants
C. Flower production
D. Promoting plantation

25. The term 'devaluation' means:
A. Reducing the value of a currency in terms of another currency
B. Increasing the value of a currency
C. Revising the value of a currency
D. None of the above

26. 'Operation Twist' is the new name given to America's Federal Bank strategy related to—
A. Increasing outsourcing activities
B. Reducing interest rates to promote long-run loans
C. Curtailing down assistance to various nations
D. Selling gold reserves in the market

27. 'Apna Khet, Apna Kaam' (i.e., Own Field, Own Work) is a new scheme under MNREGA has been initiated in the state—
A. Punjab
B. Gujarat
C. Madhya Pradesh
D. Rajasthan

28. What is 'Hawala'?
A. Full details of subject
B. Illegal transaction of foreign exchange
C. Illegal trading of shares
D. Tax evasion

29. The major aim of devaluation is to:
A. encourage imports
B. encourage exports
C. encourage both exports and imports
D. discourage both exports and imports

30. Rajeev Gandhi scheme for Empowerment of Adolescent Girls named as 'Sabla' includes the girls of the age group—
A. 9 to 12 years
B. 10 to 15 years
C. 11 to 18 years
D. 15 to 18 years

31. When was the Family Planning Programme officially started in India?
A. 1950
B. 1952
C. 1956
D. 1962

32. When was the Reserve Bank of India nationalised?
A. 1947
B. 1949
C. 1950
D. 1951

33. Which of the following is *not* a feature of the Indian economy?

A. High rate of population growth
B. Disguised unemployment
C. Lowest rate of adult literacy
D. High rate of exports

34. The 'Relative Deprivation' approach for measuring poverty has been adopted by:
A. developing countries
B. developed countries
C. under-developed countries
D. None of the above

35. 'Disinvestment' means selling the shares of the public sector units to the:
A. workers or other companies (public or private)
B. workers only
C. MNC's only
D. private sector only

36. Sustainable economic development means an increase in the rate of growth of real:
A. total and per capita product
B. total and per capita product and level of literacy rate
C. total and per capita product and life expectancy at birth
D. total and per capita product, taking into account the cost of degradation of the quality of environment in this process

37. Functional unemployment occurs when:
A. unemployed have no qualification for job
B. people frequently change their job
C. people were thrown out from job due to recession
D. None of these

38. Which among the following does **not** have a 'free trade zone'?
A. Kandla
B. Mumbai
C. Vishakhapatnam
D. Thiruvananthapuram

39. Sun Belt of USA is important for which one of the following industries?
A. Cotton textile
B. Petrochemicals
C. Hi-tech electronics
D. Food Processing

40. Commercial banking system in India is
A. unit banking
B. branch banking
C. mixed banking
D. None of the above

41. What is 'Stagflation'?
A. Inflation with growth
B. Deflation with growth
C. Inflation after deflations
D. Inflation with depression

42. Which one of the following states produce about 50 per cent of the total silk textiles in India?
A. West Bengal
B. Assam
C. Karnataka
D. Jammu and Kashmir

43. Gilt-edged market means:
A. Bullion market
B. Market of Government securities
C. Market of Guns
D. Market of pure metals

44. Which of the following is **not** a financial institution?
A. IDBI B. ICICI
C. FICCI D. HDFC

45. Major food crop of India in terms of production is:
A. Wheat
B. Rice
C. Jowar
D. Barley

46. Division of Labour is limited by:
A. hours of work
B. the number of workers
C. extent of the market
D. working space

47. The first paper mill of the country was started in 1832. Where was it located?
A. Nepanagar in Madhya Pradesh
B. Mumbai in Maharashtra
C. Sehrampore in West Bengal
D. Yamunanagar in Haryana

48. "World Development Report" is an annual publication of
A. United Nations Development Programme
B. World Trade Organisation
C. International Monetary Fund
D. International Bank of Reconstruction and Development

49. The government is preparing devolution Index which will measure social empowerment of people at the—
A. Panchayat level

B. Block level
C. District level
D. State level

50. As regard the use of international food safety standards as reference point for the dispute settlements, which one of the following does WTO collaborate with?
A. Codex Alimentarious Commission
B. International Federation of Standards Users
C. International Organisation for Standardisation
D. World Standards Cooperation

51. In India, which of the following is regulated by the Forward Markets Commission.
A. Currency Futures Trading
B. Commodities Futures Trading
C. Equity Futures Trading
D. Both Commodities Futures and Financial Futures Trading

52. With reference to India, consider the following statements:
1. The Wholesale Price Index (WPI) in India is available on monthly basis only.
2. As compared to Consumer Price Index for Industrial workers (CPI(IW)), the WPI gives less weight to food articles.

Which of the statements given above is/are correct?
A. 1 only
B. 2 only
C. Both 1 and 2
D. Neither 1 nor 2

53. What is 'NIKKEI'?
A. Share Price Index of Tokyo Share Market
B. Name of Japanese Central Bank
C. Japanese name of Country's Planning Commission
D. Foreign Exchange Market of Japan

54. First share market in India was established in—
A. Delhi
B. Kolkata
C. Mumbai
D. Chennai

55. The working of SEBI includes
A. To regulate the dealings in share market
B. To check the foul dealings in share market
C. To control the inside trading of shares
D. All of these

ANSWERS

1 C	2 B	3 A	4 D	5 D	6 D	7 A	8 C	9 D	10 C
11 B	12 B	13 B	14 A	15 A	16 C	17 C	18 D	19 B	20 D
21 C	22 D	23 D	24 B	25 A	26 B	27 D	28 B	29 B	30 C
31 B	32 B	33 D	34 A	35 A	36 D	37 B	38 D	39 D	40 C
41 D	42 C	43 B	44 C	45 B	46 B	47 C	48 D	49 A	50 A
51 B	52 B	53 A	54 C	55 D					

PLANNING IN INDIA

1. The Plans in India are reviewed and approved by the..........
   A. Union Cabinet
   B. NITI Aayog
   C. National Development Council
   D. Lok Sabha and Rajya Sabha
2. Modern economy is one of—
   A. Cash economy
   B. Credit economy
   C. Planned economy
   D. Open economy
3. Which of the following is the most important objective of Indian planning?
   A. Reducing price instability
   B. Increasing capital formation
   C. Reducing inequality of income and wealth
   D. Increasing per capita income
4. Which of the following were the principle aims of First Five-Year Plan?
   1. Self-sufficiency in food-grain production.
   2. Rehabilitate Indian economy shattered by second war and partition.
   3. Development of basic and heavy industries.
   4. Minimum Needs Programme.

   A. 1 and 2 only
   B. 3 and 4 only
   C. 1, 2 and 3 only
   D. All of these
5. Who replaced Planning Commission?
   A. NITI Aayog
   B. NIYAM Aayog
   C. NIRMAN Aayog
   D. None of these
6. The NITI Aayog of India was established in:
   A. 2014 B. 2013
   C. 2015 D. 2012
7. Sampurna Gramin Rojgar Yojana has been launched from—
   A. 1st April, 2001
   B. 25th Sept. 2001
   C. 30th Sept. 2001
   D. 2nd Oct. 2001
8. The strategy of Rolling Plan was adopted during the prime ministership of:
   A. V.P. Singh
   B. Rajiv Gandhi
   C. Morarji Desai
   D. Lal Bahadur Shastri
9. Rolling Plan was made for the period—
   A. 1971 to 1978
   B. 1980 to 1985
   C. 1978 to 1983
   D. 1992 to 1997
10. 'ABC Index' announced by the government is associated with—
    A. Health
    B. Agriculture
    C. Communication
    D. Education
11. Under which plan did the Government introduce an agricultural strategy which gave rise to Green Revolution?
    A. Sixth Five-Year Plan
    B. Second Five-Year Plan
    C. Fourth Five-Year Plan
    D. Third Five-Year Plan
12. 'Bharat Nirman Yojana' was introduced during which one of the following Five-Year Plans?
    A. 8th Five Year Plan
    B. 9th Five Year Plan
    C. 10th Five Year Plan
    D. 11th Five Year Plan
13. Pradhan Mantri Garib Kalyan Yojana (PMGKY) was announced on—
    A. March 26, 2020
    B. August 15, 2014
    C. April 1, 2017
    D. May 12, 2018
14. 'Earn while you learn' scheme has been lounched by—
    A. Ministry of Human Resource
    B. Ministry of Rural Development

C. Ministry of Tourism
D. Ministry of Youth

15. 'Rail Neer' was introduced in the railway budget of the year—
A. 2002–2003
B. 2001–2002
C. 2000–2001
D. 1999–2000

16. National Rural Health Mission (NRHM) has been launched in the country since—
A. April 1, 2005
B. April 12, 2005
C. April 1, 2006
D. April 12, 2006

17. The government's efforts to fight the menace of unemployment continue since the :
A. First Plan
B. Second Plan
C. Fifth Plan
D. Seventh Plan

18. National Income estimates in India are prepared by—
A. NITI Aayog
B. RBI
C. C.S.O.
D. Finance Ministry

19. In which year 'Make in India' Programme was launched?
A. 2014
B. 2015
C. 2016
D. 2017

20. 'Food for Work Programme' was introduced during which one of the following Five-Year Plans?
A. I
B. II
C. V
D. IX

21. Growth with social justice was the motto of which plan?
A. Fifth Plan
B. Sixth Plan
C. Seventh Plan
D. Eighth Plan

22. 'Aam Admi Bima Yojana' is an insurance scheme for rural landless house-holds introduced by—
A. National Insurance Co.
B. Life Insurance Co.
C. UTI
D. ICICI Life Pudential Co.

23. Kasturba Gandhi Education Scheme (started from July, 2004) is related to
A. Girl education
B. Adult education
C. Child Labour education
D. Tribal Women (above 18 years)

24. Which Plan aimed doubling the per capita income in ten years and achieving a growth rate of eight percent?
A. First Plan
B. Third Plan
C. Seventh Plan
D. Tenth Plan

25. Which was the first Country in the World to introduce Goods and Services Tax (GST)?
A. France
B. Italy
C. U.K.
D. Japan

ANSWERS

1 C	2 C	3 D	4 A	5 A	6 C	7 B	8 C	9 C	10 A
11 D	12 C	13 A	14 C	15 A	16 B	17 A	18 C	19 A	20 C
21 C	22 B	23 A	24 D	25 A					

INDIAN CONSTITUTION

1. Who gives recognition to political parties in India?
   A. Parliament
   B. President
   C. Supreme Court
   D. Election Commission
2. The Quorum of the Legislative Council is :
   A. one-fourth of its total membership or 10
   B. one-fourth of its membership
   C. one-tenth of its membership or ten whichever is greater
   D. 25
3. The Indian Constitution is:
   A. federal
   B. unitary
   C. a happy mixture of the federal and unitary
   D. federal in normal times and unitary in times of emergency
4. Universal adult franchise implies a right to vote to all:
   A. adult residents of the State
   B. adult male citizens of the State
   C. residents of the State
   D. adult citizens of the State
5. When a resolution prefering a charge against the President has been passed by a specified majority in the House, it is sent to the other House for investigation. If, as a result of such an investigation, a resolution is passed through a specified majority by the other House, declaring that the charge has been sustained, the President shall leave his office. The specified special majority must not be less than :
   A. two-third of the members present and voting
   B. one-third of the members present and voting
   C. three-fourth of the members present and voting and two-third of the total membership
   D. two-third of the total membership
6. Which one of the following judicial powers of the President of India has been *wrongly* listed?
   A. he appoints the Chief Justice and other judges of the Supreme Court
   B. he can remove the judges of the Supreme Court on grounds of misconduct
   C. he can consult the Supreme Court on any question of law or fact which is of public importance
   D. he can grant pardon, reprieves and respites to persons punished under Union Law
7. The Vice-president of India can be removed from his office before the expiry of his term if :
   A. the Rajya Sabha passes a resolution by a majority of its members and the Lok Sabha agrees with the resolution
   B. if the Supreme Court of India recommends his removal
   C. the President so desires
   D. None of the above
8. The Chief Justice of a High Court in India is appointed by the :
   A. Governor of the State
   B. Prime Minister of India
   C. Chief Justice of the Supreme Court
   D. President of India
9. Which of the following statements is constitutionally not true about the passing of the Union Budgets and Finance Bill in India?
   1. Under the law, Finance Bill should be adopted by both the Houses of the Parliament within 45 days of its introduction.

2. If the Finance Bill is not adopted within specified period, the government loses its authority to levy the taxes proposed in the budgets.
3. In the absence of full budget, a vote-on-account gives the power to the government to spend.
4. Government cannot raise revenues without a proper approval of the Finance Bill

A. Only 2
B. Only 3
C. Only 4
D. Only 1, 2 and 3

10. Normally, on whose advice the President's Rule is imposed in a State?
A. Chief Minister
B. Legislative Assembly
C. Governor
D. Chief Justice of High Court

11. Which Article of the Indian Constitution deals with Amendment procedure?
A. Article 368
B. Article 358
C. Article 367
D. All of these

12. Government is the agency through which the will of :
A. the state is expressed
B. the people is expressed
C. the head of the state is expressed
D. the majority is expressed

13. In a unitary system of government :
A. The centre is all powerful
B. The centre is weaker than the states
C. The centre and states stand at par
D. The states and centre are supreme in their respective spheres

14. In Cabinet system of Government the real executive authority rests with :
A. The Council of Ministers
B. The Prime Minister
C. The Constitution
D. The Parliament

15. The Head of the State under a parliamentary government:
A. is an elected representative
B. is a hereditary person
C. is a nominated person
D. may be any one of the above

16. In the event of a ministerial proposal being defeated on the floor of the legislature, under the parliamentary system :
A. the government waits for a general no-confidence motion
B. the minister concerned is taken to task by the Prime Minister
C. the minister is forced to resign
D. the whole Council of Ministers resign

17. The "due process of law" is an essential characteristic of the judicial system of:
A. UK B. France
C. USA D. India

18. Under the Constitution it is :
A. obligatory for the President to accept the advice of the Council of Ministers but is not obliged to follow it
B. obligatory for the President to accept the advice of the Council of Ministers
C. not obligatory for the President to seek or accept the advice of the Council of Ministers
D. obligatory for the President to seek the advice of the Council of Ministers if his own party is in power

19. Which one of the following statements is correct?
A. the Presiding Officer of Rajya Sabha is elected every year
B. the Presiding Officer of Rajya Sabha is elected for a term of two years at a time
C. the Presiding Officer of Rajya Sabha is elected for a term of six years
D. the Vice-President of India is the ex-officio Presiding Officer of Rajya Sabha

20. The introduction of "no confidence" motion in the Lok Sabha requires the support of at least:
A. 50 members
B. 70 members
C. 60 members
D. 80 members

21. The High Court comes under :
A. State List
B. Union List

C. Concurrent List
D. None of the above

22. Which one of the following has been wrongly listed as a Fundamental Duty of the Indian citizens?
A. to develop scientific temper, humanism and spirit of inquiry and reform
B. to work for raising the prestige of the country in the international sphere
C. to protect and improve the natural environment
D. to strive towards excellence in all spheres of individual and collective activity

23. Which one of the following is not a Fundamental Duty as outlined in Article 51A of the Constitution?
A. to abide by the Constitution and respect its ideals
B. to defend the country and render national service when called upon to do so
C. to work for the moral upliftment of the weaker sections of society
D. to preserve the rich heritage

24. The main characteristics of the Directive Principles of State Policy given in the Indian Constitution are :
A. not enforceable by any court
B. fundamental in the governance of the country
C. 'Like instruments, instructions, political manifesto and a code of moral precepts which have to guide governors of the country'
D. no law can be passed, which is opposed to these principles

25. Of the following which are true?
A. In a State, the Legislative Council is dominant with regard to non-financial bills and the Legislative Assembly with regard to financial (money) bills
B. Vidhan Parishad can virtually block legislation even if the same is passed by the Vidhan Sabha
C. In case of a tie between the two Houses, the Governor is duty-bound to call a joint session of the two Houses to have the issue settled on a majority verdict
D. If a Bill is twice approved by the Vidhan Sabha, it becomes law even if rejected by the Vidhan Parishad

26. Which one of the following types of emergency can be declared by the President?
A. Emergency due to threat of war, external aggresion or internal disturbances
B. Emergency due to break-down of constitutional machinery in a State.
C. Financial emergency on account of threat to the financial credit of India
D. all the three emergencies

27. Which state in India has a Uniform Civil Code?
A. Mizoram
B. Assam
C. Goa
D. Tamil Nadu

28. Under the administration of which one of the following is the Department of Atomic Energy?
A. Prime Ministers Office
B. Cabinet Secretariat
C. Ministry of Power
D. Ministry of Science and Technology

29. In India, the first municipal corporation was set up in which among the following?
A. Calcutta (Kolkata)
B. Madras (Chennai)
C. Bombay (Mumbai)
D. Delhi

30. If the Speaker of the State Legislative Assembly decides to resign, he should submit his resignation to the:
A. Judges of the High Court
B. Deputy Speaker
C. Chief Minister
D. Finance Minister.

31. The members of the Rajya Sabha are elected for
A. Whole life
B. Five years
C. Two years
D. Six years

32. India is a Federal State because of:
A. dual judiciary

B. dual citizenship prevalent here
C. share of power between the Centre and the States
D. written Constitution

33. Residuary Subjects are those subjects which are :
A. contained in the State list
B. contained in the Union list
C. contained in the Concurrent list
D. not covered by any of the three lists

34. Which of the following writs can be issued, by the Supreme Court, to enforce Fundamental Rights?
A. writ of Habeas Corpus
B. writ of Mandamus
C. writ of Quo-warranto
D. All of these

35. When the offices of both the President and the Vice-President of India are vacant, who will discharge their functions?
A. Prime Minister
B. Home Minister
C. Chief Justice of India
D. The Speaker

36. The Supreme Court tenders advice to the President of India on a matter of law or fact:
A. on its own
B. only when such advice is sought
C. only if the matter relates to some basic issue
D. only if the issue poses a threat to the unity and integrity of the country

37. Six months shall **not** intervene between two sessions of the Indian Parliament because :
A. it is the customary practice
B. it is the British convention followed in India
C. it is an obligation under the Constitution of India
D. None of the above

38. The States of the Indian Union can be recognised or their boundaries altered by:
A. the Union Parliament by a simple majority in the ordinary process of legislation
B. two-thirds majority of both the Houses of Parliament
C. two-thirds majority of both the Houses of Parliament and the consent of the legislatures of concerned States
D. an executive order of the Union government with the consent of the concerned State governments

39. The Basic Feature theory of the Constitution of India was propounded by the Supreme Court in the case of :
A. Minerva Mills Vs. Union of India
B. Golaknath Vs. State of Punjab
C. Menaka Gandhi Vs. Union of India
D. Keshavananda Vs. State of Kerala

40. Which one of the following writs is issued by a court in case of illegal detention of a person?
A. Habeas corpus
B. Mandamus
C. Certiorari
D. Quo-warranto

41. Sharda Act deals with:
A. Widow remarriage
B. Child marriage
C. Inter-caste marriage
D. Polygamy

42. The Vice-President discharges the duties of the President during his illness for a maximum period of:
A. three months
B. six months
C. one year
D. Indefinitely

43. Which one of the following courts can a citizen move for the enforcement of Directive Principles of State Policy?
A. The Supreme Court
B. The High Court
C. Both A and B
D. None of these

44. The party system in India can be described as:
A. Single Party
B. Bi-Party
C. Multi-Party
D. A mixture of all these

45. The Chief Minister:
A. should not be a member of the State Legislature
B. must be a member of the State Legislature
C. must be a member of the Legislative Council
D. must be a member of the Legislative Assembly

46. The Constitution of India was created:
A. a very weak centre

B. a very strong centre
C. a centre which is weak in normal times but very strong during emergencies
D. None of these

47. The recommendations of the Finance Commission are:
A. binding on the President
B. not binding on the President
C. generally accepted as a matter of convention
D. accepted or rejected by the Governments according to its convenience

48. Consider the following statements about the Attorney General of India :
1. He is appointed by the President of India.
2. He must have the same qualifications as are required for a Judge of the Supreme Court.
3. He must be a member of either House of Parliament.
4. He can be removed by impeachment by Parliament.

A. 1 and 2
B. 1 and 3
C. 2, 3 and 4
D. 3 and 4

49. The Parliament can make any law for the whole or any part of India for implementing International treaties:
A. with the consent of all the States
B. with the consent of the majority of States
C. with the consent of the States concerned
D. without the consent of any State

50. Eighth Schedule of the Constitution contains:
A. Fundamental Rights
B. List of religions
C. Laws placed beyond the Jurisdiction of courts
D. List of 22 official languages

51. Who is a non-member but can participate in the business of either of the houses of Parliament?
A. Vice-President
B. Solicitor-General
C. Attorney-General
D. Chief Justice

52. In Indian Republic the real executive authority rests with the:
A. Prime Minister
B. President
C. Bureaucrats
D. Council of Ministers

53. The mind and ideals of the framers of Indian Constitution are reflected in:
A. The Preamble
B. The Fundamental Rights
C. The Directive Principles of State Policy
D. The Independent Judiciary

54. Who can dissolve the Lok Sabha before the expiry of its normal term of 5 years?
A. the Prime Minister
B. the President at his own
C. the President on the recommendation of the Prime Minister
D. the President on the recommendation of the Speaker

55. How many times has the Preamble of the Constitution of India been amended?
A. Once B. Twice
C. Thrice D. Never

56. Reasonable restrictions on Fundamental Rights can be imposed by:
A. The Parliament
B. The President
C. The Supreme Court
D. The Prime Minister

57. What is the meaning of the word 'Secular' as used in the Preamble to the Constitution?
A. Monotheism
B. Polytheism
C. Abnegation of all religions
D. Freedom of religion and worship to all citizen

58. The Parliament is not empowered to vote on the expenditure charged on the 'Consolidated Fund of India' which includes the emoluments and allowances of:
A. Prime Minister and his Council of Ministers
B. President of India
C. Secretaries of Various Ministries
D. Armed Forces of India

59. The control of the preparation of electoral rolls for Parliament and Legislatives in India, vests with:
A. Cabinet
B. Prime Minister
C. President
D. Election Commission

60. Which one of the following Articles lays down that the State shall take steps to organise village panchayats?
A. Article 40
B. Article 26
C. Article 57
D. Article 58

61. Which language is not specified in the 8th Schedule of the Indian Constitution?
A. Sanskrit B. Sindhi
C. Urdu D. Bhojpuri

62. The Governor of State is:
A. Free from the control of the Centre
B. Controlled by the Centre and he is the agent of the President
C. Not an agent of the President
D. Not free to act in discretion in certain matters

63. Which of the following exercised the most profound influence in framing the Indian Constitution?
A. British Constitution
B. US Constitution
C. Irish Constitution
D. The Government of India Act, 1935

64. Which can be the maximum interval between two sessions of Parliament?
A. Three months
B. Four months
C. Six months
D. Nine months

65. Separation of the Judiciary from the Executive has been provided in which one of the following parts of the Indian Constitution?
A. The Preamble
B. The Fundamental Rights
C. The Directive Principles of State Policy
D. The Seventh Schedule

66. A Money Bill passed by Lok Sabha is deemed to have been passed by Rajya Sabha also when no action is taken by the Upper House within:
A. 10 days B. 14 days
C. 20 days D. 30 days

67. Which of the following is an extra-constitutional and non-statutory body?
A. Finance Commission
B. NITI Aayog
C. UPSC
D. Election Commission

68. The Judges of the Supreme Court hold office till the age of:
A. 62 years B. 65 years
C. 68 years D. 60 years

69. Election Commission is a/an:
A. legal body
B. constitutional body
C. executive committee
D. informal body

70. The greatest hallmark of personal liberty is :
A. Mandamus
B. Certiorari
C. Quo warranto
D. Habeas Corpus

71. Which one of the following Fundamental Rights has been a subject of maximum controversy and litigation?
A. right to freedom of speech
B. right to property
C. right to Constitutional remedies
D. right to religion

72. How many members can be nominated to the Rajya Sabha by the President?
A. none B. 10
C. 12 D. two

73. The framers of the Constitution borrowed the idea of judicial review from the Constitution of:
A. USA
B. France
C. United Kingdom
D. All three

74. The Electoral System in India is based on:
A. adult franchise
B. separate electorate
C. indirect election system
D. multi-vote system

75. The guardian of the Constitution of India is the:
A. Indian Parliament
B. Supreme Courts of India
C. Prime Minister of India
D. High Courts of States

76. The basic tenet of secularism as enshrined in the Constitution of India is:
A. propagation of all religions by the State
B. propagation of atheism
C. non-propagation of any religion by the State
D. None of the above

77. The word 'secular' in the Preamble of the Indian Constitution was incorporated by the:
A. 42nd amendment
B. 62nd amendment
C. 44th amendment
D. 41st amendment

78. Consider the following statements.
1. The Governor of Punjab is concurrently the Administrator of Chandigarh.
2. The Governor of Kerala is concurrently the Administrator of Lakshadweep.

Which of the above statements is/are true?
A. 1 only
B. 2 only
C. Both A and B
D. Neither A nor B

79. Which one of the following Constitutional Amendments states that the total number of ministers, including the Prime Minister, in the Council of ministers shall not exceed fifteen per cent of the total number of—
A. 90th B. 91st
C. 92nd D. 93rd

80. For which one of the following reforms was a Commission set up under the chairmanship of Veerappa Moily by the government of India?
A. Police Reforms
B. Tax Reforms
C. Reforms in Technical Education
D. Administrative Reforms

81. How many High Courts are presently in India?
A. 18 B. 20
C. 22 D. 25

82. A government that has a monarch, but one whose powers are limited by law or by a formal constitution is—
A. Constitutional Republic
B. Constitutional Monarchy
C. Authoritarian
D. Anarchism

ANSWERS

1	**2**	**3**	**4**	**5**	**6**	**7**	**8**	**9**	**10**
D	C	D	D	A	B	A	D	C	C
11	**12**	**13**	**14**	**15**	**16**	**17**	**18**	**19**	**20**
A	A	A	A	D	D	C	B	D	A
21	**22**	**23**	**24**	**25**	**26**	**27**	**28**	**29**	**30**
B	B	C	B	D	D	C	A	B	B
31	**32**	**33**	**34**	**35**	**36**	**37**	**38**	**39**	**40**
D	C	D	D	C	B	C	A	D	A
41	**42**	**43**	**44**	**45**	**46**	**47**	**48**	**49**	**50**
B	D	D	C	B	B	C	A	D	D
51	**52**	**53**	**54**	**55**	**56**	**57**	**58**	**59**	**60**
C	C	A	C	A	A	D	B	D	A
61	**62**	**63**	**64**	**65**	**66**	**67**	**68**	**69**	**70**
D	D	D	C	C	B	B	B	B	D
71	**72**	**73**	**74**	**75**	**76**	**77**	**78**	**79**	**80**
B	C	A	A	B	C	A	A	B	D
81	**82**								
D	B								

EVERYDAY SCIENCE

1. Name the instrument with the help of which a sailor in a submarine can see the objects on the surface of the sea.
   A. Telescope
   B. Periscope
   C. Gyroscope
   D. Stereoscope
2. 'Haemophilia' is the disease of ....
   A. liver B. blood
   C. brain D. bones
3. Vitamin A is abundantly found in ....
   A. Brinjal B. Tomato
   C. Carrot D. Cabbage
4. .... is not soluble in water.
   A. Vitamin A
   B. Vitamin B
   C. Vitamin C
   D. None of the above
5. The blood vessels with the smallest diameter are called ....
   A. capillaries
   B. arterioles
   C. venules
   D. lymphatics
6. Out of the following .... has the greatest elasticity.
   A. steel
   B. rubber
   C. aluminium
   D. annealed copper
7. Cooking gas is a mixture of which of the following two gases?
   A. Carbon dioxide and Oxygen
   B. Butane and Propane
   C. Carbon monoxide and Carbon dioxide
   D. Methane and Ethylene
   E. None of these
8. The substance most commonly used as a food preservative is:
   A. sodium carbonate
   B. tartaric acid
   C. acetic acid
   D. benzoic acid
9. Normally, the substances that fight against diseases in human systems are known as:
   A. dioxyribonucleic acids
   B. carbohydrates
   C. enzymes
   D. antibodies
10. The SI unit of temperature is ....
    A. Kelvin
    B. Celsius
    C. Fahrenheit
    D. None of the above
11. One of the common fungal diseases of man is :
    A. plague B. ringworm
    C. cholera D. typhoid
12. A clear sky is blue because:
    A. red light is scattered more than blue
    B. ultra violet light has been absorbed
    C. blue light is scattered more than red
    D. blue light has been absorbed
13. Jenner introduced the method of making people immune to :
    A. small pox B. rabies
    C. cholera D. polio
14. The largest cell in the human body is :
    A. Nerve cell
    B. Liver cell
    C. Muscle cell
    D. Kidney cell
15. What is the device that steps up or steps down the voltage?
    A. Dynamo
    B. Conductor
    C. Inductor
    D. Transformer
16. The protein deficiency disease is known as :
    A. Kwashiorker
    B. Cirrhosis
    C. Eczema
    D. Clycoses
17. Iron deficiency causes :
    A. rickets B. anaemia
    C. cirrhosis D. goitre
18. Blood group of an individual is controlled by:
    A. Haemoglobin
    B. Shape of RBC
    C. Shape of WBC
    D. Genes
19. In a normal man the amount of blood pumped out by the heart per minute is about :

A. 1 litre B. 3 litres
C. 4 litres D. 5 litres

20. Red/green colour blindness in man is known as :
A. Protanopia
B. Deutetanopia
C. Both A and B
D. Marfan's syndrome

21. The blue colour of the water in the sea is due to :
A. Reflection of the blue light by the impurities in sea water.
B. Reflection of the blue sky by sea water and scattering of blue light by water molecules
C. Absorption of other colours by water molecules
D. None of the above

22. The image formed on the retina of the eye is :
A. upright and real
B. larger than the object
C. small and inverted
D. enlarged and real

23. If the surface water in a lake is just going to freeze, what will be the temperature of water at the bottom?
A. 0°C
B. more than 4°C
C. 4°C
D. less than 4°C

24. Oil rises up the wick in a lamp :
A. because oil is volatile
B. due to the capillary action phenomenon
C. due to the surface tension phenomenon
D. because oil is very light

25. The 'stones' formed in human kidney consist mostly of :
A. calcium oxalate
B. sodium acetate
C. magnesium sulphate
D. calcium

26. We hear the sound later, while the light is seen earlier:
A. because light's speed is more than that of sound
B. because lights travel in a straight direction while sound in a zigzag direction
C. because sound's frequency is lower than light
D. All of the above

27. Which part of an eye is transplanted?
A. Cornea B. Retina
C. Iris D. Sciera

28. The Universal donor group of blood is:
A. O B. A
C. B D. AB

29. The green colour of the leaf is due to:
A. Presence of Chloroplast
B. Presence of Chromium
C. Presence of Leucoplast
D. Presence of excess of oxygen

30. How many calories of energy is yielded by a cup of tea?
A. 4 B. 400
C. 40 D. 1000

31. Camel uses its hump for:
A. storing water
B. storing fat
C. for balancing the body
D. temperature regulation

32. A man standing in a free falling lift releases a ball from his hand. The ball would be :
A. moving down
B. moving up
C. stationary
D. moving up and down

33. Which one of the following substances is used for preservation of food grains?
A. Sodium benzoate
B. Vinegar
C. Sodium chloride
D. Potassium permanganate

34. The disease caused by Asbestos is:
A. Emphysema
B. Paralysis
C. Diarrhoea
D. Dysentery

35. The universal law of gravitation was propounded by :
A. Kepler
B. Galileo
C. Newton
D. Copernicus

36. Bats can fly in the dark because :
A. they have a better vision in the dark
B. the pupils of their eyes are very big
C. they are guided by ultrasonic waves produced by them
D. any bird can do so

37. Blood is formed in the human adult by the :
A. heart
B. spleen
C. kidney
D. bone marrow

38. Pencil 'lead' is made up of:
A. graphite
B. charcoal
C. lead oxide
D. lampblack

39. The deficiency of which one of the following vitamins leads to bleeding of gums and loosening of teeth?
A. Vitamin D
B. Vitamin C
C. Vitamin B
D. Vitamin A

40. How much blood does a normal person have in his body?
A. 8 litres
B. 4 to 5 litres
C. 10 litres
D. 2 litres

41. Which colour of light has the longest wavelength?
A. Yellow B. Blue
C. Red D. Green

42. Petrol fire can be extinguished by:
A. Water
B. Carbon dioxide
C. Sand
D. None of these

43. Which of the following is nearest to earth?
A. Sun
B. Moon
C. Mercury
D. None of the above

44. What is the name of the instrument that measures the speed of wind?
A. Lactometer
B. Hydrometer
C. Anemometer
D. None of the above

45. Moon has no atmosphere because:
A. its surface is not smooth
B. it is quite far off
C. it does not have any living being
D. root mean square velocity of all gases is more than their escape velocity on moon's surface

46. Which one of the following is present in tobacco?
A. Nicotine
B. Heroin
C. Marijuana
D. Cocaine

47. Normal temperature of human body is :
A. 36.8°C B. 94.8°F
C. 98.6°F D. 49.8°C

48. The unit of distance used in navigation is :
A. nautical mile
B. kilometer
C. light year
D. yard

49. If the reading in a barometer shows an abrupt fall, the chances are that the weather will be :
A. very cool
B. very stormy
C. full of rains
D. calm and quiet

50. The gas which is used in cold storage plants for refrigeration is known as :
A. Chlorine
B. CO_2
C. Ammonia
D. Hydrogen

51. In the Fahrenheit scale, the number 32 corresponds to:
A. 100°C B. 23°C
C. 32°C D. 30°C

52. The term 'global warming' means:
A. quick melting of polar ice sheets
B. depletion of ozone layer
C. high temperature in torrid zone
D. general rise in temperature due to carbon dioxide

53. The pond appears shallower than it actually is, due to:
A. reflection
B. refraction
C. mirage
D. dispersion

54. The disease dropsy affects:
A. stomach
B. spinal cord
C. liver
D. kidney

55. The drug obtained from the bark of cinchona, was used for treating malaria. The synthetic drug which replaced the natural product is :
A. Chloromycetin
B. Chloroquine
C. Tetracycline
D. Ampiciline

56. When there is a decrease in the concentration of oxygen in the blood, the rate of breathing :
A. decreases
B. increases
C. does not change
D. first decreases, then increases

57. These days yellow lamps are frequently used as street light. Which one of the following gas is used in these lamps :
A. Sodium B. Neon
C. Hydrogen D. Nitrogen

58. The age of a tree, in years, can be ascertained by :
A. its weight
B. its height
C. the number of its annular rings
D. length of its root

59. Hormone secretin stimulates the secretion of
A. Bile
B. Salivary juice
C. Pancreatic juice
D. All the above

60. Extraction of sodium is done by—
A. Distal tubule
B. Proximal tubule
C. Loop of Henle
D. None of these

61. Thermal energy is an energy due to—
A. Kinetic energy of molecules
B. Potential energy of molecules
C. Both A and B
D. Neither A nor B

62. A cricket player while taking a catch lowers his hands to—
A. increase time of impulse
B. decrease time of impulse
C. take catch safely
D. increase the area of impact

63. A non-magnetic material is that which is—
A. not attracted by a magnet
B. repelled by a magnet
C. not affected even by strong magnetic fields
D. none of these

64. The largest artery in the body is—
A. Vena cava
B. Aorta
C. Ventricle
D. Capillary

65. Blood pressure is measured usually from the—
A. Branchial vein
B. Branchial artery
C. Coronary artery
D. None of these

ANSWERS

1	**2**	**3**	**4**	**5**	**6**	**7**	**8**	**9**	**10**
B	B	C	A	A	A	B	D	D	A
11	**12**	**13**	**14**	**15**	**16**	**17**	**18**	**19**	**20**
B	C	A	A	D	A	B	D	D	A
21	**22**	**23**	**24**	**25**	**26**	**27**	**28**	**29**	**30**
B	B	B	B	A	A	A	A	A	C
31	**32**	**33**	**34**	**35**	**36**	**37**	**38**	**39**	**40**
B	A	A	A	A	C	D	A	B	B
41	**42**	**43**	**44**	**45**	**46**	**47**	**48**	**49**	**50**
C	B	B	C	D	A	C	A	B	C
51	**52**	**53**	**54**	**55**	**56**	**57**	**58**	**59**	**60**
C	D	B	D	B	B	A	C	C	C
61	**62**	**63**	**64**	**65**					
C	A	C	B	B					

CULTURE

1. Match List-I with List-II and select the correct answer using the codes given below the Lists :

   List-I

   (*a*) Vishakhadatta
   (*b*) Shudraka
   (*c*) Kalidasa
   (*d*) Vatsyayana

   List-II

   1. Mrichhakatika
   2. Ritusamhara
   3. Kamasutra
   4. Devichandraguptam

   Codes :

	(*a*)	(*b*)	(*c*)	(*d*)
A.	1	4	2	3
B.	4	1	3	2
C.	1	4	3	2
D.	4	1	2	3

2. In which one of the following languages is the *Dalit* writing more conspicuous?
   A. Punjabi
   B. Assamese
   C. Marathi
   D. Odiya
3. The first writer to use Urdu as the medium of poetic expression was:
   A. Amir Khusrau
   B. Mirza Ghalib
   C. Bahadur Shah Zafar
   D. Faiz
4. The religious text of the Zoroastrians is named as:
   A. Torah
   B. The Analects
   C. Tripitika
   D. Zend Avesta
5. .... is associated with 'Videshiya' folk dance.
   A. Bihar
   B. Jharkhand
   C. Uttar Pradesh
   D. Madhya Pradesh
6. Raja Harishchandra, an early Indian film, was produced by :
   A. D.G. Phalke
   B. Ashok Kumar
   C. Ardeshir Irani
   D. None of the above
7. All films are certified by .... before they are publicly exhibited.
   A. Films Division
   B. National Film Development Corporation (NFDC)
   C. Directorate of Advertising and Visual Publicity (DAVP)
   D. Central Board of Film Certificate (CBFC)
8. Who painted the master piece 'Hamsa Damayanti'?
   A. Anjolie Ela Menon
   B. Abanindranath Tagore
   C. Amrita Shergill
   D. Raja Ravi Verma
9. Who amongst the following actresses has played the leading role in the film Elizabeth, which was very famous?
   A. Gwyneth Paltrow
   B. Cate Blanchett
   C. Simi Grewal
   D. Kim Basinger
10. The film 'Train to Pakistan' is based on the novel of the same name, written by:
    A. Bhishma Sahani
    B. Khushwant Singh
    C. Amrita Pritam
    D. Khwaja Ahmed Abbas
11. Pt. Shiv Kumar Sharma was a maestro of which one of the following instruments?
    A. Sitar
    B. Tabla
    C. Flute
    D. Santoor
12. The first feature film (talkie) to be produced in India was:
    A. Hatimtai
    B. Alam Ara
    C. Pundalik
    D. Raja Harishchandra
13. Who directed the film "Bombay"?
    A. Shyam Benegal
    B. Meera Nair
    C. Shekhar Kapoor
    D. Mani Ratnam
14. Late Iftekhar Ahmad was famous in which of the following fields?
    A. Acting
    B. Singing
    C. Music
    D. Literature

15. 'Gangaur', a religious folk dance associated with:
A. Assam
B. Himachal Pradesh
C. Haryana
D. Rajasthan

16. The character played by Jim Carrey in the movie *Man on Moon* is based on:
A. Andy Kaufman
B. Edwin Aldrin
C. John Glenn
D. Neil Armstrong

17. A popular Hindi film-based on the famous Sanskrit play *Mrichhakatika*, was titled:
A. *Meghadoot*
B. *Amrapali*
C. *Utsav*
D. *Shakuntala*

18. Who composed the song 'Zara Yad Karo Kurbani'?
A. Javed Akhtar
B. Pradeep
C. Nusrat Fateh Ali Khan
D. Raghupati Sahay 'Firaq'

19. Who was the producer of the serial 'Mahabharat'?
A. Shyam Benegal
B. B.R. Chopra
C. Ramanand Sagar
D. Mani Ratnam

20. Which of the following is a folk dance of Rajasthan?
A. Garba B. Dandya
C. Jhumar D. Kathak

21. The famous dancer Mamata Sankar is the daughter of :
A. Ravi Sankar
B. Sachin Sankar
C. Uday Sankar
D. Moni Sankar

22. Which is Maharashtra's well known folk form of musical theatre?
A. Lavni B. Nautanki
C. Tamasha D. Goatha

23. The classical Indian Music has its origin in which of the following :
A. Atharvaveda
B. Rigveda
C. Samaveda
D. Yajurveda

24. Teratali is the folk dance of:
A. Kerala
B. Rajasthan
C. Madhya Pradesh
D. Tamil Nadu

25. 'Karagam', a religious folk dance is associated with:
A. Tamil Nadu
B. Kerala
C. Andhra Pradesh
D. Karnataka

26. Consider the following statements regarding the Chakiarkoothu form of dance :
1. It is performed by Chakiar caste.
2. It cannot be traditionally witnessed by the higher caste Hindus.
3. Mizhavu is the accompanying instrument.
4. Its theatre form is called Koothambalam.

Which of these statements are correct?
A. 1, 3 and 4
B. 1, 2 and 3
C. 2, 3 and 4
D. 1, 2 and 4

27. Which of the following is a classical dance form of Kerala?
A. Kathak
B. Kuchipudi
C. Bharat Natyam
D. Kathakali

28. Which one of the following pairs of folk dance forms and states is *not* correctly matched :
A. Korku : Maharashtra
B. Jhumar : Haryana
C. Thali : Himachal Pradesh
D. Rakhal : Manipur

29. Maestro Kishan Maharaja was associated with
A. Shehnai B. Tabla
C. Santoor D. Flute

30. Sitar, Sarangi and Tabla became popular from the period of:
A. The Mughals
B. The Delhi Sultanate
C. The Vardhanas
D. The Guptas

31. Lavani is a:
A. Marathi folk song
B. Musical instrument
C. Well known player of flute
D. Treatise on percussion instruments

32. .... is associated with 'Kathakali' dance.
A. Andhra Pradesh
B. Kerala
C. Uttar Pradesh
D. Tamil Nadu

33. Which one of the following is essentially a solo dance?
A. Kuchipudi
B. Kathak
C. Manipuri
D. Mohiniattam

34. Which one of the following dance forms is associated with Samyukta Panigrahi?
A. Kathakali
B. Mohiniattam
C. Kathak
D. Odissi

35. Which of the following is the folk dance of Meghalaya?
A. Khasi
B. Loho
C. Bamboo Dance
D. Khantum

36. Kuchipudi is a dance drama of which of the following States?
A. Andhra Pradesh
B. Kerala
C. Karnataka
D. Tamil Nadu

37. Which one of the following pairs is not correctly matched?
A. Poor Man's Kathakali : *Ottanthullal*
B. Heir to Devadasi Dance : *Odissi*
C. Dance Form of Urban Origin in Karnataka : *Yakshagana*
D. Manipuri Dance : *Related to Vaishnavism*

38. Which one of the following pairs is *not* correctly matched?
A. Bharatanatyam : Tamil Nadu
B. Mohiniattam : Odisha
C. Kuchipudi : Andhra Pradesh
D. Bhangra : Punjab

39. Which among the following is also known as Jai Samhita?
A. Mahabharata
B. Ramayana
C. Satapath Brahmana
D. None of these

40. Who wrote famous book Chach Namah?
A. Al Beruni
B. Abu Bakr
C. Minhaj-us-Siraj
D. Hasan Nizami

41. Who is known as the Father of Modern Hindi Literature?
A. Makhanlal Chaturvedi
B. Tulsidas
C. Mahadevi Verma
D. Bhartendu Harish-Chandra

42. Dancing Siva is the masterpiece of which of the following art?
A. Chola Art
B. Pallava Art
C. Gupta Art
D. Rashtrakuta Art

43. Kalyana mandapam elaborated with carved pillars is the main feature of—
A. Gupta Art
B. Maurya Art
C. Vijay Nagar Art
D. Pallava Art

44. The Tomb of Salim Chisti is built at—
A. Ajmer
B. Nagaur
C. Fatehpur Sikri
D. Lahore

45. Akbar Padamsee is a famous—
A. Painter
B. Musician
C. Film Director
D. Novelist

ANSWERS

1 D	2 C	3 A	4 D	5 A	6 A	7 D	8 D	9 B	10 B
11 D	12 B	13 D	14 A	15 D	16 D	17 C	18 B	19 B	20 C
21 C	22 A	23 C	24 B	25 A	26 B	27 D	28 A	29 B	30 B
31 A	32 B	33 D	34 D	35 B	36 A	37 C	38 B	39 A	40 B
41 D	42 A	43 C	44 C	45 A					

SPORTS

1. Which Cricketer is nick named as the Pied Piper of Punjab?
A. Harbhajan Singh
B. Yuvraj Singh
C. Kapil Dev
D. Navjot Singh Sidhu

2. The term 'Grandmaster' is used in which of these games?
A. Judo B. Chess
C. Bridge D. Karate

3. The term "Derby" is related with which of the following?
A. Polo
B. Swimming
C. Racing
D. Horse Racing

4. With which game is Geet Sethi associated?
A. Basketball B. Chess
C. Snooker D. Tennis

5. The First Olympic Games were held in Olympia (Greece) in the year:
A. 300 BC B. 872 BC
C. 776 BC D. 205 AD

6. Match List-I with List-II and select the correct answer using the codes given below the Lists:

List-I	List-II
(a) Basketball	1. Lav
(b) Bridge	2. Revoke
(c) Golf	3. Pinot
(d) Tennis	4. Bunker

Codes:

	(a)	*(b)*	*(c)*	*(d)*
A.	2	3	1	4
B.	2	3	4	1
C.	3	2	1	4
D.	3	2	4	1

7. How many players are there in each side in the game of Netball?
A. 11 B. 6
C. 9 D. 7

8. Match the following:
(a) Deodhar Trophy
(b) Durand Cup
(c) Davis Cup
1. Volleyball
2. Football
3. Cricket
4. Lawn Tennis

	(a)	*(b)*	*(c)*
A.	3	2	4
B.	3	1	4
C.	2	3	1
D.	1	2	4

9. Which of the following is called 'Grand Slam'?
A. Winning the highest number of medals in the Olympic Games
B. Winning the Single's title of all the four major events in Tennis in a year, i.e.—Australian Open, French Open, Wimbledon Championship and US Open.
C. Winning the Wimbledon Singles title successively for two years
D. Winning all thirteen tricks of a deal at one time in the card games of Bridge.

10. With which game is the term 'butterfly stroke' associated?
A. Swimming B. Cricket
C. Gliding D. Skiing

11. Who is the first Indian to win the 'International Grand Master' title in Chess?
A. Anupama Abhayankar
B. Bhagyashree Sathe Thipsay
C. Vishwanathan Anand
D. D.V. Prasad

12. Arjuna Award has been instituted for outstanding contribution in the field of:
A. social service
B. literature
C. art and music
D. games and sports

13. The term 'Tee' is associated with which of the following sports?
A. Golf
B. Table Tennis
C. Polo
D. Judo

14. The term 'Penalty Kick' is used in
A. Football
B. Hockey
C. Cricket
D. None of these

15. Length of Marathan race is—
A. 20 miles 125 yards
B. 24 miles 250 yards
C. 26 miles 385 yards
D. 30 miles 400 yards

16. 'LBW' is a term related to which of the following games?
A. Golf
B. Basket ball
C. Cricket
D. Volley ball

17. Baron Pierre de Coubertin, father of the modern Olympic Games, belongs to:
A. Greece
B. USA
C. France
D. Italy

18. With which game are the terms bull's eye, muzzle and plug associated?
A. Billiards
B. Solitaire
C. Shooting
D. Rowing

19. 'Queensberry Rules' is the name given to the rules in:
A. Tennis
B. Boxing
C. Cricket
D. Hockey

20. India's National Cricket Championship is:
A. Duleep Trophy
B. Ranji Trophy
C. Irani Trophy
D. Sheesh Mahal Trophy

21. Rohinto Baria Trophy, Duleep Trophy and Charminar Challenge cup are asociated with—
A. Football
B. Hockey
C. Cricket
D. Lawn Tennis

22. Number of players in a team of Water Polo is—
A. 5 B. 7
C. 9 D. 11

23. Cricket was an Olympic event at which of the following Olympics?
A. London, 1908
B. Amsterdam, 1928
C. Paris, 1900
D. Melbourne, 1956

24. In the game of Baseball, distance between each base in a Diamond shaped ground is:
A. 90 ft
B. 80 ft
C. 72 ft
D. 56 ft

25. 'Cannon, Cue and Pot' are three terms associated with—
A. Billiards
B. Golf
C. Lawn Tennis
D. Both A and B

26. 'Green Park', where test cricket is played is located in—
A. Kolkata
B. Kanpur
C. Mohali
D. Jamshedpur

27. Who was the captain of the Indian team which played its first official Cricket Test Series against England in 1932?
A. Ranjit Singh Ji
B. The Yuvraj of Patiala
C. The Maharaja of Porbandar
D. Raja of Baroda

28. Vishwanathan Anand's name is associated with:
A. Cricket
B. Football
C. Tennis
D. Chess

29. The first winner of "Rajiv Gandhi Khel Ratna Award" (Now Major Dhyan Chand Khel Ratna Award) was:
A. Geet Sethi
B. Sachin Tendulkar
C. Vishwanathan Anand
D. Karnam Malleshwari

30. The term "Diamond" is associated with the game of:
A. Baseball
B. Bridge
C. Basketball
D. Billiards

31. What is the national game of the USA?
A. Cricket
B. Soccer
C. Baseball
D. Billiards

32. Which of the following international tennis tournaments is held on grass court?
A. US Open
B. French Open
C. Wimbledon
D. Australian Open

33. What is the diameter of a golf hole?
A. 4.25"
B. 5.5"
C. 3.5"
D. 7.5"

34. 'Merdeka Cup' is associated with ....
A. Golf B. Football
C. Squash D. Hockey

35. Baskets in the basketball game are hung at the height of:
A. 6 ft
B. 7 ft
C. 9 ft
D. 10 ft

36. The "Dronacharya Award' is associated with:
A. Eminent Surgeons
B. Famous Artists
C. Sport Coaches
D. Expert Engineers

37. Which Indian player won gold medal in Tokyo Olympic-2020?
A. P.V. Sindhu
B. Neeraj Chopra
C. Bajrang Punia
D. Ravi Kumar

38. Who among the following has become the first woman in the world to swim across seven seas?
A. Bula Chowdhury
B. Shikha Tandon
C. Amanda Beard
D. Arti Saha

39. Which Indian Sportsman is known as Hockey Wizard throughout the world?
A. A.B. Subbiah
B. Jude Felix
C. Dhyanchand
D. Ajit pal Singh

40. Number of players on each side of Volleyball, Basketball and Baseball game are respectively
A. 5, 6, 9 B. 6, 5, 9
C. 6, 9, 5 D. 6, 5, 7

41. Which of the following teams won the first one day Cricket World Cup held in 1975?
A. England
B. West Indies
C. Australia
D. Pakistan

42. When was the first SAF Games held?
A. 1984 B. 1987
C. 1952 D. 1995

43. Lionel Missi, a famous football player belongs to which country?
A. Argentina B. Italy
C. Brazil D. England

44. In which country did Tennis originate in 12th century?
A. USA
B. France
C. United Kingdom
D. Canada

45. The first Indian to win PGA title of golf is—
A. Arjun Atwal
B. Jeev Milkha Singh
C. Gaganjeet Bhullar
D. Anirban Lahini

46. Neeraj Chopra is associated with which sports?
A. Javelin Throw
B. Weightlifting
C. Wrestling
D. Badminton

ANSWERS

1	**2**	**3**	**4**	**5**	**6**	**7**	**8**	**9**	**10**
B	B	D	C	C	D	D	A	B	A
11	**12**	**13**	**14**	**15**	**16**	**17**	**18**	**19**	**20**
C	D	A	A	C	C	C	C	B	B
21	**22**	**23**	**24**	**25**	**26**	**27**	**28**	**29**	**30**
C	B	C	A	A	B	C	D	C	A
31	**32**	**33**	**34**	**35**	**36**	**37**	**38**	**39**	**40**
C	C	A	B	D	C	B	A	C	B
41	**42**	**43**	**44**	**45**	**46**				
B	A	A	B	A	A				

UNO AND WORLD

1. Which of the following countries is not a member of North Atlantic Treaty Organisation (NATO)?
   A. Norway
   B. United Germany
   C. Portugal
   D. Australia
2. Khmer Rouge is a dictatorial party of :
   A. Cambodia
   B. Indonesia
   C. Malaysia
   D. Thailand
3. Which country is not a member of SAARC?
   A. Myanmar
   B. Bangladesh
   C. Nepal
   D. Pakistan
4. The headquarters of WTO is located at :
   A. Geneva
   B. Paris
   C. The Hague
   D. Washington
5. The main function of the World Trade Organisation (WTO) is:
   A. enforcing of Uruguay Round Agreements
   B. facilitating multi-lateral trade relations of member countries and reviewing trade policies
   C. administering trade dispute settlement procedures
   D. None of the above
6. The Secretary-General of the UNO is appointed by the:
   A. General Assembly
   B. Security Council
   C. Trusteeship Council
   D. World Bank
7. The United Nations officially came into existence in 1945 on :
   A. November 24
   B. October 14
   C. October 24
   D. November 14
8. Which one of the following is true of the International Court of Justice?
   A. The Judges of the Court are appointed according to the discretion of the Secretary General
   B. No two Judges may belong to the same country
   C. The Court consists of 20 Judges
   D. The statute of the International Court of Justice is not an integral part of the UN Charter
9. Which of the following was not among the six founding countries of the European Community?
   A. Belgium B. France
   C. Germany D. UK
10. The smallest country in South America is:
    A. Ecuador B. Guyana
    C. Surinam D. Uruguay
11. In which year "Human Rights Resolution" was adopted by the U.N.?
    A. 1945 B. 1946
    C. 1947 D. 1948
12. Where is the headquarters of INTERPOL located?
    A. Berlin
    B. California
    C. Lyons
    D. Montreal
13. Parliament of which of the following countries is known as Great People's Khural?
    A. Malaysia
    B. Mongolia
    C. Thailand
    D. Indonesia
14. Which agency/organisation is not related to U.N.O.?
    A. Universal Postal Union (UPU)
    B. International Finance Corporation (IFC)
    C. World Meterological Organisation (WMO)
    D. International Confederation of Free Trade Union (ICFTU)
15. When is the UN Day celebrated?
    A. October 24
    B. January 24
    C. June 24
    D. September 24
16. The charter of the UN was signed on June 26, 1945 at:
    A. San Francisco
    B. Geneva

C. California
D. Paris

17. The members of the NAFTA include:
A. USA, Canada and Mexico
B. USA, Canada, Mexico and UK
C. USA, UK, Russia and Mexico
D. USA, Canada and Brazil

18. UNO has constituted a new cell for Gender Equality and Empowerment of Women with the name—
A. Development Women
B. UN Women
C. UN Women Empowerment
D. Division for the Advancement of the Women

19. All the Commonwealth nations were once the Colonies of:
A. France B. Germany
C. Portugal D. Britain

20. India joined the UN in:
A. 1950
B. 1947
C. 1946
D. 1945

21. The headquarters of World Intellectual Property Organisation (WIPO) is located in which of the following cities?
A. Paris
B. Madrid
C. New York
D. Geneva

22. Which of the following is the headquarters of the World Bank?
A. The Hague
B. Washington D.C.
C. Paris
D. Geneva

23. Consider the following statements about the European Union :
1. The European Union was known earlier as the European Community.
2. The Single European Act (1986) and the Maastricht Treaty were milestones in its formation.
3. Citizens of European Union countries enjoy dual citizenship.
4. Switzerland is a member of the European Union.

Which of the above statements are *correct*?
A. 2 and 4 B. 1 and 3
C. 3 and 4 D. 1, 2 and 3

24. Match List-I with List-II and select *correct* answer using the codes given below the Lists :

List-I
(*a*) WTO (*b*) IDA
(*c*) IMF (*d*) IBRD

List-II
1. Provides loans to address short-term balance of payment problems.
2. Multilateral trade negotiation body.
3. Sanction of soft loans.
4. Facilitating lendings and borrowings for reconstruction and development.

Codes :

	(*a*)	(*b*)	(*c*)	(*d*)
A.	2	3	4	1
B.	2	3	1	4
C.	3	2	4	1
D.	3	2	1	4

25. Which of these states are not signatories to the NPT?
A. Iraq
B. Israel
C. Pakistan
D. Both B and C

26. World Intellectual Property Organisation (WIPO) was formed in the year:
A. 1965 B. 1976
C. 1968 D. 1967

27. Who was the first Deputy Secretary-General of the United Nations?
A. Mark Malloch Brown
B. Louise Fréchette
C. Dr Asha-Rose
D. Abul Ahsan

28. International Criminal Court was established in the year:
A. 1995 B. 1996
C. 1997 D. 1998

29. Which country from the following is a permanent member of the UN Security Council?
A. Switzerland
B. People's Republic of China
C. Japan
D. Ukraine

30. Which of the following has been declared as a 'International non-violence day' by UNO?
A. August 2nd
B. September 2nd
C. October 2nd
D. November 2nd

31. The Headquarters of the International Monetary Fund is located at:
A. Paris
B. Vienna

C. Washington D.C.
D. Geneva

32. Bosnia-Herzegovina formed the part of:
A. Czech Republic
B. Serbia
C. Bulgaria
D. Azerbaijan

33. The Sparatly Islands over which Vietnam, Brunei, Malaysia, the Philippines and Taiwan have claims are in the:
A. South China Sea
B. Java Sea
C. Sea of Japan
D. Baring Sea

34. Where is the Headquarters of Asian Development Bank?
A. Washington D.C.
B. Paris
C. Manila
D. Canberra

35. The old name of which country was Abissinia?
A. Ethiopia B. Albania
C. Ghana D. Ukraine

36. Which is 'Country of Golden Fleece'?
A. Scotland B. Australia
C. Denmark D. Thailand

37. International 'Human Right Days' has been celebrated every year on—
A. December 7
B. December 8
C. December 9
D. December 10

38. The United Nations University is located in which of the following cities?
A. Geneva
B. New York
C. Paris
D. Tokyo

39. Which of the following countries is not a member of the South Asian Association for Regional Cooperation (SAARC)?
A. Bhutan
B. Maldives
C. Bangladesh
D. Myanmar

40. The six official languages of the UN are Russian, Chinese, English, French, Spanish and:
A. Hindi
B. Urdu
C. Arabic
D. Japanese

41. Single out the false statement pertaining to the International court of Justice:
A. Its Judges are elected
B. Its decisions are not inforceable
C. It is the Principal Judicial organ of the United Nations
D. In case of non-implementation of the decision the further redressal of national grievances is not feasible

42. The language spoken by the largest number of people in the world is:
A. Hindi
B. English
C. Mandarin
D. Spanish

43. The International Human Rights Convention adopted by the United Nations in 1990 relates to the:
A. Children
B. Migrant Workers
C. Stateless Persons
D. Disabled

44. *Majlis* is the parliament of which country?
A. Israel B. Iraq
C. Egypt D. Iran

45. Which country is known as the 'Land of Thousand Lakes'?
A. Norway B. Finland
C. Canada D. Ireland

46. The headquarters of UNESCO is situated at:
A. The Hague
B. Washington
C. New York
D. Paris

47. In the United Nations, the five Big Powers enjoy the right to Veto in the:
A. General Assembly
B. Security Council
C. Economic and Social Council
D. Trusteeship Council

48. 'MFN clause' is one of the main pillars on which:
A. WTO is based
B. IMF is based
C. IBRD is based
D. IDA is based

49. Which *one* of the following pairs takes care of the trade and economic interests of the developing countries at the international level?
A. G-15 and G-7
B. G-15 and G-77
C. G-7 and G-24
D. G-77 and G-24

50. Which of the following is the smallest country of the world?
A. Uganda
B. Bhutan
C. Vatican City
D. Sri Lanka

51. Which of the following is *not* an agency of United Nations Organisation?
A. UNDP B. OPEC
C. WTO D. UNHCR

52. In which one of the following countries is the "Head of the State" hereditary?
A. Pakistan
B. Japan
C. Canada
D. Bangladesh

53. Given below are two statements, one labelled as *Assertion (A)* and the other labelled as *Reason (R)* :
Assertion (A) : India is a member of G-77.
Reason (R) : India is a member of SAARC.
In the context of the above two statements, which one of the following is correct?
A. Both (A) and (R) are true and (R) is the correct explanation of (A)
B. Both (A) and (R) are true but (R) is not a correct explanation of (A)
C. (A) is true but (R) is false
D. (A) is false but (R) is true

54. W.T.O. came into existence in :
A. January 1997
B. January 1996
C. January 1995
D. January 1990

55. What was the major Cold War Crisis?
A. The Cuban Missile Crisis
B. The Taiwan Straits Crisis
C. The Arab-Israel War
D. All of the above

56. Agenda 21 is—
A. action plan for sustainable development
B. framework to combat climate change
C. framework convention to protect biodiversity
D. UNCED agreement to combat desertification

57. The old name of which country was 'Nippon'?
A. Myanmar
B. Japan
C. Jermany
D. None of these

58. Where was the first Nuclear Weapon Free Zone applied?
A. Africa
B. Antarctica
C. Latin America
D. Australia

59. Star Wars refers to:
A. Luke Skywalker
B. Strategic Defense Initiative
C. Space based nuclear war
D. Strategic destruction initiative

60. Which of the following is a Latin American regional institution?
A. SAARC
B. MERCOSUR
C. APEC
D. ASEAN

ANSWERS

1	**2**	**3**	**4**	**5**	**6**	**7**	**8**	**9**	**10**
D	A	A	A	B	A	C	B	D	C
11	**12**	**13**	**14**	**15**	**16**	**17**	**18**	**19**	**20**
A	C	B	D	A	A	A	B	D	D
21	**22**	**23**	**24**	**25**	**26**	**27**	**28**	**29**	**30**
D	B	D	B	D	D	B	D	B	C
31	**32**	**33**	**34**	**35**	**36**	**37**	**38**	**39**	**40**
C	B	A	C	A	B	D	D	D	C
41	**42**	**43**	**44**	**45**	**46**	**47**	**48**	**49**	**50**
D	C	A	D	B	D	B	A	B	C
51	**52**	**53**	**54**	**55**	**56**	**57**	**58**	**59**	**60**
B	B	B	C	D	A	B	C	B	B

Books and Authors

1. Who is the author of the book 'PRISON DIARY'?
   A. Bal Gangadhar Tilak
   B. Rajendra Prasad
   C. Jai Prakash Narayan
   D. Jawahar Lal Nehru
2. Who is the author of 'Satanic Verses'?
   A. Lewis Carrol
   B. Salman Rushdie
   C. Parry Mason
   D. Mulk Raj Anand
3. Who wrote 'Gitanjali'?
   A. Kalidas
   B. Gopal Das 'Neeraj'
   C. Rabindra Nath Tagore
   D. Jawahar Lal Nehru
4. Who, among the following, scholars flourishing during the Gupta Age, was the author of *Dasakumara-Charita?*
   A. Asanga B. Dignaga
   C. Dandina D. Bhattin
5. The author of *Gitagovinda* was:
   A. Halayudha
   B. Jayadeva
   C. Kalhana
   D. Jona-raja
6. "Ingenious Pain" is a book/novel written by :
   A. Andrew Miller
   B. Santa Monica
   C. Ben Johnson
   D. Bill Gates
7. Who amongst the following is the author of the famous book "An Equal Music"?
   A. Salman Rushdie
   B. Shasthivrata
   C. Vikram Seth
   D. Kamla Markandeya
8. The book 'Unto the Last' which influenced Gandhiji was authored by:
   A. Boris Yeltsin
   B. Pushkin
   C. Ruskin Bond
   D. John Ruskin
9. Who has written "Devdas"?
   A. Tarasankar Bandyopadhyay
   B. Bankim Chandra Chattopadhyay
   C. Rabindranath Tagore
   D. Sarat Chandra Chattopadhyay
10. "Ain-i-Akbari" is written by:
    A. Todar Mal
    B. Abul Fazal
    C. Sheikh Saadi
    D. Mirza Ghalib
11. "Alice in Wonderland" is written by :
    A. Lewis Carrol
    B. Chester Bowles
    C. Charles Dickens
    D. Jonathan Swift
12. "Mrichchhakatikam" is written by :
    A. Vishakhadatta
    B. Vatsyayana
    C. Sudraka
    D. Bana Bhatt
13. "My Experiments with Truth" is written by :
    A. Jawaharlal Nehru
    B. M.K. Gandhi
    C. Abul Kalam Azad
    D. Rajendra Prasad
14. Who wrote the book "India Wins Freedom"?
    A. Maulana Abul Kalam Azad
    B. Mahatma Gandhi
    C. Sir Mohammad Iqbal
    D. Abdul Gaffar Khan
15. Match List-I with List-II and select the correct answer using the codes given below the Lists :

    List-I
    (*a*) *Condition of India*
    (*b*) *Mother India*
    (*c*) *Farewell to India*
    (*d*) *Passage to India*

    List-II
    1. Edward Thompson
    2. E.M. Forster
    3. Pt. J.L. Nehru
    4. Katherine Mayo

    Codes :

	(*a*)	(*b*)	(*c*)	(*d*)
A.	2	1	4	3
B.	3	4	1	2
C.	3	1	2	4
D.	4	2	1	3

16. 'Poverty and Un British Rule in India' is written by:
    A. R.C. Dutt
    B. J.L. Nehru
    C. D.B. Naoroji
    D. S.N. Sen

17. Name the author of the book *A Passage to England:*
A. E.M. Forster
B. Nirad C. Choudhuri
C. Vikram Seth
D. Eric Segal

18. The author of the book 'The Struggle in My Life' is:
A. Mandela
B. J.L. Nehru
C. Tilak
D. Gokhale

19. Mukul and Bikhre Moti is a famous composition of—
A. Ramdhari Singh Dinkar
B. Subhadra Kumari Chauhan
C. Abul Fazal
D. Amir Khusro

20. Which of the following books is not written by Salman Rushdie?
A. The Satanic Verses
B. Shame
C. Naked Face
D. Midnight's Children

21. Who is the author of the book 'My Frozen Turbulence in Kashmir'?
A. Anita Desai
B. Kushwant Singh
C. Arun Shourie
D. Jagmohan

22. Who is the author of the book, *The God of Small Things*?
A. Mrinal Pandey
B. Shekhar Kapur
C. Arundhati Roy
D. Arun Shourie

23. *Harshcharita* was written by:
A. Banbhatt
B. Harsha Vardhan
C. Kalidas
D. Jaidev

24. Who is the author of *A Tale of Two Cities*?
A. D.H. Lawrence
B. R.L. Stevenson
C. Charles Dickens
D. William Shakespeare

25. *Long Walk to Freedom* is the autobiography of:
A. Martin Luther King
B. Nelson Mandela
C. Fidel Castro
D. Farookh Abdullah

26. "The Arctic Home of the Vedas" was written by :
A. Acharya Vinobha Bhave
B. Minoo Masani
C. S. Radhakrishnan
D. Bal Gangadhar Tilak

27. 'Neel Darpan', is a play written by:
A. Din Bandhu Mitra
B. Harish Ch. Mukherji
C. Tagore
D. Bankim Chandra

28. Who is the author of the book *'Business at the Speed of Thought'*?
A. Bill Gates
B. Robert Whiting
C. T.R. Reid
D. Peter Drunker

29. Mr. Dario Fo is the author of which of the following books?
A. News of Kidnapping
B. Taming the Waters
C. Beach Boy
D. Accidental Death of an Anarchist

30. Match the List-I with List-II and select the *correct* answer using the codes given below the Lists :

List-I
(Books)
(*a*) *The First Indian War of Independence*
(*b*) *Anand Math*
(*c*) *Life Divine*
(*d*) *Sadhana*

List-II
(Authors)
1. Rabindranath Tagore
2. Sri Aurbindo
3. Bankim Chandra Chatterji
4. Vinayak Damodar Savarkar

Codes :

	(*a*)	(*b*)	(*c*)	(*d*)
A.	4	3	2	1
B.	3	4	1	2
C.	4	3	1	2
D.	3	4	2	1

31. "In Custody" an English novel, is written by which one of the following?
A. V.S. Naipaul
B. Vikram Seth
C. Anita Desai
D. Shobha De

32. The *Tunnel of Time* is the autobiography of:
A. I.K. Gujral
B. Vishwanath Pratap Singh
C. Chandrashekhar
D. R.K. Laxman

33. *Half A Life* is the autobiography of
A. Amrita Pritam
B. V.S. Naipaul
C. Khushwant Singh
D. Dominique Loppierre

34. Who is the author of the book *Wings of Fire*?

A. Vikram Seth
B. A.P.J. Abdul Kalam
C. Arundhati Roy
D. M.J. Akbar

35. Who is the author of the lyric poetry 'Gitagovinda'?
A. Vyas
B. Lord Krishna
C. Jayadev
D. Adi Sankaracharya

36. Which of the following is not a book written by Nobel Laureate V.S. Naipaul?
A. An Area of Darkness
B. A Wounded Civilisation
C. A Bend in the River
D. Against the Grain

37. Which one of the following statements is not correct?
A. 'Neel Darpan' was a play based on the exploitation of the indigo farmers
B. The author of the play 'Ghasiram Kotwal' is Vijay Tendulkar
C. The play 'Navanna' by Nabin Chandra Das was based on the famine of Bengal
D. Urdu theatre was used to depend heavily on Parsi theatre

38. The book *Adha Likha Dastavej* is written by:
A. Indira Goswami
B. Kedarnath Singh
C. Nirmal Verma
D. Giriraj Kishore

39. The Book 'Shadow of a Princess' is a first-hand account of Princess Diana's life. It is written by:
A. Patrick Jepson
B. Byron Lord
C. Clive Ponting
D. James Jeans

40. Match the following List-I with List-II and select the correct answer from the codes given below the lists :

List-I
(Authors)
(*a*) Mahatma Gandhi
(*b*) Ram Manohar Lohia
(*c*) Dr. Rajendra Prasad
(*d*) Abul Kalam Azad

List-II
(Books)
1. India Divided
2. India Wins Freedom
3. Hind Swaraj
4. The Wheel of the History

Codes :

	(*a*)	(*b*)	(*c*)	(*d*)
A.	1	3	4	2
B.	4	3	2	1
C.	3	4	1	2
D.	2	3	4	1

41. Anand Math was written by:
A. Rabindranath Tagore
B. Bankim Chandra Chattopadhyay
C. Aurobindo Ghosh
D. Madhusudan Dutta

42. Who amongst the following is the author of the famous book "The Dark Side of Chameleot"?
A. Seymour Hersh
B. Salman Rushdie
C. Nirad C. Chaudhuri
D. Shobl. ı De
E. None of the above

43. The book "Doctor Zhivago" is written by:
A. John Gray
B. Boris Pasternak
C. Dean Ornish
D. Ardeshir Vakil

44. "A Brush with Life: An Autobiography" is written by:
A. M.F. Hussain
B. Satish Gujral
C. Sudhir Dar
D. R.K. Laxman

45. Who has written 'Hind Swaraj'?
A. Bal Gangadhar Tilak
B. Vinoba Bhave
C. Chandra Shekhar Azad
D. Mahatma Gandhi

46. Whose work is 'Bijak'?
A. Surdas
B. Kabir
C. Ravidas
D. Peepaji

47. Who wrote the novel 'Mrignayani'?
A. Vrindavan Lal Verma
B. Acharya Chatursen
C. Amrit Lal Nagar
D. Bhagwati Charan Verma

48. Who among the following wrote "Unhappy India"?
A. Lala Lajpat Rai
B. Maulana Abul Kalam Azad
C. Annie Besant
D. Mahatma Gandhi

49. Who was the eminent Tamil writer who espoused patriotic cause through his writings?
A. Subramaniam Bharati
B. Kamban
C. Niranjan
D. Shiv Ram Karanth

50. Waris Shah was the famous author of—
A. Urdu B. Hindi
C. Punjabi D. Kashmiri

51. Which among the following is not a Marathi author?
A. Hari Narayan Apte
B. Sudershan
C. Tikaram Mahay
D. Tukaram

52. Jobs for Millions is written by—
A. V.V. Giri
B. Pyare Lal
C. Sohan Singh Sital
D. Rajshekhar

53. Which famous Indian Cricketer has written Straight from the Heart?
A. Sachin Tendulkar
B. Sunil Gavaskar
C. Kapil Dev
D. Anil Kumble

54. Booker awardee book 'White Tiger' is written by—
A. Humra Qureshi
B. Arvind Adiga
C. Amitav Ghosh
D. Pawan Varma

55. Who wrote the famous book 'Life of Pi'?
A. Arindam Chaudhury
B. Vikram Seth
C. Yann Martel
D. Hari Kunzru

56. 'Non-Stop India' is a work of
A. Mark Tully
B. Aastha Aray
C. MLK Das
D. Amitav Ghosh

57. 'Out of the Blue' is written by:
A. K.P. Singh
B. Aakash Chopra
C. Yann Martel
D. Vinod Mehta

58. Whose work is 'The Inheritance of Loss'?
A. Aravind Adiga
B. J.G. Farrell
C. Kiran Desai
D. Nirmal Verma

59. 'Vernon God Little' is authored by:
A. John Banville
B. J.G. Farrell
C. Anita Desai
D. D B C Pierre

60. Who is the author of award winning book, 'The Line of Beauty'?
A. Bhagwan Das
B. Alan Hollinghurst
C. Anne Enright
D. Jhumpa Lahiri

ANSWERS

1	2	3	4	5	6	7	8	9	10
C	B	C	C	B	A	C	D	D	B
11	**12**	**13**	**14**	**15**	**16**	**17**	**18**	**19**	**20**
A	C	B	A	B	C	B	A	B	C
21	**22**	**23**	**24**	**25**	**26**	**27**	**28**	**29**	**30**
D	C	A	C	B	D	A	A	D	A
31	**32**	**33**	**34**	**35**	**36**	**37**	**38**	**39**	**40**
A	D	B	B	C	D	D	A	A	C
41	**42**	**43**	**44**	**45**	**46**	**47**	**48**	**49**	**50**
B	A	B	B	D	B	A	A	A	C
51	**52**	**53**	**54**	**55**	**56**	**57**	**58**	**59**	**60**
B	A	C	B	C	A	B	C	D	B

PERSONS

1. The different schools of modern socialism derive their strength primarily from the writings of ....
   A. Joseph Stalin
   B. Leo Tolstoy
   C. Mao Tse-tung
   D. Karl Marx
2. Baba Amte was famous as a ....
   A. Painter
   B. Singer
   C. Politician
   D. Social Worker
3. Dhrupad Dhamar style of singing was stated by:
   A. Raja Man Singh Tomar
   B. Amir Khusrau
   C. Tansen
   D. V.D. Puluskar
4. Who is the first Indian to join the Formula One League?
   A. Karun Chandok
   B. Kasam Khan
   C. N. Anbu
   D. Narain Karthikeyan
5. Sundarlal Bahuguna, a famous environmentalist, was associated with :
   A. Chipko Movement
   B. Narmada Bachao
   C. Satyagraha
   D. Anti-corruption
6. Mother Teressa's native place was :
   A. Albania B. France
   C. Greece D. Italy
7. The live polio vaccine which can be taken by mouth was developed by :
   A. Albert Sabin
   B. Edward Jenner
   C. Jonas Salk
   D. Selman Waksman
8. Which one of the following authors put forth the theory of the Drain of India's resources to England?
   A. Raja Rammohan Roy
   B. Bankim Chandra Chatterjee
   C. G.G. Agarkar
   D. Dadabhai Naoroji
9. The "Last Supper" is a famous renaissance painting. It was a master-piece of :
   A. Michael Angelo
   B. Leonardo da Vinci
   C. Titian
   D. Raphael
10. Major Dhyanchand was associated with which sports?
    A. Badminton
    B. Hockey
    C. Tennis
    D. Football
11. 'Man is born free, yet every where he is in chains'. This was said by:
    A. Voltaire
    B. John Stuart Mill
    C. Rousseau
    D. Karl Marx
12. Who among the following was a prominent social reformer?
    A. Baba Gurmukh Singh
    B. Raja Mahendra Pratap
    C. Bipin Chandra Pal
    D. Jotiba Govind Phule
13. Lord Hunt, was associated with which of the following fields?
    A. Politics
    B. Music
    C. Economics
    D. None of these
14. Who was known as "Man of Destiny"?
    A. Napoleon
    B. Nehru
    C. Hitler
    D. Mussolini
15. Who discovered that mosquito served as a carrier of malaria?
    A. Jonas Salk
    B. Ronald Ross
    C. Louis Pasteur
    D. Robert Koch
16. Who was the first woman Governor of an Indian State?
    A. Sushila Nayar
    B. Sucheta Kripalani
    C. Sarojini Naidu
    D. Sulochana Modi
17. Who among the following founded the Bhartiya Jana Sangh?
    A. Deen Dayal Upadhyaya
    B. Veer Savarkar
    C. Dr. Ram Manohar Lohia
    D. Dr. Shyama Prasad Mukherjee

18. Who among the following President of India held his office for two successive terms?
A. V.V. Giri
B. Dr. Rajendra Prasad
C. Dr. S. Radhakrishnan
D. None of these

19. Ustad Amjad Ali Khan is an exponent of:
A. Flute B. Sitar
C. Sarod D. Tabla

20. Who is the first non-Indian to receive the Bharat Ratna?
A. Martin Luther King
B. Zubin Mehta
C. Mother Teressa
D. Khan Abdul Ghaffar Khan

21. Who among of the following was an extremist?
A. Bal Gangadhar Tilak
B. Mahatma Gandhi
C. G.K. Gokhale
D. Dadabhai Naoroji

22. Who among the following Congress leaders was called the 'Grand Old Man' of India?
A. Mahatma Gandhi
B. Bal Gangadhar Tilak
C. Dadabhai Naoroji
D. Madan Mohan Malaviya

23. The first UN Secretary General was:
A. Javier Perez de Cuellar
B. U Thant
C. Tryguve Lie
D. Kurt Waldheim

24. The pioneer of Bhakti Movement in India was:
A. Kabir
B. Ramananda
C. Shankaracharya
D. Ramanuja

25. In which of the following did Sardar Vallabhbhai Patel play a leading role?
A. Bijolia Movement
B. Dandi March
C. Textile Mill workers strike at Ahmedabad
D. Bardoli Satyagraha

26. One-time associate of Mahatma Gandhi, broke off from him and launched a radical movement called 'self-respect movement'. Who was he?
A. P. Thyagaraja Shetu
B. Chhatrapati Maharaj
C. E.V. Ramaswamy Naicker
D. Jyotirao Govindrao Phule

27. Who among the following is renowned in Hindustani classical music (vocal)?
A. Shovana Narayan
B. M.S. Subbulakshmi
C. Pt. Jasraj
D. M.S. Gopalakrishnan

28. Who among the following won the Nobel Prize twice?
A. Winston Churchill
B. Madame Curie
C. Octavio Paz
D. George Choupak

29. The Greek philosopher who wrote nothing yet (who) is the most famous and that greatest figure in the world, he was:
A. Socrate
B. Marcus Aurelius
C. Plato
D. Aristotle

30. Name the person who became the first woman, the first Asian and the first Muslim to head (Secretary-General) the human rights watchdog, Amnesty International.
A. Ikno Hirayana
B. Irene Zubaida Khan
C. Gloria Arroya
D. Dame Silvia

31. Anna Hazare is known for :
A. Watershed Development
B. Rural Education
C. Tribal Development
D. Co-operative Development

32. Jayadeva, the lyricist of the Gita Govinda, adorned the court of :
A. Dharmpala
B. Devapala
C. Vijayasena
D. Lakshmansena

33. Adi Shankar who later on became Shankaracharya was born in :
A. Kashmir
B. Kerala
C. Andhra Pradesh
D. West Bengal

34. Who started vaccination?
A. Jonas E. Salk
B. Paul Muller
C. Robert Frost
D. Edward Jenner

35. The first writer to use Urdu as the medium of poetic expression was:
A. Amir Khusrau
B. Mirza Ghalib
C. Bahadur Shah Zafar
D. Faiz

36. Match *List-I* with *List-II* and select the correct answer using the codes given below the Lists :

List-I

(*a*) Pandit Vishnu Digamber Paluskar

(*b*) Venkatamahi
(*c*) Shyama Shastri
(*d*) Amir Khusrau

List-II

1. Introduced the scheme of *Raga* classification of Indian music
2. Proponent of Carnatic music
3. Proponent of the *Khayal* form of Hindustani music
4. Wrote the music for the song *Vande Mataram*

Codes :

	(*a*)	(*b*)	(*c*)	(*d*)
A.	4	1	3	2
B.	4	1	2	3
C.	1	4	3	2
D.	1	4	2	3

37. The Sufi Saint who maintained that devotional music was one way of coming close to God was:
A. Moin-ud-din Chisti
B. Baba Farid
C. Sayyid Muhammad Gesudaraz
D. Shah Alam Bukhari

38. Match List-I with List-II and select the correct answer using the codes given below the lists :

List-I

(*a*) T. Balasaraswathi
(*b*) Uma Sharma
(*c*) Indrani Rahman
(*d*) Raja and Radha Reddy

List-II

1. Kuchipudi
2. Odissi
3. Kathak
4. Bharatanatyam

Codes :

	(*a*)	(*b*)	(*c*)	(*d*)
A.	3	4	2	1
B.	2	1	4	3
C.	4	3	2	1
D.	1	2	4	3

39. Who amongst the following is associated with "Microsoft"?
A. Andrew Grove
B. Bill Gates
C. Ted Turner
D. Rupert Murdoch

40. 'Royal Asiatic Society' was founded by:
A. Sir William Jones
B. Sir John Marshall
C. R.D. Banerjee
D. Sir William Bentinck

41. Who was the Guru of Kabir?
A. Ramanuja
B. Ramananda
C. Vallabhacharya
D. Namadeva

42. The reputed musician duo, Tansen and Baiju Bawra, flourished during the reign of:
A. Jehangir
B. Bahadur Shah Zafar
C. Akbar
D. Shahjahan

43. The headquarters of the establishment of Dalai Lama is:
A. Bodh Gaya
B. Dharamshala
C. Sanchi
D. Periyar

44. Napolean was finally arrested after the battle of:
A. Borodino
B. Waterloo
C. Leipzig
D. Austerlitz

45. Who among the following personalities from the field of music is associated with Violin?
A. Pt. Bhimsen Joshi
B. Pt. V.G. Jog
C. Pt. Shiv Kumar Sharma
D. M.S. Subbulakshmi

46. "Non-violence is the law of our species as violence is the law of the brute. But where there is only a choice between cowardice and violence, I would rather have India resort to violence to defend her honour than that she should, in a cowardly manner become or remain a helpless witness to her own dishonour." This was said by:
A. Jawaharlal Nehru
B. Subhash Chandra Bose
C. Mahatma Gandhi
D. Bal Gangadhar Tilak

47. Dr. M.S. Subbulakshmi had distinguished herself in the field of:
A. Kathak
B. Bharat Natyam
C. Playing Violin
D. Vocal Music

48. The Khalsa Panth was founded by:
A. Guru Nanak Dev
B. Guru Teg Bahadur
C. Guru Hargobind
D. Guru Gobind Singh

49. 'Abinava Bharat' a secret society of revolutionaries was organised by:
A. Khudiram Bose
B. V.D. Savarkar
C. Prafulla Chaki
D. Bhagat Singh

50. Who was the first Indian Lady to became the president of congress?
A. Sarojini Naidu
B. Annie Besent
C. Nalini Sen Gupta
D. Indira Gandhi

51. Name the eminent lawyer who had debated in the INA officers trial case.
A. Moti Lal Nehru
B. Bhulabhai Desai
C. C. Rajgopalachari
D. None of these

52. Who led the protest meeting against the Rowlatt Act at Jallianwala Bagh?
A. N.B Handikar
B. Chhotu Ram
C. Saiffudin Kitchlu
D. Bhim Sen Sachar

53. Who was fondly called Rajarshi by Gandhijee?
A. Purushottam Das Tandon
B. P.M. Thevar
C. Mannathu Padmanabham
D. None of these

54. Who among the following is better known as Lokpriya?
A. Jamnalal Bajaj
B. Gopinath Bardoloi
C. B.G. Kher
D. Mazharul Haque

55. Who is known as Pahari Gandhi?
A. Baba Kanshi Ram
B. G.B. Pant
C. Hira Lal Shastri
D. None of these

56. Gadadhar Bannerjee was original name of-
A. Maharshi Dayanand
B. Ramkrishna Paramhans
C. Vivekananda
D. Rabindranath Tagore

ANSWERS

1	2	3	4	5	6	7	8	9	10
D	D	A	D	A	A	A	D	B	B
11	12	13	14	15	16	17	18	19	20
C	D	D	A	B	C	D	B	C	D
21	22	23	24	25	26	27	28	29	30
A	C	C	D	D	C	B	B	A	B
31	32	33	34	35	36	37	38	39	40
D	D	B	D	A	B	A	C	B	A
41	42	43	44	45	46	47	48	49	50
B	C	B	B	B	C	D	D	B	A
51	52	53	54	55	56				
B	C	A	B	A	B				

HONOURS AND AWARDS

1. Which of the following prizes is given by the UNESCO for popularisation of Science?
A. Visvesvarayya Award
B. UNESCO Peace Prize
C. Shanti Swaroop Bhatnagar Award
D. Kalinga Prize

2. Dr. C.V. Raman was awarded Nobel Prize in:
A. Chemistry
B. Physics
C. Literature
D. Medicine

3. Famous 'Oscar Awards' are presented by the:
A. American Motion Pictures Association
B. Academy of Motion Pictures Arts and Sciences
C. World Film Society
D. American Film Society

4. The famous Moorti Devi Award is given for excellence in which of the following fields?
A. Literature
B. Medicine
C. Science
D. Social Service

5. Pulitzer Prize is associated with:
A. Environment
B. Journalism
C. Sport
D. Cinema

6. The prestigious Ramon Magsaysay Award was instituted in the memory of Mr. Ramon Magsaysay who was:
A. The Secretary General of UN.
B. The President of the Philippines
C. The Commander of NATO in Europe
D. The President of Cambodia

7. Professor Amartya Sen has been honoured with the:
A. UNESCO Peace Prize
B. Nobel Prize in Economics
C. Bharat Ratna
D. Both B and C

8. Dhanvantari Awards are given for the best performance in the field of:
A. Space Research
B. Nuclear Sciences
C. Economics
D. Medical Science

9. Nobel Prizes are *not* given for which of the following fields?
A. Physics
B. Chemistry
C. Peace
D. Music

10. With which of the following field is B.D. Goenka award related?
A. Acting
B. Public Relations
C. Journalism
D. Cinema

11. Abel Prize is associated with:
A. Film
B. Mathematics
C. Music
D. Creative Writing

12. Jawahar Lal Nehru International Award for peace was instituted in—
A. 1970
B. 1968
C. 1965
D. 1971

ANSWERS

1	2	3	4	5	6	7	8	9	10
D	B	B	A	B	B	D	D	D	C
11	**12**								
B	C								

MISCELLANEOUS–DAYS, COMMISSIONS (WOMEN, CHILDREN ETC.)

1. Which of the following is observed as AIDS Day?
A. 1st December
B. 11th December
C. 21st December
D. 31st December

2. Which of the following is observed as "International Disabled Day"?
A. 2nd December
B. 12th December
C. 22nd December
D. None of these

3. When is the "International Women's Day" observed?
A. March 8
B. February 14
C. May 10
D. October 2

4. Pick out the wrong combination :
A. Flag Day : December 7
B. Children's Day : November 14
C. Martyrs' Day : January 30
D. Teachers' Day : December 10

5. 'National Science Day' is observed every year on:
A. February 28
B. April 5
C. November 19
D. October 2

6. Which of the following places is known as the Mecca of temple architecture?
A. Ajanta B. Khajuraho
C. Konark D. Gaya

7. On which of the following days the World Human Rights Day is celebrated?
A. December 3
B. December 10
C. December 17
D. December 25

8. Match List-I with List-II and select the correct answer using the codes given below the Lists:

List-I
(*a*) World T.B. Day
(*b*) World AIDS Day
(*c*) Anti Leprosy Day
(*d*) International Ozone Day

List-II
1. December 1
2. January 30
3. September 16
4. March 26

Codes :

	(*a*)	(*b*)	(*c*)	(*d*)
A.	4	1	2	3
B.	3	4	1	2
C.	2	3	4	1
D.	1	2	3	4

9. In Hindi literature who among the following is considered to be the harbinger of Chhaya-Vada or the new modernistic mystic note?
A. Makhan Lal Chaturvedi
B. S.H. Vatsyayan
C. Suryakanta Tripathi Nirala
D. All of the above

10. Which of the following days is observed as World Food Day?
A. September 23
B. September 15
C. October 23
D. October 16

11. Which of the following is not a Computer language?
A. Windows 98
B. PASCAL
C. C++
D. FORTRAN

12. When you call frequently "May-Day"?
A. Day of Happiness
B. Sign of Danger
C. New Year
D. First May

13. OTIS is brand name of:
A. Software
B. Shoes
C. Lift and elevators
D. Chemical and Pents

14. Dove is a symbol of :
A. MourningB. Peace
C. War D. Joy

15. Who is the Supreme Commander of the Armed Forces?

A. President
B. Prime Minister
C. General
D. Field Marshal

16. There is a traditional flower arrangement called Athapoo. In which festival is this used?
A. Onam
B. Rath Yatra
C. Teej
D. Pongal

17. Which day is celebrated as the International Labour Day?
A. 1st January
B. 21st July
B. 31st December
D. 1st May

18. The World Health Day is observed on:
A. 24th October
B. 5th September
C. 4th November
D. 7th April

19. "The World Environment Day" is observed on which of the following days?
A. June 11 B. June 30
C. June 17 D. June 5

20. Which of the following is not a site for **in situ** method of conservation of flora?
A. Biosphere Reserve
B. Botanical Garden
C. National Park
D. Wildlife Sanctuary

21. In which year Ladakh became a Union Territory?
A. 2019
B. 2018
C. 2017
D. 2016

22. SAS in computer is—
A. start along system
B. stand away system
C. stand alone system
D. None of these

23. The National project on organic farming was implemented during—
A. 10th plan B. 9th plan
C. 8th plan D. 11th plan

24. Green House Gases are
A. SO_2, NO_2, CO_2
B. N_2O, CH_4, SO_2
C. CO_2, CH_4, CFC, NO_2
D. CFC, NO_2, H_2S

25. Which one is not a fossil fuel—
A. Coal
B. Petrol
C. Uranium
D. Natural Gas

26. The smoke of tobacco contains—
A. CO_2, hydrocarbon and tar
B. CO_2 and tar
C. CO, polycyclic aromatic hydrocarbon and tar
D. CO_2, CO and tar

27. Which one is wrongly matched?
A. Veddas — Nepal
B. Papuans — New Guinea
C. Kikuyu — Kenya
D. Pygmies — Zaire

28. Name the largest railway junction in the world
A. New York
B. Boston
C. Chicago
D. Philadelphia

29. Which among the following is/are example of volcanic mountains?
1. Kilimanjaro
2. Fujiyama
3. Etna
4. Mesta
A. 1 and 2 only
B. 2 and 4 only
C. 2 and 3 only
D. 1, 2 and 3

30. Which US president launched the New Deal in 1933 to revive the US economy?
A. Herbert Hoover
B. Franklin D Roosevelt
C. John Nance Garner
D. James McReynolds

ANSWERS

1	2	3	4	5	6	7	8	9	10
A	D	A	D	A	C	B	A	C	D
11	**12**	**13**	**14**	**15**	**16**	**17**	**18**	**19**	**20**
A	D	C	B	A	A	D	D	D	B
21	**22**	**23**	**24**	**25**	**26**	**27**	**28**	**29**	**30**
A	C	A	C	C	C	A	C	D	B

ENGLISH

CHAPTER-1

Nouns & Pronouns

NOUN

A word which denotes a place, a thing, an animal or a person is said to be a noun.

1. Note the plurals of the following nouns:

Singular	*Plural*	*Singular*	*Plural*
copy	copies	cry	cries
baby	babies	duty	duties
body	bodies	country	countries
family	families	diary	diaries
fly	flies	fairy	fairies
city	cities	spy	spies
army	armies	storey	storeys
bay	bays	monkey	monkeys

2. The following nouns do not undergo any change in plural form, in general.

Singular	*Plural*	*Singular*	*Plural*
deer	deer	sheep	sheep
thousand	thousand	pair	pair
hundred	hundred	score	score
dozen	dozen	gross	gross

Note: We can write—

(*a*) thousands of men; (*b*) two pairs of shoes; (*c*) dozens of mangoes; (*d*) scores of people. etc. But—

(*a*) two thousand rupees; (*b*) three hundred men; (*c*) five dozen eggs, etc.

3. The following nouns are usually used in plural forms. They take a plural verb after them—

eatables	fetters	surroundings
riches	alms	spectacles
trousers	pants	scissors
premises	thanks	annals
congratulations	goods	shorts
tongs	pains	arms
breeches	(for troubles)	

4. The following are the nouns which are plural in appearance but are usually used in singular number. They are followed by a singular verb—

news	politics	physics
mathematics	economics	ethics
politics	classics	gallows
statistics	athletics	innings
mechanics	swnmons	mumps

5. Collective nouns often used as plurals—

public	police	cattle
audience	clergy	folk
people	poultry	nation
elite	gentry	glitterati

6. The nouns that are usually used in singular forms—

advice	hair	rice

fuel	alphabet	machinery
offspring	issue	furniture
mischief	stationery	luggage
bedding	information	abuse

7. Material nouns are always used in singular number—

gold	copper	milk
water	silk	wool

Note: They may be used in plural with a different meaning.

copper coins (coppers), chains or fetters (irons), cans made of tin (tins).

Formation of Feminine Gender from Masculine Gender

- By adding 'ess'/ 'trix'/ 'a' / 'sne' etc. *e.g.,* lion into lioness
- Placement of a word before or after noun *e.g.,* Servant into Maid-Servant; Milkman into Milkmaid
- A masculine noun containing vowel *e.g.,* Actor Avoid vowel and add 'ess' *i.e.,* Actress
- No specific note will be applied in some nouns (while changing into feminine gender) *e.g.,* Monk into Nun, Drone into Bee, Drake into Duck, Dog into Bitch.

THE PRONOUN

A pronoun is a word which is used in place of noun.

Kinds of Pronouns

1. **Personal Pronoun:** I, we, my, mine, our, ours, you, he, she, they, him, her etc.
2. **Reflexive Pronoun:** Herself, himself, myself, yourself, themselves etc.
3. **Emphatic Pronoun:** I myself, we ourselves.
4. **Demonstrative Pronoun:** This, that, there, those etc.
5. **Indefinite Pronoun:** Somebody, nobody, many, none, someone, few etc.
6. **Interrogative Pronoun:** What, who, whose, which, whom etc.
7. **Distributive Pronoun:** Neither, each, either, every, none, both etc.
8. **Relative Pronoun:** Who, which, whom etc.

MULTIPLE CHOICE QUESTIONS

Directions (Qs. 1 to 50): *In the following questions choose the correct options to fill the blanks.*

1. The place was so dirty that ..... wished to run away from there.
A. everbody B. anybody
C. few D. some

2. ..... was there to help me.
A. somebody B. anything
C. anybody D. nobody

3. Is there .... to eat?
A. some B. something
C. any D. few

4. ..... of the students were making a great noise.
A. anyone B. somebody
C. many D. nobody

5. ..... of the students can solve this sum.
A. someone B. anybody
C. somebody D. none

6. ...... of us should try our best to make India a heaven.
A. any B. somebody
C. anybody D. all

7. ...... of us do not know the real meaning of our lives.
A. any B. something
C. several D. many

8. There are not many .... in your town.
A. gentries B. gentry
C. A and B D. any of these

9. Don't write ....
A. 3's like 8's B. 3s like 8s
C. A and B D. any of these

10. I gave him ....
A. three and a half rupees
B. three rupees and a half

C. A and B
D. any of these

11. What are the .... of this place doing?
A. people B. peoples
C. pupils D. any of these

12. Whose .... are these?
A. poultries B. poultry
C. A or B D. A and B both

13. Is it a .... college?
A. girls' B. girl's
C. A or B D. A and B both

14. It is ....
A. nice poetry B. a nice poem
C. a nice poetry D. A and B both

15. Rishav is looking for a good ....
A. job B. employment
C. either A or B D. both A and B

16. Slow and steady .... the race.
A. wins B. win
C. either A or B D. both A and B

17. The road is under ....
A. repairs B. repair
C. either A or B D. both A and D

18. I do no like the .... of cricket.
A. game B. play
C. either A or B D. both A and B

19. The earthquake caused ....
A. many damages B. much damage
C. only A D. all

20. One of my .... is mad.
A. friend B. friends
C. either A or B D. both A and B

21. Please put your .... there.
A. signature B. sign
C. any of these D. both A and B

22. No news .... good news.
A. were B. was
C. both A and B D. any of these

23. My .... black.
A. hairs are B. hair is
C. hairs shall D. hair will

24. She saw two .... on the last Sunday.
A. thiefs B. theifs
C. thieves D. theives

25. My sister is a ....
A. bacheloress B. bachelor
C. unmaried D. spinster

26. One is supposed to do ....
A. our duty B. their duty
C. one's duty D. his duty

27. Take anything .... you want.
A. that B. which
C. than D. then

28. I cannot tolerate ....
A. separated you
B. your separation
C. separation from you
D. you separated

29. He is .... faithful partner.
A. Yours B. You
C. Your D. Your's

30. Ajay is more smart than ....
A. her B. hers
C. herself D. she

31. Vivek works harder than ....
A. me B. I
C. her D. his

32. They should help ....
A. the poor people B. the poor
C. the poor persons D. the poor peoples

33. .... are mad.
A. All his sons B. His all sons
C. Sons all his D. All sons his

34. The poor fellow .... to fate.
A. resigned B. resigned himself
C. resigned itself D. either A or C

35. No body will help you but ....
A. I B. me
C. ours D. his

36. It is a good chance, You must avail .... this opportunity.
A. of B. yourself of
C. for D. from

37. The person who is elected .... my relative.
A. is B. he is
C. his D. him

38. He made ....
A. yours mention B. mention of you
C. mention for you D. mention about you

39. .... I know, he is quite faithful.
A. As far as B. So far as
C. So far this D. So far so

40. It is a duty of a person to take .... for his family.
A. pain B. pains
C. either A or B D. pained

41. She does not love .... husband.
A. his B. her
C. its D. A or C

42. Let, ... work together.
A. him and me B. he and I
C. A. and B. both D. I and me

43. Copper, Silver and Gold ....
A. each will do B. either will do
C. any one will do D. A and B both

44. Jessica and Roma are very irregular .... habits.
A. in her B. in their
C. in its D. A or C

45. One likes to enjoy .... who was a great poet.
A. The sonnets of Shakespeare
B. Shakespeare's sonnets
C. Either A or B
D. A and B

46. That is the boy .... everybody loves.
A. whom B. who
C. that D. whose

47. That is the girl .... won the first prize.
A. whom B. who
C. whose D. which

48. That is the man .... purse was lost.
A. who B. whom
C. whose D. their

49. I have got .... I wanted.
A. which B. whose
C. that D. what

50. .... man has his own will.
A. All B. Any
C. Each D. Many

ANSWERS

1	**2**	**3**	**4**	**5**	**6**	**7**	**8**	**9**	**10**
A	D	B	C	D	D	D	B	A	B
11	**12**	**13**	**14**	**15**	**16**	**17**	**18**	**19**	**20**
A	B	A	D	A	A	B	A	B	B
21	**22**	**23**	**24**	**25**	**26**	**27**	**28**	**29**	**30**
A	B	B	C	D	C	A	C	C	D
31	**32**	**33**	**34**	**35**	**36**	**37**	**38**	**39**	**40**
B	B	A	B	B	B	A	B	A	B
41	**42**	**43**	**44**	**45**	**46**	**47**	**48**	**49**	**50**
B	A	C	B	A	A	B	C	D	C

CHAPTER-2

Conjunctions

A word which joins either two or more than two words/sentences is known as conjunction.

Neither .... nor (in negative sense)
Either .... or (in affirmative sense)
Both .... and
Hardly .... when/before
No sooner .... than
Scarcely .... when/before
Though .... yet

Some illustrations based on above guidelines
Illustration:

1. Yashwant is [neither] good [nor] bad.

2. It is [both] cheap [and] good.

3. [No sooner] did Ashok see the police [than] he ran away.

'Both' and 'as well as' cannot be used together in the same sentence.
Illustration: Both Bangladesh and Bhutan are poor. (✓)
Bangladesh as well as Bhutan is poor. (✓)
Both Bangladesh as well as Bhutan are poor. (×)

Never use 'that' before who, whose, whom, where, when, what, which and why.
Illustration:
The director asked Mr. S.R. Kumar that why he was late. (×)
The director asked Mr. S.R. Kumar why he was late (✓)

Not only .... but also (verb will be according to second subject)
Either .... or (verb will be according to second subject)

Illustration:

Not only (he) but also [his friends] (are) going to see the movie.

↓ S_1 ↓ S_2

'But' will be used in negative sense.

Illustration: She worked hard but failed in the examination.

S_1 + as well as + S_2

A sentence having above structure takes verb according to first subject (S_1).

Illustration: [He] [as well as] [his friends] [is] playing cricket.

↓ S_1 ↓ Conjunction ↓ S_2

Use of as if (see illustration)

Illustration:

Mr. Raj Prakash behaves [as if] he [were] the president of India.

(Note : 'As if' takes always 'were')

If two subjects are combined with 'together with' then verb will be according to first subject.

Illustration:

The captain [together with] his players [were] present in the field. (×)

↓ S_1 ↓ S_2 ↓ V

The captain [together with] his players [was] present in the field. (✓)

↓ S_1 ↓ S_2 ↓ V

MULTIPLE CHOICE QUESTIONS

Directions (Qs. 1 to 30): *In the following questions choose the correct options to fill the blanks.*

1. Neither he .... his friend is good.

A. or B. and
C. but D. nor

2. The officer asked the peon .... why he was late.

A. that B. if
C. but D. no word

3. Both Ajay .... Bijay are intelligent.

A. or B. nor
C. and D. no word

4. No Sooner did the thief see the public .... he ran away.

A. then B. and
C. but D. than

5. Abhinav .... his brothers was going to Mumbai.

A. but B. yet
C. no word D. together

6. He behaves .... he were the captain of the team.
A. as if B. as
C. no word D. that

7. Either Rupali .... Sonali is going to attend the meeting.
A. and B. but
C. nor D. or

8. Neither Nirmal .... Ashwinee is going to listen the speech of A.B. Vajpayee.
A. and B. but
C. nor D. or

9. Ravi .... Prakash are going to Kolkata.
A. or B. nor
C. but D. and

10. Rice .... curry is my usual breakfast.
A. and B. but
C. then D. than

11. Hardly had he left .... his brother came.
A. then B. than
C. when D. that

12. I would rather have a copy .... a book.
A. then B. than
C. when D. that

13. He is no other .... my friend.
A. then B. than
C. when D. but

14. He saw a snake ....he awoke.
A. then B. when
C. than D. no word

15. Ten years have passed .... my grandmother died.
A. since B. when
C. then D. than

16. She is .... good .... bad.
A. either, not B. neither, or
C. neither, nor D. neither, than

17. The cellphone is both cheap .... best.
A. than B. and
C. then D. or

18. No sooner did the thief see the police .... he ran away.
A. then B. than
C. so D. because

19. Srishti will go .... Sanju goes.
A. if B. than
C. then D. although

20. She is wise .... timid.
A. and B. yet
C. but D. however

21. Make hay .... the sun shines.
A. though B. while
C. after D. before

22. He is so weak .... he cannot walk.
A. but B. that
C. then D. so

23. Although he is rich, ... he is unhappy.
A. but B. yet
C. so D. still

24. Wait here ...... I come back.
A. till B. until
C. before D. after

25. He is my friend .... I shall help him.
A. so B. hence
C. that is why D. therefore

26. He must go away .... he will be beaten.
A. otherwise B. and
C. or D. else

27. God loves good men .... good men love God.
A. and B. or
C. that D. those

28. He was late .... he was not punished.
A. but B. yet
C. still D. therefore

29. Walk slowly ...., you may fall.
A. and B. or
C. so D. otherwise.

30. Work hard, ... you will fail.
A. and B. or
C. otherwise D. else

ANSWERS

1	2	3	4	5	6	7	8	9	10
D	D	C	D	D	A	D	C	D	A
11	**12**	**13**	**14**	**15**	**16**	**17**	**18**	**19**	**20**
C	B	B	B	A	C	B	B	A	C
21	**22**	**23**	**24**	**25**	**26**	**27**	**28**	**29**	**30**
B	B	B	A	B	C	A	C	D	D

Chapter-3

Modals & Auxiliaries

AUXILIARY VERBS

Modals are actually helping verbs. They help the finite verbs in framing sentences:

She **was** cooking food.

I **shall** guide you.

Kinds of Auxiliary Verbs

Auxiliary verbs are of two kinds:

A. Primary Auxiliaries (Modals)

B. Modal Auxiliaries (Auxiliary Modals)

(A) Primary Modals

Primary modals work both as Helping Verbs and Finite Verbs.

Be = is, am, are, was, were, being, been

Have = has, have, had, having

Do = do, does, did, done, doing

(*a*) **Usage of be/have/do as Helping verbs:**

She **is** making a cane basket.

I **have** finished my homework.

She **does** know French.

(*b*) **Usage of be/have/do as Finite verbs:**

She **was** happy.

I **have** an expensive pen.

She **is doing** her homework.

(B) Modal Auxiliaries

Shall, should, will, would, can, could, may, might, must, ought to, used to, have to, had to, dare, daren't, need needn't, mustn't are modal Auxiliaries.

Shall

'Shall' is used in the following ways:

(*a*) **With first Person Pronouns (I/we)**

I shall lend you my book.

We shall go to school together.

(*b*) **to express a suggestion**

Shall we go out for a walk?

Shall we meet the officer tomorrow?

Sometimes 'Shall' is used with Second and Third Person Pronouns as under:

(*a*) **to express a command**

You shall not tell a lie.

You shall not disturb us.

(*b*) **to express prohibition**

You shall not smoke here.

You shall not drink here.

(*c*) **to express a legal obligation**

You shall submit your sales tax return before the end of this month.

Should

'Should' is used in the following ways:

(*a*) **As Past Tense of 'shall'**
She said that she **should** settle in America.

(*b*) **to express duty and obligation**
You should do your duty honestly.

(*c*) **to express advice**
You should reach the station before time.

(*d*) **to express guess**
It should be 9 o'clock now.

(*e*) 'Should' is used with lest to express purpose.
Walk fast lest you should miss the train.

Will

'Will' is used in the following ways:

(*a*) **With Second and Third person Pronouns:**
You will dance at the party.
He will sing a song.

(*b*) **to express (Invitation/offer)**
Will you dine with me tonight?

(*c*) **to express an order**
Will you shut your big mouth?

(*d*) **to express probability**
He will come to see me tomorrow.

Sometimes 'Will' is used with 'I'

(*a*) **Determination**
I will win the first position.

(*b*) **A threat**
I will punish you.

(*c*) **A promise**
I will lend you Rs. 500/- tomorrow.

Would

'Would' is used in the following ways:

(*a*) **As Past Tense of 'will'**
He said that they would be attending the meeting the next day.

(*b*) **to express a desire or wish**
Would that I were a king!

(*c*) **to express a polite invitation**
Would you like some biscuits?

(*d*) **The usage of would in conditional sentences**
You would get good marks if you worked hard.
You would have won the race if you had run fast.

(*e*) **to express a piece of advice**
I would not meet him if I were you.

Can

'Can' is used in the following ways:

(*a*) **to express ability**
He can speak English fluently.

(*b*) **to grant permission**
You can go now.

(*c*) **to express impossibility**
Who can defeat his fate?

(*d*) **to make a request**
Can I use your motorbike?

Could

'Could' is used in the following ways:

(*a*) **As Past Tense of 'can'**
She said that she could see the sun rising.

(*b*) **to express past ability**
I could sing and dance when I was young.

(*c*) **to express a request**
Could I use your phone?

May

'May' is used in the following ways:

(*a*) **to express a request**
May I use your bicycle?

(*b*) **to seek and allow permission**
May I come in, sir?
Yes, you may.

(*c*) **to express possibility**
It may rain tonight.

(*d*) **In optative sentences**
May you live long!

Might

'Might' is used in the following ways:

(*a*) **As past tense of 'may'**
She said that her brother might come back home.

(*b*) **to express less possibility**
It might rain tonight.

(*c*) **to give and seek permission**
Might I come in, sir?
You might go home now.

Must

'Must' is used in the following ways:

(*a*) **to express duty**
You must serve your motherland.

(*b*) **to express obligation**
We must obey our elders.

(*c*) **to express advice**
You must take an umbrella before going to office.

(*d*) **to express probability**
'Must' expresses a stronger probability than may.
It must rain tonight.

Ought to

'Ought to' is used in the following ways:

(*a*) **to express obligation**
We ought to respect our teachers.

(*b*) **to express advice**
You ought to help the poor.

Used to

'Used to' is used in the following ways:

(*a*) **to express past habits**
He used to smoke.

(*b*) **to express past existence of something**
There used to be a five star hotel in this city.

Have to

'Have to' expresses compulsion in the present tense.
You have to sign the documents.

Had to

'Had to' expresses compulsion in the past time.
She had to join the office again.

Dare

'Dare' is used as a Modal only in Interrogative sentences.
How dare you touch my bag?

Dare not (Daren't)

'Dare not (Daren't)' is used in negative sentences.
She daren't complain against me.

Need

'Need' expresses an obligation/compulsion. It is used in Interrogative Sentences.
Need I say more?

Need not (Needn't)

'Need not (Needn't)' is used in negative sentences.
You needn't come here again.

Must not (Mustn't)

'Must not (Mustn't)' is the negative form of must.
You mustn't follow us.

MULTIPLE CHOICE QUESTIONS

Directions (Qs. 1 to 30): *In the following questions choose the correct options to fill in the blanks:*

1. Work hard lest you .... fail.
A. should B. may
C. can D. must

2. .... I come in, madam?
A. Can B. May
C. Will D. Must

3. It ...... rain tonight.
A. shall B. will
C. may D. can

4. You ...... love your countrymen.
A. need to B. have to
C. had to D. ought to

5. .... you like some pastries?
A. Should B. Would
C. Could D. Will

6. ...... that I were an actor!
A. Would B. Should
C. Could D. Will

7. Had you made one more effort you ...... have won the race.
A. will B. may
C. would D. shall

8. I ...... solve any sum.

A. may B. am
C. must D. can

9. ...... I smoke here?

A. Can B. Will
C. Could D. Must

10. The passengers .... keep watch on their luggage.

A. has B. have
C. should D. had

11. You .... submit your file to the authorities within a week.

A. have B. had
C. should D. would

12. ...... I use your phone?

A. Have B. Could
C. Would D. Had

13. ..... you give me your pen?

A. May B. Can
C. Must D. Dare

14. There ...... be an hospital at this place.

A. have to B. may
C. used to D. might

15. He ...... read and write when he was young.

A. would B. could
C. should D. can

16. He said that he ..... sing a song at the party.

A. should B. would
C. can D. will

17. She asked if he ...... help her.

A. should B. can
C. must D. would

18. We .... respect our elders.

A. need to B. have to
C. ought to D. had to

19. Nothing .... be done under such circumstances.

A. can B. used to
C. must D. have to

20. She ..... not ask about it.

A. has B. have
C. had D. dare

21. You .... not bring the child here.

A. have B. had
C. need D. would

22. ..... you live long!

A. Will B. May
C. Shall D. Can

23. ..... God help you!

A. Can B. Will
C. May D. Shall

24. ..... that I were a leader!

A. Would B. Should
C. Could D. Will

25. It ...... be ten o'clock now.

A. could B. would
C. should D. will

26. He ..... have reached the station by now.

A. shall B. will
C. would D. should

27. Being a receptionist, she will .... type a letter.

A. has to B. have to
C. need to D. must

28. The birds ...... fly high in the sky.

A. may B. should
C. can D. would

29. ...... I open the main gate?

A. Should B. Would
C. Could D. Must

30. If you played well, we ...... win the match.

A. would B. should
C. must D. need

ANSWERS

1	2	3	4	5	6	7	8	9	10
A	B	C	D	B	A	C	D	A	C
11	**12**	**13**	**14**	**15**	**16**	**17**	**18**	**19**	**20**
A	B	B	C	B	B	D	C	A	D
21	**22**	**23**	**24**	**25**	**26**	**27**	**28**	**29**	**30**
C	B	C	A	C	B	B	C	A	A

CHAPTER-4

Speech

Direct Speech and Indirect Speech

The words spoken by the speaker are in Direct Speech.

The words spoken by somebody expressed by someone else with some modification are known as Indirect Speech.

(*a*) Rohit says to me, "You do not understand me."

(*b*) Rohit tells me that I do not understand him.

The sentence
(*a*) shows the words spoken by Rohit. So, it is a sentence of direct speech.

The sentence
(*b*) shows the words spoken by Rohit and they have been reported with certain modification. So, it is a sentence of Indirect Speech.

Important Rules Regarding the change of Direct Speech into Indirect Speech

A. In the sentence of direct speech the verb outside the inverted commas is known as the Reporting Verb.

B. The words inside the inverted commas are known as direct speech.

C. When the sentence is indirect speech, it won't take a sign of exclamation or a sign of interrogation.

D. The Reporting Verb can be given in Present, Past or Future Tense.

E. When the Reporting Verb is in Present or Future Tense, there will be no change in the tense of direct speech while converting it into indirect speech.

F. When the Reporting Verb is in Past Tense the tense of direct speech will be changed while converting it into Indirect Speech.

G. The following adverbs and possessives should be changed as given:

(i) This into that

(ii) These into those

(iii) Here into there

(iv) Now into then

(v) Today into that day

(vi) Last night into the previous night

(vii) Tomorrow into the next day

(viii) The next day/week into the following day/week

(ix) Hence into thence.

Change of Tense

Reporting Verb	Reporting Speech	Change of Tense
Present Tense	Any Tense	No change.
Future Tense	Any Tense	No change.
Past Tense	Present/Future Tense	Change into corresponding Past Tense.
Past Tense	Past Indefinite Tense	Change into Past Perfect Tense.
Past Tense	Past Continuous Tense	Change into Past Perfect Continuous Tense
Past Tense	Past Pefect/Perfect Continuous Tense	No change.
Past Tense	Universal Truth	No change.
Past Tense	Proverb	No change.

Transformation Based on Special Rules

1. Rule Related to Interrogative Sentence

- If the answer of an interrogative sentence is possible in yes-no manner.

Illustration.

M.S. Dhoni told Rahul Dravid, "Will you help me?"

M.S. Dhoni asked Rahul Dravid whether he would help him.

(**Note :** The answer of R.S. is possible in yes-no manner)

Rule of Transformation from Direct to Indirect speech

Step I : Change R.V. into ask.

Step II : In place of comma use 'if/whether'.

Step III : Change interrogative sentence into assertive sentence.

- If the answer of an interrogative sentence is not possible in yes-no manner.

Illustration:

Rahul Dravid told Dhoni, "What do you want?"

Rahul Dravid asked Dhoni what he wanted.

(**Note :** Only in Step II, you have to avoid comma and inverted comma and rest will be same as mentioned above).

2. Rule related to Imperative Sentence

- Imperative sentence is a sentence which shows Order/Advice/Request

Illustration:

My father said to me, "Go there".

My father ordered me to go there.

Rule of Transformation from Direct to Indirect Speech

Step I : Change R.V. as per meaning/sense of R.S. into order/request/advise.

Step II : In place of comma, use 'to'.

Step III : Rest portion will be same.

3. Rule related to Optative Sentence

- Optative sentence is a sentence which exposes the feeling of bless/curse/pray/wish.

Illustration:

Mother said to me, "May you live long!"

Mother blessed me that I might live long.

Rule of Transformation from Direct to Indirect Speech

Step I : Change R.V. as per meaning/sense of R.S. into bless/curse/pray/wish.

Step II : In place of comma, use 'that'.

Step III : Change optative sentence into assertive sentence.

4. Rule related to Exclamatory Sentence

- Exclamatory sentence is a sentence which takes note of exclamatory (!) mark in that sentence showing inner feeling.

Illustration:

She said, "Alas! I am ruined".

She exclaimed with sorrow that she was ruined.

Rule of Transformation from Direct to Indirect Speech

Step I : Change R.V. as per meaning/sense of R.S. into exclaim/exclaims/exclaimed/ will or shall exclaim + joy/sorrow/ anger/surprise/applause/contempt.

Step II : Change comma into that.

Step III : Change note of exclamation (!) into full (.)

Step IV : Change exclamatory sentence into assertive sentence.

MULTIPLE CHOICE QUESTIONS

Directions (Qs. 1 to 20): *Each sentence in this assignment is followed by four options, only one is correct. Spot the correct answer.*

1. She said to me, "Keep quite and listen to my words".
A. She requested me to keep quite and listen to her words.
B. She ordered me to keep quite and listen to her words.
C. She entreated me to keep quite and listen to her words.
D. She told me to keep quite and listen to her words.

2. My brother said to me, "What are you doing here?"
A. My brother asked me that what I was doing there.
B. My brother asked me what I was doing there.
C. My brother asked me that what was I doing there.
D. My brother asked me what I was doing here.

3. Ravi said, "My father lived in this city two years ago."
A. Ravi said that his father had lived in that city two years before.
B. Ravi said that his father had lived in that city two years ago.
C. Ravi told that his father had lived in that city ago two years.
D. Ravi asked that his father had lived in that city before two years.

4. My brother said to me, "When I was young, I used to play cricket".
A. My brother told me that when I was young, I used to play cricket.
B. My brother told me that when I was young, I used to play cricket.
C. My brother told me that when he was young, I used to play cricket.
D. My brother told me that when he was young, he used to play cricket.

5. The student said, "Sir, I am not guilty".
A. The student said with respect that he was not guilty.
B. The student pleaded that he was not guilty.
C. The student pleaded with respect that he was not guilty.
D. The student said respect-fully that he was not guilty.

6. Prabha said, "I am an early-riser".
A. She regretted that she was an early-riser.
B. She said that she is an early-riser.
C. She said that she was an early-riser.
D. She regretted that she is an early-riser.

7. The police officer said to the criminal, "Speak as I tell you".
A. The police officer directed the criminal to speak as he told him.
B. The police officer told the criminal to speak as he told him.
C. The police officer advised the criminal to speak as he told him.
D. The police officer requested the criminal to speak as he told him.

8. The preacher said to me, "May God help you!"
A. The preacher prayed that God might help me.
B. The preacher prayed that God might help him.
C. The preacher requested that God might help me.
D. The preacher requested the God might help them.

9. She said to me, "Happy Diwali!"
A. She blessed me a happy Diwali.
B. She wished me a happy Diwali.
C. She prayed a happy Diwali.
D. She said to me a very happy Diwali.

10. He said, "Shall I open the gate?"
A. He asked that he should open the gate.
B. He asked if he should open the gate.

C. He ordered that he should open the gate.
D. He requested that he should open the gate.

11. I told Ravi Singh, "Do have a cup of tea".
A. I ordered Ravi Singh to have a cup of tea.
B. I advised Ravi Singh to had a cup of tea.
C. I requested Ravi Singh to have a cup of tea.
D. I said Ravi Singh to have a cup of cold tea.

12. He told me, "Shall I go to the picture?"
A. He asked that he should go to the picture.
B. He asked if he shall go to the picture.
C. He asked if he should go to the picture.
D. He requested me to go to the picture.

13. The teacher says, "Two and two makes four".
A. The teacher says that two and two made four.
B. The teacher wishes that two and two makes four.
C. The teacher advises that two and two makes four.
D. The teacher says that two and two makes four.

14. Baby said, "I will go".
A. Baby said that she will go.
B. Baby said that she could go.
C. Baby say that she will go.
D. Baby said that she would go.

15. A said to my sister, "Please, give me more money".
A. I requested my sister to give me more money.
B. I scolded my sister to give me more money.
C. I advised my sister to gave me more money.
D. I requested my sister to give her more money.

16. He said, "Bring a chair at once".
A. He ordered to bring a chair at once.
B. He requested to bring a chair at once.
C. He told to bring a chair at once.
D. He says to bring a chair at once.

17. The teacher said, "Don't make a noise".
A. The teacher says to (me/him/her) not to make a noise.
B. The teacher asked (me/him/her) not to make a noise.
C. The teacher request not to make a noise.
D. The teacher asked (me/him/her) not to made a noise.

18. My father said, "The earth is round".
A. My father said that the earth was round.
B. My father says that the earth is round.
C. My father said that the earth is round
D. My father ordered that the earth is round.

19. We said, "What a place it is!"
A. We said that it was a very fine place.
B. We said that is a very fine place.
C. We said that the place is fine.
D. We exclaimed with joy/surprise that it was a very fine place.

20. She said, "Shall I thread the needle?"
A. She asked if she should thread the needle.
B. She asked if she shall thread the needle.
C. She ordered if she should thread the needle.
D. She says that if she would thread the needle.

ANSWERS

1	2	3	4	5	6	7	8	9	10
B	B	A	D	C	C	A	A	B	B
11	**12**	**13**	**14**	**15**	**16**	**17**	**18**	**19**	**20**
C	C	D	D	A	A	B	C	D	A

CHAPTER-5

Clauses & Sentences

THE CLAUSE AND THE SENTENCE DISTINGUISHED

1. **The Sentence** is a group of words that makes complete sense. As such it contains a subject and a predicate containing a finite verb. Sometimes, it has one or more objects. It is independent and grammatically self-contained.
2. **The Clause** is a part of the predicate and has a finite verb. It also has a subject but it is dependent on the Principal (or the main) clause.

Read the following sentences:

1. He is a good player of hockey.
2. He is very rich, but he does not show off.
3. I shall work till it is evening.
4. I do not know why he has come.
5. He is the boy who wanted to see you.

BREAK-UP

1. **Sentence No. 1** has only one part. All other sentences have two parts.
2. The two parts of **Sentence No. 2** are ....
   (*a*) He .... rich, and
   (*b*) he does not show off.
3. The two parts of **Sentence No. 3** are ....
   (*a*) I .... work, and
   (*b*) it is evening.
4. The two parts of **Sentence No. 4** are ....
   (*a*) I .... know, and
   (*b*) he has come.
5. The two parts of **Sentence No. 5** are ....
   (*a*) he .... boy, and
   (*b*) (who) .... see you.

EXPLANATION

1. (*i*) **Sentence No. 1** is a fully self-contained sentence with no dependent clause on any other part of the sentence.
   (*ii*) Hence, it is a **Simple** Sentence.
2. (*i*) In **Sentence No. 2,** there are two clauses (*a*) and (*b*).
   (*ii*) Neither of these two clauses is dependent on the other.
   (*iii*) Hence, while (*a*) is the main or Principal clause, (*b*) is the coordinate clause because it is equal grammatically to the clause (*a*).
   (*iv*) Together both these clauses (*a*) and (*b*) comprise a compound sentence.
   (*v*) Clauses (*a*) and (*b*) are joined by the coordinating conjunction "but".
   (*vi*) ''He'' is the subject for both the clause (*a*) and (b).
3. (*i*) In **Sentence No. 3,** clause (*b*) is dependent on clause (*a*).

(ii) Both these clauses are joined by the subordinating conjunction "till".

(iii) Hence (b) is a subordinate Adverb clause.

4. (i) In **Sentence No. 4,** clause (b) is dependent on clause (a).

(ii) Hence it is a subordinate Noun clause.

(iii) The two clauses are joined by the subordinating conjunction "why".

(iv) The Noun clause is object to the Verb, "know".

> **NOTE:** Some grammarians regard such clauses as Adverb clauses, but that does not seem logical.

5. (i) In **Sentence No. 5,** clause (b) is dependent on clause (a).

(ii) Whereas in sentences (2) to (4), the clauses (a) and (b) have been joined by subordinating conjunctions, in sentence (5) the word "who" has a peculiarity. It acts both

(a) as a subordinating conjunction and

(b) a relative pronoun.

(iii) The implication of grammatical position is that while ....

(a) "who" joins clause (b) with clause (a).

(b) as a relative pronoun, it also becomes the subject of the Verb "wanted".

NOTE: 1. "to see" is an infinitive and should not be confused as a Verb.

2. Sentences (3) to (5) are known as complex sentences.

(iv) The who—clause in **Sentence No. 5** is a Subordinate Adjective Clause.

LOCATION OF FINITE VERBS

A detail of finite verbs of above sentences are given below:

Sentence No.	Clause (a)	Clause (b)
1.	is	....
(Note: A **Simple Sentence** has only one finite verb).		
2.	is	does (not) show
3.	shall work	is
4.	do (not) know	has come
5.	is	wanted.

THE SENTENCE

A sentence is an arrangement of words in the proper order.

(a) Santosh is a brilliant boy. (Correct)

(b) Santosh is boy a brilliant. (Incorrect)

The sentence (b) is incorrect, as the words in it have not been arranged in the proper order.

Kinds of Sentences

Usually, the sentences are considered to be of five kinds:

1. Assertive Sentence: They are of two types:

(a) **Affirmative Sentence:** A statement that affirms a fact is called an Affirmative Sentence. *e.g.,*

(i) He walks fast.

(ii) She takes a bath daily.

(b) **Negative Sentence:** A statement that makes the negative sense is called a Negative Sentence. *e.g.,*

(i) He does not like apples.

(ii) She is not a teacher.

2. Interrogative Sentence

A sentence in which a question is asked in a direct way is called an Interrogative Sentence. *e.g.,*

(*i*) Where do you live?
(*ii*) What do you want?

Interrogative sentences are also of two types:
(*a*) Passive of yes/no questions
(*b*) Wh-questions

If the answer of a question comes in 'Yes' or 'No' it is called Passive of yes/no questions, *e.g.*,

Do you know English?

In answering Wh-questions, we do not use 'Yes' or 'No'. *e.g.*,

What is your name?

3. Imperative Sentence

Sentences which show expression of request, advice, suggestion, order etc., are called Imperative Sentences. Usually, subject is not used in these sentences but it is understood, *e.g.*,

Advice:

Work hard.

Respect your elders.

Obey your parents.

Order:

Stand up.
Sit down.
Run away.
Post this letter at once.

Suggestions/Proposals:

Let's have some tea.
Let's go to theatre.
Let's sit in the shade of the tree.

Requests:

Please help me.
Kindly give me your book.

4. Exclamatory Sentence

Such a sentence expresses the sudden outburst of a strong emotion just as joy, sorrow, surprises, etc., *e.g.*,

How happy I am!
What a wonderful bird!
Alas! he is no more.
Hurrah! We have won the match.

5. Optative Sentence

Such sentences are actually an extension of exclamatory sentences. They express boon, curse, prayer, wish, etc., *e.g.*,

May you live long!
May God bless you!

MULTIPLE CHOICE QUESTIONS

Directions (Qs. 1 to 25): *In the following questions, one out of the given four alternatives is the correct transformation of the given statement, pick that one.*

1. You must be present in the meeting.
This statement can be converted into Negative as—
A. Nobody should be absent from the meeting.
B. You must not be absent from the meeting.
C. Anybody cannot be absent from the meeting.
D. You must not walk out of the meeting.

2. It is a beautiful bird.
This statement can be converted into Exclamatory as—
A. Is it a beautiful bird?
B. How is it a beautiful bird?
C. Who says it is not a beautiful bird?
D. What a beautiful bird it is!

3. It does not matter if we lose the match.
This statement can be converted into Interrogative as—
A. What does it matter if we lose the match?
B. Does it not matter if we lose the match?
C. Who says it does not matter if we lose the match?
D. How can we lose the match?

4. How happy I am!
This statement can be converted into Assertive as—
A. Am I happy?
B. I cannot say I am happy.
C. I am very happy.
D. How is it that I am happy?

5. There is none who cannot buy a bicycle.
This statement can be converted into Affirmative as—

A. Nobody can buy a bicycle.
B. Any one can buy a bicycle.
C. Some people cannot buy a bicycle.
D. It is useless to buy a bicycle.

6. You are forbidden to pluck flowers.
This statement can be converted into negative as—
A. You should not pluck flowers.
B. You are allowed to pluck flowers.
C. You are not allowed to pluck all the flowers.
D. You should give up the habit of plucking flowers.

7. He will definitely come here.
This statement can be converted into interrogative as—
A. When will he come here?
B. With whom will he come here?
C. How will he come here?
D. Will he not come here?

8. What a comfortable life he leads!
This sentence can be converted into an assertive sentence as—
A. I do not understand why he leads a comfortable life.
B. He leads a very comfortable life.
C. How does he lead a comfortable life.
D. Nobody knows how his life has become comfortable.

9. You should not absent yourself from the class any day.
This negative sentence can be converted into an affirmative one as—
A. You should be present in the class every day.
B. You should absent yourself from the class only rarely.
C. It is improper for you to be absent from the class.
D. You can come to the class any day you like.

10. What is the cause for worry?
This interrogative sentence can be converted into an assertive sentence as—
A. There is some cause for worry.
B. There is not much cause for worry.
C. There is no cause for worry.
D. Never think of a cause for worry.

11. You should give full information.
This statement can be converted into negative as—
A. Everybody should not give full information.
B. Nobody is allowed to give full information.
C. You should not hide anything.
D. You should not give full information only.

12. You dare not speak against me in public.
This statement can be converted into Interrogative as—
A. Dare you speak against me in public?
B. Is it proper for you to speak against me in public?
C. Can anybody speak against somebody in public?
D. Speaking against anybody in public is nobody's business.

13. A sailor should not be afraid of water.
This statement can be converted into Exclamatory as—
A. Should a sailor be afraid of water?
B. A sailor and afraid of water!
C. How afraid of water a sailor is!
D. A sailor cannot be afraid of water.

14. Oh! What an interesting book that was.
This statement can be converted into assertive as—
A. What an interesting book it was!
B. It was a very interesting book.
C. A very interesting book was read by me.
D. It was not an interesting book at all.

15. What can be done now?
This interrogative sentence can be converted into an assertive one as—
A. Nothing can be done now.
B. You can do everything now.
C. They can do something now.
D. Something can be done now.

16. It is useless to give any advice to an obstinate person.
This statement can be converted into negative as—
A. It is useless to ask an obstinate peson not to seek advice.
B. It is of no use giving advice to an obstinate person.

C. An obstinate person does not like the person who gives him any advice.
D. Some people do not make any use of advice given to obstinate persons.

17. Good people do not hate others.
This statement can be converted into interrogative as—
A. Do good people never hate others?
B. Why do not good people hate others?
C. When do good people say that they hate others.
D. Do good people hate others?

18. Isolation is very horrible for a child.
This statement can be converted into exclamatory as—
A. How horrible for a child isolation is !
B. How for a child isolation is horrible !
C. How horrible is for a child isolation !
D. How isolation is horrible for a child !

19. What a lame excuse !
This statement can be converted into assertive as—
A. A lame excuse it is.
B. How lame this excuse is.
C. Why do you make a lame excuse?
D. It is a very lame excuse.

20. True friends help each other not just once or twice.
This statement can be converted into affirmative as—
A. True friends help each other several times.
B. True friends help each other even unasked.
C. True friends help each other if they can.
D. True friends are helpful to each other.

21. You should refrain from smoking in public.
This statement can be converted into negative as—
A. You should not ask anybody smoking in public.
B. You should not advise anybody to smoke in public.
C. You should not smoke in public.
D. As a public servant, it is not proper for you to smoke.

22. The brave are never afraid of dangers.
This statement can be converted into interrogative as—
A. Are the brave ever afraid of dangers?
B. Do the brave ever preach against dangers?
C. Do the brave ever tell anybody to go with them at the time of dangers?
D. How do the brave manage dangers?

23. What a piece of work man is!
This exclamation can be converted into assertive as—
A. What piece of work man is?
B. Man is like a piece of work.
C. Man is a great piece of work.
D. Man is not like a piece of art.

24. Do not forget your duty wherever you go.
This negative statement can be converted into affirmative as—
A. Always remember your duty wherever you go.
B. To forget your duty wherever you go can be harmful to you.
C. Give up the habit of forgetting your duty.
D. Duty is more important than forgetfulness.

25. Who believes in ghosts these days?
This interrogative sentence can be converted into assertive as—
A. I believe in ghosts these days.
B. Nobody believes in ghosts these days.
C. You should not believe in ghosts these days.
D. There is no use believing in ghosts these days.

ANSWERS

1	**2**	**3**	**4**	**5**	**6**	**7**	**8**	**9**	**10**
B	D	A	C	B	A	D	B	A	C
11	**12**	**13**	**14**	**15**	**16**	**17**	**18**	**19**	**20**
C	A	B	B	A	B	D	A	D	A
21	**22**	**23**	**24**	**25**					
C	A	C	A	B					

CHAPTER-6

Tenses & Verbs

1. Tense indicates a point in time or period of time in the past, present, or future tense.
2. The verb may consist of a single word, or a main verb and one or more auxiliary words.
   A. The verb can indicate a state of being (What the subject is) or location.
   Bhaskar is intelligent.
   Mahesh is at work.
   B. A verb can indicate what the subject is like or becomes.
   That child **seems** frightened.
   C. A verb can indicate an action. (What the subject is doing).
   The students **will finish** in time.

The key point is that tense is related to the form of verb. There are normally three forms of the verb, say, V_1, V_2, V_3 and for convenience a fourth form V_4 as verb+ing may be assumed.

Forms of Verb

V_1	V_2	V_3	V_4
Write Read Go ...	Wrote Read Went ...	Written Read Gone ...	Writing Reading Going ...

A Comparative Chart Regarding Tenses and Verbs

Simple Present	**Simple Past**	**Simple Future**
V_1	V_2	shall/will + V_1
Present Continuous	**Past Continuous**	**Future Continuous**
is/am/are + V_4	was/were + V_4	shall/will + be + V_4
Present Perfect	**Past Perfect**	**Future Perfect**
has/have + V_3	had + V_3	shall/will + have + V_3
Present Perfect Cont.	**Past Perfect Cont.**	**Future Perfect Cont.**
has/have + been + V_4	had + been + V_4	shall/will + have been + V_4

SIMPLE PRESENT:

A. A present state of affairs.	A. My sister lives in Nagpur.
B. A general fact.	B. The sun rises in the east.
C. Habitual actions.	C. I listen to the radio in the mornings.
D. Future time-tables.	D. My flight leaves at 10:00.

PRESENT CONTINUOUS:

A. A specific action that is occurring.	A. Arvind is watching TV (right now).
B. A general activity that takes.	B. These days, I'm taking it easy.
C. Future arrangements.	C. I'm inviting Hari to the party on Friday.

SIMPLE PAST:

A. An action that began and ended at a particular time in the past.	A. The mail came early this Morning.
B. An action that occurred over a period of time but was completed in the past.	B. Dad worked in advertising in the past.
C. An activity that took place regularly in the past.	C. We jogged every morning before class.

PAST CONTINUOUS:

A. Interrupted Actions.	A. I was sewing when the telephone rang.
B. A continuous state over a period of time but was completed in the past.	B. She was looking very ill. I was meeting lots of people at that time.
C. Events planned in the past.	C. Neetu was leaving for Kolkata but had to make a last minute change
D. Expressing a future intent.	D. Jyoti is going to bring her sister tonight.
E. Predicting an event.	E. You are going to pass the test. Don't worry.

- **SIMPLE FUTURE:**

(Will):

A. Making a future decision.	A. I will call you after lunch.
B. Predicting a future event.	B. You will pass the test. Don't worry.
C. Indicating willingness to do something.	C. If I don't feel better soon, I will go to to the doctor.

FUTURE CONTINUOUS:

A. An action that will be going at a particular time in the future.	A. At noon tomorrow, I will be taking the children to their piano lessons.
B. Future actions which have already been decided.	B. I will be wearing my black dress to the dinner.

PRESENT PERFECT:

A. An action that happened at an unspecified time.	A. She has never climbed a mountain. I'm sorry. I have forgotten your Name.
B. An action that has recently occurred.	B. He's just gone to sleep.
C. An action that began in the past and continues up to the present (often used with "for" or "since").	C. Jack has lived in Chennai all his life. I have been here since Monday. He has known her for two weeks.
D. An action that happened repeatedly before now.	D. We have flown across the Pacific four times. I've failed my driver's test twice.

PRESENT PERFECT CONTINUOUS:

A. An action that began in the past and has just recently ended.
B. An action that began in the past and continues in the present.
C. An action repeated over a period of time in the past and continuing in present.

A. Have you been ringing the Bell?
B. Lokesh has been studying for two hours.
C. Suresh has been smoking since he was fifteen.

PAST PERFECT:

A. An action that occurred before another past action.
B. An action that was expected to occur in the past.

A. Tarun had left hours before we got there.
B. I had hoped to know about the job before now.

PAST PERFECT CONTINUOUS:

A. An action that occurred before another past action.
B. An action that was expected to occur in the past.

A. His eyes hurt because he had been Reading for eight hours.
B. I had been expecting a change in his attitude.

FUTURE PERFECT:

A. An action that will be completed before a particular time in the future.

A. By next July, my parents will have been married for fifty years.

FUTURE PERFECT CONTINUOUS:

A. Emphasizing the length of time that has occurred before a specific time in the future.

A. By May, my father will have been working at the same job for thirty years.

MULTIPLE CHOICE QUESTIONS

Directions (Qs. 1 to 45): *Find the correct word(s) that correctly completes the sentence.*

1. A woman came in with a baby who, she said, ... a safety pin.
A. was just swallowing
B. swallowed
C. had just swallowed
D. just swallowed

2. The telephone ..... several times before I answered it.
A. was ringing B. has rung
C. had rung D. would ring

3. An employment advertisement should ..... the number of vacancies.
A. provide B. specify
C. contain D. declare

4. A crescendo of metallic thuds arose from the market, where the iron-smiths were ..... the pieces of metals.
A. flattening B. striking
C. hammering D. thrashing

5. Ambition is one of those ..... which are never satisfied.
A. ideas B. fancies
C. passions D. needs

6. The new education policy provides a useful ..... for the planners to remove illiteracy.
A. breakup B. breakthrough
C. breakaway D. break-in

7. The family gave father a gold watch on the ..... of his fiftieth birthday.

A. time B. event
C. occasion D. celebration

8. The passengers were afraid but the captain ..... them that there was no danger.
A. promised B. assured
C. advised D. counselled

9. It's very kind of you to ..... to speak at the meeting.
A. accept B. agree
C. comply D. concur

10. I haven't seen you ..... a week.
A. within B. since
C. for D. from

11. Besides other provisions, that shopkeeper deals ..... cosmetics too.
A. with B. in
C. at D. for

12. That rule is applicable ..... everyone.
A. to B. for
C. about D. with

13. I shall take revenge ..... you.
A. from B. with
C. on D. at

14. The ruling party will have to put its own house ..... order.
A. in B. on
C. to D. into

15. ..... all intents and purposes, the manager is the master of the firm.
A. in B. upon
C. with D. to

16. Like any other country India has its ..... share of superstitions.
A. proper B. abundant
C. fair D. peculiar

17. The miser gazed ..... at the pile of gold coins in front of him.
A. avidly B. admiringly
C. thoughtfully D. earnestly

18. The pilot had been warned about the storm before he .....
A. took away B. took up
C. took over D. took off

19. On account of the dearth of grass on the arid plains the cattie became .....
A. flippant B. jubilant
C. agitated D. emaciated

20. I saw a ..... of cows in the field.
A. group B. herd
C. swarm D. flock

21. He was sent to the prison for his .....
A. sin B. vice
C. crime D. guilt

22. ..... of old paintings is a job for the experts.
A. Resurrection B. Retrieval
C. Restoration D. Resumption

23. Once he has signed the agreement, he won't be able to .....
A. back up B. back in
C. back at D. back out

24. She ..... a brief appearance at the end of the party.
A. put on B. put in
C. put across D. put up

25. The battalion operating from the mountain was able to ..... three enemy divisions.
A. tie up B. tie down
C. tie on D. tie with

26. Do you know ..... ?
A. where she comes from
B. where does she come from
C. where from she comes
D. from where does she come

27. ..... works of reference are so valuable as the Encyclopaedia Britannica.
A. A few B. Few
C. The few D. Fewe

28. The paths of glory lead ..... to the grave.
A. straight B. but
C. in D. directly

29. Walking at three o'clock, I heard the ..... of thunder.
A. crackle B. rumble
C. ripple D. clank

30. The thief ..... all the money.
A. made up B. made off with
C. made do with D. made good

31. Pakistan lost a ..... wicket just when they seemed to be doing so well, and that led to their eventual defeat.
A. critical B. crucial
C. sensitive D. providential

32. In high school many of us never realised the importance that grammar would ..... in later life.
A. figure B. portray
C. play D. exercise

33. I was astounded at his ..... lack of knowledge about the Continent of Africa.
A. abundant B. colossal
C. huge D. great

34. The ..... of the Minister's statement cannot be verified by people who have no access to official records.
A. veracity B. verbosity
C. ambiguity D. validity

35. You haven't had your lunch yet, ... you?
A. are B. aren't
C. have D. haven't

36. Life is to death as pleasure is to ......
A. poverty B. suffering
C. anguish D. pain

37. The French ..... reputed to have a very good sense of humour.
A. is B. was
C. are D. will be

38. 'Please' and 'Thank you' are the little courtesies by which we keep the ..... of life oiled and running smoothly.
A. path B. machine
C. garden D. river

39. Catching the earlier train will give us the ..... to do some shopping.
A. chance B. luck
C. possibility D. occasion

40. ..... a failure of some traffic lights, traffic is moving very slowly
A. Owing B. Due to
C. Because D. Since

41. We had ..... wonderful time at the party last night.
A. such a B. so
C. such D. very

42. Leave a two-inch ..... on each page for the teacher's remarks.
A. border B. margin
C. blank D. gap

43. I don't really know how to ..... the problem.
A. tackle B. cope
C. draw D. erase

44. What is the ..... for an airletter?
A. fare B. value
C. postage D. stamp

45. The manner in which bombs exploded in five trains within a short span of time suggests that it is a part of a .....
A. game B. conspiracy
C. villainy D. sabotage

ANSWERS

1	**2**	**3**	**4**	**5**	**6**	**7**	**8**	**9**	**10**
C	C	B	C	C	B	C	B	B	C
11	**12**	**13**	**14**	**15**	**16**	**17**	**18**	**19**	**20**
B	A	C	A	D	C	A	D	D	B
21	**22**	**23**	**24**	**25**	**26**	**27**	**28**	**29**	**30**
C	C	D	B	B	A	B	B	B	B
31	**32**	**33**	**34**	**35**	**36**	**37**	**38**	**39**	**40**
B	C	B	A	C	D	C	B	A	B
41	**42**	**43**	**44**	**45**					
A	B	A	C	B					

CHAPTER-7

Infinitives & Gerunds

Read the following sentences:

1. She has decided to resign.
2. I see a thief running.
3. She insists on my sitting beside her.

In the above sentences, the underlined words are non-finites because they are not changed with the change of the subject, *e.g.,*

They have decided to resign.

She sees a thief running.

You insist on my sitting beside you.

Non-finites are of three kinds:

1. The Infinitives (to + v_1)
2. The Participles (v_1 + ing)
3. The Gerund (v_1 + ing)

1. THE INFINITIVE

To plus first form of the verb is called an Infinitive. It is often used as a Noun.

Uses of the Infinitive

(*a*) Subject of a sentence.
To laugh loudly is good for health.
To steal is bad.

(*b*) After a transitive verb.
He loves **to eat** sweets.
She likes **to play** tennis.

(*c*) After a preposition.
They are about **to leave.**

(*d*) As a complement after the verb 'be'.
Her ambition is **to be** a teacher.
His immediate aim is **to help** her.

(*e*) As an object.
He made me **weep.**
I saw him **go.**

(*f*) After an adjective.
Honey is sweet **to taste.**
He was ashamed **to talk** to his criminal friend.

(*g*) After a noun. (often in passive)
Here is a book **to be** read carefully.

Bare Infinitive

Some Infinitives are used without 'to' and are called Bare Infinitives.

You had better **go** home.

I saw him **go.**

I heard him **sing.**

He would rather **rest** than **play.**

I can **solve** this sum.

I watched him **steal** your purse.

I watched him **open** the safe.

Let him **come** in.

You had sooner **read** your book than **play.**

NOTE: Bare Infinitives are usually used after 'causal' (or 'causative') verbs and 'modals'.

2. THE PARTICIPLE

Participles serve the purpose of Adjectives.

I heard him **singing.**

I saw him **going.**

Kinds of Participles

Participles are of the following kinds:

I. Present Participle

I watched the boy **stealing** your purse.

I saw him **climbing** the hill.

She smelt something **burning.**

Don't let me catch you **smoking.**

II. Past Participle

I got the house **painted** last week.

I had my hair **cut.**

The rose has **faded.**

He had **written** five letters.

I want the office **built** in a month.

III. Perfect Participle

Having finished cooking, she started reading a novel.

Having dusted the room, the maid began to wash the dishes.

Having written a letter to her mother, she walked out of the room.

Joining of Sentences by using Participles

(I) By using Present Participles

1. Look at the boy. He is climbing the tree.
   Look at the boy climbing the tree.
2. He was dusting the room. He found a coin.
   While dusting the room, he found a coin.
3. The child opened the box. He found a toy.
   Opening the box, the child found a toy.

3. THE GERUND

A. (verb + ing) is usually used as a Gerund. Like a Noun, it is used as under.

(*a*) As a subject of the verb.

Killing birds is not good.

Smoking is injurious to health.

(*b*) As an object of the verb.

I like **singing.**

She loves **dancing.**

(*c*) As a complement of the verb 'be'.

What I hate the most is **drinking.**

What I love the most is **playing.**

(*d*) As an object of a preposition.

I am fond of **eating.**

She was punished for **telling** a lie.

B. In some cases, instead of Gerunds Infinitives can be used.

Subject + Verb	Gerund or Infinitive
I love	singing or to sing.
He hates	smoking or to smoke.
I like	dancing or to dance.
He prefers	reading novels/to read novels.
Your bike needs	oiling or to be oiled.

C. It + be + Adjective + Gerund (Phrase).

Subject + be	Adjective/Noun	Gerund (Phrase)
It is	wrong	making so much noise.
It is	good	drinking juice in the evening.
It is	nice	walking in the moon light.

D. Subject + be + Adjective or Past Participle + Preposition + Gerund.

Subject + be	Adjective/ Past Participle	Preposition	Gerund (Phrase)
He is	fond	of	swimming.
She was	annoyed	at	his talking so loudly.
He is	capable	of	solving all the sums.

MULTIPLE CHOICE QUESTIONS

Directions (Qs. 1 to 45): *In the following questions choose the correct options to replace the words given in brackets.*

1. He came (run) to his aunt.
A. run B. running
C. to run D. in run

2. She dislikes (eat) meat.
A. eat to B. to eat
C. eating D. to eating

3. He likes (sing).
A. sing to B. singing
C. to sing D. to singing

4. We are ready (play) the match.
A. play to B. to playing
C. playing D. to play

5. (Smoke) is injurious to health.
A. Smoking B. To smoke
C. To smoking D. Smoke to

6. He loves (eat) raw vegetables.
A. eaten B. eating
C. to eating D. eat to

7. He seemed (have) finished his homework.
A. have to B. to have
C. having D. to having

8. It is not easy (achieve) this target.
A. achieve to B. achieving to
C. to achieve D. to achieving

9. It is always difficult (climb) a mountain.
A. climb to B. to climb
C. climbing to D. to climbing

10. She avoided (argue) with him.
A. argue to B. arguing
C. to arguing D. argues

11. I saw him (go).
A. to go B. to going
C. going D. gone

12. I heard him (sing).
A. to sing B. singing
C. to singing D. sung

13. She smelt something (burn).
A. burning B. to burn
C. to burning D. burn to

14. He claimed (be) the best player of hockey.
A. being to B. to be
C. been D. has been

15. We eat (live).
A. living B. to living
C. to live D. lively

16. He wanted (go) across the world.
A. go to B. to going
C. to go D. going to

17. I cannot bear (kill) birds.
A. killing B. to killing
C. to kill D. kill to

18. He wished (be) there inside the hotel.
A. being to B. to be
C. been D. been to

19. It is time (drink) some juice.
A. drinking B. to drinking
C. drink to D. to drink

20. He is too busy (take) care of his kids.
A. taking to B. to take
C. to taking D. take to

21. I forbore myself (slap) him on the face.
A. to slap B. slap to
C. slapping D. slapping to

22. She tried (open) the safe.
A. open to B. opening
C. to open D. to opening

23. It is no use (cry) over spilt milk.
A. cry to B. in crying
C. crying D. crying to

24. They enjoyed (fly) kites.
A. to fly B. fly to
C. flying D. flying to

25. It is your responsibility (keep) the accounts of every happening here.
A. keep to B. keeping to
C. to keep D. keeping

26. Please give me a pair of scissors (cut) cloth.
A. cut to B. cutting to
C. cutting D. to cut

27. She prefers (play) chess to sitting idly.
A. to playing B. playing
C. play to D. playing to

28. I prefer (talk) to the officer alone.
A. talk to B. talking to
C. to talk D. to talking

29. Would you mind your (bring) some cake for me?
A. to bring B. bring to
C. bringing to D. bringing

30. (Err) is human.
A. Err to B. Erring to
C. To erring D. To err

31. (Steal) is not good.
A. Stealing B. To steel
C. To stealing D. Stealing to

32. She heard the lion (roar).
A. to roar B. roaring
C. roar to D. to roaring

33. He is reported (be) dead.
A. be to B. to be
C. to being D. to been

34. You are ordered (bring) the file number 100.
A. bringing B. to bringing
C. bring to D. to bring

35. You are advised (take) part in sports.
A. taking to B. to taking
C. to take D. take to

36. He was sent to America (find out) the reality.
A. to find out B. finding out
C. find out to D. to finding out

37. We have decided (hold) a function on 26th of this month.
A. holding B. holding to
C. hold to D. to hold

38. He is fond of (read).
A. reading B. to reading
C. to read D. read to

39. Would you like (eat) some apples?
A. eat to B. eating to
C. to eat D. to eating

40. He was approached late at night (be) warned of the situation.
A. been B. to being
C. be to D. to be

41. He appeared (have) cast his vote in favour of us.
A. having B. to having
C. to have D. have to

42. His ambition is (become) a doctor.
A. becoming B. to becoming
C. to become D. become to

43. We are asked (be) there in the main hall.
A. being B. been
C. to be D. be to

44. Our immediate aim is (provide) financial help to the needy.
A. provide to B. providing to
C. to providing D. to provide

45. We read and write (become) civilized.
A. becoming B. becoming to
C. to become D. become to

ANSWERS

1	2	3	4	5	6	7	8	9	10
B	C	B	D	A	B	B	C	B	B
11	**12**	**13**	**14**	**15**	**16**	**17**	**18**	**19**	**20**
C	B	A	B	C	C	A	B	D	B
21	**22**	**23**	**24**	**25**	**26**	**27**	**28**	**29**	**30**
C	C	C	C	C	D	B	C	D	D
31	**32**	**33**	**34**	**35**	**36**	**37**	**38**	**39**	**40**
A	B	B	D	C	A	D	A	C	D
41	**42**	**43**	**44**	**45**					
C	C	C	D	C					

CHAPTER-8

Other Sentence Patterns

REMOVING 'TOO'

By replacing 'too' with 'so that'

1. He is too weak to walk.
   He is so weak that he cannot walk.
2. The book was too tough to comprehend.
   The book was so tough that it could not be comprehended.

> **NOTE:** Sentence No. 1 is in the Present Tense so in it 'cannot' has been used; Sentence No. 2 is in the Past Tense, so, in it 'could not' has been used.

INTERCHANGE OF DEGREE OF COMPARISON

Degree of Comparison of Adjectives

Read the following sentences:

1. She is as clever as a fox. (Positive)
   A fox is not cleverer than her. (Comparative)

> **NOTE:** In Positive Degree as is used but in Comparative Degree a Negative sentence is used. If the negative has been used with the Positive Degree, it will be removed from the comparative degree.

2. He is not so weak as his brother. (Positive)
   He is stronger than his brother. (Comparative)
3. Shimla is the coldest tourist spot in India. (Superlative)
   Shimla is colder than any other tourist spot in India. (Comparative)
   No other tourist spot is as cold as Shimla. (Positive)
4. Rohit is one of the most intelligent boys in our class. (Superlative)
   Rohit is more intelligent than most other boys in our class. (Comparative)
   Very few boys in our class are so intelligent as Rohit. (Positive)

5. Gold is not the most expensive metal. (Superlative)
A few metals are more expensive than gold. (Comparative)
Some metals are at least as expensive as gold. (Positive)
6. Lead is the heaviest of all metals. (Superlative)
Lead is heavier than any other metal. (Comparative)
No other metal is so heavy as lead. (Positive)

INTERCHANGE OF ACTIVE AND PASSIVE

A Transitive verb is usually written in Active voice or Passive voice.
He reads a book. (Active voice)
A book is read by him. (Passive voice)

CHANGING IMPERATIVE SENTENCES INTO ASSERTIVE

Read the following sentences:
1. Walk fast. (Imperative)
You are ordered to walk fast. (Affirmative)
2. Let us take a cup of tea. (Imperative)
It is proposed that we should take a cup of tea. (Affirmative)
3. Please bring me a glass of water. (Imperative)
You are requested to bring me a glass of water. (Affirmative)
4. Work hard. (Imperative)
You are advised to work hard. (Affirmative)
5. Don't smoke. (Negative imperative)
You are forbidden to smoke. (Assertive)

INTERCHANGE OF AFFIRMATIVE AND NEGATIVE SENTENCES

Read the following sentences:
1. He runs slow. (Affirmative)
He does not run fast. (Negative)
2. He loves himself the most. (Affirmative)
He does not love anybody more than himself. (Negative)
3. Mr Sharma is a busy man. (Affirmative)
Mr Sharma is not an idle man. (Negative)
4. She is as brilliant as you. (Affirmative)
You are not more brilliant than her. (Negative)
5. He spoke angrily. (Affirmative)
He did not speak calmly. (Negative)

INTERCHANGE OF INTERROGATIVE AND ASSERTIVE SENTENCES

Read the following sentences:
1. Why to speak ill of anybody? (Interrogative)
We should not speak ill of anybody. (Assertive)
2. Who can win his fate? (Interrogative)
No one can win his fate. (Assertive)
3. Where will you find such beautiful shoes? (Interrogative)
You will not find such beautiful shoes anywhere. (Assertive)

4. How can he die without paying my debt? (Interrogative)
He cannot die without paying my debt. (Assertive)
5. When will he learn manners? (Interrogative)
He will never learn manners. (Assertive)
6. What can be done now? (Interrogative)
Nothing can be done now. (Assertive)

INTERCHANGE OF EXCLAMATORY AND ASSERTIVE SENTENCES

Read the following sentences:

1. What a beautiful flower it is! (Exclamatory)
It is a very beautiful flower. (Assertive)
2. How beautiful the Taj is! (Exclamatory)
I am surprised that the Taj is very beautiful. (Assertive)
3. O for a one-rupee coin! (Exclamatory)
A one-rupee coin is urgently desired. (Assertive)
4. Would that I were rich! (Exclamatory)
I wish that I were rich. (Assertive)
5. O that I were rich! (Exclamatory)
I wish that I were rich! (Assertive)

INTERCHANGE OF PARTS OF SPEECH

Read the following sentences:

1. This way you will **minimize** the risk. (Verb)
This way you will bring the risk to the minimum level. (Adjective)
2. She fought **courageously**. (Adverb)
She showed a great **courage** in the fight. (Noun)
3. She does not speak the **truth**. (Noun)
She is not **truthful**. (Adjective)
4. He fought **bravely**. (Adverb)
He fought with **bravery**. (Noun)
5. He **ran** fast. (Verb)
He ran a fast **race**. (Noun)
6. He showed **generosity** towards his opponent. (Noun)
He was **generous** towards his opponent. (Adjective)

CHANGING OF SIMPLE SENTENCES INTO COMPOUND ONES

Read the following sentences:

1. Besides being abused he was charged with misbehaving with others. (Simple)
He was not only abused but also charged with misbehaving with others. (Compound)
2. You must run fast to catch the bus. (Simple)
Run fast or you may miss the bus. (Compound)
3. Having finished her kitchen work, Mrs Sharma sat against the T.V. set. (Simple)
Mrs Sharma finished her kitchen work and sat against the T.V. set. (Compound)

4. In spite of bitter cold, they managed to climb the hill. (Simple)
   It was bitter cold, yet they managed to climb the hill. (Compound)
5. In spite of being strong, he dare not oppose his opponents. (Simple)
   He is strong but still he dare not oppose his opponents. (Compound)

CHANGING OF SIMPLE SENTENCES INTO COMPLEX ONES

Read the following sentences:

1. In spite of being on crutches, he managed to catch the thief. (Simple)
   Though the was on crutches, he caught the thief. (Complex)
2. She is too weak in mathematics to solve even a simple sum. (Simple)
   She is so weak in mathematics that she cannot solve even a simple sum. (Complex)
3. The girl in all black is my classmate. (Simple)
   The girl, who is in all black, is my classmate. (Complex)
4. Because of/Owing to his negligence he lost his credibility. (Simple)
   He lost his credibility because he was negligent. (Complex)
5. He was happy at having been able to make an impressive speech. (Simple)
   He was happy that he was able to make an impressive speech. (Complex)
6. Put the ring at the place of your finding. (Simple)
   Put the ring where you found it. (Complex)

CHANGING OF COMPOUND SENTENCES INTO COMPLEX SENTENCES

Read the following sentences:

1. He is intelligent, but he is unkind. (Compound)
   Although he is intelligent, he is unkind. (Complex)
2. Buy a ticket or you cannot go inside the hall. (Compound)
   You cannot go inside the hall unless you buy a ticket. (Complex)
3. He could not attend the meeting, for he was ill. (Compound)
   He could not attend the meeting because he was ill. (Complex)
4. Work hard or you won't be able to earn a lot. (Compound)
   If you don't work hard, you cannot earn a lot. (Complex)
5. It was fog all around, yet he managed to cross the uneven stretch of land. (Compound)
   Although it was fog all around, he managed to cross the uneven stretch of land. (Complex)

ACTIVE VOICE – PASSIVE VOICE

Sentences containing a transitive verb can usually be written in Active as well as Passive voice. When the subject acts upon the object the sentence is written in Active voice. When the subject is acted upon, the sentence is written in Passive voice.

1. Do you read a book? (Active)
   Is a book read by you? (Passive)
2. He flies an aeroplane. (Active)
   An aeroplane is flown by him. (Passive)
3. She is unfolding the bed sheet. (Active)
   The bed sheet is being unfolded by her. (Passive)

4. Are the boys singing songs? (Active)
Are songs being sung by the boys? (Passive)
5. Mohit has forwarded your request. (Active)
Your request has been forwarded by Mohit. (Passive)
6. Have you ever seen the Taj? (Active)
Has the Taj ever been seen by you? (Passive)
7. He freed all the slaves. (Active)
All the slaves were freed by him. (Passive)
8. Did the dog bite the stranger? (Active)
Was the stranger bitten by the dog? (Passive)
9. Ajeet was helping his relatives. (Active)
His relatives were being helped by Ajeet. (Passive)
10. Was Karan grazing the horses? (Active)
Were the horses being grazed by Karan? (Passive)
11. She had gained great flesh. (Active)
Great flesh had been gained by her. (Passive)
12. Had you gripped the knob on the door? (Active)
Had the knob on the door been gripped by you? (Passive)
13. I'll hit him hard. (Active)
He will be hit hard by me. (Passive)
14. Will you imitate your brother? (Active)
Will your brother be imitated by you? (Passive)
15. You will have opened the envelope? (Active)
The envelope will have been opened by you. (Passive)
16. Will she have printed her name on the title page? (Active)
Will her name have been printed on the title page by her? (Passive)

USE OF TIME-CLAUSES

As soon as
No sooner did .... than
Hardly had .... when
Scarcely had .... when or before

These sentences are used to express two actions taking place immediately one after the other.

As soon as the cat saw the dog, it started to run.
No sooner did the cat see the dog than it started to run.
Hardly had the cat seen the dog when it started to run.
Scarcely had the cat seen the dog when it started to run.

MULTIPLE CHOICE QUESTIONS

Directions (Qs. 1 to 20): *In the following questions, one out of the given four alternatives is the correct transformation of the given statement, pick that one.*

1. You must be present in the meeting.
This statement can be converted into Negative as—
A. Nobody should be absent from the

meeting.

B. You must not be absent from the meeting.

C. Anybody cannot be absent from the meeting.

D. You must not walk out of the meeting.

2. It is a beautiful bird.

This statement can be converted into Exclamatory as—

A. Is it a beautiful bird?

B. How is it a beautiful bird?

C. Who says it is not a beautiful bird?

D. What a beautiful bird it is!

3. It does not matter if we lose the match.

This statement can be converted into Interrogative as—

A. What does it matter if we lose the match?

B. Does it not matter if we lose the match?

C. Who says it does not matter if we lose the match?

D. How can we lose the match?

4. How happy I am!

This statement can be converted into Assertive as—

A. Am I happy?

B. I cannot say I am happy.

C. I am very happy.

D. How is it that I am happy?

5. There is none who cannot buy a bicycle.

This statement can be converted into Affirmative as—

A. Nobody can buy a bicycle.

B. Any one can buy a bicycle.

C. Some people cannot buy a bicycle.

D. It is useless to buy a bicycle.

6. You are forbidden to pluck flowers.

This statement can be converted into negative as—

A. You should not pluck flowers.

B. You are allowed to pluck flowers.

C. You are not allowed to pluck all the flowers.

D. You should give up the habit of plucking flowers.

7. He will definitely come here.

This statement can be converted into interrogative as—

A. When will he come here?

B. With whom will he come here?

C. How will he come here?

D. Will he not come here?

8. What a comfortable life he leads!

This sentence can be converted into an assertive sentence as—

A. I do not understand why he leads a comfortable life.

B. He leads a very comfortable life.

C. How does he lead a comfortable life.

D. Nobody knows how his life has become comfortable.

9. You should not absent yourself from the class any day.

This negative sentence can be converted into an affirmative one as—

A. You should be present in the class every day.

B. You should absent yourself from the class only rarely.

C. It is improper for you to be absent from the class.

D. You can come to the class any day you like.

10. What is the cause for worry?

This interrogative sentence can be converted into an assertive sentence as—

A. There is some cause for worry.

B. There is not much cause for worry.

C. There is no cause for worry.

D. Never think of a cause for worry.

11. You should give full information.

This statement can be converted into negative as—

A. Everybody should not give full information.

B. Nobody is allowed to give full information.

C. You should not hide anything.

D. You should not give full information only.

12. You dare not speak against me in public. This statement can be converted into Interrogative as—

A. Dare you speak against me in public?
B. Is it proper for you to speak against me in public?
C. Can anybody speak against somebody in public?
D. Speaking against anybody in public is nobody's business.

13. A sailor should not be afraid of water. This statement can be converted into Exclamatory as—

A. Should a sailor be afraid of water?
B. A sailor and afraid of water!
C. How afraid of water a sailor is!
D. A sailor cannot be afraid of water.

14. Oh! What an interesting book that was. This statement can be converted into assertive as—

A. What an interesting book it was!
B. It was a very interesting book.
C. A very interesting book was read by me.
D. It was not an interesting book at all.

15. What can be done now? This interrogative sentence can be converted into an assertive one as—

A. Nothing can be done now.
B. You can do everything now.
C. They can do something now.
D. Something can be done now.

16. It is useless to give any advice to an obstinate person. This statement can be converted into negative as—

A. It is useless to ask an obstinate peson not to seek advice.
B. It is of no use giving advice to an obstinate person.
C. An obstinate person does not like the person who gives him any advice.
D. Some people do not make any use of advice given to obstinate persons.

17. Good people do not hate others. This statement can be converted into interrogative as—

A. Do good people never hate others?
B. Why do not good people hate others?
C. When do good people say that they hate others.
D. Do good people hate others?

18. Isolation is very horrible for a child. This statement can be converted into exclamatory as—

A. How horrible for a child isolation is !
B. How for a child isolation is horrible !
C. How horrible is for a child isolation !
D. How isolation is horrible for a child !

19. What a lame excuse ! This statement can be converted into assertive as—

A. A lame excuse it is.
B. How lame this excuse is.
C. Why do you make a lame excuse?
D. It is a very lame excuse.

20. True friends help each other not just once or twice. This statement can be converted into affirmative as—

A. True friends help each other several times.
B. True friends help each other even unasked.
C. True friends help each other if they can.
D. True friends are helpful to each other.

ANSWERS

1	2	3	4	5	6	7	8	9	10
B	D	A	C	B	A	D	B	A	C
11	**12**	**13**	**14**	**15**	**16**	**17**	**18**	**19**	**20**
C	A	B	B	A	B	D	A	D	A

CHAPTER-9

Articles & Demonstratives

Indefinite Article

'A'/ 'an' is called indefinite articles.

A. 'A' is used before a consonant sound and 'an' is used before a vowel sound.

B. The letter 'u' can have a consonant or vowel sound:
a university but an umbrella

C. The letter 'h' is sometimes not pronounced:
a horse but an hour

Uses of 'a' or 'an'

A. Before singular countable nouns when the noun is mentioned for the first Time.
I see a horse.

B. When the singular form is used to make a general statement about all people or things of that type.
A concert pianist spends many hours practicing. (All concert pianists spend many hours practicing)

C. In expressions of price, speed, and ratio.
60 miles, an hour, four times a day.

'A' or 'an' is not used

D. before plural nouns.
Flowers were growing along the river bank.

E. before non-countable nouns.
I wanted advice.

Definite Article 'The'

'The' is used:

A. before a noun that has already been mentioned:
I saw a man. The man was wearing a hat.
It is also used when it is clear in the situation in which a thing or person is referred to:
The books on the shelf are first editions.
I went to the bank. (a particular bank)

B. before singular noun that refers to a species or group.
The tiger lives in Asia. (Tigers, as a species, live in Asia)

C. before adjectives used as nouns.
The children collected money to donate to the institution for the deaf. ('the deaf' = deaf people)

D. when there is only one of something.
The sun shone down on the earth.
This is the best horse in the race.

E. before a body part in a prepositional phrase that belongs to the object in the sentence:
Someone hit me on the head. ("Me" is the object, and it is my head that was hit.) or a body part in a prepositional phrase that belongs to the subject of a passive sentence.
I was hit on the head. ("I" is the subject of the passive sentence, and it is my head that was hit.)

Note:

A possessive pronoun, rather than the article "the" is usually used with the body parts.

I hit my head. ("I" is neither the object of this sentence nor the subject of a passive sentence. Therefore a passive pronoun is used.)

Some proper names take "the" and some don't.

F. "The" is usually used with canals, deserts, forests, oceans, rivers, seas and plural islands, lakes and mountains.
the Suez Canal the Black Forest
the Hawaiian Islands the Atlantic Ocean

G. "The" is used when the name of a country or state includes the word "of", the type of government, or a plural form.
the Republic of Ireland
the United Kingdom
the Philippines

H. Otherwise, "The" is not used with:
the names of countries and states:
Japan Brazil Germany
the names of continents:
Africa Asia Europe
the names of cities:
Chicago Mexico City Hong Kong

Special Cases

A. the expression "a number of" means "several" or "many" and takes a plural verb. The expression "the number of" refers to the group and takes a singular verb.

A large number of tourists get lost because of that sign.

The number of lost tourists has increased recently.

B. the following nouns do not always take an article:

Prison	school	college
Church	bed	home
Court	jail	sea

Look at how the meaning changes:

Example: bed

No article: Jack went to bed. (=Jack walked to sleep. "Bed" refers to the general idea of sleep)

With "the", Jack went to the bed. (Jack walked over to a particular bed. The bed is referred to as a specific object.)

With "a": Jack bought a bed. (Jack purchased an object called a bed.)

C. Articles are not used with possessives Pronouns ("my", "your", etc.) or demonstratives ("this", "that", "these" and "those").

Where is my coat?

That watch was broken.

D. Non-countable nouns are used without an article to refer to something in general. Sometimes an article is used to show a specific meaning.

People all over the world want peace. (peace in general)

The peace was broken by a group of passing children. ("The peace" refers to peace at a specific time and place.)

The imparting of knowledge was the job of the elders in the community. (knowledge in general)

I have a knowledge of computers. (a specific type of knowledge.)

Demonstratives, that, these and those

A. the demonstrative adjectives and pronouns are for objects nearby the speaker:
this (singular) those (plural)
and for objects far away from the speaker.
That (singular) those (plural)

B. Demonstratives are the only adjectives that agree in number with their nouns.

That hat is nice.

Those hats are nice.

C. When there is the idea of selection, the pronoun "one"(or "ones") often follows the demonstrative.

I want a book. I 'll get this (one).

If the demonstrative is followed by an adjective, "one"(or "ones") must be used.

I want a book. I 'll get this big one.

MULTIPLE CHOICE QUESTIONS

Directions (Qs. 1 to 40): *In the following questions choose the correct options to fill the blanks.*

1. .... will have to be paid for this material.
A. Half rupee B. Half a rupee
C. A half rupee D. An half rupee

2. .... is taking keen interest in India.
A. The USA B. USA
C. An USA D. A USA

3. Only .... can save our country.
A. the Hitler B. a Hitler
C. Hitler D. an Hitler

4. I can run for ....
A. hundred miles B. the hundred miles
C. a hundred miles D. an hundred miles.

5. .... man-eater has been killed.
A. The B. A
C. An D. Either A or B

6. What .... fine idea!
A. the B. an
C. a D. no article

7. .... earth is moving around the sun.
A. An B. A
C. The D. No article

8. This is .... first example while I got.
A. the B. a
C. an D. no article

9. This is .... house which was built during earthquake.
A. a B. an
C. the D. no article

10. .... America is a rich country.
A. The B. An
C. A D. no article

11. .... U.S.A. is a developed country.
A. A B. An
C. The D. No article

12. .... Bible is a holy book.
A. A B. The
C. An D. No article

13. .... rich should help the poor.
A. The B. A
C. An D. No article

14. .... Gold is a costly metal.
A. The B. A
C. An D. No article

15. Kalidas is .... Shakespeare of India.
A. a B. an
C. the D. no article

16. I can not do .... difficult work.
A. a such B. the such
C. such the D. such a

17. How foolish .... plan it is!
A. a B. an
C. the D. no word required

18. An ink is .... useful article.
A. an B. a
C. the D. no word required

19. There are .... husband and wife.
A. a B. an
C. the D. no word required

20. He is learning .... French
A. the B. a
C. an D. no word required

21. I am going to by .... umbrella.
A. an B. a
C. the D. no word required

22. Dr. A.L. Sinha was .... University Professor.
A. the B. a
C. an D. no article

23. She is .... honest leader.
A. the B. an
C. a D. no article

24. .... lion is the king of a forest.
A. A B. No article
C. An D. The

25. The rose is .... Sweetest of all flowers.
A. an B. a
C. the D. no article

26. She caught him by .... arm.
A. the B. an
C. a D. no article

27. I know .... each boy.
A. an B. a
C. the D. no article

28. I love .... every bird.
A. a B. an
C. the D. no article

29. Mr. Rao is .... union leader.
A. a B. the
C. an D. no article

30. I am .... honest person.
A. the B. an
C. a D. no article

31. .... shirts are mine.
A. These B. That
C. This D. It

32. .... glasses belong to Mr. Jack.
A. This B. That
C. Those D. It

33. .... birds have colourful wings.
A. That B. These
C. This D. It

34. I want a car. I'll get ....one.
A. these B. this
C. those D. it

35. I need a camera. I'll get .... now.
A. it B. these
C. this D. those

36. I saw .... European in the market.
A. a B. an
C. the D. No article

37. Not .... single student was present.
A. an B. a
C. the D. No article

38. .... only person who can give some hope to a dying man is his doctor.
A. A B. An
C. The D. No article

39. Samudragupta is known as .... Napoleon of India.
A. a B. an
C. the D. No article

40. I shall board .... Flying Mail.
A. a B. an
C. the D. No article

ANSWERS

1	2	3	4	5	6	7	8	9	10
B	A	B	C	D	C	C	A	C	D
11	12	13	14	15	16	17	18	19	20
C	B	A	D	C	D	A	B	D	D
21	22	23	24	25	26	27	28	29	30
C	A	B	D	C	A	D	D	A	B
31	32	33	34	35	36	37	38	39	40
A	C	B	B	A	A	B	C	C	C

CHAPTER-10

Prepositions

A Preposition is a word which comes before a Pronoun or a Noun and expresses the relationship between Noun or Pronoun and some part of the remaining sentence.

(*a*) He is busy *with* his work.

(*b*) The boy jumped *into* the river.

(*c*) The birds are chirping *in* the trees.

In these sentences the words *with, into* and *in* show the relationship between the verbs *busy, jumped* and *chirping* with the nouns *work, river* and *trees* respectively.

Position of the Preposition

A. A Preposition usually precedes its object.

(*i*) He laughs *at* the poor.

(*ii*) He is angry *with* you.

(*iii*) She agrees *with* me.

B. In the case of Relative Pronouns.

(*i*) This is the boy whom I was looking *for*.

(*ii*) That is the pen whose mention I was making *of*.

C. In the following cases, the Preposition comes after its object.

(*i*) Where is the boy you were complaining *against*?

(*ii*) What things are there you are looking *for*?

(*iii*) Who is there, you are waiting *for*?

Omission of the Preposition

In many cases when the sentences contain Nouns of Time or Place, the Prepositions from, in and for are often omitted.

(*i*) He walked many kilometres.

(*ii*) He came to see me last year.

(*iii*) As I could not find my puppy anywhere, I looked here and there.

Prepositions are small words that show the relationship between one word and another. Prepositions in the following sentences show the position of the paper in relation to the desk, the book, his hand and the door.

The paper is "on" the desk.

The paper is "under" the book.

The paper is " in" his hand.

The paper is "by" the door.

Common Prepositions

about	at	by
in	onto	toward
above	before	concerning
inside	out	under
across	behind	despite
into	over	until
after	below	down
like	since	up
against	beneath	during
near	through	upon
along	beside	except
of	throughout	with
amid	between	for
off	till	within
among	beyond	from
on	to	without

MULTIPLE CHOICE QUESTIONS

Directions (Qs. 1 to 50): *Tick the correct Preposition for the blank in each of the following sentences.*

1. He applied ...... the manager.
A. for B. to
C. with D. by

2. Trust ...... God and do the right.
A. in B. for
C. to D. with

3. She is worthy ...... a prize.
A. with B. for
C. to D. of

4. Mr. Gomes has no taste ...... music.
A. of B. for
C. with D. to

5. You are hard ...... hearing.
A. at B. of
C. with D. for

6. He is sure ...... his success
A. for B. with
C. on D. of

7. Preeti was warned ...... the danger ahead.
A. for B. at
C. of D. None of these

8. I am thankful ...... you for a good advice.
A. for B. with
C. to D. None of these

9. Deepak would not surrender ...... the police.
A. with B. to
C. for D. on

10. The small plant in your lawn is very sensitive ...... touch.
A. on B. with
C. to D. None of these

11. Divya was sure to succeed ..... the examination.
A. for B. in
C. to D. with

12. Geeta was jealous ...... Ravina's beauty.
A. to B. with
C. for D. None of these

13. He was ignorant ..... what was happening there.
A. for B. of
C. to D. with

14. Your pen is inferior ...... mine.
A. than B. with
C. from D. to

15. Reenu is no match ...... Kanu.
A. to B. for
C. with D. upon

16. It is necessary ...... you to apply for this job.
A. on B. with
C. for D. None of these

17. Be loyal ...... your country.
A. for B. to
C. on D. with

18. Mukesh is junior ...... me.
A. than B. to
C. from D. of

19. Deepika was innocent ...... the crime.
A. of B. with
C. from D. to

20. I am desirous.... joining the Indian cricket team.
A. for B. of
C. to D. on

21. Pradeep is not eligible ...... the post.
A. to B. on
C. upon D. for

22. Does she believe ...... God?
A. to B. for
C. in D. None of these

23. Mr. Posh was charged..... the murder of his aunt.
A. for B. with
C. on D. to

24. Tagore is famous (or popular) ...... Indians.
A. for B. with
C. to D. towards

25. Kalidasa is famous ...... his drama the *Shakuntalam*.
A. for B. with
C. on D. about

26. He applied ...... the post of a teacher.
A. to B. on
C. for D. None of these

27. I differ ...... you in this matter.
A. from B. with
C. for D. above

28. My pen differs ...... yours.
A. with B. from
C. for D. upon

29. The air escaped out ...... the balloon.
A. from B. of
C. to D. under

30. I am confident ...... success.
A. of B. to
C. from D. about

31. He was deprived ...... his share and property.
A. of B. with
C. from D. about

32. He complains ...... headache.
A. about B. to
C. of D. None of these

33. My father deals ...... sugar.
A. with B. to
C. in D. None of these

34. His services were dispensed ......
A. for B. to
C. with D. None of these

35. Mohinder was born ...... a noble famly.
A. with B. about
C. towards D. in

36. He was born ...... poor parents.
A. of B. to
C. in D. on

37. A son was born ...... him.
A. to B. for
C. in D. upon

38. I was aware ...... the matter.
A. to B. of
C. in D. upon

39. He was absorbed ...... study.
A. in B. into
C. of D. under

40. The boy jumped ...... the river.
A. in B. under
C. below D. into

41. I agree ...... you.
A. upon B. to
C. with D. None of these

42. Wolves abound ...... this forest.
A. for B. in
C. with D. to

43. She did not agree ...... your proposal.
A. with B. in
C. to D. None of these

44. I was angry ...... his misconduct.
A. with B. to
C. at D. None of these

45. He is bent ...... mischief.
A. on B. of
C. to D. for

46. I complained ...... the police inspector.
A. towards B. to
C. on D. with

47. I complained ...... the policeman to the inspector.
A. to B. for
C. against D. None of these

48. Beware ...... pick-pockets.
A. about B. to
C. from D. of

49. This salesman deals ...... his customers in a polite manner.
A. in B. to
C. with D. None of these

50. This sample of liquid does not comply ...... the original.
A. to B. with
C. about D. towards

ANSWERS

1	2	3	4	5	6	7	8	9	10
B	A	D	B	B	D	D	D	B	D
11	**12**	**13**	**14**	**15**	**16**	**17**	**18**	**19**	**20**
B	D	B	D	B	D	B	B	A	B
21	**22**	**23**	**24**	**25**	**26**	**27**	**28**	**29**	**30**
D	D	B	B	A	D	B	B	A	A
31	**32**	**33**	**34**	**35**	**36**	**37**	**38**	**39**	**40**
A	D	D	D	D	A	A	B	A	D
41	**42**	**43**	**44**	**45**	**46**	**47**	**48**	**49**	**50**
D	B	D	D	A	B	D	D	D	B

CHAPTER-11

Adjectives & Adverbs

Some words tell more about another word they are called *modifiers*. There are two main kinds of modifiers: *adjectives* and *adverbs*.

Adjectives

An *adjective* modifies—tells more about—a noun or pronoun. It tells *what kind, how many,* or *which one*.

Example: *beautiful* music, *blue* sky, *large* room.

Adjectives are usually found right before a noun, right after a noun, or after a linking verb.

Note: Some adjectives, such as articles, numbers, and possessive adjectives, usually come before the noun.

Examples:

(i) **before a noun:**

This *good-looking, economical* car is your best bet.

(ii) **after a noun:**

This car, *good-looking* and *economical,* is your best bet.

Adverb

An *adverb* modifies—tells more about—a verb, adjective, or another adverb. It tells *how, when, where,* or *to what extent.*

Comparison and Adjectives

Adjectives and adverbs have three forms that show a greater or lesser degree of the characteristic of the basic word: the positive, the comparative, and the superlatives. The basic word is called the positive. The comparative is used to refer to two persons, things or groups. The superlative is used to refer to more than two persons, things or groups; it indicates the greatest or least degree of the quality named. Most adjectives of one syllable become comparative by adding "-er" to the ending and become superlative by adding "-est" to the ending. In adjectives ending with "Y", the "Y" changes to "i" before adding the endings.

Use the comparative to compare two things:

1. Mary is the more lazy of the two.
2. I've tasted creamier cheese than this.
3. James is the shorter of the two boys.
4. Of the two, I like Gail better.
5. My teacher is kinder than yours.
6. This book is more interesting than that one.

Use the superlative to compare more than two things:

1. Mary is the laziest girl I know.
2. This is the creamiest cheese I've ever tasted.

3. James is the shortest boy in the class.
4. Of those five people, I liked Gail best.
5. My teacher is the kindest in the school.
6. This book is the most interesting of the three.

There are some words to which comparison does not apply, since they already indicate the highest degree of a quality.

Here are some examples:

Immediately	**Superlative**	**First**
Last	very	unique
Uniquely	universally	perfect
Perfectly	exact	complete
Correct	dead	deadly
Preferable	round	perpendicularly
Square	third	supreme
Totally	infinitely	immortal

Errors to Avoid in Comparison

Do not combine two superlatives:

Incorrect: That was the most bravest thing he ever did.

Correct: That was the bravest thing he ever did.

Incorrect: He grew up to be the most handsomest boy in the town.

Correct: He grew up to be the most handsome boy in the town.

Do not combine two comparatives:

Incorrect: Mary was more friendlier than Susan.

Correct: Mary was friendlier than Susan.

Incorrect: The puppy was more timider last week.

Correct: The puppy was more timid last week.

MULTIPLE CHOICE QUESTIONS

Directions (Qs. 1 to 25): *In the following questions choose the correct option to fill the blank.*

1. The girl whom you met is the .... sister of Ravi Tanti.

A. eldest B. elder
C. older D. oldest

2. The historical place is ....

A. seeing worth
B. worthy of seeing
C. worth seeing
D. either A or B

3. These flowers smell ....

A. sweet
B. sweetly
C. more sweetly
D. either B or C

4. .... aspirant can not pass the UPSC examination.

A. Each B. Every
C. All D. No.

5. Harivansh Rai .... second Shakespeare.

A. is a
B. is
C. the
D. either B or C

6. .... student in the class got prizes.

A. Each and every
B. Every and each
C. Every
D. Never

7. It is .... picture than the one we saw last Monday.

A. interesting
B. much interesting
C. more interesting
D. either A or B

8. She is clever ....

A. that her mother is
B. as her mother is
C. so her mother is
D. none

9. They will get ....

A. Red, green and black paper
B. Red, green black paper
C. Red and green and black paper
D. Either B or C

10. Health is .... wealth.
A. preferable to
B. more preferable than
C. more preferable to
D. most preferable then

11. .... water that was in the jug evaporated.
A. Little B. The little
C. Small D. A small

12. He has not sung .... songs.
A. much B. most
C. more D. many

13. Srishti has searched .... office.
A. whole the B. the whole
C. a whole D. some whole

14. K.R. Dhiraj was .... best and .... famous writer.
A. a, the most B. the, a most
C. the, more D. the, the most

15. Willam Shakespeare is famous as ....
A. a poet and a dramatist
B. a poet and dramatist
C. the poet and the dramatist
D. either A or C

16. What does .... leader suggest?
A. other B. another
C. others D. anothers

17. He .... money
A. has, few B. have, few
C. has, little D. have, little

18. The .... boys are rewarded.
A. first two B. two first
C. firsts two D. two's first

19. He is .... brave.
A. stronger than
B. stronger then
C. more strong then
D. more strong than

20. No sooner said ....
A. so done B. and done
C. then done D. but done

21. She returned .... than I had thought.
A. quickly B. more quicker
C. more quickly D. quicker

22. I am .... foolish person.
A. rather the B. a rather
C. rather a D. rather

23. This pen .... rupees.
A. costs twenty
B. twenty costs only
C. costs only twenty
D. only costs twenty

24. It is .... pride.
A. nothing else but
B. nothing else than
C. else nothing than
D. but

25. This tea is .... to drink.
A. too hot B. very hot
C. enough hot D. much hot

ANSWERS

1	**2**	**3**	**4**	**5**	**6**	**7**	**8**	**9**	**10**
A	C	A	B	A	C	C	C	A	A
11	**12**	**13**	**14**	**15**	**16**	**17**	**18**	**19**	**20**
B	D	B	D	B	B	C	A	D	C
21	**22**	**23**	**24**	**25**					
C	C	C	A	A					

हिन्दी भाषा

1

समानार्थक शब्द

निर्देश (प्र.सं. 1 से 30 तक): *निम्नलिखित चार में से तीन समानार्थी शब्द हैं, जिस अक्षरांक में इनसे भिन्न शब्द दिया गया है, उसका चयन कीजिए।*

1. A. विघ्न B. बाधा C. अड़चन D. सुविधा

2. A. नासूर B. असुर C. दनुज D. दानव

3. A. यश B. कीर्ति C. निष्ठा D. गौरव

4. A. वृथा B. बेकार C. बेमतलब D. सार्थक

5. A. याचना B. जन्नत C. प्रार्थना D. विनती

6. A. चुस्त B. स्फूर्त C. सजग D. सतत

7. A. ध्वंस B. नाश C. क्षय D. निर्माण

8. A. परित्राण B. छुटकारा C. बंधन D. स्वातंत्र्य

9. A. घृणा B. प्रीति C. नफरत D. विरक्ति

10. A. आगाह B. निगाह C. नजर D. देखना

11. A. नजात B. मुक्ति C. परित्राण D. नकेल

12. A. निर्मोही B. निर्मम C. निर्दय D. सदय

13. A. दानव B. मनुज C. निशाचर D. असुर

14. A. नीरज B. राजीव C. कुंज D. नलिन

15. A. घन B. नभ C. अंबर D. आकाश

16. A. बल B. शक्ति C. विद्युत् D. उदग्र

17. A. समुच्चय B. मियाद C. चरम D. अति

18. A. अननुकूल B. उल्टा C. विरुद्ध D. व्यतिक्रम

19. A. तर B. रनिवास C. जनानखाना D. भागपुर

20. A. अल्पतम B. लघुतम C. विरलतम D. हीनतम

21. A. अंधकार B. तिमिर C. निशाकर D. अंधेरा

22. A. चर B. अस्थिर C. सजीव D. अचल

23. A. जटिल B. कठिन C. पेचीदा D. सुबोध

24. A. छली B. मासूम C. निर्दोष D. निष्पाप

25. A. अपमान B. इज्जत C. अनादर D. अवमान

26. A. खलित B. खिन्न
C. अनमना D. विमनस्क

27. A. कठिन B. दुर्जन
C. मुश्किल D. दुस्साध्य

28. A. खग B. विहग
C. पखेरू D. पाख

29. A. गीला B. आर्द्र
C. सिल D. तर

30. A. घनश्याम B. गिरिधर
C. मुरलीधर D. रसिक

31. 'आदर' का समानार्थी निम्नलिखित में से कौन-सा नहीं है?
A. सम्मान B. प्रतिष्ठा
C. इज्जत D. अवमान

32. 'विवाह' का समानार्थी निम्नलिखित में से कौन-सा नहीं है?
A. पाणिग्रहण B. परिणति
C. परिणय D. ब्याह

33. 'उचित' का समानार्थी निम्नलिखित में से कौन-सा नहीं है?
A. ठीक B. योग्य
C. कृत्य D. दुरुस्त

34. 'उदास' का समानार्थी निम्नलिखित में से कौन-सा नहीं है?
A. अनुरक्त B. दुःखी
C. विरक्त D. निरपेक्ष

35. 'परिचित' का समानार्थी है–
A. अजनबी B. अज्ञात
C. अभिज्ञ D. अनजान

36. 'विस्मय' का समानार्थी शब्द कौन-सा है?
A. गर्व B. विस्मरण
C. विस्तीर्ण D. अचंभा

37. 'चकित' का समानार्थी शब्द कौन-सा नहीं है?
A. हैरान B. उदासीन
C. विस्मित D. भौंचक्का

38. 'चहक' का समानार्थी शब्द कौन-सा नहीं है?
A. महक B. उमंग
C. कलरव D. खुशी

39. निम्न में से कौन 'आचरण' का समानार्थी है?
A. आचार
B. चाल-चलन
C. व्यवहार
D. A, B और C सभी समानार्थी हैं

40. 'विस्तार' का समानार्थी निम्नलिखित में से कौन-सा नहीं है?
A. फैलाव B. विशालता
C. लम्बाई-चौड़ाई D. निस्तार

उत्तरमाला

1	2	3	4	5	6	7	8	9	10
D	A	C	D	B	D	D	C	B	D
11	**12**	**13**	**14**	**15**	**16**	**17**	**18**	**19**	**20**
D	D	B	C	A	D	A	D	A	D
21	**22**	**23**	**24**	**25**	**26**	**27**	**28**	**29**	**30**
C	D	D	A	B	A	B	D	C	D
31	**32**	**33**	**34**	**35**	**36**	**37**	**38**	**39**	**40**
D	B	C	A	C	D	B	A	D	D

2

समास

निर्देश (प्र.सं. 1 से 5 तक): नीचे दिए गए शब्दों में प्रयुक्त समास के नाम का चयन कीजिए–

1. पीताम्बर–
A. तत्पुरुष B. अव्ययीभाव
C. बहुब्रीहि D. द्विगु

2. चरणकमल–
A. तत्पुरुष B. कर्मधारय
C. बहुब्रीहि D. अव्ययीभाव

3. घुड़सवार–
A. द्विगु B. कर्मधारय
C. तत्पुरुष D. अव्ययीभाव

4. स्वर्गप्राप्त–
A. कर्म तत्पुरुष B. करण तत्पुरुष
C. सम्प्रदान तत्पुरुष D. अपादान तत्पुरुष

5. गर्वशून्य–
A. कर्म-तत्पुरुष B. संप्रदान-तत्पुरुष
C. करण-तत्पुरुष D. अपादान-तत्पुरुष

6. 'लम्बोदर' में कौन-सा समास है?
A. तत्पुरुष B. बहुब्रीहि
C. द्विगु D. कर्मधारय

7. 'देवालय' में कौन-सा समास है?
A. तत्पुरुष B. बहुब्रीहि
C. द्विगु D. इनमें से कोई नहीं

8. 'खरा खोटा' शब्द में कौन-सा समास है?
A. द्वंद्व B. द्विगु
C. कर्मधारय D. बहुब्रीहि

9. 'निर्विवाद' में कौन-सा समास है?
A. कर्मधारय B. अव्ययीभाव
C. तत्पुरुष D. बहुब्रीहि

10. 'दहीबड़ा' में कौन-सा समास है?
A. तत्पुरुष B. द्विगु
C. बहुब्रीहि D. द्वन्द्व

11. 'चौराहा' में समास है–
A. तत्पुरुष B. द्वन्द्व
C. कर्मधारय D. द्विगु

12. 'माता-पिता' शब्द में समास है–
A. द्वन्द्व B. द्विगु
C. तत्पुरुष D. कर्मधारय

13. 'वज्रपाणि' शब्द में कौन-सा समास है?
A. तत्पुरुष B. बहुब्रीहि
C. द्वन्द्व D. द्विगु

14. 'देशभक्ति' शब्द में समास होगा–
A. अपादान तत्पुरुष B. सम्बन्ध तत्पुरुष
C. अधिकरण तत्पुरुष D. सम्प्रदान तत्पुरुष

15. 'सुनीता के बच्चे घास-फूस की तरह बढ़ रहे हैं।' उपर्युक्त वाक्य में प्रयुक्त 'घास-फूस' शब्द में समास होगा–
A. कर्मधारय B. द्वन्द्व
C. द्विगु D. अव्ययीभाव

16. निम्नलिखित शब्दों में कौन-सा शब्द बहुब्रीहि समास का उदाहरण है?
A. शूलपाणि B. यथाक्रम
C. हँसमुख D. हथकड़ी

17. इनमें से कौन-सा शब्द 'द्विगु' समास है?
A. भुजदण्ड B. माखनचोर
C. पंचशील D. लज्जाशील

18. 'प्रतिदिन' शब्द में समास होगा–
A. द्विगु B. कर्मधारय
C. तत्पुरुष D. अव्ययीभाव

19. जिन समस्त पदों में पहला शब्द संख्यावाची हो और उससे समुदाय का बोध होता हो, तो उसे कहते हैं–
A. द्विगु समास B. द्वन्द्व समास
C. कर्मधारय समास D. अव्ययीभाव समास

20. जिसमें पहला शब्द विशेषण हो और दूसरा शब्द विशेष्य, तो उसे कौन-सा समास कहेंगे?
A. द्विगु B. कर्मधारय
C. द्वन्द्व D. तत्पुरुष

21. 'पंचवटी' शब्द के लिए दिए गए विकल्प में से उपयुक्त समास कौन-सा है?
A. द्विगु B. तत्पुरुष
C. बहुव्रीहि D. कर्मधारय

22. 'बुरा-भला' शब्द में कौन-सा समास है?
A. द्वन्द्व B. द्विगु
C. कर्मधारय D. तत्पुरुष

23. 'चिड़ीमार' शब्द में कौन-सा समास है?
A. द्विगु B. कर्मधारय
C. तत्पुरुष D. अव्ययीभाव

24. 'यथोचित' शब्द में समास बताइए–
A. अव्ययीभाव B. कर्मधारय
C. बहुव्रीहि D. तत्पुरुष

25. समास कहते हैं–
A. शब्दों के मेल को
B. अक्षर के मेल को
C. स्वर-से-स्वर के मेल को
D. स्वर के साथ व्यंजन के मेल को

26. 'शिवार्पण' शब्द में कौन-सा समास है?
A. अधिकरण तत्पुरुष
B. करण तत्पुरुष
C. सम्प्रदान तत्पुरुष
D. अपादान तत्पुरुष

27. निम्नलिखित में किसमें तत्पुरुष समास है?
A. पदप्राप्त B. शताब्दी
C. चौमासा D. भाई-बहन

28. 'रसगुल्ला' में कौन-सा समास है?
A. तत्पुरुष B. बहुव्रीहि
C. द्वन्द्व D. अव्ययीभाव

29. 'भुखमरा' का समास विग्रह होगा–
A. भूख से जो मर गया B. भूख से मरा हुआ
C. भूखों मर गया जो D. भूख द्वारा मरा हुआ

30. 'दशरथ सुत' में कौन-सा समास है?
A. तत्पुरुष B. बहुव्रीहि
C. द्विगु D. द्वन्द्व

31. 'अष्टाध्यायी' में कौन-सा समास है?
A. द्वन्द्व B. द्विगु
C. तत्पुरुष D. कर्मधारय

32. 'यथाशीघ्र' में कौन-सा समास है?
A. अव्ययीभाव B. द्वन्द्व
C. कर्मधारय D. तत्पुरुष

उत्तरमाला

1	2	3	4	5	6	7	8	9	10
C	B	C	A	C	B	A	A	B	A
11	**12**	**13**	**14**	**15**	**16**	**17**	**18**	**19**	**20**
D	A	B	D	B	C	C	D	A	B
21	**22**	**23**	**24**	**25**	**26**	**27**	**28**	**29**	**30**
A	A	C	A	A	C	A	A	A	A
31	**32**								
B	A								

3

वर्तनी की शुद्धता

निर्देश (प्र.सं. 1 से 49 तक): *नीचे के प्रश्नों में एक शब्द की चार अलग-अलग वर्तनियां दी हुई हैं। इनमें से सही वर्तनी छाँटकर उस पर निशान लगाइये:*

1. A. जयोत्स्ना B. ज्योत्स्ना C. जोत्स्ना D. ज्योत्सना

2. A. कवयित्री B. कवियित्री C. कवियत्री D. कवित्री

3. A. उत्ज्वल B. उज्जवल C. ऊज्जवल D. उज्ज्वल

4. A. छः B. छह C. छह् D. छै

5. A. जिजीविषा B. जिजीवषा C. जजीवषा D. जिजिवीषा

6. A. दृश्य B. द्रश्य C. दृष्य D. दृिश्य

7. A. इतिहासिक B. ऐतिहासिक C. ऐतिहासीक D. ऐतीहासिक

8. A. बाङ्मय B. वाँङ्मय C. वांग्मय D. वांगमय

9. A. सौर्हाद्र B. सैहार्द C. सैर्हाद D. सौहार्द

10. A. आर्शीवाद B. आशिर्वाद C. आशीर्वाद D. आर्शिवाद

11. A. भूगोलिक B. भूगौलिक C. भोगौलिक D. भौगोलिक

12. A. सन्कीर्णता B. सन्कीरणता C. संर्कीणता D. संकीर्णता

13. A. परचन्ड B. प्रचण्ड C. प्रचान्ड D. परचण्ड

14. A. तार्क्रिक B. तार्किक C. ताकृिक D. ताक्रिक

15. A. इर्षा B. ईर्षा C. इर्ष्या D. ईर्ष्या

16. A. पूज्यनीय B. पुजनीय C. पूजनीय D. पुज्यनीय

17. A. अधम्र B. अध्रम C. अधर्म D. अधृम

18. A. अधिकृत B. अधिक्रित C. अधिक्रित्त D. अधिर्कित

19. A. अनुकृम B. अनुक्रम C. अनुकर्म D. अनुकम्र

20. A. अनवेषण B. अन्वेषण C. अन्वेछण D. अन्वेशण

21. A. अभिशेक B. अभिषेख C. अभिषेक D. अभीषेक

22. A. इच्छुक B. इक्षुक C. इक्छुक D. इच्छिक

23. A. इन्दिय B. इन्द्रिय C. इन्दिय D. इन्द्रिय

24. A. उतकण्ठा B. उत्कण्ठा C. उत्क्णठा D. उत्त्कन्ठा

25. A. उमृिला B. उम्रिला C. उमिर्ला D. उर्मिला

26. A. रिषि B. ऋषि
C. ऋिषि D. ऋशि्

27. A. एकागृ B. एकाग्र
C. एकार्ग D. एक्राग्र

28. A. ओजश्वि B. ओजस्वी
C. ओजश्वी D. ओजष्वी

29. A. औशधी B. औषधी
C. औषधि D. औष्धि

30. A. करम B. क्राम
C. कम्र D. कर्म

31. A. ग्रिहीत B. ग्रहीत
C. गृहीत D. गर्हित

32. A. कृतज्ञ B. क्रतज्ञ
C. क्रितज्ञ D. क्रितग्य

33. A. चतुदर्श B. चर्तुदश
C. चतुर्दश D. चतुद्रश

34. A. जर्जर B. जरर्जर
C. जज्रर D. जरजर

35. A. जघ्नय B. जघ्रय
C. जघ्न्य D. जघन्य

36. A. जेष्ठ B. ज्येश्ठ
C. ज्येष्ठ D. ज्येस्ठ

37. A. तपस्वनी B. तपस्विनी
C. तपिस्वनी D. तपिस्विनी

38. A. तादातमय B. तदात्म्य
C. तादात्म्य D. तादात्यम

39. A. तृष्णा B. तिृष्णा
C. त्रिष्णा D. तृशणा

40. A. त्रिमूर्ती B. त्रिमुर्ति
C. त्रिमूर्ति D. त्रृमूर्ति

41. A. दक्छ B. दक्च्छ
C. दक्ष D. दज्ञ

42. A. द्रर्पन B. दर्पन
C. दपर्ण D. दर्पण

43. A. दामपत्य B. दम्पत्य
C. दाम्पत्य D. दाम्पत

44. A. दीप्पित B. दीपति
C. दीप्ति D. दीप्ती

45. A. दीर्घायु B. दीरघायु
C. दीघार्यु D. दीर्घिायु

46. A. दुर्निती B. दुनीर्ति
C. दुरनीति D. दुर्नीति

47. A. दुर्दषा B. दुहशा
C. दुर्दशा D. दुद्रशा

48. A. दुर्योधन B. दुयोर्धन
C. दूरयोधन D. द्रुयोधन

49. A. दुरबुद्धि B. दुर्बुधि
C. दुबुद्धि D. दुर्बुद्धि

उत्तरमाला

1	2	3	4	5	6	7	8	9	10
B	A	D	B	A	A	B	A	D	C
11	12	13	14	15	16	17	18	19	20
D	D	B	B	D	C	C	A	B	B
21	22	23	24	25	26	27	28	29	30
C	A	D	B	D	B	B	B	C	D
31	32	33	34	35	36	37	38	39	40
C	A	C	A	D	C	B	C	A	C
41	42	43	44	45	46	47	48	49	
C	D	C	C	A	D	C	A	D	

4

विलोम

निर्देश (प्र.सं. 1 से 34 तक): *सही-सही विलोम शब्द चुनिए–*

1. अनादर
A. मान B. सम्मान
C. आदर D. सत्कार

2. अभिज्ञ
A. अज्ञानी B. अनभिज्ञ
C. अनिपुण D. मूर्ख

3. अथ
A. इति B. समाप्त
C. खत्म D. संपूर्ण

4. करुण
A. कठोर B. निष्ठुर
C. निर्दय D. कोमल

5. ऋजु
A. सीधा B. सरल
C. तिर्यक् D. वक्र

6. मौन
A. मुखर B. मूक
C. वाचाल D. प्रगल्भ

7. निर्दय
A. निर्भय B. सहृय
C. सभय D. सदय

8. तिमिर
A. प्रकाश्य B. आलोक
C. ज्योतिर्मय D. आभास

9. तीक्ष्ण
A. मंद B. तीव्र
C. प्रखर D. क्षीण

10. कृत्रिम
A. प्राकृतिक B. स्वनिर्मित
C. स्वाभाविक D. स्वचालित

11. उदात्त
A. उद्धत B. दानशील
C. अनुदात्त D. क्षमावान्

12. उदार
A. कठोर B. निर्भय
C. अपव्यय D. अनुदार

13. शुक्ल
A. काला B. कृष्ण
C. असित D. श्यामल

14. प्रस्थान
A. आगमन B. गमनागमन
C. निगम D. निर्गम

15. शूल
A. मूल B. धूल
C. फूल D. तूल

16. अपेक्षा
A. कामना B. भावना
C. अभीप्सा D. उपेक्षा

17. निरक्षर
A. शिक्षित B. अशिक्षित
C. साक्षर D. अक्षर

18. प्रकट
A. गुप्त B. लुप्त
C. सुप्त D. विलुप्त

19. उर्वर
A. उपजाऊ B. बंजर
C. गत्वर D. शस्यश्यामल

20. संधि
A. अनुग्रह B. ग्रह
C. विच्छेद D. मैत्री

21. संयोग
A. प्रयोग B. सुयोग
C. नियोग D. वियोग

22. विकास
A. सीमा B. ह्रास
C. दुबला D. नीचा

23. उत्थान
A. नमन B. पतन
C. उदय D. ध्वंस

24. क्षुद्र
A. क्षुद्रतर B. महान्
C. तुच्छ D. अवमान

25. इहलोक
A. उपकार B. पाताल
C. आदि D. परलोक

26. ज्योति
A. पुंज B. दीपक
C. तम D. रोशनी

27. यथार्थ
A. मनोवांछित B. अनुमानित
C. कल्पित D. सत्य

28. अमर
A. देवता B. मरणशील
C. मर्त्य D. दानव

29. आघात
A. अनाघात B. विस्तीर्ण
C. स्निग्ध D. डरपोक

30. व्यष्टि
A. सृष्टि B. वृष्टि
C. समष्टि D. इनमें से कोई नहीं

31. सज्जन
A. चापलूस B. व्यभिचारी
C. सहयोगी D. दुर्जन

32. उत्कर्ष
A. अपकर्ष B. परामर्श
C. संघर्ष D. विमर्श

33. क्षुधा
A. तृषा B. तृष्ण
C. तृप्ति D. मृगतृष्णा

34. सुबह
A. प्रातः B. शाम
C. रात D. दिन

उत्तरमाला

1	2	3	4	5	6	7	8	9	10
C	B	A	B	D	A	D	A	A	A
11	12	13	14	15	16	17	18	19	20
C	D	B	A	C	D	C	A	B	C
21	22	23	24	25	26	27	28	29	30
D	B	B	B	D	C	C	C	A	C
31	32	33	34						
D	A	C	B						

5

रस/छन्द

1. शांत रस का स्थायी भाव है–
A. वैराग्य B. क्षमा
C. दया D. निर्वेद

2. किस रस का स्थायी भाव 'रति' है?
A. भक्ति B. श्रृंगार
C. दोनों का D. दोनों का नहीं

3. हिन्दी काव्य-रसों की कुल संख्या कितनी है?
A. ग्यारह B. दस
C. नौ D. आठ

4. 'यशोदा हरि पालने झुलावै।
हलरावै दुलरावै मल्हावै जोइ सोइ कछु गावै॥'
इस अवतरण में कौन-सा रस है?
A. श्रृंगार B. वात्सल्य
C. शांत D. करुण

5. 'उत्साह' स्थायी भाव से किस रस की निष्पत्ति होती है?
A. शांत B. भयानक
C. रौद्र D. वीर

6. 'नभ में झपटत बाज लखि,
भूल्यो सकल प्रपंच।
कंपित तनु व्याकुल नयन,
लावक हिल्यों च रंच॥'
इस उद्धरण में कौन-सा रस है?
A. रौद्र B. वीभत्स
C. भयानक D. वीर

7. 'निसिचर हीन करहुँ महि,
भुज उठाइ पन कीन्ह।
सकल मुनिन्ह के आश्रमन,
जाइ जाइ सुख दीन्ह॥'
उपर्युक्त उद्धरण में किस रस की निष्पत्ति हुई है?
A. करुण B. वीर
C. रौद्र D. भयानक

8. "गुरु गोविंद तो एक है,
दूजा यह आकार।
आपा मेटि जीवति मरै,
तो पावै करतार॥"
उपर्युक्त दोहे में किस रस का परिपाक हुआ है?
A. श्रृंगार B. करुण
C. अद्‌भुत D. शांत

9. रौद्र रस का स्थायी भाव क्या है?
A. क्रोध B. विस्मय
C. शोक D. भय

10. पत्रा ही तिथि पाइए, वा घर के चहुं पास।
निशि दिन पूनौ ही रहत, आनन ओप उजास।।
इस दोहे में कौन-सा रस है?
A. अद्‌भुत B. हास्य
C. श्रृंगार D. वात्सल्य

11. 'जुगुप्सा' किस रस का स्थायी भाव है?
A. वीर B. भयानक
C. वीभत्स D. शांत

12. नीचे दिए गए पद्यांश में कौन-सा छन्द है?
"रसखानि कबौं इन आँखनि ते,
ब्रज के बन बाग तड़ाग निहारौं।
A. चौपाई B. दोहा
C. सवैया D. सोरठा

13. कहत, नटत, रीझत, खिझत,
मिलत, खिलत, लजियात।
भरे भौन में करत है,
नैनन ही सो बात।।

इस दोहे में कौन-सा रस है?

A. शृंगार B. वीर
C. करुण D. हास्य

14. दोहा और चौपाई कैसे छन्द हैं?

A. मात्रिक छन्द B. मुक्त छन्द
C. वार्णिक छन्द D. वर्णिक छन्द

15. 'जो अखिल कल्याणमय है व्यक्ति तेरे प्राण में
कौरवों के नाश पर है रो रहा केवल वही,
किन्तु उसके पास ही समुदायगत जो भाव हैं,
पूछ उनसे, क्या महाभारत नहीं अनिवार्य था?'

उपर्युक्त किस छन्द में लिखा गया है?

A. गीतिका B. हरिगीतिका
C. रोला D. उल्लाला

16. निम्नलिखित में कौन-सा छन्द है?

बीती नहीं यद्यपि अभी तक है निराशा की निशा,
है किन्तु आशा भी कि होगी दीप्त फिर प्राची दिशा।
महिमा तुम्हारी ही जगत में धन्य, आशे! धन्य है,
देखा नहीं, कोई कहीं अवलम्ब तुम-सा अन्य है।

A. गीतिका B. रोला
C. हरिगीतिका D. उल्लाला

17. 'हम खेले कूदे हर्षयुक्त, जिसकी प्यारी गोद में।
हे मातृभूमि तुझको निरख, मग्न क्यों न हों मोद में?'

उपर्युक्त किस छन्द में लिखा गया है?

A. हरिगीतिका B. उल्लाला
C. रोला D. गीतिका

18. निम्नलिखित में कौन-सा छन्द है?

जिसकी रज में लोट-लोट कर बड़े हुए हैं,
घुटनों के बल सरक-सरक कर खड़े हुए हैं।
परमहंस सम बाल्यकाल में सब सुख पाए,
जिसके कारण 'धूल भरे हीरे' कहलाए।

A. चौपाई B. रोला
C. गीतिका D. उल्लाला

19. वीर रस का स्थायी भाव क्या है?

A. विस्मय B. क्रोध
C. उत्साह D. जुगुप्सा

20. संचारी भावों की संख्या बताइए–

A. 10 B. 33
C. 24 D. 12

21. निम्नलिखित में कौन रौद्र रस का अनुभाव नहीं है?

A. दाँत पीसना B. पैर पटकना
C. आँखों में लाली D. छाती पीटना

22. यह देख गगन मुझमें लय है,
यह देख पवन मुझमें लय है,
मुझमें विलीन झंकार सकल,
मुझमें लय है संसार सकल।
अमरत्व फूलता है मुझमें,
संहार झूलता है मुझमें।

उपर्युक्त काव्यांश में कौन-सा रस है?

A. वीर B. रौद्र
C. अद्‌भुत D. भयानक

23. रस विवेचन से संबंधित ग्रंथ 'रस विलास' किसकी रचना है?

A. भूषण B. मतिराम
C. चिन्तामणि D. कुमारमणि

24. ज्यौं-ज्यौं पटु झटकति, हठति, हँसति नयावति नैन।
त्यौं-त्यौं निपट उदारहुँ, फगुवा देत वनै न।।

उपरोक्त पंक्तियों में कौन-सा अनुभाव है?

A. वाचिक अनुभाव B. कायिक अनुभाव
C. मानसिक अनुभाव D. सात्विक अनुभाव

25. एक ओर अजगरहिं लखि, एक ओर मृगराय।
बिकल बटोही बीच ही, पर्‌यो मूरछा खाय।।

उपरोक्त पंक्तियों में किस रस का निरूपण हुआ है?

A. भयानक B. अद्‌भुत
C. हास्य D. वीभत्स

26. मतिराम कौन-से रस का निरुपण करने वाले कवि थे?

A. शांत B. विस्मय
C. वीर D. शृंगार

27. ''ऊधव मोहिं बृज बिसरत नाहीं'' में कौन-सा रस है?
A. श्रृंगार B. हास्य
C. वीर D. करुण

28. 'उस काल मारे क्रोध के, तन काँपने उसका लगा।
मानो हवा के जोर से सोता हुआ सागर जगा।।''
प्रस्तुत पंक्तियों में कौन-सा रस है?
A. वीर B. रौद्र
C. उद्भुत D. करुण

29. ''मन पछितैहैं अवसर बीते।
दुर्लभ देह पाइ हरि पद भजु, करम, बचन अरु नीके।।''
इन पंक्तियों में कौन-सा रस है?
A. करुण B. शांत
C. भक्ति D. वात्सल्य

30. ''मूक होइ वाचाल पंगु चढ़ाइ गिरिवर गहन।
जसु कृपा सो दयाल, द्रवहु सकल कलिमय दहन।।''
प्रस्तुत पंक्तियों में कौन-सा छंद है?
A. दोहा B. चौपाई
C. सोरठा D. बरवै

31. दोहा के प्रथम और तृतीय चरण में कितनी मात्राएं होती हैं?
A. ग्यारह B. बारह
C. चौदह D. तेरह

32. दोहे और रोले को क्रम से मिलाने पर कौन-सा छंद बनता है?
A. हरिगीतिका B. कुण्डलियाँ
C. सवैया D. बरवै

33. ''अवधि शिला का उर पर था गुरु भार।
तिल-तिल काट रही थी दृग जल धार॥''
प्रस्तुत पंक्तियों में कौन-सा छंद है?
A. दोहा B. सोरठा
C. रोला D. बरवै

34. जौ तुम्हार अनुशासन पावौं।
कन्दुक इव ब्रह्माण्ड उठावौं।।
काचो घट जिम डारौं फोरी।
रोकौं मेरु मुलक जिनि तोरी।।
उपर्युक्त पंक्तियों में कौन-सा रस है?
A. वीर B. रौद्र
C. हास्य D. अद्भुत

35. वह सम मात्रिक छंद जिसके प्रत्येक चरण में 24-24 मात्राएं हों तथा प्रत्येक चरण में 11वीं एवं 13वीं मात्रा पर यति होती हो, कौन-सा छंद कहा जाएगा?
A. रोला B. सोरठा
C. सवैया D. कवित्त

36. रहिमन चुप ह्वै बैठिये, देखि दिनन का फेर।
जब नीके दिन आइहैं, बनत न लगिहैं देर।।
उपर्युक्त पंक्तियों में कौन-सा छंद है?
A. दोहा B. सोरठा
C. रोला D. चौपाई

उत्तरमाला

1	2	3	4	5	6	7	8	9	10
D	B	C	B	D	C	B	D	A	A
11	**12**	**13**	**14**	**15**	**16**	**17**	**18**	**19**	**20**
C	C	A	A	A	C	B	B	C	B
21	**22**	**23**	**24**	**25**	**26**	**27**	**28**	**29**	**30**
D	C	C	B	A	D	A	B	B	C
31	**32**	**33**	**34**	**35**	**36**				
D	B	D	A	B	A				

6

अलंकार

1. 'पत्राही तिथि पाइए, वा घर के चहुँ पास' पंक्ति में अलंकार है–
   A. अनुप्रास B. अतिशयोक्ति
   C. उत्प्रेक्षा D. ऊहा
2. 'तो पर बारौं उरबसी,
   सुन राधिके सुजान।
   तू मोहन की उरबसी,
   ह्वै उरबसी समान।।'
   इस अवतरण में कौन-सा अलंकार है?
   A. अनुप्रास B. यमक
   C. श्लेष D. रूपक
3. 'पीपर पात सरिस मनडोला', पंक्ति में अलंकार है–
   A. उत्प्रेक्षा B. उपमा
   C. रूपक D. अतिशयोक्ति
4. 'मुदित महीपति मंदिर आए।
   सेवक सचिव सुमंत बुलाए।।'
   पंक्ति में कौन-सा अलंकार है?
   A. उपमा B. रूपक
   C. अनुप्रास D. यमक
5. 'चरण धरत चिंता करत,
   चितवत चारिउ ओर।
   सुबरन को ढूँढ़त फिरत,
   कवि व्यभिचारी चोर।।'
   उपर्युक्त दोहे में कौन-सा अलंकार है?
   A. श्लेष B. यमक
   C. उपमा D. रूपक
6. 'तीन बेर खाती सो वे तीन बेर खाती हैं।' पंक्ति में अलंकार चयनित कीजिए?
   A. अनुप्रास B. श्लेष
   C. अन्योक्ति D. यमक
7. 'चरण-कमल बन्दौ हरिराई।' पंक्ति में कौन-सा अलंकार है?
   A. उपमा B. रूपक
   C. श्लेष D. अतिशयोक्ति
8. 'उस काल मारे क्रोध के,
   तन काँपने उसका लगा।
   मानों हवा के शोर से,
   सोता हुआ सागर जगा।।'
   इस उद्धरण में कौन-सा अलंकार है?
   A. अतिशयोक्ति B. उपमा
   C. उत्प्रेक्षा D. रूपक
9. निम्नलिखित विकल्पों में से शब्दालंकार को चिन्हित कीजिए–
   A. यमक B. रूपक
   C. व्यतिरेक D. प्रतीप
10. नीचे लिखे विकल्पों में से कौन-सा विकल्प रूपक अलंकार से सम्बन्धित है?
    A. इसका मुख चन्द्रमा के समान है
    B. चन्द्रमा इसके मुख के समान है
    C. इसका मुख ही चन्द्रमा है
    D. यह मुख है अथवा चन्द्रमा
11. दिए गए पद्यांश में कौन-सा अलंकार है?
    ध्वनि-मयी करके गिरि-कंदरा।
    कलित-कानन केलि-निकुंज को।।
    A. लाटानुप्रास B. छेकानुप्रास
    C. वृत्यानुप्रास D. यमक

12. 'तीर हिये मेरे पीर रघुवीर के' इस पद्यांश में कौन-सा अलंकार है?

A. विभावना B. असंगति

C. प्रतीप D. विशेषोक्ति

13. निम्नलिखित में कौन-सा अलंकार है?

'चाँद-चाँदनी चमक रहे हैं

चुपके-चुपके चम-चम से।'

A. उत्प्रेक्षा B. अनुप्रास

C. उपमा D. श्लेष

14. 'फूले कांस सकल महि छाई

जनु बरसा रितु प्रकट बुढ़ाई' में कौन-सा अलंकार है?

A. यमक B. श्लेष

C. रूपक D. उत्प्रेक्षा

15. रूपक अलंकार यहाँ होता है—

A. उपमेय उपमान की समानता में

B. उपमेय उपमान के अभेद में

C. उपमेय से उपमान की विशिष्टता में

D. उपमेय से उपमान की हीनता में

16. 'ज्यों-ज्यों बूड़े स्याम रंग, त्यों-त्यों उज्ज्वल होय' इस पंक्ति में कौन-सा अलंकार है?

A. विरोधाभास B. यमक

C. उत्प्रेक्षा D. उपमा

17. सिर झुका तूने नियति की

मान ली यह बात।

स्वयं ही मुरझा गया

तेरा हृदय—जलजात।।

इन पंक्तियों में कौन-सा अलंकार है?

A. अनुप्रास B. श्लेष

C. उत्प्रेक्षा D. रूपक

18. उपमेय में उपमान का आरोप होने पर अलंकार होता है—

A. उत्प्रेक्षा B. रूपक

C. मानवीकरण D. यमक

19. उपमेय में कल्पित उपमान की संभावना को कहते हैं—

A. उपमा B. रूपक

C. उत्प्रेक्षा D. दृष्टांत

20. उपमान और उपमेय का अभेद कहलाता है—

A. उपमा B. रूपक

C. उत्प्रेक्षा D. भ्रांतिमान

21. 'सेस महेस गनेस दिनेस सुरेसहू जाहि निरंतर गावैं — इस पंक्ति में अलंकार है—

A. रूपक B. यमक

C. अनुप्रास D. श्लेष

22. किस अलंकार में लक्षण से चमत्कार घटित होता है?

A. प्रतीप B. रूपक

C. अतिशयोक्ति D. अनन्वय

23. राम रमापति कर धनु लेहू — यहाँ कौन-सा अलंकार है?

A. वक्रोक्ति B. अनुप्रास

C. यमक D. श्लेष

24. जहाँ अनेक वर्णों की आवृत्ति केवल एक बार होती है वहाँ होता है—

A. श्लेष B. यमक

C. छेकानुप्रास D. वक्रोक्ति

25. निम्नलिखित में कौन-सा अलंकार है?

'एक कबूतर देख हाथ में पूछा कहाँ अपर है?

उसने कहा अपर कैसा? वह उड़ गया सपर है।।

A. श्लेष B. सन्देह

C. वक्रोक्ति D. विशेषोक्ति

26. आगे नदिया पड़ी अपार,

घोड़ा कैसे उतरे पार।

राणा ने सोचा इस पार,

तब तक चेतक था उस पार।

इसमें कौन-सा अलंकार है?

A. दृष्टान्त B. व्यतिरेक

C. वक्रोक्ति D. अतिशयोक्ति

27. निम्नलिखित में कौन-सा अलंकार है?

'जिन दिन देखे वे कुसुम,

गई सु बीति बहार।

अब, अलि रही गुलाब में,

अपत कँटीली डार।

A. वक्रोक्ति B. दृष्टान्त

C. उत्प्रेक्षा D. अन्योक्ति

28. निम्नलिखित पंक्तियों में कौन-सा अलंकार है?
नाक का मोती अधर की कान्ति से
बीज दाड़िम का समझ कर भ्रान्ति से
देखकर सहसा हुआ शुक मौन है
सोचता है अन्य शुक वह कौन है?
A. सन्देह B. भ्रान्तिमान
C. प्रतीप D. निदर्शना

29. निम्नलिखित पंक्तियों में कौन-सा अलंकार है?
एक म्यान में दो तलवारें कभी नहीं रह सकती हैं।
किसी और पर प्रेम नारियाँ पति का क्या सह सकती हैं?
A. दृष्टांत B. समासोक्ति
C. विभावना D. विरोधाभास

30. 'खग कुल <u>कुल-कुल</u> सा बोल रहा' रेखांकित शब्दों में अलंकार है–
A. यमक B. श्लेष
C. उपमा D. रूपक

31. शब्द की दृयर्थी योजना से कौन-सा अलंकार होता है?
A. अनुप्रास B. वक्रोक्ति
C. श्लेष D. उत्प्रेक्षा

32. जहाँ बिना कारण के कार्य का होना पाया जाए वहाँ कौन-सा अलंकार होता है?
A. विरोधाभास B. विशेषोक्ति
C. विभावना D. भ्रांतिमान

33. जहाँ उपमेय में अनेक उपमानों की शंका होती है वहाँ कौन-सा अलंकार होता है?
A. यमक B. श्लेष
C. भ्रांतिमान D. संदेह

34. "पूत कपूत तो क्यों धन संचय,
पूत सपूत तो क्यों धन संचय।।"
प्रस्तुत पंक्तियों में कौन-सा अलंकार है?
A. छेकानुप्रास B. लाटानुप्रास
C. वृत्यानुप्रास D. अन्त्यानुप्रास

35. 'उसी तपस्वी से लम्बे थे, देवदार दो-चार खड़े।'
इस पंक्ति में कौन-सा अलंकार है?
A. अनुप्रास B. प्रतीप
C. रूपक D. यमक

36. "रहिमन पुतरी श्याम, मनहु जलज मधुकर लसै।"
प्रस्तुत पंक्ति में कौन-सा अलंकार है?
A. रूपक B. उत्प्रेक्षा
C. यमक D. उपमा

37. "उदित उदय गिरि मंच पर, रघुवर बाल पतंग।
विकसे संत सरोज सब, हरषे लोचन भृंग।।"
इन पंक्तियों में प्रयुक्त अलंकार का नाम बताइए–
A. उपमा
B. उत्प्रेक्षा
C. श्लेष
D. रूपक

उत्तरमाला

1	2	3	4	5	6	7	8	9	10
B	C	B	C	A	B	B	C	A	C
11	**12**	**13**	**14**	**15**	**16**	**17**	**18**	**19**	**20**
C	B	B	D	B	A	D	B	C	B
21	**22**	**23**	**24**	**25**	**26**	**27**	**28**	**29**	**30**
C	B	A	C	C	D	D	B	A	B
31	**32**	**33**	**34**	**35**	**36**	**37**			
B	C	D	B	B	B	D			

7

पर्यायवाची शब्द

1. 'कमल' शब्द का पर्यायवाची होगा–
A. कन्दर्प B. अनंग
C. घनेश D. इन्दीवर

2. 'क्रोध' के लिए इन दिए गए पर्यायवाची शब्दों में एक गलत शब्द है, उसे चयनित कीजिए–
A. रोष B. अमर्ष
C. स्वत्व D. कोप

3. निम्नलिखित पर्यायवाची शब्दों में से जो एक शब्द 'मोर' का पर्यायवाची नहीं है, उसे चिन्हित कीजिए–
A. केकी B. कीश
C. शिखी D. शिखण्डी

4. इनमें से कौन-सा शब्द 'कृष्णा' का पर्यायवाची है?
A. राधा B. रुक्मिणी
C. द्रोपदी D. यशोदा

5. इनमें से एक शब्द 'बैल' का पर्यायवाची नहीं है, उसे चयनित कीजिए–
A. अश्म B. बृषभ
C. बलीवर्द D. गो

6. निम्नलिखित में से जो शब्द 'सौन्दर्य' का पर्यायवाची नहीं है, उसे चयनित कीजिए–
A. सुषमा B. शोभा
C. सुन्दरता D. रमणी

7. निम्नलिखित विकल्पों में से एक शब्द 'नदी' का पर्यायवाची नहीं है, उसे चयनित कीजिए–
A. तरंगिणी B. तटिनी
C. तरिणी D. सरिता

8. नीचे दिए गए विकल्पों में से एक शब्द 'घर' का पर्यायवाची नहीं है, उसे चयनित कीजिए–
A. भवन B. भुवन
C. निकेतन D. सदन

9. इनमें से कौन-सा शब्द 'पार्थ' का पर्यायवाची है?
A. भीष्म B. श्रीकृष्ण
C. युधिष्ठिर D. अर्जुन

10. 'दुःख' का पर्यायवाची शब्द निम्नलिखित में से कौन-सा है?
A. व्यथा B. पीड़ा
C. वेदना D. ये सभी पर्याय हैं

11. नीचे दिए गए शब्दों में से एक शब्द 'गीदड़' का पर्यायवाची नहीं है, उसका चयन कीजिए–
A. खगेश B. शृंगाल
C. सियार D. जम्बुक

12. निम्न में से कौन चन्द्रमा का पर्यायवाची नहीं है?
A. शशि B. हिमकर
C. शशांक D. रूपक

13. निम्न में से कौन गाय का पर्यायवाची नहीं है?
A. हेरम्ब B. गौरी
C. भद्रा D. धेनु

14. कुत्ता का पर्यायवाची शब्द निम्नलिखित में से कौन-सा है?
A. सारमेय B. क्रमेलक
C. कीर D. नागान्तक

15. आनंद का पर्यायवाची नहीं है–
A. हर्ष B. उल्लास
C. चाह D. आह्लाद

16. 'कृशानु' का पर्यायवाची शब्द है–
A. अनल B. पवन
C. दोहित्री D. अनिल

17. 'द्रौपदी' का पर्याय नहीं है–
A. द्रुपदसुता B. याज्ञसेनी
C. पांचाली D. रमणी

18. 'महादेव' का पर्यायवाची शब्द चुनिए–
A. गरुड़ध्वज B. नारायण
C. चन्द्रशेखर D. विश्वम्भर

19. 'चन्द्रमा' का पर्यायवाची शब्द चुनिए–
A. निशाकर B. निशाचर
C. तरणि D. कृशानु

20. 'धन' का पर्यायवाची जो शब्द नहीं है, उसे चुनिए–
A. द्रव्य B. द्रव
C. सम्पदा D. दौलत

21. 'पुत्री' का पर्यायवाची शब्द नहीं है–
A. तनय B. सुता
C. आत्मजा D. दुहिता

22. निम्नलिखित में से कौन-सा शब्द 'कमल' का पर्यायवाची शब्द नहीं है?
A. सरोज B. अरविन्द
C. सलिल D. पंकज

23. निम्नलिखित किस समूह में सभी शब्द 'कामदेव' के पर्यायवाची हैं?
A. कंदर्प, मदन, मनसिज, मारक
B. मदन, मन्मथ, अनंग, कंदर्प
C. मान, त्रिपुर, मन्मथ, अनंग
D. मन्मथ, मनसिज, त्रिपुर, अनंग

24. कौन-सा शब्द जंगल शब्द का पर्यायवाची नहीं है?
A. अटवी B. कान्ता
C. कान्तार D. कानन

25. कौन-सा शब्द 'अम्बर' का पर्यायवाची है?
A. आकाश B. अवनि
C. मेघ D. बादल

26. कौन-सा शब्द 'मित्र' का पर्याय नहीं है?
A. अलि B. सखा
C. सुहृद D. मीत

27. निम्नांकित में किस शब्द का अर्थ कमल होता है?
A. उत्पल B. उपल
C. जलद D. नीरद

28. निम्नलिखित में 'पुत्री' शब्द के पर्यायवाची शब्द-समूह कौन हैं?
A. भार्या, कान्ता, अबला, वनिता
B. लड़की, बेटी, अचला, वसुधा
C. सुता, धरा, वसुमती, अचला
D. तनया, आत्मजा, दुहिता, तनुजा

29. निम्नलिखित शब्द-समूह में 'बिजली' के पर्यायवाची कौन हैं?
A. ज्योति, रोशनी, चमक, प्रभा
B. विद्युत, तड़ित, चपला, दामिनी
C. उजाला, प्रभंजन, विहग, निशापति
D. मंदाकिनी, अश्म, प्रस्तर, प्रभा

30. 'जलधि' शब्द का पर्यायवाची क्या है?
A. नहर B. नाव
C. नदी D. समुद्र

31. 'पंकज' शब्द का पर्यायवाची क्या है?
A. सूर्य B. कमल
C. चन्द्रमा D. अमृत

32. 'तरकश' का पर्यायवाची शब्द है–
A. तीर B. धनुष
C. प्रत्यंचा D. निषंग

33. 'स्त्री' का पर्यायवाची शब्द नहीं है–
A. तरुणी B. प्रमदा
C. ललाम D. ललना

34. 'गणेश' का पर्यायवाची शब्द है–
A. सुधांशु B. कुबेर
C. एकदंत D. सुधाकर

35. निम्नलिखित में से कौन-सा शब्द 'तलवार' का पर्यायवाची नहीं है?
A. असि B. खड्ग
C. कृपण D. चंद्रहास

36. इनमें से कौन 'कौआ' का पर्यायवाची है?
A. वायस B. पाली
C. भद्रा D. उदक

37. निम्न में से कौन 'पत्ता' का पर्यायवाची नहीं है?
A. दल B. पर्ण
C. पल्लव D. प्रसून

38. निम्न में से कौन 'हंस' का पर्यायवाची है?

A. मराल B. सारंग
C. अनीक D. अरि

39. निम्न में से कौन 'रण' का पर्यायवाची नहीं है?

A. युद्ध B. संग्राम
C. समर D. सार

40. इनमें से कौन 'युवती' का पर्यायवाची नहीं है?

A. तरुणी B. किशोरी
C. श्यामा D. यामिनी

41. निम्न में से कौन 'इन्द्र' का पर्यायवाची नहीं है?

A. सुरपति B. मधवा
C. धनाधिप D. सुरेश

42. इनमें से कौन 'सरस्वती' का पर्यायवाची नहीं है?

A. वीणापाणि B. वाचा
C. धनद D. शारदा

43. निम्न में से कौन 'कन्या' का पर्यायवाची नहीं है?

A. तनुजा B. आत्मजा
C. नन्दिनी D. भार्या

44. इनमें से कौन 'मयूर' का पर्यायवाची नहीं है?

A. सारंग B. शिखी
C. विशिख D. केकी

45. इनमें से कौन 'शेर' का पर्यायवाची नहीं है?

A. तुरंग B. मृगेन्द्र
C. मृगराज D. व्याघ्र

46. निम्न में से कौन 'अग्नि' का पर्यायवाची है?

A. अनल B. धनद
C. सारंग D. जाह्नवी

47. 'अलंकेश' पर्यायवाची शब्द है–

A. बादल का B. कल्पवृक्ष का
C. कुबेर का D. चपला का

48. इनमें से किस शब्द के पर्यायवाची गलत हैं?

A. कमल – जलज, पंकज, सरोज
B. पुष्प – कुसुम, फूल, सुमन
C. सरस्वती – गिरा, भारती, वाणी
D. सूर्य – दिवस, याम, वासर

49. निम्नलिखित में कौन-सा शब्द 'पताका' का पर्यायवाची नहीं है?

A. झण्डा B. निशान
C. प्रस्तर D. ध्वज

50. निम्नलिखित शब्दों में से 'हनुमान' का पर्यायवाची शब्द नहीं है–

A. रामभक्त B. पवनपुत्र
C. बजरंगबली D. कपीश्वर

उत्तरमाला

1	2	3	4	5	6	7	8	9	10
D	C	D	D	A	D	C	B	D	D
11	**12**	**13**	**14**	**15**	**16**	**17**	**18**	**19**	**20**
A	D	A	A	C	A	D	C	A	B
21	**22**	**23**	**24**	**25**	**26**	**27**	**28**	**29**	**30**
A	C	B	B	A	A	A	D	B	D
31	**32**	**33**	**34**	**35**	**36**	**37**	**38**	**39**	**40**
B	D	C	C	C	A	D	A	D	D
41	**42**	**43**	**44**	**45**	**46**	**47**	**48**	**49**	**50**
C	C	D	C	A	A	C	D	C	A

4

मुहावरे/लोकोक्तियाँ

1. 'सब्जबाग दिखाना' मुहावरा का अर्थ है--
   A. बाग में घूमने जाना
   B. साग-सब्जी पैदा करना
   C. प्रलोभन देना
   D. भयभीत करना

2. 'खुदा गंजे को नाखून न दे' लोकोक्ति का अभिप्राय है–
   A. छोटे आदमी का प्रेम अस्थिर होता है
   B. लज्जित होकर दूसरे पर क्रोध न निकाले
   C. एक दोष पहले से था, दूसरा और आ गया
   D. अत्याचारी को शक्ति नहीं मिलनी चाहिए

3. 'कभी नाव गाड़ी पर कभी गाड़ी नाव पर' लोकोक्ति का सही आशय है–
   A. संघर्ष होना
   B. जीवन में उतार-चढ़ाव का क्रम
   C. भलाई करना
   D. एक-से स्वभाव वाले होना

4. 'एक हाथ से ताली नहीं बजती' लोकोक्ति का अभिप्राय है–
   A. शत्रुता दोनों पक्षों की गलती से होती है
   B. संघर्ष बराबरी वाले दो पक्षों में होना चाहिए
   C. एक आदमी से काम नहीं चलता
   D. सराहना हेतु दोनों हाथ से ताली बजाएँ

5. 'उड़ती चिड़ियों के पंख गिनना' मुहावरा का सही अर्थ होगा–
   A. अनुभवी होना   B. वाक्चतुर होना
   C. प्रतिभाशाली होना   D. असंभव कार्य करना

6. 'नक्कारखाने में तूती की आवाज' मुहावरा का अर्थ है–
   A. तूती की आवाज सबसे ऊँची होती है
   B. नक्कारखाने में तूती नहीं बोलती
   C. नकारे लोगों की सर्वत्र तूती बोलती रहती है
   D. समर्थ व्यक्ति के सामने असमर्थ व्यक्ति का प्रभाव नहीं पड़ता

7. 'आँख के अंधे नाम नयनसुख' का सही अर्थ है–
   A. गुणों के विरुद्ध नाम का होना
   B. बुद्धिहीन, किन्तु पर्याप्त धनवान
   C. अंधा आदमी प्रायः गुणवान होता है
   D. एक आँख के अंधे को भी सभी सुखद आ सकते हैं

8. 'चिकना घड़ा होना' मुहावरा का सही अर्थ है–
   A. चिकना चुपड़ा होना   B. समृद्ध होना
   C. निर्लज्ज होना   D. मधुरभाषी होना

9. 'बेटा समय रहते न पढ़े, तो भविष्य में बुरी तरह पछताओगे' – वाक्य में 'बुरी तरह पछताओगे' के स्थान पर यह मुहावरा आ सकता है–
   A. अंगारों पर लोटोगे
   B. आठ-आठ आँसू रोओगे
   C. अंचरा पसारोगे
   D. कुएँ में गिरोगे

10. "मुहावरे का प्रयोग वाक्य के अन्तर्गत होता है और लोकोक्ति पूर्ण वाक्य में होती है।" यह कथन–
    A. सही है
    B. गलत है
    C. कथन का प्रथम अंश सही है
    D. कथन का अंतिम अंश सही है

11. 'समय के अनुसार काम करना चाहिए' अर्थ की बोधक लोकोक्ति है–
    A. झूठ के पैर नहीं होते
    B. जाके पांव न फटी बिवाई, सो क्या जाने पीर पराई
    C. उँगली पकड़ कर पहुँचा पकड़ना
    D. का बरसा जब कृषि सुखाने

12. 'भारत के अतुलित धन वैभव पर अंग्रजों ने दाँत गड़ा दिए' – वाक्य में प्रयुक्त 'दाँत गड़ा दिए' का अर्थ है–

A. किसी वस्तु को गलत ढंग से पाने की गहरी चाह

B. दूसरे की वस्तु देखकर ललचा जाना

C. दूसरे की वस्तु चुराने की चेष्टा करना

D. धोखे से दूसरे की वस्तु लेना

13. 'चाँद पर थूकना' मुहावरे का आशय है–

A. असम्भव काम करना

B. निरर्थक काम करना

C. सौंदर्य का अनादर करना

D. सम्माननीय का अनादर करना

14. 'नियम विरुद्ध कार्य करना' अर्थ के अनुकूल सही मुहावरा है–

A. सूरज को दिया दिखाना

B. उल्टी गंगा बहाना

C. दाई से पेट छिपाना

D. नौ दो ग्यारह हो जाना

15. 'खाला जी का घर' मुहावरे का क्या अर्थ है?

A. आसान कार्य

B. मौसी का घर

C. भाई-भतीजावाद

D. रिश्तेदार को लाभ पहुँचाना

16. 'सिर चढ़ाना' मुहावरे का अर्थ है–

A. मनमानी करने की छूट देना

B. सिर पर बैठाना

C. सिरदर्द का बहाना करना

D. सिर पर उठा लेना

17. किस लोकोक्ति का अर्थ ''वैभव क्षणिक होता है'' होगा?

A. साँच को आँच नहीं

B. अधजल गगरी छलकत जाए

C. पाँचों उँगलियाँ बराबर नहीं होतीं

D. चार दिन की चाँदनी फिर अँधेरी रात

18. 'आँधी के आम होना' मुहावरे का अर्थ है–

A. मुफ्त उपलब्ध होना

B. संयोगवश बहुत सस्ता उपलब्ध होना

C. वैभवशाली बनना

D. अत्यन्त प्रिय होना

19. 'पाँच सात की लकड़ी, एक जने का बोझ' लोकोक्ति का अर्थ है–

A. बहुत कठिन कार्य होना

B. असम्भव बड़ी शर्त रखना

C. छोटे या कमजोर व्यक्ति की बात को कोई नहीं मानता

D. मिलकर काम करने से कठिन कार्य भी सरल हो जाता है

20. इनमें से कौन एक लोकोक्ति है?

A. अंगूठा दिखाना

B. अंधा होना

C. ऊँट के मुँह में जीरा

D. इधर-उधर की हाँकना

21. 'कलम तोड़ना' मुहावरे का क्या अर्थ है?

A. सही लिखना

B. अच्छा लिखना

C. ज्यादा लिखना

D. बेकार लिखकर प्रायश्चित करना

उत्तरमाला

1	2	3	4	5	6	7	8	9	10
C	D	B	A	A	D	A	C	B	A
11	**12**	**13**	**14**	**15**	**16**	**17**	**18**	**19**	**20**
D	A	D	B	A	A	D	B	D	C
21									
B									

9

संधि-विच्छेद

1. 'मृत्यु + उपरांत' में संधि करने से एक शब्द होगा–
   A. मृत्यूपरांत B. मृत्योपरांत
   C. मृत्युपर्यन्त D. मर्त्योपरांत
2. 'अनधिकृत' शब्द का संधि-विग्रह होगा–
   A. अन + अधिकृत B. अन् + अधिकृत
   C. अन्य + अधिकृत D. अन्नधि + कृत
3. 'कपि + ईश' का सही संधि-संयोजन कीजिए–
   A. कपिश B. कपीश
   C. कपेश D. कपिशि
4. विसर्ग के साथ स्वर अथवा व्यंजन के संयोग से जो विकार उत्पन्न होता है, उसे किस संधि के नाम से जानते हैं?
   A. स्वर संधि B. व्यंजन संधि
   C. विसर्ग संधि D. इनमें से कोई नहीं
5. 'परोपकार' शब्द का संधि-विच्छेद होगा–
   A. परा + उपकार B. परो + पकार
   C. परोप + कार D. पर + उपकार
6. 'मनः + रमा' में संधि करने से जो शब्द बनेगा, उसका सम्बन्ध किस संधि से होगा?
   A. विसर्ग संधि B. स्वर संधि
   C. व्यंजन संधि D. भाव संधि
7. 'चन्द्रोदय' में कौन-सी संधि है?
   A. यण संधि B. दीर्घ संधि
   C. वृद्धि संधि D. गुण संधि
8. निम्नलिखित में से 'वृद्धि स्वर संधि' किस शब्द में है?
   A. रजनीश B. महौषध
   C. यतीन्द्र D. शोधार्थी
9. 'सदाशय' का सही संधि-विच्छेद होगा–
   A. सद + आशय B. सतत + आशय
   C. सत् + आशय D. सदा + आशय
10. 'सन्मार्ग' में कौन-सी संधि है?
    A. स्वर संधि B. व्यंजन संधि
    C. विसर्ग संधि D. इनमें से कोई नहीं
11. 'ज्ञानोदय' में कौन-सी संधि है?
    A. स्वर संधि B. व्यंजन संधि
    C. विसर्ग संधि D. इनमें से कोई नहीं
12. 'निराधार' में कौन-सी संधि है?
    A. स्वर संधि B. व्यंजन संधि
    C. विसर्ग संधि D. इनमें से कोई नहीं
13. निम्नलिखित शब्दों में से किसमें विसर्ग संधि है?
    A. अतएव B. नरेन्द्र
    C. सज्जन D. सदैव
14. निम्नलिखित शब्दों में से किसमें व्यंजन संधि है?
    A. सप्तर्षि B. निराधार
    C. सत्कार D. हिमालय
15. 'जगन्नाथ' किस संधि का उदाहरण है?
    A. व्यंजन संधि B. विसर्ग संधि
    C. दीर्घ स्वर संधि D. यण स्वर संधि
16. निम्नलिखित शब्द का संधि-विच्छेद क्या होगा?
    भानूदय
    A. भानु + उदय B. भानू + उदय
    C. भानू + ऊदय D. भानु + ऊदय
17. 'निर्गुण' का संधि-विच्छेद होगा–
    A. निर + गुण B. नि + गुण
    C. निः + गुण D. निर + गुण

18. 'महेन्द्र' का संधि विच्छेद है–
A. मही + इन्द्र B. महो + इन्द्र
C. महा + इन्द्र D. इनमें से कोई नहीं

19. 'यद्यपि' का संधि विच्छेद है–
A. यदि + अपि B. यद् + द्यपि
C. यद्यि + अपि D. यद + अपि

20. निम्नलिखित में 'भारतेंदु' का सही संधि-विच्छेद है–
A. भारत + तेन्दु B. भार + तेन्दु
C. भारत + एन्दु D. भारत + इन्दु

21. 'उद्घाटन' शब्द का सही संधि-विच्छेद होगा–
A. उत् + घाटन B. उद् + घाटन
C. उद्ध + आटन D. इनमें से कोई नहीं

22. 'सत्कर्म' का संधि-विच्छेद है–
A. सत + कर्म B. सतत् + कर्म
C. सत् + कर्म D. सम + कर्म

23. 'अत्यन्त' शब्द का सही संधि-विग्रह है–
A. अत् + यन्त B. अति + यन्त
C. अति + अन्त D. अत् + अन्त

24. निम्नलिखित शब्द का सही संधि-विच्छेद चुनिए–
ब्रह्माण्ड
A. ब्रह्मा + अंड B. ब्रह्मण + अंड
C. बृहत् + अंड D. बृह + माण्ड

25. 'निरपेक्ष' शब्द का संधि-विच्छेद होगा–
A. निर् + पेक्ष B. नि + पेंक्ष
C. निर + पेक्ष D. निः + अपेक्ष

26. तत् + शंकर की संधि होगी–
A. तत्शंकर B. तच्छंकर
C. तक्षंकर D. उपर्युक्त में से कोई नहीं

27. 'कठोपनिषद्' का संधि-विच्छेद होगा–
A. कटु + उपनिषद् B. कठो + उपनिषद्
C. कठोप + निषद् D. कठ + उपनिषद्

28. 'भावुक' का संधि-विच्छेद होगा–
A. भाव + उक B. भो + ऊक
C. भव्य + उक D. भौ + उक

29. 'विद्यामंदिर' का विग्रह होगा–
A. विद्या का मंदिर B. विद्या के लिए मंदिर
C. विद्या और मंदिर D. विद्या के समान मंदिर

30. 'उत्कोच' का संधि विच्छेद होगा–
A. उद् + कोच B. उत् + कोच
C. उत + कोच D. उद + कोच

31. कौन-सा शब्द विसर्ग संधि का नहीं है?
A. यशोगान B. निष्कपट
C. मनोहर D. अभिषेक

32. 'मनीषा' का संधि-विच्छेद है–
A. मनि + ईषा B. मनी + ईषा
C. मनस् + ईषा D. मणि + ईशा

33. निम्नलिखित में से दीर्घ संधि का उदाहरण कौन-सा है?
A. नरेश B. नेति
C. मध्वाचार्य D. कामायनी

34. 'अति + उक्ति' शब्दों की संधि करने पर शब्द होगा–
A. अत्युक्ति B. अत्योक्ति
C. अतियुक्ति D. अतिउक्ति

35. 'निराधार' शब्द का संधि-विच्छेद है–
A. निः + आधार B. निरा + आधार
C. निरम् + आधार D. निर् + आधार

उत्तरमाला

1	2	3	4	5	6	7	8	9	10
A	A	B	C	D	A	D	B	C	B
11	**12**	**13**	**14**	**15**	**16**	**17**	**18**	**19**	**20**
A	C	A	C	A	A	C	C	A	D
21	**22**	**23**	**24**	**25**	**26**	**27**	**28**	**29**	**30**
A	C	C	A	A	B	D	D	A	B
31	**32**	**33**	**34**	**35**					
D	C	C	A	A					

10

प्रत्यय/उपसर्ग

1. प्रत्युपकार शब्द में कौन-सा उपसर्ग है?
A. प्र B. प्रत्यु
C. परि D. प्रति

2. मुख शब्द में सम उपसर्ग लगाने से बनेगा–
A. सन्मुख B. सम्मुख
C. षड्मुख D. सनममुख

3. वैज्ञानिक शब्द किस प्रत्यय से बना है?
A. निक B. अक
C. इक D. क

4. पढ़ाई शब्द में प्रत्यय है–
A. आई B. ईय
C. इ D. इनमें से कोई नहीं

5. निम्नलिखित में से उपसर्ग रहित कौन-सा शब्द है?
A. संगम B. क्रोध
C. विमोचन D. प्रत्यर्पण

6. आवरण में कौन-सा उपसर्ग लगाकर नया शब्द बनाया जा सकता है?
A. नि B. निवा
C. परि D. पर्य

7. 'कल्पना', 'शिक्षा' में इक प्रत्यय का प्रयोग करने से शब्द बनेंगे–
A. काल्पनिक, शिक्षिक B. कल्पनिक, शैक्षिक
C. कल्पनिक, शिक्षिक D. काल्पनिक, शैक्षिक

8. उपसर्ग रहित शब्द कौन-सा है?
A. सुखी B. आरुढ़
C. उपकरण D. निर्विरोध

9. 'अंध्यापिका' शब्द में प्रत्यय है–
A. का B. पिका
C. आइका D. इका

10. 'निर्धन' शब्द में कौन-सा उपसर्ग है?
A. निः B. नी
C. नि D. निर्

11. 'अत्यंत' शब्द में उपसर्ग क्या है?
A. अ B. अत्य
C. अत D. अति

12. 'अनुलेखन' शब्द में उपसर्ग है–
A. अन् B. अनु
C. अनुले D. अ

13. 'अक्लमंद' शब्द में प्रयुक्त प्रत्यय है–
A. देशज प्रत्यय B. विदेशज प्रत्यय
C. तत्सम प्रत्यय D. तद्भव प्रत्यय

14. प्रत्यक्ष में किस उपसर्ग का प्रयोग हुआ है?
A. प्रत् B. प्रती
C. प्रति D. प्रत्य

15. निम्नलिखित में से किस शब्द में अयन प्रत्यय प्रयुक्त हुआ है?
A. नारायण B. ऋणायन
C. पंडिताइन D. धनायन

16. 'सिलाई' शब्द में कौन-सा प्रत्यय है?
A. नाई B. आई
C. ई D. लाई

17. 'सबजज' शब्द के लिए सही उपसर्ग का चयन कीजिए–
A. सब B. डिप्टी
C. वाइस D. चीफ

18. दिए गए शब्द के लिए सही उपसर्ग का चयन कीजिए–
'पूर्वार्द्ध'

A. पूर्व B. पू
C. अर्द्ध D. पूर्वा

19. निम्नलिखित शब्द में उपसर्ग चुनिए–
'अभिशाप'
A. अति B. अधि
C. आ D. अभि

20. निम्नलिखित शब्द का उपसर्ग चुनिए–
'दुस्साहस'
A. दुस् B. दुर
C. दु D. स

21. निम्नलिखित शब्द का प्रत्यय बताइए–
'सजावट'
A. आव B. आवट
C. आहट D. टा

22. 'अलंकार' शब्द में कौन-सा उपसर्ग है?
A. अ B. अल
C. अलम् D. उपर्युक्त में से कोई नहीं

23. 'स्वयम्वर' शब्द में कौन-सा उपसर्ग प्रयुक्त है?
A. स्व B. स
C. स्वयं D. सम्

24. 'आ' उपसर्ग से बना निम्नलिखित में से कौन-सा शब्द समूह सही है?
A. आलू, आभा, आगमन, आसमान
B. आजन्म, आमरण, आगमन, आकर्षण
C. आरती, आमरण, आतुर, आकाश
D. आज, आखिर, आनन्द, आधा

25. अभि, अति, अधि, अनु मूलतः किस भाषा के उपसर्ग हैं?
A. उर्दू-फारसी B. हिन्दी
C. अपभ्रंश D. संस्कृत

26. बे, बंद, ला किस भाषा के उपसर्ग हैं?
A. हिन्दी B. उर्दू-फारसी
C. अपभ्रंश D. संस्कृति

27. 'पर्यावरण' शब्द में कितने उपसर्ग हैं?
A. 3 B. 2
C. 1 D. एक भी नहीं

28. रसीला, जहरीला, बर्फीला शब्द में किस प्रत्यय का प्रयोग हुआ है?
A. ला B. इला
C. आ D. ईला

29. 'उच्चारण' शब्द में उपसर्ग है–
A. उ B. उच्
C. उत् D. उच्च

30. 'कृति' शब्द का निर्माण किस प्रत्यय के योग से हुआ है?
A. क्त B. क्तिन
C. तव्य D. इनमें से कोई नहीं

31. निम्नलिखित शब्दों में से किस शब्द में उपसर्ग नहीं है?
A. अपवाद B. पराजय
C. प्रभाव D. ओढ़ना

32. 'तल्लीन' शब्द में सही उपसर्ग का विच्छेद है–
A. तल् + लीन B. तद् + लीन
C. तत + लीन D. तत् + लीन

उत्तरमाला

1	2	3	4	5	6	7	8	9	10
D	A	C	A	B	C	D	A	D	D
11	**12**	**13**	**14**	**15**	**16**	**17**	**18**	**19**	**20**
D	B	B	C	A	B	A	A	D	A
21	**22**	**23**	**24**	**25**	**26**	**27**	**28**	**29**	**30**
B	C	C	B	D	B	B	D	C	B
31	**32**								
D	D								

11

तद्भव/तत्सम

1. 'ससुर' शब्द का तत्सम रूप क्या होगा?

A. सस्वर B. स्वश्रु
C. श्वसुर D. सुसुर

2. 'पलंग' का तत्सम रूप है--

A. प्लवंग B. परमंग
C. प्लंग D. पर्यंक

3. 'ओठ' किस श्रेणी का शब्द है?

A. तद्भव B. तत्सम
C. देशज D. विदेशी

4. इनमें से तत्सम शब्द का चयन कीजिए–

A. दुग्ध B. दिन
C. बाहर D. जमुना

5. 'ईख' तद्भव शब्द का तत्सम रूप कौन-सा है?

A. गन्ना B. ईक्ख
C. इक्षु D. इक्क्षु

6. निम्नलिखित में से तद्भव शब्द 'अटारी' का तत्सम होगा–

A. अटारिका B. अटालिका
C. अटाल्लिका D. अट्टालिका

7. निम्नलिखित विकल्पों में से तद्भव शब्द का चयन कीजिए–

A. वानर B. बन्दर
C. भ्रमर D. पवन

8. 'तद्भव' से 'तत्सम' बने सही शब्द-युग्म को ज्ञात कीजिए–

A. हत्ता > हाथ B. रत्ता > रात
C. पत्ता > पत्र D. नच्चा > नाँच

9. 'कपड़ा' शब्द किस श्रेणी का शब्द है?

A. तत्सम B. तद्भव
C. देशज D. विदेशी

10. निम्नलिखित में से कौन-सा शब्द तत्सम शब्द नहीं है?

A. अग्नि B. अश्रु
C. कुआँ D. कंटक

11. निम्नलिखित में से कौन-सा शब्द तद्भव शब्द नहीं है?

A. आग B. चौदह
C. बैन D. मयूर

12. दिए गए तत्सम शब्द के लिए उचित तद्भव शब्द का चयन करें–

'शाक'

A. श्वास B. साग
C. शिर D. साँस

13. निम्न में कौन-सा शब्द विदेशी है?

A. केला B. आम
C. लीची D. नारियल

14. 'खाट' का तत्सम रूप है–

A. खट्वा B. खाट्वा
C. खाटव D. खटिया

15. 'पनही' शब्द का तत्सम रूप है–

A. ताम्बूल B. पर्ण
C. पर्णहि D. उपानह

16. 'पोखर' का तत्सम रूप है–

A. पुष्कर B. प्रखर
C. पोषक D. प्रकर

17. 'दाहिना' का तत्सम रूप है–
A. दाक्षिण्य B. दक्षिण
C. दाहिणा D. दायाँ

18. 'सुई' का तत्सम रूप है–
A. सूजी B. सूई
C. सूची D. शूचक

19. 'हस्त' का तद्भव है–
A. हांथ B. हाथी
C. हस्तिनी D. हथियार

20. निम्नलिखित में से कौन शब्द तत्सम है?
A. अग्नि B. आग
C. अगिन D. अग्नी

21. निम्नलिखित में तत्सम शब्द है–
A. मेघ B. ठेस
C. भौंरा D. जेठ

22. 'कन्धा' का तत्सम है–
A. इस्कन्ध B. स्कन्ध
C. कक्षु D. कन्धु

23. 'आँख' शब्द का तत्सम रूप है–
A. नेत्र B. लोचन
C. चक्षु D. अक्षि

24. 'अंगुली' का तद्भव रूप है–
A. अंगुल B. अंगुटी
C. उंगली D. उपर्युक्त में से कोई नहीं

25. 'गोधूम' का तद्भव है–
A. गेहूँ B. गोबर
C. गाय D. गोधन

26. 'अगहन' का तत्सम रूप कौन-सा है?
A. अग्रासन B. अग्रहण
C. आक्रमण D. अग्रहायन

27. निम्नलिखित में से कौन-सा शब्द तद्भव है?
A. उत्साह B. उछाह
C. विवाह D. उत्थान

28. 'कर्पट' का तद्भव रूप कौन-सा है?
A. कपड़ा B. कपट
C. कारपेट D. कपूर

29. निम्नलिखित में से कौन-सा शब्द तत्सम है?
A. खरा B. क्षार
C. खार D. खारा

30. निम्नलिखित में से तत्सम शब्द कौन-सा है?
A. नौकर B. नक्षत्र
C. नर्स D. नाच

31. हिन्दी के वे शब्द जो सीधे संस्कृत से आए हैं, उन्हें कहते हैं–
A. तत्सम B. तद्भव
C. देशज D. अर्द्ध-तत्सम

32. निम्न में तद्भव शब्द है–
A. अंश B. अगम्य
C. अमृत D. अमिय

33. तत्सम शब्द है–
A. अमरूद B. अमोल
C. अस्सी D. अज्ञान

34. निम्नलिखित शब्दों में से तत्सम शब्द का चयन कीजिए–
A. कलश B. कलस
C. कल्स D. कल्श

उत्तरमाला

1	2	3	4	5	6	7	8	9	10
C	D	A	A	D	D	B	C	C	C
11	**12**	**13**	**14**	**15**	**16**	**17**	**18**	**19**	**20**
D	B	C	A	D	A	A	C	A	A
21	**22**	**23**	**24**	**25**	**26**	**27**	**28**	**29**	**30**
A	B	D	C	A	D	B	A	B	B
31	**32**	**33**	**34**						
A	D	D	A						

12

अनेकार्थी शब्द

1. निम्नलिखित में से कौन एक शब्द अनेकार्थी नहीं है?
A. पत्र B. मुद्रा
C. दंड D. पुस्तक

2. कौन-सा शब्द 'अर्क' का अनेकार्थी नहीं है?
A. सूर्य B. प्रकाश किरण
C. आक का पेड़ D. ज्वाला

3. कौन-सा शब्द 'पत्र' शब्द का अनेकार्थी नहीं है?
A. पत्ता B. चिट्ठी
C. कागज D. पुष्प

4. निम्नलिखित में कौन-सा शब्द 'फल' शब्द का अनेकार्थी शब्द नहीं है?
A. परिणाम B. हल्का
C. प्रभाव D. रसयुक्त

5. निम्नलिखित में एक शब्द 'घन' का अनेकार्थी शब्द नहीं है–
A. बादल B. घना
C. घनिष्ठ D. हथौड़ा

6. निम्न में से कौन-सा शब्द 'रस' का अनेकार्थी शब्द नहीं है?
A. रूप B. स्वाद
C. पानी D. पारा

7. निम्नलिखित शब्दों में कौन एक 'वर' का अनेकार्थी नहीं है?
A. श्रेष्ठ B. वरदान
C. पति D. सुवर्ण

8. निम्नलिखित शब्दों में कौन-सा शब्द 'द्विज' का अनेकार्थी नहीं है?
A. चन्द्रमा B. पक्षी
C. दाँत D. सिंह

9. इनमें से कौन-सा शब्द 'अम्बर' का अनेकार्थी है?
A. गगन B. पृथ्वी
C. चन्द्रमा D. वायु

10. निम्नलिखित विकल्पों में से 'मत्सर' शब्द का अनेकार्थी रूप चुनिए–
A. क्रोध B. राग
C. द्वेष D. ईर्ष्या

निर्देश (प्र.सं. 11 से 13 तक): *इन प्रश्नों में प्रत्येक में चार शब्द दिए गए हैं जिनमें से तीन अनेकार्थक शब्द की श्रेणी में आते हैं। जो शब्द इस श्रेणी में नहीं आता है, उसका चयन कीजिए–*

11. A. अम्बर B. वस्त्र
C. आकाश D. किरण

12. A. मधु B. शहद
C. दूध D. शराब

13. A. इन्द्र B. सिंह
C. ब्राह्मण D. सूर्य

उत्तरमाला

1	2	3	4	5	6	7	8	9	10
D	C	D	B	C	A	D	D	A	A
11	**12**	**13**							
B	C	B							

13

शब्दार्थ

निदेश (प्र.सं. 1 से 32 तक): *नीचे दिए गए शब्दों के अर्थ को व्यक्त करने वाले सही विकल्प का चयन कीजिए–*

1. वलय
A. वृक्ष की छाल B. मृग छाल
C. घेरा D. आवरण

2. सम्पुट
A. मिश्रण B. बंधी हुई अंजलि
C. पिटारी D. मन्जूषा

3. प्रभंजन
A. अंजन B. तोड़-फोड़
C. खण्ड-खण्ड D. तेज वायु

4. पुष्कल
A. जायफल B. पुण्यफल
C. बहुत-सा D. हरा-भरा

5. प्रत्यागमन
A. परिक्रमा करना B. प्रतिरोध करना
C. बार-बार आना D. वापस आना

6. परिवाद
A. विवाद B. सम्वाद
C. निन्दा D. परिवारवाद

7. शबनम
A. शीत B. ओस
C. पाला D. कोहरा

8. नैसर्गिक
A. प्राकृतिक B. स्वर्गिक
C. पारम्परिक D. स्वर्णिम

9. अस्मिता
A. आत्म प्रशंसा B. अहंता
C. स्वार्थ D. स्वाभिमान

10. कष्ट
A. खेद B. शारीरिक असुविधा
C. दुःख D. शोक

11. कतिपय
A. अनेक B. शायद
C. थोड़ा D. कुछ

12. अपेक्षाकृत
A. अपेक्षा करके
B. किसी से अपेक्षा न करके
C. किसी से अपेक्षा करके
D. तुलना

13. अनल
A. आग B. पानी
C. धरती D. हवा

14. अनुगृहीत
A. कृपा का आभार मानने वाला
B. कृपा का आभार न मानने वाला
C. जो कृपा का पात्र न हो
D. जो सबसे कृपा का व्यवहार करे

15. उऋण
A. ऋणी B. कर्जदार
C. ऋणमुक्त D. इनमें से कोई नहीं

16. उर्मि
A. लहर B. भ्रांति
C. समूह D. वेदना

17. रज्जु
A. मछली B. मेंढक
C. रस्सी D. घोड़ा

18. सतीर्थ्य
A. सतीत्व B. तीर्थसहित
C. तीर्थ के योग्य D. सहपाठी

19. चन्द्रहास
A. चाँदनी के समान ह्रास वाला
B. तलवार
C. उदीयमान चन्द्र
D. चन्द्र का उपहास

20. वर्णिलिंगी
A. वर्ण एवं लिंग
B. वर्ण एवं लिंग वाला
C. ब्रह्मचारी के वेशवाला
D. शिव

21. कृतान्त
A. जिसका अन्त कर दिया गया
B. जिसने अन्त कर दिया
C. कृतार्थ
D. दैव

22. कृतघ्न
A. जो उपकार नहीं करता
B. जो किए हुए उपकार को नहीं मानता
C. जो शत्रु को जीत लेता है
D. जो मित्रता को नहीं मानता

23. गतानुगतिक
A. प्राचीन आदर्श के अनुसार चलने वाला
B. पीछे चलने वाला
C. अनुसरण करने वाला
D. गत को नहीं मानने वाला

24. अद्रि
A. दुःख B. गीला
C. व्यर्थ D. पर्वत

25. ऐहिक
A. दीवाना B. सांसारिक
C. एक रोग D. पागल

26. जिजीविषा
A. आय का स्रोत B. जीवित रहने की इच्छा
C. किसी से प्रेम करना D. किसी से घृणा करना

27. आभ्यांतर
A. किसी वस्तु की आभा
B. किसी वस्तु का बाहरी भाग
C. किसी वस्तु का भीतरी भाग
D. किसी वस्तु से भिन्न

28. निर्वात
A. भ्रम B. विवाद रहित
C. बिना हवा वाला D. बुराई

29. आवर्त
A. गोल B. ढक्कन
C. चाँदनी D. भँवर

30. अधिरथ
A. रथ हाँकने वाला B. रथ बनाने वाला
C. कोषाध्यक्ष D. चौकीदार

31. प्लवग
A. बन्दर B. मेंढक
C. पक्षी D. पानी

32. स्वयंभू
A. स्वावलम्बी B. स्वतः उत्पन्न
C. सर्वश्रेष्ठ D. सर्वोपरि

उत्तरमाला

1	2	3	4	5	6	7	8	9	10
C	B	D	C	D	C	B	A	B	B
11	**12**	**13**	**14**	**15**	**16**	**17**	**18**	**19**	**20**
D	D	A	A	C	A	C	D	B	C
21	**22**	**23**	**24**	**25**	**26**	**27**	**28**	**29**	**30**
B	B	B	D	B	B	C	C	D	A
31	**32**								
A	B								

14

वाक्य/वाक्यांश के लिए एक शब्द

निर्देश (प्र.सं. 1 से 34): *नीचे कुछ वाक्यांश या शब्द समूह दिए गए हैं और उसके बाद चार ऐसे शब्द दिए गए हैं, जो एक ही शब्द में वाक्यांश का या उस शब्द समूह का अर्थ प्रकट करते हैं। आपको पता लगाना है कि वह शब्द कौन-सा है, जो वाक्यांश का सही अर्थ प्रकट करता है। उस विकल्प का अक्षरांक ही आपका उत्तर है।*

1. एक स्थान से दूसरे स्थान पर जाना या ले जाना—
A. खिसका हुआ B. उखड़ा हुआ
C. स्थानच्युत D. विस्थापित

2. इंद्रियों को जीतने वाला—
A. अजातशत्रु B. इन्द्रस्वामी
C. जितेंद्रिय D. मुमुक्षु

3. एक ही कोख से जन्म लेने वाला—
A. संतति B. जातक
C. आत्मज D. सहोदर

4. अपनी इच्छा से चलने वाला—
A. स्वेच्छांचारी B. स्वच्छंद
C. अराजक D. स्वेच्छक

5. जो हर हाल में हो ही जाए—
A. होनहार B. अवश्यंभावी
C. भाग D. तत्पर

6. जो कठिनाई से समझ में आए—
A. दुर्गम B. दुर्बोध
C. दुर्लभ D. दुर्धर्ष

7. एक पर ही श्रद्धा अथवा आस्था रखने वाला—
A. एकाकी B. अलौकिक
C. अधिकारिक D. एकनिष्ठ

8. बड़ा बनने की इच्छा रखने वाला—
A. पदलोलुप B. चाटुकार
C. विवेकवान D. महत्वाकांक्षी

9. मन का दुर्भाव—
A. दृष्टिवैषम्य B. भेदभाव
C. मनोमालिन्य D. कलुषित

10. पूर्णतः स्वच्छ करना—
A. परिष्कार B. सुधार
C. आविष्कार D. पुनरोद्धार

11. जिसका जन्म उच्च कुल में हुआ हो—
A. सेठ B. अभद्र
C. अमीर D. कुलीन

12. ईश्वर को नहीं मानने वाला—
A. आस्तिक B. अधर्मवान
C. बंदा D. नास्तिक

13. उपकार मानने वाला—
A. कृतघ्न B. परोपकारी
C. अनोपचारी D. कृतज्ञ

14. किसी के पास रखी हुई दूसरे की वस्तु—
A. गिरवी B. जमानत
C. धरोहर D. सामान

15. एक स्थान से दूसरे स्थान को हटाया हुआ—
A. आंतरित B. प्रवासी
C. मुसाफिर D. स्थानांतरित

16. जिसे कठिनाई से भेदा जा सके—
A. अभेद्य B. दुर्भेद्य
C. दुर्दम्य D. अगम्य

17. जो सबको समान भाव से देखे–
A. दूरदर्शी B. क्रांतदर्शी
C. सूक्ष्मदर्शी D. समदर्शी

18. परलोक से सम्बन्धित–
A. पारलौकिक B. अलौकिक
C. इहलौकिक D. लौकिक

19. पीछे-पीछे चलने वाला–
A. अनुगामी B. प्रतिगामी
C. पश्चगामी D. अग्रगामी

20. जिसके हृदय में ममता नहीं है–
A. निर्दय B. कठोर
C. क्रूर D. निर्मम

21 जो व्यर्थ की बातें करता हो–
A. बहुभाषी B. कुवक्ता
C. वाचाल D. वाक्पटु

22. जो देखने में प्रिय लगता हो–
A. समदर्शी B. प्रियदर्शी
C. प्रियपात्र D. दर्शनप्रिय

23. अहसान न मानने वाला–
A. कृतज्ञ B. कृतघ्न
C. विश्वासघाती D. परोपजीवी

24. जिसे कठिनाई से जीता जा सके–
A. विजित B. अज्ञेय
C. अजेय D. दुर्जेय

25. बचपन और जवानी के बीच की अवस्था–
A. नवयुवा B. नवोढ़ा
C. वयःसंधि D. वयस्कता

26. पशुओं के समान व्यवहार करने वाला–
A. पाशविक B. पशुसा
C. क्रूर D. दानव

27. वह अग्नि जो जंगल में लग जाती है–
A. वनाग्नि B. दावानल
C. अनल D. प्रचंडाग्नि

28. वह वस्तु जो नाशवान है–
A. नाशक B. नासन्य
C. नासांतिक D. नश्वर

29. परिश्रम के बदले प्राप्त धनराशि–
A. मुद्रा B. करेंसी
C. पारिश्रमिक D. सिक्का

30. अधिक पढ़ी-लिखी महिला–
A. विदूषक B. विज्ञानी
C. अफसर D. विदुषी

31. दोपहर का समय–
A. अपराह्न B. पूर्वाह्न
C. अधपहर D. मध्याह्न

32. जिसके समान कोई दूसरा न हो–
A. असामान्य B. अद्वितीय
C. असाधारण D. महान्

33. जो अधिक व्यय न करता हो–
A. धन्नासेठ B. खर्चीला
C. अव्यय D. मितव्ययी

34. जो पृथ्वी से सम्बन्धित हो–
A. पार्थिव B. पृथ्वी
C. अलौकिक D. जड़

उत्तरमाला

1	2	3	4	5	6	7	8	9	10
D	C	D	A	B	B	D	D	C	A
11	12	13	14	15	16	17	18	19	20
D	D	D	C	D	B	D	A	A	D
21	22	23	24	25	26	27	28	29	30
C	B	B	D	C	A	B	D	C	D
31	32	33	34						
D	B	D	A						

15

वाक्यों की शुद्धता

निर्देश (प्र.सं. 1 से 26 तक): *नीचे दिए गए प्रश्नों में चार वाक्यों में एक वाक्य शुद्ध है और तीन अशुद्ध हैं। शुद्ध वाक्य को चुनिए।*

1. A. मैंने एक रुपए का सामान खरीदा
B. मैं एक रुपए का सामान खरीदा
C. मुझने एक रुपया का सामान खरीदा
D. मैं एक रुपया का सामान खरीदी

2. A. उसे कॉफी बनाना नहीं आता
B. उसे कॉफी बनानी नहीं आता
C. उसे कॉफी बनाना नहीं आती
D. उसे कॉफी बनाने को नहीं आते

3. A. देश का सम्मान की रक्षा करो
B. देश के सम्मान की रक्षा करो
C. देश को सम्मान की रक्षा करो
D. देश के लिए सम्मान की रक्षा करो

4. A. अतिथि को चाकू से काटकर फल खिलाओ
B. चाकू से अतिथि को काटकर फल खिलाओ
C. चाकू से फल काटकर अतिथि को खिलाओ
D. फल को काटकर चाकू से अतिथि को खिलाओ

5. A. राम ने पेट भर मिठाई खाई
B. राम ने पेट भर के मिठाई खाई
C. राम ने भरपेट मिठाई खाई
D. इनमें से सभी शुद्ध हैं

6. A. मैं आपकी सौजन्यता पर मुग्ध हूँ
B. मैं आपके सौजन्य पर मुग्ध हूँ
C. मैं आपके सुजन्य पर मुग्ध हूँ
D. इनमें से तीनों वाक्य अशुद्ध हैं

7. A. लाओ एक पानी का गिलास
B. एक पानी का गिलास लाओ
C. गिलास एक पानी का लाओ
D. एक गिलास पानी लाओ

8. A. हमारी सौभाग्यवती कन्या का विवाह होने जा रहा है।
B. हमारी आयुष्मती कन्या का विवाह होने जा रहा है।
C. हमारी सौभाग्यवती कन्या का विवाह होने जा रही है
D. इनमें से सभी शुद्ध हैं

9. A. माँ बच्चे को दूध धाय से पिला रही है
B. माँ बच्चे को दूध धाय से पिलवा रही है
C. माँ बच्चे को दूध धाय से पी रही है
D. माँ बच्चे को दूध धाय से चखा रही है

10. A. ये हमारे पास रहते हैं और वे दूर
B. वे हमारे पास रहते हैं और ये दूर
C. वे हमारे पास रहते हैं और वह दूर
D. ये हमारे पास रहते हैं और वह दूर

11. A. वेदों के छः अंग माने जाते हैं
B. वेदों में छः अंग माने जाते हैं
C. वेदों से छः अंग माने जाते हैं
D. वेदों पर छः अंग माने जाते हैं

12. A. भक्तों की सेना जा रही थी
B. भक्तों की मंडली जा रही थी
C. भक्तों की टुकड़ी जा रही थी
D. भक्तों की भीड़ जा रही थी

13. A. आपकी शंका का परिहार हुआ कि नहीं
B. आपकी शंका का निदान हुआ कि नहीं
C. आपकी शंका का समाधान हुआ कि नहीं
D. आपकी शंका निर्मूल हुई कि नहीं

14. A. यह ग्रंथ विद्वतापूर्ण लिखा गया है
B. यह ग्रंथ विद्वतापूर्वक लिखा गया है
C. यह ग्रंथ विद्वानपूर्ण लिखा गया है
D. यह ग्रंथ विद्वानपूर्वक लिखा गया है

15. A. वह टका-सा उत्तर देता है
B. वह टका-सा प्रश्न करता है
C. वह टका-सा जवाब देता है
D. इनमें से कोई नहीं

16. A. जो मिठाई पसन्द हों आप खा लो
B. जो मिठाई पसन्द हों तुम खा लो
C. जो मिठाइयाँ पसन्द हों तुम खा लो
D. जो मिठाइयाँ पसन्द हों उन्हें आप खाइए

17 A. हम बचपन में वहाँ जायेंगे
B. हम बचपन में वहाँ जाते रहे हैं
C. मैं बचपन में वहाँ जाता रहा
D. मैं बचपन में वहाँ जाऊँगा

18. A. प्रत्येक व्यक्ति कविता कर सकते हैं
B. प्रत्येक व्यक्ति कविता नहीं कर सकते हैं
C. प्रत्येक व्यक्ति कविता नहीं कर सकता
D. हर व्यक्ति कविता कर सकते हैं

19. A. हेम नरेश की पुस्तक दी
B. हेम ने नरेश को पुस्तक दी
C. हेम नरेश का पुस्तक देगा
D. हेम ने नरेश का पुस्तक दिया

20. A. मन्त्री ड्राइवर से कार चलवाता है
B. मन्त्री ड्राइवर की कार चलवाता है
C. मन्त्री ड्राइवर के लिए कार चलवाता है
D. मन्त्री ड्राइवर पर कार चलवाता है

21. A. उसकी आयु तीस वर्ष है इस समय
B. इस समय उसकी अवस्था तीस वर्ष है
C. तीस वर्ष की अवस्था है इस समय उसकी
D. इस समय तीस वर्ष की अवस्था है उसकी

22. A. रागिनी अपने आप चली गई
B. रागिनी खुद से चली गई
C. रागिनी अपने से ही चली गई
D. रागिनी आपके आप चली गई

23. A. श्याम पौधे को जल से सींच रहा है
B. पौधे को जल से सींच रहा है श्याम
C. श्याम पौधे सींच रहा है
D. जल से सींच रहा है श्याम पौधे को

24. A. वह उदद्ंडनीय है
B. वह दण्ड भोगने के योग्य है
C. वह दण्डयोग्य है
D. वह दण्ड देने के योग्य है

25. A. हमारे यहाँ तरुण नवयुवकों की शिक्षा का अच्छा प्रबन्ध है
B. हमारे यहाँ तरुण नवयुवकों का शिक्षा का अच्छा प्रबन्ध है
C. हमारे नवयुवकों की शिक्षा का यहाँ अच्छा प्रबन्ध है
D. हमारे यहाँ नवयुवकों की शिक्षा का अच्छा प्रबन्ध है

26. A. मुरझाया हुआ फूल वर्षा की फुहार से अभिसिंचित होकर पुनः खिल उठा
B. मुरझाई हुई फूल वर्षा की फुहार से अभिसिंचित होकर पुनः खिल उठा
C. मुरझाया हुआ फूल वर्षा की फुहार से अभिसिंचित होकर पुनः खिल उठी
D. मुरझाया हुआ फूल वर्षा के फुहार द्वारा अभिसिंचित होकर पुनः खिल उठे

उत्तरमाला

1	2	3	4	5	6	7	8	9	10
A	A	B	C	C	B	D	A	B	A
11	12	13	14	15	16	17	18	19	20
A	B	C	B	C	D	C	C	B	A
21	22	23	24	25	26				
B	A	C	C	D	A				

16

संज्ञा, सर्वनाम, विशेषण

1. 'सभी श्रोता **यथास्थान** बैठे थे।' व्याकरण की दृष्टि से इस वाक्य में गहरा छपा पद 'यथास्थान' क्या है?
   A. अव्यय B. संज्ञा
   C. क्रिया विशेषण D. विशेषण
2. जिन शब्दों में एक ही प्रकार की वस्तुओं अथवा व्यक्तियों का बोध हो, उन्हें कहते हैं—
   A. समूहवाचक संज्ञा B. व्यक्तिवाचक संज्ञा
   C. जातिवाचक संज्ञा D. भाववाचक संज्ञा
3. निम्नलिखित में कौन-सा शब्द पुल्लिंग है?
   A. शिक्षा B. चर्चा
   C. अर्चना D. पर्चा
4. क्रिया के रूप हैं—
   A. अनुकर्मक व अकर्मक
   B. अकर्मक व अभिकर्मक
   C. अनुकर्मक व अभिकर्मक
   D. सकर्मक व अकर्मक
5. स्त्रीलिंग शब्द है—
   A. पुराण B. पोथी
   C. काव्य D. ग्रंथ
6. 'हृदय' का विशेषण है—
   A. हृदयेश B. हार्दिक
   C. हृदयी D. इनमें से कोई नहीं
7. 'बुढ़ापा' शब्द व्याकरण के किस संज्ञा भेद से संबद्ध है?
   A. जातिवाचक संज्ञा B. भाववाचक संज्ञा
   C. व्यक्तिवाचक संज्ञा D. इनमें से कोई नहीं
8. सर्वनाम के भेद हैं—
   A. छः B. पाँच
   C. तीन D. आठ
9. जो विशेषण किसी वस्तु की मात्रा, वजन, नाप-तौल का बोध कराते हैं, उन्हें कहते हैं—
   A. सार्वनामिक विशेषण
   B. गुणवाचक विशेषण
   C. परिमाणवाचक विशेषण
   D. संख्यावाचक विशेषण
10. 'ब्राह्मणत्व' शब्द है—
    A. जातिवाचक संज्ञा B. भाववाचक संज्ञा
    C. समूहवाचक संज्ञा D. इनमें से कोई नहीं
11. संज्ञा या सर्वनाम के जिस रूप से क्रिया करने वाले का बोध हो वह है—
    A. अधिकरण कारक B. कर्त्ताकारक
    C. सम्बोधन कारक D. कर्मकारक
12. ''यह काम मैं आप कर लूँगा'' पंक्तियों में 'आप' है—
    A. सम्बन्धवाचक सर्वनाम
    B. निजवाचक सर्वनाम
    C. निश्चयवाचक सर्वनाम
    D. पुरुषवाचक सर्वनाम
13. निम्नलिखित में से कौन-सा स्त्रीलिंग में प्रयुक्त होता है?
    A. ऋतु B. पंडित
    C. हंस D. आचार्य
14. निम्नलिखित में से स्पर्श व्यंजन है—
    A. श B. छ
    C. ल D. ह
15. सर्वनाम में किस कारक का प्रयोग नहीं होता है?
    A. सम्बन्ध B. सम्बोधन
    C. सम्प्रदान D. अपादान

16. "तुम्हारे घर उस दिन, जिसे मैंने देखा, वह कौन था?" इस वाक्य में प्रश्नवाचक सर्वनाम है–

A. उस B. जिसे
C. कौन D. तुम्हारे

17. 'में' विभक्ति किस कारक की है?

A. सम्बोधन B. अधिकरण
C. सम्बन्ध D. कर्म

18. 'प्रशंसा' शब्द व्याकरणिक पद की दृष्टि से है–

A. गुणवाचक विशेषण
B. भाववाचक संज्ञा
C. जातिवाचक विशेषण
D. व्यक्तिवाचक संज्ञा

19. निम्न विकल्पों में से सकर्मक क्रिया का चयन कीजिए–

A. लेटना B. छूटना
C. पिघलना D. तड़पना

20. 'मानव' शब्द के लिए उपयुक्त भाववाचक संज्ञा का चयन कीजिए–

A. मनस्वी B. मानवता
C. मनुष्यत्व D. आदमीयत

21. निम्नलिखित में से कौन एक संयुक्त व्यंजन नहीं है?

A. क्ष B. ष
C. त्र D. ज्ञ

22. सम्बन्ध कारक का चिह्न है–

A. में, पर B. के लिए
C. -रा, -रे, -री D. से

23. तालव्य व्यंजन है–

A. च, छ, ज, झ B. ट, ठ, ड, ढ
C. त, थ, द, ध D. प, फ, ब, भ

24. य, र, ल, व – किस वर्ग के व्यंजन हैं?

A. तालव्य B. ऊष्म
C. अन्तःस्थ D. ओष्ठ्य

25. निम्न में से कौन जातिवाचक संज्ञा का उदाहरण है?

A. मालिनी B. स्त्री
C. सेना D. बचपन

26. "जो जैसा करेगा, वह वैसा भरेगा" वाक्य का सम्बन्ध किस सर्वनाम से है?

A. निजवाचक B. सम्बन्धवाचक
C. निश्चयवाचक D. पुरुषवाचक

27. 'ओ, औ' किस प्रकार के अर्थ हैं?

A. तालव्य B. मूर्धन्य
C. दन्तोष्ठ्य D. कंठोष्ठ्य

28. निम्नलिखित ईकारान्त शब्दों में एक पुल्लिंग है, उसे चयनित कीजिए–

A. पानी B. नदी
C. रोटी D. बकरी

29. 'लृट्' लकार किस काल का बोधक है?

A. वर्तमान काल का B. भूतकाल का
C. भविष्यत् काल का D. किसी काल का नहीं

30. निम्नलिखित शब्दों में किस एक का लिंग परिवर्तन हिन्दी भाषा में प्रचलित नहीं है?

A. चाचा B. बहन
C. कोयल D. भैंसा

उत्तरमाला

1	2	3	4	5	6	7	8	9	10
A	C	D	D	B	B	B	A	C	B
11	**12**	**13**	**14**	**15**	**16**	**17**	**18**	**19**	**20**
B	B	A	B	B	C	B	A	B	B
21	**22**	**23**	**24**	**25**	**26**	**27**	**28**	**29**	**30**
B	C	A	C	B	B	D	A	C	C

17

वाक्यों में त्रुटियाँ

निर्देश (प्र.सं. 1 से 35 तक): *नीचे दिया गया हर एक वाक्य चार भागों में बाँटा गया है जिन्हें (A), (B), (C) और (D) अक्षरांक दिए गए हैं। आपको यह देखना है कि वाक्य के किसी भाग में व्याकरण, भाषा, वर्तनी, शब्दों के गलत प्रयोग या इसी तरह की कोई त्रुटि तो नहीं है। त्रुटि अगर हो तो वाक्य के किसी एक भाग में ही होगी। उस भाग का अक्षरांक ही उत्तर है। अगर वाक्य त्रुटिरहित है तो उत्तर (E) दीजिए।*

1. कैक्टस के पौधे में कई चमत्कारी गुण (A)/ होते हैं लेकिन यह दुखदायी की बात (B)/ है कि हमारे देश में अभी तक इस पर (C)/ बहुत अधिक ध्यान नहीं दिया गया है। (D)/ त्रुटिरहित (E).

2. वाणिज्यिक वाहन निर्माताओं के (A)/ अनुसार, ईंधन की कीमतों में तेजी के (B)/ बावजूद बिक्री वाणिज्यिक वाहनों की (C)/ में तेजी दर्ज की गई है। (D)/ त्रुटिरहित (E).

3. जब तपती और धूल भरी (A)/ सड़कों पर मोटी-मोटी बूँदें गिरतीं तब (B)/ उमस के साथ मिट्टी की (C)/ भुनी भुनी गंध वातावरण में फैल जाती थी। (D)/ त्रुटिरहित (E).

4. औसत अगर मध्यवर्गीय (A)/ परिवार की बात करें तो उसमें (B)/ स्त्री मन को समझने की (C)/ गुंजाइश बहुत कम होती है। (D)/ त्रुटिरहित (E).

5. सुखद स्मृतियाँ चमकीले वर्तमान (A)/ से कहीं ज्यादा आनंददायक, (B)/ दुष्प्रेरणादायक और स्फूर्ति (C)/ प्रदान करने वाली होती हैं। (D)/ त्रुटिरहित (E).

6. किसी तंदरुस्त वृद्ध की देहयष्टि (A)/ देखकर लग पड़ता है (B)/ कि आयु ने उनके शरीर (C)/ पर अपना प्रभाव नहीं डाला है। (D)/ त्रुटिरहित (E).

7. कोशिश करने से मसले (A)/ समय रहते हल हो जाएं (B)/ तो ठीक वरना मन (C)/ में ग्रंथियाँ बन जाती हैं। (D)/ त्रुटिरहित (E).

8. यदि कोई विकलांग व्यक्ति (A)/ घर का मुखिया हो (B)/ तो वह गरीबी रेखा से (C)/ नीचे के दायरे में आएगा। (D)/ त्रुटिरहित (E).

9. एक मध्यवर्गीय भारतीय परिवार में पिता (A)/ काम के बोझ या दूसरे कारणों से अपने (B)/ बच्चों से कट जाता है, जिसका बच्चों (C)/ के मन पर प्रतिकूल प्रभावशाली पड़ता है। (D)/ त्रुटिरहित (E).

10. अर्थव्यवस्था विश्व के बदतर हो रहे (A)/ हालात से चिंतित वित्त मंत्री ने (B)/ कहा कि सरकार के पास नरमी (C)/ से निपटने के विकल्प सीमित हैं। (D)/ त्रुटिरहित (E).

11. बचत बैंक खातों (A)/ में बैंकों द्वारा (B)/ ब्याज की अदायगी (C)/ किया जाता है। (D)/ त्रुटिरहित (E).

12. वर्ष 2010 को आधार (A)/ बना कर राष्ट्रीय स्तर पर (B)/ नया उपभोक्ता तूल्य (C)/ सूचकांक जारी किया गया है। (D)/ त्रुटिरहित (E).

13. गुजरात की (A)/ राजरानी गांधीनगर (B)/ में एक बहुत बड़े समारोह का (C)/ आयोजन किया गया है। (D)/ त्रुटिरहित (E).

14. विमानन क्षेत्र का (A)/ नामी कम्पनी की (B)/ मुश्किलें दिनोंदिन (C)/ बढ़ती जा रही हैं। (D)/ त्रुटिरहित (E).

15. सरकार अपनी योजनाओं (A)/ का लाभ केवल कमजोर (B)/ वर्ग के लोगों तक सीमित (C)/ रखने के कक्ष में नहीं है। (D)/ त्रुटिरहित (E).

16. भारत सरकार द्वारा अर्जित (A)/ कुल राजस्व की (B)/ अधिकतम राशि आय कर (C)/ से प्राप्त होती है। (D)/ त्रुटिरहित (E).

17. दूरदर्शन के अधिकारियों (A)/ ने लोकप्रिय वाहिका (B)/ का प्रसारण बंद करने (C)/ का आदेश दिया है। (D)/ त्रुटिरहित (E).

18. राष्ट्रीय एकता तथा मानवीय (A)/ मूल्यों के मूलभूत सिद्धान्तों (B)/ को म्यान में रखकर (C)/ पाठ्य-सामग्री तैयार की गई है। (D)/ त्रुटिरहित (E).

19. दोनों देशों के वाणी (A)/ सचिवों की बैठक में (B)/ परस्पर व्यापार बढ़ाने (C)/ के लिए सहमति हो गयी। (D)/ त्रुटिरहित (E).

20. कोश के इस (A)/ नए संस्करण में बहुत (B)/ से नए शब्द (C)/ शामिल किए गए हैं। (D)/ त्रुटिरहित (E).

21. बैंक से जारी होने वाले (A)/ सभी परिपत्र, आदेश आदि (B)/ कागज के बजाय डिजिटल (C)/ माध्यमों से प्रेषित किया जाता है। (D)/ त्रुटिरहित (E).

22. नियंत्रण प्राधिकारियों से (A)/ भी अपेक्षा की गई है (B)/ कि वे प्रतिदिन प्रतिवेदन (C)/ का अध्ययन अवश्य करें। (D)/ त्रुटिरहित (E).

23. ग्लोबल वार्मिंग रूपी (A)/ शत्रु पर आक्रमण कर उसे (B)/ परस्त करने में सभी (C)/ का योगदान होना चाहिए। (D)/ त्रुटिरहित (E).

24. पेड़ नहीं सोंचते कि झोंका (A)/ आए तो झूमें या न (B)/ झूमें वे झूमते हैं और अपने (C)/ जड़ों पर यकीन रहते हैं। (D)/ त्रुटिरहित (E).

25. कितने वर्षों की अवधि (A)/ तक खाते में कोई भी लेन-देन न (B)/ होने पर खाते को (C)/ निष्कृत माना जाता है? (D)/ त्रुटिरहित (E).

26. सामाजिक कुरीतियों (A)/ का मुख्य कारण (B)/ अज्ञानता है (C)/ यह बात एकदम सही है। (D)/ त्रुटिरहित (E).

27. उसकी सौन्दर्यता (A)/ देखकर मन मयूर (B)/ नृत्य करने लगा (C)/ दिलीप ने श्याम को बताया। (D)/ त्रुटिरहित (E).

28. नगेन्द्र जी (A)/ हिन्दी के (B)/ लब्धप्रतिष्ठित (C)/ आलोचक एवं लेखक हैं। (D)/ त्रुटिरहित (E).

29. साहित्य (A)/ और जीवन का (B)/ घनघोर (C)/ सम्बन्ध है। (D)/ त्रुटिरहित (E).

30. दिल्ली से (A)/ अनेकों (B)/ पत्र-पत्रिकाओं का (C)/ प्रकाशन होता है। (D)/ त्रुटिरहित (E).

31. गाय को घास (A)/ खिलाने से और पंछी (B)/ को दाना डालने (C)/ से पूण्य मिलता है। (D)/ त्रुटिरहित (E).

32. एक संख्या का पाँच (A)/ बटा-नौ दूसरी संख्या (B)/ के पच्चीस प्रतिशत (C)/ के सम्मान है। (D)/ त्रुटिरहित (E).

33. दिनेश की मासिक (A)/ आय सुरेश की (B)/ मासिक आय से (C)/ चुगना है। (D)/ त्रुटिरहित (E).

34. इस कार की कीमत कम (A)/ होगी और कम्पनी इसमें ज्यादा से ज्यादा (B)/ भारतीय पूर्जे लगाने (C)/ की कोशिश कर रही है। (D)/ त्रुटिरहित (E).

35. कहतें हैं कि (A)/ हर दस कोश (B)/ पर बोली (C)/ बदलती है। (D)/ त्रुटिरहित (E).

उत्तरमाला

1	2	3	4	5	6	7	8	9	10
B	C	D	A	C	A	E	A	D	A
11	12	13	14	15	16	17	18	19	20
D	C	B	A	D	C	B	C	A	B
21	22	23	24	25	26	27	28	29	30
D	A	C	C	D	C	A	C	C	B
31	32	33	34	35					
D	D	D	C	B					

18

रिक्त स्थानों की पूर्ति

निर्देश (प्र.सं. 1 से 28 तक): *नीचे दिए गए प्रत्येक प्रश्न में एक रिक्त स्थान छूटा हुआ है और उसके नीचे चार शब्द सुझाए गए हैं। इनमें से कोई एक उस रिक्त स्थान पर रख देने से वह वाक्य एक अर्थपूर्ण वाक्य बन जाता है। सही शब्द ज्ञात कर उसको उत्तर के रूप में अंकित कीजिए।*

दिए गए शब्दों में से सर्वाधिक उपयुक्त का चयन करना है।

1. लोकतंत्र में बल प्रयोग करके किसी समस्या का .... करना न तो न्याय सम्मत है, न ही शोभनीय।

A. चर्चा B. बखान
C. समाधान D. कचूमर

2. गाँव जाने वाली सड़क में गड्ढों के मारे कार को इस कदर हिचकोले लग रहे थे मानो वो कोई .... हो।

A. सवारी B. साइकिल
C. शाहीगाड़ी D. बैलगाड़ी

3. हमारे शहर में .... खत्म होने के बाद अचानक गर्मी बढ़ जाती है।

A. पानी B. नदी जल
C. आर्द्रता D. ग्रीष्म

4. रविवार को सड़कों पर हाट लगने पर इतनी भीड़ हो जाती है कि .... को जगह नहीं मिलती।

A. बैठने B. तिल धरने
C. बाजार करने D. चाय पीने

5. हमारे देश में क्रिकेट को छोड़कर बाकी सभी खेलों के साथ .... व्यवहार होता है।

A. सौतेला B. अनुत्तम
C. उत्तम D. समान

6. आपसे सादर .... है कि आप हमारे समारोह में मुख्य अतिथि के रूप में पधारें।

A. कामना B. अनुरोध
C. अनुग्रह D. विनय

7. ताजमहल .... का अद्‌भुत नमूना है।

A. मूर्तिकला B. शिल्पकला
C. चित्रकला D. स्थापत्यकला

8. यहाँ की जलवायु आपके .... नहीं है।

A. योग्य B. अनुरूप
C. अनुकूल D. अनुसार

9. समय का सदुपयोग न करने वाले व्यक्तियों को बाद में .... करना पड़ता है।

A. पश्चाताप B. प्रायश्चित
C. परिष्कार D. विलाप

10. इस नाटक का .... अन्त तक बना रहा।

A. आश्चर्य B. कुतूहल
C. दर्द D. विषय

11. कोयले की दलाली में .... हाथ।

A. गंदे B. मैले
C. बिगड़े D. काले

12. एक .... सौ बीमार।

A. अनार B. सेब
C. सुनार D. वैद्य

13. एक पंथ .... काज।

A. सौ B. नौ
C. सब D. दो

14. नाम बड़े और दर्शन .... ।

A. अच्छे B. सुन्दर
C. छोटे D. सच्चे

15. डूबते को .... का सहारा।

A. राम B. तिनके

C. नैया D. खिवैया

16. इसे दुर्भाग्य ही कहा जाएगा कि भारतीय राजनीति में .... का महत्व कम नहीं हो रहा।

A. उदारता B. धर्मपरायणता

C. सदाचार D. क्षेत्रवाद

17. जनता अपना नेता इसलिए चुनती है, ताकि जनजीवन में .... आए।

A. लहर B. खुशहाली

C. मस्ती D. प्रगति

18. हमारे देश की खेल संस्थाओं को लालफीताशाही के .... से मुक्त कराना बेहद जरूरी है।

A. चंगुल B. लगाम

C. ग्रंथि D. खेल

19. हमारे देश में अभी भी दूरदराज के ऐसे कई गाँव हैं जहाँ पहुँचने के लिए अभी तक .... मार्ग नहीं बना है।

A. सवारी B. पगडंडी

C. हवाई D. सड़क

20. बड़े राज्यों को .... छोटे राज्य बनाने के फायदे भी हैं नुकसान भी।

A. जोड़कर B. कटवाकर

C. तोड़कर D. सिकोड़कर

21. सुनसान जंगल में .... धुंध के बीच वो खंडहर भुतहा इमारत जैसा लग रहा था।

A. बर्फानी B. बादली

C. घनी D. डरावनी

22. भारत में खेती और खेतिहर दोनों संकट के .... से गुजर रहे हैं।

A. व्यवधान B. रोग

C. निदान D. दौर

23. एक व्यक्ति ने कहा कि पूरा परिवार .... काम करता है तो भी महीने की कमाई पूरी नहीं पड़ती।

A. बैठकर B. जोतकर

C. जुटाकर D. मिलकर

24. आज पूरी दुनिया में आजादी और .... के लिए आंदोलन चल रहे हैं।

A. गुलामी B. लोकतंत्र

C. राजतंत्र D. तानाशाही

25. पिछले कुछ .... में भ्रष्टाचार एक अहम मुद्दे के तौर पर उभरा है।

A. वर्षो B. पलों

C. युगों D. देशों

26. तन को कपड़ा न .... को रोटी।

A. खाने B. पेट

C. भूख D. मन

27. चमड़ी जाए। पर .... न जाए।

A. इज्जत B. पैसा

C. पगड़ी D. दमड़ी

28. महात्मा बुद्ध करुणा के साक्षात्कार .... थे।

A. विग्रह B. अनुग्रह

C. परिग्रह D. अपरिग्रह

उत्तरमाला

1	**2**	**3**	**4**	**5**	**6**	**7**	**8**	**9**	**10**
C	D	C	B	A	B	D	C	A	B
11	**12**	**13**	**14**	**15**	**16**	**17**	**18**	**19**	**20**
D	A	D	C	B	D	B	A	D	C
21	**22**	**23**	**24**	**25**	**26**	**27**	**28**		
C	D	D	B	A	A	D	A		

19

परिच्छेद में रिक्त स्थानों की पूर्ति

निर्देशः *नीचे दिए गए परिच्छेदों में कुछ रिक्त स्थान छोड़ दिए गए हैं तथा उन्हें प्रश्न संख्या से दर्शाया गया है। ये संख्याएं परिच्छेद के नीचे मुद्रित हैं और प्रत्येक के सामने A, B, C, D और E विकल्प दिए गए हैं। इन पाँचों में से कोई एक इस रिक्त-स्थान को पूरे परिच्छेद के सन्दर्भ में उपयुक्त ढंग से पूरा कर देता है। आपको यह विकल्प ज्ञात करना है, और उसका अक्षरांक ही उत्तर के रूप में दर्शाना है। आपको दिए गए विकल्पों में से सबसे उपयुक्त का चयन करना है।*

परिच्छेद-1

दुनिया के अनेक देशों की तरह हमारे **...(1)...** का भी दुर्भाग्य है कि आम, केला सेब, अंगूर, अनन्नास, अनार, पपीता सरीखे लोकप्रिय और प्रचुर मात्रा में **...(2)...** होने वाले फलों के सामने बेर, करोंदा, जामुन, बेल, खिरनी, फालसा, आँवला, अंजीर, कोकम, बड़हल, शरीफा जैसे फल कम मात्रा में पैदा होते हैं और बाजार में आसानी से उपलब्ध नहीं होते हैं इसलिए लोग इनका **...(3)...** भूलते जा रहे हैं। अनुपलब्धता की व्यावसायिक वजह यही बताई जाती है कि **...(4)...** कम या नहीं के बराबर होने के कारण थोक व्यापारी इनमें रुचि नहीं लेता। इसी तरह आम का उदाहरण लें। सुदूर दक्षिण से लेकर उत्तर-पूर्व तक फैले **...(5)...** भूभाग में इसकी लगभग एक हजार प्रजातियाँ उगाई जाती रही हैं जिनके रंग, रूप, गंध और स्वाद एक-दूसरे से **...(6)...** रहे हैं। पर आज की तारीख में दशहरी, लंगड़ा, अल्फांसो जैसी भारी माँग वाली प्रजातियों ने इतने **...(7)...** ढंग से बाजार को अपनी गिरफ्त में ले लिया है कि अन्य **...(8)...** कुछ सालों बाद हाथ में दिया लेकर ढूढ़ने पर भी नहीं मिलेंगी। कहते हैं कि पुरी के भगवान् जगन्नाथ को साल के तीन सौ पैंसठ दिन तीन सौ पैंसठ प्रजातियों के भात का **...(9)...** लगाया जाता था, ताकि साल में किसी किस्म के भात की पुनरावृत्ति न हो, पर आज तो यह किसी परी कथा जैसा **...(10)...** लगता है।

1. A. देश B. बाजार C. व्यापार D. कारोबार E. विज्ञान

2. A. उगे B. सजे C. पैदा D. बिके E. मिलते

3. A. याद B. स्वाद C. कायदा D. रंग E. सुगंध

4. A. कम B. संगठन C. लदाई D. आकर्षण E. माँग

5. A. भारी B. बर्फीले C. वनीय D. विशाल E. महान्

6. A. करीब B. अलग C. विपरीत D. खट्टे E. बढ़कर

7. A. आक्रामक B. जांबाज C. उछाल D. अच्छे E. आदर्श

8. A. बाड़ियाँ B. मंडियाँ C. प्रजातियाँ D. सहजातियाँ E. उपजातियाँ

9. A. थाल B. सजाया
C. चढ़ाया D. भोग
E. तिलक

10. A. व्यवहार B. उपन्यास
C. कल्पना D. काव्य
E. किस्सा

परिच्छेद-2

रमन्ना पहलवान नदी की ओर दौड़ता हुआ जा रहा था। उसे दूसरे ...(1)... जाना था। नाव के जाने का समय हो चुका था, और वह ...(2)... ही लेट हो गया था। नदी किनारे उसे नाव ...(3)... दी। वह और जी जान लगा कर भागा और छलांग लगा कर ...(4)... के ऊपर जा चढ़ा। इस कोशिश में वो नाव में गिर पड़ा। उसके ...(5)... फट गए और उसकी कोहनी ...(6)... गई, जिसमें से खून टप-टप टपकने लगा। मगर वो ...(7)... था। उसने नाव को आखिर पकड़ लिया था। वो खुशी से उठा और चिल्लाया– मैंने नाव को पकड़ ही लिया। लेट हो गया था, मगर मुझे नाव ...(8)... मिल ही गई। पास में बैठे दूसरे यात्री ने अपना ...(9)... समेटते हुए रमन्ना को बताया– ये नाव जा नहीं रही है, बल्कि आ रही है, और अभी ही ...(10)... लगी है!

1. A. गाँव B. महल
C. घर D. दिन
E. नाले

2. A. कब का B. तब से
C. सब से D. पीछे
E. पहले

3. A. खड़ी B. दिखाई
C. चली D. दर्शन
E. पड़ी

4. A. चट्टान B. पहाड़
C. लंगर D. नाव
E. पत्थर

5. A. चादर B. कंबल
C. कपड़े D. अरमान
E. सामान

6. A. रह B. बह
C. झुक D. उठ
E. छिल

7. A. प्रसन्न B. उदात्त
C. उद्विग्न D. अधीर
E. अप्रसन्न

8. A. जाकर B. चाहे
C. सवारी D. आखिरकार
E. आकर

9. A. तशरीफ B. सामान
C. स्थान D. डंडा
E. बयान

10. A. लाने B. सुस्ताने
C. किनारे D. बहने
E. आने

उत्तरमाला

परिच्छेद-1

1	2	3	4	5
A	C	B	E	D
6	**7**	**8**	**9**	**10**
E	D	C	D	E

परिच्छेद-2

1	2	3	4	5
A	E	B	D	C
6	**7**	**8**	**9**	**10**
E	A	D	B	C

20

अर्थपूर्ण वाक्य बनाना

निर्देशः *निम्नलिखित वाक्यों (1), (2), (3), (4) तथा (5) को इस प्रकार उचित क्रम में लगाएं कि एक अर्थपूर्ण परिच्छेद बन जाए। फिर उनके नीचे दिए गए प्रश्नों के उत्तर दीजिए—*

परिच्छेद-1

(1) नाजुक बालक को देख कोई यह करने के लिए तैयार नहीं था तो बालक ने खुद एक बहुत गरम सलाख फोड़े पर लगा दी।

(2) वैद्य ने कहा फोड़ा पक नहीं रहा है इसलिए ठीक नहीं हो रहा है।

(3) एक छोटे से बालक को बाँह में एक फोड़ा हुआ था।

(4) उपाय में उसे गरम सलाख से दागने पर ठीक होगा ऐसा बताया।

(5) दर्द बहुत हो रहा था पर फोड़ा ठीक नहीं हो रहा था।

1. पहला वाक्य कौन-सा होगा?
A. (1) B. (2)
C. (3) D. (4)
E. (5)

2. दूसरा वाक्य कौन-सा होगा?
A. (1) B. (2)
C. (3) D. (4)
E. (5)

3. तीसरा वाक्य कौन-सा होगा?
A. (1) B. (2)
C. (3) D. (4)
E. (5)

4. चौथा वाक्य कौन-सा होगा?
A. (1) B. (2)
C. (3) D. (4)
E. (5)

5. अन्तिम वाक्य कौन-सा होगा?
A. (1) B. (2)
C. (3) D. (4)
E. (5)

परिच्छेद-2

निर्देशः *नीचे (1), (2), (3), (4), (5) और (6) में छः कथन दिए गए हैं। इन सभी कथनों को इस तरह व्यवस्थित कीजिए कि छहों कथनों का एक अर्थपूर्ण परिच्छेद बन जाएं। फिर उसके बाद दिए गए प्रश्नों का उत्तर दीजिए।*

(1) भारतीय नारी त्याग, बलिदान, साहस, शक्ति तथा सेवा की सजीव मूर्ति है।

(2) नारी का सम्मान करके ही पुरुष का जीवन कुसुम सुवासित होता है।

(3) उसकी शक्ति के आगे यमराज को भी हारना पड़ा।

(4) घर की व्यवस्थापिका होने के कारण वह गृहलक्ष्मी कही जाती है।

(5) सावित्री ने अपने पति सत्यवान को पुनर्जीवित करने के लिए यमराज का भी पीछा किया।

(6) सीता, सावित्री, वीरांगना लक्ष्मीबाई और तपस्विनी उर्मिला भारतीय नारियों का आदर्श हैं।

1. निम्न में से तीसरा वाक्य कौन-सा होना चाहिए?
A. (2) B. (3)
C. (5) D. (4)
E. (6)

2. अवतरण का पहला वाक्य कौन-सा है?
A. (1) B. (3)
C. (2) D. (4)
E. (5)

3. इस अवतरण का चौथा वाक्य होगा–
A. (2) B. (3)
C. (4) D. (6)
E. (1)

4. अवतरण का अन्तिम वाक्य कौन-सा होना चाहिए?
A. (4) B. (2)
C. (3) D. (5)
E. (6)

5. अवतरण का पाँचवाँ वाक्य होगा–
A. (2) B. (3)
C. (4) D. (5)
E. (6)

परिच्छेद-3

निर्देशः *नीचे (1), (2), (3), (4) तथा (5) में पाँच वाक्य दिए गए हैं। इन वाक्यों को इस तरह क्रमबद्ध कीजिए कि एक अर्थपूर्ण परिच्छेद बन जाए। उसके बाद नीचे दिए गए प्रश्नों के उत्तर दीजिए–*

(1) बहुत शोर सुनकर दोनों भाई जाग उठे, उनके कुछ देखने, समझने से पहले एक हाथी ने छोटे भाई के गले में फूलों की माला डाल दी।

(2) दो भाई रोजगार की तलाश में अपने गाँव से चले।

(3) राजा बने छोटे भाई ने बड़े भाई को अपना मंत्री बनाया और दोनों वहीं रहने लगे।

(4) चलते-चलते एक नगर की सीमा पर पहुँचे और थकावट के कारण विश्राम के लिए एक पेड़ के नीचे सो गए।

(5) इतने में जोर शोर से लोग चिल्लाने लगे–हमारे नए राजा मिल गए।

1. दूसरा वाक्य कौन-सा होना चाहिए?
A. (1) B. (2)
C. (3) D. (4)
E. (5)

2. अन्तिम वाक्य कौन-सा होना चाहिए?
A. (1) B. (2)
C. (3) D. (4)
E. (5)

3. पहला वाक्य कौन-सा होना चाहिए?
A. (1) B. (2)
C. (3) D. (4)
E. (5)

4. चौथा वाक्य कौन-सा होना चाहिए?
A. (1) B. (2)
C. (3) D. (4)
E. (5)

5. तीसरा वाक्य कौन-सा होना चाहिए?
A. (1) B. (2)
C. (3) D. (4)
E. (5)

उत्तरमाला

परिच्छेद-1

1	2	3	4	5
C	E	B	D	A

परिच्छेद-2

1	2	3	4	5
C	A	B	E	A

परिच्छेद-3

1	2	3	4	5
D	C	B	A	E

21

अवतरण पर आधारित प्रश्न

निर्देशः *निम्नलिखित अवतरणों को ध्यानपूर्वक पढ़कर उस पर आधारित दिए गए प्रश्नों के उत्तर में से सही उत्तर का चयन कीजिए–*

अवतरण-1

शरीर और मिट्टी को लेकर संसार की असारता पर बहुत कुछ कहा जा सकता है, परन्तु यह भी ध्यान देने की बात है कि जितने सारतत्व जीवन के लिए अनिवार्य हैं, वे सब मिट्टी से ही मिलते हैं। जिन फूलों को हम अपनी प्रिय वस्तुओं का उपमान बनाते हैं, वे सब मिट्टी की ही उपज हैं। रूप, रस, गंध, स्पर्श– इन्हें कौन सम्भव करता है? माना कि मिट्टी और धूल में अन्तर है, लेकिन उतना ही जितना शब्द और रस में, देह और प्राण में, चाँद और चाँदनी में। धूल वह, जिसे गोधूलि शब्द में हमने अमर कर दिया है। अमराइयों के पीछे छिपे हुए सूर्य की किरणों में जो धूलि सोने को मिट्टी कर देती है, सूर्यास्त के उपरांत लीक पर गाड़ी के निकल जाने के बाद जो रूई के बादल की तरह या ऐरावत हाथी के नक्षत्र-पथ की भाँति जहाँ की तहाँ स्थिर रह जाती है, धूल उसका नाम है।

गोधूलि पर कितने कवियों ने अपनी कलम नहीं तोड़ दी, लेकिन यह गोधूलि गाँव की अपनी सम्पत्ति है, जो शहरों के बाँटे नहीं बँटी और गाँवों में भी जिस धूलि को कवियों ने अमर किया है, वह हाथी-घोड़ों के पग-संचालन से उत्पन्न होने वाली धूल नहीं है, वरन् गो-गोपालों के पदों की धूलि है। हमारी देशभक्ति धूल को माथे से न लगाएं तो कम-से-कम उस पर पैर तो रखे। किसान के हाथ-पैर, मुँह पर छाई हुई यह धूल हमारी सभ्यता से क्या कहती है? हम काँच को प्यार करते हैं, धूलि भरे हीरे में धूल ही दिखाई देती है, भीतर की कांति आँखों से ओझल रहती है, लेकिन ये हीरे अमर हैं और एक दिन अपनी अमरता का प्रमाण भी देंगे। अभी तो उन्होंने अटूट होने का ही प्रमाण दिया है– "हीरा वही घन चोट न टूटे।" वे पलटकर चोट भी करेंगे और तब काँच और हीरे का भेद जानना बाकी न रहेगा। तब हम हीरे से लिपटी हुई धूल को भी माथे से लगाना सीखेंगे।

1. निम्नलिखित में से किससे मिट्टी और धूल शब्द युग्म की तुलना की गई है?
A. शब्द और अर्थ से
B. देह और दिमाग से
C. शब्द और रस से
D. उपर्युक्त में से किसी से नहीं

2. गद्यांश में 'गोधूलि' कहा गया है–
A. अखाड़ों की धूल
B. मोटर गाड़ियों के चलने से उड़ती धूल
C. गो-गोपालों के पदों की धूल
D. हाथी-घोड़ों के पग-संचालन से उड़ती धूल

3. 'रूई के बादल की तरह' से अलंकार है–
A. उपमा   B. वक्रोक्ति
C. उत्प्रेक्षा   D. रूपक

4. "हम काँच को प्यार करते हैं।" का क्या आशय है?
A. ऊपरी चमक-दमक ही देखते हैं
B. नकली चीजों को पसन्द करते हैं
C. धूल को पसन्द नहीं करते
D. हमें नाजुक चीजें ही पसन्द हैं

5. 'हीरा वही घन चोट न टूटे'। वस्तुतः किसके लिए प्रयुक्त है?
A. काँच के लिए   B. हीरे के लिए
C. किसानों के लिए   D. धूल के लिए

अवतरण-2

आम आदमी की कोशिश होती है कि वह आम आदमी न बना रहे, कुछ खास करके दिखाए। आम आदमी समाज में अपनी छाप नहीं छोड़ पाता। समाज की अधिकांश गतिविधियों में खास आदमी भाग लेता है। खास आदमी आम आदमी को प्रायः मूर्ख समझते हैं। ऐसा वह आम आदमी को न समझ पाने के कारण करते हैं। खास आदमी अपने कार्यों की प्रतिक्रिया आम आदमी पर परखते हैं, किन्तु आम आदमी प्रायः प्रतिक्रिया विहीन बना रहता है, आम आदमी का आम होना ही खास आदमियों को खास बनाता है। खास लोग आम आदमी को उसके बहिरंग से मापते हैं। वे आम आदमी को छिलका भर समझ लेते हैं। उसके अभ्यंतर में जो दृढ़ गुठली है, उसे नहीं पहचानते। आम आदमी को, गुठली को निगल जाना कठिन होता है। छिलका हटाने पर उसकी दम-खम प्रकट होती है। आम आदमी जब गुठली की तरह फँस जाता है, तो इतिहास को बदल डालता है। आम आदमी को आम की तरह निचोड़ डालने की भूख खास आदमी किया करते हैं। आम आदमी जब अपने को व्यक्त करता है तो समाज का मौसम बदल जाता है। तूफान उमड़ जाता है। इतिहास बदल देने के बाद आम आदमी फिर से आम होता जाता है। उसकी प्रतिक्रिया शान्त हो जाती है। खास आदमी आम आदमी के इस स्वभाव को नहीं समझ पाते। इसे समझने के लिए आम आदमी ही बनना पड़ता है।

1. आम आदमी की खास बात यही है कि–
A. वह अशान्त होता है
B. वह आम होता है
C. वह बहुत सोच-समझकर कदम उठाता है
D. वह खास आदमी से नफरत करता है

2. आम आदमी जब गुठली की तरह फँस जाता है, तो–
A. इतिहास बदल जाता है
B. खास आदमी घबरा जाता है
C. वह खास आदमी बन जाता है
D. समाज़ में उथल-पुथल मच जाती है

3. अवतरण की भाषा है–
A. सरल B. हास्यास्पद
C. कटाक्षपूर्ण D. ये सभी

4. खास आदमी किस प्रकार विशिष्ट बनते हैं?
A. अपनी योग्यताओं के कारण
B. अपने जनसम्पर्क के कारण
C. आम आदमी के आम होने के कारण
D. उपर्युक्त सभी

5. समाज-परिवर्तन का काम किसने किया है?
A. देवताओं ने B. खास आदमी ने
C. आम आदमी ने D. शासकों ने

उत्तरमाला

अवतरण-1

1	2	3	4	5
C	C	A	A	C

अवतरण-2

1	2	3	4	5
B	A	D	C	C

22

वर्तनी की त्रुटियाँ

निर्देशः *नीचे प्रत्येक प्रश्न में A, B, C और D अक्षरांक में चार शब्द दिए गए हैं। जिनमें से एक में वर्तनी सम्बन्धी त्रुटि हो सकती है। उस त्रुटियुक्त शब्द का अक्षरांक ही आपका उत्तर होगा। यदि चारों शब्दों की वर्तनी सही है तो उत्तर दीजिए E अर्थात् 'सभी सही हैं'।*

1. A. अप्रयुक्त B. अतीषयोक्ति C. अशोध्य D. सम्मति E. सभी सही हैं

2. A. अभ्युक्ति B. इष्टतम C. अपुरित D. उपस्थित E. सभी सही हैं

3. A. उत्तरजिवीता B. प्रारक्षित C. क्षैतिज D. आयातित E. सभी सही हैं

4. A. आस्थगित B. आतिथ्य C. अंतरिम D. निर्धारित E. सभी सही हैं

5. A. किफायत B. परिस्थिति C. संतुलित D. असिंचीत E. सभी सही हैं

6. A. तात्पर्य B. महोत्सव C. दंभ D. कृशक E. सभी सही हैं

7. A. लक्षण B. व्यंजन C. पगडंडी D. पारंगत E. सभी सही हैं

8. A. स्थानापन्न B. व्यावशयिक C. कोशिका D. आर्थिक E. सभी सही हैं

9. A. दांडधिकारी B. प्राधिकरण C. आदित्य D. क्रियान्वयन E. सभी सही हैं

10. A. गोपनीयता B. कार्यवाही C. उत्रदायित्व D. वयस्क E. सभी सही हैं

11. A. चूल्लु B. जीविका C. ठिठोली D. तकली E. सभी सही हैं

12. A. नजरिया B. पंडीताइ C. फरियादी D. बधाई E. सभी सही हैं

13. A. प्रकाशकीय B. फाल्गुन C. बधिर D. भोतिक E. सभी सही हैं

14. A. हौसला B. स्वीकृति C. व्यवासायिक D. लिपाई E. सभी सही हैं

15. A. फलित B. बटोही C. भजनीक D. मंडली E. सभी सही हैं

16. A. अनामिष B. अपरिहार्य C. किफायती D. गिलाफ E. सभी सही हैं

17. A. गोधुलि B. चांचल्य C. जिजीविषु D. तमोली E. सभी सही हैं

18. A. तितिक्षा B. दखलंदाजी
C. दिप्ति D. दैनिकी
E. सभी सही हैं

19. A. नजदिकी B. नियोक्ता
C. परिणीता D. पाणिग्रहण
E. सभी सही हैं

20. A. पुनीत B. प्रख्यापीत
C. फरोख्त D. बुजुर्गी
E. सभी सही हैं

21. A. अद्‌भुत B. व्यंग्य
C. अदृश्य D. समारंभ
E. सभी सही हैं

22. A. लक्षण B. महात्मन
C. सम्पर्क D. कर्तज्ञ
E. सभी सही हैं

23. A. गझिन B. आशय
C. निशपादन D. आकर्षण
E. सभी सही हैं

24. A. उत्तरीय B. स्थान्नापन
C. कुंभ D. असामान्य
E. सभी सही हैं

25. A. न्ययाधिश B. पुरस्कृत
C. वारिद D. अधिशासी
E. सभी सही हैं

26. A. चिनाई B. तंबूल
C. ठिठोली D. तन्मय
E. सभी सही हैं

27. A. अगड़ाइ B. गठीला
C. खिलाफ D. कल्पनातीत
E. सभी सही हैं

28. A. सूरत B. वैधव्य
C. लतीका D. रेगिस्तान
E. सभी सही हैं

29. A. इति B. अखिलेश
C. कबूतर D. खेरात
E. सभी सही हैं

30. A. चमत्कृत B. जिल्द
C. तमोली D. दमित
E. सभी सही हैं

31. A. प्रहसन B. तात्पर्य
C. महसूल D. पाणिगृहण
E. सभी सही हैं

32. A. मस्तिष्क B. प्रोत्साहन
C. सम्वत् D. क्रियाविधि
E. सभी सही हैं

33. A. विचारणीय B. क्रन्दन
C. पर्यावर्ण D. उपलब्धि
E. सभी सही हैं

34. A. विसतृत B. वाग्विलास
C. तात्कालिक D. अलंकार
E. सभी सही हैं

35. A. दृष्टांत B. रूढ़ि
C. सूचि D. आचमन
E. सभी सही हैं

उत्तरमाला

1	**2**	**3**	**4**	**5**	**6**	**7**	**8**	**9**	**10**
B	C	A	A	D	D	E	B	A	C
11	**12**	**13**	**14**	**15**	**16**	**17**	**18**	**19**	**20**
A	B	D	C	C	A	A	C	A	B
21	**22**	**23**	**24**	**25**	**26**	**27**	**28**	**29**	**30**
E	D	C	B	A	B	A	C	D	E
31	**32**	**33**	**34**	**35**					
D	E	C	A	C					

ARITHMETIC

1. NUMBERS

The development of the number system started with natural numbers. These are generally known as counting numbers.

Natural Numbers

Numbers which start from 1 are known as natural numbers. It is denoted by N. The smallest natural number is 1. It is written as,

$$N = \{1, 2, 3, ..., \infty\}$$

Whole Numbers

A number which starts from zero (0) is known as whole number. It is denoted by W. It is written as,

$$W = \{0, 1, 2, 3, ..., \infty\}$$

Integers

Natural numbers along with 0 and their negatives are known as integers. It is denoted by I. It is written as,

$$I = \{..., -4, -3, -2, -1, 0, 1, 2, 3, 4, ...\}$$

Even Numbers

A number which is divisible by 2 is known as even numbers.

Such as, 2, 4, 6, 10, 12, 128, 432 etc.

Odd Numbers

A number which is not divisible by 2 is known as odd numbers:

Such as, 1, 3, 5, 7, 9, 11, 13, 21, 29, 123 etc.

Prime Numbers

A number which is divided by itself is known as prime numbers. The smallest prime number is 2.

Such as, 2, 3, 5, 7, 11, 13, 17, 19, 23, ... etc.

Composite Numbers

A number which is divided by itself and others also is known as composite numbers. The smallest composite number is 4.

Such as, 4, 6, 8, 9, 10, 12, 14, 15, 16, 18, ... etc.

There are 25 prime numbers between 1 to 100.

Such as, 2, 3, 5, 7, 11, 13, 17, 19, 23, 29, 31, 37, 41, 43, 47, 53, 59, 61, 67, 71, 73, 79, 83, 89, 97.

Test, whether a given number is prime or composite: If we want to test any number more than 100, whether it is prime or not, take an integer larger than the approximate square root of that number. Let it be x. Test the divisibility of the given number by every prime number less than x. If it is not divisible by any of them, then it is prime; otherwise it is composite number.

EXAMPLE: Which of the following numbers are prime numbers?

(*i*) 421 (*ii*) 671

SOLUTION:

(*i*) The square root of 421 is nearly 21.
Prime numbers less than 21 are 2, 3, 5, 7, 11, 13, 17, 19. Clearly, 421 is not divisible by any of them. So, 421 is a prime number.

(*ii*) The square root of 671 is nearly 26.
Prime numbers less than 26 are 2, 3, 5, 7, 11, 13, 17, 19, 23. Out of these, 671 is divisible by 11. So, 671 is not a prime number. Hence it is composite number.

The formulae given below are quite useful for quick multiplication:

(*i*) $(a + b)^2 = a^2 + 2ab + b^2$

(*ii*) $(a - b)^2 = a^2 - 2ab + b^2$

(iii) $a^2 - b^2 = (a+b)(a-b)$

(iv) $a^2 + b^2 = (a+b)^2 - 2ab$

(v) $(a+b)^3 = a^3 + b^3 + 3ab(a+b)$

(vi) $(a-b)^3 = a^3 - b^3 - 3ab(a-b)$

(vii) $a^3 + b^3 = (a+b)(a^2 - ab + b^2)$

(viii) $a^3 - b^3 = (a-b)(a^2 + ab + b^2)$

EXAMPLE: Simplify the following.

(i) $\dfrac{348 \times 348 \times 348 + 252 \times 252 \times 252}{348 \times 348 - 348 \times 252 + 252 \times 252}$

(ii) $\dfrac{261 \times 261 \times 261 - 77 \times 77 \times 77}{261 \times 261 + 261 \times 77 + 77 \times 77}$

SOLUTION:

(i) $\dfrac{348 \times 348 \times 348 + 252 \times 252 \times 252}{348 \times 348 - 348 \times 252 + 252 \times 252}$

Let $348 = a$

and $252 = b$

$\therefore$ Given expression is written as

$$\frac{a \times a \times a + b \times b \times b}{a \times a - a \times b + b \times b} = \frac{a^3 + b^3}{a^2 - ab + b^2}$$

$$= \frac{(a+b)(a^2 - ab + b^2)}{(a^2 - ab + b^2)} = a + b$$

$= 348 + 252 = 600.$

(ii) $\dfrac{261 \times 261 \times 261 - 77 \times 77 \times 77}{261 \times 261 + 261 \times 77 + 77 \times 77}$

Let $261 = a$

and $77 = b$

$$\therefore \frac{a^3 - b^3}{a^2 + ab + b^2} = \frac{(a-b)(a^2 + ab + b^2)}{(a^2 + ab + b^2)} = a - b$$

$\therefore \quad 261 - 77 = 184.$

If we divide a given number by another number, then

Dividend = (Divisor × Quotient) + Remainder

EXAMPLE: On dividing 18254 by a certain number, the quotient is 289 and the remainder is 47. Find the divisor.

SOLUTION: Here, Dividend = 18254

quotient = 289

remainder = 47

$$\therefore \quad \text{Divisor} = \frac{\text{Dividend} - \text{Remainder}}{\text{Quotient}}$$

$$= \frac{18254 - 47}{289} = \frac{18207}{289} = 63$$

Hence, divisor = 63.

EXAMPLE: What least number must be subtracted from 862 to get a number exactly divisible by 31?

SOLUTION: On dividing 862 by 31, the remainder obtained is 25.

Hence, the required number = 25.

MULTIPLE CHOICE QUESTIONS

1. The face value of 8 in the numeral 458926 is:

A. 8000 B. 8

C. 1000 D. 458000

2. $106 \times 106 + 94 \times 94 = x$, the value of x is:

A. 21032 B. 20032

C. 23032 D. 20072

3. If $m \times 48 = 173 \times 240$ then the value of m is:

A. 545 B. 685

C. 865 D. 495

4. $\left(1 - \dfrac{1}{3}\right)\left(1 - \dfrac{1}{4}\right)\left(1 - \dfrac{1}{5}\right) \ldots \left(1 - \dfrac{1}{n}\right) = x$

then the value of x is:

A. $\dfrac{1}{n}$ B. $\dfrac{2}{n}$

C. $\dfrac{2(n-1)}{n}$ D. $\dfrac{2}{n(n+1)}$

5. When simplified the product

$\left(2 - \dfrac{1}{3}\right)\left(2 - \dfrac{3}{5}\right)\left(2 - \dfrac{5}{7}\right) \ldots \left(2 - \dfrac{997}{999}\right)$ is

equal to:

A. $\dfrac{5}{999}$ B. $\dfrac{1001}{999}$

C. $\dfrac{1001}{3}$ D. None of these

6. Which number should replace both the asterisks in $\left(\frac{*}{21}\right) \times \left(\frac{*}{189}\right) = 1$?

A. 21 B. 63

C. 3969 D. 147

7. In a division sum, the divisor is 12 times the quotient and 5 times the remainder. If the remainder be 48, then the dividend is:

A. 240 B. 576

C. 4800 D. 4848

8. What least number must be subtracted from 1294 so that the remainder when divided by 9, 11, 13 will leave in each case the same remainder 6?

A. 0 B. 1

C. 2 D. 3

9. If $\sqrt{\left(1+\frac{27}{169}\right)} = \left(1+\frac{x}{13}\right)$, then the value of x is:

A. 1 B. 3

C. 5 D. 7

10. If $\frac{x}{y} = \frac{3}{4}$, then the value of $\left(\frac{6}{7}+\frac{y-x}{y+x}\right)$ equals:

A. $\frac{5}{7}$ B. $1\frac{1}{7}$

C. 1 D. 2

11. The largest natural number by which the product of three consecutive even natural numbers is always divisible, is:

A. 16 B. 24

C. 48 D. 96

12. The least number of five digits which is exactly divisible by 12, 15 and 18 is:

A. 10080 B. 10800

C. 18000 D. 81000

13. The least number which when divided by 8, 9, 12, 16 and 20 leaves the same remainder 1 in each case is:

A. 712 B. 271

C. 721 D. 720

14. The value of 0.8693 + 0.092 + 0.87 + 0.4 equals:

A. 2.3213 B. 2.2331

C. 3.2313 D. 2.2313

15. The prime numbers between 1 to 50 are:

A. 8 B. 12

C. 15 D. 10

ANSWERS

1	2	3	4	5	6	7	8	9	10
B	D	C	B	C	B	D	B	A	C
11	**12**	**13**	**14**	**15**					
C	A	C	D	C					

EXPLANATORY ANSWERS

1. The face value of 8 in the numeral 458926 is 8.

2. $106 \times 106 + 94 \times 94 = x$

$\Rightarrow (106)^2 + (94)^2 = x$

$\Rightarrow (100+6)^2 + (100-6)^2 = x$

$\Rightarrow 10000 + 1200 + 36 + 10000 - 1200 + 36 = x$

$\Rightarrow 20072 = x$

$\Rightarrow x = 20072.$

3. $\because m = \frac{173 \times 240}{48} = 865.$

4. $\left(1-\frac{1}{3}\right)\left(1-\frac{1}{4}\right)\left(1-\frac{1}{5}\right)...\left(1-\frac{1}{n}\right) = x$

$\because \quad 1-\frac{1}{3} = \frac{3-1}{3} = \frac{2}{3}$

$$1-\frac{1}{4} = \frac{4-1}{4} = \frac{3}{4}$$

$$1-\frac{1}{5} = \frac{5-1}{5} = \frac{4}{5}$$

$$\vdots$$

$$1-\frac{1}{n} = \frac{n-1}{n}$$

$$\therefore \frac{2}{3}\times\frac{3}{4}\times\frac{4}{5}\times\ldots\times\frac{n-2}{n-1}\times\frac{n-1}{n} = \frac{2}{n}$$

5. $\left(2-\frac{1}{3}\right)\left(2-\frac{3}{5}\right)\left(2-\frac{5}{7}\right)\ldots\left(2-\frac{997}{999}\right)$

$$2-\frac{1}{3} = \frac{6-1}{3} = \frac{5}{3}$$

$$2-\frac{3}{5} = \frac{10-3}{5} = \frac{7}{5}$$

$$2-\frac{5}{7} = \frac{14-5}{7} = \frac{9}{7}$$

$$2-\frac{997}{999} = \frac{1998-997}{999} = \frac{1001}{999}$$

$$\therefore \frac{5}{3}\times\frac{7}{5}\times\frac{9}{7}\times\ldots\times\frac{999}{997}\times\frac{1001}{999} = \frac{1001}{3}$$

6. $\frac{*}{21}\times\frac{*}{189} = 1$

$$\frac{x^2}{21\times 189} = 1$$

$\Rightarrow \quad x^2 = 21 \times 189 = 21 \times 21 \times 9$

$\Rightarrow \quad x^2 = 21 \times 21 \times 3 \times 3$

$\Rightarrow \quad x = 21 \times 3 = 63$

7. Let quotient = Q and remainder = R

Then, divisor = 12Q = 5R

Now, R = 48

$\Rightarrow$ 12Q = 5 × 48 $\Rightarrow$ Q = 20

$\therefore$ Dividend = (20 × 240 + 48) = 4848

8. The number when divided by 9, 11, 13 leaving remainder 6 = (LCM of 9, 11, 13) + 6 = 1293

$\therefore$ Required number = (1294 – 1293) = 1

9. $\sqrt{\left(1+\frac{27}{169}\right)} = \left(1+\frac{x}{13}\right)$

$\Rightarrow \quad \sqrt{\frac{169+27}{169}} = \frac{13+x}{13}$

$\Rightarrow \quad \sqrt{\frac{196}{169}} = \frac{x+13}{13}$

$\Rightarrow \quad \frac{14}{13} = \frac{x+13}{13}$

$\Rightarrow \quad x + 13 = 14$

$\Rightarrow \quad x = 1$

10. $\because \frac{x}{y} = \frac{3}{4}$ then,

$$\frac{6}{7}+\frac{y-x}{y+x} = \frac{6}{7}+\frac{\frac{y}{y}-\frac{x}{y}}{\frac{y}{y}+\frac{x}{y}}$$

[Divide numerator and denominator by y.]

$$= \frac{6}{7}+\frac{1-\frac{3}{4}}{1+\frac{3}{4}} = \frac{6}{7}+\frac{\frac{1}{4}}{\frac{7}{4}} = \frac{6}{7}+\frac{1}{7} = \frac{7}{7} = 1$$

11. It is 2 × 4 × 6 = 48

12. Least number of 5 digits is 10000.

LCM of 12, 15, 18 is 180.

On dividing 10000 by 180, the remainder is 100.

$\therefore$ The least number = 10000 + (180 – 100) = 10080.

13. Least number = (LCM of 8, 9, 12, 16, 20) + 1

2	8,	9,	12,	16,	20
2	4,	9,	6,	8,	10
2	2,	9,	3,	4,	5
3	1,	9,	3,	2,	5
	1,	3,	1,	2,	5

$\therefore$ LCM = $2^4 \times 3^2 \times 5$ = 720

Hence, least number = (720 + 1) = 721.

14.

```
   0.8693
   0.092
   0.87
 + 0.4
   2.2313
```

$\therefore$ The value of 0.8693 + 0.092 + 0.87 + 0.4 = 2.2313.

15. The prime numbers between 1 to 50 are 2, 3, 5, 7, 11, 13, 17, 19, 23, 29, 31, 37, 41, 43, 47.

Hence, there are 15 prime numbers between 1 to 50.

2. HCF AND LCM

FACTORS

The numbers are said to be factors of a given number when they exactly divide that number.

Example: Factors of 15 are 1, 3, 5 and 15 because each of these completely divides 15.

Highest Common Factor

The HCF of two or more than two numbers is the greatest number that divides each of them exactly. The highest common factor is also known as Greatest Common Divisor or Greatest Common Measure.

EXAMPLE: Let us consider two numbers 24 and 36. All possible factors of 24 are 1, 2, 3, 4, 6, 8, 12 and 24. All possible factors of 36 are 1, 2, 3, 4, 6, 9, 12, 18 and 36. The common factors of 24 and 36 are 1, 2, 3, 4, 6, 12. The greatest factor among these common factors is 12.

Hence, 12 is the HCF of 24 and 36.

EXAMPLE: Let us consider two numbers 18 and 30.

Now, $18 = 2 \times 3 \times 3$

and $30 = 2 \times 3 \times 5$

The factors common to the two numbers are 2 and 3. Hence the required HCF $= 2 \times 3 = 6$.

There are two methods of determining the HCF of two or more numbers.

(*i*) HCF by Factorization method

(*ii*) HCF by Division method.

HCF by Factorization Method

Express each one of the given number as the product of prime factors. Now choose common factors and take the product of these factors to obtain the required HCF.

EXAMPLE: Find the HCF of 126, 396 and 5400.

SOLUTION:
$$126 = 2 \times 3 \times 3 \times 7$$
$$396 = 2 \times 2 \times 3 \times 3 \times 11$$
$$5400 = 2 \times 2 \times 2 \times 3 \times 3 \times 3 \times 5 \times 5$$

Common factors are 2, 3 and 3.

Hence, the HCF $= 2 \times 3 \times 3 = 18$.

EXAMPLE: Find the HCF of 1056, 1584 and 2178.

SOLUTION:
$$1056 = 2^5 \times 3 \times 11$$
$$1584 = 2^4 \times 3^2 \times 11$$

and $2178 = 2 \times 3^2 \times 11^2$

Hence, HCF $= (2 \times 3 \times 11) = 66$.

HCF by Division Method

Suppose we have to find the HCF of two given numbers. Divide the larger number by the smaller one. Now, divide the divisor by the remainder. Repeat the process of dividing the preceding divisor by the remainder last obtained till zero is obtained as remainder. The last divisor is the required HCF.

Suppose we have to find the HCF of three numbers. Then HCF of [(HCF of any two numbers) and (the third number)] gives the HCF of three given numbers. Similarly, the HCF of more than three numbers may be obtained.

EXAMPLE: Find the HCF of 48, 168 and 324.

SOLUTION: Firstly, we find the HCF of 48 and 168.

```
48) 1 6 8 (3
  – 1 4 4
    -------
     2 4) 4 8 (2
          4 8
          ---
           0
          ---
```

Thus, HCF of 48 and 168 = 24.

Now, we find the HCF of 24 and 324.

```
24) 3 2 4 (13
  − 2 4
    8 4
  − 7 2
    1 2) 2 4 (2
         2 4
          0
```

Thus, the HCF of 48, 168 and 324 is 12.

Lowest Common Multiple

The LCM of two or more numbers is the lowest or least number which is exactly divisible by each of them. In other words, it is the lowest number which contains each of them as a factor.

LCM by Factorization

Resolve each one of the given numbers into a product of prime factors. Then LCM is the product of highest powers of all the factors.

EXAMPLE: Find the LCM of 72, 189 and 1026.

SOLUTION: $72 = 2^3 \times 3^2$

$189 = 3^3 \times 7$

and $1026 = 2 \times 3^3 \times 19$

$\therefore$ $\text{LCM} = 2^3 \times 3^3 \times 7 \times 19$

$= 8 \times 27 \times 7 \times 19 = 28728$

EXAMPLE: Find the LCM of 12, 15, 20 and 54 by short cut method.

SOLUTION:

2	12,	15,	20,	54
2	6,	15,	10,	27
3	3,	15,	5,	27
5	1,	5,	5,	9
	1,	1,	1,	9

$\therefore \text{LCM} = 2 \times 2 \times 3 \times 5 \times 9 = 540$

FORMULA

Product of two numbers = HCF × LCM.

$$\text{LCM} = \frac{\text{Product of numbers}}{\text{HCF}}$$

$$\text{HCF} = \frac{\text{Product of numbers}}{\text{LCM}}$$

$$\text{First number} = \frac{\text{LCM} \times \text{HCF}}{\text{2nd number}}$$

$$\text{2nd number} = \frac{\text{LCM} \times \text{HCF}}{\text{First number}}$$

HCF and LCM of Fractions

(*i*) $\text{HCF} = \dfrac{\text{HCF of numerators}}{\text{LCM of denominators}}$

(*ii*) $\text{LCM} = \dfrac{\text{LCM of numerators}}{\text{HCF of denominators}}$

EXAMPLE: Find the HCF and LCM of $\frac{3}{4}, \frac{6}{8}, \frac{15}{64}$ and $\frac{12}{32}$.

SOLUTION: $\text{HCF} = \dfrac{\text{HCF of 3, 6, 15, 12}}{\text{LCM of 4, 8, 64, 32}} = \dfrac{3}{64}$

$\text{LCM} = \dfrac{\text{LCM of 3, 6, 15, 12}}{\text{HCF of 4, 8, 64, 32}} = \dfrac{60}{4}$.

MULTIPLE CHOICE QUESTIONS

1. HCF of 1485 and 4356 is:
A. 189 B. 89
C. 99 D. 83

2. LCM of 18, 24, 42, 63 is:
A. 302 B. 604
C. 504 D. 404

3. Which of the following fractions is the greatest of all?

$$\frac{7}{8}, \frac{6}{7}, \frac{4}{5}, \frac{5}{6}$$

A. $\frac{6}{7}$ B. $\frac{4}{5}$
C. $\frac{5}{6}$ D. $\frac{7}{8}$

4. Which of the following is in ascending order?
A. $\frac{5}{7}, \frac{7}{8}, \frac{9}{11}$ B. $\frac{5}{7}, \frac{9}{11}, \frac{7}{8}$
C. $\frac{7}{8}, \frac{5}{7}, \frac{9}{11}$ D. $\frac{9}{11}, \frac{7}{8}, \frac{5}{7}$

5. HCF of three numbers is 12. If they be in the ratio 1 : 2 : 3, the numbers are:
A. 12, 24, 36 B. 10, 20, 30
C. 5, 10, 15 D. 4, 8, 12

6. The largest natural number which exactly divides the product of any four consecutive natural numbers is:
A. 6 B. 12
C. 24 D. 120

7. The traffic lights at three different road crossings change after every 48 seconds, 72 seconds and 108 seconds respectively. If they all change simultaneously at 8 : 20 : 00 hrs; then they will again change simultaneously at:
A. 8 : 27 : 12 hrs B. 8 : 27 : 24 hrs
C. 8 : 27 : 36 hrs D. 8 : 27 : 48 hrs

8. The HCF of two numbers is 16 and their LCM is 160. If one of the number is 32, then the other number is:
A. 48 B. 80
C. 96 D. 112

9. The HCF of two numbers is 12 and their difference is also 12. The numbers are:
A. 66, 78 B. 70, 82
C. 94, 106 D. 84, 96

10. The largest number which exactly divides 210, 315, 147 and 161 is:
A. 3 B. 7
C. 21 D. 4410

11. The least perfect square number which is divisible by 3, 4, 5, 6 and 8 is:
A. 900 B. 1200
C. 2500 D. 3600

12. The smallest number which is divisible by 12, 15, 20 and is a perfect square, is:
A. 400 B. 900
C. 1600 D. 3600

13. The sum of two numbers is 216 and their HCF is 27. The numbers are:
A. 54, 162 B. 108, 108
C. 27, 189 D. None of these

14. The HCF and LCM of two numbers are 44 and 264 respectively. If the first number is divided by 2, the quotient is 44. The other number is:
A. 33 B. 66
C. 132 D. 264

15. The number of prime factors in $2^{222} \times 3^{333} \times 5^{555}$ is:
A. 3 B. 1107
C. 1110 D. 1272

16. The number of prime factors in the expression $(6)^{10} \times (7)^{17} \times (11)^{27}$ is:
A. 54 B. 64
C. 71 D. 81

17. Three measuring rods are 64 cm, 80 cm and 96 cm in length. The least length of cloth that can be measured exact number of times using any one of the above rod is:
A. 0.96 m B. 19.20 m
C. 9.60 m D. 96.00 m

18. The product of two numbers is 1600 and their HCF is 5. The LCM of the numbers is:
A. 320 B. 1605
C. 1595 D. 8000

19. About the number of pairs which have 16 as their HCF and 136 as their LCM, we can definitely say that:
A. Only one such pair exists
B. Only two such pairs exist
C. Many such pairs exist
D. No such pair exist

20. The total number of prime factors of the product $(8)^{20} \times (15)^{24} \times (7)^{15}$ is:
A. 59 B. 98
C. 123 D. 138

ANSWERS

1	2	3	4	5	6	7	8	9	10
C	C	D	B	A	C	A	B	D	B
11	**12**	**13**	**14**	**15**	**16**	**17**	**18**	**19**	**20**
D	D	C	C	C	B	C	A	D	C

EXPLANATORY ANSWERS

1.
```
1485) 4 3 5 6 (2
      2 9 7 0
      -------
      1 3 8 6) 1 4 8 5 (1
               1 3 8 6
               -------
                   9 9) 1 3 8 6 (14
                        9 9
                        -----
                        3 9 6
                        3 9 6
                        -----
                          0
```
$\therefore$ HCF of 1485 and 4356 is 99.

2.

2	18,	24,	42,	63
3	9,	12,	21,	63
3	3,	4,	7,	21
7	1,	4,	7,	7
	1,	4,	1,	1

LCM of 18, 24, 42, 63 = $2 \times 3^2 \times 7 \times 4 = 504$.

3. $\frac{7}{8} = 0.875$, $\frac{6}{7} = 0.857$, $\frac{4}{5} = 0.8$

$\frac{5}{6} = 0.833$

Clearly, 0.875 is the greatest of all.

Hence, $\frac{7}{8}$ is the greatest of all.

4. $\frac{5}{7} = 0.714$, $\frac{7}{8} = 0.875$, $\frac{9}{11} = 0.818$

Now, $0.714 < 0.818 < 0.875$

Hence, $\frac{5}{7} < \frac{9}{11} < \frac{7}{8}$.

5. Let the numbers be x, $2x$ and $3x$.
Then, their HCF = x
According to the question, $x = 12$
$\therefore$ The numbers are 12, 24, 36.

6. $1 \times 2 \times 3 \times 4 = 24$
$\therefore$ Required number = 24.

7. LCM of 48, 72, 108 = 432
432 seconds = 7 min 12 seconds.
So, the next simultaneous change will take place at 8 : 27 : 12 hrs.

8. Other number $= \frac{\text{LCM} \times \text{HCF}}{\text{One number}} = \frac{160 \times 16}{32} = 80$

Hence, other number = 80.

9. 12 is not the HCF of given options A, B and C. Hence, D is correct answer.
In 84, 96, 12 is HCF of 84 and 96
Difference of 96 – 84 = 12
So, required numbers are 84 and 96.

10. HCF of 210, 315, 147 and 161 = 7
Hence, the required number = 7.

11.

2	3,	4,	5,	6,	8
2	3,	2,	5,	3,	4
3	3,	1,	5,	3,	2
	1,	1,	5,	1,	2

LCM of 3, 4, 5, 6, 8 = $2 \times 2 \times 3 \times 5 \times 2$
Required number
$= (2 \times 2 \times 3 \times 3 \times 5 \times 5 \times 2 \times 2) = 3600$

12. LCM of 12, 15 and 20 = 60
Hence, required number = $60 \times 60 = 3600$.

13. HCF of 54, 162 = 54
HCF of 108, 108 = 108
HCF of 27, 189 = 27
Hence, required numbers are 27 and 189.

14. According to the question,
First number = $2 \times 44 = 88$
Other number
$= \frac{\text{LCM} \times \text{HCF}}{\text{First number}} = \frac{264 \times 44}{88} = 132$

15. The number of prime factors in the given product = (222 + 333 + 555) = 1110

16. 2, 3, 7, 11 are prime numbers in the given expression. The number of prime factors in the given expression (10 + 10 + 17 + 27) = 64

17. Required length = (LCM of 64, 80, 96) cm
= 960 cm = 9.60 m.

18. $\text{LCM} = \frac{\text{Product of numbers}}{\text{HCF}} = \frac{1600}{5} = 320$

19. HCF is always a factor of LCM. So no two numbers exist with HCF = 16 and LCM = 136.

20. Since 2, 3, 5, 7 are prime numbers and the given expression is $(2^3)^{20} \times (3 \times 5)^{24} \times (7)^{15}$ *i.e.* $2^{60} \times 3^{24} \times 5^{24} \times 7^{15}$, so the number of prime factors in the given expression
$= (60 + 24 + 24 + 15) = 123$

3. SIMPLIFICATION

Simplification means expressing in a simpler form. In order to simplify an expression we use the operations in the following order which is easily remembered as "BODMAS".

(*i*) Bracket (*ii*) Of (*iii*) Division (*iv*) Multiplication (*v*) Addition (*vi*) Subtraction.

'Of' means multiplication but it is operated even before division.

While removing brackets, first of all bar bracket '—' and after that small bracket '( )' is removed. Thereafter curley bracket '{ }' and at last square bracket '[ ]' is removed.

EXAMPLE: Simplify: $100 \div 25 \times 6 + 16 - 32$

SOLUTION: $100 \div 25 \times 6 + 16 - 32$

$= 4 \times 6 + 16 - 32$

$= 24 + 16 - 32$

$= 40 - 32 = 8$

EXAMPLE: Simplify: $54 + 24 \div 4 - 8 \times 5 + 4 \times 3$

SOLUTION: $54 + 24 \div 4 - 8 \times 5 + 4 \times 3$

$= 54 + 6 - 40 + 12$

$= 72 - 40 = 32$

EXAMPLE: Simplify: $10 - \left[6 - \left\{7 - \left(6 - \overline{8 - 5}\right)\right\}\right]$

SOLUTION: $10 - \left[6 - \left\{7 - \left(6 - 3\right)\right\}\right]$

$= 10 - [6 - \{7 - 3\}]$

$= 10 - [6 - 4] = 10 - 2 = 8.$

EXAMPLE: Simplify: $\dfrac{12 \times 12 \times 12 - 1 \times 1 \times 1}{12 \times 12 + 12 \times 1 + 1 \times 1}$

SOLUTION: Let $a = 12$ and $b = 1$

$$\therefore \quad \frac{a \times a \times a - b \times b \times b}{a \times a + a \times b + b \times b} = \frac{a^3 - b^3}{a^2 + ab + b^2}$$

$$= \frac{(a-b)(a^2 + ab + b^2)}{(a^2 + ab + b^2)}$$

$= a - b = 12 - 1 = 11$

EXAMPLE: Simplify:

$$\frac{2.33 \times 2.33 \times 2.33 + 7.67 \times 7.67 \times 7.67}{2.33 \times 2.33 - 2.33 \times 7.67 + 7.67 \times 7.67}$$

SOLUTION: Let $a = 2.33$ and $b = 7.67$

$$\frac{a^3 + b^3}{a^2 - ab + b^2} = \frac{(a+b)(a^2 - ab + b^2)}{(a^2 - ab + b^2)} = (a + b)$$

$= 2.33 + 7.67 = 10$

MULTIPLE CHOICE QUESTIONS

1. $\dfrac{48 - 12 \times 3 + 9}{12 - 9 \div 3}$ equals:

A. 3
B. 21
C. $\dfrac{7}{3}$
D. $\dfrac{1}{3}$

2. $\dfrac{69 - 14 \times 3 + 2}{9 \times 5 - (5)^2}$ equals:

A. 1.45
B. 2.75
C. 26.5
D. 265

3. If $\frac{17.28 \div x}{3.6 \times 0.2} = 2$ then, the value of x is:

A. 120 B. 1.20

C. 12 D. 0.12

4. $171 \div 19 \times 9$ equals:

A. 0 B. 1

C. 18 D. 81

5. $3120 \div 26 + 13 \times 30$ equals:

A. 2400 B. 3900

C. 536 D. None of these

6. $\frac{31}{10} \times \frac{3}{10} + \frac{7}{5} \div 20$ equals:

A. 0 B. 1

C. 100 D. $\frac{107}{200}$

7. The simplification of $1 + \cfrac{1}{2 + \cfrac{1}{1 - \cfrac{1}{3}}}$ yields the result:

A. $\frac{2}{7}$ B. $\frac{7}{9}$

C. $\frac{9}{7}$ D. $\frac{13}{7}$

8. The value of $1 + \frac{1}{4 \times 3} + \frac{1}{4 \times 3^2} + \frac{1}{4 \times 3^3}$ up to four places of decimals is:

A. 1.1202 B. 1.1203

C. 1.1204 D. None of these

9. $\dfrac{\frac{1}{2} \div 4 + 20}{\frac{1}{2} \times 4 + 20}$ equals:

A. $\frac{81}{88}$ B. $2\frac{3}{11}$

C. $\frac{161}{176}$ D. 1

10. $3 \div \left[(8-5) \div \left\{(4-2) \div \left(2 + \frac{8}{13}\right)\right\}\right]$ equals:

A. $\frac{13}{17}$ B. $\frac{68}{13}$

C. $\frac{17}{13}$ D. $\frac{13}{68}$

11. $10 - [9 - \{8 - (7 - 6)\}] - 5$ is equal to:

A. -5 B. 1

C. 3 D. 9

12. $\dfrac{\frac{1}{5} \div \frac{1}{5} \text{ of } \frac{1}{5}}{\frac{1}{5} \text{ of } \frac{1}{5} \div \frac{1}{5}}$ is equal to:

A. 1 B. 5

C. $\frac{1}{5}$ D. 25

13. The value of $1 + \cfrac{1}{1 + \cfrac{1}{1 + \cfrac{1}{9}}}$ is:

A. $\frac{29}{19}$ B. $\frac{10}{19}$

C. $\frac{29}{10}$ D. $\frac{10}{9}$

14. $\frac{3}{48}$ is what part of $\frac{1}{12}$?

A. $\frac{3}{7}$ B. $\frac{1}{12}$

C. $\frac{4}{3}$ D. None of these

15. How many $\frac{1}{8}$ s are there in $37\frac{1}{2}$?

A. 300 B. 400

C. 500 D. None of these

ANSWERS

1	2	3	4	5	6	7	8	9	10
C	A	C	D	D	B	C	B	C	A
11	**12**	**13**	**14**	**15**					
C	D	A	D	A					

EXPLANATORY ANSWERS

1. $\dfrac{48-12\times3+9}{12-9\div3}=\dfrac{48-36+9}{12-3}$

$=\dfrac{57-36}{9}=\dfrac{21}{9}=\dfrac{7}{3}.$

2. $\dfrac{69-14\times3+2}{9\times5-5^2}=\dfrac{69-42+2}{45-25}$

$=\dfrac{71-42}{20}=\dfrac{29}{20}=1.45.$

3. $17.28\div x=2\times3.6\times0.2$

$\Rightarrow \dfrac{17.28}{x}=1.44\Rightarrow 1.44\,x=17.28$

$\Rightarrow \quad x=\dfrac{17.28}{1.44}=\dfrac{1728}{144}=12.$

4. $171\div19\times9=9\times9=81.$

5. $3120\div26+13\times30=120+390=510.$

6. $\dfrac{31}{10}\times\dfrac{3}{10}+\dfrac{7}{5}\div20=\dfrac{31}{10}\times\dfrac{3}{10}+\dfrac{7}{5}\times\dfrac{1}{20}$

$=\dfrac{93}{100}+\dfrac{7}{100}=\dfrac{93+7}{100}=\dfrac{100}{100}=1$

7. $1+\dfrac{1}{2+\dfrac{1}{1-\dfrac{1}{3}}}=1+\dfrac{1}{2+\dfrac{1}{\dfrac{3-1}{3}}}$

$=1+\dfrac{1}{2+\dfrac{1}{\dfrac{2}{3}}}=1+\dfrac{1}{2+\dfrac{3}{2}}=1+\dfrac{1}{\dfrac{7}{2}}=1+\dfrac{2}{7}=\dfrac{9}{7}$

8. $1+\dfrac{1}{4\times3}+\dfrac{1}{4\times3^2}+\dfrac{1}{4\times3^3}$

$=1+\dfrac{1}{12}+\dfrac{1}{36}+\dfrac{1}{108}=\dfrac{108+9+3+1}{108}$

$=\dfrac{121}{108}=1.1203$

9. $\dfrac{\dfrac{1}{2}\div4+20}{\dfrac{1}{2}\times4+20}=\dfrac{\dfrac{1}{8}+20}{2+20}=\dfrac{\dfrac{1+160}{8}}{22}$

$=\dfrac{161}{8\times22}=\dfrac{161}{176}$

10. $3\div\left[(8-5)\div\left\{(4-2)\div\left(2+\dfrac{8}{13}\right)\right\}\right]$

$=3\div\left[3\div\left\{2\div\dfrac{34}{13}\right\}\right]$

$=3\div\left[3\div\left\{2\times\dfrac{13}{34}\right\}\right]=3\div\left[3\div\dfrac{13}{17}\right]$

$=3\div\left[3\times\dfrac{17}{13}\right]=3\div\dfrac{51}{13}=3\times\dfrac{13}{51}=\dfrac{13}{17}$

11. $10-[9-\{8-(7-6)\}]-5$

$=10-[9-\{8-1\}]-5$

$=10-[9-7]-5=10-2-5=10-7=3$

12. $\dfrac{\dfrac{1}{5}\div\dfrac{1}{5}\text{ of }\dfrac{1}{5}}{\dfrac{1}{5}\text{ of }\dfrac{1}{5}\div\dfrac{1}{5}}=\dfrac{\dfrac{1}{5}\div\dfrac{1}{25}}{\dfrac{1}{25}\div\dfrac{1}{5}}=\dfrac{\dfrac{1}{5}\times\dfrac{25}{1}}{\dfrac{1}{25}\times\dfrac{5}{1}}=\dfrac{\dfrac{5}{1}}{\dfrac{1}{5}}$

$=\dfrac{5}{1}\times\dfrac{5}{1}=25$

13. $1+\dfrac{1}{1+\dfrac{1}{1+\dfrac{1}{9}}}=1+\dfrac{1}{1+\dfrac{1}{\dfrac{10}{9}}}=1+\dfrac{1}{1+\dfrac{9}{10}}$

$=1+\dfrac{1}{\dfrac{19}{10}}=1+\dfrac{10}{19}=\dfrac{29}{19}$

14. Let x of $\dfrac{1}{12}=\dfrac{3}{48}$

$\Rightarrow \quad \dfrac{x}{12}=\dfrac{3}{48}\Rightarrow 48x=36$

$\Rightarrow \quad x=\dfrac{36}{48}=\dfrac{3}{4}.$

15. Let n times $\dfrac{1}{8}=37\dfrac{1}{2}$

$\Rightarrow \quad \dfrac{n}{8}=\dfrac{75}{2}\Rightarrow 2n=8\times75$

$\Rightarrow \quad n=\dfrac{8\times75}{2}=4\times75=300.$

4. SURDS AND INDICES

SURDS

If 'a' is a rational number and n is a positive integer such that nth root of 'a', *i.e.*, $a^{1/n}$ or $\sqrt[n]{a}$ is an irrational number, then $a^{1/n}$ is called a surd or radical.

In other words, an irrational root of a rational number is called a surd. The symbol '√' is known as surd sign or radical.

For example, $\sqrt{2} = 2^{1/2}$ = Square root of 2

$\sqrt[3]{5} = 5^{1/3}$ = Cube root of 5

Pure and Mixed Surds

Pure Surd: A surd which has unity only as rational factor, the other factor being irrational, is called a pure surd.

For example, $\sqrt{2}$, $\sqrt[3]{3}$, $\sqrt[5]{3}$ are pure surds.

Mixed Surd: A surd which has a rational factor other than unity, the other factor being irrational, is called a mixed surds.

For example, $2\sqrt{5}$ $3\sqrt[4]{7}$, $5\sqrt[3]{11}$ are mixed surds.

Rationalising Factor: When the product of two surds is a rational number, then each of them is called the rationalising factor (R.F.) of the other.

For example, $3\sqrt{5} \times \sqrt{5} = 3 \times 5 = 15$

$\therefore$ $\sqrt{5}$ is a rationalising factor of $3\sqrt{5}$.

Important Formulae Based on Surds

$\sqrt[n]{a} = a^{1/n}$ and it is called a surd of order n.

(i) $\sqrt[n]{a^n} = a$

(ii) $\sqrt[n]{ab} = \sqrt[n]{a}\sqrt[n]{b}$

(iii) $\sqrt{a} \times \sqrt{a} = a$

(iv) $\sqrt{a} \times \sqrt{b} = \sqrt{ab}$

(v) $\sqrt{a^2 b} = a\sqrt{b}$

(vi) $\left(\sqrt{a} + \sqrt{b}\right)^2 = a + b + 2\sqrt{ab}$

(vii) $\left(\sqrt{a} - \sqrt{b}\right)^2 = a + b - 2\sqrt{ab}$

(viii) $\left(\sqrt{a} + \sqrt{b}\right)\left(\sqrt{a} - \sqrt{b}\right) = a - b$ where a and b are positive rational numbers.

INDICES

Let n be a positive integer and 'a' be a real number. The continued product of n factors each equal to a *e.g.*, $a \times a \times a \times \ldots \times n$ times is written as a^n and is called "n^{th} power of a" or "a raised to the power n".

The expression a^n is termed as power function or simply power, a is called the base and n is called index or exponent of the power a^n.

For example, 2^2 = square of 2, 2^3 = cube of 2, etc.

Laws of Indices

(i) $a^m \times a^n = a^{m+n}$

(ii) $a^m \times a^n \times a^p \times \ldots = a^{m+n+p+\ldots}$

(iii) $\dfrac{a^m}{a^n} = a^{m-n}$, if $m > n$

(iv) $\dfrac{a^m}{a^n} = \dfrac{1}{a^{n-m}}$, if $m < n$

(v) $(a^m)^n = a^{mn}$

(vi) $(ab)^n = a^n b^n$

(vii) $a^0 = 1$

(viii) If $a^m = a^n$ then $m = n$

(ix) If $a^m = b^m$ then $a = b$

(x) $\dfrac{a^m}{a^m} = a^{m-m} = a^0 = 1$

MULTIPLE CHOICE QUESTIONS

1. If the infinite series is $x = \sqrt{6+\sqrt{6+\sqrt{6+...}}}$ then the value of x is:

A. 2.5 B. 3
C. 6 D. 8

2. If $\frac{9^n \cdot 3^2 \cdot 3^n - (27)^n}{3^{3m} \cdot 2^3} = \frac{1}{27}$, then the value of $(m-n)$ is:

A. 1 B. 2
C. $\sqrt{3}$ D. $\sqrt{\frac{2}{3}}$

3. If $x = \frac{\sqrt{5}+\sqrt{3}}{\sqrt{5}-\sqrt{3}}$ and $y = \frac{\sqrt{5}-\sqrt{3}}{\sqrt{5}+\sqrt{3}}$, then $(x + y)$ is equal to:

A. 8 B. 6
C. $2\sqrt{15}$ D. $2\left(\sqrt{5}+\sqrt{3}\right)$

4. $2^{x+1} + 2^{x+3} = 2560$, then x is equal to:

A. 12 B. 11
C. 8 D. 6

5. If $\frac{5+2\sqrt{3}}{7+4\sqrt{3}} = a + b\sqrt{3}$, then b is equal to:

A. –6 B. 6
C. –11 D. 11

6. If $\frac{(21)^{5.36}}{(21)^{3.47}} = (21)^x$, then the value of x is:

A. 8.88 B. 1.54
C. 9.32 D. 1.89

7. $\sqrt{24} + \sqrt{12}$ equal to:

A. $\sqrt{36}$ B. $2\sqrt{6} + 2\sqrt{3}$
C. $6\sqrt{2}$ D. $\sqrt{288}$

8. If $a^b = 64$, where a and b are positive integers then $(a - b)^{a+b-4}$ is:

A. 0 B. 1
C. 2 D. $\frac{1}{2}$

9. The value of $\frac{5^{10+n} \cdot 25^{3n-4}}{5^{7n}}$ is:

A. 5 B. 8
C. 25 D. 16

10. $3^x - 3^{x-1} = 18$, then the value of x^x is:

A. 3 B. 8
C. 27 D. 216

11. If $x = \sqrt{10+\sqrt{25+\sqrt{121}}}$, then x is equal to:

A. –2 only B. 2 only
C. ±4 D. 4 only

12. If $a^x = b^y = c^z$ and $b^2 = ac$, then y is equal to:

A. $\frac{xz}{x+z}$ B. $\frac{xz}{2(x-z)}$
C. $\frac{xz}{2(z-x)}$ D. $\frac{2xz}{x+z}$

13. $\frac{5^{n+3} - 6 \times 5^{n+1}}{9 \times 5^n - 5^n \times 2^2}$ is equal to:

A. 5 B. 19
C. 25 D. 95

14. The value of $\left(\frac{x^a}{x^b}\right)^{(a+b)} \times \left(\frac{x^b}{x^c}\right)^{(b+c)} \times \left(\frac{x^c}{x^a}\right)^{(c+a)}$ is equal to:

A. 0 B. 2
C. 1 D. 3

15. If $\sqrt{3^n} = 729$, then the value of n is:

A. 12 B. 8
C. 10 D. 6

ANSWERS

1	2	3	4	5	6	7	8	9	10
B	A	A	C	A	D	B	B	C	C
11	**12**	**13**	**14**	**15**					
D	D	B	C	A					

EXPLANATORY ANSWERS

1. $x = \sqrt{6+x}$

Squaring both sides

$$x^2 = 6 + x$$

$\Rightarrow$ $x^2 - x - 6 = 0$

$\Rightarrow$ $x^2 - 3x + 2x - 6 = 0$

$\Rightarrow$ $x(x-3) + 2(x-3) = 0$

$\Rightarrow$ $(x-3)(x+2) = 0$

$\Rightarrow$ $x = 3$ or $x = -2$

But x cannot be -2.

Hence, the required value of x is 3.

2. $$\frac{9^n \cdot 3^2 \cdot 3^n - (27)^n}{3^{3m} \cdot 2^3} = \frac{1}{27}$$

$\Rightarrow$ $\dfrac{3^{2n} \times 9 \times 3^n - 3^{3n}}{8 \times 3^{3m}} = \dfrac{1}{3^3}$

$\Rightarrow$ $\dfrac{3^{3n}(9-1)}{8\ 3^{3m}} = 3^{-3}$

$\Rightarrow$ $3^{3n-3m} = (3)^{-3}$

$\Rightarrow$ $3m - 3n = 3$

$\Rightarrow$ $3(m-n) = 3$

$\Rightarrow$ $m - n = \dfrac{3}{3} = 1$

3. $$x = \frac{\sqrt{5}+\sqrt{3}}{\sqrt{5}-\sqrt{3}} \times \frac{\sqrt{5}+\sqrt{3}}{\sqrt{5}+\sqrt{3}} = \frac{\left(\sqrt{5}+\sqrt{3}\right)^2}{5-3}$$

$\Rightarrow x = \dfrac{5+3+2\sqrt{15}}{2} = \dfrac{8+2\sqrt{15}}{2} = \dfrac{2\left(4+\sqrt{15}\right)}{2}$

$\therefore$ $x = 4 + \sqrt{15}$

Again, $y = \dfrac{\sqrt{5}-\sqrt{3}}{\sqrt{5}+\sqrt{3}} \times \dfrac{\sqrt{5}-\sqrt{3}}{\sqrt{5}-\sqrt{3}}$

$$= \frac{\left(\sqrt{5}-\sqrt{3}\right)^2}{5-3}$$

$\Rightarrow$ $y = \dfrac{5+3-2\sqrt{15}}{2}$

$$= \frac{8-2\sqrt{15}}{2} = \frac{2\left(4-\sqrt{15}\right)}{2}$$

$\Rightarrow$ $y = 4 - \sqrt{15}$

$\therefore$ $x + y = 4 + \sqrt{15} + 4 - \sqrt{15} = 8$

4. $$2^{x+1} + 2^{x+3} = 2560$$

$\Rightarrow$ $2^x \times 2 + 2^x \times 2^3 = 2560$

$\Rightarrow$ $2 \times 2^x + 8 \times 2^x = 2560$

$\Rightarrow$ $2^x(2+8) = 2560$

$\Rightarrow$ $2^x = 256 = 2^8$

$\Rightarrow$ $x = 8$

5. $\because$ $\dfrac{5+2\sqrt{3}}{7+4\sqrt{3}} = a + b\sqrt{3}$

$$\frac{5+2\sqrt{3}}{7+4\sqrt{3}} \times \frac{7-4\sqrt{3}}{7-4\sqrt{3}} = \frac{35-20\sqrt{3}+14\sqrt{3}-24}{49-48}$$

$$= \frac{11-6\sqrt{3}}{1}$$

Comparing then we get,

$a = 11$, $b = -6$

Hence, $b = -6$.

6. $$\frac{(21)^{5.36}}{(21)^{3.47}} = (21)^x$$

$\Rightarrow$ $(21)^{5.36-3.47} = (21)^x$

$\Rightarrow$ $x = 1.89$

7. $\sqrt{24} + \sqrt{12} = 2\sqrt{6} + 2\sqrt{3}$

8. $a^b = 64 = (4)^3 \Rightarrow a = 4, b = 3$

$\therefore (a-b)^{a+b-4} = (4-3)^{4+3-4} = (1)^3 = 1$

9. $$\frac{5^{10+n} \cdot 25^{3n-4}}{5^{7n}} = \frac{5^{10} \times 5^n \times (5^2)^{3n-4}}{5^{7n}}$$

$$= \frac{5^{10} \times 5^n \times 5^{6n} \times 5^{-8}}{5^{7n}}$$

$$= \frac{5^{10-8} \times 5^{7n}}{5^{7n}} = 5^2 \times 5^{7n-7n}$$

$= 25 \times 5^0 = 25 \times 1 = 25$

10. $$3^x - 3^{x-1} = 18$$

$\Rightarrow$ $3^x - 3^x \times 3^{-1} = 18$

$\Rightarrow$ $3^x\left(1 - \dfrac{1}{3}\right) = 18$

$\Rightarrow$ $3^x\left(\dfrac{2}{3}\right) = 18$

$\Rightarrow \quad 3^x = \frac{18 \times 3}{2} = 27$

$\Rightarrow \quad 3^x = (3)^3 \Rightarrow x = 3$

$\therefore \quad x^x = (3)^3 = 27$

11. $x = \sqrt{10 + \sqrt{25 + \sqrt{121}}}$

$\Rightarrow \quad x = \sqrt{10 + \sqrt{25 + 11}}$

$\Rightarrow \quad x = \sqrt{10 + \sqrt{36}}$

$\Rightarrow \quad x = \sqrt{10 + 6} = \sqrt{16}$

$\Rightarrow \quad x = 4$

12. Let $a^x = b^y = c^z = k$

then $a = k^{\frac{1}{x}},\ b = k^{\frac{1}{y}},\ c = k^{\frac{1}{z}}$

Now, $\quad b^2 = ac$

$\Rightarrow \quad \left(k^{\frac{1}{y}}\right)^2 = k^{\frac{1}{x}} \cdot k^{\frac{1}{z}}$

$\Rightarrow \quad k^{\frac{2}{y}} = k^{\frac{1}{x}+\frac{1}{z}}$

$\Rightarrow \quad \frac{2}{y} = \frac{z + x}{xz}$

$\Rightarrow \quad 2xz = y(x + z)$

$\Rightarrow \quad y = \frac{2xz}{x + z}$

13. $\frac{5^{n+3} - 6 \times 5^{n+1}}{9 \times 5^n - 5^n \times 2^2} = \frac{5^n \times 5^3 - 6 \times 5^n \times 5}{9 \times 5^n - 4 \times 5^n}$

$= \frac{5^n(125 - 30)}{5^n(9 - 4)} = 5^0 \times \frac{95}{5}$

$= 1 \times 19 = 19.$

14. $\left(\frac{x^a}{x^b}\right)^{(a+b)} \times \left(\frac{x^b}{x^c}\right)^{(b+c)} \times \left(\frac{x^c}{x^a}\right)^{(c+a)}$

$= \left(x^{a-b}\right)^{(a+b)} \times \left(x^{b-c}\right)^{(b+c)} \times \left(x^{c-a}\right)^{c+a}$

$= x^{a^2-b^2} \times x^{b^2-c^2} \times x^{c^2-a^2}$

$= x^{a^2-b^2+b^2-c^2+c^2-a^2}$

$= x^0 = 1$

15. $\sqrt{3^n} = 729 \Rightarrow 3^{n/2} = 3^6$

$\Rightarrow \quad \frac{n}{2} = 6$

$\Rightarrow \quad n = 12.$

5. RATIO AND PROPORTION

RATIO

When comparison is made by dividing one quantity by another of the same kind, the result is called ratio. If a and b are two numbers, ratio of a to b is denoted by $a : b$ or $\frac{a}{b}$. Here a is called first term and b is called the second term. The first term is also called antecedent and the second term is also called consequent.

EXAMPLE: The ratio 3 : 10 represents $\frac{3}{10}$ with antecedent 3 and consequent 10.

The multiplication or division of each term of a ratio by a same non-zero number does not effect the ratio.

PROPORTION

Equality of two ratios is called proportion. If $a : b = c : d$, then a, b, c, d are called in proportion. In a proportion $a : b : : c : d$, then a and d are called extremes and b and c are called means.

Product of extremes = Product of means

Comparison of Ratio: Suppose $\frac{a}{b} > \frac{c}{d}$ then we say that $a : b > c : d$.

Compounded Ratio: The compound ratio of the ratios $a : b$, $c : d$ and $e : f$ is $ace : bdf$.

Duplicate Ratio: The duplicate ratio of $a : b$ is $a^2 : b^2$.

Triplicate Ratio: The triplicate ratio of $a : b$ is $a^3 : b^3$.

Sub-duplicate and Sub-triplicate ratios

The sub-duplicate and Sub-triplicate ratios of ratio $a : b$ are $a^{1/2} : b^{1/2}$ and $a^{1/3} : b^{1/3}$ respectively.

Mean Proportional: Mean proportional between a and b is $\sqrt{ab}$.

Third Proportional: The third proportional to a, b is the fourth proportional to a, b, b.

Fourth Proportional: If $a : b : : c : d$ is a proportion, then d is called the fourth proportional to a, b, c.

EXAMPLE: If A : B = 3 : 4 and B : C = 8 : 9 then find A : C.

SOLUTION: $A : B = 3 : 4 \Rightarrow \frac{A}{B} = \frac{3}{4}$

$B : C = 8 : 9 \Rightarrow \frac{B}{C} = \frac{8}{9}$

$$\frac{A}{C} = \frac{A}{B} \times \frac{B}{C} = \frac{3}{4} \times \frac{8}{9} = \frac{2}{3}$$

$\Rightarrow \quad A : C = 2 : 3$

EXAMPLE: If 15% of A is the same as 20% of B, then find A : B.

SOLUTION: Given : 15% of A = 20% of B

$\Rightarrow \quad \frac{15}{100} \times A = \frac{20}{100} \times B$

$\Rightarrow \quad 3A = 4B$

$\Rightarrow \quad \frac{A}{B} = \frac{4}{3}$

$\Rightarrow \quad A : B = 4 : 3$

EXAMPLE: A stick 1.4 m long casts a shadow 1.3 m long at the same time when a pole casts a shadow 5.2 m long. Find the length of the pole.

SOLUTION: Clearly, more is the length of shadow, more is the length of the object.

Let the length of the pole be x metres.

Then, 1.3 : 5.2 : : 1.4 : x

$$\Rightarrow \quad \frac{1.3}{5.2} = \frac{1.4}{x}$$

$$\Rightarrow \quad \frac{1}{4} = \frac{1.4}{x}$$

$$\Rightarrow \quad x = 1.4 \times 4 = 5.6$$

Hence, the length of the pole is 5.6 m.

MULTIPLE CHOICE QUESTIONS

1. If A : B = 2 : 3 and B : C = 4 : 5, then C : A is equal to:

A. 15 : 8 B. 12 : 10
C. 8 : 5 D. 8 : 15

2. If 10% of x is the same as 20% of y, then $x : y$ is equal to:

A. 1 : 2 B. 2 : 1
C. 5 : 1 D. 10 : 1

3. The mean proportional to $6+\sqrt{27}$ and $6-\sqrt{27}$ is:

A. 3 B. 9
C. 10 D. $\sqrt{10}$

4. If $x : y = 9 : 11$, the value of $\frac{5x+3y}{3x+5y}$ is:

A. 45 : 55 B. 18 : 22
C. 37 : 41 D. 39 : 41

5. If $a + b : b + c : c + a = 6 : 7 : 8$ and $a + b + c = 14$, then the value of c is:

A. 14 B. 7
C. 8 D. 6

6. Two numbers are in the ratio 2 : 3. If 5 is added to each number, the ratio becomes 5 : 7. The bigger number is:

A. 30 B. 40
C. 60 D. 20

7. What should be added to each of the numbers 12, 30, 40 and 86, so that they are in proportion?

A. 6 B. 4
C. –6 D. –4

8. The ratio of males and females of a village is 5 : 3. If there are 800 males in the village, females are:

A. 240 B. 480
C. 840 D. 488

9. In a mixture of 60 litres, the ratio of ethanol to ether is 4 : 1. How much ether must be added to the mixture to make this ratio 2 : 1?

A. 10 litres B. 12 litres
C. 18 litres D. 24 litres

10. The proportion of zinc and copper in a brass piece is 4 : 5. How much zinc will be there in 180 kg of such a piece?

A. 40 kg B. 80 kg
C. 100 kg D. 120 kg

11. The prices of a scooter and a television set are in the ratio 3 : 2. If a scooter costs ₹ 6000 more than the television set, the price of the television set is:

A. ₹ 18000 B. ₹ 12000
C. ₹ 10000 D. ₹ 6000

12. The weight of a 13 metres long iron rod be 23.4 kg. The weight of 6 metres long of such rod will be:

A. 7.2 kg B. 12.4 kg
C. 10.8 kg D. 18 kg

13. The ratio between the ages of Gayatri and Savitri is 6 : 5 and the sum of their ages is 44 years. The ratio of their ages after 8 years will be:

A. 5 : 6 B. 7 : 8
C. 8 : 7 D. 14 : 13

14. Two numbers are such that the ratio between them is 3 : 5 but if each is increased by 10, the ratio between them becomes 5 : 7. The numbers are:

A. 3, 5 B. 7, 9
C. 13, 22 D. 15, 25

15. In a factory the ratio of male workers to female workers was 5 : 3. If the number of female workers was less by 40, the total number of workers in the factory was:

A. 100
B. 500
C. 160
D. 200

ANSWERS

1	2	3	4	5	6	7	8	9	10
A	B	A	D	D	A	A	B	B	B
11	**12**	**13**	**14**	**15**					
B	C	C	D	C					

EXPLANATORY ANSWERS

1. $\frac{A}{B} = \frac{2}{3}$ and $\frac{B}{C} = \frac{4}{5}$

$\Rightarrow \quad \frac{A}{B} \times \frac{B}{C} = \frac{2}{3} \times \frac{4}{5} \Rightarrow \frac{A}{C} = \frac{8}{15}$

$\Rightarrow \quad \frac{C}{A} = \frac{15}{8}$

Hence, $\quad C : A = 15 : 8.$

2. 10% of x = 20% of y

$\Rightarrow \quad \frac{10}{100}x = \frac{20}{100}y \Rightarrow \frac{x}{10} = \frac{y}{5}$

$\Rightarrow \quad \frac{x}{y} = \frac{10}{5} \Rightarrow x : y = 2 : 1$

3. Mean proportional $= \sqrt{(6+\sqrt{27})(6-\sqrt{27})}$

$= \sqrt{36-27} = \sqrt{9} = 3$

4. $\because \quad \frac{x}{y} = \frac{9}{11}$

$$\frac{5x+3y}{3x+5y} = \frac{\frac{5x}{y}+\frac{3y}{y}}{\frac{3x}{y}+\frac{5y}{y}} = \frac{5\left(\frac{x}{y}\right)+3}{3\left(\frac{x}{y}\right)+5}$$

$$= \frac{5\times\frac{9}{11}+3}{3\times\frac{9}{11}+5} = \frac{\frac{45+33}{11}}{\frac{27+55}{11}} = \frac{78}{82} = \frac{39}{41}$$

Hence, the value of $\frac{5x+3y}{3x+5y} = \frac{39}{41}$.

5. Given : $a+b = 6x,\ b+c = 7x$

and $\quad c+a = 8x \quad$ ...(*i*)

and $\quad a+b+c = 14 \quad$ ...(*ii*)

Adding Eq. (*i*)

$a+b+b+c+c+a = 6x+7x+8x$

$\Rightarrow \quad 2(a+b+c) = 21x$

$\Rightarrow \quad 2\times 14 = 21x \quad$ [from Eq. (*ii*)]

$\Rightarrow \quad x = \frac{28}{21} = \frac{4}{3}$

$\therefore \quad a+b = 6x = 6\times\frac{4}{3} = 8$

$\because \quad a+b+c = 14 \Rightarrow c = 14-8 = 6$

6. Let the two numbers are a and b

According to the question,

$\frac{a}{b} = \frac{2}{3} \Rightarrow 3a = 2b \Rightarrow b = \frac{3a}{2}$

Now, $\quad \frac{a+5}{b+5} = \frac{5}{7} \Rightarrow 7a+35 = 5b+25$

$\Rightarrow \quad 7a-5b = -10$

$\Rightarrow \quad 7a - 5\left(\frac{3a}{2}\right) = -10$

$\Rightarrow \quad 14a - 15a = -20 \Rightarrow -a = -20$

$\Rightarrow \quad a = 20,\ b = 3\times\frac{20}{2} = 30$

Hence, the bigger number is 30.

7. Let x be added to each of the numbers.

Then, $(12+x) : (30+x) :: (40+x) : (86+x)$

$\Rightarrow \quad \frac{12+x}{30+x} = \frac{40+x}{86+x}$

$\Rightarrow (12+x)(86+x) = (30+x)(40+x)$

$\Rightarrow 12\times 86 + 12x + 86x + x^2$

$= 30\times 40 + 30x + 40x + x^2$

$\Rightarrow \quad 1032 + 98x = 1200 + 70x$

$\Rightarrow \quad 28x = 168 \Rightarrow x = 6$

8. Ratio of Males : Females = 5 : 3

$\Rightarrow \quad \frac{800}{x} = \frac{5}{3} \Rightarrow 5x = 3\times 800$

$\Rightarrow \quad x = \frac{3\times 800}{5} = 3\times 160 = 480$

Hence, number of females = 480.

9. Let ethanol = $4x$ and ether = $1x$

$4x + 1x = 60 \Rightarrow 5x = 60 \Rightarrow x = 12$

Quantity of ethanol = $12 \times 4 = 48$ litres

Quantity of ether = $1 \times 12 = 12$ litres

Let m litres of ether be added to mixture to get the desired ratio. Then,

$$\frac{48}{12+m} = \frac{2}{1} \Rightarrow 24 + 2m = 48$$

$$\Rightarrow 2m = 24 \Rightarrow m = 12$$

Hence, 12 litres of ether is to be added.

10. In 9 kg of brass, zinc = 4 kg

$\therefore$ In 180 kg of brass, zinc = $\frac{4}{9} \times 180 = 80$ kg.

11. Let the prices of a scooter and a television be ₹ $3x$ and $2x$ respectively.

According to the question,

$3x - 2x = 6000 \Rightarrow x = 6000$

$\therefore$ Price of a television = 2×6000 = ₹ 12000.

12. Weight of 13 m long iron rod = 23.4 kg

Weight of 6 m long iron rod

$= \frac{23.4}{13} \times 6 \text{ kg} = 1.8 \times 6 = 10.8$ kg.

13. Let present age of Gayatri = $6x$ years and present age of Savitri = $5x$ years.

According to the question,

$$6x + 5x = 44 \Rightarrow 11x = 44 \Rightarrow x = 4$$

Gayatri's age = $6 \times 4 = 24$ years

Savitri's age = $5 \times 4 = 20$ years

After 8 years their ages will be 32 years and 28 years.

Ratio of their ages after 8 years = $\frac{32}{28} = 8 : 7$.

14. Let numbers are x and y

$$\frac{x}{y} = \frac{3}{5}$$

$$\Rightarrow 5x = 3y \Rightarrow x = \frac{3y}{5}$$

According to the question,

$$\frac{x+10}{y+10} = \frac{5}{7} \Rightarrow 7x + 70 = 5y + 50$$

$$\Rightarrow 7x - 5y = -20$$

$$\Rightarrow 7\left(\frac{3y}{5}\right) - 5y = -20$$

$$\Rightarrow 21y - 25y = -100$$

$$\Rightarrow 4y = 100 \Rightarrow y = 25$$

$$\therefore x = \frac{3 \times 25}{5} = 15$$

Hence, numbers are 15 and 25.

15. Let the number of male and female workers be $5x$ and $3x$ respectively.

According to the question,

$5x - 3x = 40 \Rightarrow 2x = 40 \Rightarrow x = 20$

$\therefore$ Number of male = $5 \times 20 = 100$

and number of female = $3 \times 20 = 60$

Hence, total number of workers = $100 + 60 = 160$.

6. PARTNERSHIP

Partnership is a form of association of two or more persons who contribute resources like money together in order to carry on a business. It may be of simple or compound type.

Simple partnership is one in which the capitals of the partners are invested for the same time. The profits or losses are divided among the partners in the ratio of their investments.

Compound partnership is one in which the capitals of the partners are invested for different periods. In such cases, equivalent capitals are calculated for each partner by multiplying their capital contributions with time. The profits or losses are then divided in the ratio of these equivalent capitals. Thus, the ratio of profits is directly proportional to both capital invested as well as time.

The partner who invests the money in the business as well as takes part in its management, is known as **Working partner**.

The partner who only invests the money in the business and does not work, is known as **Sleeping partner**.

A working partner gets either monthly payment or a share in the profit for his contribution in the management of the business. This payment is deducted from the total profit before its distribution.

EXAMPLE: A, B and C invest ₹ 15000, ₹ 20000 and ₹ 25000 respectively in a business. The profit earned is ₹ 1200. Find the share of each in the profit.

SOLUTION: This is a case of simple partnership

Ratio of investments, A : B : C

= 15000 : 20000 : 25000

= 3 : 4 : 5

Sum of the ratios = 3 + 4 + 5 = 12

Share in the profit

$$\text{For A} = \frac{3}{12} \times 1200 = ₹\ 300$$

$$\text{For B} = \frac{4}{12} \times 1200 = ₹\ 400$$

$$\text{For C} = \frac{5}{12} \times 1200 = ₹\ 500$$

- **EXAMPLE:** A and B are partners in a firm. A invests ₹ 15000 and B ₹ 25000. A is the working partner and gets 20% of the profit for his contribution in the management of the firm. B is the sleeping partner. If the profit is ₹ 475, find the share of each.

SOLUTION: First we have to deduct the payment to be made to A from the total profit for his contribution in the management of the firm.

20% of ₹ 475 = ₹ 95

Balance profit = 475 – 95 = ₹ 380

This has to be divided between A and B in the ratio of their investments *i.e.,* ₹ 15000 : ₹ 25000 = 3 : 5

$$\text{A's share} = ₹\ 380 \times \frac{3}{8} = ₹\ 142.5$$

$$\text{B's share} = ₹\ 380 \times \frac{5}{8} = ₹\ 237.5$$

Finally, A gets a total of (95 + 142.5) = ₹ 237.5 and B gets = ₹ 237.5

EXAMPLE: In a business A and B gained some amount in a certain ratio. B and C received the profit in the ratio as that of A and B. If B received ₹ 6400 and C received ₹ 10,000 then find the amount invested by B.

SOLUTION: Let the ratio of A's and B's profit be $\frac{a}{b}$.

Hence, the ratio of B's and C's profit = $\frac{a}{b}$

Thus, $A : B : C = a : b : \frac{b^2}{a}$

when A's profit, a = ₹ 6400

and C's profit, $\frac{b^2}{a}$ = ₹ 10,000

$\Rightarrow b^2 = 10{,}000 \times 6400 = 100 \times 100 \times 80 \times 80$

$\Rightarrow b = 100 \times 80 = 8000$

Hence, the amount invested by B = ₹ 8000.

MULTIPLE CHOICE QUESTIONS

1. A, B and C share the profit in the ratio of 3 : 5 : 7. If the gain is ₹ 2040, then C's share is:

A. ₹ 360 B. ₹ 600
C. ₹ 952 D. ₹ 120

2. A, B and C started a business with ₹ 47000. A puts in ₹ 5000 more than B and B ₹ 3000 more than C. The share of A out of the profit of ₹ 14100 will be:

A. ₹ 3600 B. ₹ 4500
C. ₹ 6000 D. ₹ 6300

3. A starts a business with ₹ 5000. After 4 months B joins him with a sum of ₹ 4000. In the end of the year there is a profit of ₹ 8970. The share of A in the profit will be:

A. ₹ 3120 B. ₹ 4020
C. ₹ 5850 D. ₹ 6360

4. A, B, C are three partners in a business. The profit share of A is $\frac{3}{16}$ of the profit and B's share is $\frac{1}{4}$ of the profit. If C receives ₹ 243, then the amount received by B will be:

A. ₹ 90 B. ₹ 96
C. ₹ 108 D. ₹ 120

5. A, B and C share the profit in the ratio 2 : 3 : 7. If the average gain is ₹ 8000, then B's share is:

A. ₹ 2000 B. ₹ 1000
C. ₹ 1500 D. ₹ 3000

6. Ashok started a business investing ₹ 90,000. After 3 months Shabir joined him with a capital of ₹ 1,20,000. If at the end of one year the total profit made by them was ₹ 96,000, what will be the difference between their shares?

A. ₹ 24000 B. ₹ 8000
C. ₹ 20000 D. None of these

7. Mahesh received ₹ 6000 as his share out of the total profit of ₹ 9000 which he and Ram entered at the end of one year. If Mahesh invested ₹ 20,000 for 6 months, whereas Ram invested his amount for the whole year, what was the amount invested by Ram?

A. ₹ 4000 B. ₹ 5000
C. ₹ 3000 D. ₹ 6000

8. A and B started a business jointly. A's investment was thrice the investment of B and the period of his investment was two times the period of investment of B. If B received ₹ 40,000 as profit, then their total profit is:

A. ₹ 2,40,000 B. ₹ 28000
C. ₹ 24000 D. ₹ 2,80,000

9. Anil started a business investing ₹ 70,000. After 8 months Vimal joined him with a capital of ₹ 1,80,000. In what ratio should Anil and Vimal share the profit after two years?

A. 8 : 7 B. 7 : 5
C. 7 : 6 D. None of these

10. A, B and C starts a business. A invests ₹ 3,20,000 for four months. B invests ₹ 5,10,000 for three months and C invests ₹ 2,70,000 for five months. If at the end of year there is a profit of ₹ 1,24,800, then share of B is:

A. ₹ 79000 B. ₹ 49200
C. ₹ 50000 D. ₹ 45900

11. A, B and C contract a work for ₹ 550. Together A and B are to do $\frac{7}{11}$ of the work. The share of C should be:

A. ₹ 400 B. ₹ 300
C. ₹ 200 D. ₹ $183\frac{1}{3}$

12. Jagmohan, Rooplal and Pankaj rented a video cassette for one week at a rent of ₹ 350. If they use it for 6 hrs, 10 hrs and 12 hrs respectively, the rent to be paid by Pankaj is:

A. ₹ 75 B. ₹ 125
C. ₹ 35 D. ₹ 150

13. Manoj got ₹ 6000 as his share out of the total profit of ₹ 9000 which he and Ramesh earned at the end of one year. If Manoj invested ₹ 20,000 for 6 months, whereas Ramesh invested his amount for the whole year, the amount invested by Ramesh was:

A. ₹ 60,000 B. ₹ 10,000
C. ₹ 4000 D. ₹ 5000

14. A, B and C invest ₹ 2000, ₹ 3000 and ₹ 4000 in a business. After one year A removed his money, B and C continued the business for one more year. If the net profit after 2 years be ₹ 3200, then A's share in the profit is:

A. ₹ 1000 B. ₹ 600
C. ₹ 800 D. ₹ 400

15. A and B enter into partnership investing ₹ 12000 and ₹ 16000 respectively. After 8 months, C also joins the business with a capital of ₹ 15000. The share of C in a profit of ₹ 46500 after 2 years will be:

A. ₹ 12000 B. ₹ 14400
C. ₹ 19200 D. ₹ 21200

ANSWERS

1	2	3	4	5	6	7	8	9	10
C	C	C	C	A	D	B	D	D	D
11	**12**	**13**	**14**	**15**					
C	D	D	D	A					

EXPLANATORY ANSWERS

1. C's share $= \frac{7}{15} \times 2040 =$ ₹ 952.

2. Let C's capital be ₹ x

Then B's capital = ₹ $(x + 3000)$

and A's capital = ₹ $(x + 3000 + 5000) = x + 8000$

$\Rightarrow \quad x + (x + 3000) + (x + 8000) = 47000$

$\Rightarrow \quad 3x + 11000 = 47000$

$\Rightarrow \quad 3x = 47000 - 11000 = 36000$

$\Rightarrow \quad x = 12000$

Thus, capital of A, B and C are ₹ 20000, ₹ 15000 and ₹ 12000 respectively.

∴ Profit sharing ratio = 20 : 15 : 12

∴ Profit of A $= \frac{20}{47} \times 14100 =$ ₹ 6000

3. ₹ 5000 × 12 = ₹ 60,000 for A

₹ 4000 × (12 – 4) = 4000 × 8 = ₹ 32000 for B

Ratio of profit sharing = 60000 : 32000 = 60 : 32 = 15 : 8

∴ Share of A in the profit $= \frac{15}{23} \times 8970$

$= 15 \times 390 =$ ₹ 5850

4. Let the profit be ₹ 1. Then,

$$A : B : C = \frac{3}{16} : \frac{1}{4} : \left[1 - \left(\frac{3}{16} + \frac{1}{4}\right)\right]$$

$$= \frac{3}{16} : \frac{1}{4} : \frac{9}{16}$$

$$= \frac{3}{16} : \frac{4}{16} : \frac{9}{16} \quad i.e., 3 : 4 : 9$$

when C's share is ₹ 9, then B's share = ₹ 4

when C's share is ₹ 243, then B's share

$$= \frac{4 \times 243}{9} = ₹\ 108$$

5. B's share $= \frac{3}{2+3+7} \times 8000$

$= \frac{3 \times 8000}{12} =$ ₹ 2000

6. The ratio of their investment

$= 12 \times 90000 : (12 - 3) \times 120000$

$= 12 \times 9 : 9 \times 12 = 1 : 1$

Ashok's share $= \frac{1}{1+1} \times 96000 =$ ₹ 48000

Shabir's share $= \frac{1}{1+1} \times 96000 =$ ₹ 48000

Difference between their shares

= ₹ 48000 – ₹ 48000 = 0.

7. The ratio of their profit

= ₹ 6000 : ₹ (9000 – 6000)

= ₹ 6000 : ₹ 3000 = 2 : 1

Let ₹ x be the amount invested by Ram.

The ratio of their profit = The ratio of their investment

$\Rightarrow \quad 2 : 1 = 6 \times 20000 : 12 \times x$

$$\Rightarrow \quad \frac{2}{1} = \frac{6 \times 20000}{12 \times x} \Rightarrow 2x = 10000$$

$\Rightarrow \quad x = 5000$

∴ The investment of Ram is ₹ 5000.

8. Let ₹ x be the investment of B and n years be the period of investment of B.

Given : A's investment = 3 × ₹ x = ₹ $3x$

and period of investment of A = $2n$ years

∴ The ratio of investment of A and B

= $2n \times 3x : n \times x$

= $6nx : nx = 6 : 1$

Let the total profit be ₹ y

Given B's share in profit = ₹ 40,000

$$\Rightarrow \frac{1}{6+1} \times y = ₹\, 40{,}000 \Rightarrow y = ₹\, 2{,}80{,}000$$

∴ Total profit is ₹ 2,80,000.

9. The ratio of Anil's and Vimal's share in the profit

= Ratio of their investments

= 24 × 70000 : 16 × 180000

= 24 × 7 : 16 × 18 = 7 : 12

10. The ratio of investments of A, B and C

= 4 × 320000 : 3 × 510000 : 5 × 270000

= 4 × 32 : 3 × 51 : 5 × 27

= 128 : 153 : 135

Total profit after 1 year = ₹ 124800

$$\text{Share of B} = ₹\, \frac{153}{128+153+135} \times 124800$$

$$= ₹\, \frac{153}{416} \times 124800 = ₹\, 45900$$

11. $\text{C's share} = ₹\left(550 \times \frac{4}{11}\right) = ₹\, 200$

12. Ratio of rents = 6 : 10 : 12 = 3 : 5 : 6

$\therefore \text{Pankaj's share of rent} = ₹\left(350 \times \frac{6}{14}\right) = ₹\, 150$

13. Let amount invested by Ramesh be ₹ x

∴ 20000 × 6 : 12x = 6000 : 3000

$$i.e., \frac{12x}{120000} = \frac{3000}{6000} \text{ or } x = ₹\, 5000$$

14. Ratio of investments

= (2000 × 1) : (3000 × 2) : (4000 × 2)

= 1 : 3 : 4

$\therefore \text{A's share} = ₹\left(3200 \times \frac{1}{8}\right) = ₹\, 400.$

15. Ratio of investments

= (12000 × 24) : (16000 × 24) : (15000 × 16)

= 6 : 8 : 5

$\text{C's share of profit} = ₹\left(45600 \times \frac{5}{19}\right) = ₹\, 12000$

7. AVERAGE

The sum of all the quantities of same kind divided by their number is called average (or mean) of those quantities.

FORMULAE

1. Average = $\left(\dfrac{\text{Sum of observations}}{\text{Number of observations}}\right)$
2. Sum of the first n natural numbers
$= 1 + 2 + 3 + ... + n = \dfrac{n(n+1)}{2}$
3. Sum of the squares of the first n natural numbers
$= 1^2 + 2^2 + ... + n^2 = \dfrac{n(n+1)(2n+1)}{6}$
4. Sum of the cubes of the first n natural numbers
$= 1^3 + 2^3 + ... + n^3 = \left\{\dfrac{n(n+1)}{2}\right\}^2$
5. Sum of the first n odd numbers
$= 1 + 3 + 5 + ... + (2n - 1) = n^2$
6. Distance between two stations P and Q is x km. A person covers the journey from P to Q at 'a' km/hr and returns back to P with a uniform speed of 'b' km/hr. Then the average speed of the person during the whole journey
$= \dfrac{2ab}{a+b}$ km/hr.

Different kinds of mean or average:

(*a*) Arithmetic mean

(*b*) Geometric mean

(*c*) Harmonic mean

(*a*) **Arithmetic Mean:** It is most popularly used of all the averages. For example, average income, average profit, average mileage etc. As defined earlier, it is the sum total of all values of items divided by the total number of items. For detailed discussion we will confine ourselves to Arithmetic Mean only because this is the most relevant of all the average for us.

Let $x_1, x_2, x_3, ..., x_n$ be the n values of x.

Their average is denoted by $\bar{x}$ and given by

$$\bar{x} = \frac{\text{Sum of observations}}{\text{Total number of observations}}$$

or $$\bar{x} = \frac{x_1 + x_2 + x_3 + ... + x_n}{n}$$

(*b*) **Geometric Mean :** For observations $x_1, x_2, x_3, ..., x_n$ the geometric mean denoted by G.M. is defined as:

$$\text{G.M.} = (x_1 . x_2 . x_3 \cdots x_n)^{1/n}$$

It is useful in calculating averages of ratios such as average population, growth rate, average percentage increase etc.

(*c*) **Harmonic Mean:** It is defined as

$$\text{H.M.} = \frac{n}{\frac{1}{x_1} + \frac{1}{x_2} + ... + \frac{1}{x_n}}.$$

EXAMPLE: Find the average of first ten prime numbers.

SOLUTION: First ten prime numbers are 2, 3, 5, 7, 11, 13, 17, 19, 23 and 29.

$$\therefore \text{Average} = \frac{2+3+5+7+11+13+17+19+23+29}{10}$$

$$= \frac{129}{10} = 12.9$$

EXAMPLE: If x_1, x_2, x_3, x_4, x_5 are five consecutive odd numbers then find the average of these numbers.

SOLUTION: Since x_1 is the first odd number.

$$\therefore \quad x_2 = x_1 + 2$$
$$x_3 = x_2 + 2 = x_1 + 4$$
$$x_4 = x_3 + 2 = x_1 + 6$$
$$x_5 = x_4 + 2 = x_1 + 8$$

$$\therefore \text{ Average} = \frac{x_1 + x_1 + 2 + x_1 + 4 + x_1 + 6 + x_1 + 8}{5}$$

$$= \frac{5x_1 + 20}{5} = \frac{5(x_1 + 4)}{5} = x_1 + 4$$

EXAMPLE: If the average of four consecutive even numbers is 27, then find the largest of these numbers.

SOLUTION: Let x be the first even number in the series of four consecutive even numbers.

$\therefore$ 2nd even number $= x + 2$

3rd even number $= x + 4$

4th even number $= x + 6$

$$\text{Average} = \frac{x + x + 2 + x + 4 + x + 6}{4}$$

$$\Rightarrow \quad 27 = \frac{4x + 12}{4}$$

$$\Rightarrow \quad 4x + 12 = 27 \times 4 = 108$$

$$\Rightarrow \quad 4x = 96$$

$$\Rightarrow \quad x = 24$$

Largest number in this series is $x + 6$

i.e., $24 + 6 = 30$

EXAMPLE: The average of eight numbers is 14. The average of six of these numbers is 16. What is the average of the remaining two numbers?

SOLUTION: Sum of the eight numbers $= 14 \times 8 = 112$

Sum of six of these eight numbers $= 16 \times 6 = 96$

$\therefore$ Sum of the remaining two numbers $= 112 - 96 = 16$

$\therefore$ Average of the remaining two numbers $= \frac{16}{2} = 8$

EXAMPLE: What is the average of first 30 multiples of 7?

SOLUTION: Required Average

$$= \frac{7 + 14 + 21 + ... + 210}{30}$$

$$= \frac{7(1 + 2 + 3 + ... + 30)}{30}$$

$$= \frac{7 \times 30(30 + 1)}{2 \times 30}$$

$$= \frac{7 \times 31}{2} = \frac{217}{2} = 108.5$$

EXAMPLE: The average of 11 results is 50. If the average of first six results is 49 and that of last six is 52, find the sixth result.

SOLUTION: Sum of 11 results $= 11 \times 50 = 550$

Sum of first 6 results $6 \times 49 = 294$

Sum of last 6 results $= 6 \times 52 = 312$

$\therefore$ 6th result $= 294 + 312 - 550$

$= 56$

EXAMPLE: The average age of three boys is 15 years. If their ages are in the ratio 3 : 5 : 7. What is the age of the youngest boy?

SOLUTION: Let the ages of the three boys be $3x$, $5x$ and $7x$.

$$\text{Average age} = \frac{3x + 5x + 7x}{3} = 5x$$

and $5x = 15 \Rightarrow x = 3$

The age of the youngest boy $= 3x = 3 \times 3 = 9$ years.

EXAMPLE: The average of 100 observations is 45. It was later found that two observations 19 and 31 were incorrectly recorded as 91 and 13. Find the correct average.

SOLUTION: Sum of 100 observations

$= 100 \times 45 = 4500$

New sum of 100 observations

$= 4500 + (19 + 31) - (91 + 13)$

$= 4500 + 50 - 104 = 4446$

$$\text{Correct average} = \frac{4446}{100} = 44.46$$

MULTIPLE CHOICE QUESTIONS

1. The average of first five multiples of 3 is:
A. 3 B. 9
C. 12 D. 15

2. The average of 25 results is 18, that of first 12 is 14 and of the last 12 is 17. Thirteenth result is:
A. 78 B. 85
C. 28 D. 72

3. Out of three numbers, the first is twice the second and is half of the third. If the average of the three numbers is 56, the three numbers in order are:
A. 48, 96, 24 B. 48, 24, 96
C. 96, 24, 48 D. 96, 48, 24

4. The sum of three numbers is 98. If the ratio between first and second be 2 : 3 and that between second and third be 5 : 8, then the second number is:
A. 30 B. 20
C. 58 D. 48

5. The average age of a committee of seven trustees is the same as it was 5 years ago; a young man having been substituted for one of them. The new man compared to the replaced old man, is younger in age by:
A. 5 years B. 7 years
C. 12 years D. 35 years

6. The average expenditure of a man for the first five months is ₹ 120 and for the next seven months is ₹ 130. His monthly average income if he saves ₹ 290 in that year, is:
A. ₹ 160 B. ₹ 170
C. ₹ 150 D. ₹ 140

7. The average salary of 20 workers in an office is ₹ 1900 per month. If the manager's salary is added, the average becomes ₹ 2000 per month. The manager's salary is:
A. ₹ 24000 B. ₹ 25200
C. ₹ 45600 D. None of these

8. The average temperature of first 3 days is 27°C and of the next 3 days is 29°C. If the average of the whole week is 28.5°C, the temperature of the last day is:
A. 31.5°C B. 10.5°C
C. 21°C D. 42°C

9. A cricketer scored 180 runs in the first test and 258 runs in the second. How many runs should he score in the third test so that his average score in the three tests would be 230 runs?
A. 219 B. 242
C. 334 D. None of these

10. The average of first five prime numbers is:
A. 5.0 B. 5.2
C. 5.6 D. 6.0

11. The average weight of 3 men A, B and C is 84 kg. Another man D joins the group and the average now becomes 80 kg. If another man E, whose weight is 3 kg more than that of D, replaces A, then average weight of B, C, D and E becomes 79 kg. The weight of A is:
A. 70 kg B. 72 kg
C. 75 kg D. 80 kg

12. The average age of A, B, C, D 5 years ago was 45 years. By including *x*, the present average of all the five is 49 years. The present age of *x* is:
A. 64 years B. 48 years
C. 45 years D. 40 years

13. The average height of 30 boys, out of a class of 50, is 160 cm. If the average height of the remaining boys is 165 cm, the average height of the whole class (in cm) is:
A. 161 B. 162
C. 163 D. 164

14. The average age of an adult class is 40 years. 12 new students with an average age of 32 years join the class, thereby decreasing the average of the class by 4 years. The original strength of the class was:
A. 10 B. 11
C. 12 D. 15

15. If *a, b, c, d, e* are five consecutive odd numbers, their average is:
A. $5(a+4)$ B. $\frac{abcde}{5}$
C. $5(a+b+c+d+e)$ D. None of these

16. Of the three numbers, second is twice the first and is also thrice the third. If the average of the three numbers is 44, the largest number is:
A. 24 B. 36
C. 72 D. 108

17. The average of 50 numbers is 38. If two numbers namely, 45 and 55 are discarded, the average of remaining number is:

A. 36.50 B. 37.00
C. 37.50 D. 37.52

18. The average height of 30 girls out of a class of 40 is 160 cm and that of the remaining girls is 156 cm. The average height of the whole class is:

A. 158 cm B. 158.5 cm
C. 159 cm D. 159.5 cm

19. The average of n numbers is x. If 36 is subtracted from any two numbers each, then new average is $(x - 8)$. The value of n is:

A. 6 B. 8
C. 9 D. 72

20. The average salary of male employees in a firm is ₹ 520 and that of female employees is ₹ 420. The mean salary of all the employees is ₹ 500. The percentage of female employees is:

A. 40% B. 30%
C. 25% D. 20%

ANSWERS

1	**2**	**3**	**4**	**5**	**6**	**7**	**8**	**9**	**10**
B	A	B	A	D	C	D	A	D	C
11	**12**	**13**	**14**	**15**	**16**	**17**	**18**	**19**	**20**
C	C	B	C	D	C	C	C	C	D

EXPLANATORY ANSWERS

1. Average $= \dfrac{3(1+2+3+4+5)}{5} = \dfrac{(3\times15)}{5} = 9$

2. Thirteenth result
$= [(25 \times 18) - (12 \times 14 + 12 \times 17)]$
$= [450 - (168 + 204)]$
$= 450 - 372 = 78.$

3. Let the numbers be $2x$, x and $4x$.

Average $= \dfrac{2x+x+4x}{3} = \dfrac{7x}{3}$

According to the question,

$\dfrac{7x}{3} = 56$

$\Rightarrow \quad 7x = 3 \times 56$

$\Rightarrow \quad x = \dfrac{3\times56}{7} = 24$

Hence, the numbers in order are 48, 24 and 96.

4. Let the numbers be x, y, z, then

$x + y + z = 98$

$\dfrac{x}{y} = \dfrac{2}{3}$ and $\dfrac{y}{z} = \dfrac{5}{8}$

$\therefore \quad x = \dfrac{2y}{3}$ and $z = \dfrac{8y}{5}$

So, $\dfrac{2y}{3} + y + \dfrac{8y}{5} = 98$

$\Rightarrow \quad \dfrac{10y+15y+24y}{15} = 98$

$\Rightarrow \quad 49y = 15 \times 98$

$\Rightarrow \quad y = \dfrac{15\times98}{49} = 30$

5. During these five years, the total age would have increased by $(7 \times 5) = 35$ years. But, it remains the same as it was 5 years ago.
$\therefore$ The new man is younger than the replaced old man by 35 years.

6. Total income for 12 months
= ₹ $(120 \times 5 + 130 \times 7 + 290)$
= ₹ 1800

Average monthly income = ₹$\dfrac{1800}{12}$ = ₹150

7. Total salary of 20 workers
$= 20 \times 1900 =$ ₹ 38000

Total salary of 20 workers and manager
$= 21 \times 2000 =$ ₹ 42000

Monthly salary of the manager
$= 42000 - 38000 =$ ₹ 4000.

8. Total temperature of first 3 days
$= 27 \times 3 = 81°C$

Total temperature of next 3 days
$= 29 \times 3 = 87°C$

Total temperature of 7 days

$= 28.5 \times 7 = 199.5°C$

Temperature of the last day

$= 199.5 - (81 + 87)$

$= 199.5 - 168 = 31.5°C$

9. Let runs he should score in third test be x :

Then, $\frac{180+258+x}{3} = 230$

$\Rightarrow x = 690 - 438 = 252.$

10. Average $= \frac{2+3+5+7+11}{5} = \frac{28}{5} = 5.6.$

11. Weight of D = $(80 \times 4 - 84 \times 3)$ kg = 68 kg

Weight of E = $(68 + 3)$ kg = 71 kg

(B + C + D + E)'s weight = (79×4) kg = 316 kg

$\therefore$ (B + C)'s weight

$= [316 - (68 + 71)]$ kg = 177 kg

Hence, A's weight

$= [(84 \times 3) - 177]$kg = 75 kg

12. Total age of A, B, C and D 5 years ago

$= (45 \times 4)$ years = 180 years.

Total present age of A, B, C, D and x

$= (49 \times 5)$ years = 245 years.

Present age of A, B, C and D

$= (180 + 5 \times 4)$ years = 200 years.

$\therefore$ Present age of x = 45 years.

13. Total height of 30 boys = $30 \times 160 = 4800$

Total height of 20 boys = $20 \times 165 = 3300$

Total height of 50 boys = 8100

Average height of 50 boys = $\frac{8100}{50} = 162.$

14. $40x + 12 \times 32 = (12 + x) \times 36$

$\Rightarrow 40x + 384 = 432 + 36x$

$\Rightarrow 4x = 432 - 384 = 48$

$\Rightarrow x = \frac{48}{4} = 12$

Hence, the original strength of the class was 12.

15. Average $= \frac{a+a+2+a+4+a+6+a+8}{5}$

$= \frac{5a+20}{5} = \frac{5(a+4)}{5} = a+4$

16. Let the numbers be x, $2x$ and $\frac{2x}{3}$.

Average $= \frac{x+2x+\frac{2x}{3}}{3}$

$\Rightarrow \frac{11x}{9} = 44$

$\Rightarrow x = \frac{44 \times 9}{11} = 36$

So, the numbers are 36, 72 and 24.

Hence, the largest one is 72.

17. Total of 50 numbers = $50 \times 38 = 1900$

Average of 48 numbers $= \frac{1900-(45+55)}{48}$

$= \frac{1800}{48} = 37.50$

18. The average of the whole class

$= \frac{(30 \times 160 + 10 \times 156)}{40} = \frac{4800+1560}{40}$

$= \frac{6360}{40} = 159$ cm

19. $\frac{nx - 36 - 36}{n} = x - 8$

$\Rightarrow nx - 72 = nx - 8n$

$\Rightarrow 8n = 72$

$\Rightarrow n = 9$

20. Let the total employees be 100.

n_1 = number of females = x

n_2 = number of males = $100 - x$

$\bar{x} = \frac{n_1\bar{x}_1 + n_2\bar{x}_2}{n_1 + n_2}$

$\Rightarrow 500 = \frac{x \times 420 + (100 - x) \times 520}{100}$

$\Rightarrow 500 = \frac{42x + 5200 - 52x}{10}$

$\Rightarrow 5000 = 5200 - 10x$

$\Rightarrow 10x = 200$

$\Rightarrow x = 20$ *i.e.*, 20%.

8. PROFIT AND LOSS

Cost Price (CP)

The price at which an article is purchased is called the cost price of the article.

Selling Price (SP)

The price at which an article is sold is called the selling price of the article.

Profit or Gain

If SP is greater than the CP, the seller is said to have a profit or gain.

Clearly, Gain = SP – CP

Loss

If SP is less than CP, the seller is said to have a loss.

Clearly, Loss = CP – SP

Profit or loss per cent is calculated on cost price.

$$\text{Profit \%} = \frac{\text{Profit}}{\text{CP}} \times 100$$

$$\text{Loss \%} = \frac{\text{Loss}}{\text{CP}} \times 100$$

$$\text{SP} = \frac{\text{CP} \times (100 + \text{Profit\%})}{100}, \text{ if there is gain}$$

$$\text{SP} = \frac{\text{CP} \times (100 - \text{Loss\%})}{100}, \text{ if there is loss}$$

$$\text{CP} = \text{SP} \times \left(\frac{100}{100 + \text{Profit\%}}\right), \text{ if there is gain}$$

$$\text{CP} = \text{SP} \times \left(\frac{100}{100 - \text{Loss\%}}\right), \text{ if there is loss}$$

If an article is sold at a gain of 20%,

then, SP = (120% of CP)

If an article is sold at a loss of 20%,

then, SP = (80% of CP)

Overheads

The expenses incurred on transportation, rent, personnel salary, maintenance, packaging, advertisements and the like are included under the general heading of overheads. These overhead and the profit when added to the cost price determine the selling price. If the overheads are not separately mentioned in the problem, we assume it to be zero or else these have been included in the cost price itself.

Discount

It is an offer made by the seller to the buyer for reduction in price to be paid. There are several cases where discounts are allowed. For instance, to dispose off old goods, to increase its market share when the customer is ready to pay the whole amount in cash instead of instalment and so on. It is subtracted from the original price and is usually expressed as per cent or a fraction of the marked price. The price obtained after deducting the discount from the original price is the selling price which the customer has to pay.

Example: If an article is purchased for ₹ 570 and sold for ₹ 518.70, find the lost per cent.

Solution: CP = ₹ 570

SP = ₹ 518.70

∴ Loss = CP – SP

= 570 – 518.70 = ₹ 51.30

$$\text{Loss \%} = \frac{\text{Loss}}{\text{CP}} \times 100 = \frac{51.30}{570} \times 100$$

$$= \frac{5130}{570} = \frac{513}{57} = 9\%$$

EXAMPLE: A man buys a TV for ₹ 16,000. After two years he sells it for ₹ 12800. Find his loss per cent.

SOLUTION: $\text{Loss \%} = \frac{\text{Loss}}{\text{CP}} \times 100$

$= \frac{16000 - 12800}{16000} \times 100$

$= \frac{3200}{16000} \times 100 = 20\%$

EXAMPLE: Mohan sells his watch at a loss of ₹ 500 for ₹ 1000. Find the cost price and loss per cent.

SOLUTION: CP = SP + Loss

= 1000 + 500 = ₹ 1500

$\text{Loss \%} = \frac{\text{Loss}}{\text{CP}} \times 100 = \frac{500}{1500} \times 100$

$= \frac{100}{3} = 33\frac{1}{3}\%$

EXAMPLE: Ravi buys an article for ₹ 5000 and sells it at 20% gain. Find it selling price.

SOLUTION: $\text{Profit} = 20\% \text{ of CP} = \frac{20}{100} \times 5000$

⇒ Profit = ₹ 1000

SP = CP + Profit

= 5000 + 1000

= ₹ 6000

EXAMPLE: A man sells an article at 20% gain for ₹ 3600. Find its cost price.

SOLUTION: Let CP = ₹ 100

then SP = 100 + 20 = ₹ 120

When SP ₹ 120 then CP = ₹ 100

When SP ₹ 3600 then CP = $\frac{100}{120} \times 3600$

Hence CP = ₹ 3000

EXAMPLE: The cost price of 6 pens is equal to the selling price of 4 pens. Find the profit per cent.

SOLUTION: SP of 4 pens = CP of 6 pens

SP of 2 pens = CP of $\frac{6}{4} \times 2 = 3$ pens

Profit = CP of 3 pens

investment = CP of 6 pens

$\text{Profit \%} = \frac{3}{6} \times 100 = 50\%$

Alternatively:

Let the CP of 1 pen be ₹ x.

∴ CP of 6 pens = ₹ $6x$

Also, SP of 4 pens = ₹ $6x$

∴ SP of 6 pens = $\frac{6x}{4} \times 6 =$ ₹ $9x$

Profit = SP – CP = $9x - 6x = 3x$

$\text{Profit \%} = \frac{3x}{6x} \times 100 = 50\%$

EXAMPLE: If CP of 20 tables is equal to the SP of 25 tables. Find the loss percent.

SOLUTION: Let the CP of 1 table be ₹ x.

∴ CP of 20 tables = ₹ $20x$

Also, SP of 25 tables = ₹ $20x$

∴ SP of 20 tables = ₹ $\frac{20x}{25} \times 20 =$ ₹ $16x$

Loss = $20x - 16x = 4x$

$\text{Loss \%} = \frac{\text{Loss}}{\text{CP}} \times 100$

$= \frac{4x}{20x} \times 100 = 20\%$

EXAMPLE: Ram sold a book at a profit of 6%. Had he sold it for ₹ 2 more he would have gained 10%. Find the cost price of the book.

SOLUTION: (10% – 6%) of CP = 4% of CP = ₹ 2

⇒ $\frac{4}{100} \times \text{CP} = 2$

⇒ $\text{CP} = \frac{200}{4} =$ ₹ 50

EXAMPLE: An article is sold for ₹ 4600 at a gain of 15%. What would be the profit or loss per cent if it is sold for ₹ 3600?

SOLUTION: CP = $4600 \times \frac{100}{115} =$ ₹ 4000

$\text{Loss \%} = \frac{4000 - 3600}{4000} \times 100 = 10\%$

MULTIPLE CHOICE QUESTIONS

1. A loss of 5% was suffered by selling a plot for ₹ 4085. The cost price of the plot was:
A. ₹ 4350 B. ₹ 4259.25
C. ₹ 4200 D. ₹ 4300

2. On selling an article for ₹ 240, a trader loses 4%. In order to gain 10%, he must sell that article for:
A. ₹ 264.00 B. ₹ 273.20
C. ₹ 275.00 D. ₹ 280.00

3. A man purchased a watch for ₹ 400 and sold it at a gain of 20% of the selling price. The selling price of the watch is:
A. ₹ 300 B. ₹ 320
C. ₹ 440 D. ₹ 500

4. If 5% more is gained by selling an article for ₹ 350 than by selling it for ₹ 340, the cost of the article is:
A. ₹ 50 B. ₹ 160
C. ₹ 200 D. ₹ 225

5. Profit after selling a commodity for ₹ 425 is same as loss after selling it for ₹ 355. The cost of the commodity is:
A. ₹ 385 B. ₹ 390
C. ₹ 395 D. ₹ 400

6. The cost price of an article, which on being sold at a gain of 12% yields ₹ 6 more than when it is sold at a loss of 12%, is:
A. ₹ 30 B. ₹ 25
C. ₹ 20 D. ₹ 24

7. The CP of an article which is sold at a loss of 25% for ₹150, is:
A. ₹ 125 B. ₹ 175
C. ₹ 200 D. ₹ 225

8. When the price of pressure cooker was increased by 15%, its sale fell down by 15%. The effect on the money receipt was:
A. no effect B. 15% decrease
C. 7.5% increase D. 2.25% decrease

9. A man sells 320 mangoes at the cost price of 400 mangoes. His gain per cent is:
A. 10% B. 25%
C. 15% D. 20%

10. By selling 12 oranges for one rupee a man loses 20%. How many for a rupee should he sell to get a gain of 20%?
A. 5 B. 8
C. 10 D. 15

11. A man sells a car to his friend at 10% loss. If the friend sells it for ₹ 54000 and gains 20%, the original CP of the car was:
A. ₹ 25000 B. ₹ 37500
C. ₹ 50000 D. ₹ 60000

12. The loss incurred on selling an article for ₹ 270 is as much as the profit made after selling it at 10% profit. The CP of the article is:
A. ₹ 90 B. ₹ 110
C. ₹ 363 D. ₹ 300

13. An item costing ₹ 200 is being sold at 10% loss. If the price is further reduced by 5%, the selling price will be:
A. ₹ 179 B. ₹ 175
C. ₹ 171 D. ₹ 170

14. A trader lists his articles 20% above CP and allows a discount of 10% on cash payment. His gain per cent is:
A. 10% B. 6%
C. 8% D. 5%

15. A discount series of 10%, 20% and 40% is equal to a single discount of:
A. 50% B. 56.80%
C. 70% D. 70.28%

ANSWERS

1	2	3	4	5	6	7	8	9	10
D	C	D	C	B	B	C	D	B	B
11	**12**	**13**	**14**	**15**					
C	D	C	C	B					

EXPLANATORY ANSWERS

1. Loss = 5%, SP = ₹ 4085

Let CP = ₹ 100

$\therefore$ SP = ₹ 100 – 5 = ₹ 95

When SP ₹ 95 then CP = ₹ 100

When SP ₹ 4085 then CP = $\frac{100}{95} \times 4085$

= 4300

Hence, the cost price of the plot was ₹ 4300.

2. Loss = 4%, SP = ₹ 240

Let CP = ₹ 100

$\therefore$ SP = 100 – 4 = 96

When SP ₹ 96 then CP = ₹ 100

When SP ₹ 240 then CP = $\frac{100}{96} \times 240$ = ₹ 250

Again 100 + 10 = 110

When CP 100 then SP = ₹ 110

When CP 250 then SP = $\frac{110}{100} \times 250$ = ₹ 275

3. Let SP = ₹ x

then, profit = $\frac{20}{100} \times x$ = ₹ $\frac{x}{5}$

CP = SP – profit = $x - \frac{x}{5}$ = ₹ $\frac{4x}{5}$

According to the question,

$\frac{4x}{5} = 400 \Rightarrow 4x = 2000$

$\Rightarrow \quad x = 500$

Hence, selling price of the watch = ₹ 500.

4. Let CP = ₹ x

Then, if SP = ₹350

Profit = SP – CP = ₹ $(350 - x)$

if SP = ₹ 340 then, profit = ₹ $(340 - x)$

$\therefore (350 - x) - (340 - x) = \frac{5}{100}x$

$\Rightarrow 10 = \frac{5}{100}x \quad \Rightarrow x = 200$

Hence, the cost of the article = ₹ 200.

5. Let CP = ₹ x,

then, $425 - x = x - 355 \Rightarrow 2x = 780$

$\Rightarrow x = 390$

Hence, the cost of commodity is ₹ 390.

6. Let CP of the article = ₹ x

Then, SP when profit is 12%

$= \left(\frac{12x}{100} + x\right) = \frac{112x}{100}$

$\therefore \frac{112x}{100} - \frac{88x}{100} = 6$

$\Rightarrow \quad 24x = 600$

$\Rightarrow \quad x = \frac{600}{24} = 25$

$\therefore$ CP of the article is ₹ 25.

7. 100 – 25 = 75

When SP 75 then CP = ₹ 100

When SP 150 then CP = ₹ $\frac{100}{75} \times 150$ = ₹ 200

8. Let the original cost of each cooker be ₹ 1 and let the number sold originally be 100.

Total sale proceed = ₹ (100 × 1) = ₹ 100

New rate = (115% of ₹ 1) = ₹ 1.15

Number sold now = 85

$\therefore$ Sale proceed now = ₹(1.15 × 85) = ₹ 97.75

So, there is a decrease of 2.25% in the money receipt.

9. Let CP of each mango be ₹ 1.

Then, CP of 400 mangoes = ₹ 400

$\therefore$ CP of 320 mangoes = ₹ 320

SP of 320 mangoes = ₹ 400

Profit = 400 – 320 = ₹ 80

Profit% = $\frac{80}{320} \times 100$ = 25%

10. SP = ₹ 1, Loss = 20%

$\Rightarrow$ CP = $\left(\frac{100}{80} \times 1\right) \Rightarrow$ CP = ₹ $\frac{5}{4}$

Now, CP = ₹ $\frac{5}{4}$, gain, 20%

$\Rightarrow$ SP = $\frac{120}{100} \times \frac{5}{4}$ = ₹ $\frac{3}{2}$

For ₹$\frac{3}{2}$, he must sell 12 oranges

For ₹ 1, he must sell $\left(12 \times \frac{2}{3}\right)$ = 8 oranges.

11. SP = ₹ 54000 and gain earned = 20%

CP = ₹$\left(\frac{100}{120} \times 54000\right)$ = ₹ 45000

Now, SP = ₹ 45000 and Loss = 10%

∴ CP = ₹$\left(\frac{100}{90} \times 45000\right)$ = ₹ 50000

12. Let CP be ₹ x. Then,

$$x - 270 = 10\% \text{ of } x = \frac{x}{10}$$

$$\Rightarrow \quad x - \frac{x}{10} = 270$$

$$\Rightarrow \quad 9x = 10 \times 270$$

$$\Rightarrow \quad x = \frac{10 \times 270}{9}$$

$$\Rightarrow \quad x = 300$$

∴ CP of the article is ₹ 300.

13. SP = 90% of ₹ 200 = ₹ 180

Further, SP = (95% of ₹180) = ₹ 171

14. Let CP = ₹ 100. Then, MP = ₹ 120.

SP = 90% of ₹ 120 = $\frac{90}{100} \times 120$ = ₹ 108

Profit = SP – CP = 108 – 100 = ₹ 8

Profit % = $\frac{\text{Profit}}{\text{CP}} \times 100 = \frac{8}{100} \times 100 = 8\%$

15. Let original price = ₹ 100

Price after 1st discount = ₹ 90

Price after 2nd discount

= ₹$\left(\frac{80}{100} \times 90\right)$ = ₹ 72

Price after 3rd discount

= ₹$\left(\frac{60}{100} \times 72\right)$ = ₹ 43.20

∴ Single discount = 100 – 43.20 = 56.8%.

9. SIMPLE AND COMPOUND INTEREST

In any money transaction there is a **lender** who gives money, and a **borrower** who receives money. The amount of loan borrowed, is called the principal (P). The borrower pays a certain amount for the use of this money. This is called **Interest (I)**. Interest is always calculated on the principal borrowed. The borrowing is for a specified **Time (t)** and on specified terms. The specified term is expressed as per cent of the principal and is called rate of interest.

The sum of the principal and the interest is called the **Amount (A)**. In general, the rate of interest may be yearly, half yearly, quarterly or monthly as mutually agreed upon by both parties at the time of transaction. Depending upon the period of rate of interest, time is expressed in multiples of this period.

Interest is of two kinds—**Simple Interest and compound Interest**. If the interest is calculated only, on a certain sum borrowed it is called Simple Interest.

The simple interest (SI) on a principal P at R% per annum for T years is given by:

$$SI = \frac{P \times R \times T}{100}$$

$$\therefore \quad P = \frac{SI \times 100}{R \times T}$$

$$\therefore \quad R = \frac{SI \times 100}{P \times T}$$

$$\therefore \quad T = \frac{SI \times 100}{P \times R}$$

Compound Interest differs from Simple Interest that in CI the interest for the future period is calculated not only on the principal but also on the interest earned until the previous period. Thus, the total interest earned in case of CI is not uniformly distributed over time units whereas in Simple Interest it is uniformly distributed. The interest due at the end of the first unit of time is added to the principal and the amount so obtained becomes the principal for the second unit. Similarly, the amount after the 2nd unit of time becomes the principal for the third unit of time and continues till the last unit of time.

The difference between the final amount (A) obtained at the last unit of time and the original principal is called the **Compound Interest**.

Important Relations

Principal = ₹ P (in rupees)

Rate = R % (in per cent per annum)

Time period = T years (in years)

Amount = ₹ A (in rupees)

I. When interest is compounded annually,

$$A = P\left[1 + \frac{R}{100}\right]^T$$

II. When interest is compounded half-yearly,

$$A = P\left[1 + \frac{R/2}{100}\right]^{2T} = P\left[1 + \frac{R}{200}\right]^{2T}$$

[R is divided by 2 and T is multiplied by 2.]

III. When interest is compounded quarterly,

$$A = P\left[1+\frac{R/4}{100}\right]^{4T} = P\left[1+\frac{R}{400}\right]^{4T}$$

[R is divided by 4 and T is multiplied by 4.]

IV. When interest is $R_1\%$ for first year, $R_2\%$ for 2nd year and $R_3\%$ for third year;

$$A = P\left[1+\frac{R_1}{100}\right]\left[1+\frac{R_2}{100}\right]\left[1+\frac{R_3}{100}\right]$$

V. CI = A – P

EXAMPLE: Find the simple interest on ₹ 1000 for 3 years at 10% p.a.

SOLUTION: $SI = \frac{P\times R\times T}{100} = \frac{1000\times 10\times 3}{100} = ₹\,300$

EXAMPLE: Find the amount of ₹ 600 in 4 years at 3% p.a.

SOLUTION: $SI = \frac{P\times R\times T}{100} = \frac{600\times 3\times 4}{100} = ₹\,72$

∴ Amount = P + SI = 600 + 72 = ₹ 672

EXAMPLE: In what time will ₹ 7000 give ₹ 3675 as interest at the rate of 7% p.a. simple interest?

SOLUTION: $T = \frac{SI\times 100}{P\times R} = \frac{3675\times 100}{7000\times 7}$

$= \frac{15}{2} = 7\frac{1}{2}$ years.

EXAMPLE: At what rate per annum will a sum of ₹ 5000 amount to ₹ 6000 in 4 years?

SOLUTION: SI = A – P = 6000 – 5000 = ₹ 1000

$R = \frac{SI\times 100}{P\times T} = \frac{1000\times 100}{5000\times 4} = 5\%$

EXAMPLE: In how many years will a sum of money double itself at 5% rate of interest?

SOLUTION: A sum doubles itself when amount of interest becomes equal to the principal

SI = P, R = 5%

∴ $T = \frac{100\times P}{P\times 5} = 20$ years

EXAMPLE: A certain sum amounts to ₹ 115200 in 2 years and to ₹ 165888 in 4 years. Find the sum and rate per cent.

SOLUTION: Here, amount on ₹ 115200 for 2 years at CI is ₹ 165888

∴ $115200\left(1+\frac{R}{100}\right)^2 = 165888$

$\left(1+\frac{R}{100}\right)^2 = \frac{165888}{115200} = 1.44$

∴ $1+\frac{R}{100} = 1.2$

$\frac{R}{100} = 1.2-1 = 0.2$

⇒ R = 0.2 × 100 = 20%

Amount after 2 years is ₹ 115200

∴ $P\left(1+\frac{20}{100}\right)^2 = 115200$

⇒ $P = \frac{115200}{\left(1+\frac{20}{100}\right)^2} = \frac{115200}{1.44} = 80000$

∴ Principal = ₹ 80000

EXAMPLE: A sum of money doubles itself at CI in 15 years. In how many years will it become eight times?

SOLUTION: $P\left(1+\frac{R}{100}\right)^{15} = 2P$

⇒ $\left(1+\frac{R}{100}\right)^{15} = 2$

Let T be the required number of years that makes the principal 8 times of it.

∴ $P\left(1+\frac{R}{100}\right)^{T} = 8P$

⇒ $\left(1+\frac{R}{100}\right)^{T} = 8 = (2)^3$

⇒ $\left(1+\frac{R}{100}\right)^{T} = \left[\left(1+\frac{R}{100}\right)^{15}\right]^3$

⇒ $\left(1+\frac{R}{100}\right)^{T} = \left(1+\frac{R}{100}\right)^{45}$

⇒ T = 45 years

Hence, required number of years is 45 years.

EXAMPLE: The difference between simple and compound interest on a sum of money at 5% p.a. for 2 years is ₹ 25. Find the sum.

SOLUTION: Let P = ₹ 100

$$SI = \frac{P \times R \times T}{100} = \frac{100 \times 5 \times 2}{100} = ₹\ 10$$

$$A = P\left(1 + \frac{R}{100}\right)^T = 100\left(1 + \frac{5}{100}\right)^2$$

$$= \frac{100 \times 21 \times 21}{400} = ₹\ \frac{441}{4}$$

$$CI = A - P = \frac{441}{4} - 100 = ₹\ \frac{41}{4}$$

$$CI - SI = \frac{41}{4} - 10 = \frac{41 - 40}{4} = ₹\ \frac{1}{4}$$

When difference ₹ $\frac{1}{4}$ then P = ₹ 100

When difference ₹ 25 then P = 100 × 4 × 25
= ₹ 10000

Hence, sum = ₹ 10000.

MULTIPLE CHOICE QUESTIONS

1. The simple interest on ₹ 500 for 6 years at 5% p.a. is:
A. ₹ 250 B. ₹ 150
C. ₹ 140 D. ₹ 120

2. A certain sum of money at SI amounts to ₹ 1012 in $2\frac{1}{2}$ years and to ₹ 1067.20 in 4 years. The rate of interest per annum is:
A. 2.5% B. 3%
C. 4% D. 5%

3. ₹ 1200 amounts to ₹ 1632 in 4 years at a certain rate of simple interest. If the rate of interest is increased by 1%, it would amount to how much?
A. ₹ 1635 B. ₹ 1644
C. ₹ 1670 D. ₹ 1680

4. A man will get ₹ 87 as simple interest on ₹ 725 at 4% per annum in:
A. 3 years B. 3½ years
C. 4 years D. 5 years

5. At simple interest, a sum doubles after 20 years. The rate of interest per annum is:
A. 5% B. 10%
C. 20% D. Data inadequate

6. A lent ₹ 600 to B for 2 years and ₹ 150 to C for 4 years and received altogether from both ₹ 90 as simple interest. The rate of interest is:
A. 12% B. 10%
C. 5% D. 4%

7. Interest on a certain sum of money for $2\frac{1}{3}$ years at $3\frac{3}{4}$% per annum is ₹ 210. The sum is:
A. ₹ 2800 B. ₹ 1580
C. ₹ 2400 D. None of these

8. A certain sum of money at simple interest amounts to ₹ 1260 in 2 years and to ₹ 1350 in 5 years. The rate per cent per annum is:
A. 2.5% B. 3.75%
C. 5% D. 7.5%

9. A sum of money doubles itself in 5 years. It will become 4 times itself in:
A. 10 years B. 12 years
C. 15 years D. 20 years

10. The simple interest on a sum of money will be ₹ 600 after 10 years. If the principal is trebled after 5 years, the total interest at the end of 10 years will be:
A. ₹ 600 B. ₹ 900
C. ₹ 1200 D. Data inadequate

11. ₹ 800 amounts to ₹ 920 in 3 years at simple interest. If the interest rate is increased by 3%, it would amount to how much?
A. ₹ 1056 B. ₹ 1112
C. ₹ 1182 D. ₹ 992

12. A sum of money at simple interest amounts to ₹ 2240 in 2 years and ₹ 2600 in 5 years. The sum is:
A. ₹ 1880 B. ₹ 2000
C. ₹ 2120 D. Data inadequate

13. If ₹ 7500 are borrowed at CI at the rate of 4% per annum, then after 2 years the amount to be paid is:
A. ₹ 8082 B. ₹ 7800
C. ₹ 8100 D. ₹ 8112

14. Simple interest on a sum at 4% per annum is ₹ 80 in 2 years. The compound interest on the same sum for the same period is:
A. ₹ 81.60 B. ₹ 160
C. ₹ 1081.60 D. None of these

15. ₹ 800 at 5% per annum compound interest will amount to ₹ 882 in:
A. 1 year B. 2 years
C. 3 years D. 4 years

ANSWERS

1	2	3	4	5	6	7	8	9	10
B	C	D	A	A	C	C	A	C	C
11	**12**	**13**	**14**	**15**					
D	B	D	A	B					

EXPLANATORY ANSWERS

1. $SI = \frac{P \times R \times T}{100} = \frac{500 \times 5 \times 6}{100} = ₹ 150$

2. SI for $1\frac{1}{2}$ years $= 1067.20 - 1012 = ₹ 55.20$

SI for $2\frac{1}{2}$ years $= 55.20 \times \frac{2}{3} \times \frac{5}{2} = ₹ 92$

$\therefore$ Principal = ₹ (1012 – 92) = ₹ 920

$R = \frac{SI \times 100}{P \times T} = \frac{92 \times 100 \times 2}{920 \times 5} = 4\%$

3. $R = \frac{SI \times 100}{P \times T} = \frac{432 \times 100}{1200 \times 4} = 9\%$

New rate = (9 + 1)% = 10%

$SI = \frac{P \times R \times T}{100} = \frac{1200 \times 10 \times 4}{100} = ₹ 480$

Amount = P + SI = 1200 + 480 = ₹ 1680

4. $T = \frac{SI \times 100}{P \times R} = \frac{87 \times 100}{725 \times 4} = 3$ years

5. Let P be ₹ x then A = ₹ $2x$

SI = A – P = $2x - x$ = ₹ x

$R = \frac{SI \times 100}{P \times T} = \frac{x \times 100}{x \times 20} = 5\%$

6. $SI = \frac{P \times R \times T}{100} = \frac{600 \times R \times 2}{100} = 12R$

Again $SI = \frac{P \times R \times T}{100} = \frac{150 \times R \times 4}{100} = 6R$

Total SI = 12R + 6R = 18R

According to the question,

$18R = 90 \Rightarrow R = \frac{90}{18} = 5\%$

7. $T = 2\frac{1}{3} = \frac{7}{3}$ years,

$R = 3\frac{3}{4}\% = \frac{15}{4}\%$

$P = \frac{SI \times 100}{P \times T} = \frac{210 \times 100}{\frac{15}{4} \times \frac{7}{3}}$

$= \frac{210 \times 100 \times 4 \times 3}{15 \times 7} = ₹ 2400$

8. SI for 3 years = ₹ 1350 – ₹ 1260 = ₹ 90

SI for 1 year $= \frac{90}{3} = ₹ 30$

SI for 2 years = ₹ 30 × 2 = ₹ 60

P = A – SI = 1260 – 60 = ₹ 1200

$R = \frac{SI \times 100}{P \times T} = \frac{60 \times 100}{1200 \times 2} = \frac{5}{2} = 2.5\%$

9. Let P be ₹ x, A = ₹ $2x$,

SI = $2x - x$ = ₹ x

$$R = \frac{SI \times 100}{P \times T} = \frac{x \times 100}{x \times 5} = 20\%$$

Again, P = ₹ x, A = $4x$,

SI = $4x - x = 3x$

$$T = \frac{SI \times 100}{P \times R} = \frac{3x \times 100}{x \times 20} = 15 \text{ years}$$

10. Let P be ₹ x

SI = ₹ 600, T = 10 years.

$$R = \frac{SI \times 100}{P \times T} = \frac{600 \times 100}{x \times 10} = \frac{6000}{x}\%$$

$$\text{SI for first 5 years} = \frac{x \times 5 \times 6000}{100 \times x} = ₹\,300$$

$$\text{SI for last 5 years} = \frac{3x \times 5 \times 6000}{100 \times x} = ₹\,900$$

Total interest at the end of 10 years

= 900 + 300 = ₹ 1200.

11. P = ₹ 800, SI = 920 – 800 = ₹ 120

T = 3 years

$$R = \frac{SI \times 100}{P \times T} = \frac{120 \times 100}{800 \times 3} = 5\%$$

New rate = 8% (increase 3%)

$$SI = \frac{P \times R \times T}{100} = \frac{800 \times 8 \times 3}{100} = ₹\,192$$

$\therefore$ A = P + SI = 800 + 192 = ₹ 992.

12. SI for 3 years = 2600 – 2240 = ₹ 360

$$\text{SI for 2 years} = \frac{360}{3} \times 2 = ₹\,240$$

$\therefore$ Sum = 2240 – 240 = ₹ 2000

13. $$A = P\left(1 + \frac{R}{100}\right)^T = 7500\left(1 + \frac{4}{100}\right)^2$$

$$= 7500 \times \frac{26}{25} \times \frac{26}{25} = ₹\,8112$$

14. $$P = \frac{SI \times 100}{T \times R} = \frac{80 \times 100}{4 \times 2} = ₹\,1000$$

$$A = P\left(1 + \frac{R}{100}\right)^T = 1000\left(1 + \frac{4}{100}\right)^2$$

$$= 1000 \times \frac{26}{25} \times \frac{26}{25} = 1081.60$$

CI = A – P = 1081.60 – 1000 = ₹ 81.60

15. Let time = x years

$$A = P\left(1 + \frac{R}{100}\right)^T$$

$$882 = 800\left(1 + \frac{5}{100}\right)^x$$

$$\Rightarrow \frac{882}{800} = \left(\frac{21}{20}\right)^x$$

$$\Rightarrow \left(\frac{21}{20}\right)^2 = \left(\frac{21}{20}\right)^x \Rightarrow x = 2$$

$\therefore$ Time = 2 years

10. TIME AND WORK

Performing or doing work of any amount involves efforts of person (S) over a period of time. Therefore, the number of persons (P), the quantity of work (W) and the period of time (T) are important variables in problems related to "Time and Work". Moreover time (T) taken to do a work depends not only on how many persons are employed to do it but also on how efficient they are. Efficiency here means rate of doing same work. This aspect comes into picture when the problem involves comparison of work done by different categories of persons. For instance, efficiencies of man, woman, boy, girl in general are different. Even efficiency of one man may not be same as that of other; but unless otherwise specifically stated in the problem, all men or women working in a group are assumed to do work with equal efficiency.

The problems on Time and Work can be solved by following two methods:

(*i*) Ratio and proportion method

(*ii*) Unitary method

(*i*) **Ratio and Proportion Method:** Since problems concerning to Time and Work have proportional relation, these can be solved by this method. We have tried to solve questions based on Time and Work in the chapter mentioned.

(*ii*) **Unitary Method:** This is a very simple and useful method. The term 'Unitary' is self-evident. In this method, we first proceed to reduce the problem to either work done by one person or work done in 1 day and so on as per the requirement of the problem. Let us try to understand it.

(*a*) If a man can do a piece of work in 10 days he will do $\frac{1}{10}$ of the work in 1 day. Conversely, if a man can do $\frac{1}{10}$ of the work in 1 day, he will do the work in 10 days.

(*b*) If the number of men engaged to do a piece of work be changed in the ratio 5 : 4, the time required for the work will be changed in the ratio 4 : 5.

(*c*) If A is x times as good a workman as B, then A will take $\frac{1}{x}$ of the time that B takes to do a certain work.

All the above points can be summarised into one and can be written in the following form:

If M_1 persons can do W_1 works in D_1 days and M_2 persons can do W_2 works in D_2 days then we have a very general formula in the relationship of

$$M_1 D_1 W_2 = M_2 D_2 W_1$$

The above relationship can be taken as a very basic and all-in-one formula we also derive:

(*i*) More men less days and conversely more days less men.

(*ii*) More men more work and conversely more work more men.

(*iii*) More days more work and conversely more work more days.

$$M_1 D_1 T_1 W_2 = M_2 D_2 T_2 W_1$$

Example: 5 men can prepare 10 toys in 6 days working 6 hrs a day. How many days can 12 men prepare 16 toys working 8 hrs a day?

Solution: $M_1 D_1 T_1 W_2 = M_2 D_2 T_2 W_1$

$$5 \times 6 \times 6 \times 16 = 12 \times D_2 \times 8 \times 10$$

$$D_2 = \frac{5 \times 6 \times 6 \times 16}{12 \times 8 \times 10} = 3 \text{ days.}$$

EXAMPLE: A can reap a field in 8 days, which B alone can reap in 12 days. In how many days, both together, can reap this field?

SOLUTION: A's 1 day's work $= \frac{1}{8}$

B's 1 day's work $= \frac{1}{12}$

(A + B)'s 1 day's work $= \left(\frac{1}{8}+\frac{1}{12}\right)$

$= \frac{3+2}{24} = \frac{5}{24}$

∴ Both together can reap the field in $\frac{24}{5}$ days

$= 4\frac{4}{5}$ days.

EXAMPLE: A and B together can do a piece of work in 12 days, B alone can finish it in 30 days. In how many days can A alone finish the work?

SOLUTION: (A + B)'s 1 day's work $= \frac{1}{12}$

B's 1 day's work $= \frac{1}{30}$

∴ A's 1 day's work $= \frac{1}{12} - \frac{1}{30}$

$= \frac{5-2}{60} = \frac{3}{60} = \frac{1}{20}$

Hence, A alone can finish the work in 20 days.

EXAMPLE: A and B can do a piece of work in 12 days, C and A in 20 days and B and C in 15 days. In how many days will they finish it together and separately?

SOLUTION: (A + B)'s 1 day's work $= \frac{1}{12}$

(B + C)'s 1 day's work $= \frac{1}{15}$

(C + A)'s 1 day's work $= \frac{1}{20}$

Adding, 2(A + B + C)'s 1 day's work

$= \left(\frac{1}{12}+\frac{1}{15}+\frac{1}{20}\right) = \frac{5+4+3}{60}$

$= \frac{12}{60} = \frac{1}{5}$

or (A + B + C)'s 1 day's work $= \frac{1}{10}$

∴ A, B, C together can finish the work in 10 days.

Now, C's 1 day's work $= \frac{1}{10} - \frac{1}{12} = \frac{1}{60}$

∴ C alone can finish the work in 60 days.

Similarly B's 1 day's work $= \frac{1}{10} - \frac{1}{20} = \frac{1}{20}$

∴ B alone can finish the work in 20 days.

A's 1 day's work $= \frac{1}{10} - \frac{1}{15} = \frac{1}{30}$

∴ A alone can finish the work in 30 days.

EXAMPLE: A can do a piece of work in 25 days and B can finish it in 20 days. They work together for 5 days and then A goes away. In how many days will B finish the work?

SOLUTION: (A + B)'s 5 days work $= 5\left(\frac{1}{25}+\frac{1}{20}\right) = \frac{9}{20}$

Remaining work $= 1 - \frac{9}{20} = \frac{11}{20}$

Now, $\frac{1}{20}$ work is finished by B in 1 day

∴ $\frac{11}{20}$ work will be finished by B in $\left(\frac{20 \times 11}{20}\right)$ = 11 days.

EXAMPLE: A is thrice as good a workman as B and is therefore able to finish a piece of work in 60 days less than B. Find the time in which they can do it, working together.

SOLUTION: Ratio of work done by A and B in the same time = 3 : 1

Ratio of time taken by A and B = 1 : 3

Suppose B takes x days to finish a work then, A takes $(x - 60)$ days

∴ $\frac{x-60}{x} = \frac{1}{3}$ or $3(x-60) = x \Rightarrow x = 90$

∴ B can finish the work in 90 days.

A can finish the work in (90 – 60) = 30 days

Both finish the work $= \left[\frac{1}{30}+\frac{1}{90}=\frac{2}{45}\right]$

$= \frac{45}{2} = 22\frac{1}{2}$ days.

EXAMPLE: A certain number of men complete a piece of work in 60 days. If there were 8 men more, the work could be finished in 10 days less. How many men were originally there?

SOLUTION: Let the original number of men be x.

Now, x men can finish the work in 60 days

and $(x + 8)$ men can finish it in $(60 – 10)$ *i.e.*, 50 days.

$$\therefore \quad x + 8 : x :: 60 : 50$$

$$\Rightarrow \quad \frac{x+8}{x} = \frac{60}{50} = \frac{6}{5}$$

$$\Rightarrow \quad 6x = 5x + 40 \Rightarrow x = 40$$

Hence, the original number of men = 40.

EXAMPLE: If 4 men or 6 boys can finish a piece of work in 20 days, in how many days can 6 men and 11 boys finish it?

SOLUTION: 4 men = 6 boys

$$\therefore \quad 6 \text{ men} = \frac{6}{4} \times 6 = \frac{36}{4} = 9 \text{ boys}$$

6 men + 11 boys = 9 + 11 = 20 boys

Now, 6 boys can finish a work in 20 days.

1 boy can finish the same work in 6×20 days.

20 boys can finish the same work in $\frac{6 \times 20}{20}$

= 6 days.

EXAMPLE: If 12 men can build a wall 360 m long in 54 days, how many days will it take to build a similar wall 160 m long, if 16 men working on it?

SOLUTION: 12 men can build 360 m long wall in 54 days.

1 man can build 360 m long wall in 54×12 days.

1 man can build 1 m long wall in $\frac{54 \times 12}{360}$ days

16 men can build 1 m long wall in $\frac{54 \times 12}{360 \times 16}$ days

16 men can build 160 m long wall in $\frac{54 \times 12 \times 160}{360 \times 16}$ days

= 18 days.

EXAMPLE: If 3 persons weave 168 carpets in 7 days, how many carpets will 8 persons weave in 5 days?

SOLUTION: 3 persons can weave in 7 days 168 carpets

1 person can weave in 7 days = $\frac{168}{3}$ carpets

1 person can weave in 1 day = $\frac{168}{3 \times 7}$ carpets

8 persons can weave in 1 day = $\frac{168 \times 8}{3 \times 7}$ carpets

8 persons can weave in 5 days = $\frac{168 \times 8 \times 5}{3 \times 7}$ carpets

= 320 carpets

EXAMPLE: Mukesh can do a job in 12 days while Manoj can do the same job in 15 days. They undertake to complete the job for ₹ 5400. What will be the share of each in the income?

SOLUTION: Mukesh's 1 day's work = $\frac{1}{12}$

Manoj's 1 day's work = $\frac{1}{15}$

Ratio of their 1 day's work = $\frac{1}{12} : \frac{1}{15} = 5 : 4$

$\therefore$ Mukesh's share = ₹ $\frac{5}{9} \times 5400$ = ₹ 3000

Manoj's share = ₹ $\frac{4}{9} \times 5400$ = ₹ 2400

MULTIPLE CHOICE QUESTIONS

1. A and B can together do a piece of work in 15 days. B alone can do it in 20 days. In how many days can A alone do it?

A. 30 days B. 40 days

C. 45 days D. 60 days

2. A can do a piece of work in 30 days while B can do it in 40 days. A and B working together can do it in:

A. 70 days B. $42\frac{3}{4}$ days

C. $27\frac{1}{7}$ days D. $17\frac{1}{7}$ days

3. A can do $\frac{1}{3}$ of the work in 5 days and B can do $\frac{2}{5}$ of the work in 10 days. In how many days both A and B together can do the work?

A. $7\frac{3}{4}$ days
B. $8\frac{4}{5}$ days
C. $9\frac{3}{8}$ days
D. 10 days

4. A, B and C can do a piece of work in 6, 12 and 24 days respectively. They altogether will complete the work in:

A. $3\frac{3}{7}$ days
B. $\frac{7}{24}$ days
C. $4\frac{4}{5}$ days
D. $\frac{5}{24}$ days

5. A, B and C contract a work for ₹ 550. Together A and B are to do $\frac{7}{11}$ of the work. The share of C should be:

A. ₹ $183\frac{1}{3}$
B. ₹ 200
C. ₹ 300
D. ₹ 400

6. A and B finish a job in 12 days while A, B and C can finish it in 8 days. C alone will finish the job in:

A. 20 days
B. 14 days
C. 24 days
D. 16 days

7. 12 men can complete a work in 8 days. Three days after they started the work, 3 more men joined them. In how many days will all of them together complete the remaining work?

A. 2
B. 4
C. 5
D. 6

8. Mahesh and Umesh can complete a work in 10 and 15 days respectively. Umesh starts the work and after 5 days Mahesh joins him. In all, the work would be completed in:

A. 9 days
B. 7 days
C. 11 days
D. None of these

9. Sunil completes a work in 4 days whereas Dinesh completes the work in 6 days. Ramesh works $1\frac{1}{2}$ times as fast as Sunil. How many days it will take for the three together to complete the work?

A. $\frac{7}{12}$
B. $1\frac{5}{12}$
C. $1\frac{5}{7}$
D. None of these

10. A can complete a work in 6 days and B in 5 days. They work together, finish the job and receive ₹ 220 as wages. B's share should be:

A. ₹ 120
B. ₹ 110
C. ₹ 100
D. ₹ 90

11. 12 men and 8 children can finish a piece of work in 9 days. If each child takes twice the time taken by a man to finish the work, in how many days will 12 men finish the same work?

A. 8 days
B. 15 days
C. 9 days
D. 12 days

12. A, B and C together earn ₹ 150 per day while A and C together earn ₹ 94 and B and C together earn ₹ 76. The daily earning of C is:

A. ₹ 75
B. ₹ 56
C. ₹ 34
D. ₹ 20

13. If 5 men or 9 women can finish a piece of work in 19 days, 3 men and 6 women will do the same work in:

A. 10 days
B. 12 days
C. 13 days
D. 15 days

14. A can do a piece of work in 12 days. B is 60% more efficient than A. The number of days, it takes B to do the same piece of work, is:

A. $7\frac{1}{2}$ days
B. $6\frac{1}{4}$ days
C. 8 days
D. 6 days

15. A and B can do a piece of work in 45 and 40 days respectively. They began the work together, but A leaves after some days and B finished the remaining work in 23 days. After how many days did A leave?

A. 6 days
B. 8 days
C. 9 days
D. 12 days

ANSWERS

1	2	3	4	5	6	7	8	9	10
D	D	C	A	B	C	B	A	D	A
11	**12**	**13**	**14**	**15**					
D	D	D	A	C					

EXPLANATORY ANSWERS

1. (A + B)'s 1 day's work = $\frac{1}{15}$

B's 1 day's work = $\frac{1}{20}$

A's 1 day's work = $\frac{1}{15} - \frac{1}{20} = \frac{4-3}{60} = \frac{1}{60}$

$\therefore$ A can do this work alone in 60 days.

2. A's 1 day's work = $\frac{1}{30}$

B's 1 day's work = $\frac{1}{40}$

(A + B)'s 1 day's work

$= \frac{1}{30} + \frac{1}{40} = \frac{4+3}{120} = \frac{7}{120}$

$\therefore$ Both together will finish the work in $\frac{120}{7}$

$= 17\frac{1}{7}$ days.

3. $\frac{1}{3}$ of the work is done by A in 5 days.

$\therefore$ Whole work will be done by A in 3 × 5

= 15 days

$\frac{2}{5}$ of the work is done by B in 10 days.

Whole work will be done by B in $\left(10 \times \frac{5}{2}\right)$

= 25 days

(A + B)'s 1 day's work = $\frac{1}{15} + \frac{1}{25} = \frac{5+3}{75} = \frac{8}{75}$

$\therefore$ Both together can finish it in $\frac{75}{8} = 9\frac{3}{8}$ days.

4. A's 1 day's work = $\frac{1}{6}$

B's 1 day's work = $\frac{1}{12}$

C's 1 day's work = $\frac{1}{24}$

(A + B + C)'s 1 day's work = $\frac{1}{6} + \frac{1}{12} + \frac{1}{24}$

$= \frac{4+2+1}{24} = \frac{7}{24}$

$\therefore$ They all together will complete the work in

$\frac{24}{7}$ days = $3\frac{3}{7}$ days

5. Work to be done by C = $\left(1 - \frac{7}{11}\right) = \frac{4}{11}$

$\therefore$ (A + B) : C = $\frac{7}{11} : \frac{4}{11} = 7 : 4$

$\therefore$ C's share = ₹$\frac{4}{11} \times 550$ = ₹ 200

6. (A + B)'s 1 day's work = $\frac{1}{12}$

(A + B + C)'s 1 day's work = $\frac{1}{8}$

C's 1 day's work = $\frac{1}{8} - \frac{1}{12} = \frac{3-2}{24} = \frac{1}{24}$

Hence, C will complete the work in 24 days.

7. 1 man's 1 day's work = $\frac{1}{96}$

12 men's 3 day's work = $\frac{12}{96} \times 3 = \frac{3}{8}$

Remaining work = $\left(1-\frac{3}{8}\right) = \frac{5}{8}$

15 men's 1 day's work = $\frac{15}{96}$

Now, $\frac{15}{96}$ work is done by them in 1 day

$\therefore$ $\frac{5}{8}$ work will be done by them in $\frac{96}{15} \times \frac{5}{8}$
= 4 days

8. Umesh's 5 day's work = $\frac{5}{15} = \frac{1}{3}$

Remaining work = $\left(1-\frac{1}{3}\right) = \frac{2}{3}$

Now, $\left(\frac{1}{10}+\frac{1}{15}\right)$ work is done by A and B in 1 day.

$\therefore$ $\frac{2}{3}$ work will be done by A and B in $6 \times \frac{2}{3}$
= 4 days.

So, the work would be completed in (5 + 4)
= 9 days.

9. Time taken by Ramesh alone = $\frac{2}{3} \times 4 = \frac{8}{3}$ days

$\therefore$ Their 1 day's work = $\left(\frac{1}{4}+\frac{1}{6}+\frac{3}{8}\right)$

$= \frac{6+4+9}{24} = \frac{19}{24}$

So, together they can finish the work in $\frac{24}{19}$ days

$= 1\frac{5}{19}$ days.

10. Ratio of time taken by A and B = 6 : 5
Ratio of work done in same time = 5 : 6
So, the money is to be divided among A and B in the ratio 5 : 6.

$\therefore$ B's share = ₹ $\frac{6}{11} \times 220$ = ₹ 120

11. 2 children = 1 man
$\therefore$ 8 children + 12 men = 4 + 12 = 16 men
Now, less men, more days

12 : 16 : : 9 : x $\Rightarrow \frac{12}{16} = \frac{9}{x} \Rightarrow x = 12$ days

12. B's daily earning = ₹ (150 – 94) = ₹ 56
A's daily earning = ₹ (150 – 76) = ₹ 74
C's daily earning = ₹ [150 – (56 + 74)] = ₹ 20

13. 5 men = 9 women $\Rightarrow$ 1 man = $\frac{9}{5}$ women

$\therefore$ 3 men + 6 women = $\left(3 \times \frac{9}{5} + 6\right) = \frac{57}{5}$ women

Now, 9 women can do the work in 19 days

$\therefore$ $\frac{57}{5}$ women can do it in $\frac{9 \times 19 \times 5}{57}$ = 15 days

14. A's 1 day's work = $\frac{1}{12}$

B's 1 day's work = $\frac{1}{12}$ + 60% of $\frac{1}{12} = \frac{2}{15}$

Hence, B can do the whole work in $\frac{15}{2}$

$= 7\frac{1}{2}$ days.

15. B's 23 day's work = $\frac{23}{40}$

Remaining work = $\left(1-\frac{23}{40}\right) = \frac{17}{40}$

Now, (A + B)'s 1 day's work = $\left(\frac{1}{45}+\frac{1}{40}\right) = \frac{17}{360}$

$\frac{17}{360}$ work is done by A and B in 1 day

$\frac{17}{40}$ work is done by A and B in $\frac{360}{17} \times \frac{17}{40}$
= 9 days.

Hence, A left after 9 days.

11. AREA AND PERIMETER

The area of any figure is the amount of surface enclosed within its boundary lines. It is measured by the number of square metres or square centimetres or square inches (or some other units of square measure) it contains.

Perimeter

Perimeter of a geometrical figure is the total length of the sides enclosing the figure.

Triangle

A triangle is a plane figure bounded by three sides. It includes three angles. It is denoted by the symbol Δ. The sum of angles of a triangle is 180°.

(*i*) **Equilateral Triangle:** A triangle in which all sides are equal is called an equilateral triangle.

(*ii*) **Isosceles Triangle:** A triangle in which two sides are equal is called an isosceles triangle.

(*iii*) **Scalene Triangle:** A triangle in which all sides are different or unequal is called scalene triangle.

(*iv*) **Right Angled Triangle:** A triangle having one of the angles equal to 90° is called a right angled triangle. The side opposite to the right angle of a triangle is called its hypotenuse.

Quadrilateral

A plane figure bounded by four straight lines is called a quadrilateral.

Various Types of Quadrilaterals:

(*i*) **Rectangle:** A quadrilateral whose opposite sides are equal and all angles are at right angles. The diagonals of a rectangle are equal.

(*ii*) **Square:** A rectangle having all sides are equal is called a square.

(*iii*) **Parallelogram:** A quadrilateral whose opposite sides are equal and parallel is called parallelogram.

(*iv*) **Rhombus:** A parallelogram having all the sides equal is called a rhombus. Diagonals of a rhombus are not equal and they bisect each other at right angles.

(*v*) **Trapezium:** A quadrilateral having one pair of opposite sides parallel, is called a trapezium.

Circle

The path traced by a point which moves in such a way that its distance from a fixed point is always same, is called a circle. The fixed point is called its centre and fixed distance is called its radius. The length of the whole path of a circle is called its circumference.

(*i*) **Arc:** Any part of the circumference of a circle is called an arc.

(*ii*) **Chord:** The straight line joining the ends of an arc of a circle is called a chord.

(*iii*) **Diameter:** The chord passing through the centre of a circle is called its diameter.

The diameter of a circle divides the circle into two equal parts, each one of which is called a semi-circle.

(*iv*) **Segment:** The area enclosed by an arc and a chord is called a segment.

(*v*) **Sector:** The area bounded by an arc and two radii is called a sector.

Formulae for Area of Various Figures:

(*i*) **Rectangle:**

Area of rectangle = $l \times b$

Perimeter of rectangle = $2(l + b)$.

(ii) **Square:**

Area of square = $(\text{side})^2$

Perimeter of square = $4 \times$ side

Area of room = $l \times b$

Area of 4 walls of a room = $2(l + b) \times h$

(iii) **Parallelogram:**

Area of $11^{gm} = b \times h$

Area of rhombus = $\frac{1}{2} \times d_1 \times d_2$.

(iv) **Trapezium:**

Area of trapezium = $\frac{1}{2}$(sum of parallel sides) $\times$ (distance between them)

(v) **Triangle:**

(a) Area of right triangle = $\frac{1}{2} \times b \times h$

(b) Area of equilateral triangle = $\frac{\sqrt{3}}{4} \times (\text{side})^2$

(c) Area of scalene triangle

$$= \sqrt{s(s-a)(s-b)(s-c)}$$

where, $s = \frac{a+b+c}{2}$

(vi) **Circle:**

(a) Area of circle = πr^2

(b) Circumference of a circle = $2\pi r$

(c) Length of arc = $\frac{\theta}{360} \times 2\pi r$

(d) Area of sector = $\frac{\theta}{360} \times \pi r^2$

Polygon

A polygon is plane figure bounded by multiple number of sides. Normally, it is used for figures enclosed by more than four sides: *e.g.*, pentagon, hexagon, octagon etc.

Regular Polygon

It is a polygon whose all sides are equal.

For a regular polygon of n equal sides, its vertex angle θ is given by

$$\theta = \left(\frac{n-2}{n}\right) \times 180°$$

Example: Find the area and perimeter of a rectangle whose length is 25 m and breadth is 15 m.

Solution: Area of rectangle $= l \times b$

$= 25 \times 15 = 375 \text{ m}^2$

Perimeter of rectangle $= 2(l + b)$

$= 2(25 + 15) = 80$ m

Example: Find the area of a rectangle whose one side is 6 m and the diagonal is 10 m.

Solution: Another side of rectangle $= \sqrt{(10)^2 - (6)^2}$

$= \sqrt{100-36} = \sqrt{64} = 8$ m

Area of rectangle $= l \times b = 8 \times 6 = 48 \text{ m}^2$

Example: Find area and perimeter of a square whose each side is 12 cm.

Solution: Area of square $= (\text{side})^2 = (12)^2 = 144 \text{ cm}^2$

Perimeter of square $= 4 \times \text{side} = 4 \times 12 = 48$ cm

Example: Find the area of a parallelogram whose base is 35 m and altitude 18 m.

Solution: Area of parallelogram $= b \times h$

$= 35 \times 18 = 630 \text{ m}^2$

Example: Find the area of a rhombus one side of which measures 20 cm and one diagonal 24 cm.

Solution: Since the diagonals of a rhombus bisect at right angles, so one side and half of each of the diagonals form a right angled triangle. In this right angled triangle,

One side = 20 cm, another side $= \frac{24}{2} = 12$ cm

Third side $= \sqrt{(20)^2 - (12)^2} = \sqrt{400-144}$

$= \sqrt{256} = 16$ cm

Hence other diagonal $= 16 \times 2 = 32$ cm

Area of rhombus $= \frac{1}{2} \times d_1 \times d_2$

$= \frac{1}{2} \times 24 \times 32 = 12 \times 32$

$= 384 \text{ cm}^2$

Example: Find the area of an equilateral triangle each of whose sides measures 12 cm.

Solution: Area of equilateral triangle

$= \frac{\sqrt{3}}{4}(\text{side})^2 = \frac{\sqrt{3}}{4} \times (12)^2$

$$= \frac{\sqrt{3}}{4} \times 144 = 36\sqrt{3} \text{ cm}^2$$

$$= 36 \times 1.73 = 62.28 \text{ cm}^2$$

EXAMPLE: Find the area of a triangle whose sides are 40 cm, 41 cm and 9 cm respectively.

SOLUTION: $s = \frac{a+b+c}{2} = \frac{9+40+41}{2}$

$$= \frac{90}{2} = 45 \text{ cm}$$

$$\text{Area of triangle} = \sqrt{s(s-a)(s-b)(s-c)}$$

$$= \sqrt{45(45-9)(45-40)(45-41)}$$

$$= \sqrt{45 \times 36 \times 5 \times 4}$$

$$= \sqrt{225 \times 144}$$

$$= 15 \times 12 = 180 \text{ cm}^2$$

EXAMPLE: Find the circumference and the area of a circle of radius 3.5 cm.

SOLUTION: Circumference $= 2\pi r$

$$= 2 \times \frac{22}{7} \times 3.5 = 22 \text{ cm}$$

$$\text{Area of circle} = \pi r^2 = \frac{22}{7} \times 3.5 \times 3.5$$

$$= 38.5 \text{ cm}^2$$

EXAMPLE: In a circle of radius 35 cm, an arc subtends an angle of 72° at the centre. Find the length of the arc and the area of the sector.

SOLUTION: Length of arc $= \frac{\theta}{360} \times 2\pi r$

$$= \frac{72}{360} \times 2 \times \frac{22}{7} \times 35$$

$$= 44 \text{ cm}$$

$$\text{Area of the sector} = \frac{\theta}{360} \times \pi r^2$$

$$= \frac{72}{360} \times \frac{22}{7} \times 35 \times 35$$

$$= 770 \text{ cm}^2$$

EXAMPLE: Find the area of a trapezium whose parallel sides are 77 cm, 60 cm and the other sides are 25 cm and 26 cm.

SOLUTION:

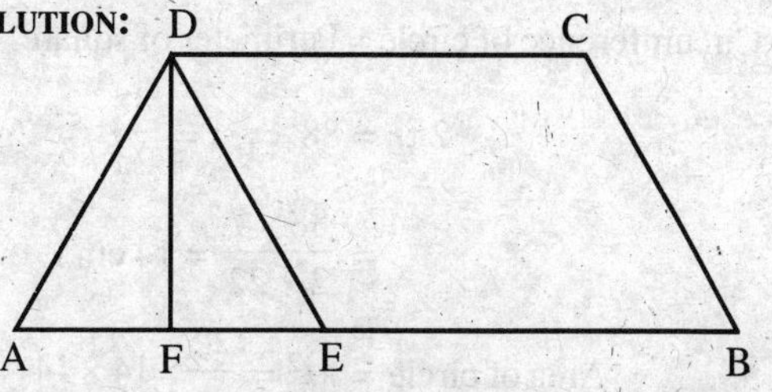

Let ABCD be the given trapezium in which AB = 77 cm, CD = 60 cm, BC = 25 cm, AD = 26 cm.

Draw DE || BC and DF ⊥ AB

Now, DE = BC = 25 cm

AE = AB – EB = AB – CD

= 77 – 60 = 17 cm

In ΔDAE, $s = \frac{17+25+26}{2} = \frac{68}{2} = 34 \text{ cm}$

$$\text{Area of } \Delta DAE = \sqrt{34(34-17)(34-25)(34-26)}$$

$$= \sqrt{34 \times 17 \times 9 \times 8} = 204 \text{ cm}^2$$

$$\text{Again area of } \Delta DAE = \frac{1}{2} \times AE \times DF$$

$$204 = \frac{1}{2} \times 17 \times DF$$

$$\Rightarrow \quad DF = \frac{2 \times 204}{17} = 24 \text{ cm}$$

$$\therefore \text{ Area of trapezium ABCD} = \frac{1}{2}(AB + CD) \times DF$$

$$= \frac{1}{2}(77 + 60) \times 24$$

$$= \frac{1}{2} \times 137 \times 24$$

$$= 1644 \text{ cm}^2$$

EXAMPLE: A copper wire when bent in the form of a square, encloses an area of 484 cm^2. If the same wire is bent in the form of circle, find the area enclosed by it.

SOLUTION: Area of the square = 484 cm^2

$$\text{Side} = \sqrt{484} = 22 \text{ cm}$$

Length of wire = Perimeter of square

= 4 × side = 4 × 22

= 88 cm

Let r be the radius of the circle.

∴ Circumference of circle = Perimeter of square

$$\therefore \quad 2\pi r = 88 \Rightarrow r = \frac{88}{2\pi}$$

$$= \frac{88 \times 7}{2 \times 22} = 14 \text{ cm}$$

$$\text{Area of circle} = \pi r^2 = \frac{22}{7} \times 14 \times 14$$

$$= 616 \text{ cm}^2$$

EXAMPLE: A bicycle wheel makes 5000 revolutions in moving 11 km. Find the diameter of the wheel.

SOLUTION: Distance covered by the wheel in 1 revolution

$$= \frac{\text{Distance covered}}{\text{Number of revolutions}} = \frac{11}{5000} \text{ km}$$

$$= \frac{11 \times 1000 \times 100}{5000} \text{ cm} = 220 \text{ cm}$$

∴ Circumference of the wheel = 220 cm

$$2\pi r = 220 \Rightarrow 2 \times \frac{22}{7} \times r = 220$$

$$\Rightarrow \quad r = \frac{220 \times 7}{44} = 35 \text{ cm}$$

Hence, diameter of the wheel = 35 × 2 = 70 cm

EXAMPLE: The perimeter of a square is 44 cm and circumference of a circle is 44 cm. Which area is greater and by how much?

SOLUTION: Side of square $= \frac{44}{4} = 11$ cm

$$\text{Area of square} = (11)^2 = 121 \text{ cm}^2$$

Circumference of a circle $= 2\pi r$

$$\Rightarrow \quad 44 = 2 \times \frac{22}{7} \times r$$

$$\Rightarrow \quad r = \frac{44 \times 7}{44} = 7 \text{ cm}$$

$$\text{Area of circle} = \pi r^2$$

$$= \frac{22}{7} \times 7 \times 7 = 154 \text{ cm}^2$$

Clearly, area of circle > area of square

Difference = 154 – 121 = 33 cm^2.

EXAMPLE: A sheet of paper is in the form of a rectangle ABCD in which AB = 40 cm and AD = 28 cm. A semi-circular portion with BC as diameter is cut off. Find the area of the remaining paper.

SOLUTION:

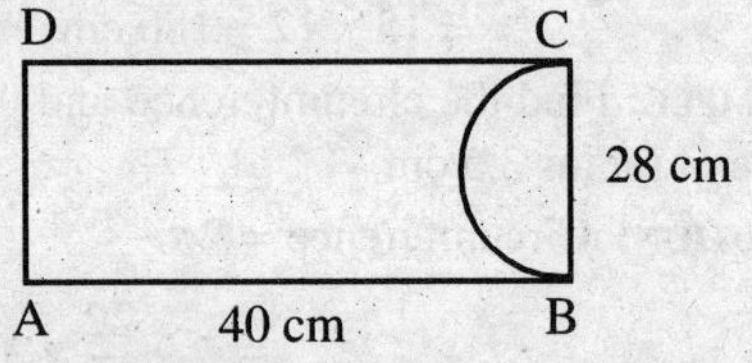

$$\text{Area of ABCD} = 40 \times 28 = 1120 \text{ cm}^2$$

$$\text{Area of semicircle} = \frac{1}{2}\pi r^2$$

$$= \frac{1}{2} \times \frac{22}{7} \times 14 \times 14$$

$$= 22 \times 14 = 308 \text{ cm}^2$$

Area of the remaining paper = 1120 – 308 = 812 cm^2

MULTIPLE CHOICE QUESTIONS

1. The length of a plot is four times its breadth. A playground measuring 1200 square metres occupies a third of the total area of the plot. What is the length of the plot, in metres?
   A. 20 B. 30
   C. 60 D. None of these

2. The width of a rectangular hall is $\frac{3}{4}$ of its length. If the area of the hall is 300 m^2, then the difference between its length and width is:
   A. 3 m B. 4 m
   C. 5 m D. 15 m

3. The length and breadth of a rectangular piece of land are in ratio of 5 : 3. The owner spent ₹ 3000 for surrounding it from all the sides at ₹ 7.50 per metre. The difference between its length and breadth is:
   A. 50 m
   B. 100 m
   C. 150 m
   D. 200 m

4. A room 8 m × 6 m is to be carpeted by a carpet 2 m wide. The length of carpet required is:

A. 12 m B. 36 m

C. 24 m D. 48 m

5. The length of a rectangle is increased by 60%. By what per cent would the width have to be decreased to maintain the same area?

A. $37\frac{1}{2}\%$ B. 60%

C. 75% D. 120%

6. A man walked 20 m to cross a rectangular field diagonally. If the length of the field is 16 m, the breadth of the rectangle is:

A. 4 m

B. 16 m

C. 12 m

D. Cannot be determined

7. If the ratio of the areas of two squares is 9 : 1, the ratio of their perimeters is:

A. 9 : 1 B. 3 : 1

C. 3 : 4 D. 1 : 3

8. The perimeter of both, a square and a rectangle are each equal to 48 m and the difference between their areas is 4 m². The breadth of the rectangle is:

A. 10 m B. 12 m

C. 14 m D. None of these

9. Area of a square with side x is equal to the area of a triangle with base x. The altitude of the triangle is:

A. $\frac{x}{2}$ B. x

C. $2x$ D. $4x$

10. If only the length of the rectangular plot is reduced to $\frac{2}{3}$rd of its original length, the ratio of original area to reduced area is:

A. 2 : 3 B. 3 : 2

C. 1 : 2 D. None of these

11. If the radius of a circle be reduced by 50%, its area is reduced by:

A. 25% B. 50%

C. 75% D. 100%

12. The perimeter of a rhombus is 52 m while its longer diagonal is 24 m. Its other diagonal is:

A. 5 m B. 10 m

C. 20 m D. 28 m

13. The circumference of a circle is 352 m, then its area in m² is:

A. 9856 B. 8956

C. 6589 D. 5986

ANSWERS

1	2	3	4	5	6	7	8	9	10
D	C	A	C	A	C	B	A	C	B
11	**12**	**13**							
C	B	A							

EXPLANATORY ANSWERS

1. Area of the plot = 3 × 1200 = 3600 m²

Let breadth be x m. Then length = $4x$ m

According to the question,

$4x \times x = 3600 \Rightarrow x^2 = 900 \Rightarrow x = 30$

Hence, length of the plot = 4 × 30 = 120 m.

2. Let length be x m, then breadth = $\frac{3x}{4}$ m

Area of the hall = $x \times \frac{3x}{4} = \frac{3x^2}{4}$

According to the question,

$\frac{3x^2}{4} = 300 \Rightarrow x^2 = 400 \Rightarrow x = 20$

Length = 20 m and breadth = $\frac{3}{4} \times 20 = 15$ m

Difference = 20 – 15 = 5 m

3. Let length = $5x$ m and breadth = $3x$ m

Perimeter of rectangle = $2(5x + 3x) = 16x$ m

But perimeter = $\frac{\text{Total cost}}{\text{Rate}} = \frac{3000}{7.50} = 400$ m

Now, $16x = 400 \Rightarrow x = 25$

$\text{length} = 5x = 5 \times 25 = 125 \text{ m}$

$\text{breadth} = 3x = 25 \times 3 = 75 \text{ m}$

$\text{Difference} = 125 - 75 = 50 \text{ m}$

4. Length of the carpet $= \dfrac{8 \times 6}{2} = 24$ m.

5. Initially, let length $= x$ and breadth $= y$

Let new breadth $= z$.

Then new length $= \dfrac{160x}{100} = \dfrac{8x}{5}$

$\therefore \quad \dfrac{8x}{5} \times z = xy \Rightarrow z = \dfrac{5y}{8}$

Decrease in breadth $= \left(y - \dfrac{5y}{8}\right) = \dfrac{3y}{8}$

$\therefore$ Decrease per cent $= \dfrac{3y}{8} \times \dfrac{1}{y} \times 100$

$= \dfrac{75}{2} = 37.5\% =$

6. Breadth $= \sqrt{(20)^2 - (16)^2}$

$= \sqrt{400 - 256} = \sqrt{144} = 12$ m.

7. Let the areas of the squares be $(9x^2)$ m^2 and (x^2) m^2

Then, their sides are $3x$ m and x m respectively

Ratio of their perimeters $= \dfrac{12x}{4x} = 3 : 1$

8. Let length of rectangle $= x$ m

and breadth of rectangle $= y$ m

Also, let the side of the square be z m

According to the question,

$2(x + y) = 4z = 48$

$x + y = 24$ and $z = 12$

Also, $\quad z^2 - xy = 4$

$\Rightarrow \quad (12)^2 - 4 = xy$

$\Rightarrow \quad xy = 140$

$\because \quad x + y = 24$ and $xy = 140$

$(x - y)^2 = (x + y)^2 - 4xy$

$\Rightarrow \quad (x - y)^2 = (24)^2 - 4(140)$

$\Rightarrow \quad (x - y)^2 = 576 - 560 = 16$

$\Rightarrow \quad x - y = 4$

Now, $\quad x + y = 24$

$x - y = 4$

Solving and get $x = 14$, $y = 10$

Hence, breadth of rectangle $= 10$ m.

9. According to the question,

$x^2 = \dfrac{1}{2} \times x \times h$

$\Rightarrow \quad h = \dfrac{2x^2}{x} = 2x$

10. Let length $= x$ and breadth $= y$

New length $= \dfrac{2}{3}x$

$\therefore \quad \dfrac{\text{Original area}}{\text{Reduced area}} = \dfrac{xy}{\dfrac{2}{3}xy} = \dfrac{3}{2} = 3 : 2$

11. Original area $= \pi r^2$, New area $= \pi\left(\dfrac{r}{2}\right)^2 = \dfrac{\pi r^2}{4}$

Reduction in area $= \pi r^2 - \dfrac{\pi r^2}{4} = \dfrac{3\pi r^2}{4}$

Reduction per cent $= \dfrac{3\pi r^2}{4} \times \dfrac{1}{\pi r^2} \times 100 = 75\%$

12. Side of rhombus $= \dfrac{52}{4} = 13$ m

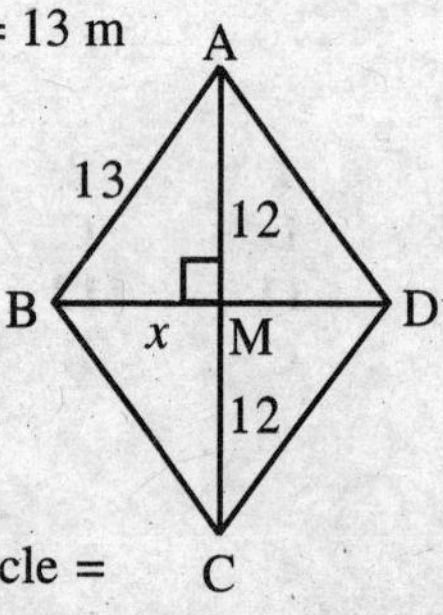

In ΔABM,

$x^2 = (13)^2 - (12)^2$

$x^2 = 169 - 144$

$x^2 = 25$

$\Rightarrow \quad x = 5$ m

$\therefore$ Another diagonal

$= 2 \times 5 = 10$ m

13. Circumference of a circle $= 2\pi r$

$\Rightarrow \quad 352 = 2 \times \dfrac{22}{7} \times r$

$\Rightarrow \quad r = \dfrac{352 \times 7}{44} = 56$ m

Area of circle $= \pi r^2 = \dfrac{22}{7} \times 56 \times 56$

$= 9856 \text{ m}^2$

12. VOLUME AND SURFACE AREA

We know that every real object occupies some space. It is usually specified by its three dimensions—length, breadth and depth (or height or thickness). It may be a solid or a hollow object. In case of circular, cylindrical and spherical object the specifying dimensions may change to radius, angle etc. The amount of space occupied by the object is called its volume. Its unit of measurement is m^3, cm^3, $(\text{inches})^3$ etc. The area of the surfaces (plane/curved) of the object is called its surface area.

A Cuboid and A Cube

The solid like wooden boxes, tea containers, match box etc. which have six faces, each of which is a rectangle, are called cuboids. It has 12 edges.

A cuboid in which every face is a square is called a cube. Length of each face of a cube is called its edge.

Prism

A right prism is a solid in which the two ends are congruent parallel figures and the side faces are rectangles. The total area of side faces of a prism is called the lateral surface of the prism.

Cylinder

The solid generated by the revolution of a rectangle about one of its sides as axis is called a cylinder.

Pyramid

A solid whose base is a plane rectilinear figure having the side faces as triangles meeting at a common vertex is called a pyramid. When the base of a pyramid is a triangle, the pyramid is called a tetrahedron.

Cone

The solid generated by the revolution of a right angled triangle about one of the sides containing the right angle as the axis is called a right circular cone.

The perpendicular distance from the vertex to the base is called the height of the cone and the length of slant face from vertex to the base is called the slant height of the cone.

Frustum

If a cone is cut by a plane parallel to the base so as to divide the cone into two parts, then the lower part is called the frustum of the cone.

Sphere

When a semicircle moves about its diameter, the solid generated is called a sphere.

Formulae

Cuboid:

Volume of cuboid $= l \times b \times h$ cubic units

Whole surface area $= 2(lb + bh + hl)$ square units

Diagonal of cuboid $= \sqrt{l^2 + b^2 + h^2}$ units

Area of 4 walls of a room $= 2(l + b) \times h$ square units

Cube:

Volume of cube $= a^3$ cubic units

Side of cube $= \sqrt[3]{\text{Volume}}$

Lateral surface area $= 4a^2$ square units

Total surface area $= 6a^2$ square units

Diagonal of the cube $= \left(\sqrt{3}\,a\right)$ units

Cylinder:

Volume of cylinder = $\pi r^2 h$ cubic units

Lateral surface area = $2\pi rh$ square units

Total surface area = $2\pi r(h + r)$ square units

Cone:

Volume of cone = $\frac{1}{3}\pi r^2 h$ cubic units

Lateral surface area = πrl square units

Total surface area = $\pi r(l + r)$ square units

Slant height (l) = $\sqrt{r^2 + h^2}$

Sphere:

Volume of sphere = $\frac{4}{3}\pi r^3$ cubic units

Surface area = $4\pi r^2$ square units

Hemisphere:

Volume = $\frac{2}{3}\pi r^3$ cubic units

Lateral surface area = $2\pi r^2$ square units

Total surface area = $3\pi r^2$ square units

Frustum:

Volume = $\frac{1}{3}\pi h(r_1^2 + r_1 r_2 + r_2^2)$ cubic units

Curved surface area = $\pi(r_1 + r_2) \times l$ square units

Total surface area = $\pi\left[r_1^2 + r_2^2 + (r_1 + r_2)l\right]$ square units

Pyramid:

Volume = $\frac{1}{2}$ × (area of base) × height cubic units

EXAMPLE: The dimensions of a metallic cuboid are 100 cm × 80 cm × 64 cm. It is melted and recast into cube. Find the total surface area of the cube.

SOLUTION: Volume of cuboid = $l \times b \times h$

$= 100 \times 80 \times 64$

$= 512000 \text{ cm}^3$

Volume of cube = a^3

According to the question,

$a^3 = 512000$

$\Rightarrow \quad a^3 = 8 \times 8 \times 8 \times 10 \times 10 \times 10$

$\Rightarrow \quad a = 8 \times 10 = 80 \text{ cm}$

Total surface area of cube = $6a^2 = 6 \times 80 \times 80 = 38400$

Hence, total surface area of cube is 38400 cm^2.

EXAMPLE: Three cubes whose edges measure 3 cm, 4 cm and 5 cm respectively form a single cube. Find the total surface area of the new cube.

SOLUTION: Let the edge of new cube = x cm

$x^3 = 3^3 + 4^3 + 5^3$

$= 27 + 64 + 125 = 216 \text{ cm}^3$

$\Rightarrow \quad x^3 = 6 \times 6 \times 6 \Rightarrow x = 6 \text{ cm}$

Total surface area of cube = $6(x)^2 = 6 \times 6 \times 6 = 216 \text{ cm}^2$

Hence, total surface area of new cube = 216 cm^2.

EXAMPLE: The capacity of a cylindrical tank is 6160 m^3. If the radius of its base is 14 m, find the depth of the tank.

SOLUTION: Volume of cylinder = $\pi r^2 h$

$\pi r^2 h = 6160$

$\Rightarrow \quad \frac{22}{7} \times 14 \times 14 \times h = 6160$

$\Rightarrow \quad h = \frac{6160}{44 \times 14} = 10 \text{ m}$

Hence, depth of the tank is 10 m.

EXAMPLE: How many bullets can be made out of a lead cylinder 28 cm high and 6 cm radius, each bullet being 1.5 cm in diameter?

SOLUTION: Number of bullets

$= \frac{\text{Volume of cylinder}}{\text{Volume of 1 bullet}}$

$= \frac{\pi \times 6 \times 6 \times 28}{\frac{4}{3} \times \pi \times 0.75 \times 0.75 \times 0.75}$

$= \frac{6 \times 6 \times 28 \times 3}{4 \times \frac{3}{4} \times \frac{3}{4} \times \frac{3}{4}} = \frac{6 \times 6 \times 28 \times 4 \times 4 \times 3}{3 \times 3 \times 3}$

$= 1792$

EXAMPLE: A metal sphere of diameter 42 cm is dropped into a cylindrical vessel, which is partly filled with water. The diameter of the vessel is 1.68 metres. If the sphere is completely submerged, find by how much the surface of water will rise.

SOLUTION: Radius of the sphere = 21 cm

Volume of sphere = $\frac{4}{3}\pi r^3$

$= \frac{4}{3} \times \frac{22}{7} \times 21 \times 21 \times 21$

$= 38808 \text{ cm}^3$

Volume of water displaced by sphere = 38808 cm^3

Let water rise by h cm.

$$\text{Volume of cylinder} = \pi r^2 h$$

$$\frac{22}{7} \times 84 \times 84 \times h = 38808$$

$$\Rightarrow \quad h = \frac{38808 \times 7}{22 \times 84 \times 84} = \frac{7}{4} = 1.75 \text{ cm}$$

EXAMPLE: A tent is in the form of a right circular cylinder surmounted by a cone. The diameter of cylinder is 24 m. The height of the cylindrical portion is 11 m while the vertex of the cone is 16 m above the ground. Find the area of the canvas required for the tent.

SOLUTION: Lateral surface area of cylinder = $2\pi rh$

$$= 2 \times \frac{22}{7} \times 12 \times 11 = \frac{5808}{7} \text{ m}^2$$

Height of cone = 16 – 11 = 5 m

Radius of cone = 12 m

$$\text{Slant height } l = \sqrt{r^2 + h^2} = \sqrt{12^2 + 5^2}$$

$$= \sqrt{169} = 13 \text{ m}$$

Lateral surface area of cone = πrl

$$= \frac{22}{7} \times 12 \times 13 = \frac{3432}{7} \text{ m}^2$$

$$\text{Area of canvas} = \frac{5808}{7} + \frac{3432}{7}$$

$$= \frac{9240}{7} = 1320 \text{ m}^2$$

EXAMPLE: The slant height of the frustum of a cone is 20 cm and the height of the frustum is 16 cm. The radius of the smaller circle is 8 cm. Find the volume and total surface area of the frustum.

SOLUTION: $l = \sqrt{h^2 + (R - r)^2} = \sqrt{16^2 + (R - 8)^2}$

$$\Rightarrow \quad 20 = \sqrt{256 + R^2 - 16R + 64}$$

$$= \sqrt{R^2 - 16R + 320}$$

$\Rightarrow$ $R^2 - 16R + 320 = 400$

$\Rightarrow$ $R^2 - 16R - 80 = 0 \Rightarrow R = 20$ cm

$$\text{Volume of frustum} = \frac{1}{3}\pi h(R^2 + r^2 + Rr)$$

$$= \frac{1}{3} \times \frac{22}{7} \times 16(400 + 64 + 160)$$

$$= \frac{73216}{7} \text{ cm}^3$$

Total surface area = $\pi(R^2 + r^2 + Rl + rl)$

$$= \frac{22}{7}(400 + 64 + 400 + 160)$$

$$= \frac{22}{7} \times 1024 = \frac{22528}{7}$$

$$= 3218.28 \text{ cm}^2$$

EXAMPLE: The length of a garden roller is 2 m and diameter is 1.4 m. How much area will it cover in 10 revolutions?

SOLUTION: Area covered

= Curved surface × no. of revolutions

= $2\pi rh \times 10$

$$= 2 \times \frac{22}{7} \times 0.7 \times 2 \times 10 = 88 \text{ m}^2$$

EXAMPLE: A cylinder is made by lead whose radius is 4 cm and height is 10 cm. By melting it how many spheres of radius 2 cm can be made?

SOLUTION: Given, radius of the cylinder = 4 cm

and height of the cylinder = 10 cm

$\therefore$ Volume of the cylinder = $\pi r^2 h = \pi(4)^2 \times 10$

$= 160\pi \text{ cm}^3$

$$\text{Volume of sphere} = \frac{4}{3}\pi r^3 = \frac{4}{3}\pi(2)^3$$

$$= \frac{32}{3}\pi \text{ cm}^3$$

$$\therefore \quad \text{Number of spheres} = \frac{\text{Volume of cylinder}}{\text{Volume of one sphere}}$$

$$= \frac{160\pi}{\frac{32}{3}\pi} = \frac{160 \times 3}{32} = 15$$

Hence, number of spheres that can be made are 15.

MULTIPLE CHOICE QUESTIONS

1. The surface area of a cube is 726 m^2. The volume of cube is:

A. 1300 m^3 B. 1331 m^3
C. 1452 m^3 D. 1542 m^3

2. Sum of the length, width and depth of a cuboid is s and its diagonal is d. Its surface area is:

A. s^2 B. d^2
C. $s^2 - d^2$ D. $s^2 + d^2$

3. A wooden box of dimensions 8 m × 7 m × 6 m is to carry rectangular boxes of dimensions 8 cm × 7 cm × 6 cm. The maximum number of boxes that can be carried in 1 wooden box is:

A. 1200000 B. 1000000
C. 9800000 D. 7500000

4. The length of the longest rod that can be placed in a room 30 m long, 24 m broad and 18 m high is:

A. 30 m B. $15\sqrt{2}$ m
C. 60 m D. $30\sqrt{2}$ m

5. If the volume of two cubes are in the ratio 8 : 1, the ratio of their edges is:

A. 8 : 1 B. $2\sqrt{2} : 1$
C. 2 : 1 D. None of these

6. A metal sheet 27 cm long 8 cm broad and 1 cm thick is melted into a cube. The difference between the surface areas of two solids will be:

A. 284 cm^2 B. 296 cm^2
C. 286 cm^2 D. 300 cm^2

7. If each edge of a cube is increased by 50%, the percentage increase in surface area is:

A. 50% B. 75%
C. 100% D. 125%

8. If a right circular cone of vertical height 24 cm has a volume of 1232 cm^3, then the area of its curved surface in cm^2 is:

A. 1254 B. 704
C. 550 D. 154

9. Two cubes have volumes in the ratio 1 : 27. The ratio of their surface areas is:

A. 1 : 3 B. 1 : 8
C. 1 : 9 D. 1 : 18

10. If the volumes of two cones are in the ratio 1 : 4 and their diameters are in the ratio 4 : 5, then the ratio of their heights is:

A. 1 : 5 B. 5 : 4
C. 5 : 16 D. 25 : 64

11. The radius of a wire is decreased to one-third. If volumes remains the same, length will increase:

A. 1 time B. 3 times
C. 6 times D. 9 times

12. A cylindrical piece of metal of radius 2 cm and height 6 cm is shaped into a cone of same radius. The height of cone is:

A. 18 cm B. 14 cm
C. 12 cm D. 8 cm

13. If 1 cubic cm of cast iron weight 21 g then the weight of a cast iron pipe of length 1 m with a bore of 3 cm and in which the thickness of the metal is 1 cm, is:

A. 21 kg B. 24.2 kg
C. 26.4 kg D. 18.6 kg

14. The number of solid spheres, each of diameter 6 cm, that could be moulded to form a solid metal cylinder of height 45 cm and diameter 4 cms, is:

A. 3 B. 4
C. 5 D. 6

15. A right cylinder and a right circular cone have the same radius and the same volume. The ratio of the height of the cylinder to that of the cone is:

A. 3 : 5 B. 2 : 5
C. 3 : 1 D. 1 : 3

ANSWERS

1	2	3	4	5	6	7	8	9	10
B	C	B	D	C	C	D	C	C	D
11	**12**	**13**	**14**	**15**					
D	A	C	C	D					

EXPLANATORY ANSWERS

1. Surface area of cube = $6a^2$

$6a^2 = 726 \Rightarrow a^2 = \frac{726}{6} = 121 \Rightarrow a = 11$ m

Volume of cube = $a^3 = 11 \times 11 \times 11 = 1331$ m^3

2. $l + b + h = s$

and $\sqrt{l^2 + b^2 + h^2} = d \Rightarrow l^2 + b^2 + h^2 = d^2$

$(l + b + h)^2 = s^2$

$\Rightarrow l^2 + b^2 + h^2 + 2(lb + bh + hl) = s^2$

$\Rightarrow d^2 + 2(lb + bh + hl) = s^2$

$\Rightarrow 2(lb + bh + hl) = s^2 - d^2$

$\therefore$ Surface area = $(s^2 - d^2)$.

3. Number of boxes = $\frac{800 \times 700 \times 600}{8 \times 7 \times 6} = 1000000$

4. Diagonal of cuboid = $\sqrt{l^2 + b^2 + h^2}$

$\therefore$ Length of longest rod = $\sqrt{30^2 + 24^2 + 18^2}$

$= \sqrt{900 + 576 + 324} = \sqrt{1800}$

$= \sqrt{30 \times 30 \times 2} = 30\sqrt{2}$ m

5. Let their volumes be $8x^3$ and x^3.
Then, their sides are $2x$ and x
$\therefore$ Ratio of their edges = 2 : 1

6. Volume of sheet = $27 \times 8 \times 1 = 216$ cm^3
Volume of cube formed = 216 cm^3

Side of cube = $\sqrt[3]{216} = 6$ cm
Surface area of cuboid = $2(lb + bh + hl)$
$= 2(27 \times 8 + 8 \times 1 + 1 \times 27) = 502$ cm^2
Surface area of cube = $6(\text{side})^2 = 6 \times 36 = 216$ cm^2
Difference in areas = $502 - 216 = 286$ cm^2

7. Let original length of cube = x
then, its surface area = $6x^2$

New edge = $\left(\frac{150}{100}x\right) = \frac{3}{2}x$

New surface area = $6 \times \left(\frac{3}{2}x\right)^2$

$= 6 \times \frac{9}{4}x^2 = \frac{27}{2}x^2$

Increase in surface area = $\left(\frac{27}{2} - 6\right)x^2 = \frac{15}{2}x^2$

$\therefore$ Increase % = $\frac{15x^2/2}{6x^2} \times 100$

$= \frac{15x^2}{12x^2} \times 100 = 125\%$

8. Volume of cone = 1232

$\Rightarrow \frac{1}{3}\pi r^2 h = 1232$

$\Rightarrow \frac{1}{3} \times \frac{22}{7} \times r^2 \times 24 = 1232$

$\Rightarrow r^2 = \frac{3 \times 7 \times 1232}{22 \times 24} = 49 \Rightarrow r = 7$ cm

$\Rightarrow l = \sqrt{r^2 + h^2} = \sqrt{7^2 + 24^2} = \sqrt{625} = 25$ cm

Lateral surface area of cone = πrl

$= \frac{22}{7} \times 7 \times 25 = 22 \times 25 = 550$ cm^2

9. Let their volumes are x^3 and $27x^3$.
Then, their sides are x and $3x$.

Ratio of their surface areas = $\frac{6x^2}{6(3x)^2} = \frac{x^2}{9x^2}$

$= 1 : 9$

10. Let the diameters of the bases of the cones be $4r$ and $5r$. Let their heights be h and H.

then, $\frac{\frac{1}{3}\pi \times \left(\frac{4r}{2}\right)^2 \times h}{\frac{1}{3}\pi\left(\frac{5r}{2}\right)^2 \times H} = \frac{1}{4}$

$\Rightarrow \frac{16}{25} \times \frac{h}{H} = \frac{1}{4}$

$\Rightarrow \frac{h}{H} = \frac{25}{64}$

11. Let original radius = r

and original length = h

$$\text{New radius} = \frac{1}{3}r$$

Let new length = H

then, $$\pi r^2 h = \pi\left(\frac{1}{3}r\right)^2 \times H = \frac{\pi r^2 H}{9}$$

$\therefore$ $$H = 9h$$

Thus length becomes 9 times.

12. Volume of cone = Volume of cylinder

$$\frac{1}{3}\pi r^2 h = \pi r^2 h$$

$$\Rightarrow \frac{1}{3} \times \frac{22}{7} \times 2 \times 2 \times h = \frac{22}{7} \times 2 \times 2 \times 6$$

$$\Rightarrow \frac{h}{3} = 6 \Rightarrow h = 18 \text{ cm}$$

$\therefore$ Height of cone = 18 cm

13. Diameter = 3 cm, h = 1 m = 100 cm

$$\therefore \text{Radius} = \frac{3}{2} \text{ cm} = 1.5 \text{ cm}$$

thickness = 1 cm

$\therefore$ R = 1.5 + 1 = 2.5 cm

r = 1.5 cm

$$\text{Volume of metal} = \pi(R^2 - r^2) \times h$$
$$= \pi[(2.5)^2 - (1.5)^2] \times 100$$
$$= \pi[4] \times 100 = \pi \times 400 \text{ cm}^3$$

$\because$ $1 \text{ cm}^3 = 21$ g

$\therefore$ $\pi \times 400 \text{ cm}^3 = 21 \times \pi \times 400$ g

$$= 21 \times \frac{22}{7} \times \frac{400}{1000} \text{ kg}$$

$$= 26.4 \text{ kg}$$

14. $$\text{Number of spheres} = \frac{\text{Volume of cylinder}}{\text{Volume of sphere}}$$

$$= \frac{\pi \times 2 \times 2 \times 45}{\frac{4}{3}\pi \times (3)^3} = \frac{4 \times 45 \times 3}{4 \times 27} = 5$$

15. Volume of cylinder = Volume of cone

$$\pi r^2 h = \frac{1}{3}\pi r^2 H$$

$$\Rightarrow 3h = H \Rightarrow \frac{h}{H} = \frac{1}{3}$$

13. DATA INTERPRETATION

The collection of figures and facts in every field is called the statistical data. There are three types of statistical data.

(*a*) **Primary data:** The data collected by the investigator or the statistician to be used or integrated himself are called primary data. It is more reliable and relevant because it is collected by the investigator himself for the first time for his study.

(*b*) **Secondary data:** The data which are collected originally by someone else and used and interpreted by others for statistical analysis are called secondary data.

(*c*) **Grouped data:** When primary data is arranged in classes or groups to bring out certain sailent feature of the data is called grouped data.

Graphical Representation of Data

A graph is a visual form for presentation of data, highlighting their basic facts and relationship.

The word graph, chart and diagram are used interchangeably for the pictorial representation of data. However, the visual form made by using rectangular coordinate system is called a graph. In general, the other pictorial representation in which the coordinate system is not used are called diagrams or charts.

Variate: The quantity that we measure from observation-to-observation is called a variate.

Class-Interval: Every data is generally divided into small group using some interval is said to be in class-interval, *e.g.*, 0–5, 5–10, 10–15 etc.

Class-Size: The difference between the true upper limit and true lower limit of a class gives the size of a class-interval, *e.g.*, class-size of the class-interval 0–5 is 5.

Mid Value: The variable value which is mid-way between the lower and upper limit of a class is called its mid-value, *e.g.*, mid-value of class-interval 0–5 is $\frac{0+5}{2} = 2.5$.

Frequency: The number of observations corresponding to particular class is said to be the frequency of that class, *e.g.*, frequency of the inteı val 5–10 is 6. It means 6 persons have got 5 or more articles but less than 10.

Cumulative Frequency: The sum of the preceding frequencies is called cumulative frequency. Last frequency of cumulative frequency column is equal to the sum of the frequencies.

Class Limit: Every interval has two limits. Lower number of the interval is called lower limit while upper number of the interval is called upper limit, *e.g.*, in class-interval 0–5, 0 is lower limit while 5 is the upper limit.

Histogram

A statistical graph that represents by the height of a rectangular column the number of times that each class of result occurs in a sample or experiment, *e.g.*, the following table represents the number of matured persons in age group (15–20) in a city.

Age Group	Number of persons
15–20	200
20–25	350
25–30	475
30–35	600
35–40	750
40–45	900
45–50	100

Then the histogram of the data is given below:

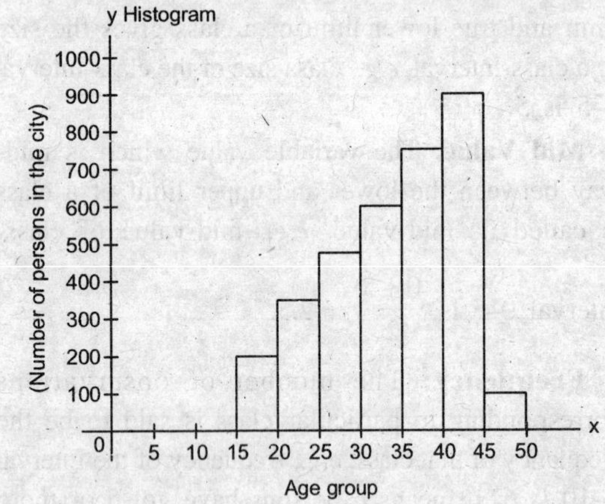

Bar Chart

A graph consisting of bars whose lengths are proportional to quantities in a set of data. It can be used when one axis cannot have a numerical scale, *e.g.*, to show how many different columns of flowers grow from a packet of mixed seeds, *e.g.*,

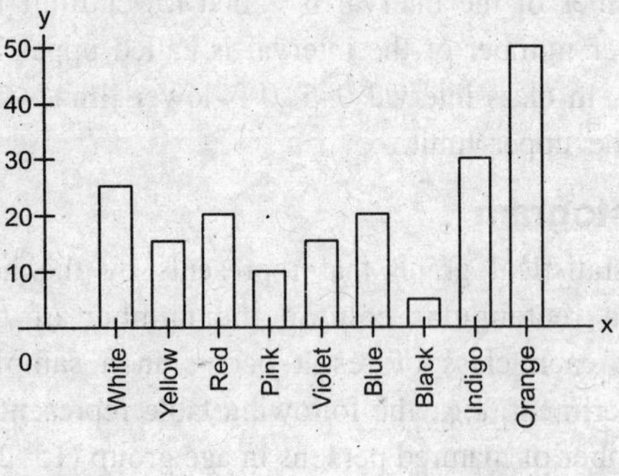

Pie Chart

A diagram in which proportions are illustrated as sectors of a circle. The relative area of the sectors representing the different proportions, *e.g.*, if out of 100 military personnels 25 personnels use tank, 30 personnels use warship, 40 personnels use aircraft and rest of them use rifles. Then pie-chart of the above data is

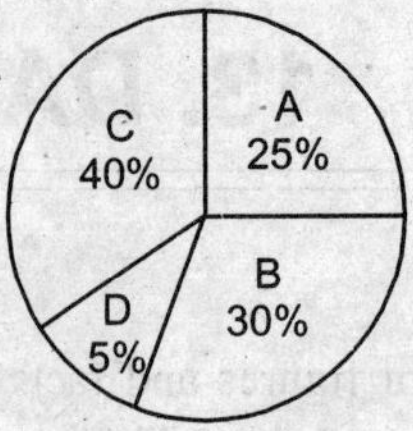

$$\text{A uses tank} = \frac{25}{100} \times 360 = 90°$$

$$\text{B uses warship} = \frac{30}{100} \times 360 = 108°$$

$$\text{C uses aircraft} = \frac{40}{100} \times 360 = 144°$$

$$\text{D uses rifles} = \frac{5}{100} \times 360 = 18°$$

EXAMPLE: Find out the marks obtained in different subjects from the following pie-diagram, if the total marks be 540.

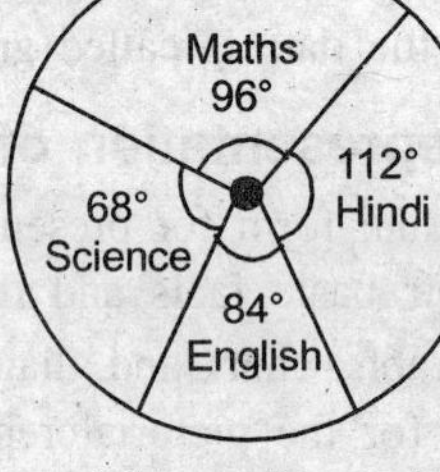

SOLUTION: Sum of the angles at the centre of circle = 360°

Total marks = 540

$$\therefore \text{ Marks obtained in Hindi} = \frac{112}{360} \times 540 = 168$$

$$\text{Marks obtained in English} = \frac{84}{360} \times 540 = 126$$

$$\text{Marks obtained in Science} = \frac{68}{360} \times 540 = 102$$

$$\text{Marks obtained in Maths} = \frac{96}{360} \times 540 = 144$$

MULTIPLE CHOICE QUESTIONS

Directions (Qs. 1 to 5): *Answers the questions on the basis of the following table:*

Assume all colleges sent equal number of candidates in all subjects for the examination.

Percentage of results for Subjects

College	Maths	Physics	Chemistry	Zoology	Botany
A	52	65	62	47	40
B	47	62	52	35	38
C	53	70	46	54	39
D	35	72	58	62	57

1. Taking all the colleges into account which subject has shown highest percentage result?
   A. Chemistry
   B. Maths
   C. Zoology
   D. Physics

2. Taking the performance in all the subjects into account which college has shown highest level of percentage results?
   A. D B. A
   C. B D. C

3. Seeing the performance of all the four colleges together which combination of groups has shown lowest level of percentage results?
   A. Zoology and Botany
   B. Physics and Chemistry
   C. Maths and Physics
   D. Chemistry and Botany

4. Taking all the colleges into account which subject has shown lowest percentage result?
   A. Maths
   B. Physics
   C. Chemistry
   D. Botany

5. Taking the performance in all subjects into account which college has shown lowest level?
   A. A B. B
   C. C D. D

Directions (Qs. 6 to 10): *These questions refer to the following circle graph showing the expenditure distribution of a certain family. The family spends ₹6500 per month.*

Expenditure Distribution of a Certain Family

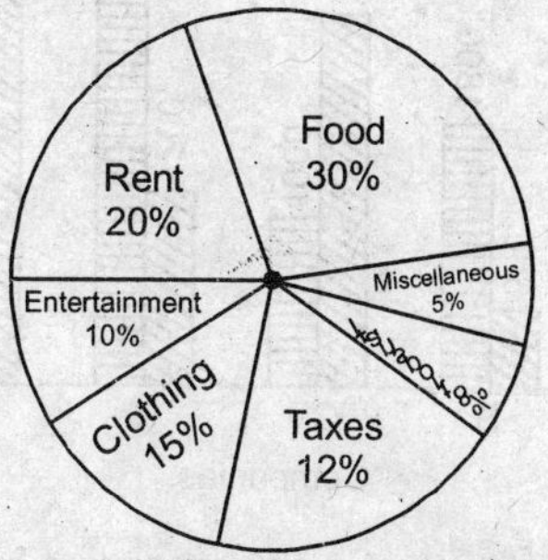

6. How much it spends on food per month?
   A. ₹ 1950
   B. ₹ 2950
   C. ₹ 4850
   D. ₹ 850

7. How much are its annual taxes?
   A. ₹ 6500 B. ₹ 9360
   C. ₹ 8900 D. ₹ 9500

8. How many degrees should there be in the central angle showing clothing, taxes and transportation combined?
   A. 100 B. 115
   C. 118 D. 126

9. How much more money per month is spent by the family on food as compared to the rent?
   A. ₹ 650 B. ₹ 750
   C. ₹ 550 D. ₹ 850

10. If the expenditure budget of the family is raised to ₹ 8000 per month and distribution on various items remain the same, then the monthly expenses on both, the entertainment and the transport, will be:
    A. ₹ 1700
    B. ₹ 1650
    C. ₹ 1440
    D. ₹ 1320

Directions (Qs. 11 to 15): *Study the following graph carefully and answer the following questions.*

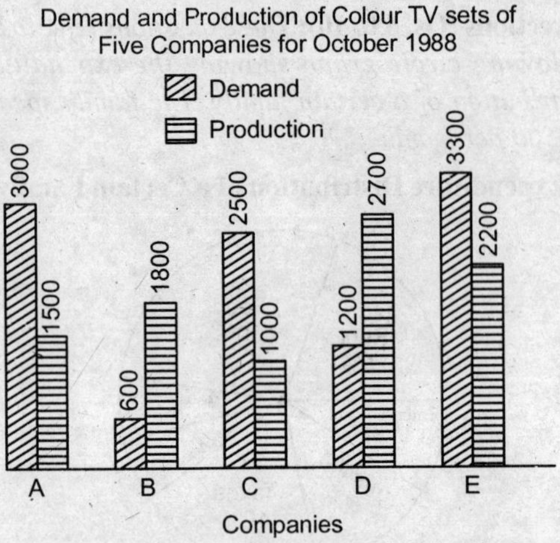

11. What is the ratio of companies having more demand than production of those having more production than demand?

A. 2 : 3 B. 4 : 1

C. 2 : 2 D. 3 : 2

12. What is the difference between average demand and average production of the five companies taken together?

A. 1400 B. 400

C. 280 D. 138

13. The production of Company 'D' is approximately how many times that of the production of the Company A?

A. 1.8 B. 4.5

C. 2.5 D. 4.9

14. The demand for Company 'B' is approximately what per cent of the demand for Company 'C'?

A. 4% B. 24%

C. 20% D. 60%

15. If Company A desires to meet the demand by purchasing surplus TV sets from a single company, which one of the following companies can meet the need adequately?

A. B B. C

C. D D. None of these

Directions (Qs. 16 to 20): *Study the following graph to answer the given questions.*

Per cent profit earned by two companies over the given years

$$\% \text{ Profit} = \frac{\text{Income} - \text{Expenditure}}{\text{Expenditure}} \times 100$$

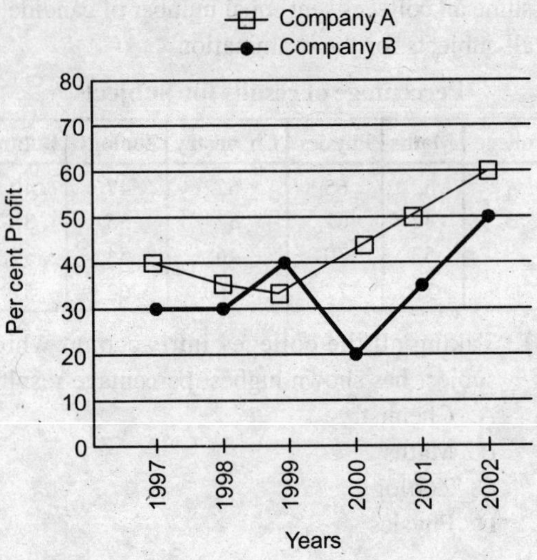

16. If the expenditure of Company B in 2000 was ₹ 200 crores, what was its income?

A. ₹ 240 crores B. ₹ 220 crores

C. ₹ 160 crores D. ₹ 180 crores

17. If the income of Company A in 2002 was ₹ 600 crores, what was its expenditure?

A. ₹ 360 crores B. ₹ 480 crores

C. ₹ 375 crores D. ₹ 320 crores

18. If the income of Company B in 1998 was ₹ 200 crores, what was its profit in 1999?

A. ₹ 21.5 crores

B. ₹ 153 crores

C. ₹ 46.15 crores

D. Cannot be determined

19. If the incomes of the two companies in 1998 were equal, what was the ratio of their expenditure?

A. 1 : 2 B. 26 : 27

C. 4 : 5 D. 100 : 67

20. What is the per cent increase in per cent profit for Company B from year 2000 to 2001?

A. 75 B. 175

C. 160 D. 150

ANSWERS

1	2	3	4	5	6	7	8	9	10
D	A	A	D	B	A	B	D	A	C
11	**12**	**13**	**14**	**15**	**16**	**17**	**18**	**19**	**20**
D	C	A	B	C	A	C	D	B	A

EXPLANATORY ANSWERS

1. Maths : $52 + 47 + 53 + 35 = 187$
Physics : $65 + 62 + 70 + 72 = 269$
Chemistry : $62 + 52 + 46 + 58 = 218$
Zoology : $47 + 35 + 54 + 62 = 198$
Botany : $40 + 38 + 39 + 57 = 174$
Clearly, Physics has shown highest percentage result.

2. A : $52 + 65 + 62 + 47 + 40 = 266$
B : $47 + 62 + 52 + 35 + 38 = 234$
C : $53 + 70 + 46 + 54 + 39 = 262$
D : $35 + 72 + 58 + 62 + 57 = 284$
Clearly, college D has shown highest level of percentage result.

3. Zoology and Botany of groups has shown lowest level of percentage result.

4. Total marks of Botany = 174 which shows lowest percentage result.

5. College B has shown lowest level because its total percentage result in all five subjects is 234 which is lowest.

6. Food 30% of ₹ 6500 = $\frac{30}{100} \times 6500$ = ₹ 1950

7. Taxes = 12% of ₹ 6500

= $\frac{12}{100} \times 6500$ = ₹ 780/month

= ₹ 780 × 12 = ₹ 9360/year

∴ Annual taxes = ₹ 9360

8. Clothing, taxes and transportation combined are 35%.

Now, $100\% = 360°$

$35\% = \frac{360°}{100} \times 35 = 126°$

9. 10% of ₹ 6500 = $\frac{10}{100} \times 6500$ = ₹ 650/month

10. 18% of ₹ 8000 = $\frac{18}{100} \times 8000$ = ₹ 1440

11. The companies having more demand than production are A, C and E *i.e.* their number is 3.
The companies having more production than demand are B and D *i.e.* their number is 2.
So, the required ratio is 3 : 2.

12. Average demand

$= \frac{1}{5}(3000 + 600 + 2500 + 1200 + 3300)$

$= \frac{10600}{5} = 2120$

Average production

$= \frac{1500 + 1800 + 1000 + 2700 + 2200}{5}$

$= \frac{9200}{5} = 1840$

∴ Difference between average demand and average production = 2120 – 1840 = 280

13. Let $K(1500) = 2700$

$\Rightarrow \quad K = \frac{2700}{1500} = \frac{9}{5} = 1.8.$

14. Let x% of (demand for C) = (demand for B)

$\Rightarrow \quad \frac{x}{100} \times 2500 = 600$

$\Rightarrow \quad x = \frac{600 \times 100}{2500} = 24\%$

15. Since Company D produces highest number of TV sets and Company A desires to meet the demand by purchasing surplus TV sets from a single Company.
Clearly, D can meet the demand of A.
∴ Correct answer is C.

16. Let the income be ₹ x crores

$$\therefore \quad 20 = \frac{x - 200}{200} \times 100$$

$$\Rightarrow \quad 40 = x - 200$$

$$\Rightarrow \quad x = 240$$

$\therefore$ Income = ₹ 240 crores

17. The income of Company A in 2002

= ₹ 600 crores

% Profit = 60

Let the expenditure be ₹ x crores.

$$\therefore \quad 60 = \frac{600 - x}{x} \times 100$$

$$\Rightarrow \quad x = \frac{600 - x}{60} \times 100$$

$$\Rightarrow \quad x = \frac{(600 - x)5}{3}$$

$$\Rightarrow \quad 3x = 3000 - 5x$$

$$\Rightarrow \quad 8x = 3000$$

$$\Rightarrow \quad x = \frac{3000}{8} = 375$$

Hence, expenditure = ₹ 375 crores.

18. It cannot be determined as Income and Expenditure of respective year is not known.

19. Let their equal incomes be ₹ 1 crore. Also, let expenditure of Company A be ₹ E_1 crores and that of Company B be ₹ E_2 crores.

Now, $$35 = \frac{1 - E_1}{E_1} \times 100$$

$$35\,E_1 = 100 - 100\,E_1$$

$$135\,E_1 = 100 \qquad ...(i)$$

Similarly $$30 = \frac{1 - E_2}{E_2} \times 100$$

$$130\,E_2 = 100 \qquad ...(ii)$$

From (*i*) and (*ii*)

$$135\,E_1 = 130\,E_2$$

$$\Rightarrow \quad \frac{E_1}{E_2} = \frac{130}{135} = \frac{26}{27}$$

$$\therefore \quad E_1 : E_2 = 26 : 27$$

20. Required percentage = $\frac{35 - 20}{20} \times 100$

$$= \frac{15}{20} \times 100 = 75.$$

GENERAL SCIENCE

PHYSICS

1. When a body is stationary
- A. there is no force acting on it
- B. the combination of forces acting on it balance each other
- C. the force acting on it are not in contact with it
- D. the body is in vacuum

2. Newton's first law of motion gives the concept of
- A. energy
- B. work
- C. momentum
- D. inertia

3. Newton's second law gives a measure of
- A. acceleration
- B. force
- C. momentum
- D. angular momentum

4. A man in a lift will weigh more when
- A. lift accelerated upward
- B. lift accelerates downward
- C. lift descends freely
- D. the lift going up in slowing down

5. Three equal weights of mass 2 kg. each are hanging on a string passing over a fixed pully as shown in figure. What is the tension in the string connecting the weight *B* and *C*?

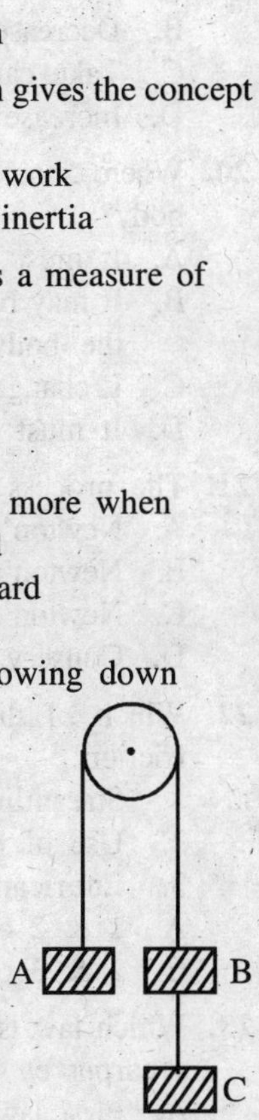

- A. zero
- B. 13 N
- C. 3.3 N
- D. 19.6 N

6. A body is accelerated by applying a force of 30 N. The momentum of the body after 2 sec.
- A. 7.5 kg-m/s
- B. 30 kg-m/s
- C. 120 kg-m/s
- D. 60 kg-m/s

7. With what minimum acceleration can a fireman slide down a rope whose breaking strength is 3/4th of his weight?
- A. 1/4 g
- B. 1/2 g
- C. 3/4 g
- D. zero

8. Conservation of linear momentum is equivalent to
- A. Newton's 1st law of motion
- B. Newton's 2nd law of motion
- C. Newton's 3rd law of motion
- D. None of the above

9. If the net force acting on a body is doubled, the acceleration of the body is
- A. halved
- B. doubled
- C. unchanged
- D. quadrupled

10. A jet plane flies in air because
- A. the thrust of the jet compensates the force of gravity
- B. the weight of air whose volume is equal to the volume of the plane is more than the weight of the plane
- C. the flow of air and the wings causes an upward force which compensates for the force of gravity
- D. the gravity does not act on body moving with high speed

11. The passengers in a boat are not allowed to stand because:
A. this will raise the centre of gravity and the boat will be rocked
B. this will lower centre of gravity and the boat will rocked
C. the effective weight of system increases
D. of surface tension effects

12. A person presses the earth least where he is:
A. sitting
B. standing
C. running
D. lying on the ground

13. One litre of cool air weighs heavier than one litre of hot air because of the:
A. increased number of collisions between the molecules
B. increased number of molecules at high temperature
C. greater energy of molecules at high temperature
D. lower energy of molecules at high temperature

14. A bomb is dropped from an aeroplane moving horizontal at constant speed. When air resistance is taken into consideration, then the bomb:
A. flies with the aeroplane
B. falls on earth ahead of the aeroplane
C. falls on earth behind aeroplane
D. falls on earth exactly below the aeroplane.

15. A ball is thrown upwards in a train which is accelerating. The ball will fall
A. Ahead of the thrower
B. Behind the thrower
C. In the hands of thrower
D. Data inadequate

16. The flying of birds is a proof of Newton's:
A. first law
B. second law
C. third law of motion
D. both second and third law

17. A moving bullet hits a solid target resting on a frictionless surface and gets embedded in it. What is conserved in this process?
A. both momentum and kinetic energy
B. kinetic energy alone
C. momentum alone
D. neither momentum nor kinetic energy

18. Fat can be separated from milk in a cream-separator because of:
A. cohesive force
B. gravitational force
C. centrifugal force
D. centripetal force

19. A cricket player while taking a catch lowers his hands to
A. Increase time of impulse
B. Decrease time of impulse
C. Take catch safely
D. Increase the area of impact

20. Where should be the centre of gravity of a body?
A. It must lie within the body
B. It may be near but not essentially within the body
C. It changes its position from time to time
D. It must be outside the body

21. The process of walking involves
A. Newton's first law of motion
B. Newton's second law of motion
C. Newton's third law of motion
D. Conservation of momentum

22. Which of the following is used to reduce friction
1. Streamlines
2. Use of ball bearings
3. Lubrication
A. 1 & 2 only B. 1 & 3 only
C. 2 & 3 only D. 1, 2 & 3

23. Which law is involved in the act of cleaning a carpet by beating it with a stick?
A. First law of motion.
B. Second law of motion.
C. Law of conservation of energy.
D. Law of conservation of mass.

24. When a body is taken from the earth to the moon:
A. Its weight increases
B. Its weight decreases
C. Its weight remains unchanged
D. It becomes completely weightless

25. Which of the following is the cause of weightlessness experienced while orbiting around earth on a spaceship ?
A. Inertia B. Zero gravity
C. Acceleration D. Centre of gravity

26. The weight of an object would be minimum when it is placed:
A. at the North Pole
B. at the South Pole
C. at the Equator
D. at the Centre of the Earth

27. As the train starts moving, a man sitting inside leans backwards because of:
A. inertia of rest
B. inertia of motion
C. moment of inertia
D. conservation of mass

28. Electrons revolve round the nucleus because of:
A. cohesive force B. adhesive force
C. centripetal force D. centrifugal force

29. If the speed of a particle in circular motion is doubled and its radius is halved, then the centripetal force will
A. increase six times
B. increase eight times
C. increase four times
D. remain the same

30. If velocity of a particle is uniform, then its acceleration would be
A. positive B. negative
C. very low D. zero

31. The speed of the earth is highest when it is
A. farthest from the sun
B. nearest to the sun
C. passing through the month of September
D. none of the above

32. Slopes are made on the road in order to
A. help the driver to drive slowly
B. reduce friction
C. help the vehicle to get the centripetal force
D. help the driver to retain balance while driving

33. If a body is sent with a velocity of ....km sec^{-1}, it would leave the earth forever.
A. 11.9 B. 11.6
C. 11.4 D. 11.2

34. In the motion of the planets,
A. the angular velocity is constant
B. the linear momentum is constant
C. the angular momentum is constant
D. none of the above

35. The value of g
A. increases with increase in depth
B. decreases with decrease in depth
C. remains same regardless of the depth
D. depends upon the mass of the object

36. The path traced by a satellite launch vehicle is
A. a hyperbola B. a circle
C. a parabola D. none of these

37. If the speed of rotation of the Earth increases, the weight of the body at the equator will
A. increase
B. remain the same as before
C. be zero
D. decrease

38. If the distance of the Sun from the Earth is doubled, then the gravitational attraction between the Sun and the Earth will be
A. 1/3rd of the value at present
B. 1/4th of the value at present
C. 1/6th of the value at present
D. none of the above

39. An iron ball and a wooden ball are released from a height in vacuum. The speed of the iron ball would be
A. same to the speed of the wooden ball
B. more than the speed of the wooden ball
C. lesser than the speed of the wooden ball
D. none of these

40. A freely falling body
A. is weightless
B. has double the weight, which it actually possesses
C. is likely to gain weight as it moves towards the Earth
D. none of the above

41. Moment of inertia of thin uniform rod of length l is equal to
A. $\frac{ml^2}{6}$ B. $\frac{ml^2}{12}$
C. $\frac{ml^2}{4}$ D. $\frac{ml^2}{24}$

42. The inertial force acts in a
A. opposite direction to that of acceleration force
B. same direction as that of accelerating force
C. perpendicular direction to that accelerating force
D. none of the above

43. The earth's gravitational force field is said to be conservative force field because
A. the value of gravitational force rise fixed
B. the direction of gravitational force is fixed
C. the work acted by the earth's gravitational field on a particle is independent on the path traced out by the particle
D. the work acted by the earth's gravitational field will cause same path for all particles irrespective of their mass

44. The maximum frictional force that comes into play when a body just begins to slide over the surface of another body is known as
A. Dynamic friction
B. Rolling friction
C. Kinetic friction
D. Limiting friction

45. The limiting force of friction is
A. the value of frictional force which stops the movement of the body
B. the value of frictional force which can not exceed under a situation
C. the frictional force acting when the body is just about to move
D. the frictional force acting on a body when it is in motion

46. A car is moving at 100 km/h. If the mass of the car is 950 kg, its kinetic energy is:
A. 367 J B. 0.367 J
C. 3.67 MJ D. 3.67 J

47. Einstein got his Nobel Prize for:
A. His theory of relativity
B. Explanation of Photoelectric effect
C. His theory of atomic heats of solids
D. None of the above

48. If a body moves along a frictionless horizontal surface its weight:
A. does work B. does not work
C. work partially D. none of these

49. A car and a lorry both are moving with equal kinetic energies. If equal breaking force is applied on both, then before coming to rest:
A. the car will cover a greater distance
B. lorry will cover a greater distance
C. both will cover the same distance
D. the distance covered by them will depend only on their respective velocities.

50. The work done by a force:
A. is independent of the frame of reference
B. is same in all reference-frames
C. is same in all inertial frames
D. none of these

51. Identify the correct statement of Work-Energy Theorem:
A. Work done by all the forces on a particle to displace it is equal to its change in kinetic energy.
B. Work done by all the forces on a particle is equal to its change in mechanical energy.
C. Work done by all the forces acting on a particle is equal to change in its potential energy.
D. Work done by a force on a particle is equal to change in its kinetic energy.

52. Which of the following statement is true?
A. Kinetic energy and momentum both are conserved in all types of motion.
B. Momentum is conserved in elastic collision but not in inelastic collision.
C. Total kinetic energy is not conserved but momentum is conserved in inelastic collision.
D. Kinetic energy is conserved in elastic collision but not in inelastic collision.

53. Thermal energy is a energy due to:
A. Kinetic energy of molecules
B. Potential energy of molecules
C. Both (A) and (B)
D. None of these

54. The internal energy of a gas:
A. is the sum total of kinetic and potential energies.
B. is the total transitional kinetic energies.
C. is the total kinetic energy of randomly moving molecules.
D. is the total kinetic energy of gas molecules.

55. Power is measured in—
A. Joules per second
B. Joules per minute
C. Joules per square second
D. None of these

56. A rifle bullet loses 1/20th of its velocity in passing through a plank. Assuming constant resistive force, the least number of such planks required just to stop the bullet is:
A. 5 B. 10
C. 11 D. 20

57. Absolute zero is
A. –273°C B. –273°F
C. –273°K D. none of these

58. Which one of the following statements is correct.
A. It is the temperature at which, saturated vapour pressure of a liquid equals the atmospheric pressure
B. It is the temperature below which, evaporation of the liquid occurs very rapidly
C. It is the temperature above which, a gas cannot be liquified.
D. It is the temperature at which the states of solid, liquid and gas co-exit.

59. When the temperature of body is equal to that of atmosphere, then
A. heat transfer between body and atmosphere continues
B. there is no exchange of heat
C. the body is in unstable equilibrium
D. none of the above

60. Good absorbers of heat are
A. poor emitters of heat
B. good emitters of heat
C. only black bodies
D. none of these

61. How many calories of heat are required by 1 gram of water at 99°C to boil off?
A. 530 B. 640
C. 540 D. 500

62. The mean kinetic energy of a gas molecule is proportional to
A. $\sqrt{T}$ B. T^2
C. T D. None of the above

63. The temperature, to which a gas must be cooled before it can be liquified by pressure alone, is known as its
A. saturation point
B. freezing point
C. liquification temperature
D. critical temperature

64. What is Latent Heat?
A. It is the heat given to a body and simultaneously the body releases it to the atmosphere
B. It is the heat given to a body to heat it by 1°C
C. It is the heat given to body to change its state at constant temperature
D. None of the above

65. In case of negative work, the angle between the force and displacement is:
A. 0° B. 45°
C. 90° D. 180°

66. The work done on an object does not depend on the:
A. displacement
B. angle between force and displacement
C. force applied
D. initial velocity of the object

67. Water stored in a dam possesses:
A. no energy B. electrical energy
C. kinetic energy D. potential energy

68. Which of the following does not possess the ability to do work not because of motion?
A. a sparrow flying in the sky
B. a sparrow moving slowly on the ground
C. a sparrow in the nest on a tree
D. a squirrel going up a tree

69. When an object falls freely towards the earth, then its total energy:
A. increases
B. decreases
C. remains constant
D. first increases and then decreases

70. Which one of the following is not the unit of energy?
A. joule B. newton-metre
C. kilowatt D. kilowatt-hour

71. Which of the following energy change involves frictional force?
A. chemical energy to heat energy
B. kinetic energy to heat energy
C. potential energy to sound energy
D. chemical energy to kinetic energy

72. An object is falling freely from a height x. After it has fallen a height $x/2$, it will possess:
A. only potential energy
B. only kinetic energy
C. half potential and half kinetic energy
D. less potential and more kinetic energy

73. The commercial unit of energy is:
A. watt B. watt-hour
C. kilowatt-hour D. kilowatt

74. The device which converts mechanical energy into energy which runs our microwave oven is:
A. electric motor B. alternator
C. turbine D. electric heater

75. Kinetic energy of a body is directly proportion to its:
A. Weight B. Speed
C. Mass D. Velocity

76. Internal energy of a gas increases when
A. the change is cyclic
B. it absorbs heat
C. the change is adiabatic
D. none of these

77. The power of a water jet flowing through an office of radius 10 cm with a velocity 5 ms^{-1} is
A. 196 watt B. 1960 watt
C. 19.6 watt D. 1.96 watt

78. Which of the following statements is wrong?
A. Sound travels in straight line
B. Sound travels as waves
C. Sound is a form of energy
D. Sound travels faster in vacuum than in air

79. Sound waves do not show in air:
A. polarisation B. diffraction
C. refraction D. reflection

80. With the rise of temperature, the velocity of sound:
A. decreases
B. remains the same
C. increases
D. is independent of temperature

81. Velocity of sound will be:
A. smaller in moist air than in dry air
B. greater in moist air than in dry air
C. same in moist and dry air
D. independent of its density

82. The apparent wavelength of light from a star moving away from the earth is 0.02% more than actual wavelength. What is the velocity of the star.
A. 30 kms^{-1} B. 60 kms^{-1}
C. 90 kms^{-1} D. none of these

83. Buzzing of a mosquito is:
A. loud sound B. shrill sound
C. flat sound D. sweet sound

84. The frequency of the third harmonic of a closed organ pipe is equal to which of the overtone

A. first   B. second

C. fourth   D. none of these

85. Pitch of sound depends upon it:

A. wavelength

B. frequency

C. amplitude

D. periodicity and regularity

86. Doppler's effect of sound is produced when the source and the observer are:

A. moving

B. in relative motion

C. stationary

D. resonance phenomenon

87. The Doppler effect is applicable for:

A. light waves only

B. sound waves only

C. both light and sound waves

D. none of the above

88. To a stationary man the frequency of a sound source moving towards the man appears to be:

A. lower than the original frequency

B. same as the original frequency

C. higher than the original frequency

D. lower as well higher than the original frequency depending upon the speed of the source

89. The same notes being played on the Sitar and Veena differ in:

A. pitch

B. quality

C. both pitch and quality

D. neither pitch nor quality

90. Two closed organ pipes, when sounded together give five beats per second. Their lengths are in the ratio of 100 : 101. The fundamental notes (in Hz.) produced by them are

A. 245, 250   B. 250, 255

C. 495, 500   D. 500, 505

91. When we hear a sound, we can identify its source from:

A. amplitude of sound

B. intensity of sound

C. wavelength of sound

D. absorb sound

92. Consider the following statements:

Assertion A: The velocity of sound in the air increases due to presence of moisture in it.

Reason R: The presence of moisture in air lowers the density of air.

Of these statements,

A. both (A) and (R) are true and (R) is the correct explanation of (A).

B. both (A) and (R) are true but (R) is not the correct explanation of (A).

C. (A) is true but (R) is false.

D. (A) is false but (R) is true.

93. To hear a clear echo what should be the minimum distance between the reflecting surface and the observer?

A. 165 metre   B. 165 feet

C. 16.5 metre   D. 16.5 feet

94. Why does radio reception improve slightly during the night?

A. The outside noise is reduced very much at night.

B. Unlike the daytime, only a few radio stations broadcast during the night.

C. Sunlight affects radio broadcasts to some extent during the day.

D. The magnetic field of the earth acts with reduced intensity during the night, thereby reducing its impact on broadcasts.

95. An air-box attached to a musical instrument increases the:

A. pitch of the sound

B. intensity of the sound

C. quality of the sound

D. shrillness of the sound

96. An astronaut can't hear his companion at the surface of the moon because:
A. produced frequencies are above the audio frequency
B. there is no medium for sound propagation
C. temperature is too low during night and too high during day.
D. there are too many craters on the surface of the moon

97. The difference between musical sound and noise is due to:
A. musical instruments
B. wave lengths
C. pitch
D. intensity

98. Why the auditorium walls are provided with cardboard panels and porons wall furnishings?
A. So that the sound from the stage may be heard properly
B. So that the echo effect may be minimised
C. So that the sound may appear to be pleasing on the ears of the listeners
D. All of the above

99. A musical sound is the one that is produced
A. at regular intervals
B. in quick succession
C. Both (A) and (B)
D. None of (A) and (B)

100. Which relationship, out of those given below, represents the velocity of sound wave?
A. $v = \frac{\lambda}{n}$ B. $v = nl$
C. $v = \frac{n}{\lambda}$ D. $v = nl + 1$

CHEMISTRY

1. Volume of a gas at NTP is 1.12×10^{-7} cc. Calculate the number of molecules in it.
A. 3.01×10^{12} B. 3.01×10^{20}
C. 3.01×10^{24} D. 30.1×10^{23}

2. The element present in the largest amount in rocks and minerals is
A. Silicon B. Carbon
C. Hydrogen D. Gold

3. The average K.E. of an ideal gas per molecule in SI units at 25°C will be
A. 6.17×10^{-21} kJ B. 6.17×10^{-21} J
C. 6.17×10^{-20} J D. 7.16×10^{-20} J

4. The alloy of steel containing chromium to resist rusting, is known as:
A. wrought iron B. cast iron
C. hard steel D. stainless steel

5. The number of atoms in 100 g of an F.C.C. crystal with density d = 10 gm cm^{-3} and cell edge as 200 pm is equal to
A. 3×10^{25} B. 5×10^{24}
C. 1×10^{25} D. 2×10^{25}

6. Which of the following is a chemical change?
A. Evaporation B. Precipitation
C. Dissolution D. Oxidation

7. Which of the following substance consists of only one element?
A. Diamond B. Glass
C. Marble D. Sand

8. Why is tungsten used in the manufacture of electric bulbs?
A. It is cheaper than other metals
B. It is both durable and economical
C. It has high melting-point
D. It makes the bulb light brighter

9. If rate of diffusion of A is 5 times that of B, what will be the density ratio of A and B?
A. $\frac{1}{25}$ B. $\frac{1}{5}$
C. 25 D. 5

10. Which is the lightest element in the universe?
A. Helium B. Hydrogen
C. Nitrogen D. Silicon

11. Gun-powder is a mixture of:
A. nitrates of potassium and sodium
B. sulphates of potassium and mangnesium
C. charcoal, sulphur and potassium nitrate
D. potassium sulphate and charcoal

12. For protection against gamma radiations, the shields should be made of:
A. Iron B. Lead
C. Copper D. Tin

13. Which of the following statement is correct?
I. German silver is an alloy of silver and copper and zinc.
II. There is no zinc in brass
III. Bronze is an alloy of copper and tin
A. I, II and III B. Only III
C. I and III D. I and II

14. The metal generally mixed with gold while making ornaments is:
A. zinc B. iron
C. silver D. copper

15. Magnalium is an alloy of
A. Magnesium and Copper
B. Aluminium and Copper
C. Magnesium and Aluminium
D. None of these

16. When a crystal of potassium permanganate is placed at the bottom of water in a beaker, the water in the whole beaker turns purple on its own, even without stirring. This is an example of:
A. distribution B. intrusion
C. diffusion D. effusion

17. Choose the correct statement in respect of fluids.
A. only gases behave as fluids
B. gases and solids behave as fluids
C. gases and liquids behave as fluids
D. None of these

18. Which one of the following represents the correct arrangement in the increasing order of forces of attraction between their particles?
A. water, air, oxygen
B. air, sugar, oil
C. oxygen, water, sugar
D. None of these

19. If 4 g of oxygen diffuse through a very narrow hole, how much hydrogen would have diffused under identical conditions?
A. 16 g B. 1 g
C. $\frac{1}{4}$g D. 64 g

20. The best evidence for the existence and movement of particles in liquids was provided by:
A. John Dalton B. Thomas Edyson
C. J.J. Thomson D. Robert Brown

21. Which form of matter has no fixed shape but it has a fixed volume?
A. krypton B. kerosene
C. carbon steel D. oxygen

22. When a gas jar full of air is placed upside down on a gas jar full of bromine vapours, the red-brown vapours of bromine from the lower jar go upward into the jar containing air. In this experiment:
A. bromine cannot be heavier than air because it is going upwards against gravity
B. both air and bromine have the same density
C. bromine is heavier than air
D. air is heavier than bromine

23. Which one of the following statements is not true?
A. the molecules in a solid vibrate about a fixed position
B. the molecules in a liquid are arranged in a regular pattern
C. the molecules in a gas exert negligibly small forces on each other, except during collisions
D. the molecules of a gas occupy all the space available

24. Which one of the following does not undergo sublimation?
A. iodine
B. sodium chloride
C. ammonium chloride
D. None of these

25. If the temperature of an object of 268 K, it will be equivalent to:
A. –5°C B. –50°C
C. –15°C D. –25°C

26. The boiling point of ethane is, –88°C. This temperature will be equivalent to:
A. 285 K B. 218 K
C. 185 K D. –185 K

27. When heat is constantly supplied by a gas burner with small flame to melt ice, then the temperature of ice during melting:
A. increases very slowly
B. does not increase at all
C. first remain constants then decreases
D. None of these

28. When water at 0°C freezes to form ice at the same temperature of 0°C, then it:
A. absorbs some heat
B. releases some heat
C. neither absorbs nor releases heat
D. Both A and B

29. The latent heat of vaporisation of water is:
A. 2.25×10^6 J/kg
B. 2.25×10^8 J/kg
C. 22.5×10^4 J/kg
D. 22.5×10^{-6} J/kg

30. Which of the following represent the suitable conditions for the liquefaction of gases?
A. low temperature, low pressure
B. high temperature, low pressure
C. low temperature, high pressure
D. high temperature, high pressure

31. During summer days, water kept in an earthen pot (pitcher) becomes cool because of the phenomenon of:
A. radiation B. transpiration
C. osmosis D. evaporation

32. The conversion of a solid vapours without passing through the liquid state is called:
A. osmosis B. fusion
C. sublimation D. evaporation

33. Which of the following energy is absorbed during the change of state of a substance?
A. specific heat B. latent heat
C. heat capacity D. heat of solution

34. During respiration, glucose and oxygen enter our body cells and waste products carbon dioxide and water leave the body cells by the process of:
A. evaporation B. osmosis
C. diffusion D. plasmolysis

35. Which of the following is not an element?
A. graphite B. germanium
C. silica D. silicon

36. Which one of the following substances is neither a good conductor of electricity nor an insulator?
A. gallium B. germanium
C. chromium D. potassium

37. The element which is not common between the compounds called baking soda and soda ash is
A. nitrogen B. hydrogen
C. oxygen D. sulphur

38. Which elements are normally exist in the liquid state?
A. iodine and mercury
B. mercury and chlorine
C. bromine and iodine
D. bromine and mercury

39. On the basis of composition of matter, milk is considered to be:
A. a pure substance
B. an impure substance
C. an element
D. a compound

40. Which of the following does not have fixed melting point/boiling point?
A. gold B. ethanol
C. air D. oxygen

41. Which is the most effective method of separating mixtures of miscible volatile liquids?
A. Fractional distilliation
B. Simple distillation
C. Chromatography
D. Filtration

42. Brittleness is a property of solid due to which—
A. they break into small pieces
B. the solid does not back to its original shape
C. solid regains its original shape
D. None of these

43. The purification of a substance in which it eva-porates without melting can be carried out by:
A. Crystallization
B. Distillation
C. Steam distillation
D. Sublimation

44. Stainless steel is an alloy of:
A. Iron and nickel
B. Iron, chromium and nickel
C. Iron, chromium and zinc
D. Iron and manganese

45. Out of the following, an example of matter which can be termed as fluid is:
A. carbon B. sulphur
C. oxygen D. phosphorus

46. An aqueous solution of an acid is characterised by the presence of
A. H^+ ions B. H_2^+ ions
C. H_4O^+ ions D. H_3O^+ ions

47. Which of the following acid is used as a dehydrating and drying agent?
A. Acetic B. Hydrochloric
C. Nitric D. Sulphuric

48. A substance which behaves both as an acid and base is
A. Amphoteric B. Alkali
C. Salt D. Hygroscope

49. Soda water contains:
A. Carbonic acid B. Sulphuric acid
C. Carboxylic acid D. Nitrous acid

50. The main use of salt in the diet is to:
A. make the taste of food better
B. produce in small amounts the hydrochloric acid required for the digestion of food.
C. ease the process of cooking
D. increase the solubility of food particles in water

51. The acid that can be used as a hypnotic is:
A. tartaric acid B. benzoic acid
C. barbituric acid D. butanoic acid

52. When milk is converted into curd, the sour taste is due to:
A. Acetic acid B. Citric acid.
C. Lactic acid D. Tartaric acid

53. Match the following :

	List-I		List-II
I.	Sodium bicarbonate	a.	Double salt
II.	Alum	b.	Mixed salt
III.	Bleaching Powder	c.	Acidic salt
IV.	Sodium chloride	d.	Normal salt

A. I-c, II-a, III-b, IV-d
B. I-a, II-d, III-b, IV-c
C. I-d, II-a, III-c, 1V-b
D. I-c, II-b, III-a, IV-d

54. All acids essentially contain the element:
A. oxygen B. chlorine
C. sulphur D. hydrogen

55. The acid generally stored in batteries is:
A. sulphuric acid B. nitric acid
C. hydrochloric acid D. acetic acid

56. Ants have .... acid.
A. glutaric B. citric
C. acetic D. formic

57. Acid precipitation is now regarded as a serious problem in some European and Asian countries. Its major cause or source is:
A. discharge of acidic effluents onto neutral or slightly alkaline land where the acidic components precipitate.
B. emission of sulphur oxides and nitrogen oxides from thermal power plants and burning of fossil fuels; these oxides dissolve in atmospheric water vapour and fall back on earth as acid rain.
C. natural carbon dioxide released during respiration of living organisms dissolves in water, forming carbonic acid which

is the chief contributor to acidity in rain water.

D. None of the above

58. Weakest acid among the following is:

A. CH_3COOH B. C_6H_5OH

C. H_2O D. C_2H_2

59. Vinegar contains:

A. 10 to 20% acetic acid

B. 10% acetic acid

C. 6 to 10% acetic acid

D. 100% acetic acid

60. Formic acid is not representative member of carboxylic acids because

A. it does not contain alkyl group

B. it contains an aldehydic group while the other acids do not

C. it is the first member of the series

D. it is a gas

61. Baking soda is a/an:

A. Acidic substance

B. Basic substance

C. Neutral substance

D. None of these

62. Which of the following is acidic:

A. Milk B. Lemon

C. Salt solution D. Sugar solution

63. Which of the following substance has bitter taste?

A. Milk B. Amla

C. Soap solution D. Salt solution

64. Which of the following is a base according to Lowry-Bronsted concept?

A. I^- B. H_3O^-

C. HCl D. NH_4^+

65. Name the substance which makes the fruits sour:

A. Acids B. Bases

C. Salts D. None of these

66. When a particular quantity of a hydrochloric acid solution is mixed with a particular quantity of sodium hydroxide solution, one gets a:

A. Half acidic solution

B. Acidic solution

C. Neutral solution

D. Basic solution

67. Acids and bases react to produce:

A. Water and oxygen gas

B. Salt and hydrogen gas

C. Salt and water

D. None of these

68. What happens when bases are dissolved in water?

A. H^+ ions are formed

B. OH^- ions are formed

C. O^- ions are formed

D. None of these

69. What does the acid in water contain?

A. H^+ ions B. OH^- ions

C. O^- ions D. 2OH ions

70. For an acidic solution:

A. $[H^+] = [OH^-]$ B. $[H^+] < [OH^-]$

C. $[H^+] > [OH^-]$ D. $[H^+] = 2OH$

71. Which compound is used as an antacid?

A. Soda ash

B. Baking soda

C. Nitrous oxide

D. Magnesium carbonate

72. Which compound is used for disinfecting water?

A. Soda ash

B. Sodium carbonate

C. Bleaching powder

D. Hydrogen oxide

73. A salt whose aqueous solution will have a pH of more than 7 will be:

A. K_2CO_3 B. K_2SO_4

C. NaCl D. NH_4Cl

74. Chemical formula of baking soda is:

A. Na_2CO_3 B. $Na_2CO_3 10H_2O$

C. $Na_2CO_3 . 2H_2O$ D. $NaHCO_3$

75. Which of the following salts will give an aqueous solution having pH of almost 7?

A. NH_4NO_3 B. NH_4Cl

C. $CaCl_2$ D. KCl

76. According to Arrhenius theory acids are those compounds which give
A. Oxygen ions B. Hydrogen ions
C. Hydroxide ions D. None of these

77. Which is the strong base?
A. NaOH B. $Mg(OH)_2$
C. NH_4OH D. None of these

78. According to Bronsted Lowry concept, the relative strengths of the bases CH_3COO^-, OH^- and Cl^- are in the order
A. $OH^- > CH_3COO^- > Cl^-$
B. $Cl^- > OH^- > CH_3OO^-$
C. $CH_3COO^- > OH^- > Cl^-$
D. $OH^- > Cl^- > CH_3COO^-$

79. A solution reacts with marble chips to produce a gas which turns lime water milky. The solution contains:
A. Na_2SO_4 B. $CaSO_4$
C. H_2SO_4 D. K_2SO_4

80. Which one of the following is not an organic acid?
A. ethanoic acid B. formic acid
C. citric acid D. carbonic acid

81. Which property is not shown by acids?
A. they have sour taste
B. they feel soapy
C. they turn litmus red
D. None of these

82. The discomfort caused by indigestion due to over-eating can be cured by taking:
A. vinegar B. lemon juice
C. baking soda D. caustic soda

83. Which property is common between vinegar and curd?
A. have sweet taste B. have bitter taste
C. are tasteless D. have sour taste

84. Which indicator produces a pink colour in an alkaline solution?
A. methyl orange B. turmeric paper
C. phenolphthalein D. litmus paper

85. Fresh milk has pH of 6. When milk changes into curd, the pH value will:
A. become 7
B. become less than 6
C. become more than 7
D. remain unchanged

86. Wasp stings can be treated with:
A. baking soda B. vinegar
C. washing soda D. milk of magnesia

87. The colour of methyl orange indicator in a solution is yellow. The pH of this solution is likely to be:
A. 7 B. less than 7
C. 0 D. more than 7

88. Which of the following is a Lewis acid?
A. Cl^- B. H_3O^+
C. BF_3 D. C_2H_5OH

89. Bee sting contains:
A. an acidic liquid
B. a salt solution
C. an alkaline liquid
D. an alcohol

90. Wasp sting contains:
A. a sugar solution B. an acidic liquid
C. a salt solution D. an alkaline liquid

91. One of the following does not inject an acidic liquid into the skin through its sting. This is:
A. honey bee B. ant
C. wasp D. nettle leaf hair

92. The salt which will give an acidic solution on dissolving in water is:
A. KCl B. NH_4Cl
C. Na_2CO_3 D. CH_3COONa

93. One of the following salts will give an alkaline solution on dissolving in water. This is:
A. Na_2CO_3 B. Na_2SO_4
C. NaCl D. $(NH_4)_2SO_4$

94. The number of molecules of water of crystallisation present in washing soda crystals is:
A. five B. two
C. ten D. seven

95. The aqueous solution of one of the following salts will turn phenolphthalein indicator pink.

This salt is:

A. KCl B. K_2SO_4

C. K_2CO_3 D. KNO_3

96. Which of the following can adsorb largest volume of hydrogen gas?

A. Finely divided platinum

B. Finely divided nickel

C. Colloidal solution of palladium

D. Colloidal Hydroxide

97. A basic oxide will be formed by the element:

A. K B. S

C. P D. Kr

98. An acidic oxide is produced by the element:

A. Na B. C

C. Ca D. H

99. Which among the following is most reactive metal:

A. aluminium B. copper

C. tin D. calcium

100. The least reactive metal among the following is:

A. sodium B. silver

C. copper D. lead

BIOLOGY

1. The structure which constitutes the basic structural and functional unit of living beings is:

A. Atoms B. Cell

C. Molecule D. None of the above

2. Chloroplast is a/an:

A. organelle B. cell

C. tissue D. organ

3. The scientist who stated that plants and animal's body is consisted of cells was:

A. Leeuwenhoek B. Robert Brown

C. Dutrochet D. None of the above

4. Cell theory was proposed by:

A. Einstein

B. J. Schwann & R. Schleiden

C. Robert Hooke

D. All the above

5. Largest cell in the human body is:

A. Nerve cell B. Liver cell

C. Epithelial cell D. None of the above

6. Cell of Amoeba is:

A. Spindle shaped B. Broad shaped

C. Spherical in shape D. Indefinite in shape

7. The factor which influences unicellular organisms to keep spherical shape is:

A. Surface tension B. Osmosis

C. Viscosity D. Protoplasm

8. Which unicellular organism of the following does not possess the organised nucleus?

A. Bacteria B. Amoeba

C. Chlamydomonas D. None of the above

9. Cells of multicellular organism are usually:

A. Triangular B. Rectangular

C. Polyhedral D. None of the above

10. The difference between protoplasm and cell sap was given by:

A. Huxley B. Purkinje

C. Hugo Von Mohl D. None of these

11. Nucleolus mainly contain:

A. RNA B. DNA

C. ADP D. ATP

12. Which is substitution of mitochondria in *E.coli?*

A. Mesomes B. Golgi body

C. Ribosome D. Glyoxysomes

13. Middle lamella is mainly made up of:

A. Chlorophyll

B. Na, H_2 and P compounds

C. NaCl

D. Calcium pectate compounds

14. Cell membrane surrounds the:

A. Nucleoplasm B. Cell wall

C. Protoplasm D. None of the above

15. Which is present in a bacterial cell?
A. Nucleoid B. Prochromosome
C. Genophore D. All above

16. In plants, respiration occurs in:
A. growing tissues B. all living cells
C. cell wall D. xylem and phloem

17. The longest cell in the plant kingdom is:
A. sieve tube B. vessel
C. sclerenchyma fibre D. tracheid

18. Plastids are present only in:
A. Animal cells B. Animals
C. Plant cells D. None of the above

19. Centrosome is found only in:
A. Animal cells B. Plant cells
C. Both A and B D. None of the above

20. The living matter of an organism is:
A. Nucleus B. Protoplasm
C. Cell D. Nucleoplasm

21. *Amoeba* consists of:
A. Many cells B. One cell
C. Two cells D. Four cells

22. The power house of a cell is:
A. Golgi complex B. Ribosomes
C. Mitochondria D. None of the above

23. The organelle of a cell concerned digestion is:
A. Golgi Complex B. Mitochondria
C. Ribosomes D. Lysosomes

24. The organelle associated with protein synthesis in a cell is:
A. Mitochondria B. Lysosomes
C. Ribosomes D. Chromosomes

25. Biological oxidation of enzymes occur in:
A. Golgi complex B. Ribosomes
C. Mitochondria D. None of the above

26. Golgi bodies are the sites of a cellular:
A. respiration B. digestion
C. secretion D. diamorphism

27. The plasma membrane of animal cells is elastic due to the presence of:
A. lipids B. carbohydrates
C. proteins D. water

28. The group of cells having similar origin, structure and function are called:
A. Organ B. Tissues
C. Cell membrane D. None of the above

29. The meristematic tissue is found in:
A. growing regions B. vascular bundles
C. leaves D. None of the above

30. Vascular layers of plant body shows:
A. Protective tissue B. Epithelia tissue
C. Meristematic tissue D. None of the above

31. Which tissue is found in pith and cortex of stem and roots?
A. Sclerenchyma B. Parenchyma
C. Collenchyma D. None of the above

32. In higher animals, the skin is made up of:
A. Epithelial tissue B. Connective tissue
C. Nerve tissue D. None of the above

33. Blood is a:
A. Connective tissue B. Muscular tissue
C. Epithelial tissue D. None of the above

34. Connective tissues are present in:
A. Spinal cord
B. Nerves
C. Bones and cartilage
D. None of the above

35. Which of the following is cell wall protein?
A. HRGP B. PRP
C. GRP D. All the above

36. Which of the following have cartilaginous skeleton?
A. Man B. Dear
C. Shark D. None of the above

37. Bacteria is an example of:
A. Eukaryotic cell B. Prokaryotic cell
C. Connective tissue D. Muscular tissue

38. Which of the following cellular organelles extracts energy from carbohydrates and form ATP molecules?
A. Mitochondria B. Chloroplast
C. Ribosomes D. Nucleus

39. The outermost part of a plant cell is:
A. Plasma membrane B. Cell wall
C. Epidermis D. Cuticle

40. True nucleus is absent in:
A. Bacteria B. Algae
C. Fungi D. None of the above

41. Centre of autonomic nervous system is located in:
A. hypothalamus
B. medulla oblongata
C. cerebellum
D. both A and B

42. Central nervous system is consists of:
A. Brain
B. Spinal cord
C. Nerves and ganglia
D. Both A. and B.

43. The centre for the control of all activities of an animal is:
A. Heart B. Brain
C. Liver D. Stomach

44. Diencephalon has centres for the control of:
A. Metabolism of fats and carbohydrates
B. Regulation of genital function
C. Sleep
D. All the above

45. When the person is alert, with open eyes and actively trying to solve some complex problem, the EEG shows-waves:
A. alpha B. beta
C. delta D. gamma

46. The system which consists of nerves arising from the brain the spinal cord is called:
A. Peripheral nervous system
B. Central nervous system
C. Autonomous nervous system
D. None of the above

47. The number of cranial nerves in a frog are:
A. 10 pairs B. 15 pairs
C. 12 pairs D. 4 pairs

48. In frog the auditory nerve arises from:
A. Medulla B. Pharynx
C. Internal ear D. Tongue

49. Which one of the following is a motor nerve?
A. Facial B. Abducens
C. Vagus D. Olfactory

50. Which of the following cranial nerve of man is both sensory and motor?
A. Optic B. Auditory
C. Olfactory D. Trigeminal

51. Which structure helps a person to maintain his equilibrium?
A. Cochlea
B. Hammer
C. Semicircular canals
D. None of these

52. Receptors for hearing and balance are called:
A. Photoreceptors
B. Tangoreceptors
C. Statoacoustic receptors
D. Olfactoreceptors

53. Sclerotic, cloroid and retina are the layers of:
A. Intestine B. Eyeball
C. Stomach D. Oesophagus

54. Which of the following have solid optic lobes?
A. Frog B. Snake
C. Man D. Bird

55. Deficiency of vitamin A in the body results in insufficient rhodopsin in the rods which leads to:
A. colour blindness B. total blindness
C. night blindness D. myopia

56. Human temperature is set at:
A. 47.5°C B. 37°C
C. 37°F D. 98.4°C

57. The sensory ganglion concerned with spinal reflex is located in:
A. Dorsal root of spinal nerve
B. Ventral root of spinal nerve
C. Both A and B
D. None of the above

58. Jacobson's organs are concerned with .... in amphibians:
A. taste B. smell
C. touch D. taste and vision

59. Constriction of the pupil is function of:
A. Parasympathetic system

B. Hypothalamus
C. Thalamus
D. None of the above

60. Brain is produced by:
A. mesoderm
B. ectoderm
C. endoderm
D. both mesoderm and ectoderm

61. Which among the following nerves carry the impulse to the spinal cord?
A. Reflex Action B. Central Nerves
C. Motor D. Sensory nerves

62. The stimulus of the plant due to certain chemicals is called:
A. Phototropism B. Chemotropism
C. Geotropism D. Arthrotopism

63. Memory is related to
A. Cerebellum B. Cerebrum
C. Medulla D. Olfactory lobes

64. Plant hormones are:
A. Physical substances
B. Chemical substances
C. Photo Chemical substances
D. Both A and B

65. Central nervous system consists of:
A. Brain and spinal cord
B. Brain and visceral nerves
C. Cranial and sympathetic nervous system
D. Spinal and visceral nerves

66. The function of control and coordination performed in plants by:
A. Plant hormones B. Photosynthesis
C. Respiration D. Osmosis

67. Which of the following is the bony cover box in the skull that protects the brain?
A. Outer Brain B. Mid brain
C. Cranium D. Fore brain

68. Reflex actions in man are controlled by:
A. Brain B. Spinal cord
C. Sense glands D. Hormones

69. What is the other name of the endocrine glands?
A. Ducting gland B. Normal
C. Ductless gland D. Oesophagus

70. Which of the following is the regulating centre for swallowing, coughing, sneezing and vomiting?
A. Cerebellum
B. Medulla oblongata
C. Pons
D. Spinal cord

71. Which of the following is a gaseous hormone:
A. Gibberellin B. Ethylene
C. Cytokinin D. Auxin

72. Name the instrument which can record electrical activity of brain:
A. X-ray B. ECG
C. EEG D. Ultrasound

73. The endocrine gland situated on the top of the either side of kidney is:
A. Thymus gland
B. Pituitary gland
C. Adrenal gland
D. Parathyroid gland

74. Insulin and glucagon hormone is secreted by:
A. Pituitary gland B. Adrenal gland
C. Pancreas D. Thyroid gland

75. Calcitrin is secreted from:
A. Thyroid gland B. Adrenal gland
C. Parathyroid gland D. Pituitary gland

76. Nervous tissue is made up of:
A. Neurons B. Nerve fibres
C. Neuroglia D. All the above

77. A nerve is composed of:
A. Muscular tissue
B. Nerve fibre bundles
C. Bundle sheaths
D. None of the above

78. The secretion of adrenal glands called:
A. Aldrin B. Adrenalin
C. Sympathin D. None of these

79. Temperature control centre is located in the:
A. Hypophysis B. Hypothalamus
C. Diencephalon D. None of these

80. Number of spinal nerves in rabbit are:
A. 32 pairs B. 23 pairs
C. 73 pairs D. 37 pairs

81. Semon consists of an enzyme:
A. seminase B. hyaluronidase
C. vasciulase D. ligase

82. Vernalization is related to:
A. Plant growth B. Flowers
C. Stems D. Leaves

83. Auxin promotes:
A. Growth of stems
B. Elongation and growth of stems and roots
C. Enlargement of fruits
D. Both A and C

84. Which of the following promotes cell division in vascular cambium?
A. Gibberellin
B. Cytokinin
C. Auxin
D. None of the above

85. Which of the following can retard the ageing of plant organs?
A. Auxin
B. Ethylene
C. Cytokinin
D. None of the above

86. Which of the following growth hormone is act as a stress hromone?
A. IAA
B. 2, 4 D
C. ABA
D. None of the above

87. Which of the following is capable of delaying yellowish of leaves?
A. Gibberelic acid B. IAA
C. ABA D. Cytokinins

88. Phytochrome is found in:
A. Fungi B. Algae
C. Pteridophytes D. Angiosperms

89. Corpus luteum is developed from:
A. left over oocyte
B. nephrostome
C. left over Graafian follicle after release of ovum
D. none of these

90. The development of embryo inside an egg is called:
A. Vivipery B. Carnivorous
C. Omnivorous D. Ovipery

91. The type of fertilization occur in frog is:
A. Internal
B. External
C. Both A and B
D. None of the above

92. The only haploid stage in an animal life cycle is the:
A. Zoospores
B. Spores
C. Gametes
D. None of the above

93. The common method of reproduction in yeast is:
A. Fission
B. Binary fission
C. Budding
D. Sexual reproduction

94. Oblique ovary is found in:
A. Solanaceae B. Palmaceae
C. Poaceae D. Liliaceae

95. Most of the plant's auxin is produced in its:
A. Root tips B. Buds
C. Leaves D. Shot apex

96. A fruit developed from the wall of the:
A. Style B. Androecium
C. Ovary D. None of these

97. The rate of cleavage in a zygote depends upon:
A. amount of yolk
B. amount of cytoplasm
C. size of nucleus
D. all above

98. The meiotic process by which homologous are paired during prophase I is called:
A. Chasma B. Crossing over
C. Duplication D. Synapsis

99. Growth is maximum in the zone of:
A. Tracheds B. Sieve tubes
C. Cell elongation D. Companion cells

100. At what stage does cytokinesis begin?
A. Anaphase B. Prophase
C. Telephase D. None of these

ANSWERS

PHYSICS

1	**2**	**3**	**4**	**5**	**6**	**7**	**8**	**9**	**10**
B	D	B	A	B	D	A	C	B	A
11	**12**	**13**	**14**	**15**	**16**	**17**	**18**	**19**	**20**
A	D	B	C	B	C	C	C	A	C
21	**22**	**23**	**24**	**25**	**26**	**27**	**28**	**29**	**30**
C	D	A	B	B	D	A	C	B	D
31	**32**	**33**	**34**	**35**	**36**	**37**	**38**	**39**	**40**
B	C	D	C	B	C	D	B	A	A
41	**42**	**43**	**44**	**45**	**46**	**47**	**48**	**49**	**50**
B	A	C	D	C	B	B	B	C	D
51	**52**	**53**	**54**	**55**	**56**	**57**	**58**	**59**	**60**
A	D	C	C	A	C	B	C	A	B
61	**62**	**63**	**64**	**65**	**66**	**67**	**68**	**69**	**70**
C	C	D	A	D	D	D	C	C	C
71	**72**	**73**	**74**	**75**	**76**	**77**	**78**	**79**	**80**
B	C	C	B	C	C	B	D	A	C
81	**82**	**83**	**84**	**85**	**86**	**87**	**88**	**89**	**90**
B	B	B	A	B	B	C	C	B	D
91	**92**	**93**	**94**	**95**	**96**	**97**	**98**	**99**	**100**
D	A	A	C	B	B	C	B	D	A

CHEMISTRY

1	**2**	**3**	**4**	**5**	**6**	**7**	**8**	**9**	**10**
A	A	B	D	B	D	A	C	A	B
11	**12**	**13**	**14**	**15**	**16**	**17**	**18**	**19**	**20**
C	B	B	D	C	C	C	C	A	D
21	**22**	**23**	**24**	**25**	**26**	**27**	**28**	**29**	**30**
B	C	B	B	A	C	B	B	A	C
31	**32**	**33**	**34**	**35**	**36**	**37**	**38**	**39**	**40**
D	C	B	C	C	B	B	D	B	C
41	**42**	**43**	**44**	**45**	**46**	**47**	**48**	**49**	**50**
A	A	D	B	C	D	D	A	A	B
51	**52**	**53**	**54**	**55**	**56**	**57**	**58**	**59**	**60**
C	A	A	D	A	D	B	D	C	B

61	**62**	**63**	**64**	**65**	**66**	**67**	**68**	**69**	**70**
B	B	C	A	A	C	C	B	A	C
71	**72**	**73**	**74**	**75**	**76**	**77**	**78**	**79**	**80**
B	C	A	D	D	B	A	A	C	D
81	**82**	**83**	**84**	**85**	**86**	**87**	**88**	**89**	**90**
B	C	D	C	B	B	D	C	A	D
91	**92**	**93**	**94**	**95**	**96**	**97**	**98**	**99**	**100**
C	B	A	C	C	C	A	B	D	B

BIOLOGY

1	**2**	**3**	**4**	**5**	**6**	**7**	**8**	**9**	**10**
B	A	C	B	A	D	A	A	C	C
11	**12**	**13**	**14**	**15**	**16**	**17**	**18**	**19**	**20**
A	A	D	C	D	B	C	C	A	B
21	**22**	**23**	**24**	**25**	**26**	**27**	**28**	**29**	**30**
B	C	D	C	C	C	A	B	A	A
31	**32**	**33**	**34**	**35**	**36**	**37**	**38**	**39**	**40**
B	A	A	C	D	C	B	A	B	A
41	**42**	**43**	**44**	**45**	**46**	**47**	**48**	**49**	**50**
D	D	B	D	B	A	A	A	B	D
51	**52**	**53**	**54**	**55**	**56**	**57**	**58**	**59**	**60**
C	C	B	C	C	B	A	B	A	C
61	**62**	**63**	**64**	**65**	**66**	**67**	**68**	**69**	**70**
D	B	B	B	A	A	C	B	C	B
71	**72**	**73**	**74**	**75**	**76**	**77**	**78**	**79**	**80**
B	C	A	C	D	D	B	B	B	D
81	**82**	**83**	**84**	**85**	**86**	**87**	**88**	**89**	**90**
B	B	D	B	C	C	D	D	C	D
91	**92**	**93**	**94**	**95**	**96**	**97**	**98**	**99**	**100**
B	C	C	A	D	C	A	D	C	A

GENERAL INTELLIGENCE & REASONING

1. Letter Series

In letter series, the letters follow a definite order. The given series of letters can be in natural order or in reverse order or combination of both. The letters may be skipped or repeated or consecutive. The given series may be single or may even comprise of two different series merged at alternate positions. While attempting questions on letter series one should note the pattern of alphabet series.

Alphabets in natural series are :

A B C D E F G H I J K L M N O P Q R S T U V W X Y Z

E ↓ 5th, J ↓ 10th, O ↓ 15th, T ↓ 20th, Y ↓ 25th; A ↓ 1st

Alphabets in reverse series are :

Z Y X W V U T S R Q P O N M L K J I H G F E D C B A

Z ↓ 1st, V ↓ 5th, Q ↓ 10th, L ↓ 15th, G ↓ 20th, B ↓ 25th

Note : On reaching Z, the series restarts from A and on reaching A, it restarts from Z.

EXERCISE

Directions : *In each of the following series determine the order of the letters. Then from the given options select the one which will complete the given series.*

1. B Y C X D W E ?
(*a*) S (*b*) T
(*c*) U (*d*) V

2. B A F E J I P O ? U
(*a*) V (*b*) T
(*c*) S (*d*) Q

3. B A D C ? H G J I
(*a*) EF (*b*) FE
(*c*) FG (*d*) DF

4. ADG, XVT, BEH, WUS, ?
(*a*) VTR (*b*) CFI
(*c*) DFJ (*d*) STU

5. GMSY, IOUA, KQWC, ?
(*a*) MSYE (*b*) NSYE
(*c*) MTYE (*d*) MSYF

6. ADG, GJM, ?, SVY
(*a*) MPS (*b*) MQR
(*c*) MQS (*d*) SPM

7. XYZ, UVW, ?, OPQ
(*a*) RST (*b*) STU
(*c*) QRS (*d*) TUV

8. JOBS, KMEO, LKHK, ?, NGNC
(*a*) MJLH (*b*) LIKG
(*c*) MIKG (*d*) MNGM

9. AZ, GT, MN, ?, YB
(*a*) KF (*b*) TS
(*c*) RX (*d*) SH

10. BMY, DNW, FOU, ?
(*a*) HPT (*b*) HPS
(*c*) HQS (*d*) GPS

11. AZ, CX, EV, ?
(*a*) HU (*b*) GS
(*c*) GT (*d*) HT

12. DMP, FLN, HKL, JJJ, ?
(*a*) MIH (*b*) III
(*c*) LIH (*d*) MII

13. ECA, JHF, OMK, ?, YWU
(*a*) TRP (*b*) LNP
(*c*) QPN (*d*) RPT

14. ABP, CDQ, EFR, ?
(*a*) GHS (*b*) HGS
(*c*) GHR (*d*) GHT

15. BEH, KNQ, TWZ, ?
(*a*) IJL (*b*) BDF
(*c*) CFI (*d*) ADG

16. EJO, TYD, INS, XCH, ?
(*a*) MRW (*b*) NRV
(*c*) MRV (*d*) NRW

17. ABP, CDQ, EFR,?
(*a*) GHS (*b*) GIS
(*c*) GGS (*d*) GJS

18. NRA, PRC, RRE, TRG, ?
(*a*) USI (*b*) VRI
(*c*) WRJ (*d*) TRI

19. FJKP, ILMQ, LNOR, OPQS, ?
(*a*) RQTV (*b*) RQSS
(*c*) RRST (*d*) RTTU

20. DQCP, EPEN, FOGL, GNIJ, ?
(*a*) HNLG (*b*) HLJG
(*c*) HOMI (*d*) HMKH

21. DFST, FSTD, STDF, ?
(*a*) TSFD (*b*) FDTS
(*c*) TDFS (*d*) SFDT

22. IXT, MAV, QDX, ?
(*a*) WGX (*b*) VHY
(*c*) UGZ (*d*) YHZ

23. QYK, ?, ISG, EPE
(*a*) NWJ (*b*) MVI
(*c*) NVI (*d*) MVJ

24. JMC, CLT, KND, ?, LOE, GPX
(*a*) ENV (*b*) DMX
(*c*) EOU (*d*) DRX

25. ZDV, XGS, VJP, ?
(*a*) SNM (*b*) TMM
(*c*) TNR (*d*) SNT

EXPLANATORY ANSWERS

1. (*d*) : There are two alternate series.

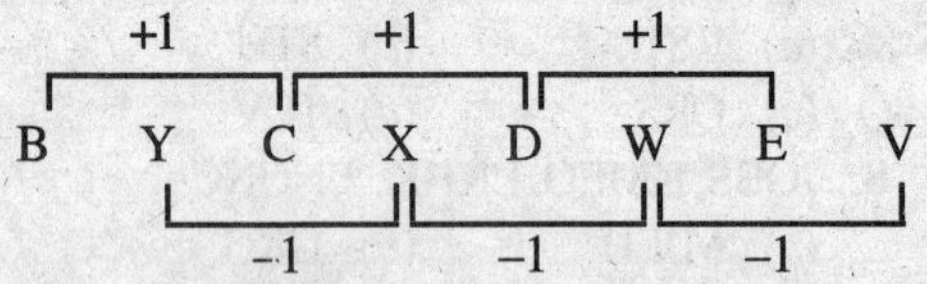

Series I : BCDE (natural order)
Series II : YXWV (reverse order)

2. (*a*) : Each vowel (AEIOU) is preceded by the letter that comes next to it in the natural alphabetical series.

3. (*b*) : The letters in natural series are divided into sections of two letters each. The letters in each section are written backward.
<u>BA</u> <u>DC</u> <u>FE</u> <u>HG</u> <u>JI</u>

4. (*b*) : There are two alternate series.

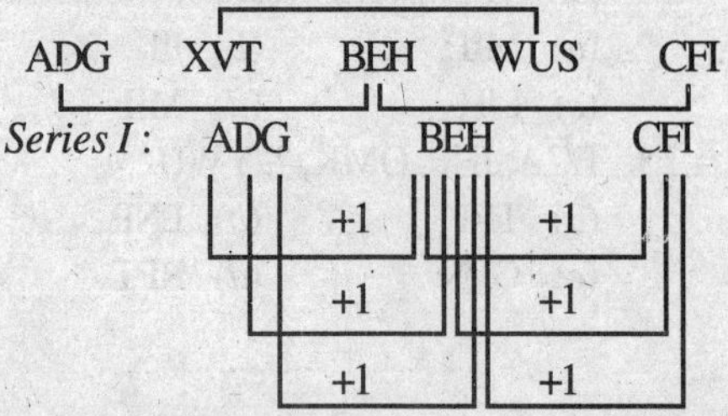

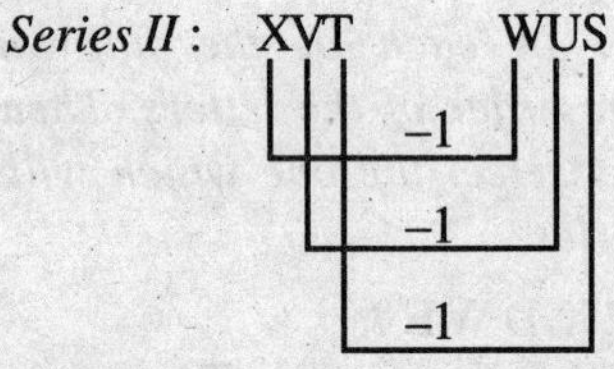

5. (*a*) : The series is formed by moving each letter two steps forward from one group to the next.

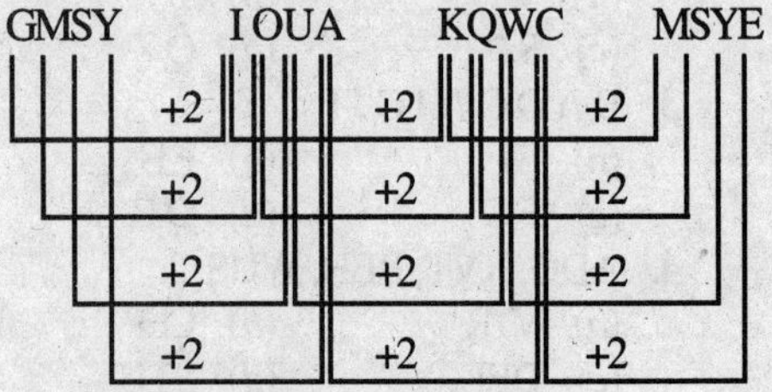

(The series restarts from A on reaching Z)

6. (*a*) : In each group of three letters the alphabet is in the succession of +3. The next group begins with the last alphabet of the previous group.

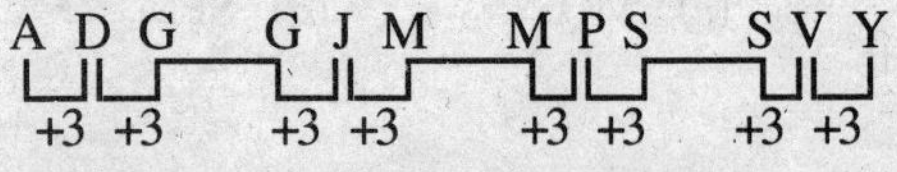

7. (*a*) : The alphabet from one group to the next are in recession of –3, *i.e.,*

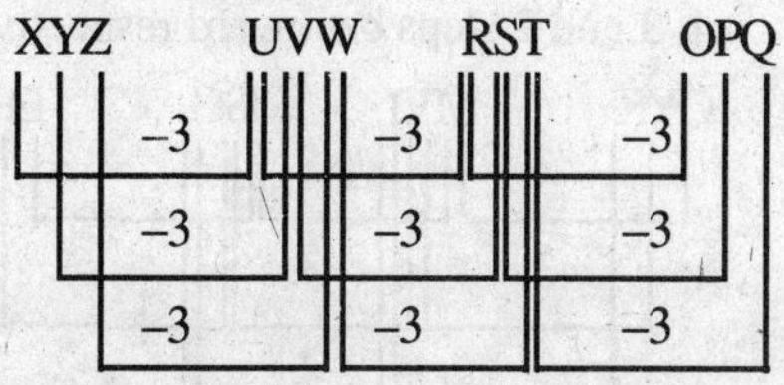

8. (*c*) : The alphabets in each group follow the pattern +1, –2, +3 and –4 respectively from one group to the next group.

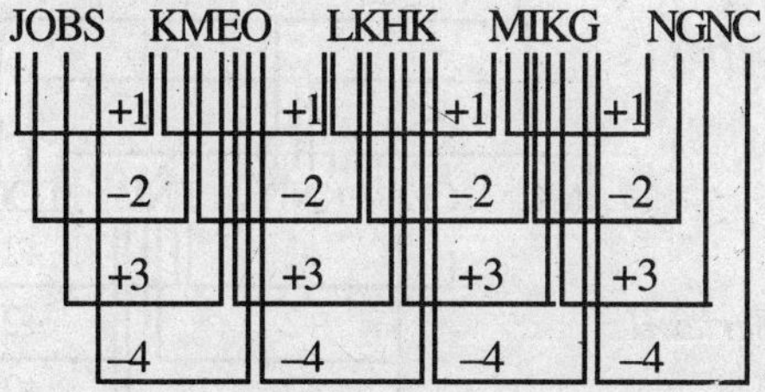

9. (*d*) : The letters in one group correspond to the letters in the next group in the manner +6, –6 respectively, *i.e.,*

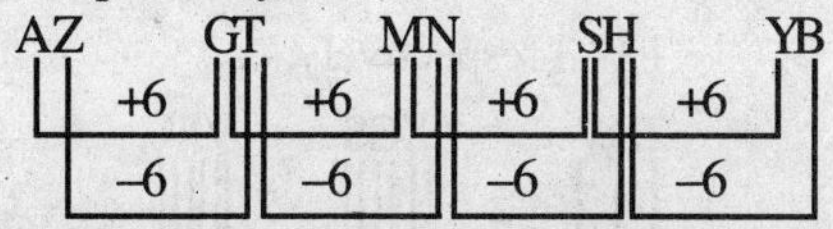

10. (*b*) : The letters in one group correspond to the letters in the next group in the manner +2, +1, -2 respectively, *i.e.,*

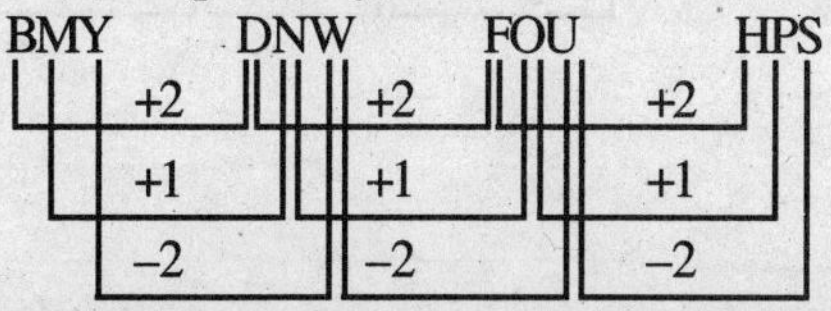

11. (*c*) : The letters in each group correspond to the letters in the next group in the manner +2, –2 respectively, *i.e.,*

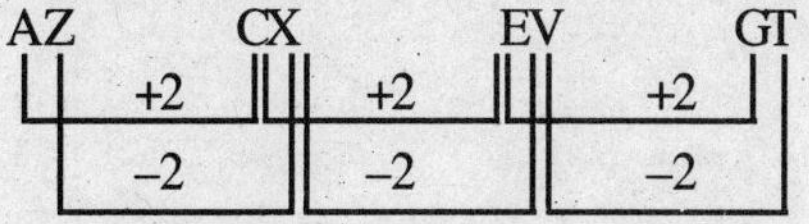

12. (*c*) : The alphabets in each group correspond to the alphabets in the next group in the manner +2, –1, –2 respectively, *i.e.,*

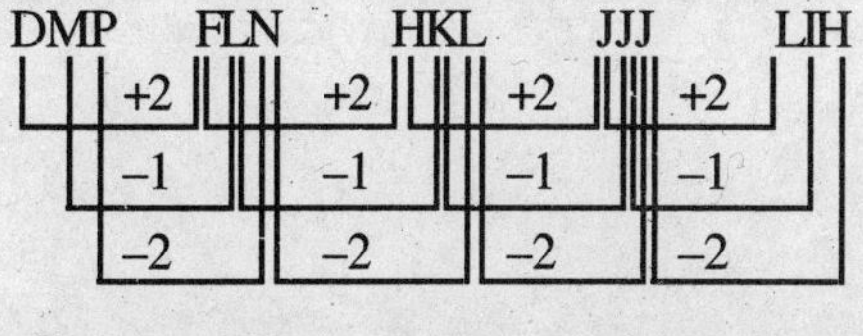

13. (*a*) : The alphabets in each group are moved five steps forward, *i.e.,*

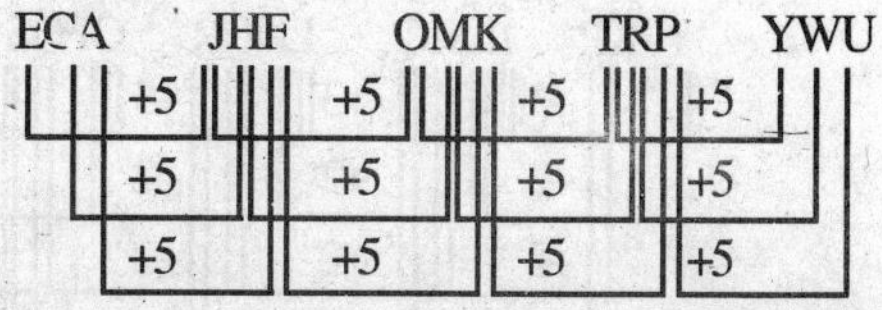

14. (*a*) : The letters in one group correspond to the letters in the next group in the manner +2, +2, +1 respectively, *i.e.,*

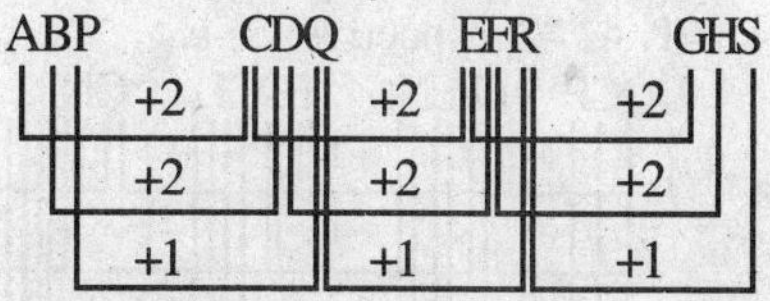

15. (*c*) : All the letters in each group are moved nine steps forward.

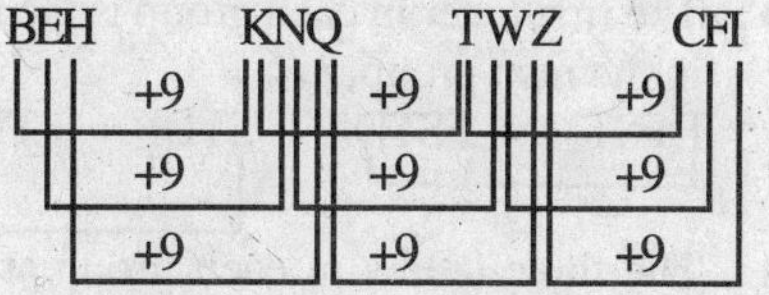

16. (*a*) : There are two alternate series :

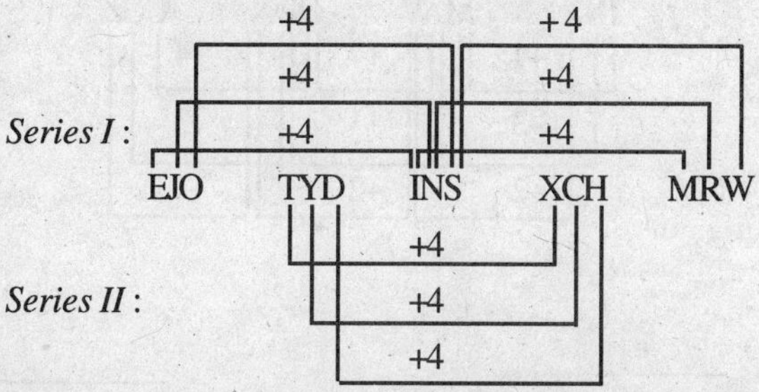

17. (*a*) : The letters in one group correspond to the letters in the next group in the manner +2, +2, +1 respectively, *i.e.,*

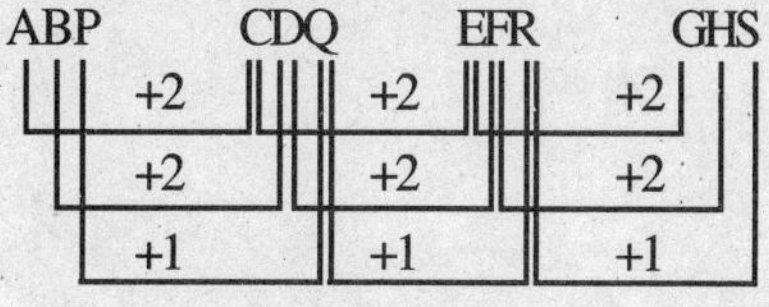

18. (*b*) : The first and third letters are moved two steps forwards while the middle letter remains unchanged, *i.e.,*

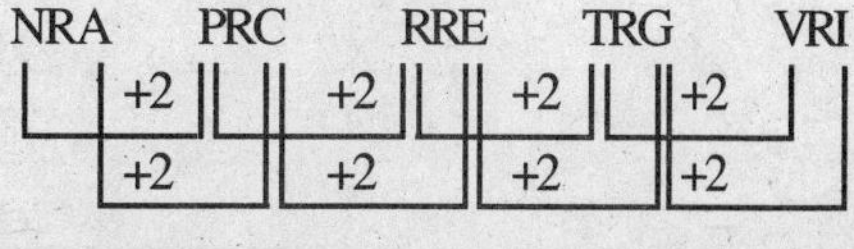

19. (*c*) : The four letters are moved 3, 2, 2, 1 steps forward respectively, *i.e.,*

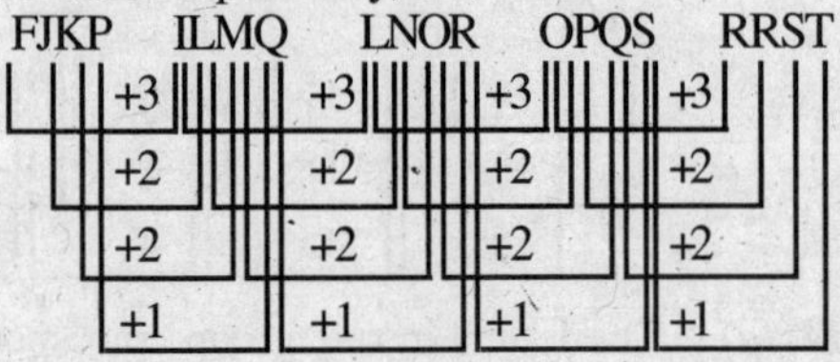

20. (*d*) : The letters in one group correspond to the letters in the next group in the manner, +1, –1, +2 –2 respectively, *i.e.,*

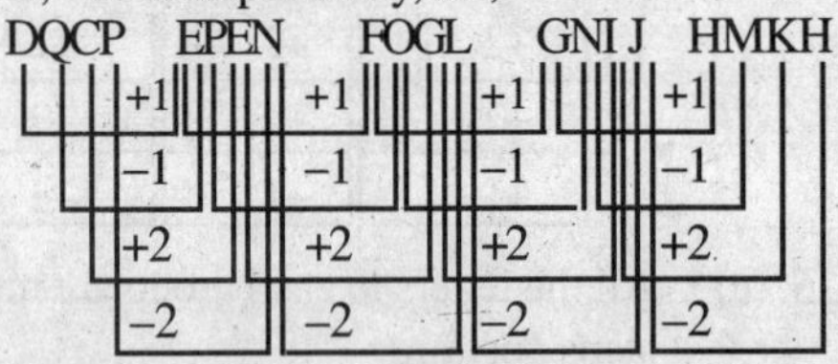

21. (*c*) : The first letter in each group is the last letter in the next group, *i.e.,*

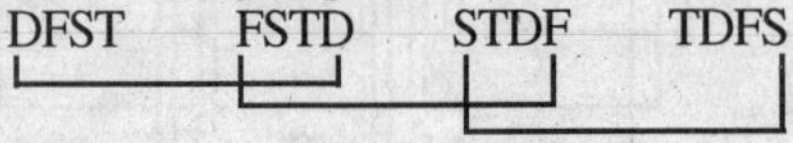

22. (*c*) : The three letters in each group are moved 4, 3 and 2 steps forward respectively, *i.e.,*

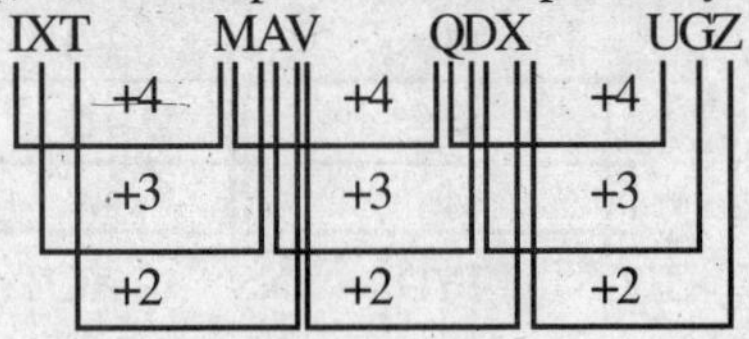

23. (*b*) : The three letters in each group are moved 4, 3 and 2 steps backward respectively, *i.e.,*

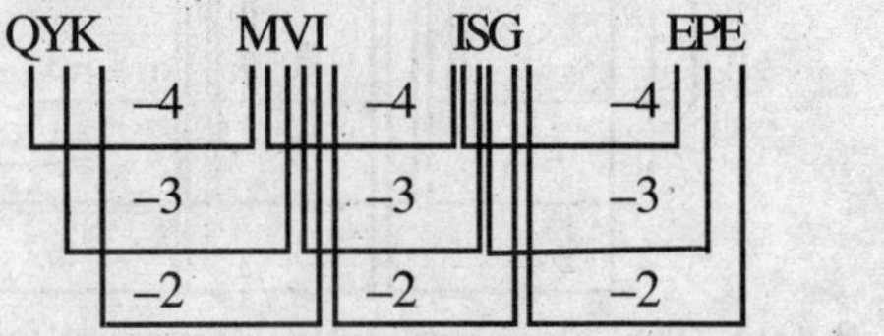

24. (*a*) : There are two alternate series :

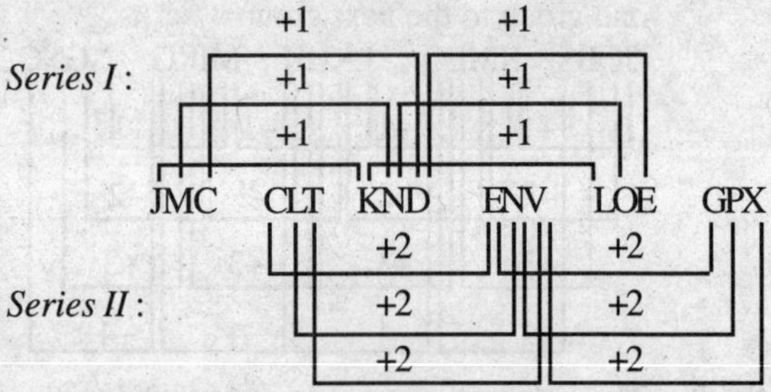

25. (*b*) : The letters in one group correspond to the letters in the next group in the manner –2, +3 –3 respectively, *i.e.,*

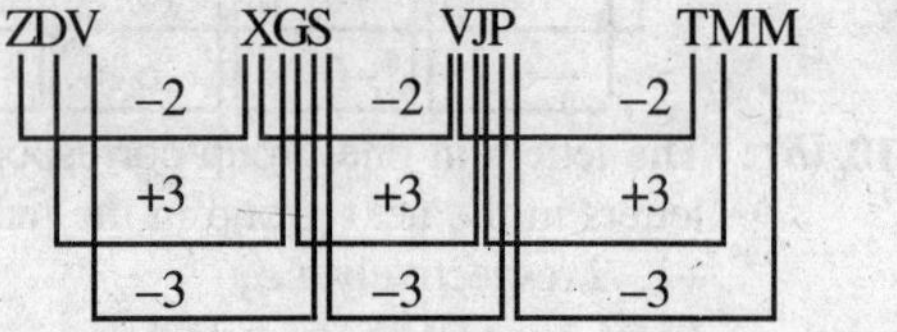

2. WRONG LETTER SERIES

In this type of series, the candidates are not required to find the letter or group of letters which will complete the given series but, they have to identify the letter or number which is wrong or misfit in the given series.

SOLVED EXAMPLE

1. Which of the following letters in the given series is wrong?

J M P T V Y

(*a*) J (*b*) P (*c*) T (*d*) Y

Ans. (*c*) : The letters in this series are moved three steps forward, *i.e.*,

J M P S V Y

+3 +3 +3 +3 +3

Letter 'T' should have been 'S'.

EXERCISE

Directions : *Which letter(s) in each of the following series is wrong or is misfit in the series?*

1. AEHOU
(*a*) U (*b*) O
(*c*) H (*d*) E

2. CHMSWB
(*a*) C (*b*) S
(*c*) B (*d*) W

3. XSNICY
(*a*) Y (*b*) C
(*c*) S (*d*) I

4. ZAWBXC
(*a*) D (*b*) C
(*c*) X (*d*) W

5. MLONQPR
(*a*) R (*b*) O
(*c*) Q (*d*) L

6. DKRYFL
(*a*) L (*b*) D
(*c*) R (*d*) Y

7. LNQTWZCF
(*a*) C (*b*) Q
(*c*) L (*d*) F

8. XW, DC, CB, NM, PQ
(*a*) NM (*b*) CB
(*c*) PQ (*d*) XW

9. BEINSAI
(*a*) A (*b*) E
(*c*) S (*d*) I

10. ZTPKHF
(*a*) Z (*b*) P
(*c*) T (*d*) F

EXPLANATORY ANSWERS

1. (*c*) : The series is made with vowels only. AEIOU. I should be in place of H.

2. (*b*) : The letters in the series are moved five steps forward.

C H M R W B

+5 +5 +5 +5 +5

R should be in place of S

(The series restarts from A on reaching Z)

3. (*b*) : The pattern in the series is –5, *i.e.*,

X S N I D Y

–5 –5 –5 –5 –5

D should be in place of C.

4. (*d*) : There are two alternate series

+1 +1

Z A Y B X C

−1 −1

Series I : ZYX (reverse series)
Series II : ABC (natural series)
Y should be in place of W.

5. (*a*) : Two consecutive letters are written backwards.

ML ON QP SR

S should be in place of R.

6. (*a*) : The pattern in this series in moving the letters seven steps forward.

D K R Y F M

+7 +7 +7 +7 +7

M should be in place of L.

7. (*c*) : The pattern in the series is +3

K N Q T W Z C F

+3 +3 +3 +3 +3 +3 +3

K should be in place of L.

8. (*c*) : The series is made with any two consecutive letters written backwards.

XW DC CB NM QP
← ← ← ← ←

Q should come before P in the series.

9. (*c*) : The difference between the letters is increased by one at each step.

B E I N T A I

+3 +4 +5 +6 +7 +8

T should be in place of S.

10. (*b*) : The difference between the letters is decreased by one at each step.

Z T O K H F

−6 −5 −4 −3 −2

O should be in place of P.

3. Repeat Series

In this type of series, small letters of the alphabet are used to make a set of letters which are repeated. The candidate has to find the set of letters which will fit the blanks left in the given series in such a manner that one section of the series is further repeated in the same manner.

SOLVED EXAMPLE

1. Which of the following groups of letters will complete the given series?
ba-b-aab-a-b
(*a*) baab (*b*) abba (*c*) abaa (*d*) babb
Ans. (*b*) : The series is baab, baab, baab. Here the section 'baab' is repeated in the series.

***Solving steps* :** The candidate has to look for clues to solve such series pattern. 'aab' in the Series indicates that 'b' in this series is preceded by two 'a' so, the first blank and the last blank will be filled by 'a'. Now the first set is formed, *i.e.,* 'baab' in the beginning. This set is repeated, so the second and third blanks will have 'b' filling them. Now, solve the exercise given below to know the different ways in which these series are formed.

EXERCISE

Directions : *Which of the following groups of letters will complete the given series?*

1. ab---b-bbaa-
(*a*) babba (*b*) abaab
(*c*) abbab (*d*) baaab

2. aa-ab--aaa-a
(*a*) baaa (*b*) abab
(*c*) aaab (*d*) aabb

3. -baa-aab-a-a
(*a*) baab (*b*) abab
(*c*) aaba (*d*) aabb

4. -a cca-ccca-acccc-aaa
(*a*) ccaa (*b*) acca
(*c*) caac (*d*) caaa

5. c-bbb--abbbb-abbb-
(*a*) abccb (*b*) bacbb
(*c*) aabcb (*d*) abacb

6. ac-cab-baca-aba-acac
(*a*) bcbb (*b*) aacb
(*c*) babb (*d*) acbc

7. --aba--ba-ab
(*a*) abbab (*b*) bbaba
(*c*) baabb (*d*) abbba

8. --babbba-a--
(*a*) bbaba (*b*) babbb
(*c*) baaab (*d*) ababb

9. k-mk-lmkkl-kk-mk
(*a*) lklm (*b*) lkmk
(*c*) lkmm (*d*) lkml

10. abc-d-bc-d-b-dd
(*a*) decdb (*b*) dadac
(*c*) cdabe (*d*) bacde

11. b-abbc-bbca-bcabb-ab
(*a*) acba (*b*) acaa
(*c*) cacc (*d*) cabc

12. aca-ac--a-ac
(*a*) babc (*b*) aaac
(*c*) cacc (*d*) caca

13. ba-cb-b-bab-?
(*a*) acbb (*b*) bcaa
(*c*) cabb (*d*) bacc

14. ab-aa-caab-aab-a
(*a*) bcbc (*b*) bbca
(*c*) cbcc (*d*) caba

15. -bbcaa-bcaa-bc-a-bca
(*a*) bacab (*b*) abbab
(*c*) abcba (*d*) bcaab

16. a-bccb-ca-cca-baab-c
(*a*) accab (*b*) abcaa
(*c*) bacaa (*d*) ababc

17. b-dabbcd-b-c-ab
(*a*) cabd (*b*) bcad
(*c*) dcba (*d*) acbd

18. a-ba-caacb-bc-
(*a*) acbb (*b*) cbab
(*c*) cbaa (*d*) cbba

19. c-baa-aca-cacab-acac-bca
(*a*) acbaa (*b*) cbaac
(*c*) bccab (*d*) bbcaa

20. -bcc-ac-aabb-ab-cc
(*a*) bacab (*b*) abaca
(*c*) aabca (*d*) bcaca

21. ab-ccca-bccc-bbcc-
(*a*) abbc (*b*) bbac
(*c*) bbca (*d*) cabc

22. -cbc-a-bcaac-ca
(*a*) aaba (*b*) caab
(*c*) bcab (*d*) aacb

23. ab-ba--ba-
(*a*) abba (*b*) baab
(*c*) baba (*d*) abab

24. yx-yx-yxz-xzy-zyxz
(*a*) zzyx (*b*) xxzy
(*c*) yyzx (*d*) yzxz

25. xxxy-y-xxy-yxx-
(*a*) xyxy (*b*) yxyx
(*c*) yyxx (*d*) xxyy

EXPLANATORY ANSWERS

1. (*d*) : The series is abbaab, abbaab.
2. (*c*) : The series is aaaaba, aaaaba.
3. (*b*) : The series is aba, aba, aba, aba.
4. (*d*) : The series is c,a,cc,aa, ccc, aaa, cccc, aaaa.
5. (*a*) : The series is cabbbb, cabbbb, cabbbb.
6. (*b*) : The series is acac, abab, acac, abab, acac.
7. (*a*) : The series is ab, ab, ab, ab, ab, ab.
8. (*b*) : The series is bababb, bababb.
9. (*d*) : The series is klmk, klmk, klmk, klmk.
10. (*b*) : The series is abcdd, abcdd, abcdd.
11. (*d*) : The series is bcab, bcab, bcab, bcab, bcab.
12. (*c*) : The series is ac, ac, ac, ac, ac, ac.
13. (*d*) : The series is babc, babc, babc.
14. (*c*) : The series is abca, abca, abca, abca.
15. (*b*) : The series is abbca, abbca, abbca, abbca.
16. (*d*) : The series is aabcc, bbcaa, ccabb, aabcc.
17. (*a*) : The series is bcdab, bcdab, bcdab.
18. (*c*) : The series is acbabca, acbabca.
19. (*a*) : The series is cabaac, acabca, cabaac, acabca.
20. (*a*) : The series is bbccaa, ccaabb, aabbcc.
21. (*b*) : The series is abbccc abbccc.
22. (*d*) : The series is acbca acbca acbca.
23. (*d*) : The series is ab ab ab ab ab.
24. (*a*) : The series is yxz yxz yxz yxz yxz yxz.
25. (*b*) : The series is xxx yyy xxx yyy xxx.

4. Number Series

In this type of series, the set of given numbers in a series are related to one another in a particular pattern or manner. The relationship between the numbers may be (i) consecutive odd/even numbers; (ii) consecutive prime numbers; (iii) squares/cubes of some numbers with/without variation of addition or subtraction of some number; (iv) sum/product/difference of preceding numbers; (v) addition/subtraction/multiplication/division by some number; and (vi) many more combinations of the relationships given above.

EXERCISE

Directions : *In the following questions, select the number(s) from the given options for completing the given series.*

1. 7776, 1296, 216, 36, 6, ?
(*a*) 6 (*b*) 0
(*c*) 3 (*d*) 1

2. 29282, 2662, 242, 22, ?
(*a*) 1 (*b*) 2
(*c*) 0 (*d*) 11

3. 1, 2, 2, 4, 16, ?, 65536
(*a*) 276 (*b*) 64
(*c*) 256 (*d*) 198

4. 3, 5, 9, 15, 23, ?, 45
(*a*) 37 (*b*) 35
(*c*) 31 (*d*) 33

5. 7, 21, 35, 49, 63, ?
(*a*) 70 (*b*) 77
(*c*) 81 (*d*) 108

6. 10, 14, 23, 39, 64, ?, 149
(*a*) 78 (*b*) 128
(*c*) 103 (*d*) 100

7. 6, 24, 29, 116, 121, ?, 489
(*a*) 468 (*b*) 484
(*c*) 243 (*d*) 363

8. 5, 50, 45, 450, 445, ?, 4445
(*a*) 4450 (*b*) 4600
(*c*) 4550 (*d*) 4500

9. 6.25, 9, 12.25, 16, 20.25, 25, 30.25?
(*a*) 36 (*b*) 32
(*c*) 28.25 (*d*) 40.25

10. 243, 5, 81, 15, 27, 45, 9, ?
(*a*) 5 (*b*) 15
(*c*) 135 (*d*) 27

11. 2, 7, 14, 23, ?, 47
(*a*) 31 (*b*) 38
(*c*) 28 (*d*) 34

12. 0, 1, 8, 27, 64, ?
(*a*) 125 (*b*) 128
(*c*) 256 (*d*) 121

13. 37, 47, 58, ?, 79, 95
(*a*) 71 (*b*) 69
(*c*) 68 (*d*) 67

14. 4, –8, 14, –22, 32, ?
(*a*) –44 (*b*) 42
(*c*) –42 (*d*) 44

15. 6, 7, 9, 11, 15, 15, 24, 19, ?
(*a*) 32 (*b*) 34
(*c*) 36 (*d*) 37

16. 2, 6, 12, 20, 30, ?
(*a*) 42 (*b*) 36
(*c*) 41 (*d*) 40

17. 1, 4, 5, 11, 9, 18, ?, 25
(*a*) 12 (*b*) 13
(*c*) 19 (*d*) 23

18. 27, 45, 9,15, 3, 5, ?
(*a*) 1 (*b*) 1/3
(*c*) 1/5 (*d*) 1/9

19. 3, 1/3, 14, 1/14, 25, 1/25, ?
(*a*) 1/36 (*b*) 34
(*c*) 35 (*d*) 36

20. 1/2, 3/4, 5/8, 7/16, ?
(*a*) 10/17 (*b*) 9/32
(*c*) 11/34 (*d*) 12/35

21. 4, 8, 7, 14, 12, 22, 19, ?, 28
(*a*) 12 (*b*) 24
(*c*) 28 (*d*) 32

22. 96, 90, 78, ?, 36, 6
(*a*) 60 (*b*) 72
(*c*) 48 (*d*) 54

23. 6, 3, 11, 8, 18, 15, 27, 24, ?, ?
(*a*) 36, 33 (*b*) 36, 35
(*c*) 38, 35 (*d*) 38, 34

24. 1, 6, 15, ?, 45, 66, 91
(*a*) 25 (*b*) 26
(*c*) 27 (*d*) 28

25. 1, 2, 5, 12, 27, 58, 121, ?
(*a*) 246
(*b*) 247
(*c*) 248
(*d*) 249

EXPLANATORY ANSWERS

1. (*d*) : The numbers in this sequence are divided by 6 each time.

2. (*b*) : The numbers in the series are divided by 11 at each step.

3. (*c*) : The number in the series is product of all the numbers preceding it.

1 2 2 4 16 256 65536

(1×2) (1×2×2) (1×2×2×4) (1×2×2×4×16) (1×2×2×4×16×256)

4. (*d*) : The difference between consecutive numbers increases by 2 at each step.

3 5 9 15 23 33 45

+2 +4 +6 +8 +10 +12

5. (*b*) : The series is multiplication of 7 by odd numbers starting from 3.

7 21 35 49 63 77

×3 ×5 ×7 ×9 ×11

6. (*d*) : The number plus the square of numbers in natural order starting from 2 gives the next number in the series.

10 14 23 39 64 100 149

$+2^2$ $+3^2$ $+4^2$ $+5^2$ $+6^2$ $+7^2$

7. (*b*) : The sequence in the series is ×4, +5, which is repeated.

8. (*a*) : The sequence in the series is ×10, –5, which is repeated.

9. (*a*) : There are two alternate series :

+6 +8 +10

6.25 9 12.25 16 20.25 25 30.25 36

+7 +9 +11

Series I : 6.25, 12.25, 20.25, 30.25 (sequence is +6, +8, +10)

Series II : 9, 16, 25, 36 (sequence is +7, +9, +11)

10. (*c*) : There are two alternate series :

÷3 ÷3 ÷3

243 5 81 15 27 45 9 135

×3 ×3 ×3

Series I : 243, 81, 27, 9 (division by 3)

Series II : 5, 15, 45, 135 (multiplication by 3)

11. (*d*) : The difference between two consecutive numbers is increasing by 2 starting from 5.

2 7 14 23 34 47

+5 +7 +9 +11 +13

12. (*a*) : The numbers are cubes of numbers in natural order.

13. (*a*) : The sum of the digits of the number is added to the number to obtain the next number in the series.

37 47 58 71 79 95

+(3+7) +(4+7) +(5+8) +(7+1) +(7+9)

14. (a) : Alternate numbers are marked positive and negative, but the difference between their magnitude increases by 2 at each step.

4 −8 14 −22 32 −44

4 6 8 10 12

15. (c) : There are two alternate series :

+3 +6 +9 +12

6 7 9 11 15 15 24 19 36

+4 +4 +4

Series I : 6, 9, 15, 24, 36 (sequence is +3, +6, +9, +12)

Series II : 7, 11, 15, 19 (addition of 4 at each step)

16. (a) : The difference between the consecutive numbers in the series increases by 2 at each step.

2 6 12 20 30 42

+4 +6 +8 +10 +12

17. (b) : There are two alternate series :

+4 +4 +4

1 4 5 11 9 18 13 25

+7 +7 +7

Series I : 1, 5, 9, 13 (addition of 4)

Series II : 4, 11, 18, 25 (addition of 7)

18. (a) : There are two alternate series :

÷3 ÷3 ÷3

27 45 9 15 3 5 1

÷3 ÷3

Series I : 27, 9, 3, 1 (division by 3)

Series II : 45, 15, 5 (division by 3)

19. (d) : Two consecutive numbers form a pair. The difference between the numbers placed at odd places increases by 11 and the second number is the fraction part of the number.

$3 \quad \frac{1}{3} \quad 14 \quad \frac{1}{14} \quad 25 \quad \frac{1}{25} \quad 36$

+11 +11 +11

20. (b) : In this fraction series the numbers on the top are increased by 2 and at the bottom, multiplied by 2.

21. (d) : There are two alternate series :

+3 +5 +7 +9

4 8 7 14 12 22 19 32 28

+6 +8 +10

Series I : 4, 7, 12, 19, 28 (sequence is +3, +5, +7, +9)

Series II : 8, 14, 22, 32 (sequence is +6, +8, +10)

22. (a) : The series is formed by multiples of 6 in this manner :

6×16	$= 96$	
6×15	$= 90$	$(16 - 1) = 15$
6×13	$= 78$	$(15 - 2) = 13$
6×10	$= 60$	$(13 - 3) = 10$
6×6	$= 36$	$(10 - 4) = 6$
6×1	$= 6$	$(6 - 5) = 1$

23. (c) : There are two alternate series :

+5 +7 +9 +11

6 3 11 8 18 15 27 24 38 35

+5 +7 +9 +11

Series I : 6, 11, 18, 27, 38

Series II : 3, 8, 15, 24, 35

(Both series follow the pattern +5, +7, +9, +11)

24. (d) : The difference between the numbers in this series is increased by 4 at each step.

1 6 15 28 45 66 91

+5 +9 +13 +17 +21 +25

25. (c) : The sequence in this series is number into 2 plus the numbers in natural order starting from 0.

1 2 5 12 27 58 121 248

(1×2)+0 (2×2)+1 (5×2)+2 (12×2)+3 (27×2)+4 (58×2)+5 (121×2)+6

5. Wrong Number Series

In this type of series, the given series may be complete but what needs to be identified is the number in the given completed series which is disturbing the sequential pattern of that series and does not fit in with the relationship shared between the other numbers.

EXERCISE

Directions : *In the given series find the number which is wrong.*

1. 5, 25, 120, 625, 3125, 15625
(*a*) 15625 (*b*) 625
(*c*) 120 (*d*) 5

2. 4, 8, 11, 22, 18, 36, 24, 50
(*a*) 8 (*b*) 22
(*c*) 36 (*d*) 24

3. 2, 4, 12, 24, 72, 142, 432
(*a*) 432 (*b*) 12
(*c*) 142 (*d*) 72

4. 2, 3, 4, 4, 6, 8, 9, 12, 16
(*a*) 3 (*b*) 9
(*c*) 6 (*d*) 12

5. 97, 91, 86, 83, 79, 77, 76, 76
(*a*) 86 (*b*) 76
(*c*) 91 (*d*) 83

6. 7, 11, 11, 9, 15, 7, 19, 5, 23, 1
(*a*) 5 (*b*) 7
(*c*) 1 (*d*) 9

7. 3, 7, 12, 28, 48, 118, 192, 448
(*a*) 12 (*b*) 118
(*c*) 28 (*d*) 7

8. 10, 100, 1100, 11000, 111000, 1210000
(*a*) 1210000 (*b*) 11000
(*c*) 100 (*d*) 111000

9. 24576, 6144, 1536, 386, 96, 24
(*a*) 386 (*b*) 6144
(*c*) 96 (*d*) 1536

10. 11, 13, 15, 17, 19, 23, 29, 31, 37
(*a*) 13 (*b*) 23
(*c*) 15 (*d*) 31

11. 36, 43, 49, 54, 60, 61, 63, 64
(*a*) 60 (*b*) 63
(*c*) 54 (*d*) 43

12. 3, 10, 41, 206, 1236, 8660
(*a*) 10 (*b*) 41
(*c*) 206 (*d*) 1236

13. 17, 25, 37, 50, 65, 82, 101
(*a*) 25 (*b*) 17
(*c*) 101 (*d*) 65

14. 12, 20, 38, 42, 56, 72
(*a*) 20 (*b*) 38
(*c*) 56 (*d*) 72

15. 5, 6, 11, 22, 42, 88, 176
(*a*) 5 (*b*) 42
(*c*) 176 (*d*) 11

16. 905, 180, 175, 35, 30, 6, 1
(*a*) 6 (*b*) 1
(*c*) 175 (*d*) 905

17. 5040, 840, 160, 42, 14, 7
(*a*) 7 (*b*) 160
(*c*) 14 (*d*) 840

18. 3, 32, 363, 3993, 43923
(*a*) 363 (*b*) 3
(*c*) 32 (*d*) 43923

19. 3, 18, 38, 78, 123, 178, 243
(*a*) 78 (*b*) 3
(*c*) 123 (*d*) 18

20. 0, 1, 2, 2, 4, 4, 6, 8, 8, 10
(*a*) 6 (*b*) 0
(*c*) 1 (*d*) 10

21. 5, 12, 16, 24, 27
(*a*) 12 (*b*) 16
(*c*) 24 (*d*) 27

22. 27, 36, 45, 60, 71, 99
(*a*) 27 (*b*) 45
(*c*) 60 (*d*) 71

23. 81, 64, 49, 35, 25, 16
(*a*) 64 (*b*) 35
(*c*) 25 (*d*) 16

24. 625, 125, 25, 5, 0
(*a*) 0 (*b*) 125
(*c*) 5 (*d*) 625

25. 25, 19, 17, 13, 11, 7
(*a*) 25 (*b*) 17
(*c*) 13 (*d*) 7

EXPLANATORY ANSWERS

1. (*c*) : The numbers in the series are multiplied by 5 to get the next number.
∴ 125 should be in place of 120.

2. (*d*) : Two numbers form a pair. The first number increases by 7 for the next pair and the second number is the double of first number.

4 8 11 22 18 36 25 50
×2 ×2 ×2 ×2
+7 +7 +7

∴ 25 should be in place of 24.

3. (*c*) : There are two alternate series and in each series, the numbers are multiplied by 6 to get the next number.

×6 ×6 ×6
2 4 12 24 72 144 432
×6 ×6

∴ 144 should be in place of 142.

4. (*b*) : There are three alternate series and in each series, the numbers are multiplied by 2 to get the next number.

×2 ×2
2 3 4 4 6 8 8 12 16
×2 ×2
×2 ×2

Series I : 2, 4, 8
Series II : 3, 6, 12
Series III : 4, 8, 16
∴ 8 should be in place of 9.

5. (*d*) : The difference between the consecutive numbers in the series decreases by 1 at each step.

97 91 86 82 79 77 76 76
−6 −5 −4 −3 −2 −1 −0

∴ 82 should be in place of 83.

6. (*c*) : There are two alternate series :

+4 +4 +4 +4
7 11 11 9 15 7 19 5 21 3
−2 −2 −2 −2

Series I : 7, 11, 15, 19, 23 (addition of 4)
Series II : 11, 9, 7, 5, 3 (subtraction of 2)
∴ 3 should be in place of 1.

7. (*b*) : There are two alternate series and in each series, the numbers are multiplied by 4 to get the next number.

×4 ×4 ×4
3 7 12 28 48 112 192 448
×4 ×4 ×4

∴ 112 should be in place of 118.

8. (*d*) : The numbers in this series are multiplied by 10 and 11 alternately is, *i.e.*, × 10, × 11.

10 100 1100 11000 121000 1210000
×10 ×11 ×10 ×11 ×10

∴ 121000 should be in place of 111000.

9. (*a*) : The numbers in this series are divided by 4 to get the next number.

24576 6144 1536 384 96 24
÷4 ÷4 ÷4 ÷4 ÷4

∴ 384 should be in place of 386.

10. (*c*) : The series comprises of prime numbers in increasing order. Only 15 is an exception.

11. (*a*) : The difference between two consecutive numbers is decreasing by 1 at each step.

36 43 49 54 58 61 63 64

+7 +6 +5 +4 +3 +2 +1

∴ 58 should be in place of 60.

12. (*d*) : The sequence followed in this series is :

$3 \times 3 + 1 = 10$
$10 \times 4 + 1 = 41$
$41 \times 5 + 1 = 206$
$206 \times 6 + 1 = 1237$; and
$1237 \times 7 + 1 = 8660$

∴ 1237 should be in place of 1236.

13. (*a*) : The numbers in the series are 1 plus the squares of numbers in natural order starting from 4.

17	26	37	50	65	82	101
↓	↓	↓	↓	↓	↓	↓
4^2+1	5^2+1	6^2+1	7^2+1	8^2+1	9^2+1	10^2+1

∴ 26 should be in place of 25.

14. (*b*) : The sequence followed in this series is :

$3 \times 4 = 12$
$4 \times 5 = 20$
$5 \times 6 = 30$
$6 \times 7 = 42$
$7 \times 8 = 56$
$8 \times 9 = 72$

∴ 30 should be in place of 38.

15. (*b*) : The numbers in the series are the sum of all the numbers preceding them.

5 6 11 22 44 88 176

(5 + 6)
(5 + 6 + 11)
(5 + 6 + 11 + 22)
(5 + 6 + 11 + 22 + 44)
(5 + 6 + 11 + 22 + 44 + 88)

∴ 44 should be in place of 42.

16. (*d*) : The sequence followed in the series is ÷ 5, – 5 which is repeated.

900 180 175 35 30 6 1

÷5 –5 ÷5 –5 ÷5 –5

∴ 900 should be in place of 905.

17. (*b*) : The numbers in the series are divided by numbers in reverse order starting from 6 to get the next number.

5040 840 168 42 14 7

÷6 ÷5 ÷4 ÷3 ÷2

∴ 168 should be in place of 160.

18. (*c*) : The numbers in this series are multiplied by 11 to get the next number.

3 33 363 3993 43923

×11 ×11 ×11 ×11

∴ 33 should be in place of 32.

19. (*b*) : 3 is the only prime number in the series.

20. (*d*) : There are two alternate series :

+2 +2 +2 +2

0 1 2 2 4 4 6 8 8 16

×2 ×2 ×2 ×2

Series I : 0, 2, 4, 6, 8, (addition of 2)
Series II : 1, 2, 4, 8, 16 (multiplication by 2)

∴ 16 should be in place of 10.

21. (*c*) : The sequence in the series is +7, +4 which is repeated, *i.e.*,

5 12 16 23 27

+7 +4 +7 +4

∴ 23 should be in place of 24.

22. (*d*) : All other numbers are divisible by 3.

23. (*b*) : The sequence is the square of the number in decreasing order starting from 9, *i.e.*,

$9^2 = 9 \times 9 = 81$
$8^2 = 8 \times 8 = 64$
$7^2 = 7 \times 7 = 49$
$6^2 = 6 \times 6 = 36$
$5^2 = 5 \times 5 = 25$
$4^2 = 4 \times 4 = 16$

∴ 36 should be in place of 35.

24. (*a*) : The number in the series are divided by 5 to get the next number

625 125 25 5 1

÷5 ÷5 ÷5 ÷5

∴ 1 should be in place of 0 digit.

25. (*a*) : Other numbers are prime numbers.

6. WORD ANALOGY

In Analogy Tests, the relationship between two given words is established and then applied to the other words. The type of relationship may vary, so while attempting such questions the first step is to identify the type of relationship, which can be any one of the following.

EXERCISE

Directions : *In the questions given below one term is missing. Based on the relationship of the two given words find the missing term from the given options.*

1. HUNGER : FOOD : : THIRST : ?
(*a*) Water (*b*) Drink
(*c*) Tea (*d*) Coffee

2. HUNTER : GUN : : WRITER : ?
(*a*) Book (*b*) Pen
(*c*) Poem (*d*) Page

3. WOOL : SHEEP : : SILK : ?
(*a*) Saree (*b*) String
(*c*) Silkworm (*d*) Moth

4. FOOD : STOMACH : : FUEL : ?
(*a*) Engine (*b*) Automobile
(*c*) Rail (*d*) Aeroplane

5. WATER : SAND : : OCEAN : ?
(*a*) Island (*b*) River
(*c*) Desert (*d*) Waves

6. ADULT : BABY : : FLOWER : ?
(*a*) Seed (*b*) Bud
(*c*) Fruit (*d*) Butterfly

7. WRITER : READER : : PRODUCER : ?
(*a*) Creator (*b*) Contractor
(*c*) Creature (*d*) Consumer

8. ENTRANCE : EXIT : : LOYALTY : ?
(*a*) Treachery (*b*) Patriotism
(*c*) Fidelity (*d*) Reward

9. MOTHER : MATERNAL : : FATHER : ?
(*a*) Eternal (*b*) Detrimental
(*c*) Paternal (*d*) Formidable

10. PEARL : NECKLACE : : FLOWER : ?
(*a*) Plant (*b*) Garden
(*c*) Petal (*d*) Bouquet

11. ALPHABET : WORD : : WORD : ?
(*a*) Sound (*b*) Music
(*c*) Sentence (*d*) Dictionary

12. LIFE : DEATH : : HOPE : ?
(*a*) Cry (*b*) Pain
(*c*) Despair (*d*) Sad

13. GOOD : BAD : : VIRTUE : ?
(*a*) Blame (*b*) Sin
(*c*) Despair (*d*) Vice

14. BIRD : FLY : : SNAKE : ?
(*a*) Timid (*b*) Clatter
(*c*) Crawl (*d*) Hole

15. CAT : MOUSE : : BIRD : ?
(*a*) Cage (*b*) Trap
(*c*) Eagle (*d*) Worm

16. STATE : EXILE
(*a*) Police : Arrest
(*b*) Judge : Convict
(*c*) Constitution : Amendment
(*d*) Church : Excommunicate

17. CAPRICIOUSNESS : RELIABILITY
(*a*) Extemporaneous : Predictability
(*b*) Unreliable : Inhuman
(*c*) Tenacious : Practicality
(*d*) Arbitrary : Whimsical

18. LOATH : COERCION
(*a*) Detest : Caressing
(*b*) Irritate : Caressing
(*c*) Irate : Antagonism
(*d*) Reluctant : Persuasion

19. SCALES : FISH
(*a*) Lady : Dress (*b*) Tree : Leaves
(*c*) Bird : Feather (*d*) Skin : Man

20. TREE : SAPLING
(*a*) Hut : Mansion
(*b*) Giant : Dwarf
(*c*) Horse : Foal
(*d*) Ant : Elephant

21. CHALK : BLACKBOARD
(*a*) Door : Handle
(*b*) Table : Chair
(*c*) Ink : Paper
(*d*) Type : Paint

22. PRIMEVAL : MEDIEVAL
(*a*) Dinosaur : Dragon
(*b*) Gorilla : Soldier
(*c*) Evolution : Revelation
(*d*) Thorn : Rose

23. TRILOGY : NOVEL
(*a*) Rice : Husk
(*b*) Milk : Cream
(*c*) Fabric : Weaving
(*d*) Serial : Episode

24. PEDANT : ERUDITION
(*a*) Prude : Modesty
(*b*) Blunt : Politician
(*c*) Diplomats : Tactless
(*d*) Enemy : Friendly

25. FURY : IRE
(*a*) Convulsion : Spasm
(*b*) Amusement : Happiness
(*c*) Joke : Laugh
(*d*) Dispassion : Emotion

26. BaBy : TaTa : : LiLy : ?
(*a*) PooL (*b*) ROse
(*c*) HaNd (*d*) DoWN

27. BCDA : STUR : : KLMJ : ?
(*a*) VWXU (*b*) EFHG
(*c*) SRTU (*d*) QSRP

28. AEI : LPT : : CGK : ?
(*a*) OSV (*b*) RUY
(*c*) TXC (*d*) FJN

29. RUX : TRP : : BEH : ?
(*a*) SQN (*b*) QON
(*c*) QOM (*d*) QNL

30. CART : ART : : FOUR : ?
(*a*) RUN (*b*) TWO
(*c*) QUE (*d*) OUR

31. FIK : JGO : : DFR : ?
(*a*) BIO (*b*) HDV
(*c*) GCU (*d*) FLP

32. LJH : KKI : : CIA : ?
(*a*) BJB (*b*) DHB
(*c*) BJC (*d*) BBJ

33. ACE : HIL : : MOQ : ?
(*a*) SVW (*b*) TUX
(*c*) RTW (*d*) WUS

34. BCDE : WVUT : : QRST : ?
(*a*) EFHG (*b*) JIHG
(*c*) POML (*d*) GEDC

35. PNLJ : IGEC : : USQO : ?
(*a*) HJLN (*b*) LNJH
(*c*) NLJH (*d*) JHNL

36. DIMO : DMIO : : JUVR : ?
(*a*) JVRU (*b*) JRVU
(*c*) JVUR (*d*) JUVR

EXPLANATORY ANSWERS

1. (*a*) : Hunger is satiated by food, thirst by water.

2. (*b*) : Weapon of a hunter is a gun, weapon of a writer is a pen.

3. (*c*) : Wool is obtained from sheep, silk is obtained from silkworm.

4. (*a*) : Food is consumed in stomach, fuel is consumed in engine.

5. (*c*) : The related words are near opposites.

6. (*b*) : The youngone of an adult is a baby and that of a flower is a bud.

7. (*d*) : A writer aims to please the readers by his writings, a producer aims to please the consumers by his products.

8. (*a*) : The related words are opposites.

9. (*c*) : Relations on the mother's side are maternal and on the father's side paternal.

10. (d) : Many pearls make a necklace, many flowers make a bouquet.

11. (c) : More than one alphabet make a word, more than one word make a sentence.

12. (c) : The related words are opposites.

13. (d) : The related words are opposites.

14. (c) : Birds fly, snakes crawl.

15. (d) : Cat chases the mouse, bird chases the worm.

16. (d) : Punishment of leaving the State is exile, punishment of leaving the Church is excommunication.

17. (c) : The related words are antonyms.

18. (d) : Loathing is the result of constant coersion, reluctance is the result of constant persuasion.

19. (d) : Covering of the fish is scales, covering of man is skin.

20. (c) : Young tree is a sapling, young horse is a foal.

21. (c) : Chalk is used to write on blackboard, ink is used to write on paper.

22. (a) : The related words represent almost the same time period and answer option represents almost the same sized creatures.

23. (d) : Trilogy is section of a novel, episode is a section of a serial.

24. (a) : The related words are synonyms.

25. (b) : Fury causes ire, amusement causes happiness.

26. (c) : In each group the alternate letters are capitals.

27. (a) : In each group the first three letters are consecutive and they follow the fourth letter.

ABCD : RSTU :: JKLM : UVWX

28. (d) : In each group the letters jump three letters between them, *i.e.,* they are moving to the fourth letter.

AEI : LPT :: CGK : FJN

+4 +4   +4 +4   +4 +4   +4 +4

29. (c) : The letters in first set are jumping two letters, *i.e.,* moving three steps forward and in the second they are jumping one letter, *i.e.* moving two steps backward.

RUX : TRP :: BEH : QOM

+3 +3   –2 –2   +3+3   –2 –2

30. (d) : The first set of letters drop the first letter to get the second set.

CART : ART :: FOUR : OUR

31. (b) : The three letters in first set are moved +4, –2, and +4 steps respectively.

FIK : JGO :: DFR : HDV

+4, –2, +4   +4, –2, +4

32. (a) : The letters in the first set are moved –1, +1 and +1 steps respectively.

LJH : KKI :: CIA : BJB

–1, +1, +1   –1, +1, +1

33. (b) : The three letters are moved +7, +6 and +7 steps forward respectively.

ACE : HIL :: MOQ : TUX

+7, +6, +7   +7, +6, +7

34. (b) : The consecutive letters in the first set are in natural order and in the second set, they are in reverse order.

BCDE : WVUT :: QRST : JIHG

→ ← → ←

35. (c) : The letters are moved seven steps backwards.

PNLJ : IGEC :: USQO : NLJH

–7, –7, –7, –7   –7, –7, –7, –7

36. (c) : Only the middle letters are reversed to obtain the second set of letters.

DIMO : DMIO :: JUVR : JVUR

7. NUMBER ANALOGY

In number analogy also, the relationship between the given numbers is detected and then applied to the second part to find the missing numbers. This relationship between the numbers can be based on any of the following patterns : *(i)* numbers can be odd/even/prime numbers; *(ii)* numbers can be multiples of one number; *(iii)* numbers can be squares/cubes of different numbers; *(iv)* some numbers can be added to/ subtracted from/multiplied to/divided into the first number to get the second number; *(v)* the second number can be the sum/product/difference of the digits of first number; and *(vi)* combinations of any mathematical calculations given above can apply to the relationship between the two given numbers.

EXERCISE

Directions : *In the following questions, select the number from the given options which follows the same relationship as shared between the first two numbers.*

1. 1 : 11 : : 2 : ?
(*a*) 20 (*b*) 22
(*c*) 24 (*d*) 44

2. $\frac{1}{7} : \frac{1}{14} :: \frac{1}{9} : ?$
(*a*) $\frac{1}{88}$ (*b*) $\frac{1}{80}$
(*c*) $\frac{1}{81}$ (*d*) $\frac{1}{18}$

3. 0.16 : 0.0016 : : 1.02 : ?
(*a*) 10.20 (*b*) 0.102
(*c*) 0.0102 (*d*) 1.020

4. 663 : 884 : : 221 : ?
(*a*) 332 (*b*) 554
(*c*) 773 (*d*) 442

5. 16 : 0.16 : : ?
(*a*) 2 : 0.02 (*b*) 7 : 0.007
(*c*) 1.3 : 0.13 (*d*) 0.01 : 0.001

6. $3 : \frac{1}{3} :: ?$
(*a*) 6 : 12 (*b*) 5 : 2/15
(*c*) 8 : 1/8 (*d*) 9 : 27

7. 65 : 13 : : 180 : ?
(*a*) 93 (*b*) 36
(*c*) 133 (*d*) 102

8. 125 : 27 : : 343 : ?
(*a*) 729 (*b*) 64
(*c*) 216 (*d*) 512

9. 357 : 73 : : ?
(*a*) 429 : 94 (*b*) 201 : 21
(*c*) 138 : 38 (*d*) 93 : 39

10. 731 : 902 : : 655 : ?
(*a*) 646 (*b*) 800
(*c*) 793 (*d*) 556

11. 162 : 9 : : 310 : ?
(*a*) 33 (*b*) 27
(*c*) 16 (*d*) 4

12. 13 : 17 : : 15 : ?
(*a*) 19 (*b*) 11
(*c*) 21 (*d*) 16

13. 225 : 15 : : 256 : ?
(*a*) 26 (*b*) 16
(*c*) 20 (*d*) 28

14. 46 : 48 : : 54 : ?
(*a*) 59 (*b*) 40
(*c*) 67 (*d*) 62

15. 33 : 36 : : 21 : ?
(*a*) 9 (*b*) 18
(*c*) 25 (*d*) 32

16. 123 : 149 : : 201 : ?
(*a*) 202 (*b*) 404
(*c*) 401 (*d*) 227

17. 7 : 105 : : 5 : ?
(*a*) 97 (*b*) 83
(*c*) 75 (*d*) 61

18. 11 : 101 : : 73 : ?
(*a*) 153 (*b*) 330
(*c*) 543 (*d*) 703

19. 4 : 32 : : 8 : ?
(*a*) 34 (*b*) 68
(*c*) 92 (*d*) 128

20. 94 : 26 : : 62 : ?
(*a*) 16 (*b*) 22
(*c*) 39 (*d*) 48

EXPLANATORY ANSWERS

1. (*b*) : The first number is repeated to obtain the second number.

2. (*d*) : The first fraction is multiplied by half to obtain the second fraction.

$\frac{1}{7} : \frac{1}{14} :: \frac{1}{9} : \frac{1}{18}$

$\times\frac{1}{2}$ $\times\frac{1}{2}$

3. (*c*) : The decimals are divided by 100.

0.16 : 0.0016 :: 1.02 : 0.0102

÷ 100 ÷ 100

4. (*d*) : The digits at tens and hundreds place is same but the digit at the units place is half the other identical digits.

663 : 884 :: 221 : 442

5. (*a*) : Of the two related numbers, the second number is the result of first number divided by 100.

16 : 0.16 :: 2 : 0.02

÷ 100 ÷ 100

6. (*c*) : Of the two related numbers, the second number is the part fraction of the first number, *i.e.* 3 is related to one-third $\left(\frac{1}{3}\right)$. Similarly, 8 will be related to one-eighth $\left(\frac{1}{8}\right)$.

7. (*b*) : The first number is divided by 5 to get the second number.

65 : 13 :: 180 : 36

÷ 5 ÷ 5

8. (*a*) : The numbers are cubes of different odd numbers.

125 : 27 :: 343 : 729

↓ ↓ ↓ ↓

5^3 3^3 7^3 9^3

9. (*a*) : The central digit of the first number is left out and the corner digits written in reverse order to get the second number.

357 : 73 :: 429 : 94

10. (*a*) : The sum of the digits of both the numbers is same.

$731 : 902 \rightarrow 7 + 3 + 1$
$= 9 + 0 + 2$ *i.e.* $11 = 11$

$655 : 646 \rightarrow 6 + 5 + 5$
$= 6 + 4 + 6$ *i.e.* $16 = 16$

11. (*d*) : The sum of the digits of the first number is the second number.

162 : 9 :: 310 : 4

$1 + 6 + 2$ $3 + 1 + 0$

12. (*a*) : First number plus 4 gives the second number.

13 : 17 :: 15 : 19

+4 +4

13. (*b*) : The root of first number is the second number.

225 : 15 :: 256 : 16

$\sqrt{225}$ $\sqrt{256}$

14. (*b*) : The product of the digits of first number is multiplied by 2 to get the second number.

46 : 48 :: 54 : 40

$(4 \times 6)\,2$ $(5 \times 4)\,2$

15. (a) : The square of the sum of the digits of the first number is the second number.

33 : 36 :: 21 : 9

$(3+3)^2$ $(2+1)^2$

16. (c) : Each digit of the first number are squared to get the digits of the second number.

123 : 149 :: 201 : 401

1^2 2^2 3^2 2^2 0^2 1^2

17. (c) : The first number is multiplied by 15 to get the second number.

7 : 105 :: 5 : 75

$\times 15$ $\times 15$

18. (d) : Zero is inserted in between the digits of the first number to get the second number.

11 : $1\underline{0}1$ :: 73 : $7\underline{0}3$

19. (d) : Double the first number multiplied by the number itself gives the second number.

4 : 32 :: 8 : 128

$(4\times 2)\,4$ $(8\times 2)\,8$

20. (a) : The sum of the digits of the first number multiplied by two gives the second number.

94 : 26 :: 62 : 16

$(9+4)\times 2$ $(6+2)\times 2$

8. ODD ONE OUT

In this type of classification, four words are given out of which three are almost same in matter or meaning and only one word is different from the common three. One has to find out the word which is different from the rest.

EXERCISE

Directions : *In each of the following questions, three words are alike in some manner. Spot the odd one out.*

1. (*a*) Green (*b*) Red (*c*) Colour (*d*) Orange

2. (*a*) Stable (*b*) Hole (*c*) Canoe (*d*) Sty

3. (*a*) Nose (*b*) Eyes (*c*) Skin (*d*) Teeth

4. (*a*) Venus (*b*) Moon (*c*) Pluto (*d*) Mars

5. (*a*) Happy (*b*) Gloomy (*c*) Lively (*d*) Cheerful

Directions : *Three of the following four in each question are alike in a certain way and so form a group. Select the group of letters that does not belong to that group.*

6. (*a*) ACE (*b*) LOR (*c*) GIK (*d*) VXZ

7. (*a*) TSR (*b*) LKJ (*c*) PQO (*d*) HGF

8. (*a*) EF LM (*b*) KJ SR (*c*) XW HG (*d*) ED YX

9. (*a*) JOPK (*b*) BOPC (*c*) QOPR (*d*) TOPS

10. (*a*) DfH (*b*) MoQ (*c*) UwY (*d*) lnO

Directions : *In each of the following questions, there are four options. Three numbers, in these options, are alike in certain manner. Only one number does not fit in. Choose the one which is different from the rest.*

11. (*a*) 1948 (*b*) 2401 (*c*) 966 (*d*) 1449

12. (*a*) 182 (*b*) 169 (*c*) 130 (*d*) 158

13. (*a*) 129 (*b*) 130 (*c*) 131 (*d*) 132

14. (*a*) 3215 (*b*) 9309 (*c*) 4721 (*d*) 2850

15. (*a*) 1776 (*b*) 2364 (*c*) 1976 (*d*) 3776

Directions : *In the following questions select the pair which is different from the other three.*

16. (*a*) Chair - Furniture
(*b*) Shirt - Garment
(*c*) Necklace - Jewellery
(*d*) Bogie - Engine

17. (*a*) Crayon - Paper
(*b*) Pencil - Lead
(*c*) Pen - Ink
(*d*) Brush - Paint

18. (*a*) War - Peace
(*b*) Real - Natural
(*c*) Premiere - First
(*d*) Wrath - Anger

19. (*a*) Finger - Thimble
(*b*) Head - Cap
(*c*) Waist - Tiara
(*d*) Foot - Shoe

20. (*a*) Day - Night
(*b*) Clever - Foolish
(*c*) Clear - Blurred
(*d*) Arrive - Come

Directions : *In the following questions, which of the following pair of letters is different from the other three?*

21. (*a*) FGH - HIJ (*b*) PQR - RST (*c*) MNO - OPQ (*d*) CDE - DEF

22. (*a*) JuM - jUm (*b*) iLo - Ilo (*c*) PSa - psA (*d*) ZeX - zEx

23. (*a*) NQT - JMP (*b*) CFI - RUX (*c*) ADG - FGH (*d*) SVY - ORU

24. (*a*) DXD - XDX (*b*) KUK - UKU (*c*) FHF - EHE (*d*) RSR - SRS

25. (*a*) AYT - BZU (*b*) FNG - EMF (*c*) RWO - QVN (*d*) HJD - GIC

Directions : *Which of the following pair of numbers is different from the other three pairs?*

26. (*a*) 28, 4 (*b*) 63, 7 (*c*) 56, 8 (*d*) 35, 5

27. (*a*) 3, 11 (*b*) 8, 16 (*c*) 5, 13 (*d*) 14, 24

28. (*a*) 13, 156 (*b*) 12, 144 (*c*) 15, 180 (*d*) 16, 176

29. (*a*) 32, 13 (*b*) 46, 20 (*c*) 51, 24 (*d*) 72, 45

30. (*a*) 5, 25 (*b*) 9, 81 (*c*) 4, 64 (*d*) 6, 36

31. (*a*) 91, 10 (*b*) 57, 12 (*c*) 69, 15 (*d*) 72, 13

32. (*a*) 20, 10 (*b*) 45, 27 (*c*) 15, 12 (*d*) 30, 18

33. (*a*) 7, 3 (*b*) 13, 9 (*c*) 11, 7 (*d*) 17, 8

34. (*a*) 10, 20 (*b*) 40, 50 (*c*) 30, 40 (*d*) 50, 60

35. (*a*) 16, 26 (*b*) 3, 4 (*c*) 26, 24 (*d*) 27, 25

EXPLANATORY ANSWERS

1. (*c*) : All others are types of colour.

2. (*c*) : Canoe is a boat. Others are resting places of birds/animals.

3. (*d*) : All others are sense organs.

4. (*b*) : All others are planets.

5. (*b*) : All others are expressions of joy.

6. (*b*) : The sequence in each group is +2. Only option (*b*) has sequence in +3, *i.e.*,

ABCDE: A→C +2, C→E +2 LMNOPQR: L→O +3, O→R +3

GHIJK: H→J +2, J→K +2 VWXYZ: W→Y +2, Y→Z +2

7. (*c*) : The sequence of alphabet in each group is in reverse order. Only option (*c*) has sequence in disturbed order.

8. (*a*) : Two consecutive alphabet in each group are in reverse sequence (–1), *i.e.*,

KJ SR; XW HG; ED YX
–1 –1 –1 –1 –1 –1

Only in option (*a*) the sequence is in natural order (+1), *i.e.*,

EF +1 LM +1

9. (*d*) : In each group, letters 'OP' are common. The two corner alphabet are in natural order (+1); *i.e.*,

JOPK (J, K +1); BOPC (B, C +1); QOPR (Q, R +1)

Only in option (*d*) they are in reverse order (–1); *i.e.*,

TOPS (T, S –1)

10. (*d*) : In other groups, only the alphabet in the centre is of lower case. In this option letter 'L' on the left is also in lower case.

11. (*a*) : Other numbers are divisible by 7.

12. (*d*) : Other numbers are multiples of 13.

13. (*c*) : 131 is a prime number.

14. (*b*) : In other numbers, no digit is repeated.

15. (*b*) : In other numbers, the last two digits are same.

16. (*d*) : Bogie is a part of train which is a type of conveyance. Chair, Shirt and Necklace are types of furniture, garment and jewellery respectively.

17. ***(a)*** **:** The medium used for writing with pencil is lead, with pen it is ink and with brush, it is paint. With crayon it should be wax.

18. ***(a)*** **:** The pair of words are opposite. Other pairs are synonyms.

19. ***(c)*** **:** Tiara is worn on the head.

20. ***(d)*** **:** Other words are opposite to each other.

21. ***(d)*** **:** In all other groups, the letters are in natural series and the last letter of first part is the first letter of the second part.

22. ***(b)*** **:** In all other groups, only the vowel is in lower case in the first part and in second part the case is reversed.

23. ***(c)*** **:** In all other groups, the letters jump two letters in between them.

24. ***(c)*** **:** In all other groups, the single letter in first part is repeated in the second and vice versa.

25. ***(a)*** **:** In all other groups, the letters in the first part are one step forward than the corresponding letters in the second part.

26. ***(b)*** **:** In all other pairs 7 times the second number is the first number. In this option 9 times 7 is the first number.

27. ***(d)*** **:** In all other groups, the difference between the two numbers is 8.

28. ***(d)*** **:** In other groups 12 times, the first number is the second number. In this option 11 times the first number is the second number.

29. ***(a)*** **:** 13 is a prime number.

30. ***(c)*** **:** In all other pairs, the second number is a perfect square of the first.

31. ***(d)*** **:** In all other pairs, the second number is the sum of the digits of the first number.

32. ***(a)*** **:** In all other pairs, the numbers are divisible by 3.

33. ***(d)*** **:** In other groups, the difference between the numbers is 4.

34. ***(a)*** **:** In this option, the second number is double the first number. In other groups the difference between the two numbers is 10.

35. ***(a)*** **:** In other groups, the first digits of the two numbers are same (consider 3 and 4 as 03 and 04).

9. Coding and Decoding

Coding is a secretive language which is used to change the representation of the actual term/word/value. This coded language can be framed by *(i)* moving the letters one or more steps forward or backward; *(ii)* substituting numbers for letters and vice–versa; *(iii)* writing the letters of the given word in reverse order in part or in whole; and *(iv)* replacing the letters in their natural series by the same positioned letters in their reverse series.

There is variety in ways of coding. Coding language is not only for words and numbers but also for hiding a group of words, statements or even sentences. This form of coding pattern may appear to be confusing but after solving only a few questions it is very easy to understand. Questions based on this coding pattern require no moving of steps or straining efforts of calculations, but only quick tallying or comparing ability. The codes can be letters or numbers.

EXERCISE

Directions : *In the following questions select the right option which indicates the correct code for the word or letter given in the question.*

1. If MUSK is coded as 146816, then ZERO will be coded as :
   (*a*) 113811 (*b*) 122912
   (*c*) 15915 (*d*) 2651815
2. If BAD is coded as 7, HIS as 9, LOW will be coded as :
   (*a*) 50 (*b*) 8
   (*c*) 23 (*d*) 5
3. In a certain code LIBERATE is written as 56403170, TRIBAL will be written in the same code as :
   (*a*) 734615 (*b*) 736415
   (*c*) 136475 (*d*) 034615
4. In certain military code, SYSTEM is written as SYSMET, and NEARER as AENRER, what will be the code for FRACTION?
   (*a*) CRAFNOIT (*b*) FRCAITNO
   (*c*) CARFNOIT (*d*) FRACNOIT
5. If CRUDE is written as BSTED, then MOIST will be coded as :
   (*a*) NNJRU (*b*) LNHRS
   (*c*) NPJTU (*d*) LPHTS
6. In a certain code ALPACA is written as ACAPLA. How will ANIMAL be written in that code?
   (*a*) LAMINA (*b*) ALAMIN
   (*c*) LAMNIA (*d*) AAMLIN
7. In a certain code FINGER is written as DGLECP. What will be the code for KIDNEY?
   (*a*) IGBLCW (*b*) IGCLBW
   (*c*) IBCGLE (*d*) IGBKCV
8. In a certain code QUESTION is written as NXBVQLLQ. How will REPLY be coded?
   (*a*) YHMOV (*b*) OBMVI
   (*c*) VHSOB (*d*) OHMOV
9. If in a certain code SKEW is coded as PNCY, then what will JXQV will stand for?
   (*a*) MUTS (*b*) MUST
   (*c*) MTSU (*d*) STUM
10. In a certain code LONDON is written as MPOEPO. What will IVOHSZ mean in the same code?
    (*a*) HUNGRY (*b*) HUNDRY
    (*c*) GRUNHY (*d*) HONDUS
11. In a certain code language 8514 is a code for HEAD, 3945 for RIDE and 057 for BEG. What will be the code for GRADE?
    (*a*) 71345 (*b*) 73415
    (*c*) 74135 (*d*) 73145

12. If MOTHERLAND is coded as 9501623748, how will DREAM be coded?
(*a*) 82697 (*b*) 86297
(*c*) 82769 (*d*) 82679

13. If OATH is coded in a certain language as TEYL, then how will WORD be coded?
(*a*) BWRH (*b*) HRWB
(*c*) BSWH (*d*) CSXI

14. If FINANCE is coded as GKQESIL, then how will BANK be coded in the same manner?
(*a*) CBOL (*b*) CDRP
(*c*) CCQO (*d*) CCPN

15. PLANNING is coded in a certain language as UFFHSCSA. How will AUTHORITY be coded in the same language?
(*a*) FOYBTLNND
(*b*) FYOTBNNLT
(*c*) FBOYTLNTN
(*d*) FBOYTNLTN

Directions : *In the following questions study the coded patterns and then select the right option from the given alternatives.*

16. In a certain language, (a) 'go ju mi' stands for 'plenty of money'; (b) pao ju go nei vu' for 'money creates lots of problems'; (c) 'kol vu nei' for 'problems create tension'; and (d) 'sol tun ju haw' for 'still money is needed'. Which of the following words stand for 'money'?
(*a*) nei (*b*) ju
(*c*) haw (*d*) go

17. In a certain language, (a) 'FOR' stands for 'old is gold'; (b) 'ROT' stands for 'gold is pure'; (c) 'ROM' stands for 'gold is costly'. How will 'pure old gold is costly' be written?
(*a*) TFROM (*b*) FOTRM
(*c*) FTORM (*d*) TOMRF

18. In a certain code '415' means 'milk is hot'; '18' means 'hot soup'; and '895' means 'soup is tasty'. What number will indicate the word 'tasty'?
(*a*) 9 (*b*) 8
(*c*) 5 (*d*) 4

19. In a certain code '643' means 'she is beautiful', '593' means 'he is handsome', and '567' means 'handsome meets beautiful'. What number will indicate the word 'meets'?
(*a*) 5 (*b*) 3
(*c*) 7 (*d*) 6

20. In a certain code language, (a) 'dugo hui mul zo' stands for 'work is very hard'; (b) 'hui dugo ba ki' for 'Bingo is very smart'; (c) 'nano mul dugo' for 'cake is hard', and (d) 'mul ki qu' for 'smart and hard'. Which of the following words stand for 'Bingo'?
(*a*) jalu (*b*) dugo
(*c*) ki (*d*) ba

Directions : *Read the given coded information and choose the correct answer from the given options.*

21. If 'water' is called 'blue', 'blue' is called 'red', 'red' is called 'white', 'white' is called 'sky', 'sky' is called 'rain', 'rain' is called 'green', 'green' is called 'air' and 'air' is called 'table', which of the following is the colour of milk?
(*a*) white (*b*) rain
(*c*) sky (*d*) green

22. If 'light' is called 'dark', 'dark' is called 'green', 'green' is called 'blue', 'blue' is called 'red', 'red' is called 'white' and 'white' is called 'yellow', what is the colour of blood?
(*a*) red (*b*) dark
(*c*) white (*d*) yellow

23. If 'sky' is called 'sea', 'sea' is called 'water', 'water' is called 'air', 'air' is called 'cloud' and 'cloud' is called 'river', then what do we drink when thirsty?
(*a*) sky (*b*) air
(*c*) water (*d*) sea

24. If 'yellow' means 'red', 'white' means 'green', 'red' means 'orange', 'blue' means 'white' and 'green' means 'blue', then the colour of sky is :
(*a*) white (*b*) green
(*c*) blue (*d*) yellow

25. If 'land' is called 'sky', 'sky' is called 'air', 'air' is called 'water', 'water' is called 'sand' and 'sand' is called 'solid', where do fishes swim?
(*a*) air (*b*) sky
(*c*) water (*d*) sand

EXPLANATORY ANSWERS

1. *(b)* : The coded number signifies the position of the alphabet in its reverse order of the alphabetical series (ZYXW...)

M U S K → MUSK
↓ ↓ ↓ ↓
14th 6th 8th 16th → 146816

Similarly,

Z E R O → ZERO
↓ ↓ ↓ ↓
1st 22nd 9th 12th → 122912

2. *(d)* : The coded number is the sum of number digits signifying the position of the alphabet in the natural order.

B A D
↓ ↓ ↓
2nd 1st 4th *i.e.,* 2 + 1 + 4 = 7

Similarly,

H I S
↓ ↓ ↓
8th 9th 19th *i.e.,* 8 + 9 + 19 = 36
further, 3 + 6 = 9

Also,

L O W
↓ ↓ ↓
12th 15th 23rd *i.e.,* 12 + 15 + 23 = 50
further, 5 + 0 = 0

3. *(b)* : The letters of the word TRIBAL are picked from LIBERATE. So will be the coded numbers.

L I B E R A T E → given word
5 6 4 0 3 1 7 0 → codes

Similarly,

T R I B A L → word to be coded
7 3 6 4 1 5 → answer codes

4. *(c)* : The word is divided into two equal parts and the letters of each part are written in reverse order.

SYS TEM SYS MET NEA RER AEN RER

Similarly,

FRAC TION CARF NOIT

5. *(d)* : The code is formed by moving the letters one step backwards and one step forward alternately.

CRUDE BSTED
−1
+1
−1
+1
−1

Similarly,

MOIST LPHTS
−1
+1
−1
+1
−1

6. *(a)* : The letters of the word are written backwards.

ALPACA ACAPLA

Similarly,

ANIMAL LAMINA

7. *(a)* : The word is coded by moving the letters two steps backwards.

FINGER DGLECP
−2
−2
−2
−2
−2
−2

Similarly,

KIDNEY IGBLCW
−2
−2
−2
−2
−2
−2

8. *(d)* : The letters of the word are coded by moving three steps backward and three steps forward alternately.

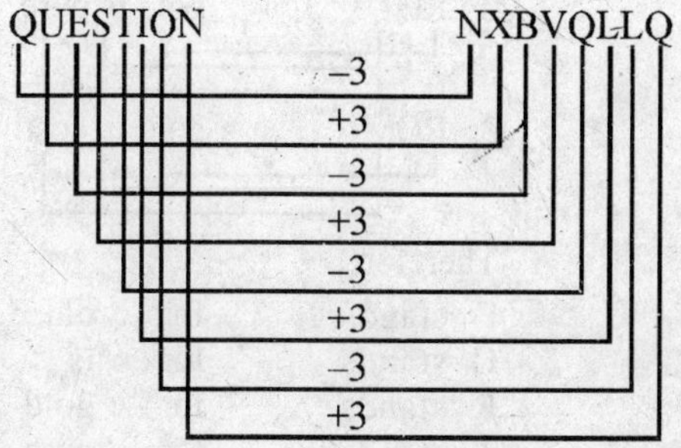

Similarly,

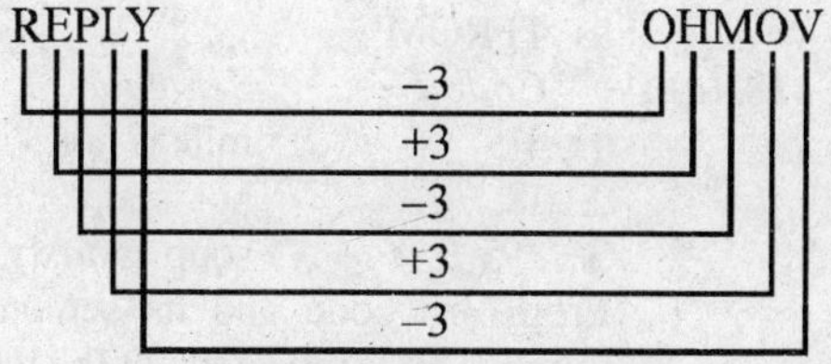

9. *(b)* : The letters are decoded by moving the letters +3, –3, +2 and –2 steps respectively.

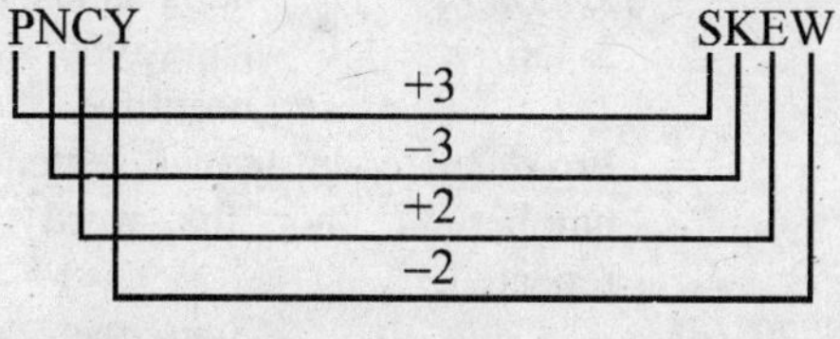

Similarly,

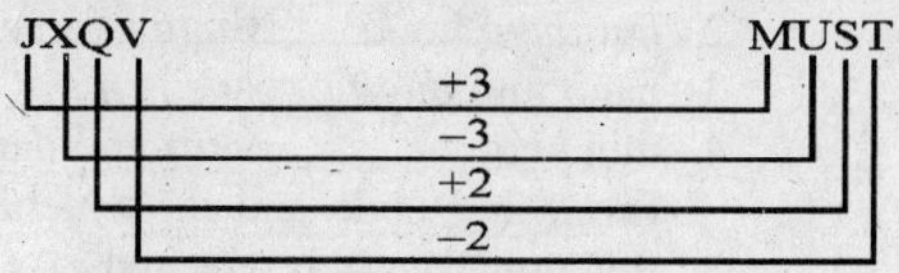

10. *(a)* : The letters of the coded word are moved one step backward.

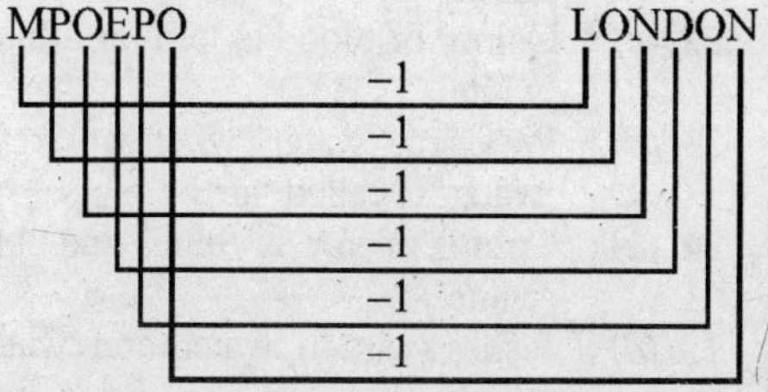

Similarly,

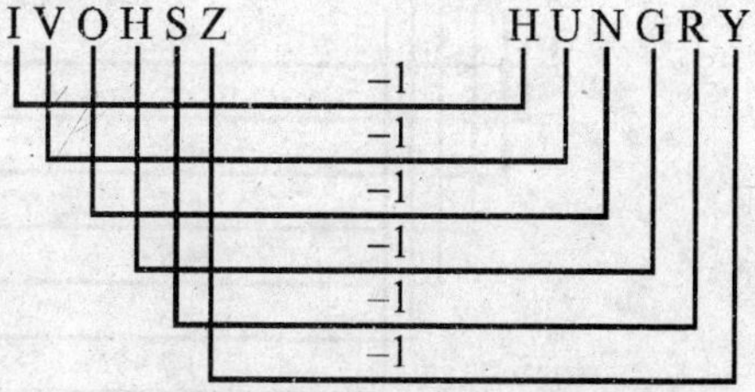

11. *(d)* : The word GRADE is framed by letters in the given words. So, in order to find the code for GRADE select the respective number codes.

H E A D R I D E B E G → letters
8 5 1 4 3 9 4 5 0 5 7 → codes

So,

G R A D E →letters
7 3 1 4 5 →answer codes

12. *(d)* : The letters of the word are coded by numbers. So to find the code for DREAM select the respective numbers.

M O T H E R L A N D → letters
9 5 0 1 6 2 3 7 4 8 → codes

So, D R E A M → letters
8 2 6 7 9 → answer codes

13. *(c)* : The letters are coded by moving five and four steps forward alternately.

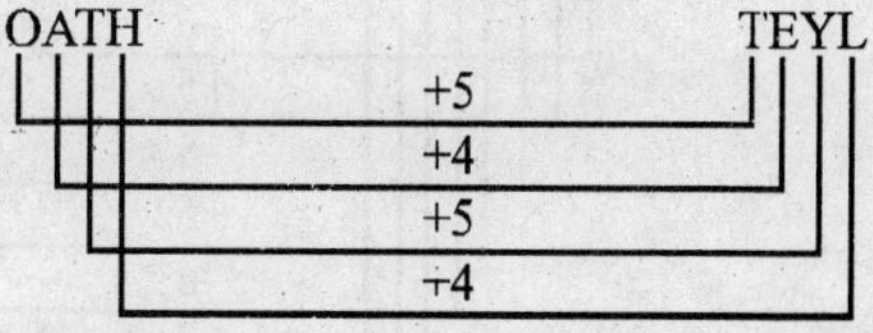

Similarly,

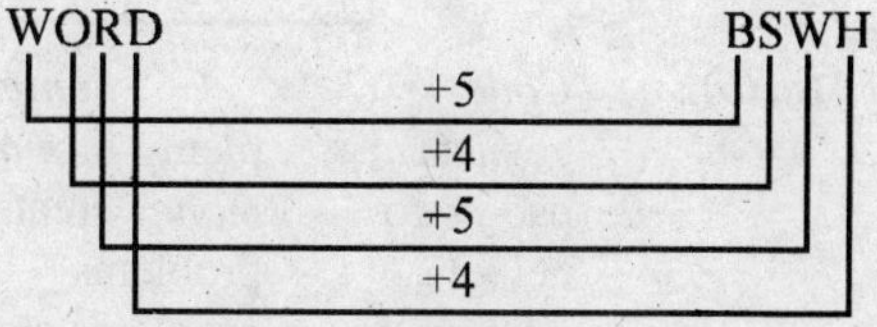

14. *(c)* : The letters of the word are coded by moving one step ahead and increasing the difference by one.

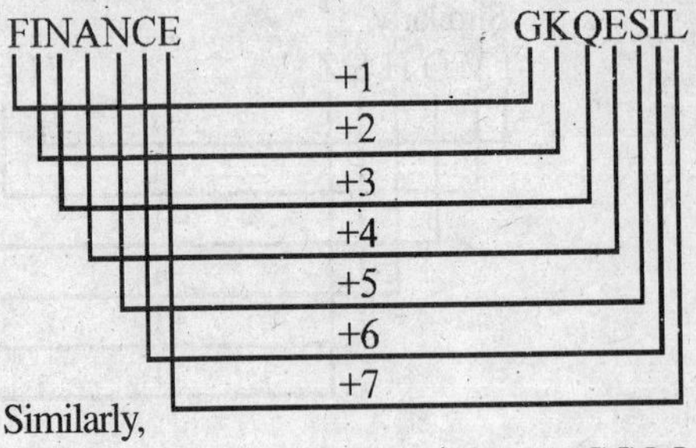

Similarly,

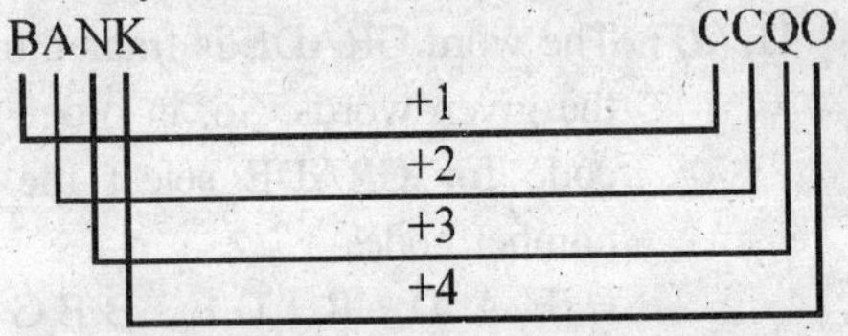

15. *(a)* : The letters of the word are coded by moving five steps forward and six steps backward alternately.

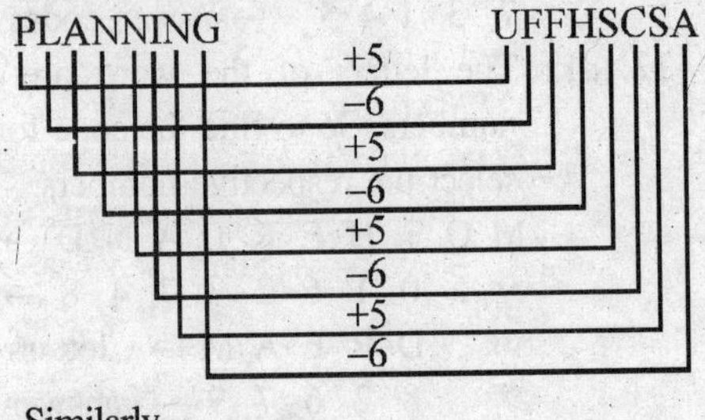

Similarly,

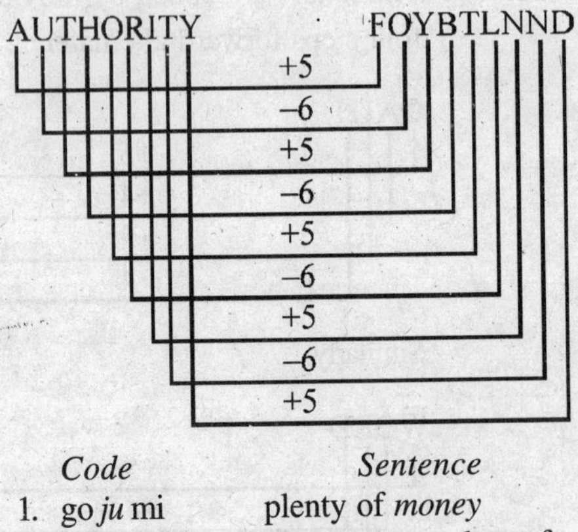

16. *(b)* :

Code	*Sentence*
1. go *ju* mi	plenty of *money*
2. pao *ju* go nei vu	*money* creates lots of problems
3. kol vu nei	problems create tension
4. sol tun *ju* haw	still *money* is needed

In 1st, 2nd and 4th codes and their sentences the word 'ju' is repeated and so is 'money'.

17. *(a)* :

Code	*Sentence*
1. FOR	old is gold
2. ROT	gold is pure
3. ROM	gold is costly

Therefore,

F stands for old
O stands for is
R stands for gold
T stands for pure
M stands for costly

So, 'pure old gold is costly' will be written as 'TFROM'.

18. *(a)* :

Code	*Sentence*
1. 415	milk is hot
2. 18	hot soup
3. 895	soup is *tasty*

From 3rd code and its sentence neither number '9' is repeated nor the word 'tasty'.

19. *(c)* :

Code	*Sentence*
1. 643	she is beautiful
2. 593	he is handsome
3. 567	handsome *meets* beautiful

From 3rd code and its sentence, neither number '7' nor the word 'meets' is repeated.

20. *(d)* :

Code	*Sentence*
1. *dugo hui* mul zo	work *is very* hard
2. *hui dugo* **ba** *ki*	**Bingo** *is very smart*
3. nano mul *dugo*	cake is *hard*
4. mul *ki* qu	*smart* and hard

From 2nd code and its sentence, neither 'ba' nor 'Bingo' is repeated.
(Words repeated are in italics)

21. *(c)* : Colour of milk is 'white' and 'white' is called 'sky'.

22. *(c)* : Colour of blood is 'red' and 'red' is called 'white'.

23. *(b)* : We drink 'water' when we are thirsty and 'water' is called 'air'.

24. *(a)* : Colour of sky is 'blue' and 'blue' means 'white'.

25. *(d)* : Fishes swim in 'water' and 'water' is called 'sand'.

10. Statement Analysis

In these type of questions, a few statements are given. Certain facts are broken up and mentioned in these statements. What is required is to analyse the statements, arrange and sort out the given facts and then answer the questions related to the given statements.

EXERCISE

1. Among five friends, A is heavier than B; C is lighter than D; B is lighter than D but heavier than E. Who among them is the heaviest?

(*a*) B (*b*) C

(*c*) A (*d*) Can't say

2. Pune is bigger than Jhansi, Sitapur is bigger than Chittor. Raigarh is not as big as Jhansi, but is bigger than Sitapur. Chittor is not as big as Sitapur. Which is the smallest?

(*a*) Jhansi (*b*) Pune

(*c*) Chittor (*d*) Sitapur

3. Ajay works more than Ram. Alok works as much as Raju. Pankaj works less than Alok. Ram works more than Alok. Who works the most of all?

(*a*) Ajay (*b*) Ram

(*c*) Alok (*d*) Raju

4. Among five friends P, Q, R, S and T, who is the youngest? To arrive at the answer which of the following information given in the statements (A) and (B) is sufficient?

(A) R is younger than P and T.

(B) S is younger than Q.

(*a*) Only A alone is sufficient

(*b*) Either A or B is sufficient

(*c*) Both A and B together are needed

(*d*) Both A and B together are not sufficient

5. A is elder to B while C and D are elder to E who lies between A and B. If C be elder to B, which one of the following statements is necessarily true?

(*a*) E is elder to B

(*b*) A is elder to C

(*c*) C is elder to D

(*d*) D is elder to C

6. Suresh is as much older than Kamal as he is younger than Prabodh. Navin is as old as Kamal. Which of the following statements is wrong?

(*a*) Suresh is older than Navin

(*b*) Kamal is younger than Suresh

(*c*) Prabodh is not the oldest

(*d*) Navin is younger than Prabodh

Directions (Qs. 7 to 9) : *Ram, Sohan and Mohan play football, hockey and cricket. Ram, Ramesh and Mohan play hockey, cricket and basketball. Ram, Sohan, Rahim and Mohan play football and cricket. Now answer the following questions based on the above statements :*

7. Which game is played by all the boys?

(*a*) Football (*b*) Hockey

(*c*) Cricket (*d*) Basketball

8. Which two boys play all the games?

(*a*) Ram, Sohan (*b*) Ram, Ramesh

(*c*) Sohan, Mohan (*d*) Ram, Mohan

9. Who does not play football?

(*a*) Ramesh (*b*) Sohan

(*c*) Rahim (*d*) Mohan

Directions (Qs. 10 to 12) : *Read the following directions and answer the questions given below :*

There are five persons in a group. Out of these two are men. Only three persons know swimming, of which one is a man. There is a couple, of which the husband knows swimming. A is the younger sister of D and B is the husband of E. C is a swimming champion.

10. Who is the other man in the group?
(*a*) C (*b*) B
(*c*) A (*d*) D

11. The two women who know how to swim are:
(*a*) A and C (*b*) C and D
(*c*) D and E (*d*) A and E

12. The two persons who do not know how to swim are :
(*a*) B and D (*b*) D and E
(*c*) A and E (*d*) A and D

Directions (Qs. 13 to 15) : *Read the following statements and answer the questions given below :*

Rajat, Sushil and Nagesh play football, hockey and cricket. Rajat, Ramu and Nagesh play hockey, cricket and basketball. Rajat, Sushil, Mayank and Nagesh play football and cricket.

13. Which game is played by all the boys?
(*a*) Hockey (*b*) Basketball
(*c*) Football (*d*) Cricket

14. Who does not play football?
(*a*) Rajat (*b*) Nagesh
(*c*) Sushil (*d*) Ramu

15. Which of the following two boys play all the games?
(*a*) Nagesh, Rajat
(*b*) Mayank, Ramu
(*c*) Ramu, Nagesh
(*d*) Sushil, Mayank

Directions (Qs. 16 to 20) : *Read the following information and answer the questions given below:*

(*i*) P, Q, R, S, T and U are six members in a family in which there are two married couples.
(*ii*) T a teacher is married to the doctor who is mother of R and U.
(*iii*) Q the lawyer is married to P.
(*iv*) P has one son and one grandson.
(*v*) Of the two married ladies one is a housewife.
(*vi*) There is also one student and one male engineer in the family.

16. Who among the following is the housewife?
(*a*) Q (*b*) P
(*c*) S (*d*) T

17. Which of the following represents the group of females in the family?
(*a*) QTR (*b*) PSR
(*c*) PSU (*d*) Data inadequate

18. Which of the following is true about the granddaughter in the family?
(*a*) She is a student
(*b*) She is an engineer
(*c*) She is a lawyer
(*d*) Data Inadequate

19. How R is related to U?
(*a*) Brother
(*b*) Sister
(*c*) Brother or Sister
(*d*) Data inadequate

20. How is P related to R?
(*a*) Grandfather (*b*) Mother
(*c*) Sister (*d*) Grandmother

EXPLANATORY ANSWERS

1. (*d*) : The five friends in descending order of weight are : A/D, B/C, E or A/D, B, C/E. Either A or D is the heaviest.

2. (*c*) : The order of cities in descending order of size is : Pune, Jhansi, Raigarh, Sitapur, Chittor.

3. (*a*) : On the basis of doing work, the descending order will be : Ajay, Ram, Alok/Raju, Pankaj.

4. (*d*) : Statements are not inter-related.

5. (*a*) : The order in descending seniority will be : A/C/D, E, B.

6. (*c*) : On the basis of age the descending order will be : Prabodh, Suresh, Kamal/Navin.

Chart for Answers 7 to 9

Boy	*Games Played*
Ram	Football, Hocky, Cricket, Basketball
Sohan	Football, Hockey, Cricket
Mohan	Football, Hockey, Cricket, Basketball
Ramesh	Hockey, Cricket, Basketball
Rahim	Football, Cricket.

7. *(c)* **8.** *(d)* **9.** *(a)*

For Answers 10 to 12 the information chart will be :

A. Woman ((younger sister of D); knows swimming.

B. Man (husband of E); knows swimming

C. Woman; Swimming champion

D. Man (brother of A)

E. Woman (wife of B)

From the couple B & E, B (husband) knows swimming. C is a swimming champion. Three persons know how to swim of which only B is a man. So, the two women who know how to swim are C and A (the younger sister of D). There are two men in the group of five. One is B and the other will be D.

10. *(d)* **11.** *(a)* **12.** *(b)*

Chart for Answers 13 to 15

Boy	*Games Played*
Rajat	— Football, Hockey, Cricket, Basketball
Sushil	— Football, Hockey, Cricket, Basketball
Nagesh	— Football, Hockey, Cricket, Basketball
Ramu	— Hockey, Cricket, Basketball
Mayank	— Football, Cricket

13. *(d)* **14.** *(d)* **15.** *(a)*

Chart for Answers 16 to 20

P (female/housewife) — Q (male/lawyer) *Grandparents*

T (male/teacher) — S (female/doctor) *Parents*

R, U (of R and U, one is a male engineer and one is a student) Children

16. *(b)* **:** One married lady S who is mother of R and U is a doctor. Q the lawyer is married to P. Of the two married ladies one is a house-wife. As Q is a lawyer the other married lady who is a housewife should be P.

17. *(d)* **:** Sex of R and U is not given.

18. *(a)* **:** P has one son T and one grandson either R or U one of whom is an engineer. So, the granddaughter is a student.

19. *(c)* **:** Sex of R and U is not given, but as both are children of S and one is a male engineer, the relationship between the two is of brother and sister.

20. *(d)*

11. PLACE ARRANGEMENT

Place arrangement generally refers to the positioning of persons or objects in a manner indicated by set of information given. One has to understand the order of placement and then attempt questions following the given information.

EXERCISE

Directions : *In the following questions, understand the arrangement pattern and then select the right answer from the given options :*

1. Five boys are sitting in a row. Raghu is not adjacent to Shyam or Amit. Ajay is not adjacent to Shyam. Raghu is adjacent to Mayank. If Mayank is at the middle in the row, then Ajay is adjacent to whom out of the following?
   (*a*) Amit (*b*) Raghu
   (*c*) Mayank (*d*) Shyam
2. Mini is to the right of Rajni but to the left of Ananta. Saya is to the right of Mini but to the left of Jaya. Who is on the extreme left if all the girls are facing North?
   (*a*) Jaya (*b*) Mini
   (*c*) Rajni (*d*) Saya
3. O, P, Q, R, S and T are standing on a bench according to their height. P is taller than O but shorter than S. Only S is taller than T. R is shorter than P but taller than Q. Who is the shortest?
   (*a*) O (*b*) Q
   (*c*) P (*d*) Cannot be said
4. Five personalities are living in a multistoried building. Mr. Effortless lives in a flat above Mr. Active, Mr. Charge lives in a flat below Mr. Diligent, Mr. Active lives in a flat above Mr. Diligent and Mr. Behaved lives in a flat below Mr. Charge. Who lives in the topmost flat?
   (*a*) Mr. Charge (*b*) Mr. Diligent
   (*c*) Mr. Effortless (*d*) Mr. Behaved
5. Six friends are sitting in a circle and playing cards. Kenny is to the left of Danny. Michael is in-between Bob and John. Roger is in between Kenny and Bob. Who is sitting to the right of Michael?
   (*a*) Danny (*b*) John
   (*c*) Kenny (*d*) Bob
6. Four girls A, B, C and D are sitting in a circle. B and C are facing each other. Which of the following is definitely true?
   (*a*) A is to the left of C
   (*b*) D is to the left of C
   (*c*) A and D are facing each other
   (*d*) A is not between B and C
7. Brijesh, Jayesh, Amar and Praveer are playing a game of cards. Amar is to the right of Jayesh who is to the right of Brijesh. Who is to the right of Amar?
   (*a*) Brijesh
   (*b*) Praveer
   (*c*) Brijesh or Praveer
   (*d*) Jayesh
8. In a pile of 10 books there are 3 of History, 3 of Hindi, 2 of Maths, and 2 of English. Taking from above there is an English book between a History and Maths book, a History book between a Maths and an English book, a Hindi book between an English and a Maths book, a Maths book between two Hindi books, and two Hindi books between a Maths and a History book. Book of which subject is at the sixth position from the top?
   (*a*) English (*b*) Hindi
   (*c*) History (*d*) Maths

9. Five persons A, B, C, D and E are sitting in a row facing you such that D is on the left of C and B is on the right of E. A is on the right of C and B is on the left of D. If E occupies a corner position, then who is sitting in the centre?
(*a*) A (*b*) B
(*c*) C (*d*) D

10. Six friends A, B, C, D, E and F are standing in a circle. B is between F and C; A is between E and D; F is to the left of D. Who is between A and F?
(*a*) C (*b*) B
(*c*) D (*d*) E

EXPLANATORY ANSWERS

1. (*b*) : The order of sitting is :
Amit, Shyam, Mayank, Ajay, Raghu
or
Ajay, Raghu, Mayank, Amit, Shyam

2. (*c*) : The order in which the girls are positioned is :
Rajni, Mini, Ananta, Saya, Jaya
or
Saya, Jaya, Ananta
or
Saya, Ananta, Jaya

3. (*d*) : In descending order of height, the standing positions are :

S		S
T		T
P	*or*	P
R		R
O		Q
Q		O

Either O or Q is the shortest. The informa-tion given is not enough to clarify the answer.

4. (*c*) : The personalities living in flats in multi-storied building are in order given below :
Mr. Effortless
Mr. Active
Mr. Diligent
Mr. Charge
Mr. Behaved

5. (*d*) : The order in which the friends are sitting is :

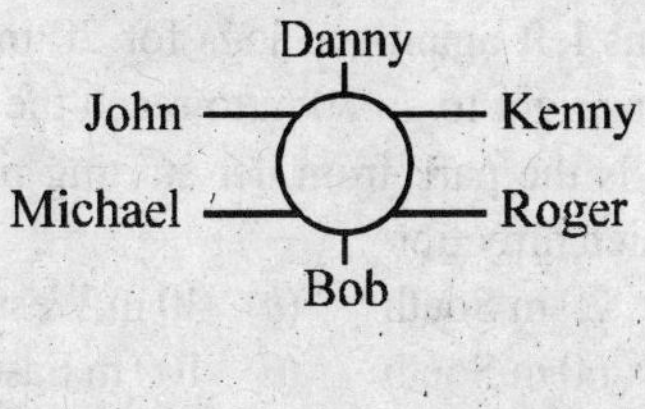

6. (*c*) : The sitting positions are :

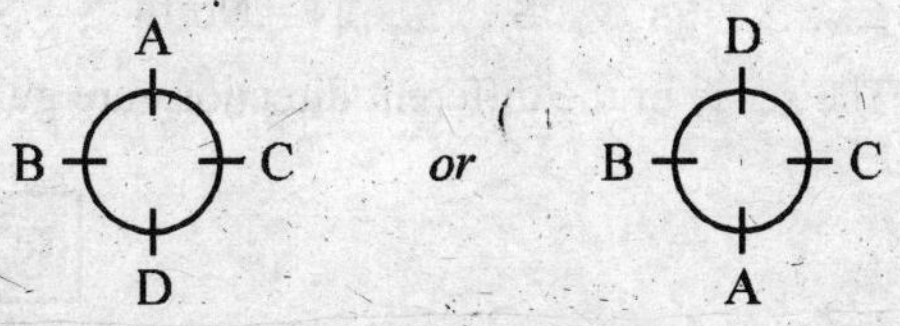

7. (*b*) : The order from left to right is :
Brijesh, Jayesh, Amar, Praveer

8. (*b*) : The pile of books is in the order :
1st — History
English
Maths
History
English
6th — Hindi
Maths
Hindi
Hindi
10th — History

9. (*d*) : Sitting order while facing us is :
A, C, D, B, E

10. (*c*) : The pattern of standing is :

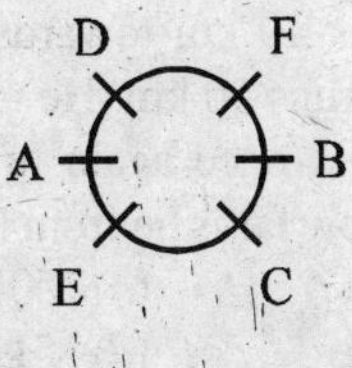

12. Direction Sense

In these type of tests, the directions in questions needs to be perceived. Such questions are based on the direction chart.

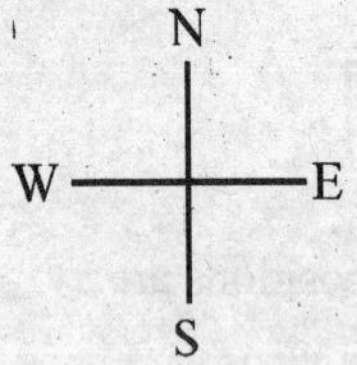

N = North S = South E = East W = West

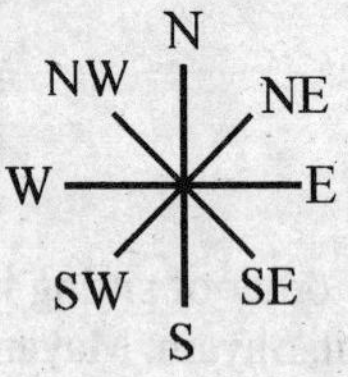

The sense of the different directions are guided by the left and right turns or angular turns.

EXERCISE

Directions : *In the following questions, select the right answer from the given options to depict the correct direction/distance.*

1. Kittu walks towards East and then towards South. After walking some distance he turns towards West and then turns to his left. In which direction is he walking now?
   (*a*) North (*b*) South
   (*c*) East (*d*) West
2. A person is driving towards West. What sequence of directions should he follow so that he is driving towards South?
   (*a*) left, right, right
   (*b*) right, right, left
   (*c*) left, left, left
   (*d*) right, right, right
3. Richa drives 8 km to the South, turns left and drives 5 km. Again, she turns left and drives 8 km. How far is she from her starting point?
   (*a*) 3 km (*b*) 5 km
   (*c*) 8 km (*d*) 13 km
4. Dingi runs 40 km towards North then turns right and runs 50 km. He turns right and runs 30 km, and once again turns right and runs 50 km. How far is he from his starting point?
   (*a*) 90 km (*b*) 50 km
   (*c*) 10 km (*d*) 5 km
5. If North is called North-West, North-West is called West, West is called South-West and so on. What will South-East be called?
   (*a*) East (*b*) West
   (*c*) North-East (*d*) South-East
6. A man travels 100 km towards South. From there he turns right and travels 100 km and again turns right to travel 50 km. Which direction is he in from his starting point?
   (*a*) North (*b*) North-East
   (*c*) East (*d*) South-West
7. A train runs 120 km in West direction, 30 km in South direction and then 80 km in east direction before reaching the station. In which direction is the station from the train's starting point?
   (*a*) South-West (*b*) North-West
   (*c*) South-East (*d*) South
8. Facing the West direction, Priya jogs for 20 m, turns left and goes further 40 m. She turns left again and jogs for 20 m. Then she turns right to go 20 m to reach the park. How far is the park from her starting point and in which direction?
   (*a*) 20 m South (*b*) 40 m West
   (*c*) 60 m South (*d*) 100 m East

9. If all the directions are rotated, *i.e.*, if North is changed to West and East to North and so on, then what will come in place of North-West?
(*a*) South-West (*b*) North-East
(*c*) East-North (*d*) East-West

10. A and B start together from one point. They walk 10 km towards North. A turns left and covers 5 km whereas B turns right and covers 3 km. A turns left again and covers 15 km whereas B turns right and covers his 15 km. How far is A from B?
(*a*) 18 km (*b*) 10 km
(*c*) 5 km (*d*) 8 km

11. Tarun is walking towards East. What direction he should not follow if he should walk towards North?
(*a*) right, right, left, right, right
(*b*) right, right, left, left, left
(*c*) right, right, right
(*d*) right, left, right, left

12. Sony and Moni start walking from a point. Sony walks in West direction and Moni in South direction. After covering 20 km, Soni turns left and walks 15 km. Moni walks 10 km, turns left and walks 5 km. Soni, then turns left again and walks 25 km, whereas Moni turns right and walks 5 km. How far are Sony and Moni from each other?
(*a*) 5 km
(*b*) They are back at the starting point
(*c*) They are at same place at the finishing point
(*d*) Data is insufficient

13. I was walking in South-East direction. After a while I turned 90° to the right and walked ahead. Later I turned 45° to the right. In which direction am I walking now?
(*a*) North (*b*) North-East
(*c*) South-West (*d*) East

14. Two friends Jack and Bunny start a race, and together they run for 50 mts. Jack turns right and runs 60 mts while Bunny turns left and runs 40 mts. Then Jack turns left and runs 50 mts while Bunny turns right and runs 50 mts. How far are the two friends now from each other?
(*a*) 60 mts (*b*) 100 mts
(*c*) 20 mts (*d*) 150 mts

15. A policeman left his police post and proceeded south 4 km, after hearing a loud sound from point A. On reaching the place he heard another sound and proceeded 4 km to his left to the point B, only to find that the sound was coming from left of B. From B he proceeded left to reach that place 4 km away. In which direction he has to go to reach his police post?
(*a*) North (*b*) South
(*c*) East (*d*) West

EXPLANATORY ANSWERS

1. (*b*) :
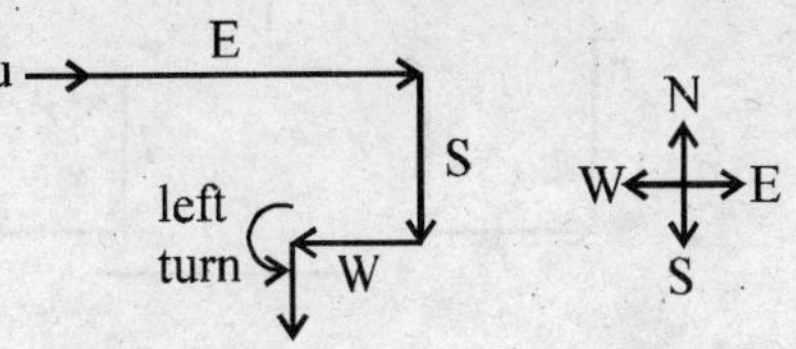

2. (*d*) :
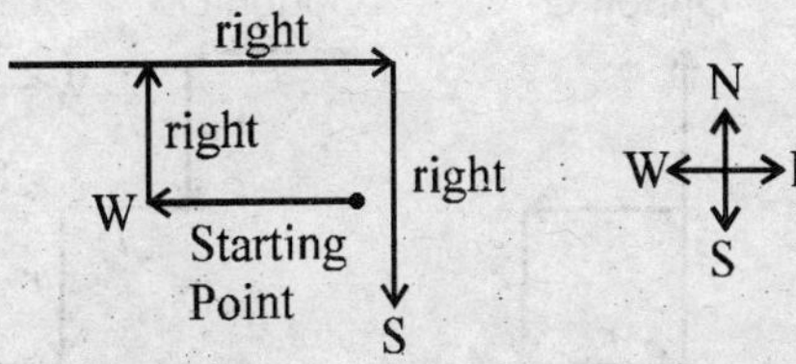

3. (*b*) :
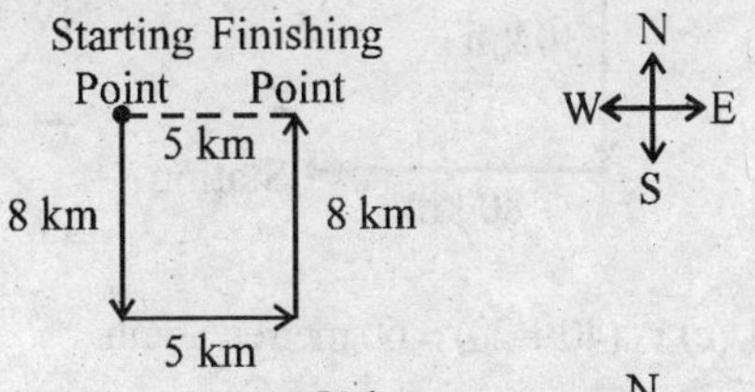

4. (*c*) :
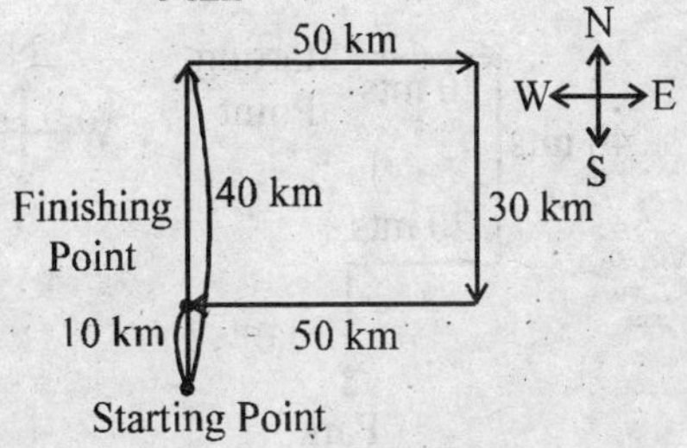

5. (a) : **Original Directions**

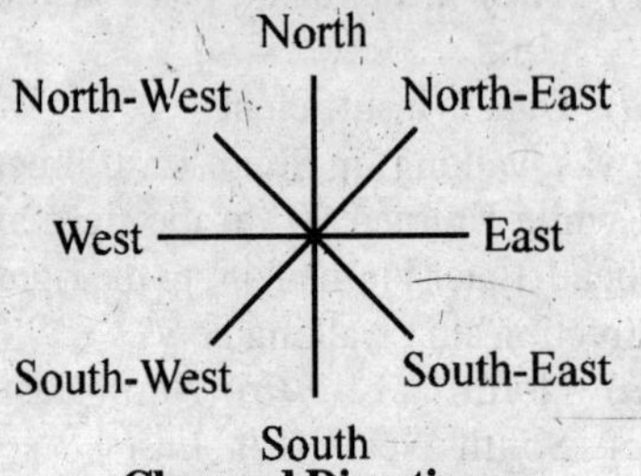

Changed Directions

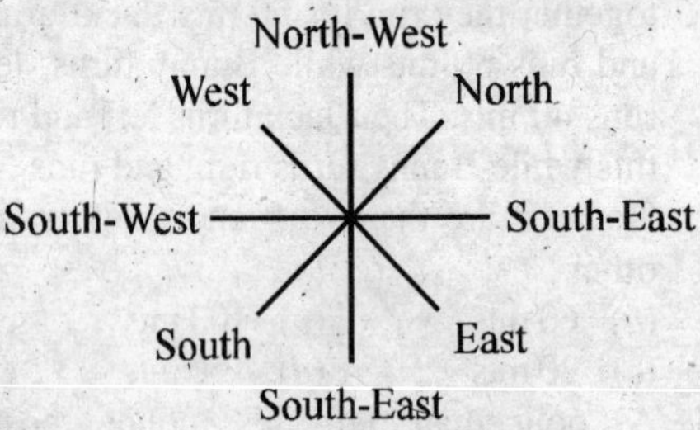

6. (d) :

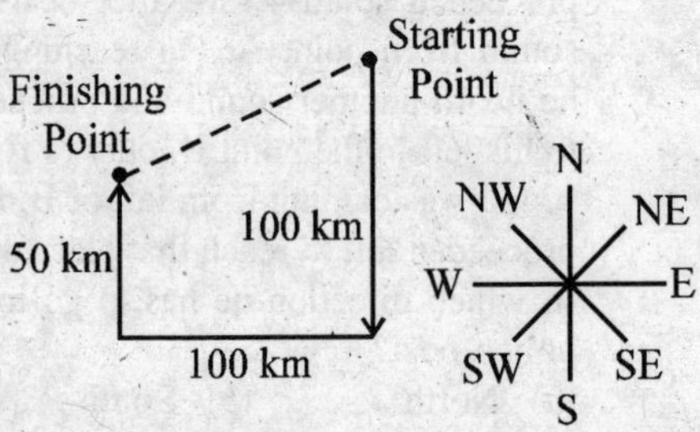

7. (a) :

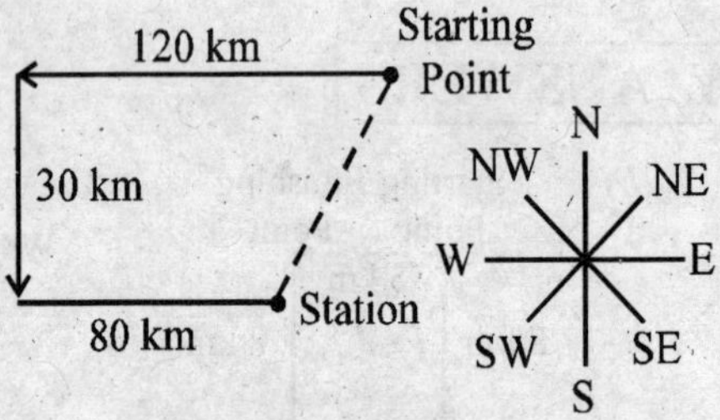

8. (c) : (40 + 20) = 60 metres South

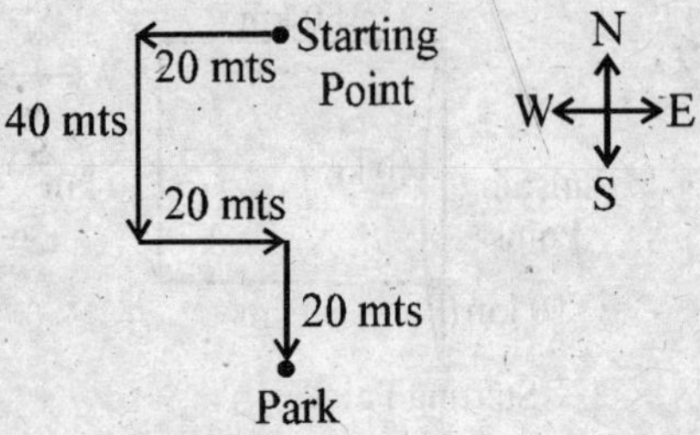

9. (a) : **Original Directions**

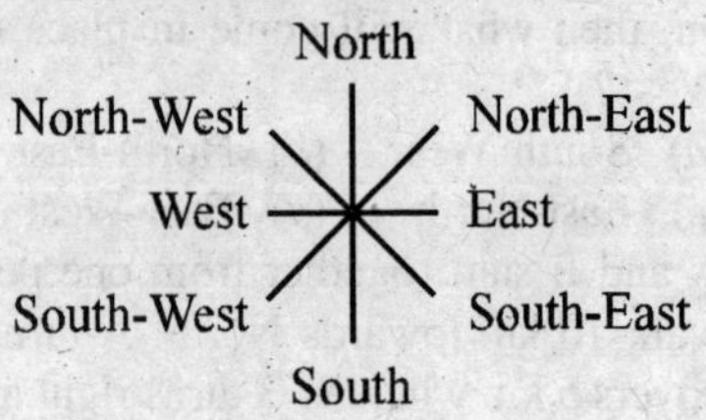

Changed Directions

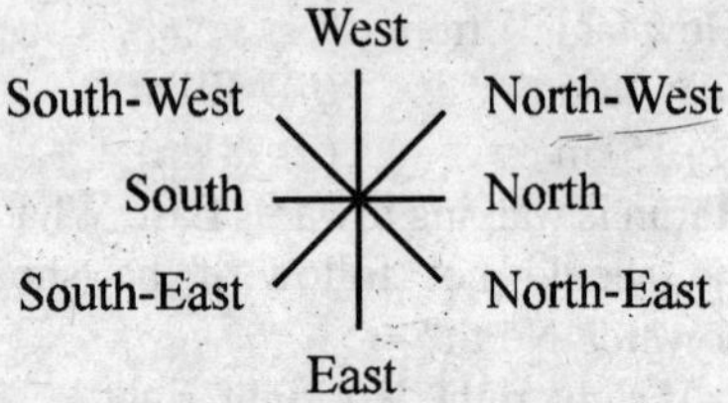

10. (d) :

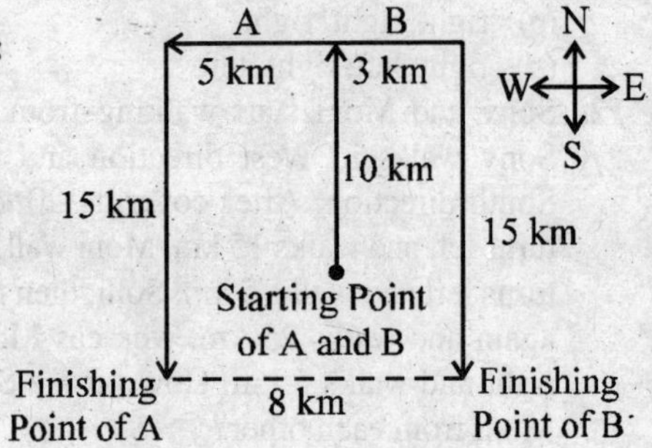

11. (d) :

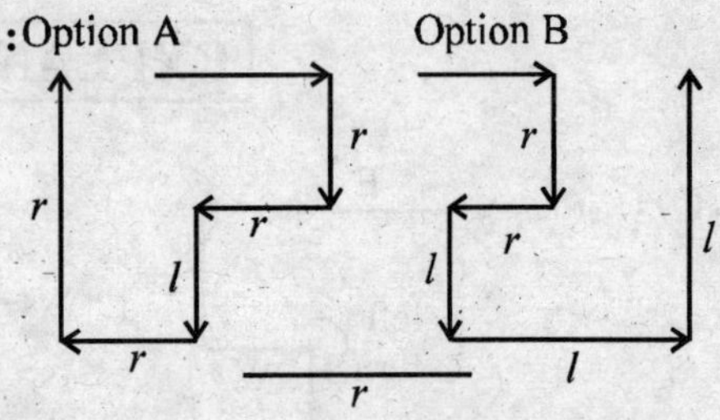

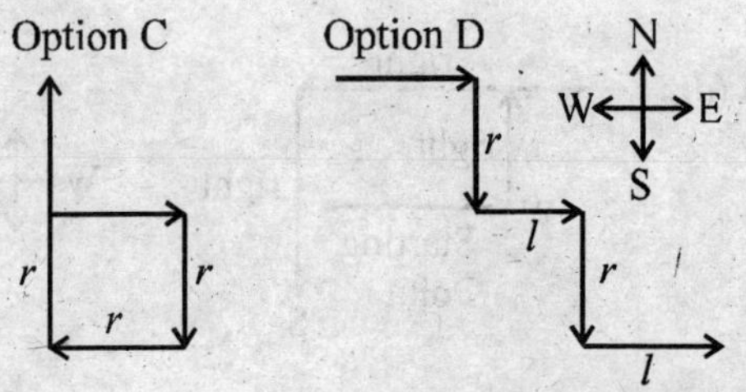

12. *(c)* :

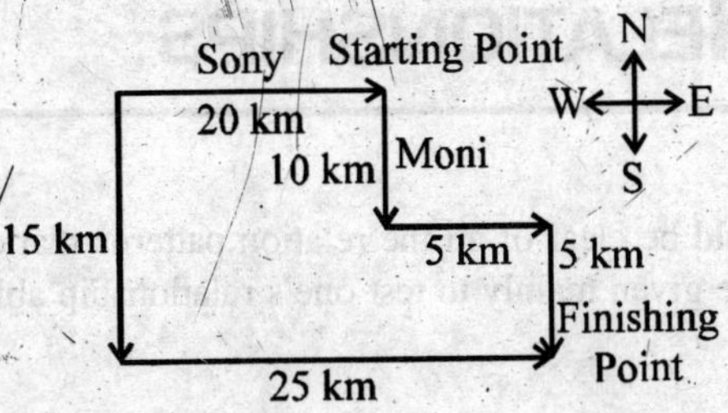

13. *(a)* : The direction of the movement is :

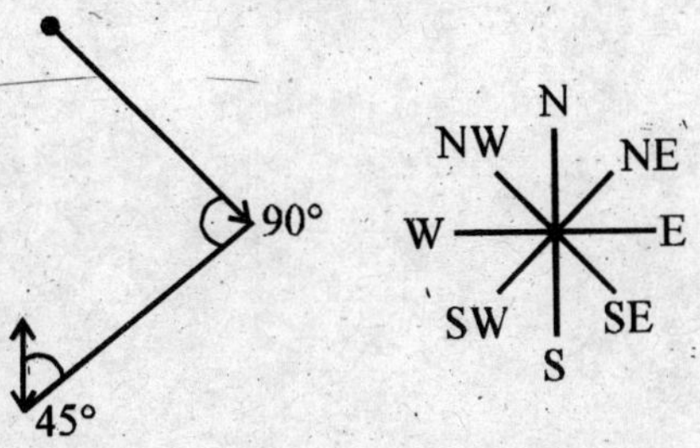

14. *(b)* : The track of both the friends is :

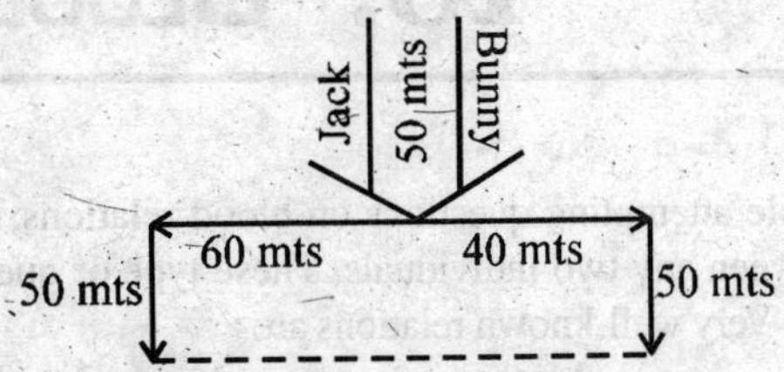

The two friends are 60 + 40 = 100 mts apart

15. *(d)* :

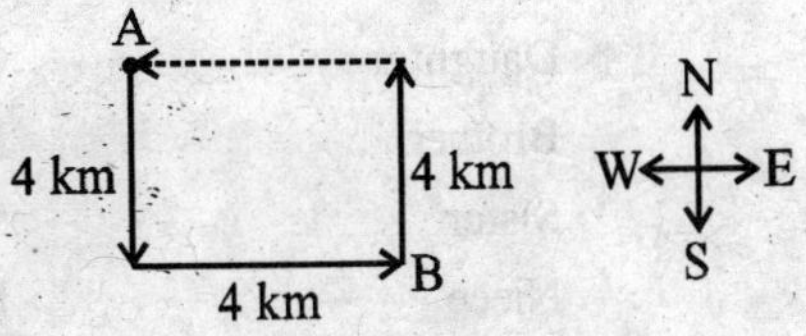

13. Blood Relationships

While attempting questions on blood relations, one should be clear of all the relation patterns that can exist between any two individuals. These type of questions are given mainly to test one's relationship ability.

Very well-known relations are :

Mother	Grandmother
Father	Grandfather
Son	Grandson
Daughter	Granddaughter
Brother	Brother-in-law
Sister	Sister-in-law
Niece	Father-in-law
Nephew	Mother-in-law
Uncle	Son-in-law
Aunt	Daughter-in-law
Husband	Cousin
Wife	

The patterns of some relationships which help in solving questions in these tests are :

Father's *or* Mother's Father	—	Grandfather (Paternal *or* Maternal)
Father's *or* Mother's Mother	—	Grandmother (Paternal *or* Maternal)
Father's *or* Mother's Son	—	Brother
Father's *or* Mother's Daughter	—	Sister
Father's Brother	—	Paternal Uncle
Father's Sister	—	Paternal Aunt
Mother's Brother	—	Maternal Uncle
Mother's Sister	—	Maternal Aunt
Uncle *or* Aunt's Son *or* Daughter	—	Cousin
Son's Wife	—	Daughter-in-law
Daughter's Husband	—	Son-in-law
Husband's *or* Wife's Brother	—	Brother-in-law
Husband's *or* Wife's Sister	—	Sister-in-law
Brother's Wife	—	Sister-in-law
Sister's Husband	—	Brother-in-law
Brother's Son	—	Nephew
Brother's Daughter	—	Niece

EXERCISE

Directions : *In each of the following questions keenly study the relationship mentioned between the persons, and then from the given options select the right relationship as the answer.*

1. A lady said, "The person standing there is my grandfather's only son's daughter". How is the lady related to the standing person?
(*a*) Sister
(*b*) Mother
(*c*) Aunt
(*d*) Cousin

2. Ajay is the brother of Vijay. Mili is the sister of Ajay. Sanjay is the brother of Rahul and Mehul is the daughter of Vijay. Who is Sanjay's Uncle?
(*a*) Rahul
(*b*) Ajay
(*c*) Mehul
(*d*) Data inadequate

3. A man introduced the boy coming with him as "He is son of the father of my wife's daughter". What relation did the boy bear to the man?
(*a*) Son-in-law
(*b*) Son
(*c*) Brother
(*d*) Father

4. If Amit's father is Billoo's father's only son and Billoo has neither a brother nor a daughter, what is the relationship between Amit and Billoo?
(*a*) Uncle — Nephew
(*b*) Father — Daughter
(*c*) Father — Son
(*d*) Cousins

5. Pointing to a woman in the photograph a man said, "She is the daughter of my grand-mother's only son. How is the woman related to the man?
(*a*) Mother (*b*) Daughter
(*c*) Sister-in-law (*d*) Sister

6. Pointing to a photograph, a woman said, "She is the only daughter of my mother's father." How is the woman related to the person in the photograph?
(*a*) Mother
(*b*) Grandmother
(*c*) Daughter
(*d*) Cannot be determined

7. Ram is the brother of Shyam and Mahesh is the father of Ram. Jagat is the brother of Priya and Priya is daughter of Shyam. Who is the uncle of Jagat ?
(*a*) Shyam
(*b*) Mahesh
(*c*) Ram
(*d*) Data insufficient

8. Introducing a man, a woman said, "His wife is the only daughter of my father". How is the man related to the woman?
(*a*) Husband
(*b*) Father
(*c*) Father-in-law
(*d*) Brother

9. If Maya is the only daughter of Richa's grandmother's brother, how is Maya's daughter related to Richa?
(*a*) Niece
(*b*) Cousin
(*c*) Aunt
(*d*) Mother

10. Pointing to a woman, a man said, "Her husband's mother is the wife of my father's only son". How is the man related to the woman?
(*a*) Son
(*b*) Brother-in-law
(*c*) Uncle
(*d*) Father-in-law

EXPLANATORY ANSWERS

1. (a) :

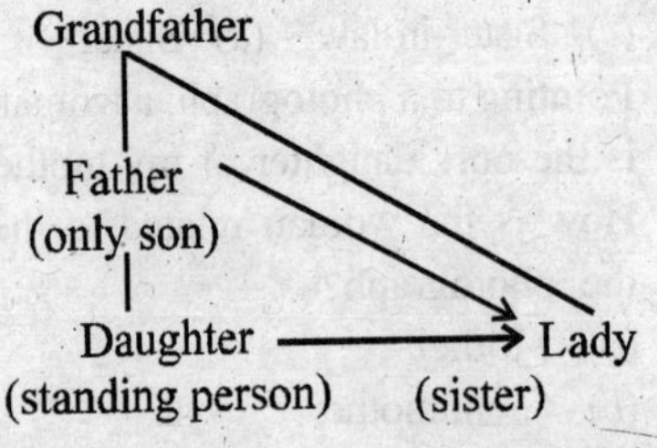

Lady's grandfather's son is lady's father and father's daughter will only be lady's sister.

2. (d) :

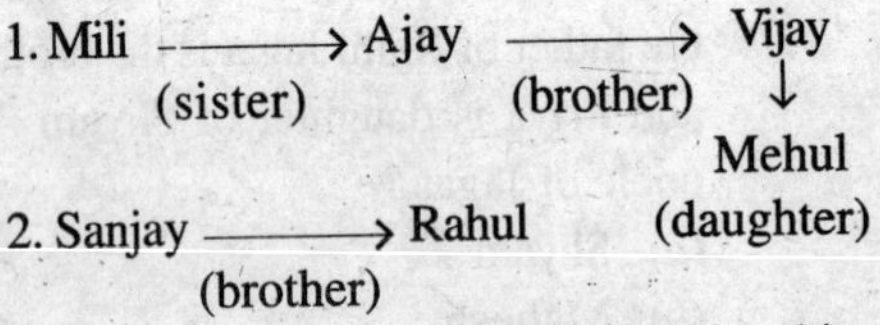

There are two sets of relationship. Information given is incomplete and no relation can be established between the two sets.

3. (b) : The relationship chart based on problem is :

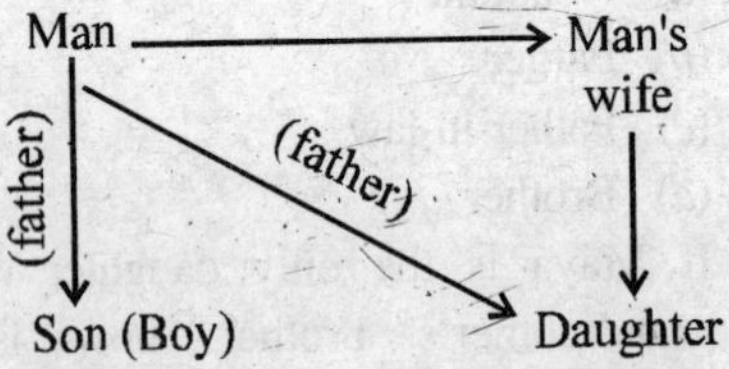

'Father of the man's wife's daughter' is the man himself and the boy in question is the man's son.

4. (c) : The relationship chart based on problem is :

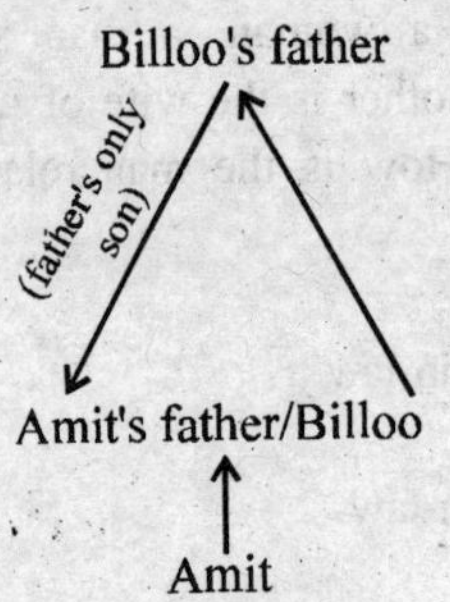

Amit's father is Billoo's father's only son means Billoo is the only son in question also, he is the father of Amit. It must be noted that Billoo has no brother which means he is single and also, when he has no daughter, Amit is his only son.

5. (d) :

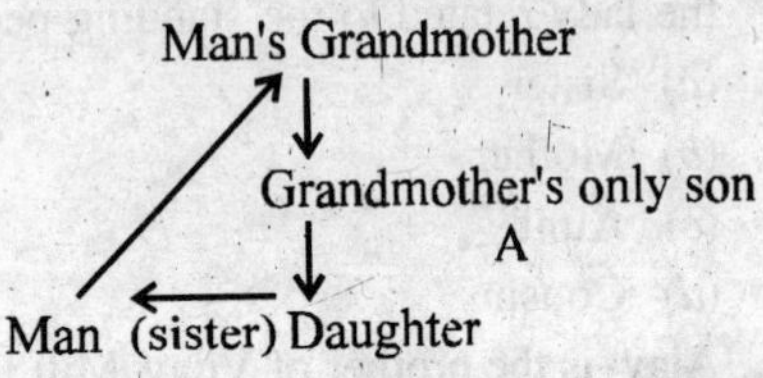

'My grandmother's only son' is the father of the man, and 'daughter of my grandmother's only son' is the sister of the man.

6. (c) :

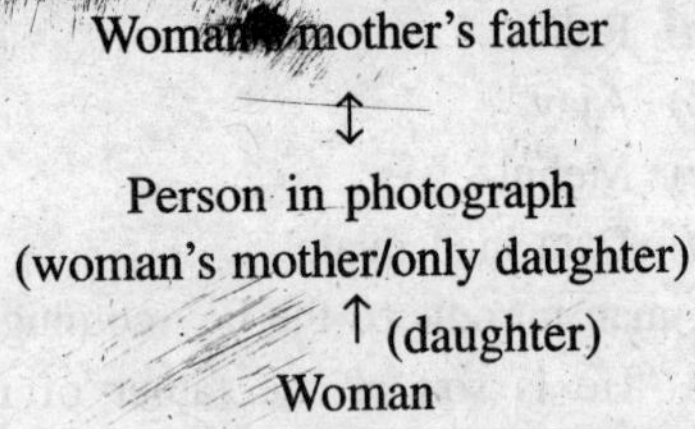

'Only daughter of my mother's father' is the person in the photograph and she is also the mother of the woman. So, the woman is the daughter of the person in the photograph.

7. (c) :

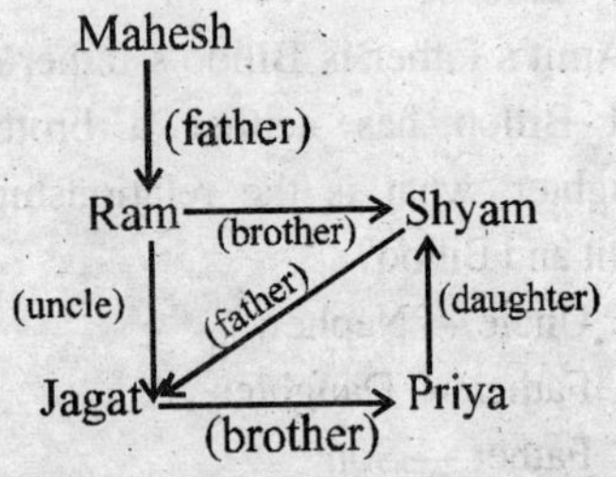

Jagat is brother of Priya and Priya daughter of Shyam. So Shyam is also the father of Jagat. Ram is the brother of Shyam. So, Jagat's father's brother Ram the uncle of Jagat.

8. (*a*) :

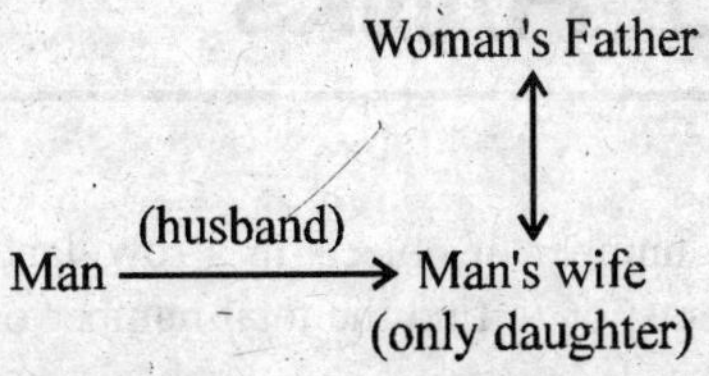

'Only daughter of my father' is the woman herself and the man is her husband.

9. (*b*) :

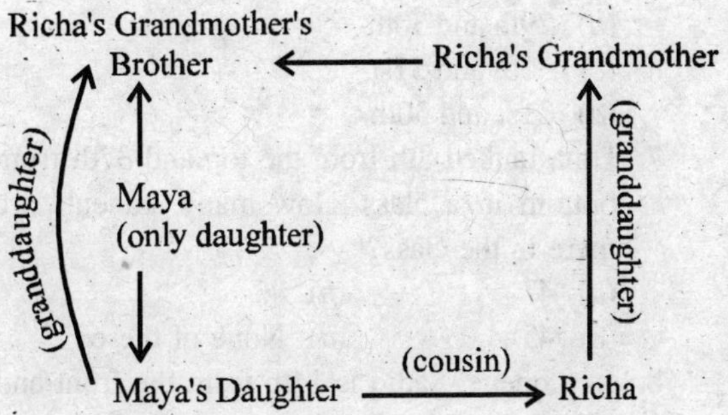

Both Maya's Daughter and Richa are granddaughters of a brother and a sister respectively. So Maya's daughter is the cousin of Richa.

10. (*d*) :

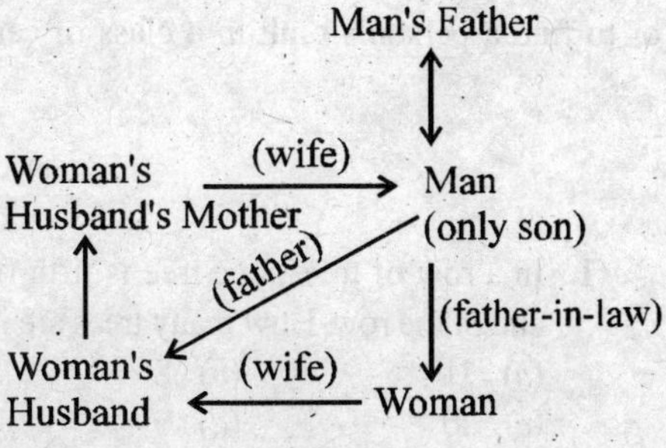

'My father's only son' is the man himself. 'Her husband's mother' is the wife of the man and so the man is the father of the woman's husband. As the woman is the wife of man's son, the man is the father-in-law of the woman.

14. Rows and Ranks

These type of problems need easy calculations to find out the number of objects in a row, lane or queue or to find a person's rank in a class of certain number of students; or to find the total number of students.

EXERCISE

1. In a row of trees, one tree is fifth from either end of the row. How many trees are in the row?

(*a*) 11 (*b*) 8
(*c*) 10 (*d*) 9

2. Jaya ranks 5th in a class of 53. What is her rank from the bottom in the class?

(*a*) 49th (*b*) 48th
(*c*) 47th (*d*) 50th

3. Mohan ranks twenty-first in a class of sixty-five students. What will be his (Mohan's) rank if the lowest candidate is assigned rank 1?

(*a*) 44th (*b*) 45th
(*c*) 46th (*d*) Data inadequate

4. If Rahul finds that he is 12th from the right in a line of boys and 4th from the left, how many boys should be added to the line such that there are 28 boys in the line?

(*a*) 12 (*b*) 14
(*c*) 20 (*d*) 13

5. In a row of boys, Rajan is tenth from the right and Suraj is tenth from the left. When Rajan and Suraj interchange their positions, Suraj will be twenty-seventh from the left. Which of the following will be Rajan's position from the right?

(*a*) Tenth
(*b*) Twenty-sixth
(*c*) Twenty-ninth
(*d*) None of these

6. Mahesh and Suresh are ranked 11th and 12th respectively from the top in a class of 41 students. What will be their respective ranks from the bottom?

(*a*) 32nd and 33rd
(*b*) 29th and 30th
(*c*) 30th and 31st
(*d*) 31st and 30th

7. Uma ranked 8th from the top and 37th from bottom in a class. How many students are there in the class?

(*a*) 47 (*b*) 46
(*c*) 45 (*d*) None of these

8. In a queue, Sadiq is 14th from the front and Joseph is 17th from the end, while Jane is in between Sadiq and Joseph. If Sadiq be ahead of Joseph and there be 48 persons in the queue, how many persons are there between Sadiq and Jane?

(*a*) 5 (*b*) 6
(*c*) 7 (*d*) 8

9. Rohan ranked eleventh from the top and twenty-seventh from the bottom among the students who passed the annual examination in a class. If the number of students who failed in the examination was 12, how many students appeared for the examination?

(*a*) 48
(*b*) 49
(*c*) 50
(*d*) Cannot be determined

10. Some boys are sitting in a row. P is sitting fourteenth from the left and Q is seventh from the right. If there are four boys between P and Q, how many boys are there in the row?

(*a*) 19 (*b*) 21
(*c*) 25 (*d*) 23

EXPLANATORY ANSWERS

1. (*d*):

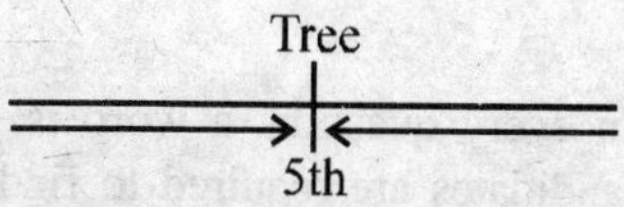

Total number of trees in the row are :
$(5+5)-1=9$.

2. (*a*) :

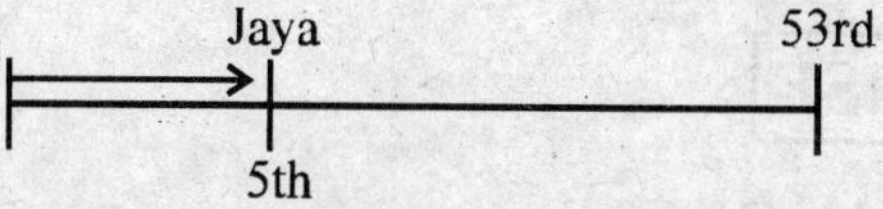

Jaya's rank from the bottom is :
$(53-5)+1=49$th.

3. (*b*) :

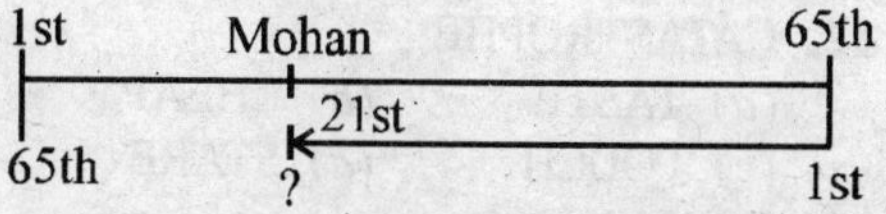

Note : Mohan's rank from the last or the question asked means the same.

Mohan's rank is $(65-21)+1=45$th.

4. (*d*) :

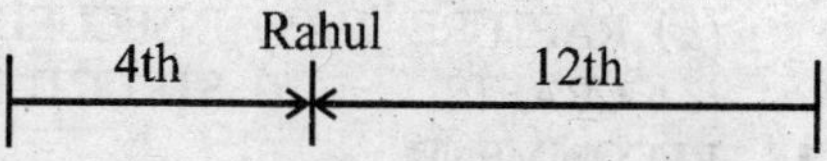

The number of boys in the line are :
$(4+12)-1=15$
To make a line of 28 boys, $(28-15)$ *i.e.* 13 more boys are needed.

5. (*d*) :

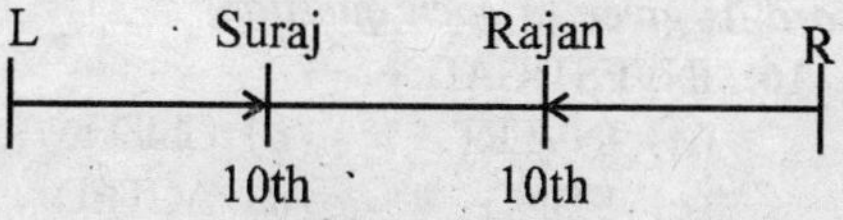

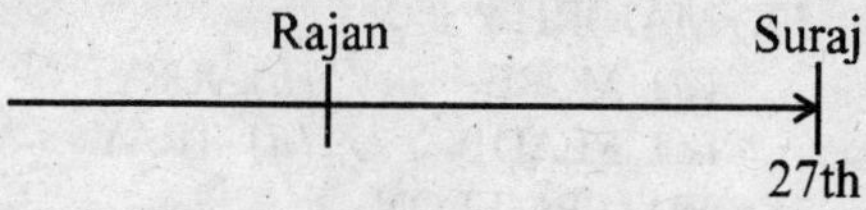

As the position of boys is equal from both ends, Rajan will also be 27th from the right after changing positions.

6. (*d*) :

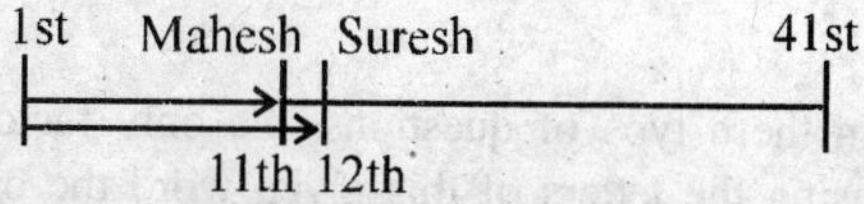

Mahesh's position from bottom is :
$(41-11)+1=31$st
Suresh's position from bottom is :
$(41-12)+1=30$th.

7. (*d*) :

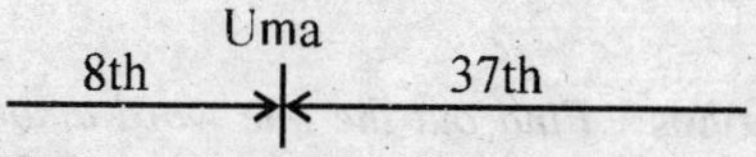

Total number of students in the class are :
$(8+37)-1=44$.

8. (*d*) :

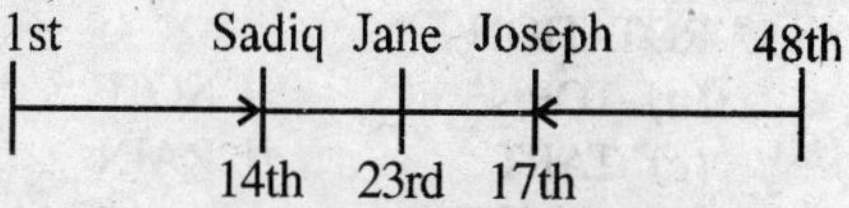

Sadiq's position from front : 14th
Joseph's position from last :
17th or $48-17+1=32$nd from front.
Middle postion between Sadiq & Joseph

$$= \frac{(32-14)}{2}+14 = 23 \text{ rd.}$$

Hence, Jane position is 23rd from front
Person between Sadiq & Jane
$= 23-14-1=8$.

9. (*b*) :

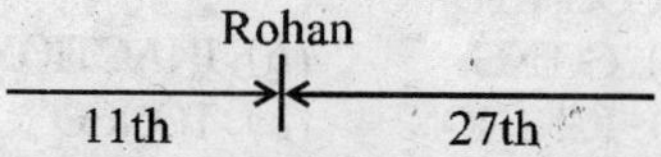

Number of students who passed the examination $(11+27)-1=37$
Those who failed = 12
Total number of students who appeared in the examination $= 37+12=49$.

10. (*c*) :

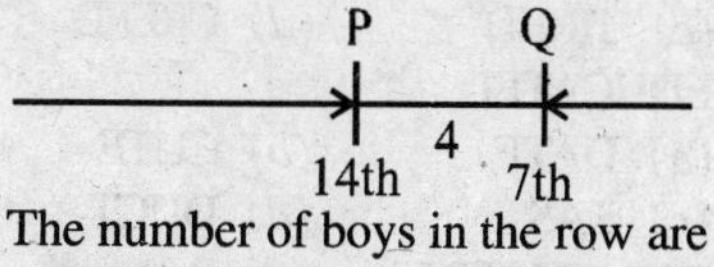

The number of boys in the row are :
$(14+4+7)=25$.

15. PERMUTATIONS AND COMBINATIONS

In these type of questions, the only factor essential is alertness. In every question, a word is given. By using the letters of this given word the options are formed. The candidates are required to find from the given options the word *(i)* which cannot be formed by using the letters of the given word or *(ii)* which can be formed by using the letters of the given word.

EXERCISE

Directions : *Find out the one word among the options which cannot be formed by using the letters of the word as given in each question.*

1. ROTATION
   (*a*) TORN (*b*) NOTE
   (*c*) TART (*d*) RAIN
2. PHILOSOPHY
   (*a*) SOIL (*b*) SHIP
   (*c*) SOLO (*d*) SPIN
3. SLAVATION
   (*a*) SNORT (*b*) LATVIA
   (*c*) SALIVA (*d*) AVAIL
4. ACADEMY
   (*a*) DEMY (*b*) MACE
   (*c*) DIRE (*d*) MADE
5. INCOGNITO
   (*a*) GOING (*b*) INACTION
   (*c*) IGNITION (*d*) TONGO
6. JUDICIARY
   (*a*) INJURY (*b*) CADDY
   (*c*) DICY (*d*) ACRID
7. DOCTRINE
   (*a*) CRUST (*b*) DOCTOR
   (*c*) TIRED (*d*) CREED
8. EDUCATED
   (*a*) DATE (*b*) CUTE
   (*c*) EAST (*d*) DUCT
9. INSUFFICIENT
   (*a*) ENTICE (*b*) SCENT
   (*c*) SUFFICE (*d*) THENCE
10. DECEMBER
    (*a*) REDEEM (*b*) DECREE
    (*c*) BRACED (*d*) MEMBER
11. FUGITIVE
    (*a*) EXIT (*b*) FIVE
    (*c*) GIVE (*d*) GIFT
12. CATASTROPHE
    (*a*) TASTE (*b*) CHEAP
    (*c*) POUCH (*d*) STARE
13. TORRENTIAL
    (*a*) TRAIL (*b*) MENTAL
    (*c*) LEARN (*d*) RETAIL
14. INFRASTRUCTURE
    (*a*) RAPTURE (*b*) INSECURE
    (*c*) CRAFTS (*d*) STRUCTURE
15. RECOMMEND
    (*a*) MEND (*b*) ROME
    (*c*) CANE (*d*) OMEN

Directions : *Find out the one word among the options which can be formed by using the letters of the word as given in each question.*

16. INVESTIGATE
    (*a*) INVERT (*b*) GLIDE
    (*c*) STING (*d*) ACTED
17. MAJORITY
    (*a*) MORE (*b*) JURY
    (*c*) READ (*d*) TRAY
18. WATERMELON
    (*a*) MAKER (*b*) WRITE
    (*c*) TOWER (*d*) NOVEL
19. PREDICTION
    (*a*) DESIRE (*b*) CREDIT
    (*c*) ACTION (*d*) PICKED
20. BARGAIN
    (*a*) GRAIN (*b*) BARGE
    (*c*) ANGRY (*d*) TRING

21. THERMOSTAT
(*a*) MOTHER (*b*) STAMEN
(*c*) THRUST (*d*) HOIST

22. LEARNED
(*a*) DREAM (*b*) CLEAR
(*c*) ELDER (*d*) DRAPE

23. ADVENTURE
(*a*) AWARE (*b*) EVENT
(*c*) TRUCE (*d*) DRIED

24. THANKSGIVING
(*a*) AVENGE (*b*) HAUNTS
(*c*) GRAINS (*d*) SAVING

25. NOCTURNAL
(*a*) CRUST (*b*) TRAIL
(*c*) CORAL (*d*) OCEAN

ANSWERS

1	2	3	4	5	6	7	8	9	10
(*b*)	(*d*)	(*a*)	(*c*)	(*b*)	(*a*)	(*a*)	(*c*)	(*d*)	(*c*)
11	**12**	**13**	**14**	**15**	**16**	**17**	**18**	**19**	**20**
(*a*)	(*c*)	(*b*)	(*a*)	(*c*)	(*c*)	(*d*)	(*c*)	(*b*)	(*a*)
21	**22**	**23**	**24**	**25**					
(*a*)	(*c*)	(*b*)	(*d*)	(*c*)					

16. Symbol Substitution

Questions in these category are easy to attempt. Candidates must be quick in substituting symbols and calculations. The common pattern of questions asked are given below.

EXERCISE

1. If "+" means "–"; "–" means "×"; "×"means "÷" and "÷" means "+", then
$15 \times 5 \div 10 + 5 - 3 = ?$
(a) 9.5 (b) 0
(c) –2 (d) 24

2. If "+" means "×"; "–" means "÷"; "÷"means "+" and "×" means "–", then what will be the value of $20 \div 40 - 4 \times 5 + 6 = ?$
(a) 60 (b) 1.67
(c) 150 (d) 0

3. If × stands for addition, < for subtraction, + stands for division, > for multiplication, – stands for equal to, ÷ for greater than, and = stands for less than, state which of the following is true?
(a) $5 \times 3 < 7 \div 8 + 4 \times 1$
(b) $3 \times 4 > 2 - 9 + 3 < 3$
(c) $5 > 2 + 2 = 10 < 4 \times 8$
(d) $3 \times 2 < 4 \div 16 > 2 + 4$

4. If → stands for subract, ← stands for add, ↑↑ stands for multiply, ↓↓ stands for divide, ↔ for greater than, ⟷ stands for equal to, then which of the following alternatives is true?
(a) 4 ← 6 ↑↑ 2 ⟷ 3 → 12 ← 12
(b) 10 ↓↓ 5 ↑↑ 5 ⟷ 9 → 3 ← 4
(c) 15 ↑↑ 2 → 5 ⟷ 12 ↓↓ 4 ← 3
(d) 13 ↓↓ 13 ← 1 ↔ 20 → 5 ↑↑ 2

5. If Δ denotes =; + denotes >, – denotes <, □ denotes ≠, × denotes > and ÷ denotes < then a + b – c denotes
(a) b Δ c □ a
(b) b □ a ÷ c
(c) a ÷ b × c
(d) b – a + c

6. If '✱' denotes '×', 'Δ' denotes '÷', '□' denotes '–', '●' denotes '+', 'α' denotes '=' and 'β' denotes ≠, then which of the following euations is correct?
(a) 2 □ 10 ✱ 4 Δ 5 α 5 ● 12 Δ 6
(b) 27 Δ 9 ● 6 β 3 ✱ 6 □ 9
(c) 4 Δ 2 ✱ 0 α 7 Δ 1 ✱ 0
(d) 5 ● 6 Δ 3 □ 2 α 8 Δ 4 ✱ 3

7. If ↓ stands for '÷', ↑ stands for '×', → stands for '+' and ← stands for '–', then
25 ↓ 5 → 3 ↑ 6 ← 8 = ?
(a) 9 (b) 12
(c) 16 (d) 15

8. If the + and × signs of the following equations are interchanged, which will be the correct equation?
(a) $7 \times 5 + 3 = 20$
(b) $4 + 9 \times 1 = 42$
(c) $6 \times 5 + 8 = 46$
(d) $2 + 11 \times 4 = 28$

9. If '+' stands for multiplication, '×' stands for addition, '÷' stands for subtraction and '–' stands for division, then what will be the result of the following equation?
$7 \times 4 \div 10 \times 2 + 5 = ?$
(a) 7 (b) 0
(c) 11 (d) 15

10. If 'A' means '÷', 'B' means '+', 'C' means '×' and 'D' means '–', then
12 C 4 A 24 D 10 B 1 = ?
(a) $11\frac{1}{3}$ (b) 23
(c) –7 (d) $16\frac{4}{5}$

EXPLANATORY ANSWERS

1. (*c*) : $15 \div 5 + 10 - 5 \times 3$
$3 + 10 - 15 = -2$

2. (*d*) : $20 + 40 \div 4 - 5 \times 6$
$20 + 10 - 30 = 0$

3. (*c*) : (*a*) $5 + 3 - 7 > 8 \div 4 + 1$
$1 > 3$
(*b*) $3 + 4 \times 2 = 9 \div 3 - 3$
$11 = 0$
(*c*) $5 \times 2 \div 2 < 10 - 4 + 8$
$5 < 14$
(*d*) $3 + 2 - 4 > 16 \times 2 \div 4$
$1 > 8$

4. (*b*) : (*a*) $4 + 6 \times 2 = 3 - 12 + 12$
$16 = 3$
(*b*) $10 \div 5 \times 5 = 9 - 3 + 4$
$10 = 10$
(*c*) $15 \times 2 - 5 = 12 \div 4 + 3$
$25 = 6$
(*d*) $13 \div 13 + 1 > 20 - 5 \times 2$
$2 > 10$

5. (*d*) : What is given is a > b < c
The equations are :
(*a*) b = c ≠ a which is wrong
(*b*) b ≠ a < c which is wrong
(*c*) a < b > c which is wrong
(*d*) b < a > c which is correct
Therefore, (*d*) is the answer.

6. (*c*) : The solved equations will be :
(*a*) $2 - 10 \times 4 \div 5 = 5 + 12 \div 6$
$2 - 8 = 5 + 2$
$-6 = 7$ which is wrong
(*b*) $27 \div 9 + 6 \neq 3 \times 6 - 9$
$3 + 6 \neq 18 - 9$
$9 \neq 9$ which is wrong
(*c*) $4 \div 2 \times 0 = 7 \div 1 \times 0$
$2 \times 0 = 7 \times 0$
$0 = 0$ which is correct
(*d*) $5 + 6 \div 3 - 2 = 8 \div 4 \times 3$
$5 = 6$ which is wrong

7. (*d*) : $25 \div 5 + 3 \times 6 - 8$
$5 + 18 - 8 = 15$

8. (*c*) : After interchanging the signs the equations are :
(*a*) $7 + 5 \times 3 = 22$ which is wrong
(*b*) $4 \times 9 + 1 = 37$ which is wrong
(*c*) $6 + 5 \times 8 = 46$ which is correct
(*d*) $2 \times 11 + 4 = 26$ which is wrong

9. (*c*) : $7 + 4 - 10 + 2 \times 5$
$7 + 4 - 10 + 10 = 11$

10. (*c*) : $12 \times 4 \div 24 - 10 + 1$
$2 - 10 + 1 = -7$

17. MISSING NUMBERS

Playing with numbers and mathematical skills are needed to attempt these type of tests. The candidates have to work out the right combination of arithmetical symbols to arrive at the answer options which will take the place of the interrogation sign in the given questions.

EXERCISE

Directions: *In each question given below which one number can be placed at the sign of interrogation?*

1.

(*a*) 693 (*b*) 939
(*c*) 981 (*d*) 993

2.

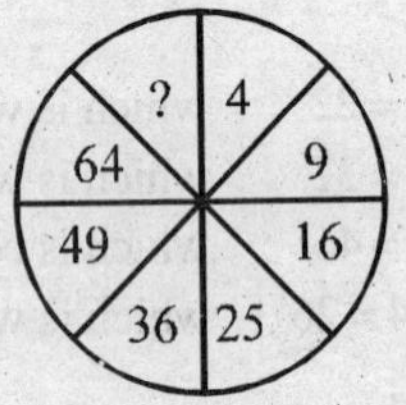

(*a*) 68 (*b*) 100
(*c*) 72 (*d*) 81

3.

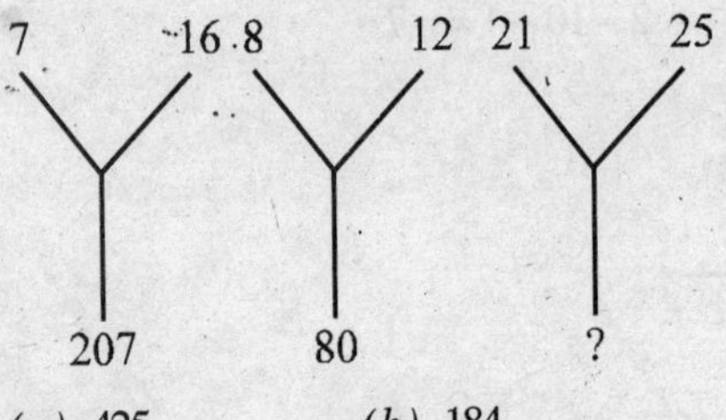

(*a*) 425 (*b*) 184
(*c*) 241 (*d*) 210

4.

(*a*) 35 (*b*) 37
(*c*) 45 (*d*) 48

5.

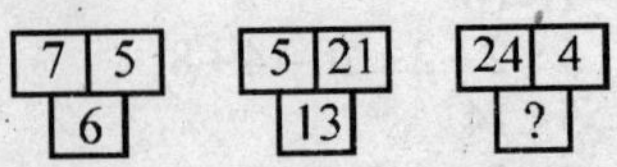

(*a*) 4 (*b*) 8
(*c*) 20 (*d*) 14

6.

14	9	4
12	7	2
10	5	0
16	11	?

(*a*) 9 (*b*) 6
(*c*) 3 (*d*) 7

7.

(*a*) 69 (*b*) 49
(*c*) 50 (*d*) 60

8.

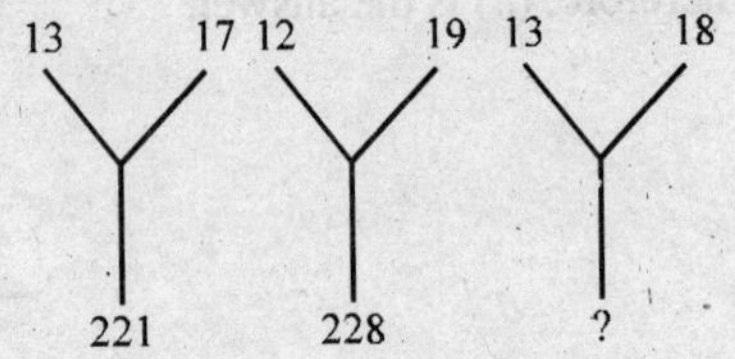

(*a*) 31 (*b*) 229
(*c*) 234 (*d*) 312

9.

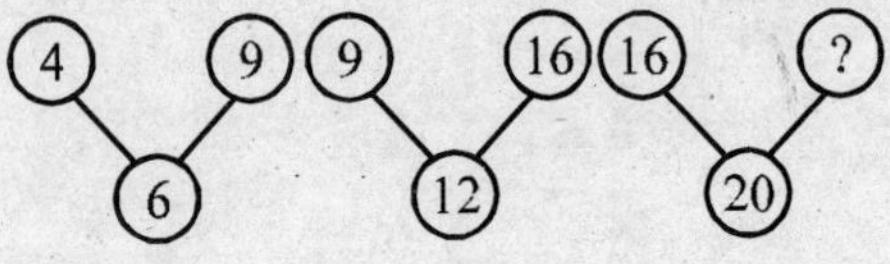

(*a*) 21 (*b*) 25
(*c*) 50 (*d*) 60

10.

51	(11)	61
64	(30)	32
35	(?)	43

(*a*) 25 (*b*) 27
(*c*) 32 (*d*) 37

11.

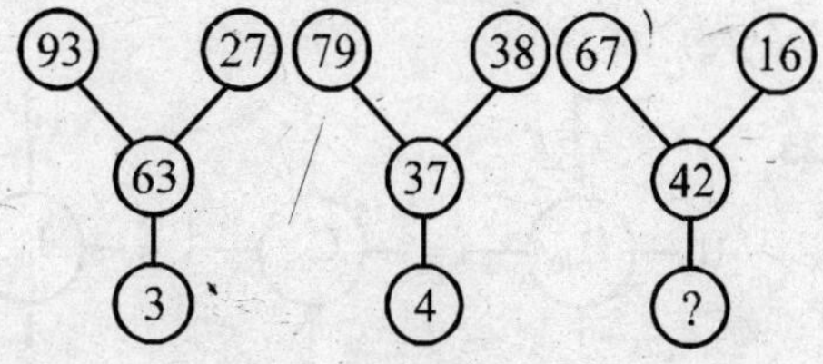

(*a*) 5 (*b*) 6
(*c*) 8 (*d*) 9

12.

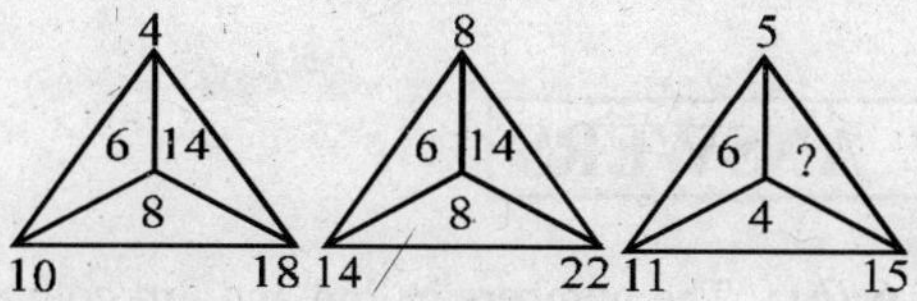

(*a*) 8 (*b*) 14
(*c*) 10 (*d*) 6

13.

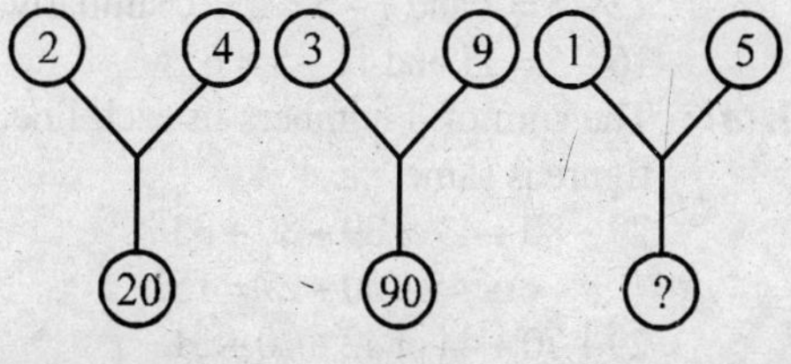

(*a*) 20 (*b*) 25
(*c*) 26 (*d*) 75

14.

27	22	50
13	12	26
9	2	?

(*a*) 12 (*b*) 39
(*c*) 18 (*d*) 24

15.

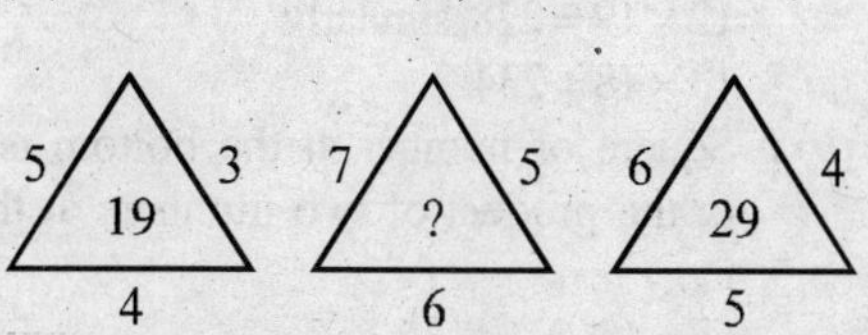

(*a*) 25 (*b*) 47
(*c*) 37 (*d*) 41

16.

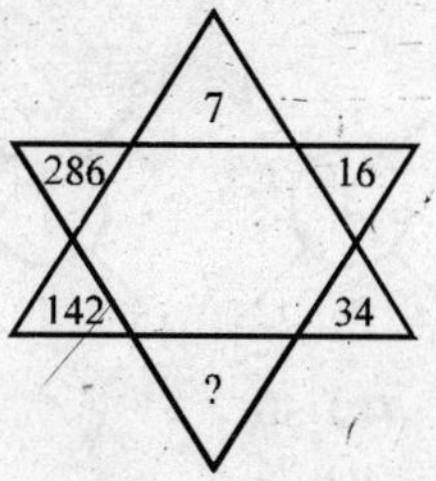

(*a*) 70 (*b*) 68
(*c*) 56 (*d*) 92

17.

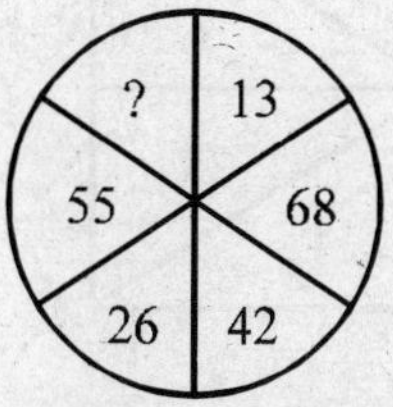

(*a*) 41 (*b*) 37
(*c*) 29 (*d*) 25

18.

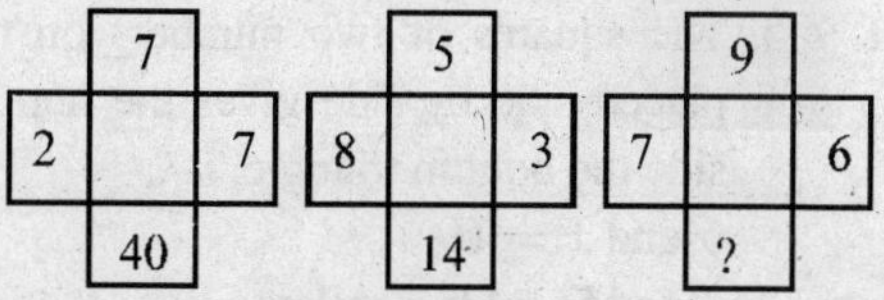

(*a*) 72 (*b*) 68
(*c*) 82 (*d*) 96

19.

42	(21)	22
78	(?)	84
162	(18)	99

(*a*) 12 (*b*) 13
(*c*) 60 (*d*) 72

20.

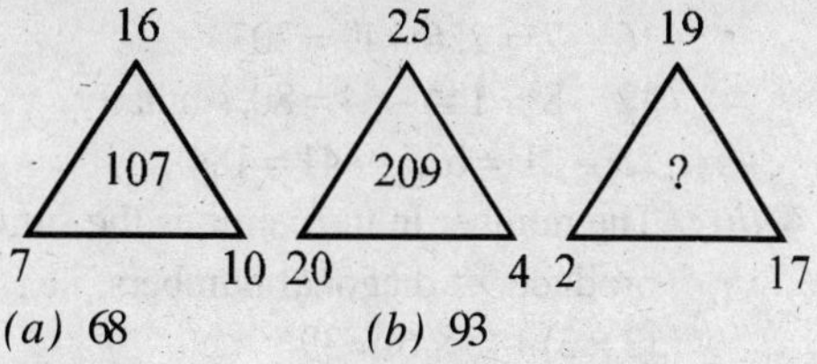

(*a*) 68 (*b*) 93
(*c*) 175 (*d*) 217

21.

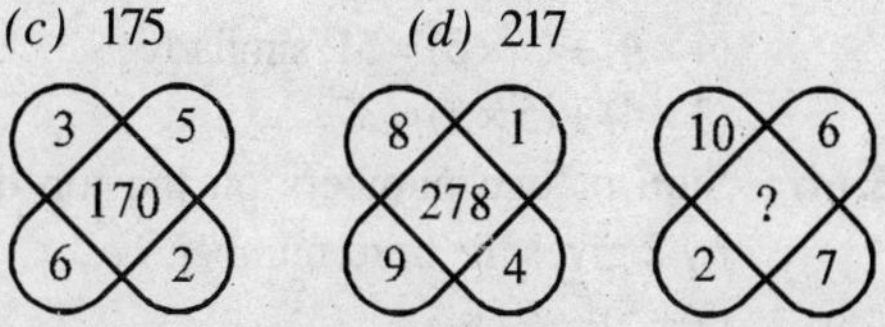

(*a*) 960 (*b*) 628
(*c*) 830 (*d*) 492

22. 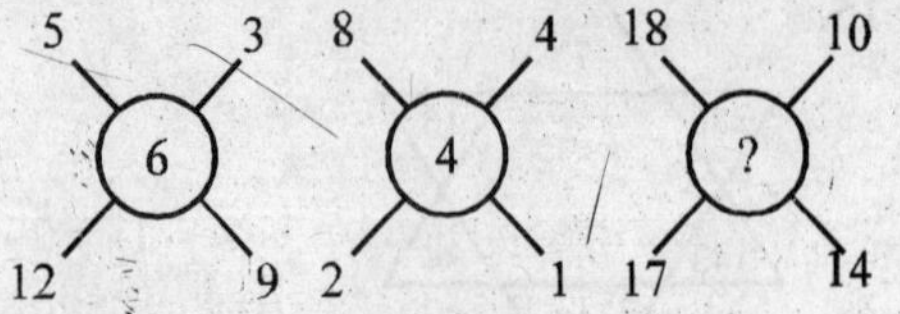

(a) 18 (b) 10

(c) 36 (d) 24

23. 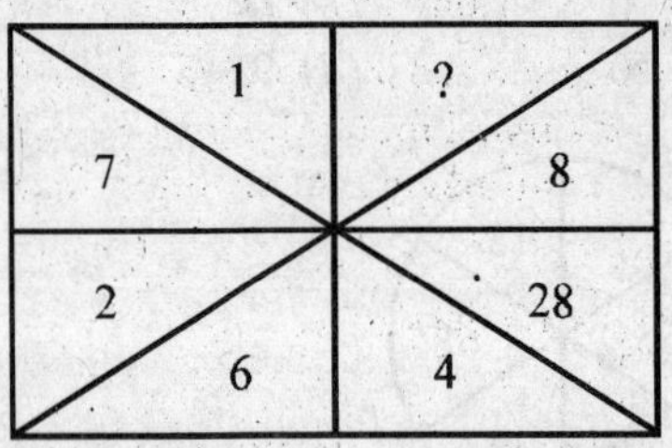

(a) 24 (b) 10

(c) 32 (d) 12

24.

6	(40)	4
3	(12)	3
7	(?)	2

(a) 51 (b) 36

(c) 22 (d) 4

25. 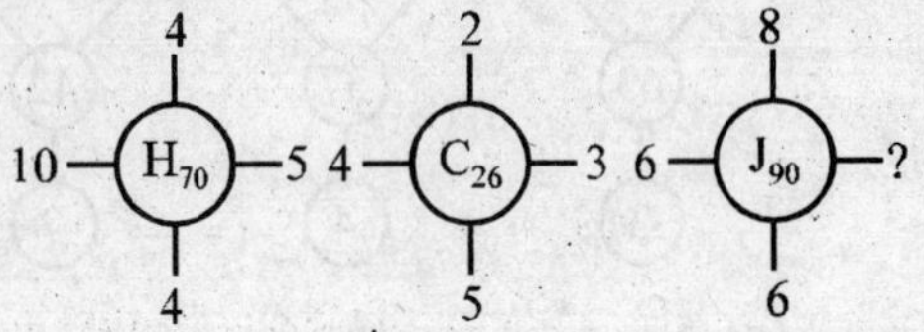

(a) 5 (b) 4

(c) 2 (d) 1

EXPLANATORY ANSWERS

1. (c) : The squares of two numbers on the top placed side by side gives the number inside the bottom triangle, *i.e.*,
6^2 and $3^2 = 369$
2^2 and $5^2 = 425$, similarly
3^2 and $9^2 = 981$.

2. (d) : Starting from number 4 the numbers are the squares of numbers in natural order *i.e.*, $2^2 = 4, 3^2 = 9, 4^2 = 16 \ldots\ldots 9^2 = 81$.

3. (b) : The number at the bottom is the difference of the squares of two numbers at the top, *i.e.*,
$16^2 - 7^2 = 256 - 49 = 207$
$12^2 - 8^2 = 144 - 64 = 80$, similarly
$25^2 - 21^2 = 625 - 441 = 184$.

4. (b) : The number in the centre is the sum of the products of diagonal numbers, *i.e.*,
$(3 \times 3) + (5 \times 6) = 39$
$(4 \times 4) + (7 \times 5) = 51$, similarly
$(3 \times 4) + (5 \times 5) = 37$.

5. (d) : Sum of two numbers on the top divided by 2 gives the third number, *i.e.*,
$(7 + 5) \div 2 = 6$
$(5 + 21) \div 2 = 13$, similarly
$(24 + 4) \div 2 = 14$.

6. (b) : The numbers in 2nd and 3rd columns are 5 less than the nunbers in 1st and 2nd columns respectively, *i.e.*,
$14 - 5 = 9$ and $9 - 5 = 4$
$12 - 5 = 7$ and $7 - 5 = 2, \ldots$ similarly
$16 - 5 = 11$ and $11 - 5 = 6$.

7. (a) : The sum of 3 numbers in each line in one figure is same, *i.e.*,
$29 + 80 + 43$ or $39 + 80 + 33$
or $45 + 80 + 27 = 152$
$29 + 70 + 44$ or $42 + 70 + 31$
or $43 + 70 + 30 = 143$,
similarly $59 + 80 + 20$ or $39 + 80 + 40 = 159$.
The missing number is :
$159 - (80 + 10) = 69$.

8. (c) : The number at the bottom is the product of two numbers at the top, *i.e.*,
$13 \times 17 = 221$
$12 \times 19 = 228$, similarly
$13 \times 18 = 234$.

9. (b) : Square of number at the bottom is equal to the product of two numbers at the top, *i.e.*,
$6^2 = 4 \times 9$, *i.e.*, 36
$12^2 = 9 \times 16$, *i.e.*, 144, similarly
$20^2 = 16 \times ?$, *i.e.*, 400. The missing number is $400 \div 16 = 25$.

10. *(b)* : The sum of the products of the digits of numbers in 1st and 3rd columns is the number in the 2nd column, *i.e.,*
$(5 \times 1) + (6 \times 1) = 11$
$(6 \times 4) + (3 \times 2) = 30$, similarly
$(3 \times 5) + (4 \times 3) = 27$.

11. *(d)* : The sum of numbers on right and centre subtracted from the number on the left gives the number at the bottom, *i.e.,*
$93 - (27 + 63) = 3$
$79 - (38 + 37) = 4$, similarly
$67 - (16 + 42) = 9$.

12. *(c)* : The number inside each triangle is the difference of the numbers at its base *i.e.*
$10 - 4 = 6$, $18 - 4 = 14$ and $18 - 10 = 8$
$14 - 8 = 6$, $22 - 8 = 14$ and $22 - 14 = 8$, similarly
$11 - 5 = 6$, $15 - 5 = 10$ and $15 - 11 = 4$.

13. *(c)* : The sum of squares of two numbers at the top gives the third number below, *i.e.,*
$2^2 + 4^2 = 20$
$3^2 + 9^2 = 90$, similarly
$1^2 + 5^2 = 26$.

14. *(a)* : The sum of numbers in 1st and 2nd column plus 1 is the number in the 3rd column, *i.e.,*
$27 + 22 + 1 = 50$
$13 + 12 + 1 = 26$, similarly
$9 + 2 + 1 = 12$.

15. *(d)* : The product of numbers on either side of the triangle plus the number at the base is the number inside the triangle, *i.e.,*
$(5 \times 3) + 4 = 19$
$(6 \times 4) + 5 = 29$, similarly
$(7 \times 5) + 6 = 41$.

16. *(a)* : Clockwise starting from number 7, the next number is obtained by doubling the number and adding 2, *i.e.,*
$(7 \times 2) + 2 = 16$
$(16 \times 2) + 2 = 34 \ldots$, similarly
$(34 \times 2) + 2 = 70$
$(70 \times 2) + 2 = 142$
$(142 \times 2) + 2 = 286$.

17. *(c)* : The difference between the numbers in opposite sectors is 13, *i.e.,*
$26 - 13 = 13$
$68 - 55 = 13$, similarly
The missing number is $42 - 13 = 29$
($42 + 13 = 55$ is not given as option).

18. *(b)* : The number at the bottom is obtained by subtracting the sum of two numbers in the centre grid line from the square of the number at the top, *i.e.,*
$7^2 - (2 + 7) = 40$
$5^2 - (8 + 3) = 14$, similarly
$9^2 - (7 + 6) = 68$.

19. *(b)* : The number inside the brackets is obtained by multiplying the number on the left by 2 and then dividing the product by the sum of digits of number on the right, *i.e.,*
$(42 \times 2) \div (2 + 2) = 21$
$(162 \times 2) \div (9 + 9) = 18$, similarly
$(78 \times 2) \div (8 + 4) = 13$.

20. *(a)* : Subtracting the sum of squares of two numbers at the base from the square of number at the apex gives the number inside the triangle, *i.e.,*
$16^2 - (7^2 + 10^2) = 107$
$25^2 - (20^2 + 4^2) = 209$, similarly
$19^2 - (2^2 + 17^2) = 68$.

21. *(c)* : The number in the centre is the product of all the 4 numbers minus 10, *i.e.,*
$(3 \times 5 \times 2 \times 6) - 10 = 170$
$(8 \times 1 \times 4 \times 9) - 10 = 278$, similarly
$(10 \times 6 \times 7 \times 2) - 10 = 830$.

22. *(d)* : The number inside the circle is the product of difference of two numbers above and difference of two numbers below, *i.e.,*
$(5 - 3)(12 - 9) = 6$
$(8 - 4)(2 - 1) = 4$, similarly
$(18 - 10)(17 - 14) = 24$.

23. *(a)* : Starting from number 1 anticlockwise the number in the diagonally opposite section is its multiplication by 4, *i.e.,*
$1 \times 4 = 4$, $7 \times 4 = 28$, $2 \times 4 = 8$, similarly
$6 \times 4 = 24$.

24. *(a)* : Square of the number on the left plus the number on the right is the number within brackets, *i.e.,*

$6^2+4=40$

$3^2+3=12$, similarly

$7^2+2=51$.

25. *(b)* : Letter H is 8th in order of alphabetical series. Taking the sum of numbers placed vertically outside the circle + 8; multiplying it by the number on the right; then subtracting from the product the number on the left, gives the number inside the circle, *i.e.,*

Step I $\rightarrow$ $4+8+4 = 16$

Step II $\rightarrow$ $16\times5 = 80$

Step III $\rightarrow$ $80-10 = 70$

Letter C is 3rd in order, so

Step I $\rightarrow$ $2+3+5 = 10$

Step II $\rightarrow$ $10\times3 = 30$

Step III $\rightarrow$ $30-4 = 26$

Similarly, J is 10th in order, so

Step I $\rightarrow$ $8+10+6 = 24$

Step II $\rightarrow$ $24\times ?$

Step III $\rightarrow$ $(24\times ?)-6=90$

Simplifying the above equation :

$24\times ? = 90+6$, *i.e.,* 96

$? = 96\div24=4$.

18. ALPHABET PROBLEMS

Alphabet problems are fun to attempt. They are based on alphabetical series in natural as well as reverse order.

Natural Order

A B C D E F G H I J K L M N O P Q R S T U V W X Y Z

Reverse Order

Z Y X W V U T S R Q P O N M L K J I H G F E D C B A

Note : The series starts from A on reaching Z and from Z on reaching A. Of these A E I O U are vowels and the rest are consonants.

EXERCISE

1. Which letter should be ninth letter to the left of ninth letter from the right if the first half of the alphabet is reversed?

(*a*) I (*b*) D
(*c*) F (*d*) E

2. Starting from the fifth letter from the left, if twelve letters are written in reverse order, then which letter will be the seventh to the left of the fourteenth letter from the right?

(*a*) N (*b*) H
(*c*) L (*d*) O

3. What letter will come in the centre of sixth letter from the right and thirteenth letter from the left?

(*a*) Q (*b*) R
(*c*) P (*d*) S

4. If in the word "DISTURBANCE", the first letter is interchanged with the last letter, the second letter is interchanged with the tenth letter and so on, which letter would come after the letter "T" in the newly formed word?

(*a*) I (*b*) U
(*c*) N (*d*) S

5. If it is possible to make a meaningful word with the third, the fifth, the seventh and the tenth letters of the word PROJECTION. If no such word can be made, give 'O' as the answer. If more than one such word can be made, give 'M' as the answer.

(*a*) T (*b*) N
(*c*) O (*d*) M

6. A meaningful word is made if we take the first, fourth, fifth, seventh, tenth, eleventh and the twelfth letters of the word "FELICITATIONS". Which of the following will be the fifth letter of that word from the right end of that word?

(*a*) T (*b*) C
(*c*) N (*d*) I

7. On rearranging the jumbled spelling of the word SKARTINS, a language is obtained. What is the fifth letter from the right of the rearranged word?

(*a*) N (*b*) K
(*c*) R (*d*) S

8. If the 1st, 3rd, 5th, 7th, 10th and 13th letters of the word "ENTERTAINMENT" are used to make a meaningful word, then what two letters will come in the centre?

(*a*) AM (*b*) TT
(*c*) RE (*d*) NA

9. On rearranging the jumbled spelling of the word GRUBY a sport is obtained. What is the letter in the centre?

(*a*) R (*b*) B
(*c*) G (*d*) U

10. If the letters 'ERVSECI' can be rearranged to form a meaningful word what will be the fifth letter from the right?

(a) R *(b)* V
(c) E *(d)* None of these

11. From the word HASTEN how many independent meaningful English words can be made without changing the order of the letters and using each letter only once?

(a) 1 *(b)* 2
(c) 3 *(d)* 4

EXPLANATORY ANSWERS

1. *(d)* : MLKJIGHFEDCBANOPQRSTUVWXYZ

9th 9th

2. *(d)* : ABCDPONMLKJIHGFEQRSTUVWXYZ

7th 14th

3. *(a)* :

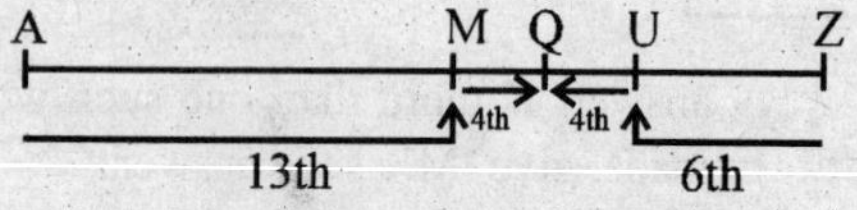

13th letter from left is 'M' and 6th letter from right is 'U'. The letter in the centre of 'M' and 'U' is 'Q'.

4. *(d)* : ECNABRUTSID

5. *(d)* : PROJECTION

The 3rd, 5th, 7th and 10th letters are OETN.

The words formed are TONE and NOTE.

6. *(b)* : FELICITATIONS

The 1st, 4th, 5th, 7th, 10th, 11th and 12th lettes are FICTION.

The word is FICTION and 5th letter from right is 'C'.

7. *(d)* : The word is SANSKRIT and 5th letter from right is 'S'.

8. *(b)* : ENTERTAINMENT

The 1st, 3rd, 5th 7th, 10th and 13th letters are ETRAMT.

The word formed is MATTER.

9. *(c)* : The sport is RUGBY. The letter in the centre is 'G'.

10. *(a)* : The word is SERVICE and fifth letter from right is 'R'.

11. *(b)* : The words formed are : HAS, TEN.

19. Logical Diagram

In these type of questions, a set of five different figures is given as options. Each figure represents a logical pattern of certain groups of related words wherein each word represents a class. One has to identify the most appropriate logical figure for the set of words given. Some of the relationships represented by these diagrams are given below. Understand the relationship patterns and then attempt the exercise following the explanation.

EXERCISE

Directions : *From the five logical Diagrams, select one which best illustrates the relationship among three given classes in the questions 1 to 10.*

(a)

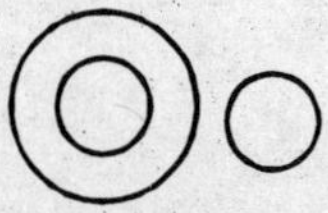

(b)

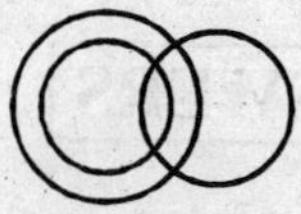

(c)

(d)

(e)

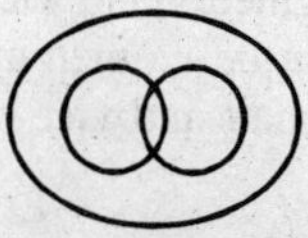

1. Birds, fruits, mangoes
2. Criminals, lawyers, bandits
3. Swimmers, bachelors, men
4. Smart, engineers, women
5. Vegetables, potatoes, brinjals
6. Grapes, sweet, fruit
7. Doctors, architects, humans
8. Scholars, people, Indians
9. Children, naughty, studious
10. Pens, pencils, stationery

Directions : *From the five logical diagrams select one which best illustrates the relationship among three given classes in questions 11 to 20.*

(a)

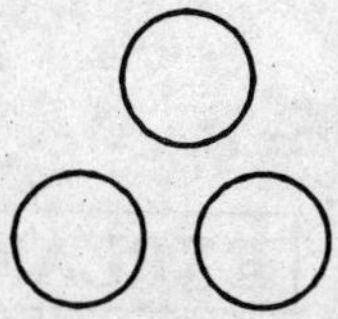

(b)

(c)

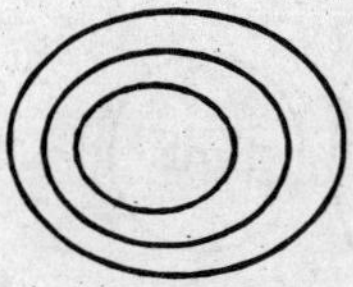

(d)

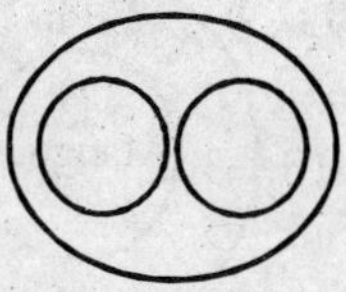

(e)

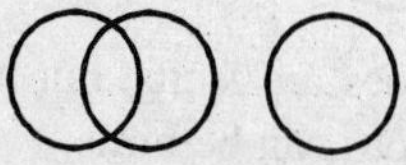

11. Ink, crayons, red
12. Canines, dogs, pups
13. Table, chair, stool
14. Ripe, mangoes, basket
15. Scholars, studious, illiterates
16. Cars, ships, means of conveyance
17. Age, number, thirteen
18. Country, state, continent
19. Father, parent, mother
20. Iron, metal, mercury

Directions : *From the five logical diagrams select one which best illustrates the relationship among three given classes in the questions 21 to 30.*

(a)

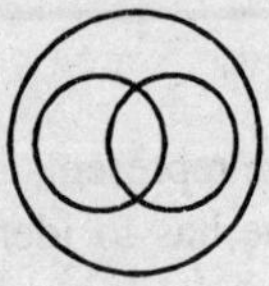

(b)

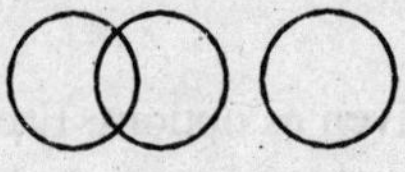

(c)

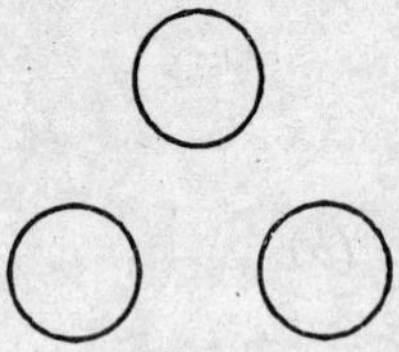

(d)

(e)

21. Lizards, Reptiles, Crocodiles
22. Whales, Tortoise, Fishes
23. Birds, Crows, Parrots
24. Sisters, Women, Mothers
25. Plants, Scientists, Men
26. Novels, Album, English
27. Sentences, Words, Paragraph
28. Beef, Mutton, Flesh
29. Principal, Student, Parent
30. Lily, Rose, Flower.

EXPLANATORY ANSWERS

1. ***(a)*** **:**

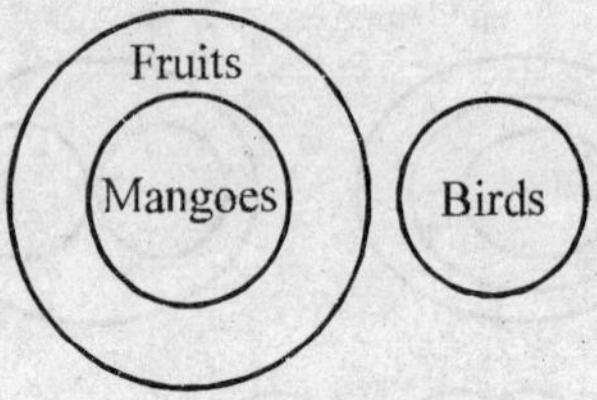

All mangoes are fruits, but neither fruits, nor mangoes can be birds.

2. ***(a)*** **:**

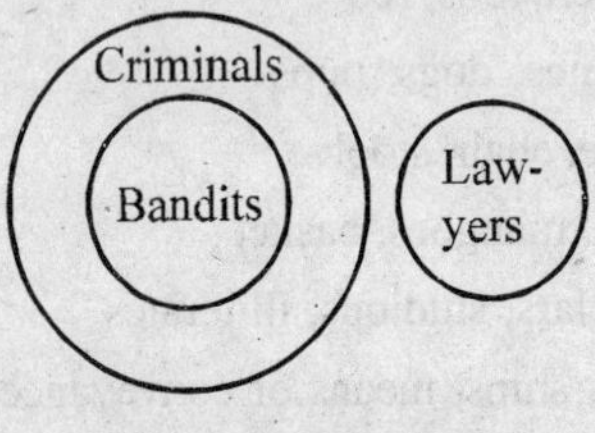

All bandits are criminal, but neither criminals nor bandits can be lawyers.

3. ***(b)*** **:**

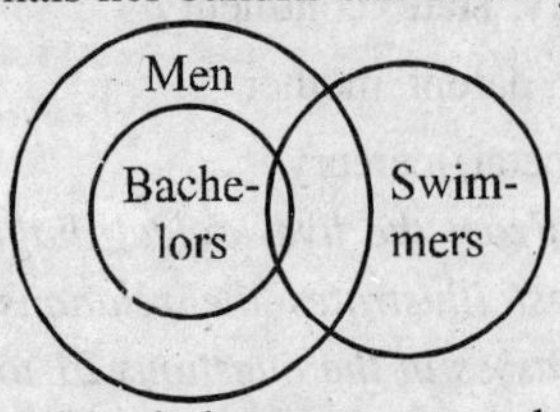

All bachelors are men and some men and bachelors can be swimmers.

4. ***(c)*** **:**

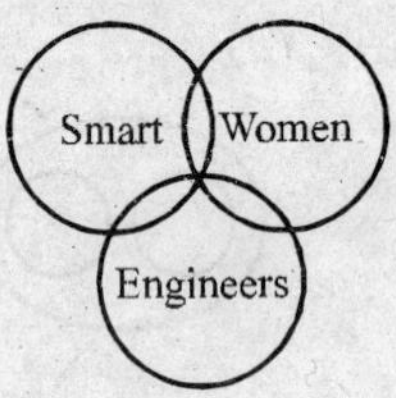

Some women can be smart and some women can be engineers and vice–versa. Some engineers can be women and some engineers can be smart and vice–versa.

5. ***(d)*** **:**

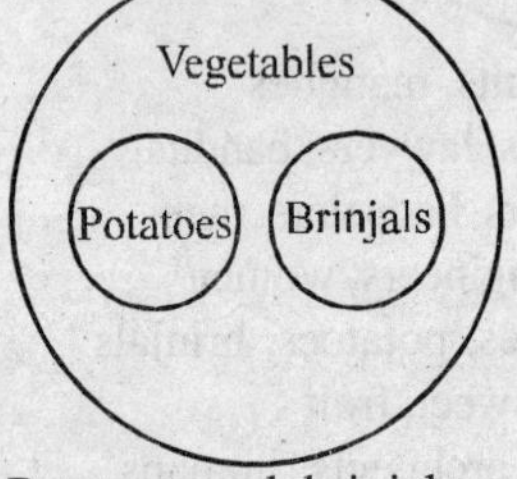

Potatoes and brinjals are vegetables but they have nothing in common. Some vegetables are potatoes and some are brinjals.

6. ***(b)*** **:**

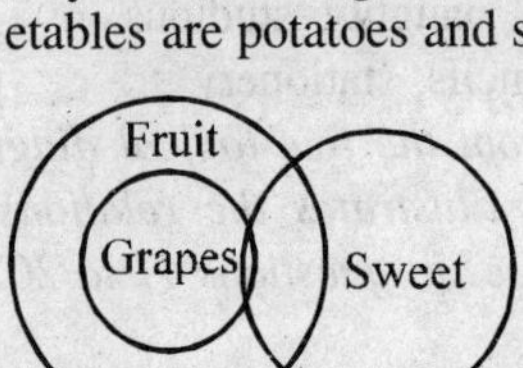

Some grapes are sweet and all grapes are fruit. But not all that is sweet is fruit.

7. ***(d)*** **:**

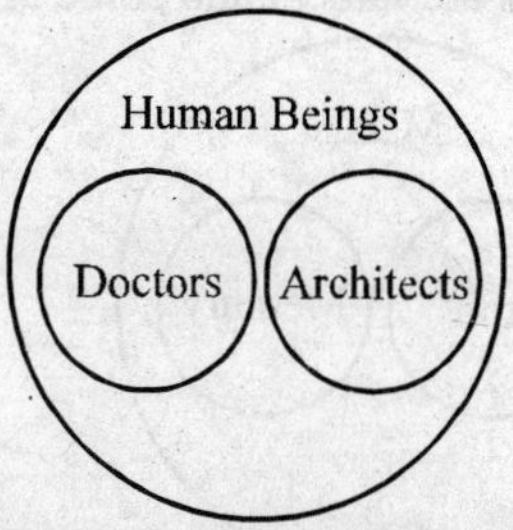

Doctors and architects are two separate classes, but all doctors and architects are humans and some humans are either doctors or architects.

8. ***(e)*** **:**

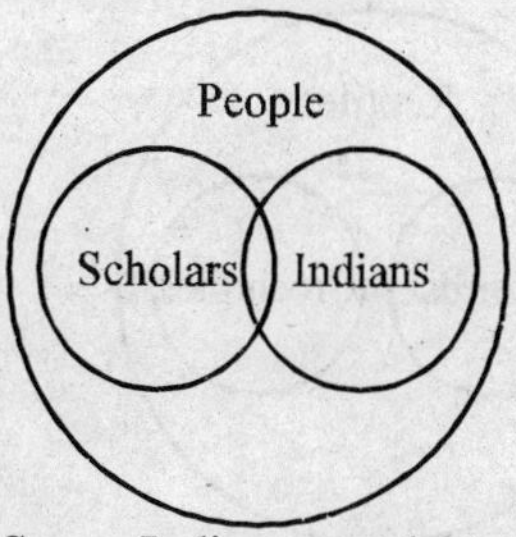

Some Indians can be scholars and some scholars can be Indians. All scholars and Indians are people.

9. ***(c)*** **:**

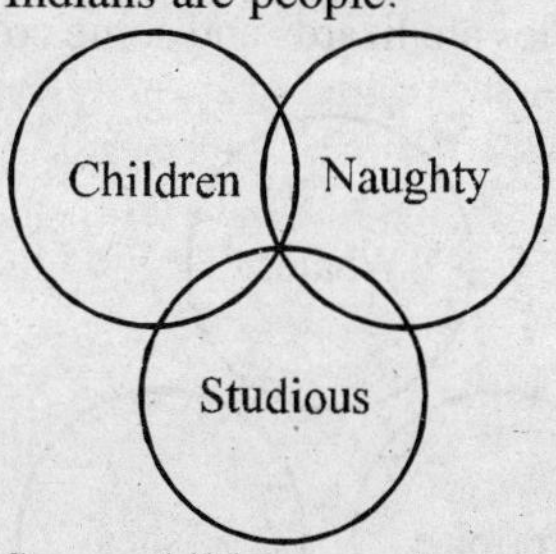

Some children can be naughty and some can be studious, some studious can be children and some naughty. Some naughty can be studious and some children.

10. ***(d)*** **:**

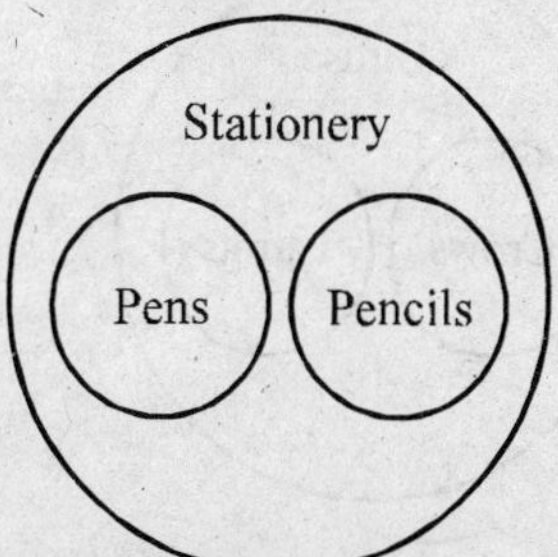

Pens and pencils both are items of stationery and some stationery is pens and pencils, but pens and pencils are two separate classes.

11. ***(b)*** **:**

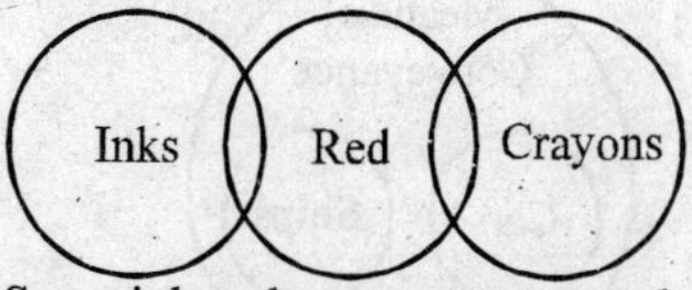

Some ink and some crayons can be red and some red units can be inks and crayons, but ink and crayon have nothing in common.

12. ***(c)*** **:**

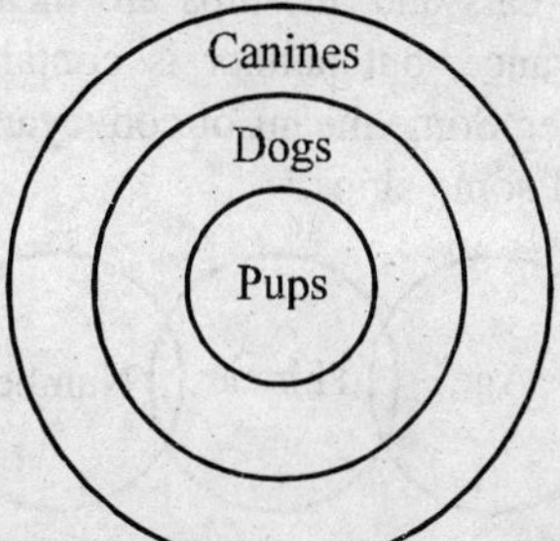

All pups are dogs and all dogs are canines. Some canines are dogs, of which some are pups.

13. ***(a)*** **:**

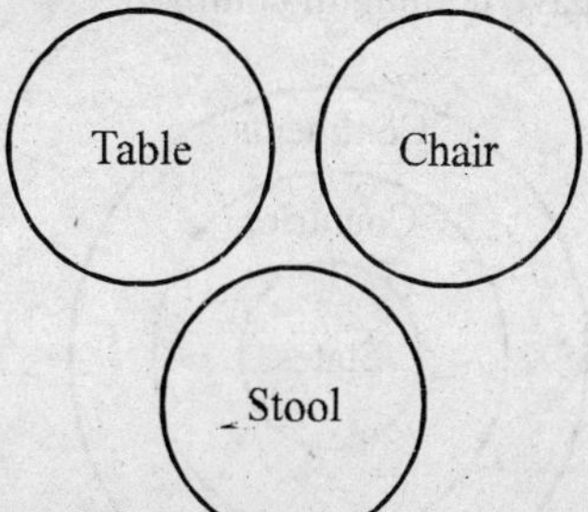

All three are different classes.

14. ***(e)*** **:**

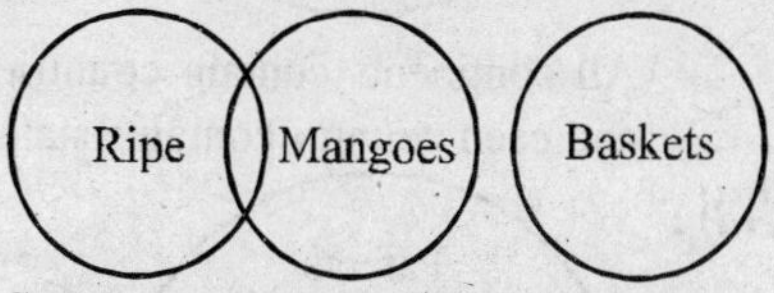

Some mangoes are ripe and some ripe units are mangoes, but neither ripe units nor mangoes can be baskets.

15. ***(e)*** **:**

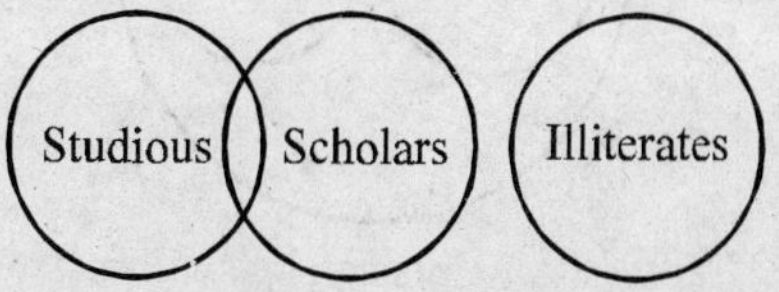

Some studious can be scholars and some scholars can be studious, but neither studious nor scholars can be illiterates.

16. *(d)* :

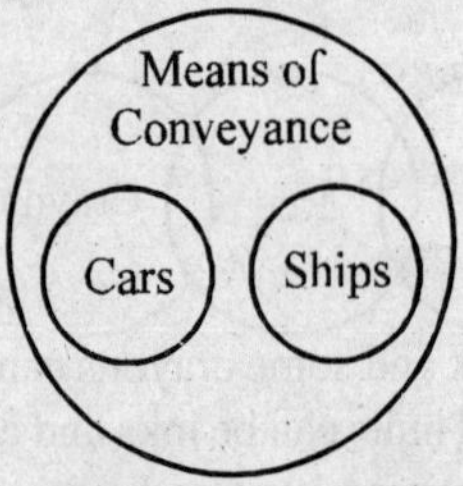

All cars and all ships are means of conveyance, but neither is contained in the other. Some means of conveyance are cars and some ships.

17. *(b)* :

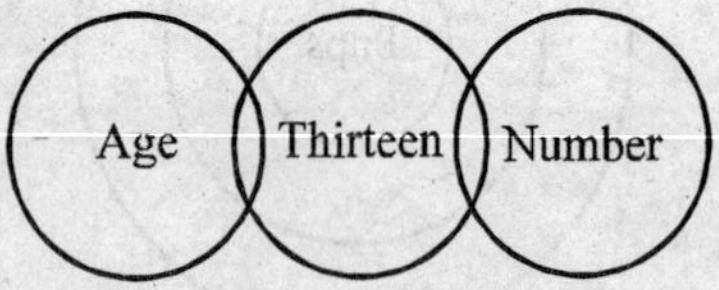

Some are aged thirteen and some numbers are thirteen. Some thirteen units are numbers and some ages. Age and number have nothing in common.

18. *(c)* :

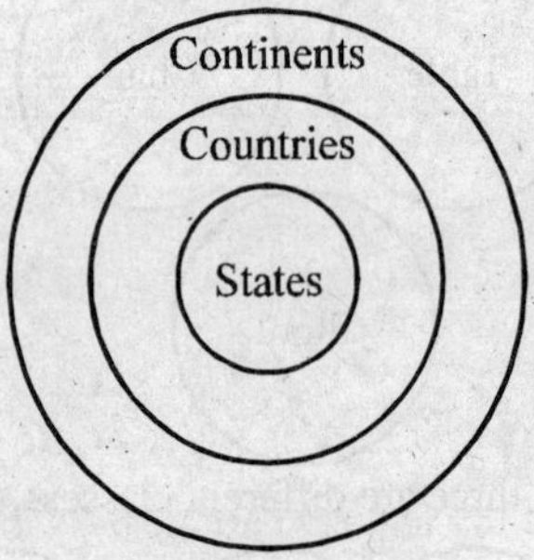

All continents contain countries within it and each country contains states within it.

19. *(d)* :

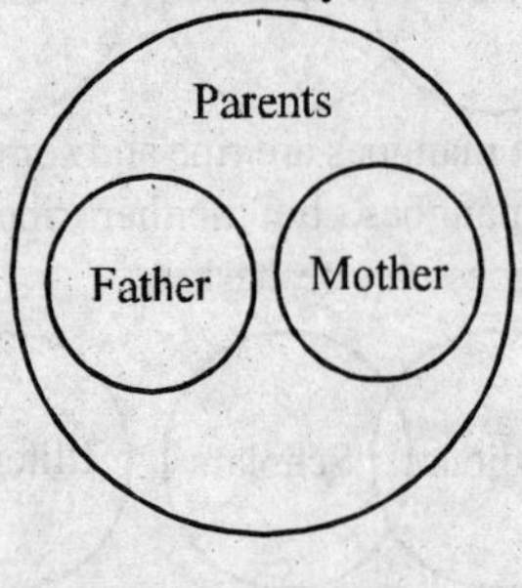

All fathers and mothers are parents, but they are two separate classes. Some of the parents are fathers and some are mothers.

20. *(d)* :

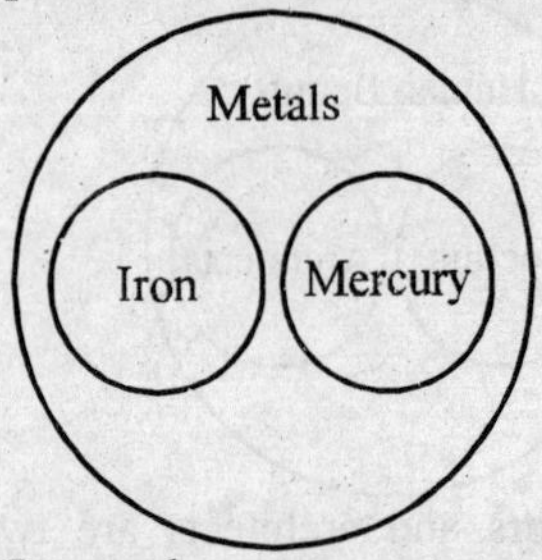

Iron and mercury are metals, but they have nothing in common. Some metals are iron and some mercury.

21. *(d)* :

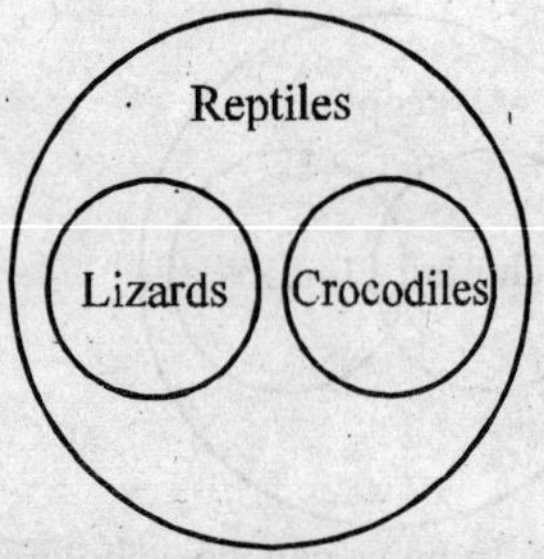

All lizards and crocodiles are reptiles, but neither is contained in the other. Some reptiles are lizards and some crocodiles.

22. *(c)* :

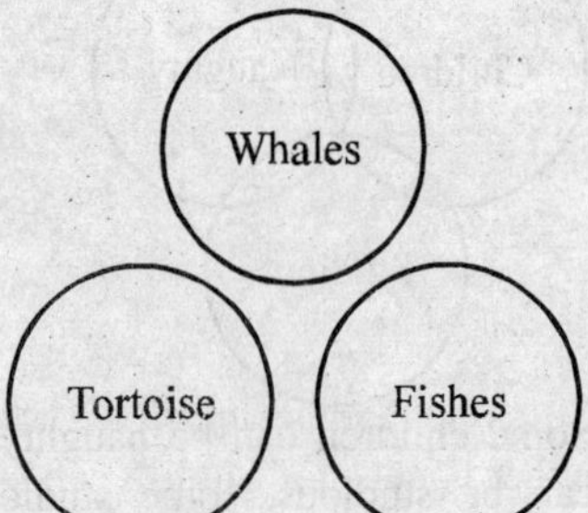

All three are different classes.

23. *(d)* :

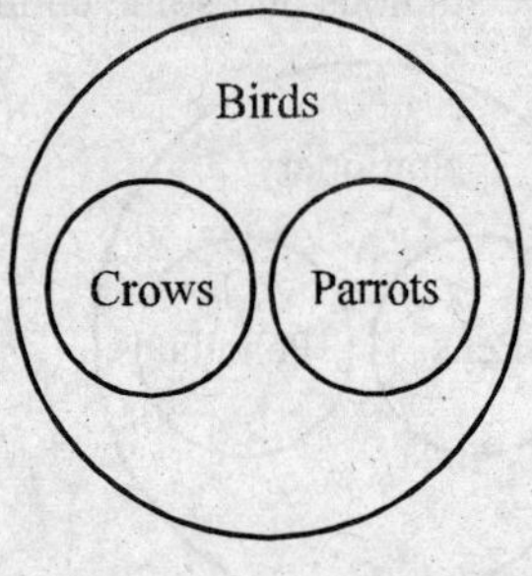

All crows and parrots are birds but neither is contained in the other. Some birds are crows and some parrots.

24. *(a)* :

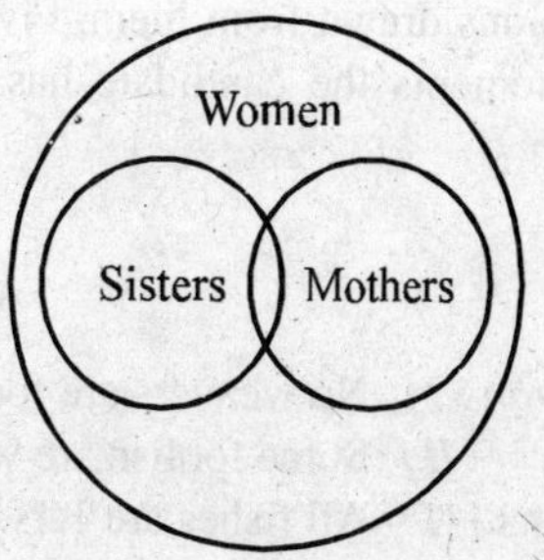

Some sisters can be mothers and some mothers can be sisters. All sisters and mothers are women.

25. *(b)* :

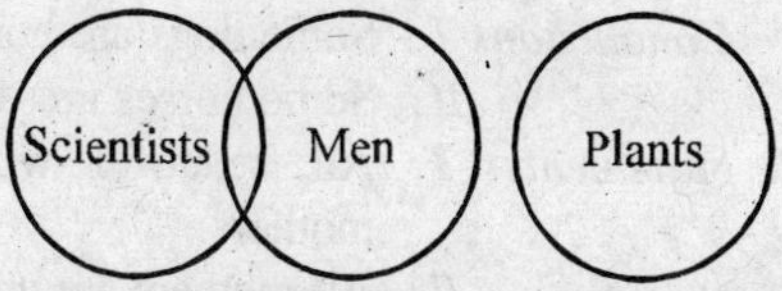

Some scientists can be men and some men can be scientists, but neither scientists nor men can be plants.

26. *(b)* :

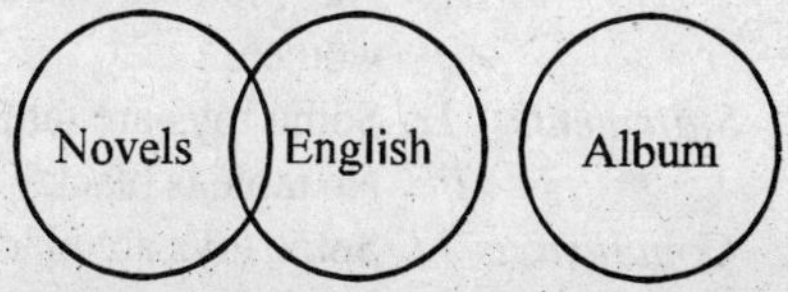

Some novels can be in English and some written material in English can be novels, but neither novels nor English can be album.

27. *(e)* :

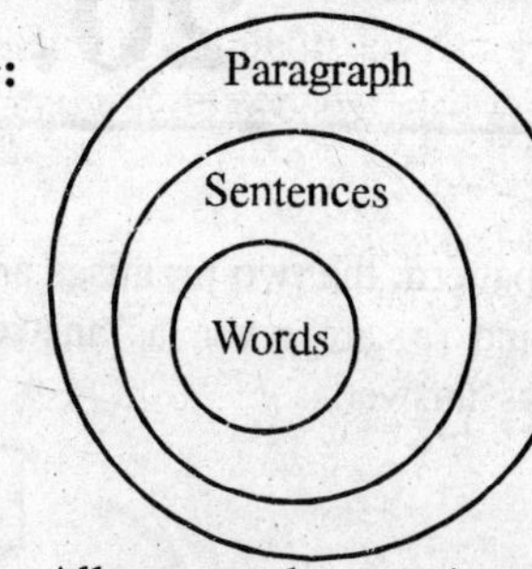

All paragraphs contain sentences within it and all sentences contain words within it.

28. *(d)* :

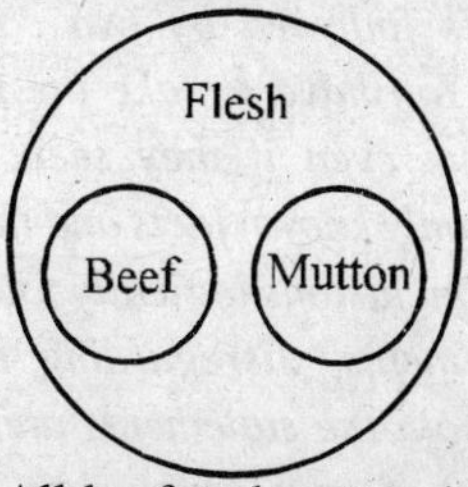

All beef and mutton is flesh of some animals. Some flesh is beef and some mutton.

29. *(b)* :

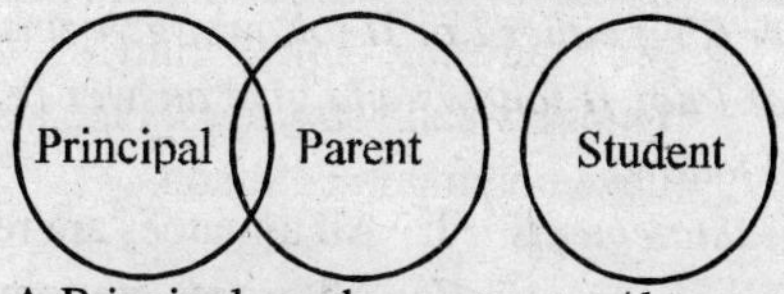

A Principal can be a parent and parent can be a principal. A student is a different class.

30. *(d)* :

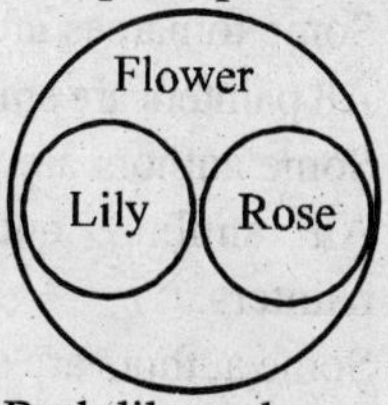

Both lily and rose are flowers. But neither is contained in the other.

20. SYLLOGISM

In this reasoning pattern, the two premises are followed by two conclusions drawn from them. Five options *(a)*, *(b)*, *(c)*, *(d)* and *(e)* are given as answers. Based on the two statements the candidate has to select the right option as answer.

EXERCISE

Directions (Qs. 1-10): *In each question below are given two statements followed by two conclusions numbered I and II. You have to take the two given statements to be true even if they seem to be at variance from commonly known facts and then decide which of the given conclusions logically follows from the two given statements, disregarding commonly known facts. Read both the statements and—*

Give answer (a) if only conclusion I follows; give answer (b) if only conclusion II follows; give answer (c) if either I or II follows; give answer (d) if neither I nor II follows and give answer (e) if both I and II follows.

1. *Statements* *I:* All tomatoes are red.
II: All grapes are tomatoes.
Conclusions *I:* All grapes are red.
II: Some tomatoes are grapes.

2. *Statements* *I:* All painters are smilling.
II: Some authors are painters.
Conclusions *I:* All smiling authors are painters.
II: Some authors are smiling.

3. *Statements* *I:* All peons in this office are efficient.
II: Ramu is not efficient.
Conclusions *I:* Ramu is not peon in this office.
II: Ramu should be more efficient.

4. *Statements* *I:* All weavers are hard working.
II: No hard working men are foolish.
Conclusions *I:* No weavers are foolish.
II: Some foolish are weavers.

5. *Statements* *I:* All fishes are cars.
II: All cars are vegetables.
Conclusions *I:* Some vegetables are cars.
II: Some vegetables are fishes.

6. *Statements* *I:* Some dogs are pups.
II: All horses are pups.
Conclusions *I:* Some dogs are horses.
II: Some horses are dogs.

7. *Statements* *I:* All beautiful women are mothers.
II: All mothers are understanding.
Conclusions *I:* All beautiful women are understanding.
II: All mothers are beautiful women.

8. *Statements* *I:* Some toys are tables.
II: No table is black.
Conclusions *I:* Some toys are black.
II: Some toys are not black.

9. *Statements* *I:* All rivers are mountains.
II: Some rivers are deserts.
Conclusions *I:* Some mountains are deserts.
II: Some deserts are not mountains.

10. *Statements* *I:* All men are horses.
II: All horses are elephants.
Conclusions *I:* All men are elephants.
II: All elephants are men.

Directions (Qs. 11-15): *In the following questions, select the set of conclusion which logically follows from the given statements.*

11. *Statements* *I* : All foxes are plates.
II : All plates are trees.
Conclusions *I* : All foxes are trees.
II : All trees are foxes.
III : Some trees are foxes.
IV : Some trees are plates.
(*a*) All conclusions are correct.
(*b*) Only conclusions I, III, and IV follow.
(*c*) Only conclusions II, III, and IV follow.
(*d*) Only conclusions I and IV follow.
(*e*) None of the above.

12. *Statements* *I* : Some cubes are squares.
II : All squares are circles.
Conclusions *I* : All cubes are circles.
II : Some circles are cubes.
III : Some circles are squares.
IV : All squares are cubes.
(*a*) Only conclusion I follows.
(*b*) Only conclusion I, II and III follow.
(*c*) All conclusions are correct.
(*d*) Only conclusions II and III follow.
(*e*) None of the above.

13. *Statements* *I* : All cups are goats.
II : All goats are tins.
Conclusions *I* : All goats are cups.
II : All tins are goats.
III : No cups are tins.
IV : No tins are cups.
(*a*) Only conclusions III and IV follow.
(*b*) Only conclusios I and II follow.
(*c*) Only conclusions I, II and III follow.
(*d*) All conclusions are correct.
(*e*) None of the above.

14. *Statements* *I* : All bombs are bags.
II : Some bags are jets.
Conclusions *I* : All bombs are jets.
II : All jets are bombs.
III : Some jets are bombs.
IV : Some bombs are jets.
(*a*) Only conclusion III follows.
(*b*) Only conclusions I and II follow.
(*c*) All conclusions are correct.
(*d*) Only conclusions III and IV follow.
(*e*) None of these.

15. *Statements* *I* : Some thorns are jackets.
II : Some jackets are boats.
Conclusions *I* : No thorns are boats.
II : All jackets are boats.
III : Some boats are thorns.
IV : No jackets are thorns.
(*a*) Either conclusion I or IV follows.
(*b*) Either conclusion I or II follows.
(*c*) Either conclusion I or III follows.
(*d*) No conclusion is correct.
(*e*) All conclusions are correct.

EXPLANATORY ANSWERS

1. (*e*) : When all tomatoes are red and all grapes are tomatoes, then all grapes are also red. When all grapes are tomatoes, then some tomatoes must be grapes. Therefore, both conclusions I and II are correct.

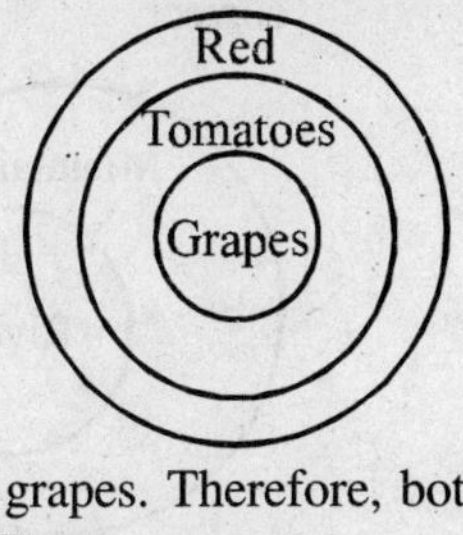

2. (*b*) : When all painters are smiling and some authors are painters, then some authors are smiling. Therefore, only conclusion II is correct.

3. (*a*) : When all the peons of the office are efficient, then Ramu cannot be a peon in this office. Therefore, only conclusion I is correct.

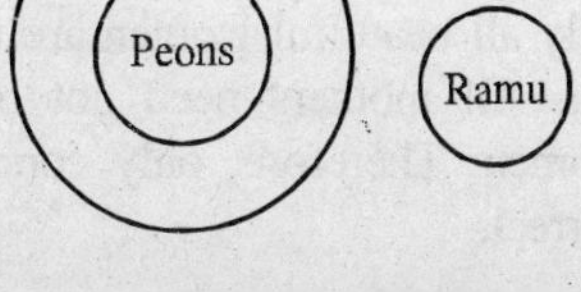

4. *(a)* : When all weavers are hardworking and no hardworking men are foolish, then no weavers are foolish. Therefore, only conclusion I is correct.

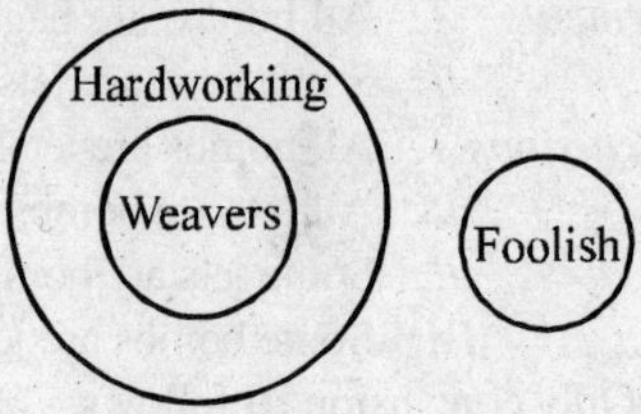

5. *(e)* : When all fishes are cars and all cars are vegetables, then all fishes will naturally be vegetables. This means that some vegetables are fishes. And when all cars are vegetables, then some vegetables will be cars naturally. Therefore, both the conclusions I and II are correct.

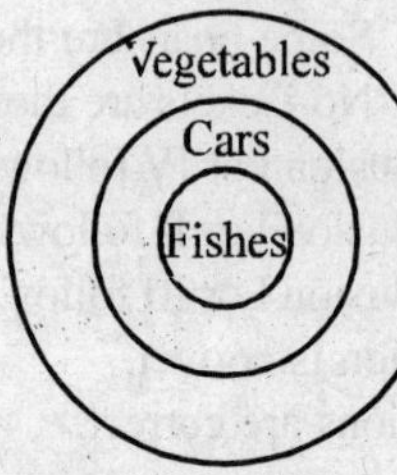

6. *(d)* : No relationship can be established between the two statements. Therefore, neither conclusion I nor conclusion II is correct.

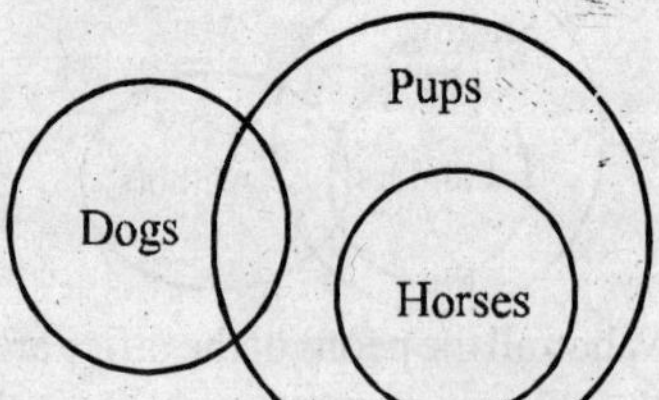

7. *(a)* : When all beautiful women are mothers and all mothers are understanding, then naturally all beautiful women are understanding. All mothers need not be beautiful women. Therefore, only conclusion I is correct.

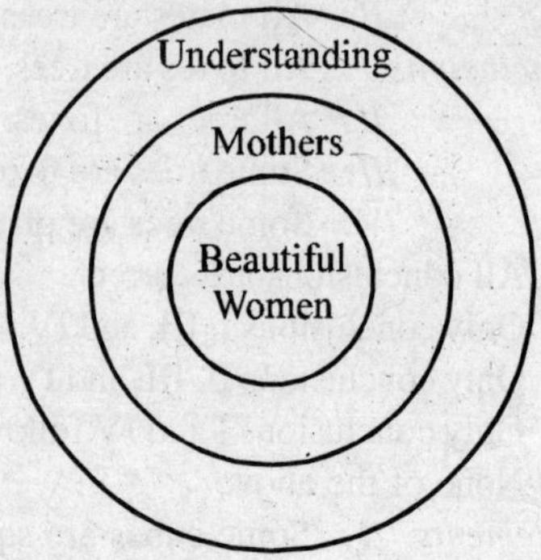

8. *(c)* : When some toys are tables and no table is black, then it is indicated that some toys can be black, as all toys are not tables. On the other hand, some toys may not be black. Therefore, there is a possibility that some toys may or may not be black. As such, either conclusion I or conclusion II can be correct.

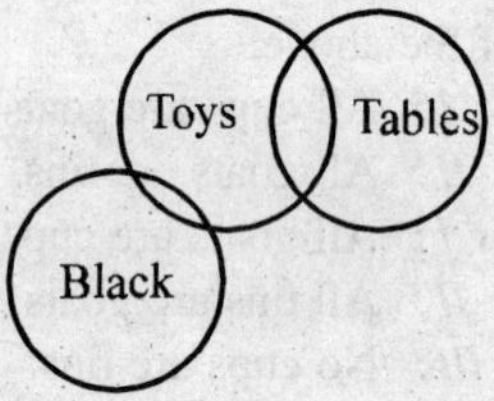

9. *(e)* : When all rivers are mountains and some rivers are deserts, then some deserts cannot be mountains and also, some mountains need not be deserts. Therefore, both conclusion I and conclusion II are correct.

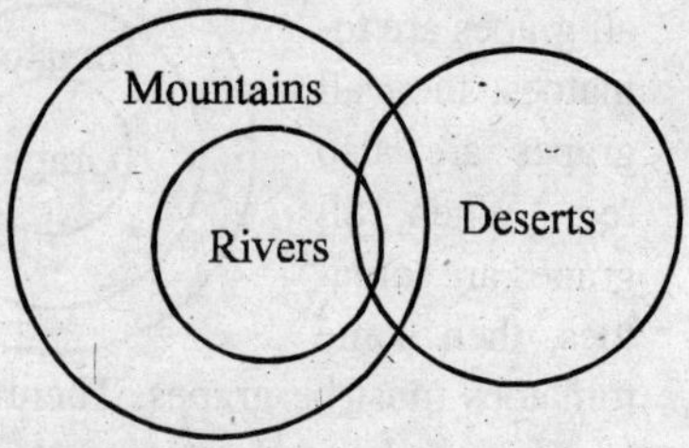

10. *(a)* : When all men are horses and all horses are elephants then, naturally all men are elephants, but all elephants need not be men. Therefore, only conclusion I is correct.

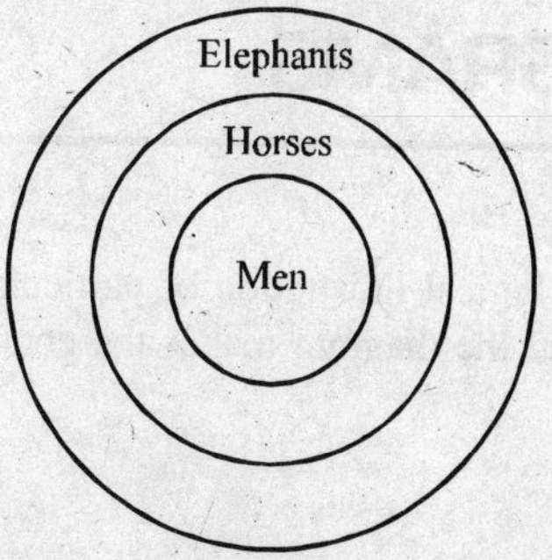

11. ***(b)*** **:**

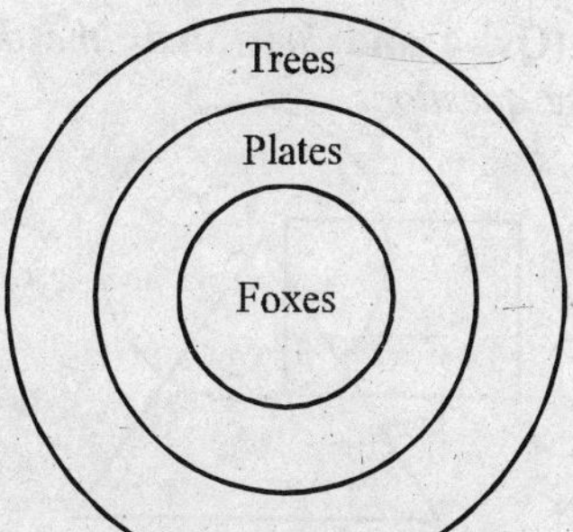

When all foxes are plates and all plates are trees, then naturally all foxes will be trees and some trees will then have to be foxes. And when all plates are trees then some trees will have to be plates. Therefore, only conclusions I, III and IV are correct.

12. ***(d)*** **:** When it is given that some cubes are squares and all squares are circles, then some cubes will naturally be circles, though all cubes cannot be circles. When some cubes are circles, then some circles will have to be cubes. And when all squares are circles, then some circles will have to be squares. As per given statement II, all squares are circles. Therefore all squares cannot be cubes. As such only conclusions II and III are correct.

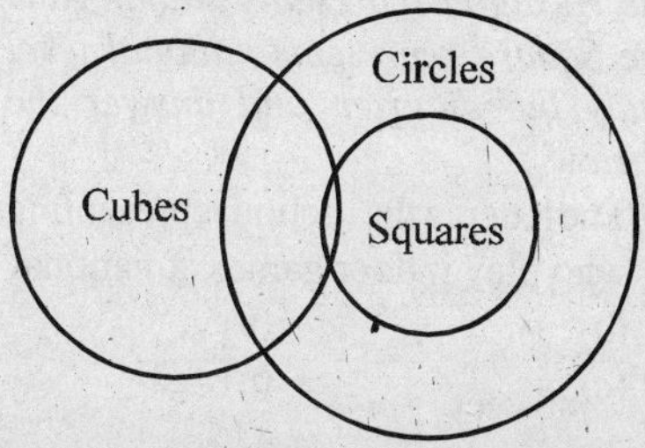

13. ***(e)*** **:** When all cups are goats, then only some goats can be cups. When all goats are tins, then only some tins can be goats. When all cups are goats and all goats are tins, then naturally all cups are tins and some tins must be cups. Therefore, all the conclusions are incorrect.

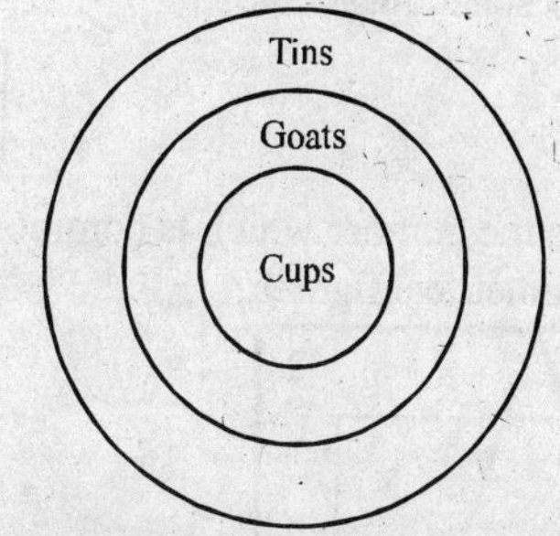

14. ***(e)*** **:** When all bombs are bags and some bags are jets then all bombs cannot be jets. 'Some bags' indicate that there is no chance of some bombs being jets, or some jets being bombs. Further all jets cannot be bombs. Therefore, all conclusions are incorrect.

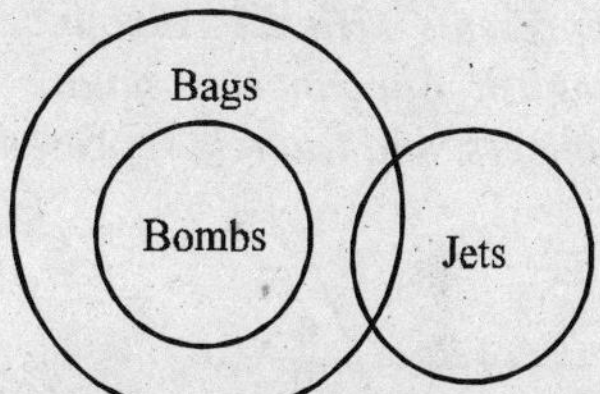

15. ***(d)*** **:** When some thorns are jackets and some jackets are boats, then some thorns may be boats but some boats cannot be thorns. As per Statement I, some thorns are jackets, some jackets need to be thorns. When Statement II conveys that some jackets are boats, then it is clear that all jackets cannot be boats. Therefore, no particular given conclusion can be drawn from the given statements.

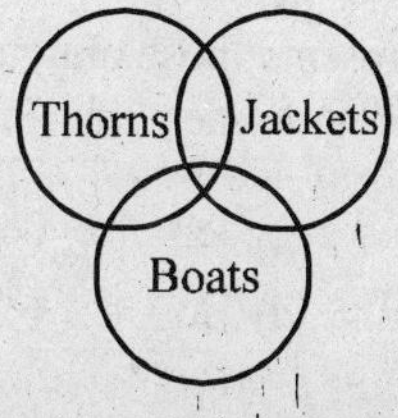

21. VENN DIAGRAMS

In these type of questions, diagrammatic representation presents a logical illustration of particular class or statements based on which the questions are asked. A clear view of the diagram makes the concepts clear for attempting such questions.

EXERCISE

1. What is the number which is common to only two geometrical figures?

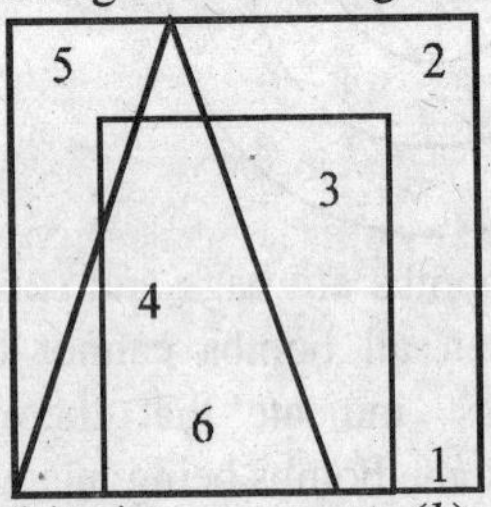

(a) 4 (b) 3
(c) 5 (d) 2

Directions (Qs. 2 and 3) : *In the following diagram, rectangle represents Hindi Announcers, circle represents English Announcers, square represents French Announcers, and triangle represents German Announcers.*

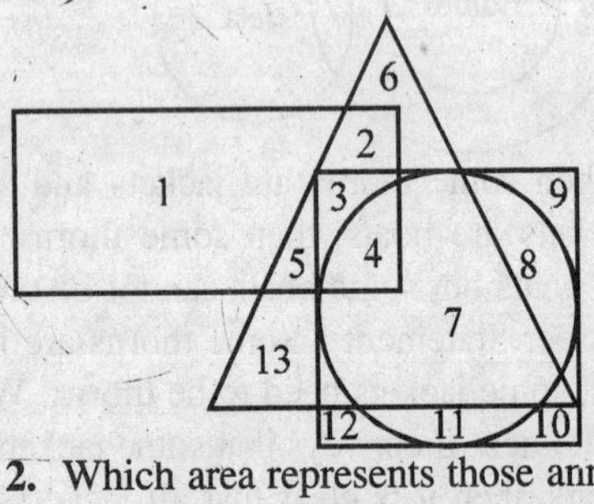

2. Which area represents those announcers who can present programmes in Hindi, French and German only?
(a) 1 (b) 2
(c) 3 (d) 4

3 Which area represents those announcers who can present programmes in French and English only?
(a) 7 (b) 9
(c) 11 (d) 13

Directions (Qs. 4 and 5) : *Study the diagram to answer these questions.*

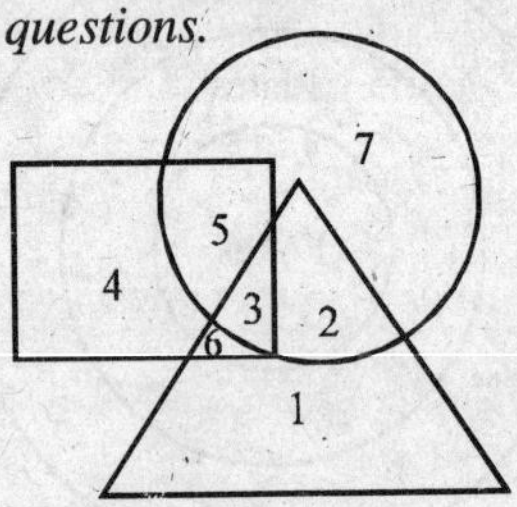

4. Which number is in all the geometrical figures?
(a) 5 (b) 6
(c) 2 (d) 3

5. Number 6 is in :
(a) Rectangle and triangle
(b) Circle and traingle
(c) Rectangle and circle
(d) Rectangle only

Directions (Qs. 6 to 9) : *In the following diagram*

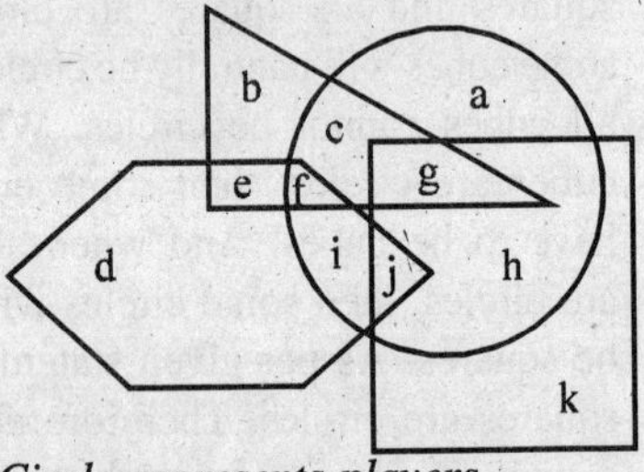

The Circle represents players
The Triangle represents outdoor games
The Hexagon represents indoor games and
The Square represents national level players
Study the diagram and answer the questions given below :

6. The letter in the section representing the players who play indoor games at national level is :
(a) f (b) i
(c) j (d) g

7. The letter representing the section of outdoor as well as indoor game players who do not play at the national level is :

(*a*) c (*b*) f

(*c*) e (*d*) i

8. The section representing national level players who do not play either outdoor or indoor games but still come under the category of players is :

(*a*) k (*b*) g

(*c*) c (*d*) h

9. Persons who play outdoor games but do not come under the category of players are represented in the section marked :

(*a*) b (*b*) c

(*c*) a (*d*) d

Directions (Qs. 10 to 13) : *Study the diagram given below.*

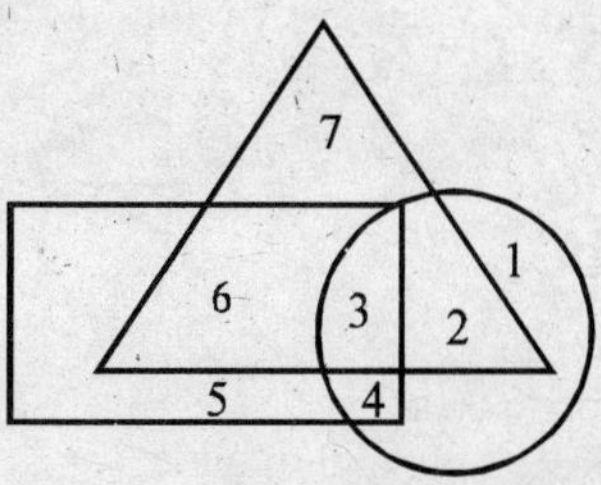

A college provides three different activities, students union represented by triangle, literary society represented by rectangle and social service league represented by circle.

10. Those who take part in both literary society and social service league but not in students union are represented by :

(*a*) 3 & 4 (*b*) 5 & 6

(*c*) 5 & 1 (*d*) 4

11. Those who take part in students union but not in social service league are represented by :

(*a*) 2 & 7 (*b*) 6 & 7

(*c*) 6 (*d*) 7

12. Those students who are members of literary society only and not of any other activity are represented by :

(*a*) 2 (*b*) 5

(*c*) 3 & 4 (*d*) 3

13. Those students who are members of all three groups are represented by :

(*a*) 2 (*b*) 3

(*c*) 4 (*d*) 6

EXPLANATORY ANSWERS

1. ***(b)*** **:**

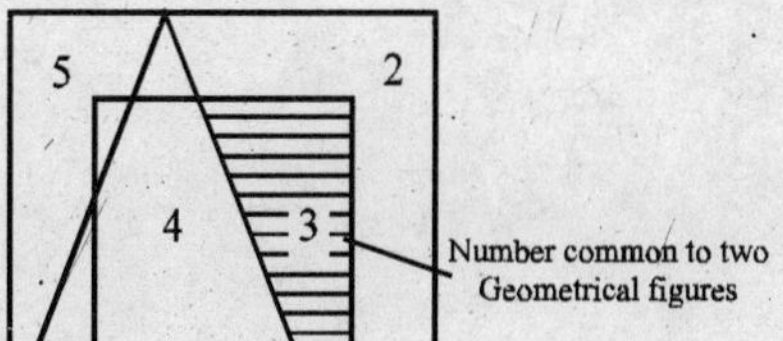

Note : Numbers 4 and 6 are common to all three geometrical figures.

2. ***(c)***, **3.** ***(c)*** **:**

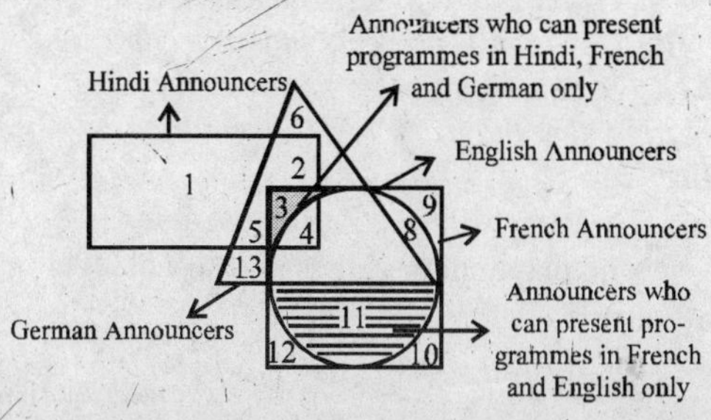

4. ***(d)***, **5.** ***(a)*** **:**

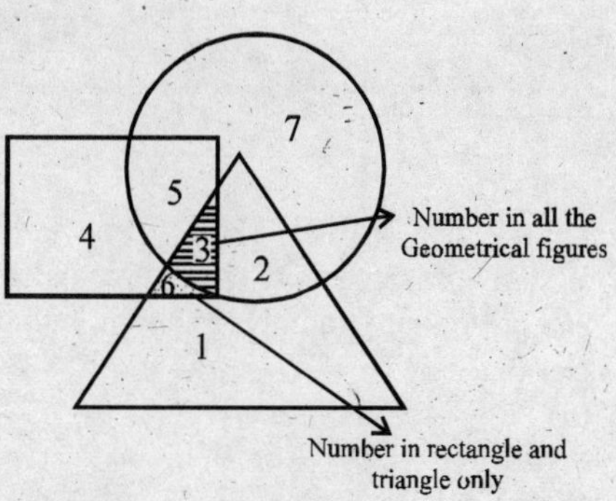

6. ***(c)***,

7. ***(b)***,

8. ***(d)***,

9. ***(a)*** **:**

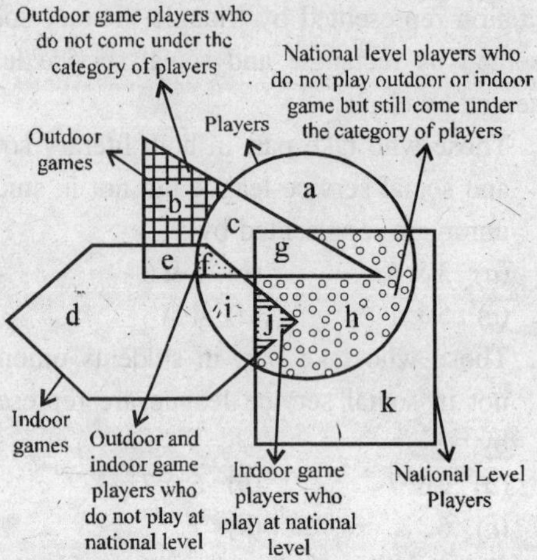

10. *(d)*, **11.** *(b)*, **12.** *(b)*, **13.** *(b)* :

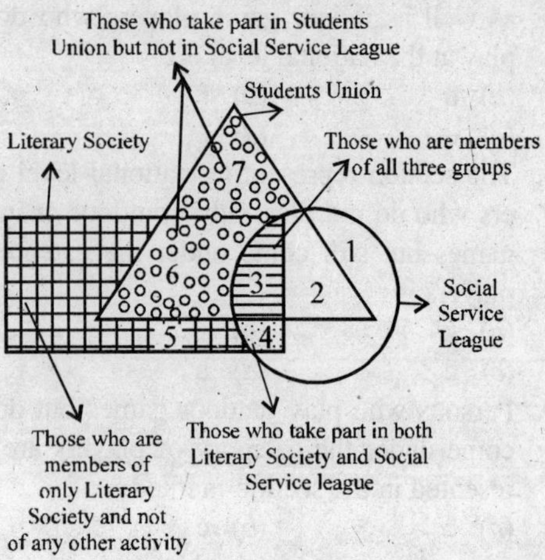

22. Non-Verbal Series

EXERCISE

Directions (Q. 1–10) : *In each of the following questions which one of the five answer figures given below should come after the problem figures if the sequence are continued?*

Problem Figures | **Answer Figures**

1.  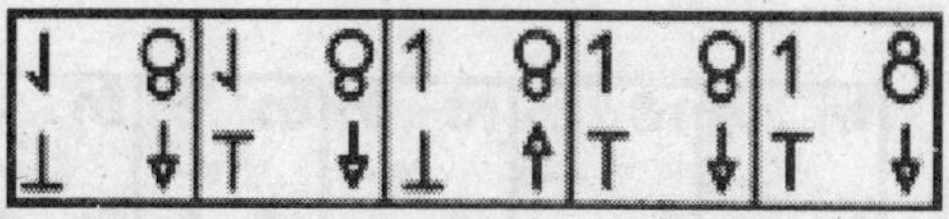

(a) *(b)* *(c)* *(d)* *(e)*

2. 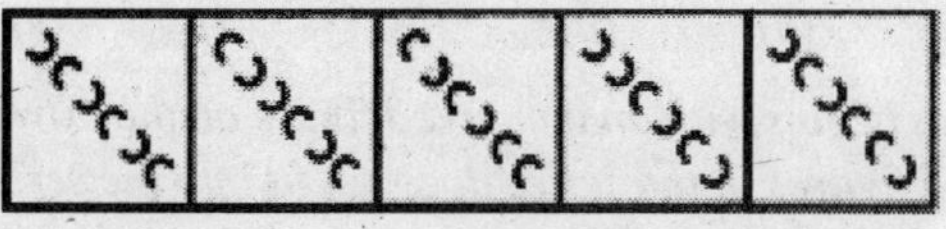 

(a) *(b)* *(c)* *(d)* *(e)*

3. 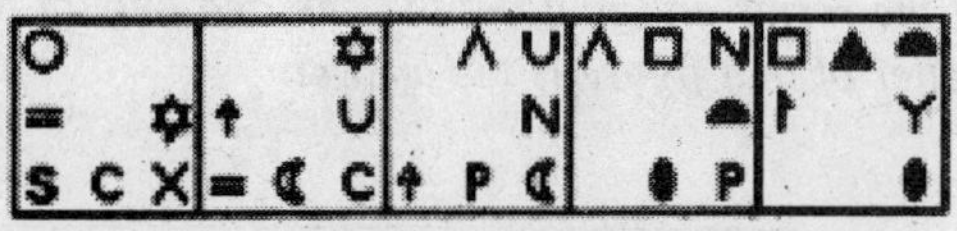 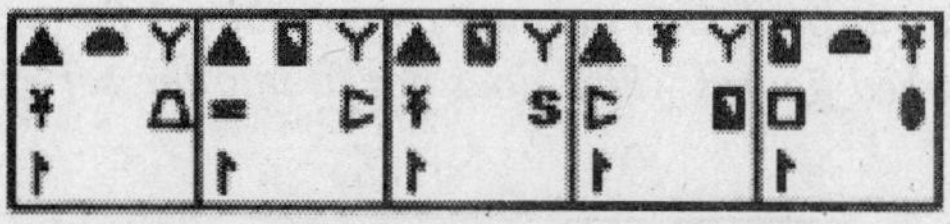

(a) *(b)* *(c)* *(d)* *(e)*

4.  

(a) *(b)* *(c)* *(d)* *(e)*

5.  

(a) *(b)* *(c)* *(d)* *(e)*

6. 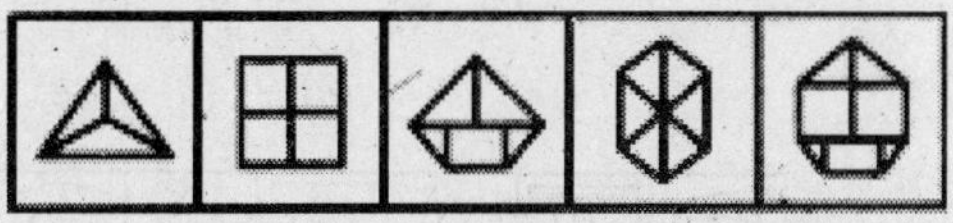 

(a) *(b)* *(c)* *(d)* *(e)*

7.  

(a) *(b)* *(c)* *(d)* *(e)*

Problem Figures **Answer Figures**

8.

(a) (b) (c) (d) (e)

9.

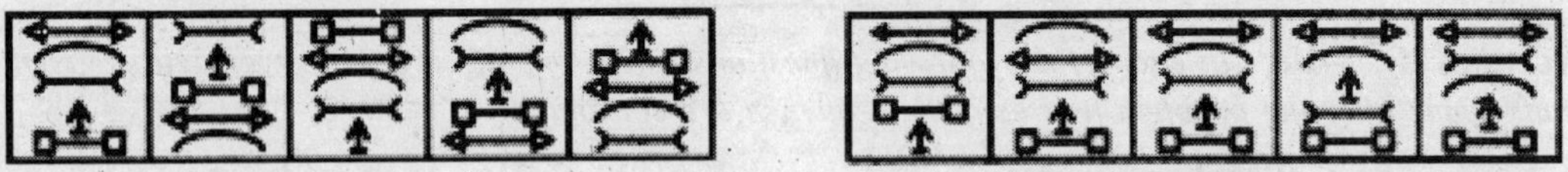

(a) (b) (c) (d) (e)

10.

(a) (b) (c) (d) (e)

Directions (Q. 11-20) : *In each of these questions, a series begins with an unmarked figure on the extreme left in the row of figures. One and only one of the five lettered figures in the series does not fit into the series. The two unmarked figures, one on the extreme left and the other on the extreme right fit into the series. Take as many aspects into account as possible of the figures in the series and find out the one and only of the five marked figures which does not fit into the series. The letter of that figure is the answer.*

11.

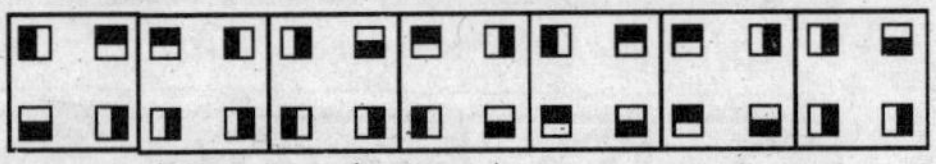

(a) (b) (c) (d) (e)

12.

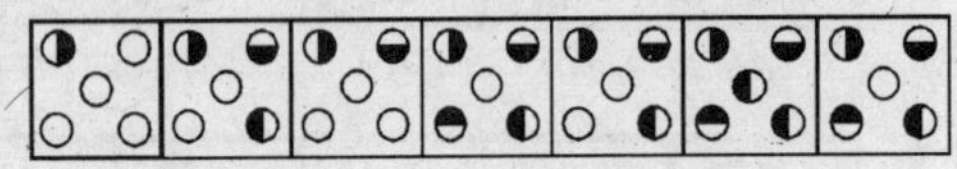

(a) (b) (c) (d) (e)

13.

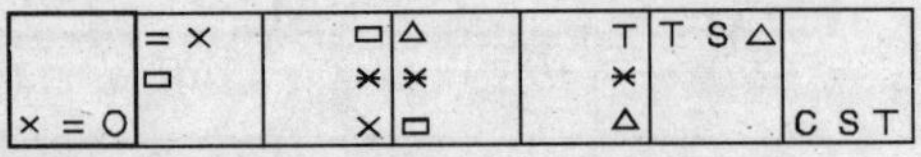

(a) (b) (c) (d) (e)

14.

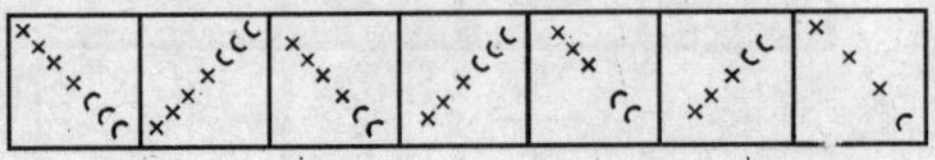

(a) (b) (c) (d) (e)

15.

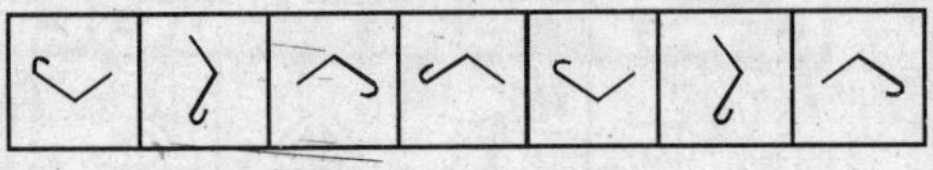

(a) (b) (c) (d) (e)

16.

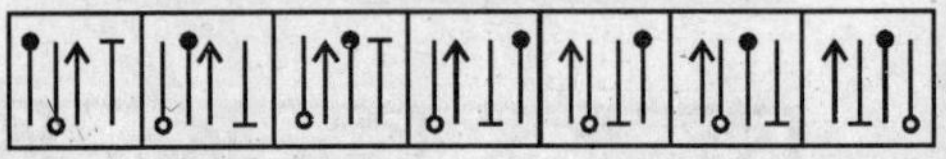

(a) (b) (c) (d) (e)

17.

(a) (b) (c) (d) (e)

18.

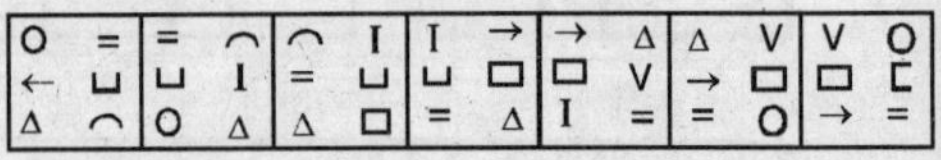

(a) (b) (c) (d) (e)

19.

(a) (b) (c) (d) (e)

20.

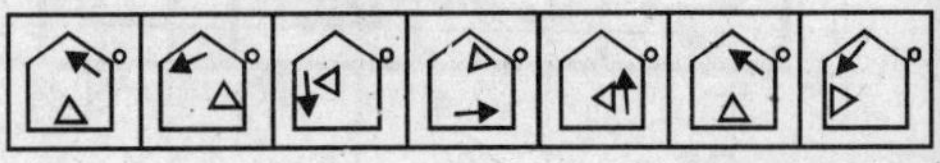

(a) (b) (c) (d) (e)

Directions (Q. 21–30) : *Each of the following questions consist of problem figures followed by answer figures. Select a figure from amongst the answer figures which will continue the same series or pattern as established by the problem figures.*

Problem Figures | **Answer Figures**

21.
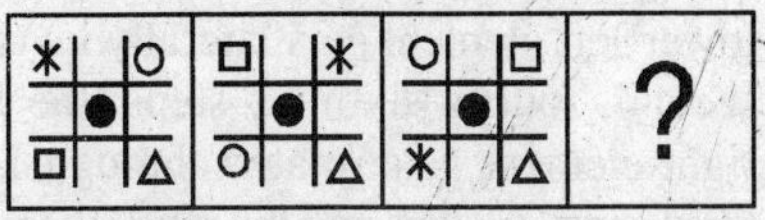
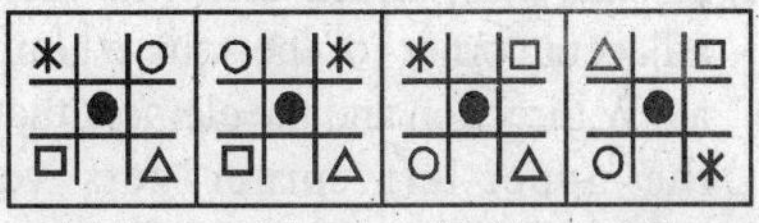
(a) (b) (c) (d)

22.
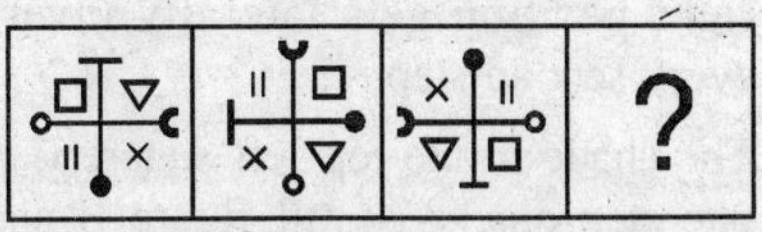
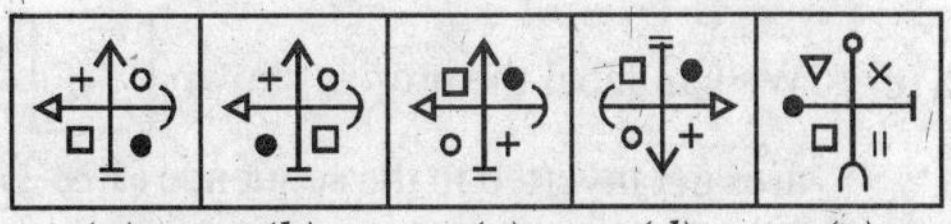
(a) (b) (c) (d) (e)

23.
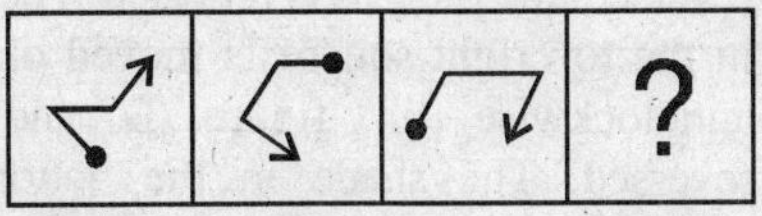
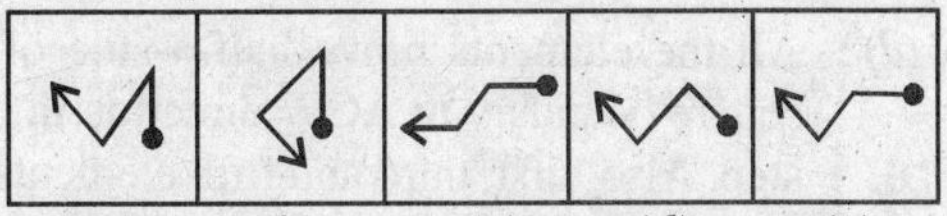
(a) (b) (c) (d) (e)

24.
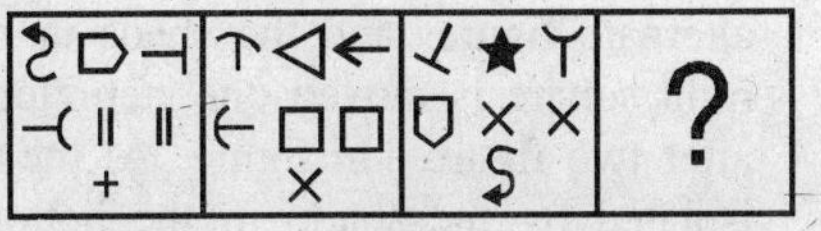
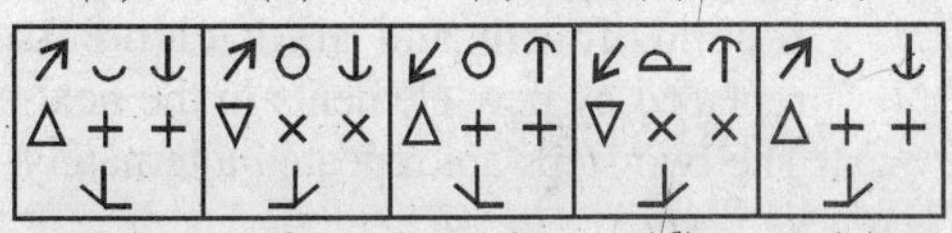
(a) (b) (c) (d) (e)

25.
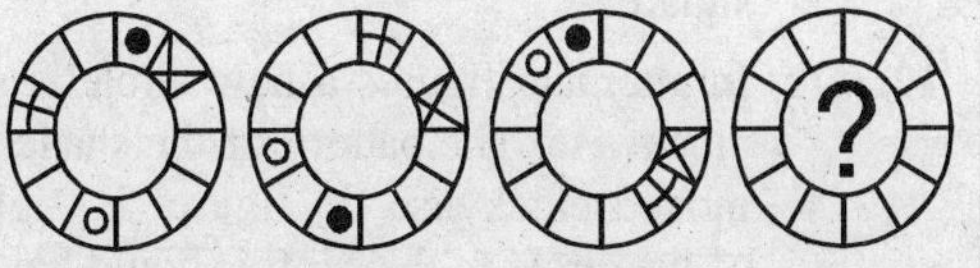
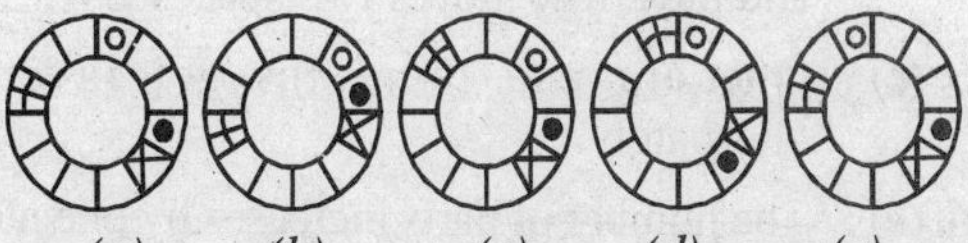
(a) (b) (c) (d) (e)

26.
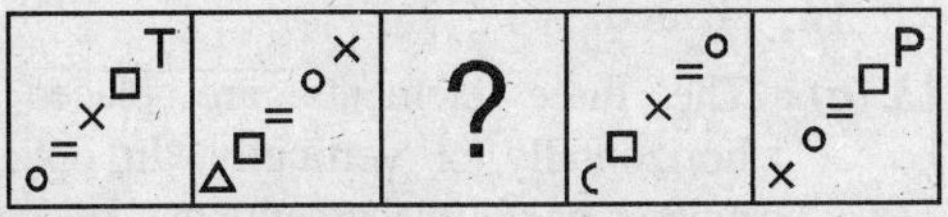
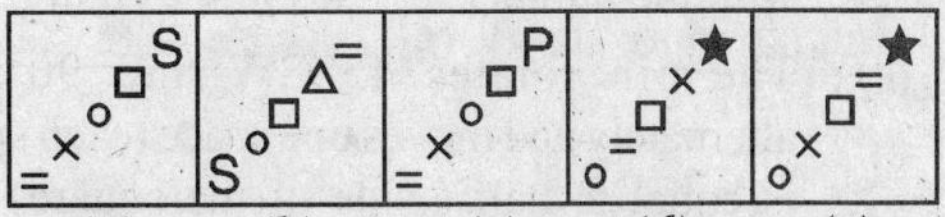
(a) (b) (c) (d) (e)

27.
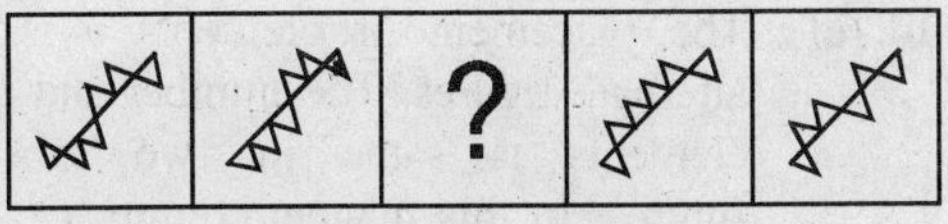
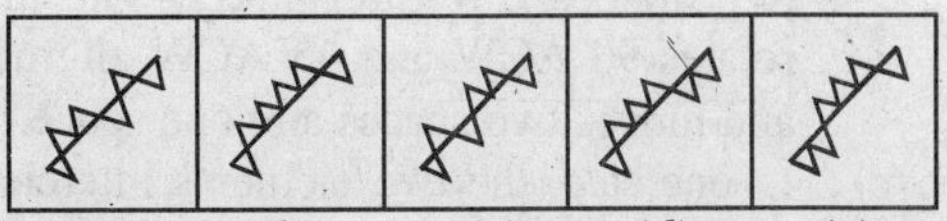
(a) (b) (c) (d) (e)

28.
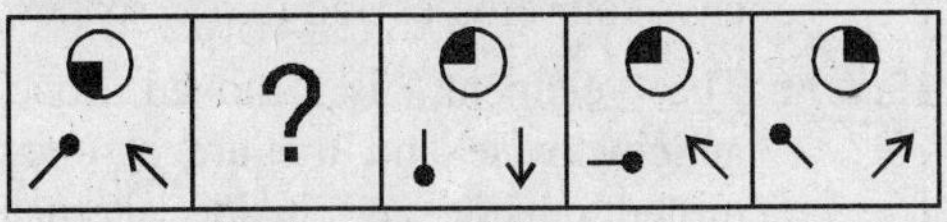
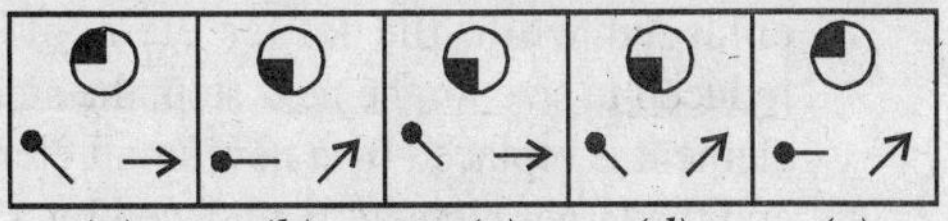
(a) (b) (c) (d) (e)

29.
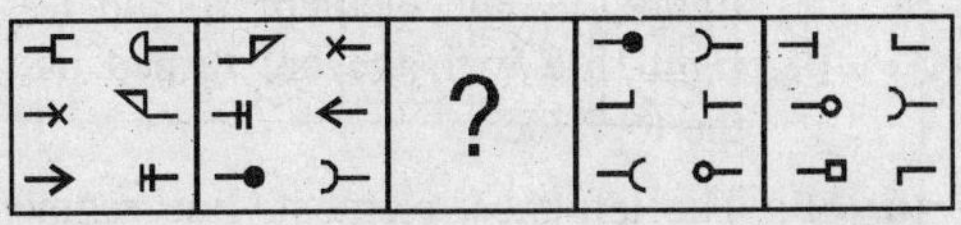
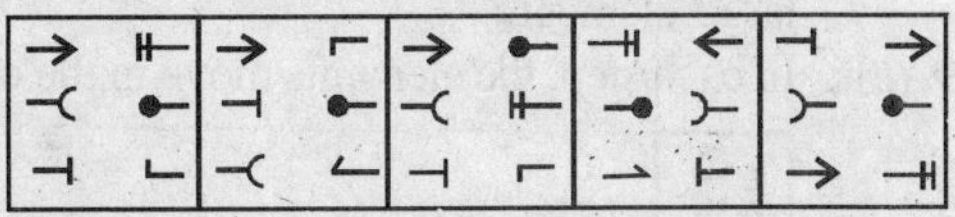
(a) (b) (c) (d) (e)

30.
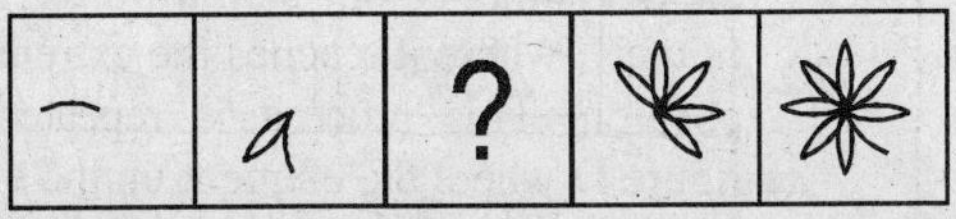
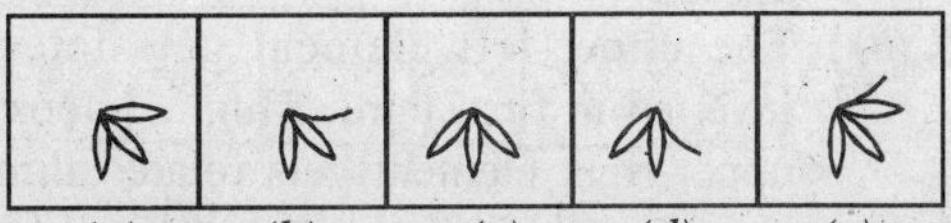
(a) (b) (c) (d) (e)

EXPLANATORY ANSWERS

1. (*d*) : In each step, all the elements move to the adjacent corner (of the square boundary) in a CW direction and the element that reaches the upper-left corner gets vertically inverted.

2. (*c*) : We can label the arcs as shown 

. The arcs get inverted in the sequence (1 & 2), (3, 4 & 5), (6 & 1), (2, 3 & 4), (5 & 6), ...

3. (*d*) : All the elements move half-a-side of the square boundary in ACW direction in each step. Also, first, third and fifth elements are replaced by new elements in one step and second, fourth and sixth elements are replaced by new elements in the next step. The two steps are repeated alternately.

4. (*a*) : In each step, the dot moves one space CW and the arrow moves two spaces CW.

5. (*c*) : One arc and four arcs get inverted alternately.

6. (*e*) : The number of parts increases by one along with the number of sides in the figure.

7. (*c*) : The pin rotates 45°CW and 90°CW alternately and moves one space (each space is equal to half-a-side of the square) and two spaces CW alternately. The arrow rotates 90°ACW and 45°ACW alternately and moves two spaces and one space.

8. (*e*) : In one step, the two elements interchange positions and the smaller element gets enlarged while the larger element gets reduced in size. In the next step, the smaller element is replaced by a new small element and the larger element is replaced by a new large element.

9. (*c*) : In each step, the elements move in the order

.

10. (*b*) : The upper-left element gets laterally inverted in first, third, fifth. .... steps; the upper-right element gets rotated through 180° is first, fourth, seventh,.... steps; the lower-left element gets laterally inverted in second, fourth, sixth, ... steps; the lower-right element gets rotated through 180° in third, sixth,... steps and the pin at the middle-right position gets laterally inverted in every second step.

11. (*a*) : The shade in the top left square is moved one step clockwise till figure B and then reversed, the process is repeated. The shade in the top right square is moved one step anticlockwise till figure D and then reversed. The shade in the bottom left square is moved one step clockwise in alternate figures and the shade in bottom right square is moved one step clockwise after two figures. In figure 'A' the rule is isolated by the shade in the bottom left square.

12. (*e*) : In alternate figures a new circle is shaded clockwise. The pattern of the shade is also moved clockwise. In figure 'E' right half of the circle in the centre should have been shaded.

13. (*a*) : The three elements are placed either horizontally or vertically. In option 'A' neither of the placements can be applied.

14. (*c*) : The placement of elements is same in alternate figures. The number and type of elements is same in two subsequent figures. In this manner, figure 'C' should have four crosses and two C shapes.

15. (*c*) : The element is moved one step anticlockwise and the arc at one end is turned outside and inside alternately. In figure 'C' the element should be on the right side with the arc turned outside on the top side.

16. (*e*) : The left most element, line segment with the dot is moved one step towards right till figure C where it reaches the extreme right position. This process is repeated from figure D where the element on the extreme left, line segment with a circle, is moved. In figure 'E' the placement of the elements does not follow the rule of the series.

17. (e) : The 'T' line is rotated 45° clockwise and the line with the circle 45° anticlockwise. The 'Y' shape and the arrow are repeated twice after two figures. In option E, the 'T' shape and the line with the circle are rotated by 90°.

18. (e) : First the elements in the four corners are moved one step anticlockwise, next the four elements from the top are moved one step anticlockwise and then the four elements from the bottom are moved one step anticlockwise. Of the remaining two elements, the one on the left is made new each time and then their places are interchanged. This process is repeated from figure D. In option 'E' open square should have been in place of circle to continue the series.

19. (a) : At each step the outermost figure is removed and a new figure is placed right in the centre of other two figures. In option 'A' the triangle is turned upside down, which violates the rule of the series.

20. (a) : The arrow is moved one step anticlockwise and the triangle one step clockwise. In figure 'A' the triangle should have been on the left side of the figure.

21. (a) : The places of star, circle and square are moved one step clockwise at each step.

22. (e) : The elements in the four quadrants are moved one step clockwise and the elements at the ends of the cross are moved one step anticlockwise in this series.

23. (a) : In alternate figures, the line with the dot is turned 90° clockwise and the arrow 180° clockwise.

24. (e) : In alternate figures, the element in the top left position is horizontally inverted and moved one and half steps anticlockwise, the top middle element is turned 90° clockwise and moved one step anticlockwise, the top right element is turned 135° clockwise and moved one step anticlockwise, the element at the bottom is replaced by a new element and moved to the top middle position, and the two identical elements are replaced by two new identical elements.

25. (a) : The cross and the circle move one and two steps clockwise respectively (at each step), the plus moves 3, 4 and 5 steps clockwise, and the dot 6, 5 and 4 steps clockwise.

26. (a) : At first step, the fifth or the bottom most element is moved to the second place from top, the second element moved to the fourth place, the fourth element is moved to the third place, the third element is moved to the first or the topmost place and the element on the top, which is made new, is moved to the last or the fifth place. At second step i.e., from second problem figure to third problem figure the above process is reversed. The bottom most element is the first and the top most element is the last or fifth. Hereafter, the process is repeated from the beginning. Option 'A' is the right answer.

27. (c) : Starting from the bottom, one triangle is moved to the opposite side at each step in upward order. Option 'C' fits into the question marked space.

28. (c) : The shade inside the circle is rotated clockwise in alternate figures; the line segment with a dot is rotated 135° clockwise in alternate figures and the arrow is rotated 135° anticlockwise in alternate figures. By this process answer figure 'C' completes the series.

29. (a) : At each step the elements are moved diagonally upward and then laterally inverted, and the top two elements are made new and placed at the bottom line. By this process, option figure 'A' completes the series.

30. (a) : The number of arcs making the petals of the flower are increased by one, one and half, two, two and half respectively at each step. Also, the flower is turned 45° anticlockwise. By this process, option 'A' is the right answer.

23. Non-Verbal Analogy

EXERCISE

TYPE-I

Directions (Q. 1-15): *The second figure in the first unit of the Problem Figures bears a certain relationship to the first figure. Similarly, one of the figures in the Answer Figures bears the same relationship to the first figures in the second unit of the Problem Figures. Locate the figure which would fit the questions marks.*

Problem Figures | **Answer Figures**

1. 
1 2 3 4
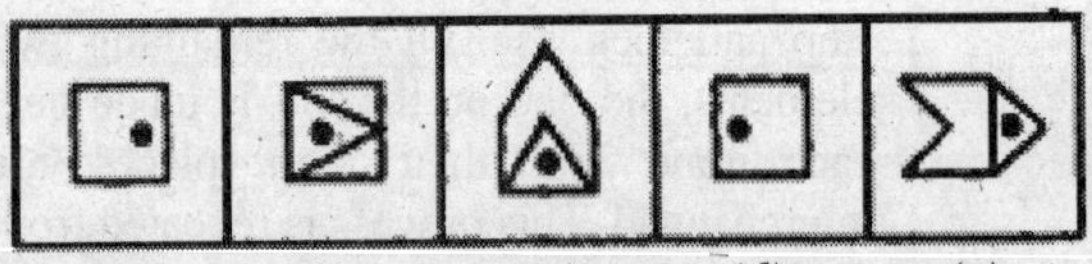
(a) (b) (c) (d) (e)

2. 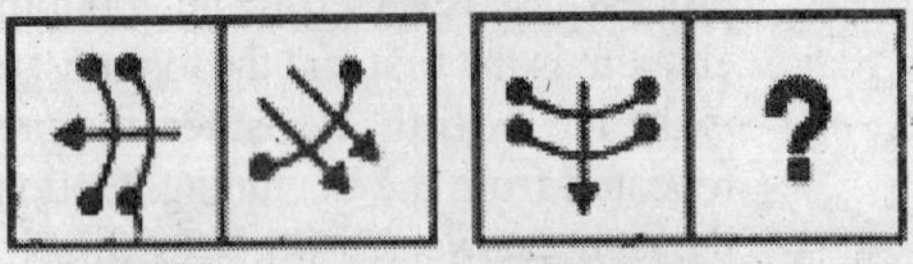
1 2 3 4

(a) (b) (c) (d) (e)

3. 
1 2 3 4
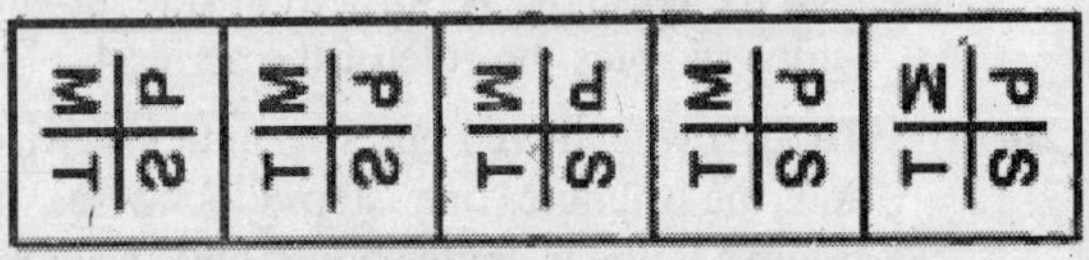
(a) (b) (c) (d) (e)

4. 
1 2 3 4

(a) (b) (c) (d) (e)

5. 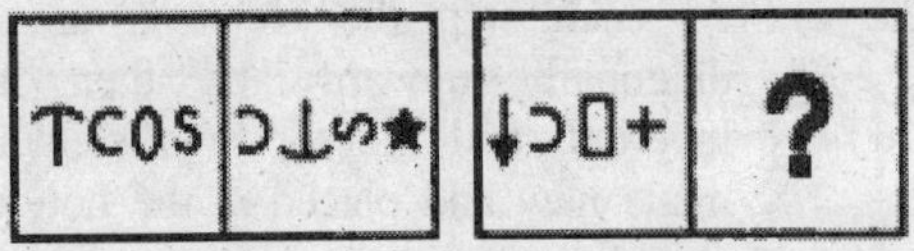
1 2 3 4
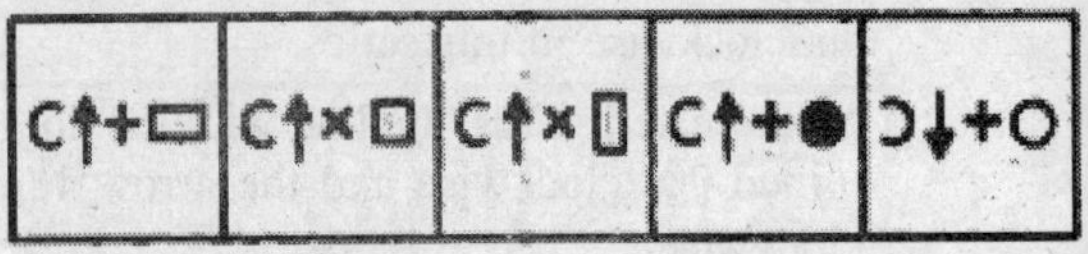
(a) (b) (c) (d) (e)

6. 
1 2 3 4

(a) (b) (c) (d) (e)

Problem Figures | **Answer Figures**

7.
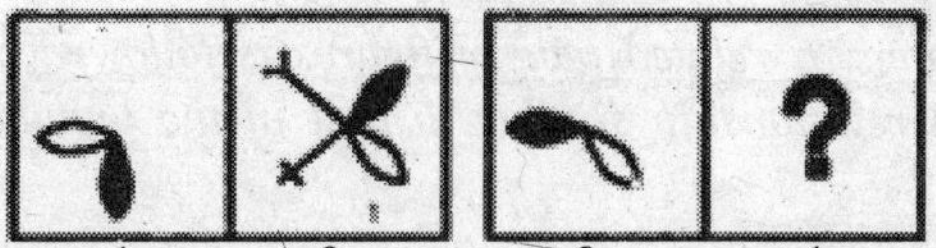
1 2 3 4

(a) (b) (c) (d) (e)

8.

1 2 3 4

(a) (b) (c) (d) (e)

9.
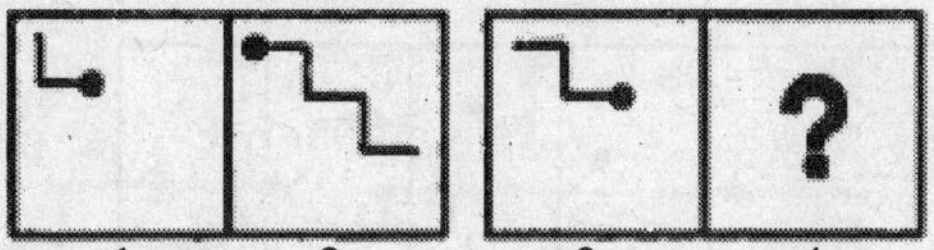
1 2 3 4
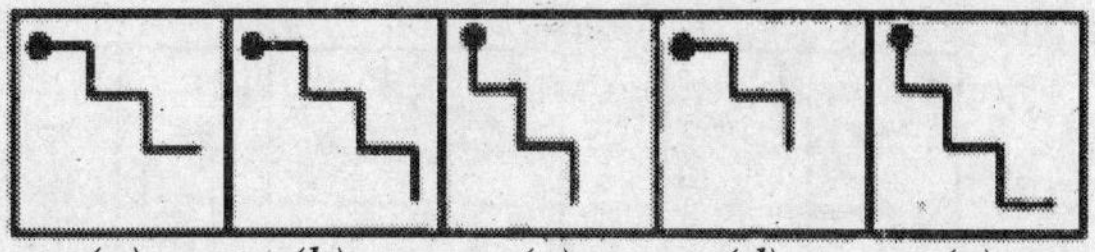
(a) (b) (c) (d) (e)

10.
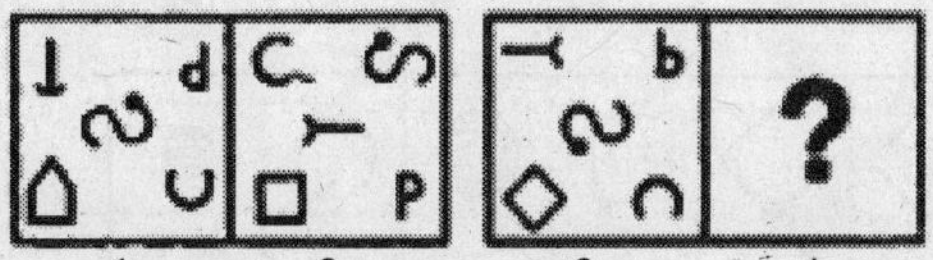
1 2 3 4
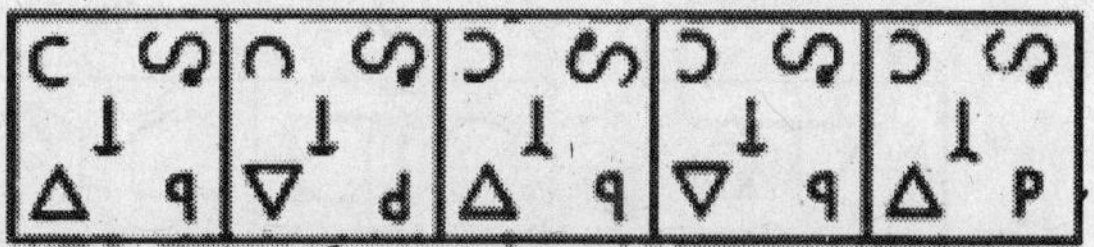
(a) (b) (c) (d) (e)

11.

1 2 3 4

(a) (b) (c) (d) (e)

12.
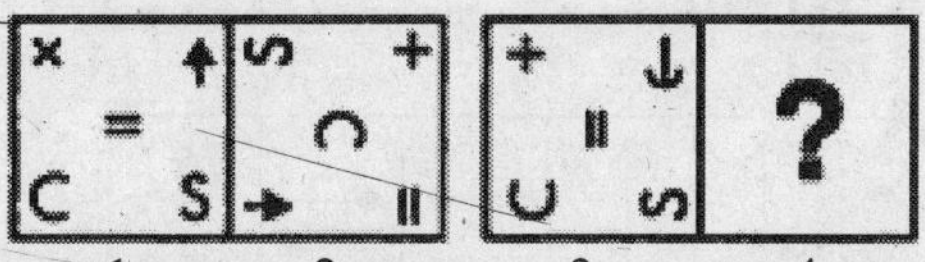
1 2 3 4
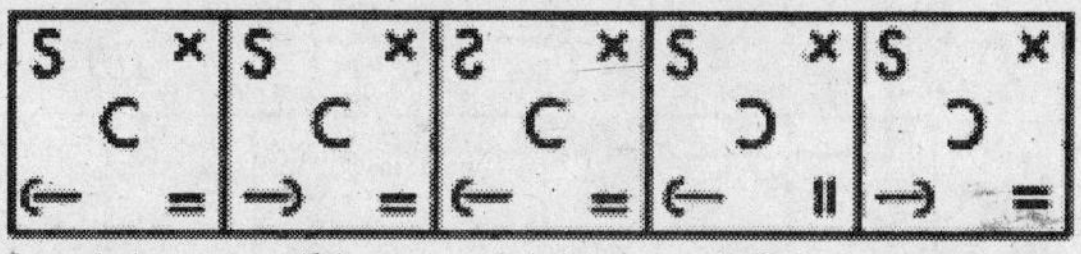
(a) (b) (c) (d) (e)

13.

1 2 3 4

(a) (b) (c) (d) (e)

14.
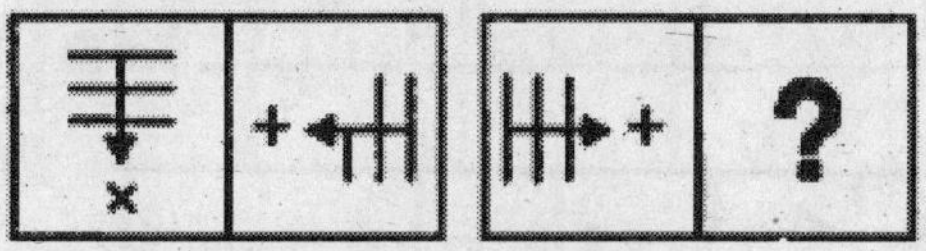
1 2 3 4
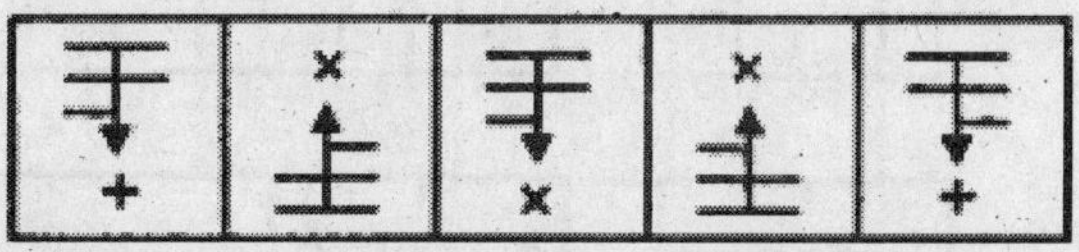
(a) (b) (c) (d) (e)

15.
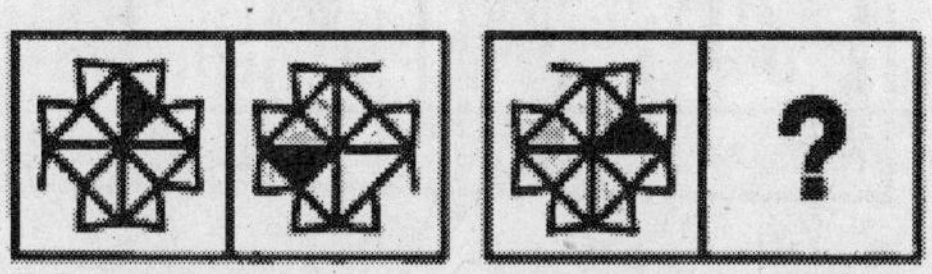
1 2 3 4

(a) (b) (c) (d) (e)

TYPE-II

Directions (Q. 16–30): *In each of the following questions, a related pair of figures is followed by five numbered pairs of figures. Select the pair that has a relationship* ***similar*** *to that in the unnumbered pair.*

Problem Figure **Answer Figures**

16.
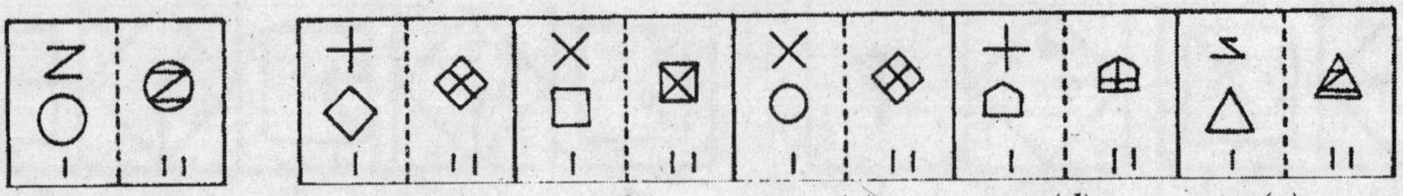
(a) (b) (c) (d) (e)

17.
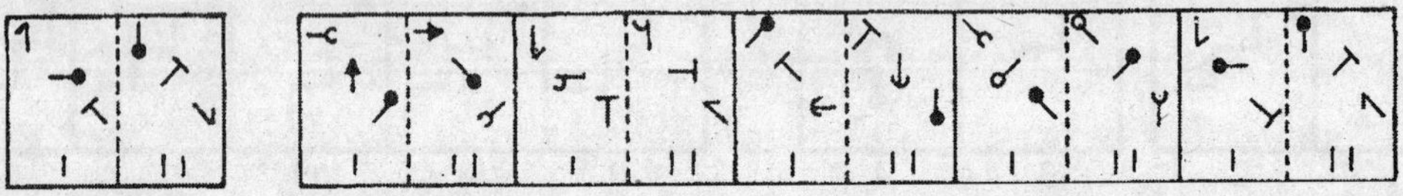
(a) (b) (c) (d) (e)

18.
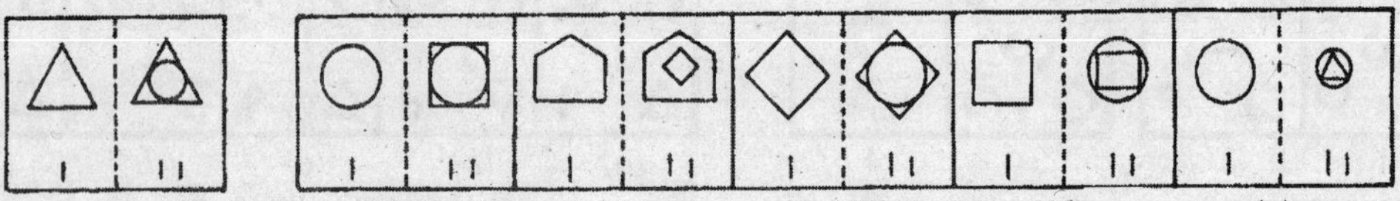
(a) (b) (c) (d) (e)

19.
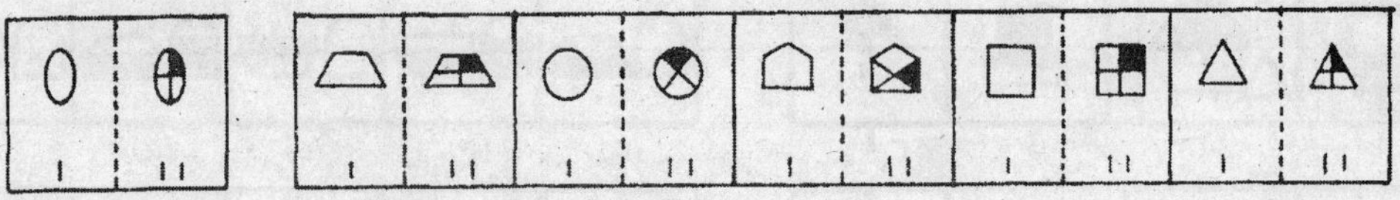
(a) (b) (c) (d) (e)

20.
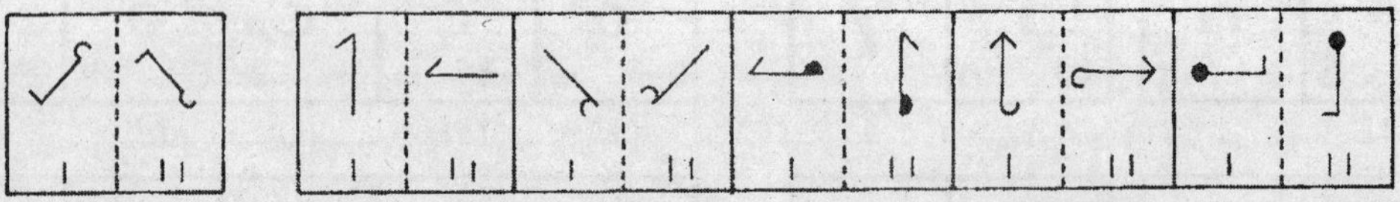
(a) (b) (c) (d) (e)

21.
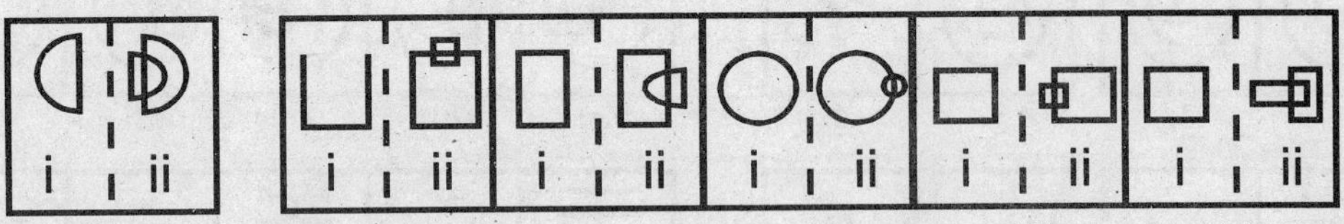
(a) (b) (c) (d) (e)

22.
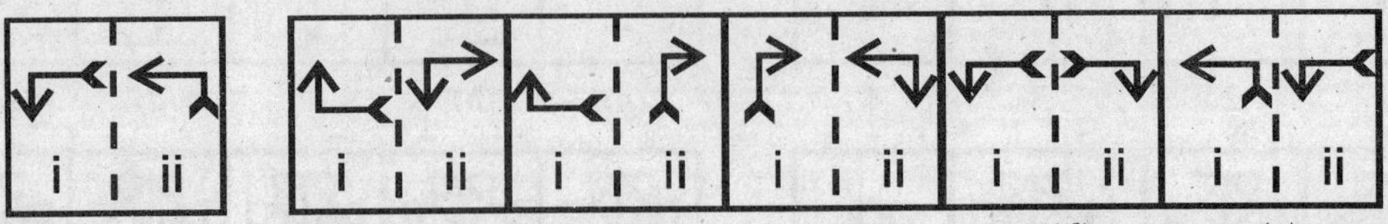
(a) (b) (c) (d) (e)

Problem Figure **Answer Figures**

23. 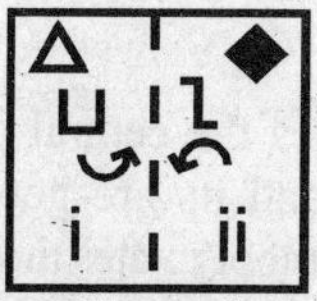 

(a) (b) (c) (d) (e)

24. 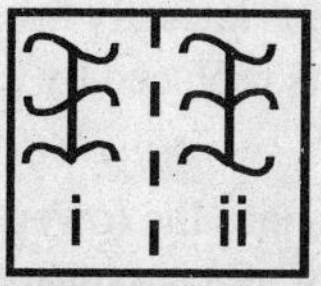 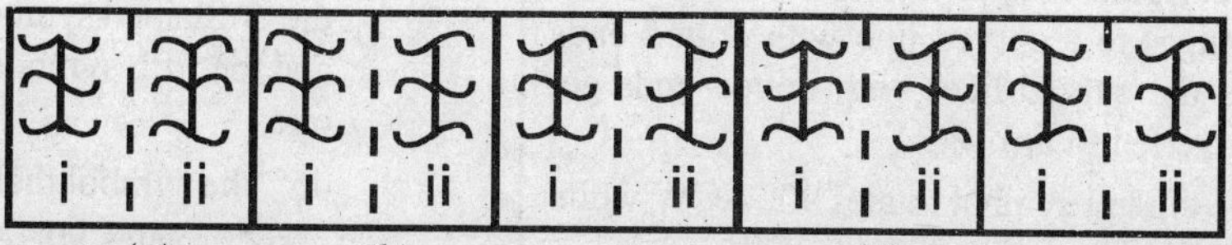

(a) (b) (c) (d) (e)

25. 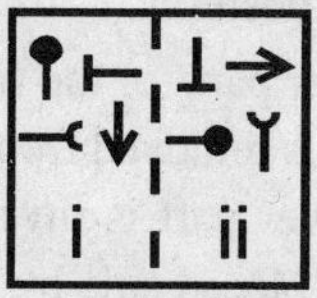 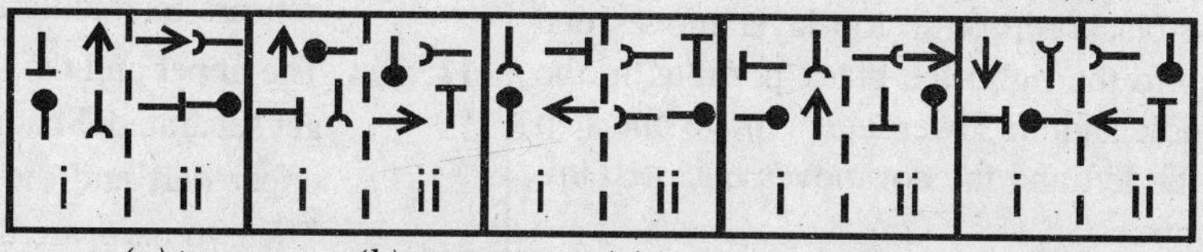

(a) (b) (c) (d) (e)

26. 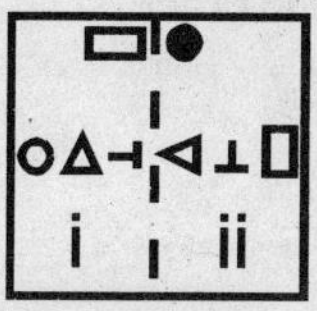 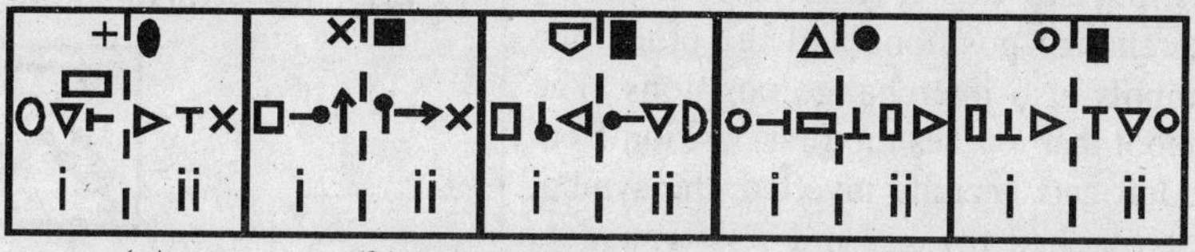

(a) (b) (c) (d) (e)

27. 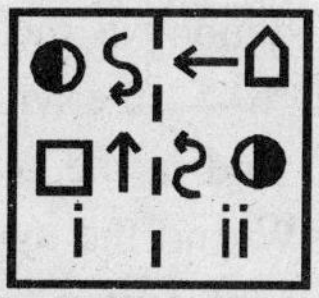 

(a) (b) (c) (d) (e)

28. 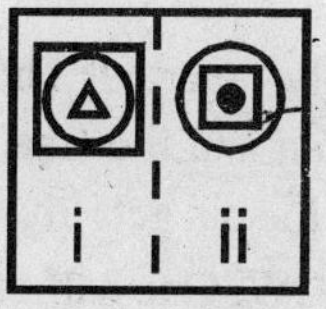 

(a) (b) (c) (d) (e)

29.  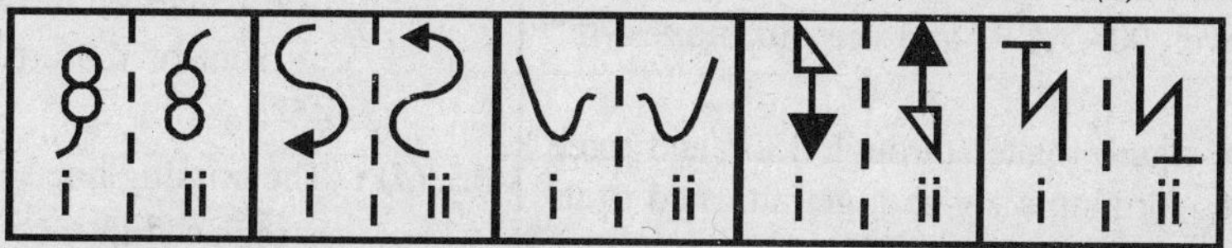

(a) (b) (c) (d) (e)

30. 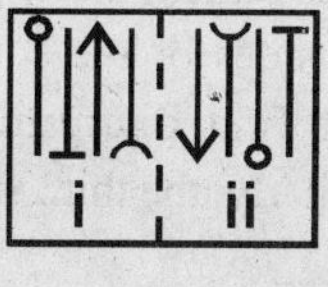 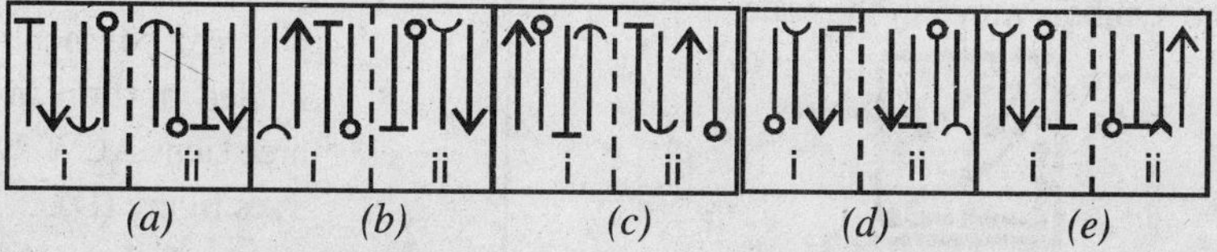

(a) (b) (c) (d) (e)

EXPLANATORY ANSWERS

1. (*b*) : The R.H.S. figure is fitted into the L.H.S. figure and the resulting figure is rotated 90° CW.

2. (*b*) : The figure rotates 45° ACW, the arrow changes to a curved line with dotted ends and the curved lines with dotted ends get converted to arrows.

3. (*d*) : The top left symbol rotates 90° ACW while all other symbols rotate 90° CW.

4. (*e*) : The black portion in top layer moves one step to the right; the black portions in the middle and the lower layers move one step to the left and the dot moves one step upwards.

5. (*d*) : The first and second symbols from the left interchange positions and the other two symbols also interchange positions. The symbol that reaches the first position from the left gets laterally inverted; the symbol that reaches the second position gets inverted, the third symbol rotates 90° CW and the fourth symbol gets replaced by a new one.

6. (*d*) : The single figure is replaced by a figure similar to the double figures and the double figures are replaced by figures similar to the single figure.

7. (*e*) : The figure rotates 135° ACW; a 'T' appears diagonally opposite to the black leaf and a 'Y' appears diagonally opposite to the white leaf.

8. (*c*) : The square rotates through 45°. The arrow moves 90° ACW and the pin moves 45° ACW.

9. (*b*) : The figure rotates through 180° and three lines forming a zig-zag, get attached to its lower end.

10. (*d*) : The symbols move in the order

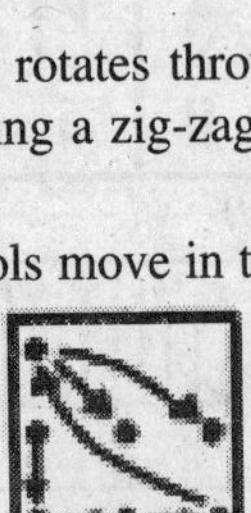

The symbol that reaches the central position rotates 90° CW and its arc gets inverted; the 'P' shaped symbol rotates through 180°; the 'C' shaped symbol rotates 90° CW; the 'S' Shaped symbol gets laterally inverted and the fifth symbol gets replaced by a new one.

45°, the symbol that reaches the lower right corner rotates 90° ACW and a new symbol appears in middle-left position.

11. (*e*) : The upper and the lower parts of the figure get separated. Shading is removed from the upper part and the lower part is inverted. The two parts are then placed side by side.

12. (*a*) : The symbols move in the order

The symbol that reaches the top-left corner rotates 90° ACW; the symbol in the top-right corner rotates through 45°; the symbols in the lower-left corner and in the central positions rotates 90° CW and the symbol that reaches the lower-right corner rotates through 90°.

13. (*e*) : The figure gets laterally inverted. The dot on the larger arc, the pin and the small arc rotate 90° ACW. Also, the pin gets inverted.

14. (*c*) : The figure rotates 90° CW. One half of one of the lines on the arrow is lost. The figure in front of the arrowhead rotates through 45°.

15. (*d*) : The missing line segment in the first figure is replaced in second. Then moving ACW, the third line segment is removed along the two next consecutive sides of the square. Shaded portion in the first figure moves three steps ACW. Similarly, the third figure gives figure (D).

16. (b) : The uppermost design enters into innerside side of the lower design from Ist figure to the IInd figure.

17. (a) : In element I to II upper left design comes at lower right rotating 135° C.W. Middle design goes to upper left and rotates 90° CW. While lower right design goes to middle and it also rotates 90° C.W. The same changes occur in option A.

18. (e) : In element I to II and ellipse is put in the triangle. Similarly in option E a triangle is put in the ellipse.

19. (d) : From first figure to IInd figure, design is divided into four equal parts and right side of the upper portion becomes shaded.

20. (e) : From Ist figure to IInd figure, design is reversed after moving 90° anticlockwise direction.

21. (d) : The figure in the first part is laterally inverted and a similar but smaller design is placed on its left side in the second part.

22. (e) : The element in first part is moved by 90° and the places of short and long line segments are interchanged.

23. (c) : The number of sides making the top left figure is increased by one and a new figure is made, shaded and moved to the top right position. The element in the centre is turned 90° anticlockwise and the small line on the other side is turned by 180°. The element in the bottom right is turned upside down and moved to the bottom left position.

24. (a) : The direction of both arcs on the top, are on the middle right and arc on the bottom left in first part are turned to the other side in the second part.

25. (b) : From part one to part two, the element in the top left is turned 90° clockwise and the other three 90° anticlockwise, also the elements are moved one step anticlockwise.

26. (b) : From part one to part two, the top right element is turned by 90° and moved down, the lower right and middle elements are turned 90° clockwise and 90° anticlockwise respectively and moved to the left and the lower left element is shaded and moved up.

27. (a) : All the four elements exchange place diagonally and in doing so the top left element is laterally inverted, the top right element is horizontally inverted, the bottom right element is turned 90° anticlockwise and the number of lines making the element in bottom left is increased by one.

28. (e) : The innermost figure is removed and the new innermost figure also encloses the other two figures. The innermost and smallest figure is then shaded.

29. (b) : The design in the first part is horizontally inverted in the second.

30. (b) : All the elements in the first part are turned upside down and then 1st, 2nd, 3rd and 4th positioned elements become 3rd, 4th, 1st and 2nd elements in the second part.

24. Odd Man Out

In this type of reasoning a statement is followed by inferences drawn from it. From these inferences only one definitely follows which is the hidden proposition of the sentence and it is the right answer to the question.

EXERCISE

Directions (Q. 1–10) : *In each question below five figures are given. Four are similar in a certain way and so form a group. The question is— which one of the figures* **does not** *belong to that group?*

1. 

(a) (b) (c) (d) (e)

2. 

(a) (b) (c) (d) (e)

3. 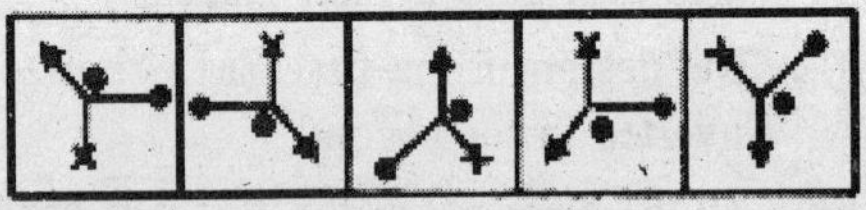

(a) (b) (c) (d) (e)

4. 

(a) (b) (c) (d) (e)

5. 

(a) (b) (c) (d) (e)

6. 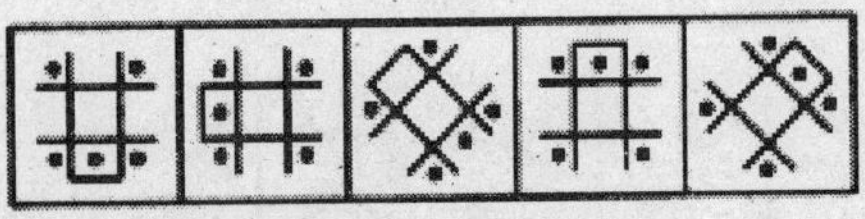

(a) (b) (c) (d) (e)

7. 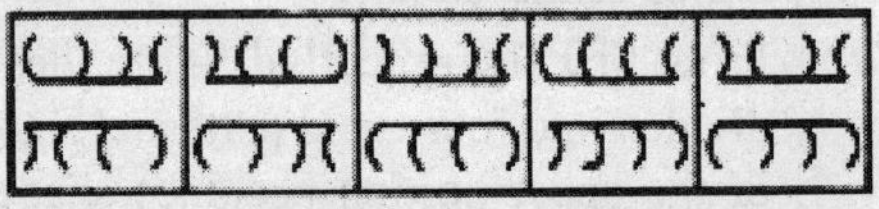

(a) (b) (c) (d) (e)

8. 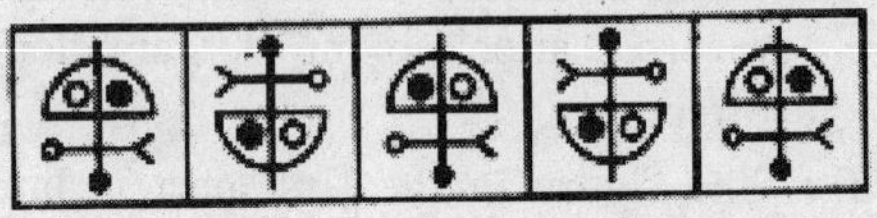

(a) (b) (c) (d) (e)

9. 

(a) (b) (c) (d) (e)

10. 

(a) (b) (c) (d) (e)

Directions (Q. 11–20) : *In each of the following questions, in four out of the five figures, element I is related to element II in the same particular way. Find out the figure in which the element I is* **not** *so related to element II.*

11. 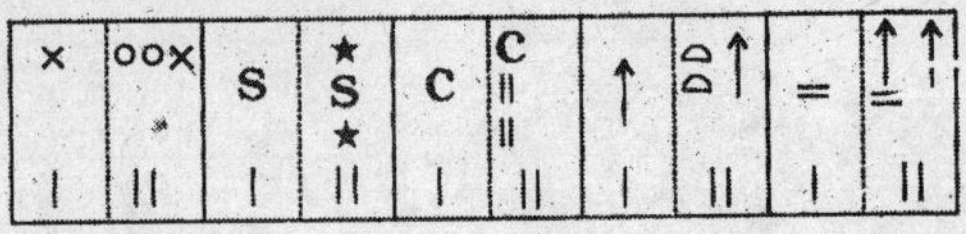

(a) (b) (c) (d) (e)

12. 

(a) (b) (c) (d) (e)

13. 

(a) (b) (c) (d) (e)

14. 

(a) (b) (c) (d) (e)

15. 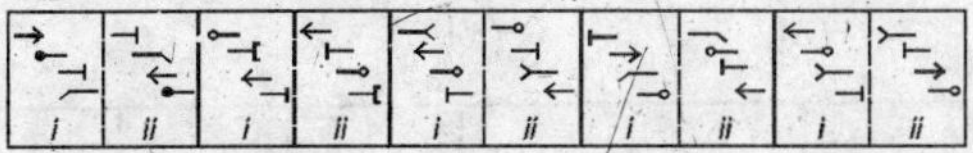

(a) (b) (c) (d) (e)

16. 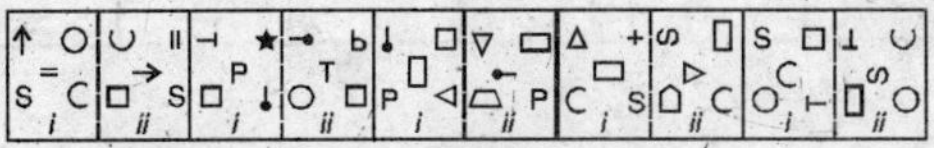

(a) (b) (c) (d) (e)

17. 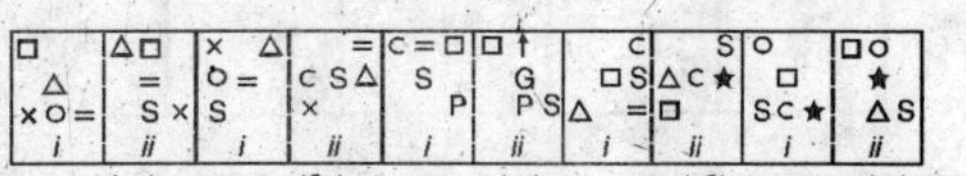

(a) (b) (c) (d) (e)

18. 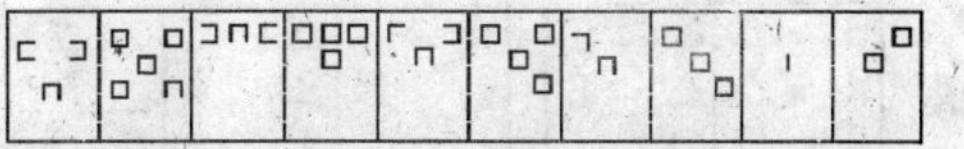

(a) (b) (c) (d) (e)

19. 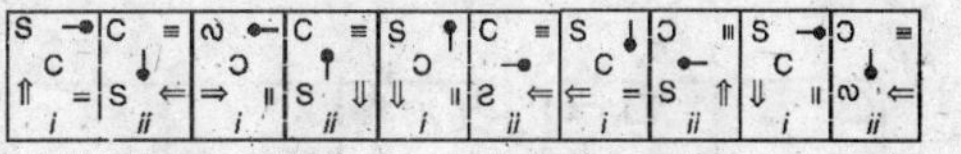

(a) (b) (c) (d) (e)

20. 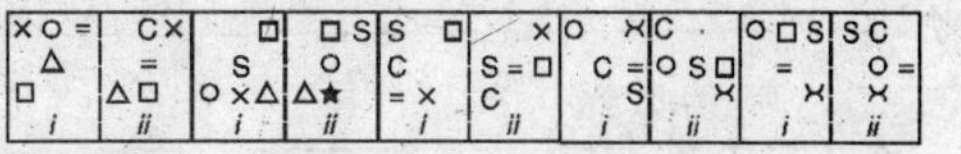

(a) (b) (c) (d) (e)

Directions (Q. 21–30) : *In each of the following questions, a related pair of figures (unnumbered) is followed by five numbered pairs of figures. Out of these five, four have relationship similar to that in the unnumbered pair. Only one pair of figures does not have similar relationship. Select that pair of figures which does not have a similar relationship to that in the unnumbered pair. Number of that pair is your answer.*

21. 

(a) (b) (c) (d) (e)

22. 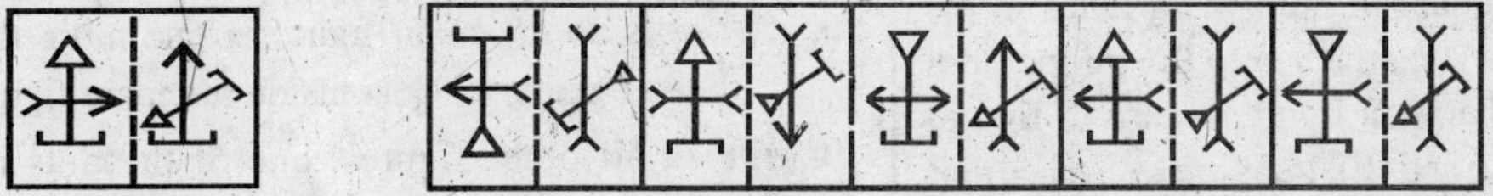

(a) (b) (c) (d) (e)

23. 

(a) (b) (c) (d) (e)

24. 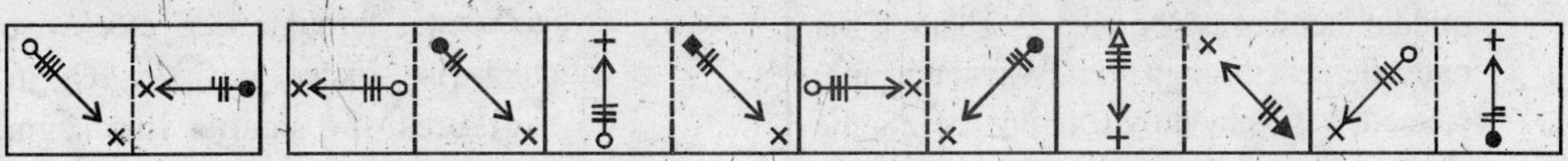

(a) (b) (c) (d) (e)

25. 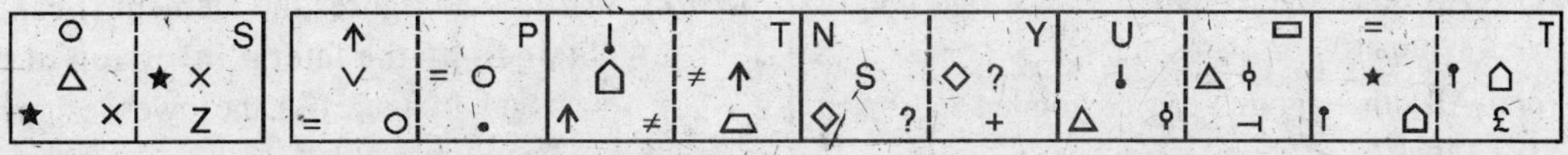

(a) (b) (c) (d) (e)

26. 

(a) (b) (c) (d) (e)

27. 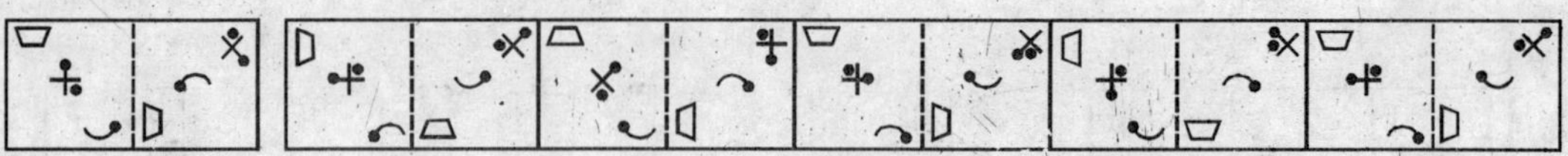

(a) (b) (c) (d) (e)

28. 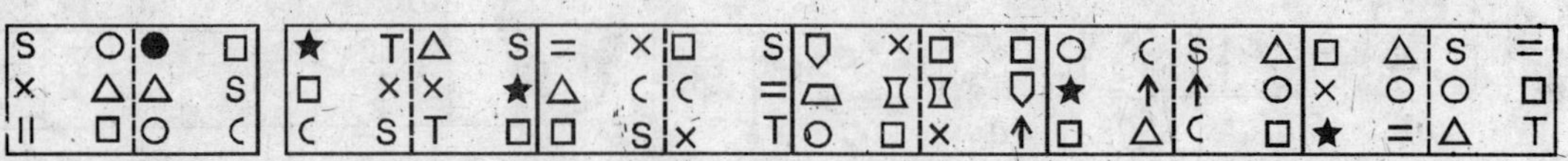

(a) (b) (c) (d) (e)

29. 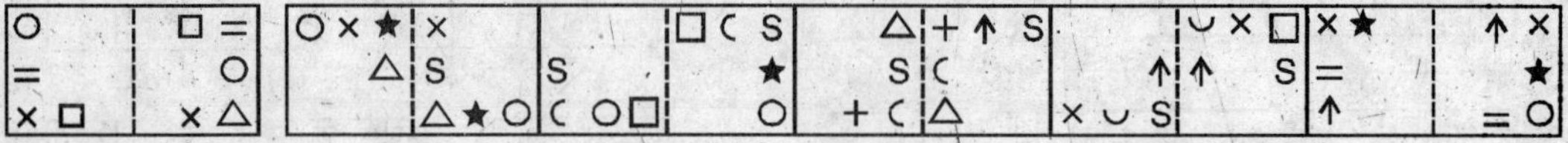

(a) (b) (c) (d) (e)

30. 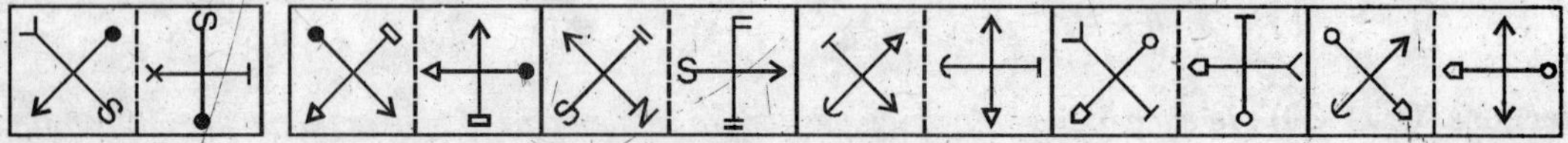

(a) (b) (c) (d) (e)

EXPLANATORY ANSWERS

1. *(d)* : In all other figures, the arrow and the + sign lie towards the black end of the main figure.

2.*(a)* : The pins, equal in number of sides in the main figure are attached to the midpoint of a side of the main figure in case of figures (B), (C), (D) and (E). In figure (A), these pins are attached to a vertex of the main figure.

3.*(c)* : In all other figures, the dot appears in the angle formed between the arrow and the pin.

4.*(a)* : All other figures can be rotated into each other. (In each figure except figure (A), the middle element is obtained by rotating the outer element through 90° CW and the inner element is obtained by rotating the middle element through 90° CW).

5.*(c)* : All other figures have at least one line of symmetry.

6.*(c)* : All other figures can be rotated into each other.

7.*(e)* : In each one of the other four figures, four arcs are curved towards the left and four other arcs are curved towards the right.

8.*(c)* : All other figures can be rotated into each other.

9.*(d)* : In all other figures, the number of dots outside the main figure is one more than the number of dots inside the main figure.

10.*(a)* : In all other figures, one of the dots lies outside the triangle as well as the circle.

11.*(e)* : Except in figure (B), in all other figures, from element I to II two new designs are added in one side of the main design.

12.*(c)* : In each figure from element I to II the main design rotates through 135° clockwise or anticlockwise. Except in figure (C), in all other figures, the smaller line segment moves to other side from element I to II.

13.*(a)* : In all other figures the element II can be obtained by the lateral inversion of the element I. In figure (A), the lower design has not been inverted.

14.*(b)* : In figure (B), the small segment is on the same side as that of the half shaded circle in both the elements.

15.(*d*) : The first design is inverted and moved to third place, the second design is moved to the fourth place, third design to the first place and fourth design is inverted and moved to the second place. Option (D) violates this.

16.(*b*) : In all other options the top-left element is moved to the centre with 90° clockwise rotation. Here, it is rotated anticlockwise.

17.(*d*) : All the designs are shifted in a set pattern one behind the other. The fourth design in all others is changed and placed in the last. Here, the fifth and last designs are changed.

18.(*a*) : In all other pair of figures, all incomplete squares in the first elements are completed and an extra square is added in the second element.

19.(*a*) : From element I to element II, the 'S' shape is turned 90° clockwise and moved down, the double arrow shape '⇒' is turned 90° clockwise and moved to the right, the two parallel lines one turned by 90°; one parallel line is added and all three lines are moved up, the line with a dot is turned 90° clockwise and moved to the centre and the 'C' shape in the centre is turned by 180° and moved to top left position. Here, the double arrow is turned anticlockwise.

20.(*c*) : Starting from one unit, all units are moved in a set pattern, the places of last two units moved are interchanged and the last unit is then made new. Here, no changes are made in the last two units.

21.(*d*) : From element I to element II clockwise the first unit is moved 2 steps forward, the second unit 1 step forward, the third unit 2½ steps forward and the fourth unit 3 steps forward. In option 'D' the third unit violates the rule.

22.(*e*) : From element I to element II, the horizontal bar is turned 135° anticlockwise and the unit at the lower end is turned by 180°. The vertical bar is turned 90° anticlockwise and the unit at the lower end is turned by 180°. In option 'E' one more unit at the top is turned by 180°.

23.(*e*) : In element II, the shade is moved two sections clockwise and shifted from the centre to the base. In option 'E' it is not so.

24.(*a*) : In element II, the arrow is turned 135° clockwise. In option 'A' it is turned anticlockwise.

25.(*b*) : From element I to element II, the bottom right unit and bottom left unit are moved to the centre and middle left position respectively. The other two units are removed and two new elements are placed in the top right and bottom centre position respectively. In option 'B' the placement of bottom right and left elements is not right.

26.(*c*) : In element II, the shades are shifted one petal clockwise. In option 'C' one of the shades is not moved.

27.(*b*) : From element I to element II, the unit on the top left is turned 90° anticlockwise and moved to the bottom right corner position, the unit in the centre is turned 135° anticlockwise and moved to the top right position, and the unit in the bottom right is turned by 180° and moved to the centre. In option 'B', the middle unit is turned 135° clockwise.

28.(*a*) : From element I to element II, a new unit is placed in the top left position, the top left unit is moved to the middle right position, the middle right unit is moved to the left position, the middle left unit is replaced by a new unit and placed in bottom right position, the bottom right unit is moved to the top right position, and the top right unit is moved diagonally to replace the bottom left unit. In option 'A', the middle left unit is not changed when moved to the bottom right position.

29.(*e*) : From element I to element II starting anticlockwise, the first and second units are moved 1½ steps clockwise respectively, the third unit ½ step anticlockwise, the fourth unit 2 steps clockwise, and a new unit is placed ahead of the first unit. Option 'E' violates the rules.

30.(*e*) : In element II, the cross is turned 135° clockwise and then the positions of left and top units on the cross are interchanged In option 'E' it is not so.

R. Gupta's®

ENGLISH IMPROVEMENT BOOKS

Book Name	Code	Price (₹)
General English for Competitive Exams (Objective MCQs)	R-1762	90
The English Enhancement Book	R-1720	180
Common Errors in English (English-Hindi)	R-1709	195
Spoken English	R-1654	195
All About English	R-1391	240
Treasury of Synonyms & Antonyms (Words with Hindi Meanings)	R-1348	180
All Time English	R-1100	120
The Right & Wrong English (Volume-I)	R-1076	140
The Right & Wrong English (Volume-II)	R-1077	140
The Right & Wrong English (Volume-III)	R-1078	140
Dealing with English Made Easy	R-1042	70
Popular English Grammar for Competitions	R-938	95
Popular English-Grammar (with Hindi Explanation)	R-204	140
English Grammar	R-611	195
English Grammar & Composition	R-783	130
English Grammar & Comprehension	R-705	120
Pocket English Grammar	R-676	40
A Concise English Grammar	R-269	60
General Grammar & Interactive English	R-452	140
English Literature & Grammar	R-378	110
English Reading Comprehension	R-303	160
Gloria English Speaking Course (Hindi-English)	R-218	280
English Improvement Course	R-358	240
Dictionary of Synonyms & Antonyms	R-205	140
Dictionary of Prepositions	R-270	80
Handbook of Idioms & Phrases	R-473	60
Idioms, Phrases & Proverbs (with Hindi Meanings & Usage) (English-Hindi)	R-353	65
Handbook of Proverbs	R-514	95
Common Errors in English	R-305	160
Spoken & Communicative English	R-670	240
Key to Spoken & Communicative English	R-671	45
Words Commonly Confused	R-576	110
Writing Correct English	R-541	95
Write English Right	R-578	110
How to Write Correct English (Hindi-English)	R-451	120
Exploring English	R-503	110
Multiple Uses of Words	R-721	70
Handbook of Quotations	R-190	120
Art of Communication in English	R-419	110
Modern English Usage	R-388	110
Objective General English	R-229	140
Advance General English	R-230	130
General English (With Multiple-Choice Questions)	R-311	150
Test of English Language	R-310	120
Improve Your Vocabulary	R-389	95

For Cash on Delivery (COD)

E-mail your order to: **order@rameshpublishinghouse.com**

1603

Ramesh Publishing House, 4457, Nai Sarak, Delhi-6

TO PURCHASE ONLINE LOG ON TO **www.rameshpublishinghouse.com**